GW00707397

PEDIGREES OF LEADING WINNERS 1960 – 1980

compiled by

MARTIN PICKERING and MICHAEL ROSS

J. A. ALLEN & CO. LTD.,
1 Lower Grosvenor Place,
Buckingham Palace Road, London SW1W 0EL

1981

The publishers wish to extend their grateful thanks to the Thoroughbred Breeders' Association, also to Weatherbys for permission to make use of copyright material from the *General Stud Book*.

© Martin Pickering & Michael Ross

ALL RIGHTS RESERVED
No part of this book may be reproduced, stored in a retrieval system or transmitted in any form or by any means, electronic, mechanical, photocopying, recording or otherwise, without the prior permission of the publishers.

British Library Cataloguing in Publication Data
Pickering, Martin
   Pedigrees of Leading Winners, 1960-1980
   1. Horse Breeding 2. Race Horses
   1. Title 11. Ross, Michael
   636. '2 SF291

   ISBN 0-85131-372-8

Published in 1981 by J. A. Allen & Company Ltd. 1 Lower Grosvenor Place, London SW1W 0EL.

Printed at the Grange Press, Butts Road, Southwick, Sussex

PREFACE

In 1960 the Thoroughbred Breeders' Association published a collection of 837 pedigrees under the title 'Pedigrees of Leading Winners, 1912-1959', the compilation having been undertaken by Mr. F. L. Birch and by his son Mr. Franklin E. Birch, who succeeded him as Secretary to the T.B.A.

Six years later the Association published a second volume containing 214 pedigrees which covered the years 1960-1965. That volume has long since been out of print and, in an attempt to produce a really comprehensive and up-to-date collection of international pedigrees Martin Pickering, who was also for several years Secretary of the T.B.A. before becoming Manager of the Stud Book Department at Weatherbys, has joined forces with Michael Ross, the Editor of 'Pattern Races' and of the 'Directory of the Turf'.

This new edition of 'Pedigrees of Leading Winners' contains the pedigrees and summarized racing records of 1,056 top performers in Great Britain, Ireland, France, Germany, Italy, the United States and Canada, and is believed to be the largest number of four-generation pedigrees ever collected in one volume. The starting point for it was the 214 pedigrees contained in the 1960-1965 edition and these have been brought up-to-date and, in the case of the overseas winners, been expanded to four generations. Since then, for the years 1966 to 1980 inclusive, the winners of all Group I races in Great Britain, Ireland, France, Germany and Italy have been included, as have also the winners of 13 of the British Group II events – the Coronation Stakes at Royal Ascot, the Coventry Stakes, the Flying Childers Stakes (which for many years was Group I), the Gimcrack Stakes, the Great Voltigeur Stakes, the Hardwicke Stakes, the King Edward VII Stakes, the Nassau Stakes, the Park Hill Stakes, the Prince of Wales's Stakes, the Ribblesdale Stakes, the St. James's Palace Stakes and the William Hill Sprint Championship (formerly the Nunthorpe Stakes).

It was more difficult to draw up a satisfactory list of qualifying races for North America. However the winners from 1966 to 1980 inclusive of 9 top-class events all appear in the book, these races being the Kentucky Derby, the Preakness Stakes, the Belmont Stakes, the Coaching Club American Oaks, the Marlboro Cup, the Jockey Club Gold Cup, the Woodward Stakes, the Washington D.C. International and the Hollywood Gold Cup. In addition, the compilers have used their discretion in including many other distinguished winners in the U.S.A. and Canada to bring the total representation for these two countries to over 100 horses.

In the European countries, also, many celebrated horses which did not win any of the qualifying races have been included and it would have been only too easy to have gone on adding to this list, but a line had to be drawn somewhere. Racing records have been taken up to December 31, 1980.

The index has been made more comprehensive than in the previous editions, inasmuch as it now contains not only the winners and their parents and grandparents, but also their third and fourth dams. It is hoped that this will make it easier to trace any notable winners from a particular branch of a family.

April, 1981   MARTIN PICKERING and MICHAEL ROSS

CONVERSION RATES 1960–1980

Foreign earnings have been converted to £ sterling using the following rates. These appeared in the Statistical Abstract from 1960–1971 and from 1972–1980 the Statistical Record conversion rates have been used.

These conversion rates should not be used for penalties under Jockey Club Rules of Racing. For that purpose reference must be made to Rule No 101, or equivalent.

Year	French franc	German Deutsche mark	Italian lire	N. American dollar (U.S.A. & Canada)
1960	13.75	12.00	1741.00	2.79
1961	13.75	12.00	1745.00	2.82
1962	13.76	11.00	1743.00	2.82
1963	13.76	11.00	1743.00	2.80
1964	13.76	11.00	1743.00	2.80
1965	13.76	11.00	1743.00	2.80
1966	13.76	11.00	1743.00	2.80
1967	13.76	11.00	1743.00	2.80
1968	11.86	9.65	1500.00	2.40
1969	Jan 1–Aug 10 11.86 then 13.25	Jan 1–Oct 27 9.65 then 8.83	1500.00	2.40
1970	13.25	8.83	1500.00	2.40
1971	13.25	8.83	1500.00	2.40
1972	13.30	8.35	1515.00	2.55
1973	12.00	7.50	1370.00	2.35
1974	10.88	6.28	1410.50	2.32
1975	10.42	5.66	1519.00	2.35
1976	9.04	5.29	1384.00	2.03
1977	8.43	4.01	1487.00	1.70
1978	8.98	4.02	1669.50	1.91
1979	8.50	3.71	1688.00	2.04
1980	9.06	3.86	1811.25	2.26

INDEX

to the selected winners, to the horses appearing in the first two generations of their pedigrees and to their third and fourth dams. The names and numbers in bold type refer to the pedigrees and racing records of the selected winners.

April View 105, 322
Arabella (by Buchan) 659, 828
Arabella (by Wallenstein) 62
Arachné 300
Aralia (by Alchimist) 53, 521
Aralia (by Asterus) 539
Aralina 53
Aranda 48
Arandena 48, 1022
Arantelle 50
Arbar 44, 201
Arbe 551
Arbencia 219
Arbitrator 46, 150, 648
Archduchess 558
Arcola 390
Arcola II 87
Arcor 44
Arctic Blue 57
Arctic Night 160, 871
Arctic Prince 21, 279, 527, 685, 839
Arctic Rullah 57
Arctic Star 45, 47, 181, 439, 818, 822
Arctic Storm 45
Arctic Sun 57, 279
Arctic Tern 46
Arctic Time 47
Arctic Vale 47
Arctic Villa 332
Arctrullah 57
Ardale 48, 1022
Ardan 107, 339
Ardeen 714
Ardelle 684
Ardent Dancer 49
Ardent Range 669
Ardue 904
Arena 159, 954
Argentée 300
Argentina 73
Argument 50
Ariana 889
Arietta 514, 811
Aristareta 41, 780
Aristophanes 313, 314, 316, 415, 518, 720, 963
Arjon 51
Arkebuse 53
Ark Royal 399
Armageddon 8
Armistice III 52, 773, 1003
Armond 390
Armos 684
Aroma 473, 772
Arona 18
Around the Roses 125
Arratos 53
Arroche 298
Ars Divina 803
Artaius 54
Artemisa 606
Arthur 55
Artistic 724
Artistic Rose 31, 109
Artists Proof 213
Art Paper 704, 705, 748
Arts and Letters 56, 191, 1038
Art Style 57
Aryenne 58
Ascona 25
Asgard 62
Asharaz 861
Ash Blonde 371
Asheratt 443, 730
Ashleen 443, 730
Ashmore 59
Ash Plant 63, 172, 412, 747
Asian Princess 713
Aspertina 39

Asphodele 615
Aspidistra 256, 981
Assignation 856, 883
Astaire 154
Astana 201
Astaria 737
Astec 60, 267
Aster 53
Asterios 18, 410
Astese 61
Asti Spumante 916
Astral II 51
Astrentia 306
Astrid 509, 510, 633, 935, 937
Astrid Wood 509, 510, 633, 935, 937
Astronomie 44
Astrophel 746
Astuce 443
Atalante 18
Atan 477, 868, 870
Athanasius 286
Athasi 600, 1046
Athena 723
Athenagoras 62
Athene 790
Athenia 884
Athens Wood 63
Atherstone Wood 64
Atilla 65
Atout Maitre 87, 653
Atrevida 380
Attica 351, 443, 485, 649, 884
Attica Meli 66
Atys 595
Auditing 610
Auld Alliance 342
Aunt Chaney 1006
Aunt Clara 777, 839, 840
Aunt Edith 67
Aunt May 536, 571
Aurabella 68
Aurelius 69
Aureole 26, 42, 68, 69, 70, 137, 163, 193, 202, 285, 399, 419, 432, 580, 583, 590, 636, 669, 687, 692, 698, 702, 744, 809, 828, 880, 922, 1001, 1015, 1024
Auriban 539
Aurora 20, 24, 172, 371, 398, 416, 495, 557, 599, 995
Aurore Boreale 513, 695, 893, 894
Aurore Polaire 513, 893, 894
Authi 70, 1024
Autobiography 71
Avanti 1019
Avatar 72
Avella 708, 833
Avena 591, 600, 1046
Avenida 62
Averof 73
Avonbeg 673
A Wind is Rising 442
Azalea 799
Azeez 655
Azincourt 74
Aziyade 52
Azzurrina 75

Baalim 76
Babucon 412
Babur 694
Baby Doll 710, 915, 972
Baby League 122, 655
Babylon 827
Baby Polly 1015
Bacona 939
Bacuco 77
Badalona 104
Badine 82

Bagheera 664
Bahama 614
Bairam II 675, 676
Bakou 82
Bala 1009
Balaclava 953
Balaklava 104
Bald Eagle 281, 409, 838
Baldric II 78, 291, 436
Baletta 83
Balidar 79, 118, 1047
Balladier 205
Balla Tryst 645
Ballechin 424
Ballili 953
Ballingham Lady 865
Ballisland 783
Bally Ache 80
Ballydam 80
Bally Free 1038
Ballylinan 816
Ballymiss 310
Ballymore 81, 603
Ballymoss 12, 33, 83, 108, 152, 261, 509, 510, 578, 582, 686, 820, 821, 910, 937
Ballynash 673, 697, 804, 1029
Ballynulta 783
Ballyogan 49, 80, 81
Ballyogan Queen 144
Bally's Mil 582
Ballywellbroke 673, 697
Balthazar 104
Balto 82
Baly Rockette 83
Bandarilla 829, 836, 952
Banditry 2
Band Practice 154
Banish Fear 211, 444
Bank Account 645
Bankline 996
Bannerette 1011
Banquet Bell 179, 519
Banta 101
Bantam 356
Barbara 84
Barbara Burrini 825
Barbare 84, 718
Barbarona 520
Barba Toni 61
Barberybush 796
Barbieri 85
Barbizonnette 246
Barchester 367
Bardia 874
Barina 104
Bar Le Duc 35
Barley Corn 248, 292, 323, 345, 429, 482, 483, 654, 698, 805, 841, 844
Barley Mow 743
Bar Nothing 215
Barn Pride 112, 115, 221, 1023
Barquerolle 153
Barra 535, 638
Barsine 282
Basalt 86
Bases Full 116
Bashful 299
Bastia 731, 788, 795, 796, 825, 830, 837
Batitu 87
Baton 151
Baton Rouge 383
Battle Eve 672
Battlefield 56
Battle Joined 8, 1049
Battle Law 804
Battle Queen 804
Bayan Kara 338, 357, 587, 1049
Bayborough 442

Bay Express 88
Bayora 123, 952
Bayou 190
Bayrose 31, 109
Bayuk 119, 126
Beactive 881
Beadah 353
Be a Honey 727
Be Ambitious 213, 373
Beaming Beauty 215
Bean Feast 133
Beatitude 74
Beau Charmeur 89
Beaugency 90
Beaukiss 768
Beau Prince II 4, 493, 539, 806
Beau Sabreur 737, 739
Beausite 1023
Beautiful Girl 803
Beautillion 940, 1052
Bebe Grande 710, 972
Bebopper 957
Becassine 360
Becti 312, 405
Bee Bee Bee 91
Be Faithful 117, 213, 373, 628
Be Friendly 92
Begum 532, 1048
Behistoun 93
Bel Agnes 288
Bel Baraka 462, 1009
Bel Bolide 94
Belbroughton 367
Beldale Flutter 95
Belgio 96
Believe Me 270
Belinda 356
Belinda Blue Eyes 356
Bella II 338, 357, 587, 1049
Belladonna 100
Bella Mourne 786
Bella Paola 717
Bellatrix II 775
Bella Zetta 358
Belle Angevine 338, 357, 587, 1049
Belle Femme 228
Belle Ferronniere (by Bruleur) 93
Belle Ferronniere (by Cosmos) **97**
Belle Histoire 71
Belle Musique 391, 555
Belle of All 702
Belle of Athens 63
Belle of Ireland 464
Belle of the Ball 464
Belle of Troy 232, 303, 750
Belle Sauvage 521, 1001
Belle Sicambre 98
Bellesoeur 391, 555
Belle Travers 860
Bellezza (by Solario) 93
Bellicent 161
Bellini 121, 294, 546, 959
Beloved 761
Be My Guest 99
Benane 1021
Bench Game 769
Ben Marshall 100
Bent Twig 981
Beotie 93
Bereitschaft 86
Bernborough 865
Bernera 865
Bernie Bird 740
Bernina 121
Besieged 865
Bessarona 520
Best in Show 990
Best Risk 690
Best Turn 225

Bete à Bon Dieu 136
Better Bee 91
Better Half 544, 893
Better Self 256
Betty Dalme 644
Betty Loraine 155
Betwixt 176
Bey 1007
B. Flat 714
Bibibeg 813
Bibi Mah 615
Bibi Toori 675, 813
Big Game 16, 339, 378, 401, 557, 605, 683, 892, 959, 965
Big Hurry 23, 703, 819, 923
Big Spruce 101
Bill and Coo 761
Billings 182
Binnacle 80
Binse 86
Biobelle 90, 124
Biologie 507
Birdbrook 133
Bird Nest 27, 315
Bireme 102
Birkhahn 18, 25, 53, 475, 500, 625, 726, 926, 933, 1037, 1040
Birthday Bouquet 81
Birthday Wood 81
Biscayne 103
Bishopscourt 276, 460
Bizkorra III 729
Blabla 104
Black Betty 463
Black Brook 438
Black Domino 282, 338
Blackmail 751
Black Ray 279, 1041
Black Rock 315
Black Satin 105
Black Tarquin 982
Blade of Time 215
Blakeney 106, 453, 454, 860, 999
Blanchisseuse 879
Blanco 916
Blanding 45
Blank Day 564
Blaue Adria 76
Blaue Blume 76
Blaue Donau 252
Blaustrumpf 76
Bleebok 802
Bleep-Bleep 107
Blenheim 185, 461
Blessed Again 108
Bleu Azur 26, 188
Blini 356
Blockhaus 788
Blois 810
Bloodroot 117, 213, 373, 628
Blue Banner 317, 467
Blue Bear 89, 428
Blue Blur 441
Blue Cashmere 108
Blue Cross 873
Blue Delight 28, 318, 668
Blue Denim 226, 369, 684, 735, 795
Blue Gem 166, 306, 730, 767, 890, 931, 984
Blue Girl 984
Blue Grouse 441
Bluehaze 316
Blue Jeans 450
Blue Kiss 89, 428
Blue Mark 492
Blue Missy 677
Blue Moon 85
Blue Peter 39, 100, 400, 859
Blue Prelude 26, 188

Blue Prince II 226, 490, 667, 735, 1025
Blue Range 669, 671
Blue Sash 611
Blue Swords 383
Blue Tom 109
Blue Train 460, 492
Blue Tzar 505
Blushing Groom 110
Bodicee 93
Bohemienne 97
Bois Roussel 273, 536, 686, 705, 762, 777, 840, 922, 1031
Bolaris 465
Bold and Brave 116
Bold Bidder 94, 111, 150, 242, 609, 815, 907
Boldboy 112
Bold Commander 264, 431, 564
Bold Enchantress 313
Bold Experience 921
Bold Fascinator 113
Bold Fay 465
Bold Forbes 114
Bold Front 315
Bold Irish 823
Bold Lad (IRE) 112, 115, 221, 781, 1023
Bold Lad (USA) 113, 341, 550, 885
Bold Lily 315
Bold Maid 285, 565
Bold 'n Determined 116
Boldnesian 855, 932
Bold Reason 117
Bold Reasoning 855, 932
Bold Ruler 1, 71, 94, 111, 112, 113, 114, 115, 116, 147, 150, 171, 213, 221, 264, 312, 313, 333, 341, 415, 418, 431, 437, 441, 455, 478, 550, 609, 680, 720, 752, 787, 815, 823, 856, 885, 907, 927, 935, 954, 983, 1020, 1023
Bold Venture 742
Bolero 740, 1056
Bolkonski 118
Bombazine 134
Bona 86
Bonconte di Montefeltro 119
Bon Marché 136, 145
Bon Mot (by Beresford) 127
Bon Mot III (by Worden II) 120, 497, 900
Bonnard 121
Bonne Bouche 15
Bonny Bush 394
Bonny Jet 394
Bonus 168
Book Debt 421
Book Law 175
Bootless 231, 747
Boran 707
Border Bounty 144, 266, 714
Boreale 986
Borealis 156, 398, 403, 500, 846
Bornastar 801
Born Fool 35
Borobella 426, 659
Borrow 140
Boscage 757
Bosnia 300
Bossuet 185
Botany Bay 438
Botticelli 39, 100, 327, 626, 859
Boucher 122
Bouclette 82
Boudoir 155, 208, 331, 361, 409, 463, 543
Bouillabaisse 312
Bounteous 2, 123, 714

Bouquet 324
Bourbon 124
Bourlon Reel 1030
Bourtai 101, 190, 576, 876
Bowl Game 125
Boxeuse 501
Boys I'm It 35
Bozzetto 77, 300, 1012
Brabantia 88
Braccio da Montone 126
Bracey Bridge 127
Bramalea 802, 901
Bramouse 18, 726
Brantome 973, 1002
Brave Array 315
Brave City 869
Brave Empress 54
Brave Henriette 128
Brave Johnny 128
Bravely Go 640
Brazen Molly 130
Breakspear II 983
Breath O'Morn 740, 741
Breton 129
Breughel 97
Bridal Colors 710
Bride Elect 106, 401, 405
Bridgemount 590
Bridle Way 979
Brief Candle 973
Brigadier Gerard 130, 512
Bright Lady 578
Bright News 166, 849
Bright Set 230, 471, 852
Bright Spot 578
Brig O'Doon 1047
Brilliant Green 432
Brinda 957
Bringley 131
Broad Ripple 351
Broadway 441, 787, 823
Broadway Dancer 132
Broadway Melody 132
Brolly 880
Brook 133
Brown Baby 72, 392
Brown Berry 72, 392
Brown Princess 430
Brulette 521, 1001
Brumeux 245, 398
Brunhild 459
Bruni 134
Brunoro 610
Bryan G. 185
Bubbles 429, 501
Bubbling Beauty 46
Buchaness 880
Buckeye 915
Buckpasser 135, 190, 592, 752, 990
Buckskin 136
Bucolic 825
Buisson Ardent 49, 64, 167, 669, 853, 867, 882
Buisson d'Or 1004
Bula 385
Bull Dandy 1030
Bull Lea 562, 750, 857
Bull Page 632
Bullpoise 288
Bunch Grass 86
Bunworry 121
Buonamica 39, 100, 121, 859
Buontalenta 119, 126
Buoy 137
Bura 405
Burgonet 378, 605
Burgoo Maid 522
Busaca 138
Busanda 135, 752
Businesslike 135, 610

Busiris 139
Busted 138, 140, 141, 180, 267, 911, 987, 1026
Bustino 141
Busy Fairy 465

Cabalistique 196
Cabhurst 142
Cabrella 142
Cadmus 362
Caergwrle 143
Caerlissa 292, 309, 686, 922
Caerphilly 143
Cagire II 499, 743
Caida 953
Cairn Rouge 144
Calash 567
Caldarello 145
Caldarium 142
Calgary 938
Caliban 146
California 394, 938
Callais 539
Calliopsis 1018
Callisto 406
Calluna 63, 118, 241, 1018
Calve 147
Camargue II 255
Cambremont 58
Cambyses 822
Camelina 359
Camenae 407, 976, 986
Cameo 691, 758
Cameronian 294
Camlarg 1051
Campanette 63, 241
Campanula (by Ansitz) 196
Campanula (by Blandford) 63, 118, 1018
Canalette 104, 120, 970, 1029
Canary Seed 725
Candida 942, 987, 999
Candy Cane 144
Candy Dish 148
Candy Spots 148
Candytuft 718
Canfli 486
Canidia 406, 1016
Canina 1011
Canisbay 149, 662, 1027
Cannonade 150
Canonero II 151
Cantadora 341, 455
Cantata 924
Canterbury Belle 852
Cantora 157
Canvas 194
Canvas Shoe 695
Cap and Bells 485
Capelet 789
Capital Issue 481
Capo Bon 152
Cappellina 85
Captain's Fancy 260
Captain's Gig 547
Captivation 264
Carabella 153
Caracalla II 1042
Caracol 154
Caracolero 155
Caralline 136, 145
Caramel 649
Caran D'Ache 302
Cardington King 156
Card King 156
Careless 231, 232, 247, 303, 722, 747
Careless Nora 231, 747
Caretta 959
Carlos Primero 157
Carmarthen 158

Ergina 424, 757
Erica Fragrans 525, 560, 964
Erimo Hawk 276
Erin 823
Erisca 614
Eroica 320, 975
Escasida 606
Escort 277
Escutcheon 190, 576, 876
Esmeralda 652
Esperance 649
Espresso 827, 1014
Esquire Girl 530
Esterelle 142
Etalon Or 36
Ethane 390, 391, 395
Ethel Dear 741
Ethel Gray 305
Ethel Walker 8
Ethyl 390
Etiquette 409
Etoile de France 439, 651
Etoile Filante 107
Etona 939
Etonian 957
Eufrosina 723
Euridice 737
Euroclydon 737
Evening 763
Evening Belle 672, 763
Evening Out 672
Evening Thrill 376
Everget 667
Example 278
Exar 279
Exbury 207, 278, **280**, 283, 554, 894
Exceller 281
Excelsa 279, 1041
Exchange 282
Exclusive 11, 342
Exclusive Native 11, 342
Exit Smiling 637
Expansive 283
Experience II 523
Extravaganza 368
Eyeshadow 545
Eyewash 48, 762

Faberge II 268, 336, 343, 790
Faggot 432
Faiblesse 302
Fainne Oir 368
Fair Alycia 115
Fair Angela 582
Fair Arabella 284
Fair Bid 249, 254
Fair Charmer 855
Fair Cop 744, 982
Fair Dame 413
Fair Dolly 4
Fair Ease 776
Fair Edith 67
Fair Edwine 115
Fair Emma 6, 398, 402
Fairey Fulmar 568, 875
Fairfax 1017
Fair Flame 158
Fair Freedom 453, 454, 847, 909, 1038
Fair Greek 864
Fairholme 487
Fair Isle 834
Fair Linda 459
Fair Line 472
Fairly Hot 744, 982
Fair Maid of Perth 1009
Fair Perdita 490
Fair Ranger 538, 609
Fair Salinia 284
Fair Share 459, 956

Fair Simone 158
Fair Spoken 776
Fair Terms 304
Fair Trial 32, 65, 84, 277, 368, 424, 704, 705, 748, 973
Fair Venus 6, 42, 398, 402
Fairway 365, 492, 998
Fair Winter 285, 565
Fairy Godmother 254
Fairy Palace 56
Fairy Prince 397
Fairy's Love 505
Faizebad 259
Faktotum 9
Falcon 870
Fallaha 786
False Evidence 209
Fama 32
Family Honour 771
Fancy Free 1036
Fancy Girl 764
Fancy Racket 185
Fanfar 286
Fanghorn 253
Fantan II 81, 146, 604, 759, 760, 842
Fante 61, 410, 962
Fantomas 287
Fara 146
Faramoude 559
Farandole 4
Farandole II 167, 559
Faraway Son 288, 1025
Farce 550
Farceuse 96
Fargo 311
Farhana 289
Farizade 52
Farmerette 801, 886
Farthing Damages 613, 688, 831
Fascinating 716
Fasciola 1020
Fast Beauty 425
Fast Fox 447, 926
Fast Lady 319
Fast Line 297, 541, 555, 660
Fastnet 37, 447
Fastnet Rock 814, 888
Fast Turn 8, 1049
Fatusael 290
Faubourg II 319
Faustina 311
Faustitas 302, 311
Faustoper 302
Faustsage 302
Favilla 311
Favoletta 291
Favorite 719
Fazeley 356
Feather Bed 180
Feather Time 148
Fee Esterel 443, 730
Feemoss 509, 510, 593, 861, 937
Feevagh 509, 510, 633, 935, 937
Feira de Rio 379
Felicio 292
Feliza 96
Felsetta 102, 137, 399, 557, 867, 874
Felucca 102, 137, 399, 557, 850, 867
Feola 100, 403, 497
Feria 379
Feronia 68
Festoon 65
Fete Royale 4
Ficelle 400
Fidalgo 181, 323, 529, 785, 822
Fidgette 501
Fidra 513, 894
Fidyi 293

Field Mouse 986
Fighting Charlie 294
Fighting Don 27, 315, 766
Fighting Edie 292, 309
Fighting Fox 27, 315
Fighting Ship 295
Figliastra 345
Figonero 296
Fiji 304
Filasse 1039
Filastic 1039
Filiberto 297, 555
Filigrana 542
Fille d'Amour 447
Fille de Poète 487, 728
Fille de Salut 375
Fille des Chaumes 298
Fille de Soleil 286, 375, 775
Fille du Vent II 298
Fils d'Eve 298
Final Straw 299
Fin Bon 300
Fine Art 300, 301, 833, 977
Fine Feathers II 296
Fine Pearl 301
Fine Top 244, 260, 300, 301, 360, 589, 833, 924, 977
Fior d'Orchidea 662, 665 671
Fire Falls 623
Firefly 1011
Firelight 230, 471
Firestreak 420, 889, 942
Firetop 632
Firle 526, 890, 1032
First Feather 188, 824
First Flight 294
First House 701
First Landing 798, 824
First Lord 302
First Love 431
Fisherman's Bridge 194
Fitz's Fancy 182
Flagette 41, 101, 668, 854, 972
Flag of Truce 487
Flambette 1033
Flame Tamer 1
Flaming Page 12, 168, 369, 427, 632, 635, 637, 733, 754, 968
Flaming Swords 316
Flaming Top 632, 968
Flaneur 690
Flaring Top 632, 968
Flash On 422
Flatter 423, 548
Flattered 548
Flattering 423
Fleche d'Amour 788
Fleet 303
Fleet Diver 623
Fleet Nasrullah 35, 270, 304, 308, 328, 353
Fleet Rings 211
Fleet Wahine 304
Fleur 968
Fleur des Neiges 462, 1009
Flicka de Saint-Cyr 293
Flight of the Heron 294
Flight's Daughter 71
Flighty Falls 531
Flirting 563
Flirting Around 305
Flitter Flutter 95
Flivver 486
Floradora 75
Floralie 259, 307
Florence Dombey 388
Floribunda 306, 671
Florida 286
Floride 504
Flossy 307
Flower 439

Flower Bed 361
Flower Bowl 72, 155, 361, 370, 467, 655, 742
Flowing Lava 590
Flush Royal 889
Flute Enchantée 59, 329, 375, 484, 533, 598, 772, 779, 800
Fly Away 507
Flyaway Home 486
Fly High 505
Flying Colours 983
Flying home 487
Flying Paster 308
Flying Sally 42
Flying Tammie 537
Flying Water 309
Folastra 293
Foliage 17
Folie Douce 910
Folle Nuit 815, 910
Folle Passion 815, 910
Folle Rousse 310
Fontanus 311
Fontenay 222, 627, 695
Foolishness 176
Foolish Pleasure 312
Fool-Me-Not 312
Fordham 313
Forecourt 961
Forego 314
Foretaste 497
Forfeit 667
Forli 299, 313, 314, 316, 415, 444, 518, 720, 899, 963, 964
Forlorn River 315, 766
For Love 667
Formentera 309
Formidable 316
Formosa 286
Forsythia 286
Forteresse 802
Fortino II 160, 162, 210, 340, 538, 626, 709, 836, 864, 966, 988
Fortlin 836
Fort Marcy 317
Fortunate Lady 516
Fortunedale 516
Forward Pass 318
Fossette 504
Fossinette 504
Fotheringay 759
Four Fires 230, 471
Foxcraft 447, 1020
Foxhunter 42, 507
Foxtrot 464, 529, 765
Foxy Tetra 362
Fragrance 99, 446, 896
Fragrant View 324
Fraicheur 678
Fran 663, 992
Francia 457
Francis S. 442
Frankly 173
Free Flowing 940
Free for All 256
Free Man 854, 1029
French Beige 75, 536, 570, 571
French Bird 713
French Cream 319
French Duchess 623
French Fern 866
French Kin 323, 658, 785
French Kiss 866, 913
French Moss 679
French Vamp 228
Frère Basile 320
Fresco 701
Fresh as Fresh 528, 545
Friar's Carse 881
Fric 287, 432
Friedrichsdorf 286

12

14

Miraloma 585
Miranda 32
Mirawala 32, 405
Mirnaya 552, 566
Misleading 95
Miss Barbara 520
Miss Barberie 236, 263
Miss Bula 385
Miss Carmie 183
Miss Coventry 774
Miss Cracknel 499
Miss Dan 585
Miss Disco 111, 115, 147, 333, 856, 927, 1020
Miss Fairfax 161
Miss Florida 504
Miss France 103, 181, 439, 651, 822
Miss Gammon 939
Miss Grillo 466, 572
Miss Honor 123, 952
Missile 586
Missile Belle 586
Missinaibi 485
Mississipian 587
Miss Kid 522
Miss Know All 826
Miss Larksfly 749, 763, 994
Miss Minx 371, 629, 1027
Miss Nasrullah 444
Miss Onslow 967
Miss Pecksniff 388
Miss Petard 588
Miss Pinkerton 993
Miss Protege 555
Miss Remaid 1052
Miss Spy 307
Miss Stephen 230, 471, 852
Miss Upward 588
Miss Winston 10, 899, 989
Missy Baba 337, 455
Mist 591, 814
Mister Sic Top 589
Misti IV 427, 591, 812, 814
Mistigo 590
Mistigri 591
Mistress Ann 249
Mistress Ford 84
Mistress Gwynne 420, 445
Misty Morn 113, 341, 550, 885, 927
Miswaki 592
Mitidja II 625
Mitraille 323, 785
Mitrailleuse 323, 658, 785
Mixed Blessing 245, 384
Mixed Marriage 473, 868
Miz Carol 819
M-Lolshan 593
Mobola 559
Moccasin 40
Mock Orange 258
Moiety Bird 870
Moira II 217
Moleca 61
Molinka 508
Molly Adare 130, 674, 683
Molly Desmond 130
Molvedo 186, 508, 540, **594,** 662, 771, 983
Monade 595
Monarchia 996
Monet 558
Money for Nothing 613, 688
Mon Fils 596
Mongo 597
Monrovia 484
Monsoon 65, 800
Montagnana 429, 501, 533
Montana 474
Montcontour 598

Montebella 68
Monterrico 599
Monteverdi 600
Montez 776
Monticella 900
Montorselli 601
Mooncreek 395
Moonmadness 242, 538, 609
Moonrise 408, 452, 618
Moonstone 643, 711, 749
Moorestyle 602
Morana 217
More So 603
Morkande 585, 595
Morland 199, 440, 498
Mormyre 585, 595
Morston 604, 1035
Mortagne 585, 595
Moskvitchka 598
Moslem Chief 235
Moss Bank 605

Mossborough 33, 133, 136, 152, 200, 227, 280, 484, 556, 574, 578, 598, 605, 642, 679, 684, 686, 821, 827, 848, 866, 913, 928, 1044
Moss Rose 484
Mot d'Amour 900
Mother 652
Mother Goose 46, 648
Motherland 834
Mother Wit 753
Mots d'Or 239
Moubariz 606
Moulines 607
Moulton 449, **608,** 919
Mountain Fastness 669
Mountain Mint 590
Mountain Path 181, 423, 556, 827, 848, 905, 956, 1042
Mount Hagen 242, **609**
Mount Marcy 72
Mourne 87, 349, 358, 771, 786, 804
Mousson 897
Moutiers 1029
Mr. Busher 297
Mr. Jinks 15
Mr. Prospector 394, 442, 592
Mr. Right 610
Mrs. Cidyns 1009
Mrs. Dent 899
Mrs. Gail 899
Mrs. Green 432
Mrs. McArdy 611
Mrs. Mops 536, 571
Mrs. Penny 612
Mrs. Pumpkin 254
Mrs. Swan Song 1042
Mr. Trouble 715, 884
Muci 594
Mulattin 899
Mulberry Harbour 173
Mulligatawny 448
Multijuga 448
Mummy's Pet 613
Mumtaz Begum 262, 380, 446, 456, 622, 628, 817, 961
Mumtaz Mahal 705, 961
Murcia 594, 830
Murrayfield 334, **614**
Musaka 606
Muscida 770
Muscosa 663
Music Boy 570, **615**
Musician 766
Music Maestro 616
Musidora 417
Mustang 943
Mwanza 611, 984

My Babu 66, 67, 215, 254, 333, 519, 530, 532, 544, 545, 691
My Charmer 855
My Dear Girl 235, 434, 473
My Game 563
My Goodness Me 617
My Margaret 499
My Mascot 719
My Recipe 373, 434
Myrobella 419, 889
Myrtle Charm 855
Myrtle Green 553, 601
Myrtlewood 997
Mysterious 618
My Swallow 619
My Swanee 936

Nacelle 193
Nachtviole 624
Nadika 678, 679
Nadir 489
Nadjar 620
Nafah 439, 651
Nagaika 193, 194
Nagami 335, 666
Naic 539
Naim 193
Nairn 237
Nakamuro 594
Nalee 576
Namagua 523, 627
Namedy 646
Namesake 627
Nan 230, 852
Nanaia 240, 243, 779, 1034
Nandine 269
Nanette (by Arjaman) 646
Nanette (by Worden II) 621
Nanon 620, 626
Nantahala 656
Nantallah 40, 139, 151, 373, 470. 518, 656, 886, 963
Nanticious (by Nantallah) 373
Nanticious (by Northfields) **621**
Nantua 156, 269
Narcisse 615
Narrative 71
Narrator 631, 653
Narrow Escape 835
Nashua 466, 576, 655, 738, 802, 876
Nasram II 62, **622,** 1056
Nasrullah 31, 62, 110, 111, 115, 122, 147, 166, 222, 245, 251, 304, 306, 310, 318, 333, 378, 445, 446, 452, 466, 481, 483, 495, 498, 568, 581, 622, 628, 629, 630, 673, 730, 738, 758, 767, 773, 799, 838, 856, 876, 890, 903, 904, 911, 927, 931, 946, 981, 984, 994, 1020, 1045, 1046, 1054, 1056
Nassau 614
Natalma 99, 132, 535, 632, 647, 648, 650, 920, 968, 990
Natasha 370
Natashka 370
Native Charger 404, 929
Native Dancer 28, 208, 216, 219, 331, 344, 351, 352, 404, 422, 461, 494, 511, 543, 585, 648, 761, 823, 843, 851, 857, 868, 881, 929
Native Diver 623
Native Gal 11
Native Glitter 351
Native Partner 316
Native Prince 14, 713
Native Valor 11
Nato 749
Naujwan 343

Naurica 85
Naval Patrol 1039
Navarino 624
Naxos 626
Nearco 16, 24, 29, 45, 73, 177, 200, 212, 234, 275, 317, 319, 321, 330, 372, 430, 440, 446, 534, 583, 597, 605, 622, 628, 631, 642, 645, 648, 653, 675, 687, 872, 875, 913, 930, 961, 979, 1001, 1044, 1055
Nearctic 99, 132, 465, 535, 632, 645, 647, 648, 650, 920, 968, 990, 1038
Nearis 465
Nearly 233, 257, 259, 307, 621
Neartic 716
Nearula 481, 608
Nebbiolo 625
Nebelwerfer 196, 479, 1037
Neberna 106, 604, 1036
Nebos 626
Necelia 790
Neckar 53, 62, 86, 252, 302, 413, 479, 708, 912, 945, 950, 971, 1019, 1051
Necklace II 709
Nelcius 523, **627**
Nelion 770
Nella 583, 590, 669, 687, 809
Nella da Gubbio 620
Nellie Flag 114, 314, 329
Nellie Fleet 329
Nellie L. 114
Nellie Morse 114
Nellie Park 685
Nell K 489
Nell's Joy 489
Neocracy 26, 163, 202, 580
Neola 727
Neolight 170
Neomenie 193
Nepenthe 172
Neptune's Doll 50
Neriad 192
Nerissa 606
Nesta 164
Nestoi 164
Netherton Maid 401, 411, 765, 991
Neutron 184, 199, 572
Never Again II 656
Never Bend 5, 236, 350, 355, 426, 438, 452, 581, **628,** 718, 799, 873
Never Cross 629
Never Say 629
Never Say Die 66, 170, 232, 245, 303, 495, 591, 607, 629, 630, 820, 1032
Never Too Late II 630
New Moon 393
New Pin 163
New Providence 920
Nica 120, 960, 970, 1029
Niccolina 175
Niccolo Dell'Arca 121, 175, 282, 534, 542, 546, 579, 682, 745
Nick of Time 276
Nicolaus 276
Night Attire 643
Night Off 631
Night Sound 448
Nigromante 148
Nigua 148
Nijinsky 12, 58, 168, 369, 427, **632,** 635, 637, 733, 754
Nikoli 633
Niksar 634
Nile Lily 799
Nimbus 13, 367

Tierceron **971**
Tiffauges 589
Tiller 972
Tilly Kate 256
Tilly Rose 256
Tillywhim 413
Timandra 973
Time and Chance 529, 765
Time Call 204, 406, 565, 751, 874
Time-Honoured 809
Timid Tilly 599
Timour 96
Tim Tam 225, 473, 537
Tina II 813
Tip the Wink 167
Tip-toe 943
Tissot 290, 666
Tiziano 1005
Toblerone 269
Tofanella 121, 294, 340, 546, 959, 971
Tokamura 340, 553
Tolosana 340
To Market 111, 908
Tom Fool 109, 135, 169, 312, 485, 531, 538, 572, 609, 752, 879, 895
Tompion 109, 699
Tom Rolfe 22, 125, 188, 257, 414, 635, 824, **974**
Tonala 597
Tonina 962
Tonnera 975
Too Bald 281
Too Much Honey 938
Topaz 711
Tophorn 179, 519
Top Ville 976
Topyo 977
Toque Rose 163
Torbella III 733
Torbido 551
Torpenhow 7
Tosca 320, 975
Tosta 96
Toulouse Lautrec 251, 379, 390, 494, 553
Toupie 300, 301, 833, 977
Tourbillon 715
Tourment 74, 293, 301, 484, 833
Tourzima 5, 44
Toute Belle II 346, 386
Tout Sweet Twenty 598
Tower Walk 978
Town Crier 209
Track Spare 769, **979**
Traffic 789, 1016
Traffic Judge 226, 789, 940, 1052
Traffic Light 892
Traghetto 39, 61, 77, 551, 579, 962
Transtevere 243
Transworld 980
Traverse 232, 247, 303, 722
Travos 540, 947
Treasure Chest 350
Tree of Knowledge 981
Treiberwehr 945, 950
Treibjagd 945, 950
Trelawny 982
Trepan 983
Très Bonne 37
Trevisa 313, 314, 316, 415, 518, 720, 963
Trevisana 971, 1005
Trial by Fire 658
Trial Ground 167
Tribal Chief 611, **984**
Trick Chick 660
Trig 163
Trillion 985

Trinity Term 664
Triomphe 414
Triple First 986
Triplicate 91
Trip to the Moon 366
Trixie from Tad 689, 721, 958
Trojan Lass 328
Tromos 987
Trophae 945, 950
Tropical Cream 988
Tropical Sun 274, 521, 1001
Tropicaro 988
Tropic Star 451, 988
Tropique 695
Troublepeg 715
Troy 989
True Bearing 838
True Picture 105, 516, 702
Trustful 905, 984
Try My Best 990
Try Try Again 971
Tsianina 108, 631
Tudenham 991
Tudor Fair 776
Tudor Gleam 349, 355
Tudor Jinks 282
Tudor Melody 108, 132, 259, 354, 388, 457, 460, 513, 542, 563, 607, 663, 664, 941, 955, 991, 992, 1028, 1035
Tudor Minstrel 13, 73, 79, 99, 206, 354, 388, 397, 460, 499, 542, 606, 613, 756, 811, 898, 917, 947, 955, 991, 992, 1028
Tudor Music 658, 663, **992**
Tudor Romp 1035
Tularia 418
Tuleg 996
Tulyar 418, 985
Tumbledownwind 993
Tumble Wind 993
Tumbling 22
Turkhan 1015
Turkish Blood 1001, 1015
Turn-to 8, 117, 182, 225, 231, 328, 381, 382, 383, 409, 547, 556, 561, 690, 703, 741, 798, 802, 848, 883, 884, 923, 985
T.V. Lark 183, 211, 362, 749, 763, **994**
Twenty-one Plus 699
Twice Over 183
Twilight Alley 995
Twilight Hour 643
Two Bob 183
Two Cities 78, 291, 436
Two Lea 318
Two Rings 647
Twosy 183
Two to Paris 996
Tycoon II 389
Typecast 997
Typha 654
Typhoon 998
Tyrant 935
Tyrnavos 999

Uags 904
Uccello 725
Udaipur 289
Ufa 139
Ulrika Eleonora 379
Ultima Ratio 59
Ultimate Fancy 185
Ulupi's Sister 593
Umberto 914
Umidwar 6, 386, 503, 982
Una 227, 368
Una Felina 379
Undaunted II 285
Under Canvas 898

Unforgettable 341, 455
Unfurl 880
Un Kopeck 1000
Unterwegs 524
Untidy 163
Upadee 1017
Upper Case 921
Up Spirits 182
Up the Hill 22, 270
Urbinella 390
Urca 139
Urshalim 291, 483, 903
U Time 494
Utrillo 524
Utrillo II 390, 391, 395
Uvira 337

Vacillate 55
Vagrancy 370, 982
Vaguely Noble 7, 214, 258, 272, 281, 337, 357, 433, 587, 638, 640, 641, 908, **1001**, 1006
Valadier 713
Val d'Assa 517, 1013
Val de Loir 90, 175, 192, 217, 369, 488, 491, 960, **1002**, 1003
Val de l'Orne 1003
Vale 1018
Valerullah 229
Vali 90, 175, 192, 488, 491, 493, 806, 960, 1002, 1003, 1005
Valiant Heart 1004
Valkyr 78, 370
Valoris 1005
Valour 1006
Valse 78
Valse Folle 336
Valtellina 643
Vampa 1007
Vanda Cerulea 80
Vandale II 6, 41, 48, 52, 101, 126, 287, 360, 668, 706, 854, 943, 949, 972
Vaneuse 236, 263
Vanikoro 951
Vanille 6, 126, 943
Vanossa 319
Varano 1007
Vareta 456, 620, 636, 861, 1054
Varingo 1008
Varna II 1007
Varsoviana 1007
Vasco de Gama 1009
Vatellor 319, 501
Vauchellor 639
Vela 1010
Vellada 108
Venante 187
Veneta 207
Venetian Way 1011
Venturesome 423, 445, 548
Verbena 517, 1013
Verdict 526, 890
Verdura 405
Verity 516
Veronese 293, **1012**
Veronica C 996
Veronique 570, 615
Veronique II 861, 1054
Verrieres 1018
Versicle 526, 890, 1032
Vers l'Amour 462
Verso II 55, 74, 104, 504, 506, 725
Vertencia 187, 277
Vertex 528, 545
Vervain 1013
Verve 482
Vervelle 949
Vestal Girl 55, 397, 527
Vestalia 397
Victoria Cross 203, 433

Victoriana 465
Victoria Park 465, 650, 968
Victrix II 82, 796
Vieille Canaille 210, 400
Vieille Maison 210, 400, 1002
Vieille Pierre 210, 400
Vielle 1014
Vienna (by Aureole) 7, 214, 258, 272, 281, 337, 357, 433, 587, 638, 640, 641, 908, 1001, 1006, **1015**
Vienna (by Menow) 78
Vieux Manoir 90, 175, 192, 280, 384, 443, 488, 491, 634, 764, 774, 804, 960, 1002, 1003, 1012
Vific 1016
Vigogne 1016
Village Beauty 702
Village Green 702
Villainy 332
Villa Medici 385
Villarrica 791
Vilmoray 619
Vilmorin 898, 1054
Vimadee 1017
Vimy 140, 407, 468, 472, 517, 1013, 1017
Vimy Line 472
Violet Bank 79, 118, 1047
Violetta III 291
Violon d'Ingres 484
Virelle 273
Virginia Hills 635
Virginia L. 258, 734
Virginia Water 581
Virtuous (by Above Suspicion) 70, 260, 387, 1024
Virtuous (by Gallant Man) 342
Visor 762
Vitiges 1018
Vixenette 219, 344, 585, 851, 881
Vocation 577
Volage 1007
Voleuse 82
Volubilis 861, 1054
Voute Celeste 513, 893
Vraiment 1008
Vulpina 397

Wafer 339
Waffenart 1024
Waffles 121, 339
Waidmann 945
Waidmannsheil 410
Waidwerk 1019
Wait and Take 1024
Wajima 1020
Wake Atoll 1056
Wake Island 266
Walburga 1019
Waldcanter 524
Waldmeister 1021
Waldrun 410, 945, 1019, 1037
Wale 1022
Wallonin 1024
Wally 1019
Waltzing Matilda 559
War Admiral 135, 376, 414
War Duck 229
War East 798
War Glory 228
War Kilt 881
Warning 277
War Path III 1025
War Plume 229
War Relic 382, 586, 710
Warrior Lass 798
Wassia 1040
Waterloo 1023
Waterval 374, 978
Watling Street 51

21

1   **ABEER** 1 (ch.f., January 18, 1977)

Bred by Mr. and Mrs. Darrell Brown in U.S.A.

Won 3 races, placed 4, £44,252, in England, at 2 and 3 years, incl. Flying Childers Stakes, Queen Mary Stakes; 2nd Cherry Hinton Stakes; 3rd William Hill Cheveley Park Stakes.

DEWAN (b. 1965)	Bold Ruler (b. 1954)	Nasrullah	Nearco / Mumtaz Begum
		Miss Disco	Discovery / Outdone
	Sunshine Nell (ch. 1948)	Sun Again	Sun Teddy / Hug Again
		Nellie Flag	American Flag / Nellie Morse
FLAME TAMER (br. 1965)	Court Martial (ch. 1942)	Fair Trial	Fairway / Lady Juror
		Instantaneous	Hurry On / Picture
	Marta (br. 1947)	Haltal	The Porter / False Modesty
		Jessie Gladys	Pharamond / Mad Passion

2   **ABERGWAUN** 4 (b.f., March 3, 1968)

Bred by D. Hefin Jones.

Won 13 races, placed 8, £54,326, in Ireland, England and France, from 2 to 5 years, incl. Diadem Stakes, Prix Maurice de Gheest, Challenge Stakes, Vernons Sprint Cup, Prix de Seine-et-Oise, King's Stand Stakes; 2nd King's Stand Stakes, Prix de l'Abbaye de Longchamp; 3rd Prix du Petit Couvert.

BOUNTEOUS (b. 1958)	Rockefella (br. 1941)	Hyperion	Gainsborough / Selene
		Rockfel	Felstead / Rockliffe
	Marie Elizabeth (ch. 1948)	Mazarin	Mieuxce / Boiarinia
		Miss Honor	Mr. Jinks / Bayora
DUGO (b. 1959)	Dumbarnie (br. 1949)	Dante	Nearco / Rosy Legend
		Lost Soul	Solario / Orlass
	Golden Happiness (b. 1953)	Golden Cloud	Gold Bridge / Rainstorm
		Doll's Delight	Nearco / Banditry

3   **ABERMAID** 12 (gr.f., March 16, 1959)

Bred by Sir Percy Loraine and R. More O'Ferrall.

Won 4 races, placed 3, £26,156, in England and Ireland, at 2 and 3 years, incl. 1,000 Guineas Stakes, New Stakes; 2nd Jersey Stakes; 3rd Irish 1,000 Guineas Stakes, Falmouth Stakes.

ABERNANT (gr. 1946)	Owen Tudor (br. 1938)	Hyperion	Gainsborough / Selene
		Mary Tudor II	Pharos / Anna Bolena
	Rustom Mahal (gr. 1934)	Rustom Pasha	Son-in-Law / Cos
		Mumtaz Mahal	The Tetrarch / Lady Josephine
DAIRYMAID (ch. 1947)	Denturius (ch. 1937)	Gold Bridge	Swynford or Golden Boss / Flying Diadem
		La Solfatara	Lemberg / Ayesha
	Laitron (ch. 1932)	Soldennis	Tredennis / Soligena
		Chardon	Aldford / Thistle

4   **ACACIO D'AGUILAR** 1 (ch.c., May 22, 1969)

Bred by J. de Souza-Lage, in France.

Won 4 races, placed 13, 849,785 fr., in France, Germany, Italy and U.S.A. from 3 to 5 years, incl. Preis von Europa; 2nd Prix Maurice de Nieuil; 3rd Gran Premio del Jockey Club; 4th Premio Roma, Grosser Preis von Nordrhein-Westfalen and Grosser Preis von Baden.

REFORM (b. 1964)	Pall Mall (ch. 1955)	Palestine	Fair Trial / Una
		Malapert	Portlaw / Malatesta
	Country House (br. 1955)	Vieux Manoir	Brantome / Vieille Maison
		Miss Coventry	Mieuxce / Coventry Belle
ALVORADA (ch. 1960)	Beau Prince II (ch. 1952)	Prince Chevalier	Prince Rose / Chevalerie
		Isabelle Brand	Black Devil / Isabelle d'Este
	Fair Dolly (b. 1945)	Hierocles	Abjer / Loika
		Farandole	Mon Talisman / Fete Royale

5   **ACAMAS** 13 (b.c., May 2, 1975)

Bred by Marcel Boussac, in France.

Won 3 races, placed 2, 1,615,000 fr., in France at 2 and 3 years, incl. Prix du Jockey-Club and Prix Lupin; 2nd Prix Greffulhe; 3rd Grand Criterium.

MILL REEF (b. 1968)	Never Bend (b. 1960)	Nasrullah	Nearco / Mumtaz Begum
		Lalun	Djeddah / Be Faithful
	Milan Mill (b. 1962)	Princequillo	Prince Rose / Cosquilla
		Virginia Water	Count Fleet / Red Ray
LICATA (b. 1969)	Abdos (br. 1959)	Arbar	Djebel / Astronomie
		Pretty Lady	Umidwar / La Moqueuse
	Gaia (br. 1962)	Shantung	Sicambre / Barley Corn
		Gloriana	Pharis II / Tourzima

6   **ACCRALE** 19 (b.c., February 3, 1962)

Bred by Limestone Stud, in England.

Won 4 races, placed 5, 38,848,000 L., in Italy at 3 years, incl. Gran Premio d'Italia and Gran Premio di Milano; 3rd Premio Ambrosiano.

VANDALE II (b. 1943)	Plassy (b. 1932)	Bosworth	Son-in-Law / Serenissima
		Pladda	Phalaris / Rothesay Bay
	Vanille (b. 1929)	La Farina	Sans Souci II / Malatesta
		Vaya	Beppo / Waterhen
ACCRUED (b. 1953)	Umidwar (b. 1931)	Blandford	Swynford / Blanche
		Uganda	Bridaine / Hush
	Fair Emma (ch. 1943)	Solario	Gainsborough / Sun Worship
		Fair Venus	Fairway / Wings of Love

7   ACE OF ACES 8 (b.c., March 21, 1970)

Bred by John R. Gaines, in U.S.A.

Won 6 races, placed 11, £65,347, in France, England, Germany and U.S.A., at 3 and 4 years, incl. Sussex Stakes, Prix du Chemin de Fer du Nord, Oettingen-Rennen; 2nd Prix de la Porte Maillot, Prix de l'Abbaye de Longchamp; 3rd Prix Eugene Adam; 4th Prix du Moulin de Longchamp.

VAGUELY NOBLE (b. 1965)	Vienna (ch. 1957)	Aureole	Hyperion
			Angelola
		Turkish Blood	Turkhan
			Rusk
	Noble Lassie (b. 1956)	Nearco	Pharos
			Nogara
		Belle Sauvage	Big Game
			Tropical Sun
SOFARSOGOOD (b. 1952)	Revoked (b. or br. 1943)	Blue Larkspur	Black Servant
			Blossom Time
		Gala Belle	Sir Gallahad III
			Bel Tempo
	Apogee (b. 1934)	Pharamond	Phalaris
			Selene
		Summit	Ultimus
			Torpenhow

8   ACK ACK 9 (b.c., February 24, 1966)

Bred by Capt. H. F. Guggenheim, in U.S.A.

Won 19 races, placed 8, $636,641, in U.S.A. from 2 to 5 years, incl. Hollywood Gold Cup, Santa Anita H., Arlington Classic, Withers Stakes, Los Angeles H., American H., San Antonio Stakes, San Carlos H. and San Pasqual H.; 2nd Jersey Derby.

BATTLE JOINED (b. 1959)	Armageddon (b. 1949)	Alsab	Good Goods
			Winds Chant
		Fighting Lady	Sir Gallahad III
			Lady Nicotine
	Ethel Walker (b. 1953)	Revoked	Blue Larkspur
			Gala Belle
		Ethel Terry	Reaping Reward
			Mary Terry
FAST TURN (b. 1959)	Turn-to (b. 1951)	Royal Charger	Nearco
			Sun Princess
		Source Sucree	Admiral Drake
			Lavendula II
	Cherokee Rose (b. 1951)	Princequillo	Prince Rose
			Cosquilla
		The Squaw II	Sickle
			Minnewaska

9   ADEN 8 (b.c., February 14, 1975)

Bred by Voskhod Stud, in U.S.S.R.

Won 4 races, placed 7, 322,160 DM and 13,020 points, in Germany, U.S.S.R. and Poland at 2 and 3 years, incl. Preis von Europa and Prize of the Congress, Warsaw; 2nd Preis des Landes Nordrhein-Westfalen and Budapest Prize; 3rd Russian Derby.

DERZKIY (ch. 1954)	Douglas (b. 1944)	Granit II	Tagor
			Glitsinia
		Drofa	Fairbairn
			Dahe
	Zapoved' (ch. 1945)	Press Gang	Hurry On
			Fifinella
		Zambezi	Ekonomist
			Zigota
ALFA (b. 1964)	Faktotum (br. 1952)	Harlekin	Magnat
			L'Heure Bleue
		Fruhlingssonne	Lampos
			Fruhlingsfee
	Akrobatika (ch. 1957)	Baltic Baron	Blanc
			Baalbek
		Anapa	Agregat
			Pantera II

10   ADMETUS 1 (ch.g., April 17, 1970)

Bred by Ballymacoll Stud Farm Ltd, in France.

Won 12 races, placed 11, £146,120, in England, France and U.S.A. from 3 to 6 years, incl. Prince of Wales Stakes, Prix Maurice de Nieuil, Grand Prix d'Evry, Washington D.C. International; 2nd Prix Dollar, Grand Prix de Deauville; 3rd Prix Exbury.

REFORM (b. 1964)	Pall Mall (ch. 1955)	Palestine	Fair Trial
			Una
		Malapert	Portlaw
			Malatesta
	Country House (br. 1955)	Vieux Manoir	Brantome
			Vieille Maison
		Miss Coventry	Mieuxce
			Coventry Belle
LA MILO (ch. 1963)	Hornbeam (ch. 1953)	Hyperion	Gainsborough
			Selene
		Thicket	Nasrullah
			Thorn Wood
	Pin Prick (b. 1955)	Pinza	Chanteur II
			Pasqua
		Miss Winston	Royal Charger
			East Wantleye

11   AFFIRMED 23 (ch.c., February 21, 1975)

Bred by Harbor View Farm, in U.S.A.

Won 22 races, placed 6, $2,393,818 in U.S.A. from 2 to 4 years, incl. Kentucky Derby, Preakness Stakes, Belmont Stakes, Santa Anita Derby, Hollywood Derby, Hopeful Stakes, Futurity Stakes, Laurel Futurity, Hollywood Juvenile Championship, Sanford Stakes, Jim Dandy Stakes, San Felipe H., Jockey Club Gold Cup, Hollywood Gold Cup, Santa Anita H., Woodward Stakes, Californian Stakes and Charles H. Strub Stakes; 2nd Marlboro Cup, Travers Stakes, Champagne Stakes and San Fernando Stakes; 3rd Malibu Stakes.

EXCLUSIVE NATIVE (ch. 1965)	Raise a Native (ch. 1961)	Native Dancer	Polynesian
			Geisha
		Raise You	Case Ace
			Lady Glory
	Exclusive (ch. 1953)	Shut Out	Equipoise
			Goose Egg
		Good Example	Pilate
			Parade Girl
WON'T TELL YOU (b. 1962)	Crafty Admiral (b. 1948)	Fighting Fox	Sir Gallahad III
			Marguerite
		Admiral's Lady	War Admiral
			Boola Brook
	Scarlet Ribbon (b. 1957)	Volcanic	Ambrose Light
			Hot Supper
		Native Valor	Mahmoud
			Native Gal

12   AFRICAN DANCER 7 (b.f., March 28, 1973)

Bred by Hascombe and Valiant Studs.

Won 2 races, placed 3, £31,269, in England, at 2 and 3 years, incl. Cheshire Oaks, Park Hill Stakes; 2nd Yorkshire Oaks; 3rd Oaks Stakes, Lancashire Oaks.

NIJINSKY (b. 1967)	Northern Dancer (b. 1961)	Nearctic	Nearco
			Lady Angela
		Natalma	Native Dancer
			Almahmoud
	Flaming Page (b. 1959)	Bull Page	Bull Lea
			Our Page
		Flaring Top	Menow
			Flaming Top
MIBA (b. 1962)	Ballymoss (ch. 1954)	Mossborough	Nearco
			All Moonshine
		Indian Call	Singapore
			Flittemere
	Stop Your Tickling (bl. 1949)	Jock II	Asterus
			Naic
		Senatrix	King Salmon
			Romulea

13   AFRICAN SKY 6 (b.c., March 3, 1970)

Bred by New England Stud, in England.

Won 6 races, placed 1, 661,619 fr., in France at 2 and 3 years, incl. Prix de la Foret, Prix du Palais Royal, Prix Quincey and Prix de Fontainebleau; 4th Poule d'Essai des Poulains.

SING SING (b. 1957)	Tudor Minstrel (br. 1944)	Owen Tudor	Hyperion / Mary Tudor II
		Sansonnet	Sansovino / Lady Juror
	Agin the Law (b. 1946)	Portlaw	Beresford / Portree
		Revolte	Xandover / Sheba
SWEET CAROLINE (b. 1954)	Nimbus (b. 1946)	Nearco	Pharos / Nogara
		Kong	Baytown / Clang
	Lackaday (b. 1947)	Bobsleigh	Gainsborough / Toboggan
		Lackadaisy	Felstead / Complacent

14   AFRICAN SONG 12 (b.c., March 19, 1977)

Bred by W. Moloney.

Won 2 races, placed 2, £37,131, in England, at 3 years, incl. King's Stand Stakes; 3rd Duke of York Stakes.

AFRICAN SKY (b. 1970)	Sing Sing (b. 1957)	Tudor Minstrel	Owen Tudor / Sansonnet
		Agin the Law	Portlaw / Revolte
	Sweet Caroline (b. 1954)	Nimbus	Nearco / Kong
		Lackaday	Bobsleigh / Lackadaisy
GOLDWYN PRINCESS (b. 1970)	Native Prince (b. 1964)	Native Dancer	Polynesian / Geisha
		Sungari	Eight Thirty / Swabia
	Goldwyn Girl (ch. 1953)	Court Martial	Fair Trial / Instantaneous
		Zolotaia	Gold Bridge / Thamar

15   AGGRAVATE 11 (b.f., May 11, 1966)

Bred by Worksop Manor Stud Farm.

Won 3 races, placed 3, £7,962, in England, at 2 and 3 years, incl. Park Hill Stakes; 2nd Musidora Stakes; 4th Oaks Stakes.

AGGRESSOR (b. 1955)	Combat (br. 1944)	Big Game	Bahram / Myrobella
		Commotion	Mieuxce / Riot
	Phaetonia (ch. 1945)	Nearco	Pharos / Nogara
		Phaetusa	Hyperion / Saddle Tor
RAVEN LOCKS (bl. 1945)	Mr. Jinks (gr. 1926)	Tetratema	The Tetrarch / Scotch Gift
		False Piety	Lemberg / St. Begoe
	Gentlemen's Relish (bl./br. 1926)	He	Santoi / She
		Bonne Bouche	Buchan / Dinner

16   AGGRESSOR 10 (b.c., March 6, 1955)

Bred by Someries Stud.

Won 11 races, placed 4, £37,282, in England, from 2 to 5 years, incl. King George VI and Queen Elizabeth Stakes, John Porter Stakes, Hardwicke Stakes, Cumberland Lodge Stakes.

COMBAT (br. 1944)	Big Game (b. 1939)	Bahram	Blandford / Friar's Daughter
		Myrobella	Tetratema / Dolabella
	Commotion (b. 1938)	Mieuxce	Massine / L'Olivete
		Riot	Colorado / Lady Juror
PHAETONIA (ch. 1945)	Nearco (br. 1935)	Pharos	Phalaris / Scapa Flow
		Nogara	Havresac II / Catnip
	Phaetusa (ch. 1937)	Hyperion	Gainsborough / Selene
		Saddle Tor	Hurry On / Leighon Tor

17   AHONOORA 1 (ch.c., April 12, 1975)

Bred by Wyld Court Stud

Won 7 races, placed 7, £86,589, in England, from 2 to 4 years, incl. William Hill Sprint Championship, King George Stakes; 2nd King's Stand Stakes, Vernons Sprint Cup, Temple Stakes.

LORENZACCIO (ch. 1965)	Klairon (b. 1952)	Clarion III	Djebel / Columba
		Kalmia	Kantar / Sweet Lavender
	Phoenissa (b. 1951)	The Phoenix	Chateau Bouscaut / Fille de Poete
		Erica Fragrans	Big Game / Jennydang
HELEN NICHOLS (ch. 1966)	Martial (ch. 1957)	Hill Gail	Bull Lea / Jane Gail
		Discipliner	Court Martial / Edvina
	Quaker Girl (gr. 1961)	Whistler	Panorama / Farthing Damages
		Mayflower	Borealis / Foliage

18   AKARI 16 (b.c., April 12, 1966)

Bred by Gestüt Ebbesloh, in Germany.

Won 5 races, placed 10, 174,990 DM., in Germany, from 2 to 4 years, incl. Aral-Pokal and Union-Rennen; 2nd Grosser Preis von Nordrhein-Westfalen; 3rd Spreti-Rennen; 4th Aral-Pokal.

BIRKHAHN (br. 1945)	Alchimist (br. 1930)	Herold	Dark Ronald / Hornisse
		Aversion	Nuage / Antwort
	Bramouse (b. 1936)	Cappiello	Apelle / Kopje
		Peregrine	Phalaris / Clotho
ARONA (b. 1958)	Asterios (b. 1947)	Oleander	Prunus / Orchidee II
		Astarte	Janitor / Arabeske
	Alte (b. 1946)	Lampos	Fervor / Lady Love
		Aktinie	Herold / Atalante

19   **ALARICH** 2 (b.c., March 19, 1957)

Bred by Gestüt Rösler, in Germany

Won 4 races, placed 11, 112,600 DM., in Germany, from 2 to 5 years, incl. Deutsches Derby; 2nd Preis des Winterfavoriten; 3rd Union-Rennen.

MANGON (br. 1949)	Gundomar (br. 1948)	Alchimist	Herold / Aversion
		Grossularia	Aurelius / Grollenicht
	Mainkur (b. 1940)	Janus	Buchan / Jane Pierney
		Makrone	Graf Ferry / Makrele
ALMA MATER (b. 1950)	Ticino (b. 1939)	Athanasius	Ferro / Athanasie
		Terra	Aditi / Teufelsrose
	Alex (ch. 1939)	Louqsor	Aethelstan / Lapis Lazuli
		Tiara	Flying Orb / Donnetta

20   **ALCAEUS** 16 (ch.c., May 20, 1957)

Bred by Banstead Manor Stud Ltd.

Won 2 races, placed 3, £8,887, in England and Ireland, from 2 to 4 years, incl. Dee Stakes, Ormonde Stakes; 2nd Derby Stakes, Irish Derby Stakes.

ALYCIDON (ch. 1945)	Donatello II (ch. 1934)	Blenheim	Blandford / Malva
		Delleana	Clarissimus / Duccia di Buoninsegna
	Aurora (ch. 1936)	Hyperion	Gainsborough / Selene
		Rose Red	Swynford / Marchetta
MARTELINE (ch. 1948)	Court Martial (ch. 1942)	Fair Trial	Fairway / Lady Juror
		Instantaneous	Hurry On / Picture
	Meraline (ch. 1939)	Mieuxce	Massine / L'Olivete
		Merina	Chateau Bouscaut / Merry Legend

21   **ALLANGRANGE** 5 (ch.c., March 8, 1967)

Bred by Joseph McGrath, jun.

Won 5 races, £16,146, in Ireland, at 2 and 3 years, incl. Irish St. Leger.

LE LEVANSTELL (b. 1957)	Le Lavandou (b. 1944)	Djebel	Tourbillon / Loika
		Lavande	Rustom Pasha / Livadia
	Stella's Sister (ch. 1950)	Ballyogan	Fair Trial / Serial
		My Aid	Knight of the Garter / Flying Aid
SILKEN PRINCESS (ch. 1956)	Arctic Prince (br. 1948)	Prince Chevalier	Prince Rose / Chevalerie
		Arctic Sun	Nearco / Solar Flower
	Silken Slipper (b. 1943)	Bois Roussel	Vatout / Plucky Liege
		Carpet Slipper	Phalaris / Simon's Shoes

22   **ALLEGED** 2 (b.c., May 4, 1974)

Bred by Mrs. June H. McKnight, in U.S.A.

Won 9 races, placed 1, £338,614, in England, Ireland and France, from 2 to 4 years, incl. Prix de l'Arc de Triomphe (twice), Great Voltigeur Stakes, Gallinule Stakes, Royal Whip Stakes (twice), Prix du Prince d'Orange; 2nd St. Leger Stakes.

HOIST THE FLAG (b. 1968)	Tom Rolfe (b. 1962)	Ribot	Tenerani / Romanella
		Pocahontas	Roman / How
	Wavy Navy (b. 1954)	War Admiral	Man o'War / Brushup
		Triomphe	Tourbillon / Melibee
PRINCESS POUT (b. 1966)	Prince John (ch. 1953)	Princequillo	Prince Rose / Cosquilla
		Not Afraid	Count Fleet / Banish Fear
	Determined Lady (b. 1959)	Determine	Alibhai / Koubis
		Tumbling	War Admiral / Up The Hill

23   **ALLEZ FRANCE** 1 (b.f. May 24, 1970)

Bred by Bieber-Jacobs Stable, in U.S.A.

Won 13 races, placed 5, 6,254,162 fr., in France and England, from 2 to 5 years, incl. Prix de l'Arc de Triomphe, Prix de Diane, Poule d'Essai des Pouliches, Prix Vermeille, Prix Ganay (twice), Criterium des Pouliches, Prix d'Ispahan, Prix d'Harcourt, Prix Dollar and Prix Foy (twice); 2nd Prix de l'Arc de Triomphe and Champion Stakes (twice); 3rd Prix d'Ispahan.

SEA BIRD II (ch. 1962)	Dan Cupid (ch. 1956)	Native Dancer	Polynesian / Geisha
		Vixenette	Sickle / Lady Reynard
	Sicalade (b. 1956)	Sicambre	Prince Bio / Sif
		Marmelade	Maurepas / Couleur
PRICELESS GEM (b./br. 1963)	Hail to Reason (br. 1958)	Turn-to	Royal Charger / Source Sucree
		Nothirdchance	Blue Swords / Galla Colors
	Searching (b. 1952)	War Admiral	Man o'War / Brushup
		Big Hurry	Black Toney / La Troienne

24   **ALMIRANTA** 1 (ch.f., April 15, 1959)

Bred by Lord Howard de Walden.

Won 2 races, placed 1, £11,010, in England, at 3 years, incl. Park Hill Stakes, Princess Elizabeth Stakes; 2nd Yorkshire Oaks.

ALYCIDON (ch. 1945)	Donatello II (ch. 1934)	Blenheim	Blandford / Malva
		Delleana	Clarissimus / Duccia di Buoninsegna
	Aurora (ch. 1936)	Hyperion	Gainsborough / Selene
		Rose Red	Swynford / Marchetta
ROSARIO (b. 1954)	Nearco (br. 1935)	Pharos	Phalaris / Scapa Flow
		Nogara	Havresac II / Catnip
	Sanlinea (ch. 1947)	Precipitation	Hurry On / Double Life
		Sun Helmet	Hyperion / Point Duty

25   ALPENKÖNIG 2 (b.c., April 3, 1967)

Bred by Gestüt Schlenderhan, in Germany.

Won 7 races, placed 4, 426,700 DM., in Germany, at 2 and 3 years, incl. Deutsches Derby, Grosser Preis von Nordrhein-Westfalen, Aral-Pokal and Grosser Preis von Baden; 2nd Preis der Winterfavoriten; 3rd Union-Rennen.

TAMERLANE (br. 1952)	Persian Gulf (b. 1940)	Bahram	Blandford / Friar's Daughter
		Double Life	Bachelor's Double / Saint Joan
	Eastern Empress (b. 1944)	Nearco	Pharos / Nogara
		Cheveley Lady	Solario / Lady Marjorie
ALPENLERCHE (br. 1962)	Birkhahn (br. 1945)	Alchimist	Herold / Aversion
		Bramouse	Cappiello / Peregrine
	Ascona (b. 1956)	Mangon	Gundomar / Mainkur
		Alma mater	Ticino / Alex

26   ALTESSE ROYALE 1 (ch.f., April 25, 1968)

Bred by Colonel and Mrs. F. R. Hue-Williams.

Won 4 races, placed 1, £76,884, in England and Ireland, at 2 and 3 years, incl. Oaks Stakes, Irish Guinness Oaks, 1,000 Guineas Stakes; 2nd Nell Gwyn Stakes.

SAINT CRESPIN III (ch. 1956)	Aureole (ch. 1950)	Hyperion	Gainsborough / Selene
		Angelola	Donatello II / Feola
	Neocracy (b. 1944)	Nearco	Pharos / Nogara
		Harina	Blandford / Athasi
BLEU AZUR (ch. 1959)	Crepello (ch. 1954)	Donatello II	Blenheim / Delleana
		Crepuscule	Mieuxce / Red Sunset
	Blue Prelude (br. 1951)	Blue Peter	Fairway / Fancy Free
		Keyboard	Bois Roussel / Keystone

27   ALTHREY DON 1 (gr.c., March 20, 1961)

Bred by J. Leavy.

Won 6 races, £7,638, in England, from 2 to 5 years, incl. Nunthorpe Stakes.

FIGHTING DON (b. 1942)	Fighting Fox (b. 1935)	Sir Gallahad III	Teddy / Plucky Liege
		Marguerite	Celt / Fairy Ray
	Bird Nest (b. 1929)	Mad Hatter	Fair Play / Madcap
		Tree Top	Ultimus / Thirty-third
SLAINTE (gr. 1953)	Magic Red (gr. 1941)	Link Boy	Pharos / Market Girl
		Infra Red	Ethnarch / Black Ray
	Salvia (br. 1939)	Sansovino	Swynford / Gondolette
		Love in the Mist	Buchan / Ecstasy

28   ALYDAR 9 (ch.c., March 23, 1975)

Bred by Calumet Farm, in U.S.A.

Won 14 races, placed 10, $957,195, in U.S.A., from 2 to 4 years, incl. Florida Derby, Champagne Stakes, Sapling Stakes, Blue Grass Stakes, Flamingo Stakes, Travers Stakes, Whitney Stakes, Arlington Classic Invitational H. and Nassau H.; 2nd Kentucky Derby, Preakness Stakes, Belmont Stakes, Futurity Stakes, Hopeful Stakes, Remsen Stakes, Laurel Futurity, Carter H. and Oaklawn H.; 3rd Suburban H.

RAISE A NATIVE (ch. 1961)	Native Dancer (gr. 1950)	Polynesian	Unbreakable / Black Polly
		Geisha	Discovery / Miyako
	Raise You (ch. 1946)	Case Ace	Teddy / Sweetheart
		Lady Glory	American Flag / Beloved
SWEET TOOTH (b. 1965)	On-and-On (b. 1956)	Nasrullah	Nearco / Mumtaz Begum
		Two Lea	Bull Lea / Two Bob
	Plum Cake (ch. 1958)	Ponder	Pensive / Miss Rushin
		Real Delight	Bull Lea / Blue Delight

29   AMBERGRIS 22 (ch.f., February 3, 1958)

Bred by Sir Percy Loraine and R. More O'Ferrall.

Won 6 races, placed 4, £16,120, in Ireland and England, at 2 and 3 years, incl. Irish Oaks, Champagne Stakes, Musidora Stakes; 2nd Oaks Stakes, 1,000 Guineas Stakes; 3rd Coronation Stakes.

SICAMBRE (br. 1948)	Prince Bio (b. 1941)	Prince Rose	Rose Prince / Indolence
		Biologie	Bacteriophage / Eponge
	Sif (br. 1936)	Rialto	Rabelais / La Grelee
		Suavita	Alcantara II / Shocking
QUARTERDECK (b. 1947)	Nearco (br. 1935)	Pharos	Phalaris / Scapa Flow
		Nogara	Havresac II / Catnip
	Poker Chip (ch. 1937)	The Recorder	Captain Cuttle / Lady Juror
		Straight Sequence	Stratford / Little Flutter

30   AMBEROID 8 (b. or br.c., April 8, 1963)

Bred by Dr. Horace N. Davis, in U.S.A.

Won 7 races, placed 15, $491,716, in U.S.A., from 2 to 4 years, incl. Belmont Stakes, Wood Memorial Stakes and Queen's County H., 2nd Remsen Stakes, New Hampshire Sweepstakes, Travers Stakes, Fountain of Youth Stakes, Amory L. Haskell H., Gulfstream Park H. and Grey Lag H.; 3rd Preakness Stakes, Garden State Stakes and Pimlico Futurity.

COUNT AMBER (b. 1957)	Ambiorix II (b. 1946)	Tourbillon	Ksar / Durban
		Lavendula	Pharos / Sweet Lavender
	Quick Touch (ch. 1946)	Count Fleet	Reigh Count / Quickly
		Alms	St. Brideaux / Bonus
SPENCERIAN (b. 1956)	Destino (br. 1947)	Beau Pere	Son-in-Law / Cinna
		Sun Lady	Sun Teddy / Lady Lark
	Script (b. 1950)	Bimelech	Black Toney / La Troienne
		Inscribe	Brazado / Inscoelda

31   AMBER RAMA 1 (ch.c, April 30, 1967)

Bred by Mrs. P. A. B. Widener II, in U.S.A.

Won 4 races, placed 3, £49,313, in France and England, at 2 and 3 years, incl. Prix Robert Papin, Prix Morny, King's Stand Stakes; 2nd Prix de Seine-et-Oise; 4th 2,000 Guineas Stakes.

JAIPUR (b. 1959)	Nasrullah (b. 1940)	Nearco	Pharos
			Nogara
		Mumtaz Begum	Blenheim
			Mumtaz Mahal
	Rare Perfume (b. 1947)	Eight Thirty	Pilate
			Dinner Time
		Fragrance	Sir Gallahad III
			Rosebloom
PINK SILK (ch. 1957)	Spy Song (br. 1943)	Balladier	Black Toney
			Blue Warbler
		Mata Hari	Peter Hastings
			War Woman
	Bayrose (b. 1949)	Sir Gallahad III	Teddy
			Plucky Liege
		Artistic Rose	Challenger II
			Dogana

32   AMPNEY PRINCESS 14 (b.f., March 4, 1960)

Bred by Park Farm Stud.

Won 5 races, placed 10, £6,195, in England, from 2 to 6 years, incl. Diadem Stakes; 3rd Chesham Stakes.

WILWYN (b. 1948)	Pink Flower (b. 1940)	Oleander	Prunus
			Orchidee II
		Plymstock	Polymelus
			Winkipop
	Saracen (b. 1943)	Donatello II	Blenheim
			Delleana
		Lovely Rosa	Tolgus
			Napoule
FAMA (b. 1950)	Fair Trial (ch. 1932)	Fairway	Phalaris
			Scapa Flow
		Lady Juror	Son-in-Law
			Lady Josephine
	Seed (br. 1940)	Solario	Gainsborough
			Sun Worship
		Mirawala	Phalaris
			Miranda

33   ANCASTA 9 (ch.f., February 2, 1961)

Bred by F. W. Burmann

Won 3 races, placed 2, £14,506, in England and Ireland, at 2 and 3 years, incl. Irish Guinness Oaks, Pretty Polly Stakes (Curragh); 2nd Park Hill Stakes; 3rd Yorkshire Oaks.

BALLYMOSS (ch. 1954)	Mossborough (ch. 1947)	Nearco	Pharos
			Nogara
		All Moonshine	Bobsleigh
			Selene
	Indian Call (ch. 1936)	Singapore	Gainsborough
			Tetrabbazia
		Flittemere	Buchan
			Keysoe
ANYTE II (ch. 1950)	Pharis II (br. 1936)	Pharos	Phalaris
			Scapa Flow
		Carissima	Clarissimus
			Casquetts
	Theano (b. 1940)	Tourbillon	Ksar
			Durban
		Souryva	Gainsborough
			L'Esperance

34   ANCIENT REGIME 15 (gr.f., April 4, 1978)

Bred by General Agricultural Services Ltd., in U.S.A.

Won 2 races, placed 2, 382,600 fr., in France and England at 2 years, incl. Prix Morny; 2nd Prix Robert Papin; 4th Queen Mary Stakes.

OLDEN TIMES (b. 1958)	Relic (bl. 1945)	War Relic	Man o'War
			Friar's Carse
		Bridal Colors	Black Toney
			Vaila
	Djenne (b. 1950)	Djebel	Tourbillon
			Loika
		Teza	Jock II
			Torissima
CATERINA (gr. 1963)	Princely Gift (b. 1951)	Nasrullah	Nearco
			Mumtaz Begum
		Blue Gem	Blue Peter
			Sparkle
	Radiopye (gr. 1954)	Bright News	Stardust
			Inkling
		Silversol	Solenoid
			Silver Lady

35   ANCIENT TITLE 8 (b./br.g., April 19, 1970)

Bred by Mr. and Mrs. William Kirkland, in U.S.A.

Won 24 races, placed 20, $1,252,791, in U.S.A. from 2 to 8 years, incl. Hollywood Gold Cup, Californian Stakes (twice), Charles H. Strub Stakes, Whitney Stakes, San Antonio Stakes, Del Mar Invitational H., Bel Air H., Caballero H., San Carlos H., San Fernando Stakes, San Vicente Stakes, Los Angeles H., Malibu Stakes, Sunny Slope Stakes and San Pasqual H.; 2nd Santa Anita H. (twice), Hollywood Gold Cup, Californian Stakes, Caballero H., Will Rogers H., San Antonio Stakes, San Felipe H. and San Jacinto Stakes; 3rd Californian Stakes, Oak Tree Invitational, Marlboro Cup, Governor Stakes, American H. and San Antonio Stakes.

GUMMO (b. 1962)	Fleet Nasrullah (b. 1955)	Nasrullah	Nearco
			Mumtaz Begum
		Happy Go Fleet	Count Fleet
			Draeh
	Alabama Gal (b. 1957)	Determine	Alibhai
			Koubis
		Trojan Lass	Priam III
			Rompers
HI LITTLE GAL (b. 1963)	Bar Le Duc (ch. 1953)	Alibhai	Hyperion
			Teresina
		Boudoir II	Mahmoud
			Kampala
	Salma (br. 1954)	Salmagundi	Hash
			Manatella
		Born Fool	Bull Lea
			Boys I'm It

36   ANILIN 27 (b.c., January 31, 1961)

Bred by Voskhod Stud, in U.S.S.R.

Won 22 races, placed 3, 738,835 DM., in U.S.S.R., Germany, East Germany and U.S.A. from 2 to 6 years, incl. Preis von Europa (3 times), Grand Prize of the Socialist Countries (twice) and Russian Derby; 2nd Washington D.C. International; 3rd Washington D.C. International.

ELEMENT (b. 1952)	Etalon Or (ch. 1936)	Massine	Consols
			Mauri
		La Savoyarde	Filibert de Savoie
			La Balladeuse
	Margaritka (b. 1944)	Gainslaw	Winalot
			Margaret Burr
		Macedonja	Mah Jong
			Cylicja
ANALOGICHNAYA (ch. 1953)	Agregat (b. 1943)	Artist's Proof	Gainsborough
			Clear Evidence
		Abeba	Balbinus
			Az A Hired
	Giurza (ch. 1938)	Zator	Tagor
			Zia
		Gagara II	Getman Ney
			Gortenzja

37   ANNE LA DOUCE 1 (b.f., February 13, 1958)

Bred by P. Boyriven, in France.

Won 3½ races, placed 6, £12,944, in France and England, at 2 and 3 years, incl. Prix Vermeille (dead-heat); 2nd Prix de Pomone; 3rd Oaks Stakes.

```
                        ┌ Fastnet         ┌ Pharos          ┌ Phalaris
SILNET                  │ (b. or br. 1933)│                 └ Scapa Flow
(b. 1949)               │                 └ Tatoule         ┌ Alcantara II
                        │                                   └ Titanite
                        │                 ┌ King Salmon     ┌ Salmon-Trout
                        └ Silver Jill      │                └ Malva
                          (b. 1939)        └ Jilt           ┌ Obliterate
                                                            └ Amourette

                        ┌ Tehran          ┌ Bois Roussel    ┌ Vatout
SWEET ANNE              │ (b. 1941)        │                └ Plucky Liege
(ch. 1950)              │                 └ Stafaralla      ┌ Solario
                        │                                   └ Mirawala
                        └ Cheerful Anne   ┌ Bahram          ┌ Blandford
                          (b. 1939)        │                └ Friar's Daughter
                                          └ Anne of Brittany┌ Diligence
                                                            └ Tres Bonne
```

38   ANNE'S PRETENDER 1 (ch.c., March 17, 1972)

Bred by Sir Charles Clore, in U.S.A.

Won 6 races, placed 16, £162,245, in England, Ireland, France and U.S.A., from 2 to 5 years, incl. Prince of Wales Stakes, Brigadier Gerard Stakes, Prix Niel, Century H.; 2nd Ladbroke Derby Trial Stakes, Prix Eugene Adam, American H., San Marcos H.; 3rd Irish Sweeps Derby, Joe Coral Eclipse Stakes, Queen Elizabeth II Stakes, Hollywood Invitational H., San Luis Obispo H.; 4th Derby Stakes, San Juan Capistrano Invitational H.

```
                        ┌ Endeavour II    ┌ British Empire  ┌ Colombo
PRETENSE                │ (br. 1942)       │                └ Rose of England
(b./br. 1963)           │                 └ Himalaya        ┌ Hunter's Moon
                        │                                   └ Partenope
                        └ Imitation       ┌ Hyperion        ┌ Gainsborough
                          (ch. 1951)       │                └ Selene
                                          └ Flattery        ┌ Winalot
                                                            └ Fickle

                        ┌ Silnet          ┌ Fastnet         ┌ Pharos
ANNE LA DOUCE           │ (b. 1949)        │                └ Tatoule
(b. 1958)               │                 └ Silver Jill     ┌ King Salmon
                        │                                   └ Jilt
                        └ Sweet Anne      ┌ Tehran          ┌ Bois Roussel
                          (ch. 1950)       │                └ Stafaralla
                                          └ Cheerful Anne   ┌ Bahram
                                                            └ Anne of Brittany
```

39   ANTELAMI 7 (b.c., 1959)

Bred by Razza Dormello-Olgiata, in Italy.

Won 8 races, placed 4, 49,500,000 L., in Italy from 2 to 4 years, incl. Derby Italiano, Gran Premio d'Italia and Premio Presidente della Repubblica; 2nd Premio Emanuele Filiberto.

```
                        ┌ Blue Peter      ┌ Fairway         ┌ Phalaris
BOTTICELLI              │ (ch. 1936)       │                └ Scapa Flow
(b. 1951)               │                 └ Fancy Free      ┌ Stefan the Great
                        │                                   └ Celiba
                        └ Buonamica       ┌ Niccolo Dell'Arca ┌ Coronach
                          (b. 1943)        │                  └ Nogara
                                          └ Bernina         ┌ Pharos
                                                            └ Bunworry

                        ┌ Traghetto       ┌ Cavaliere d'Arpino ┌ Havresac II
ALLEGRA                 │ (ch. 1942)       │                    └ Chuette
(ch. 1949)              │                 └ Talma           ┌ Papyrus
                        │                                   └ Tolbooth
                        └ Aspertina       ┌ Ortello         ┌ Teddy
                          (ch. 1938)       │                └ Hollebeck
                                          └ Nuwara Eliya    ┌ Craig an Eran
                                                            └ Alista
```

40   APALACHEE 5 (b.c., February 8, 1971)

Bred by Claiborne Farm, in U.S.A.

Won 4 races, placed 1, £40,754, in Ireland and England, at 2 and 3 years, incl. Observer Gold Cup, Gladness Stakes; 3rd 2,000 Guineas Stakes.

```
                        ┌ Princequillo    ┌ Prince Rose     ┌ Rose Prince
ROUND TABLE             │ (b. 1940)        │                └ Indolence
(b. 1954)               │                 └ Cosquilla       ┌ Papyrus
                        │                                   └ Quick Thought
                        └ Knight's Daughter ┌ Sir Cosmo     ┌ The Boss
                          (b. 1941)          │              └ Ayn Hali
                                            └ Feola         ┌ Friar Marcus
                                                            └ Aloe

                        ┌ Nantallah       ┌ Nasrullah       ┌ Nearco
MOCCASIN                │ (b. 1953)        │                └ Mumtaz Begum
(ch. 1963)              │                 └ Shimmer         ┌ Flares
                        │                                   └ Broad Ripple
                        └ Rough Shod      ┌ Gold Bridge     ┌ Swynford or Golden Boss
                          (b. 1944)        │                └ Flying Diadem
                                          └ Dalmary         ┌ Blandford
                                                            └ Simon's Shoes
```

41   APPIANI II 4 (b.c., May 20, 1963)

Bred by Razza Dormello-Olgiata, in Italy.

Won 7 races, placed 6, 55,632,623 L., in Italy and England, from 2 to 4 years, incl. Derby Italiano and Premio Presidente della Repubblica; 2nd Gran Premio di Milano; 3rd Eclipse Stakes; 4th King George VI and Queen Elizabeth Stakes and Gran Premio d'Italia.

```
                        ┌ Vandale II      ┌ Plassy          ┌ Bosworth
HERBAGER                │ (b. 1943)        │                └ Pladda
(b. 1956)               │                 └ Vanille         ┌ La Farina
                        │                                   └ Vaya
                        └ Flagette        ┌ Escamillo       ┌ Firdaussi
                          (ch. 1951)       │                └ Estoril
                                          └ Fidgette        ┌ Firdaussi
                                                            └ Boxeuse

                        ┌ Rockefella      ┌ Hyperion        ┌ Gainsborough
ANGELA RUCELLAI         │ (br. 1941)       │                └ Selene
(b. 1954)               │                 └ Rockfel         ┌ Felstead
                        │                                   └ Rockliffe
                        └ Aristareta      ┌ Niccolo Dell'Arca ┌ Coronach
                          (ch. 1947)       │                  └ Nogara
                                          └ Acquaforte      ┌ Blenheim
                                                            └ Althea
```

42   APPRENTICE 19 (ch.g., April 4, 1960)

Bred by H.M. The Queen.

Won 2 races, placed 4, £7,023, in England, from 3 to 8 years, incl. Yorkshire Cup, Goodwood Cup; 2nd Queen Alexandra Stakes (twice); 3rd Queen's Vase.

```
                        ┌ Hyperion        ┌ Gainsborough    ┌ Bayardo
AUREOLE                 │ (ch. 1930)       │                └ Rosedrop
(ch. 1950)              │                 └ Selene          ┌ Chaucer
                        │                                   └ Serenissima
                        └ Angelola        ┌ Donatello II    ┌ Blenheim
                          (b. 1945)        │                └ Delleana
                                          └ Feola           ┌ Friar Marcus
                                                            └ Aloe

                        ┌ Foxhunter       ┌ Foxlaw          ┌ Son-in-Law
YOUNG ENTRY             │ (ch. 1929)       │                └ Alope
(ch. 1945)              │                 └ Trimestral      ┌ William the Third
                        │                                   └ Mistrella
                        └ Fair Venus      ┌ Fairway         ┌ Phalaris
                          (b. 1937)        │                └ Scapa Flow
                                          └ Wings of Love   ┌ Gay Crusader
                                                            └ Flying Sally
```

43   APPROVAL 1 (ch.c., February 20, 1967)

Bred by Newsells Stud Co.

Won 2 races, placed 2, £23,223, in England, at 2 and 3 years, incl. Observer Gold Cup, Dante Stakes.

ALCIDE (b. 1955)	Alycidon (ch. 1945)	Donatello II	Blenheim / Delleana
		Aurora	Hyperion / Rose Red
	Chenille (br. 1940)	King Salmon	Salmon-Trout / Malva
		Sweet Aloe	Cameronian / Aloe
SUCCESS (b. or br. 1955)	Arctic Prince (br. 1948)	Prince Chevalier	Prince Rose / Chevalerie
		Arctic Sun	Nearco / Solar Flower
	Lake Success (b. 1946)	Hyperion	Gainsborough / Selene
		Lucerne	Sansovino / Lake Leman

44   ARCOR 13 (b.c., March 17, 1959)

Bred by Marcel Boussac, in France.

Won 3 races, placed 2, £18,370, in England and France, at 3 and 4 years, incl. Prix du Conseil Municipal; 2nd Derby Stakes, Grand Prix de Marseille.

ARBAR (b. 1944)	Djebel (b. 1937)	Tourbillon	Ksar / Durban
		Loika	Gay Crusader / Coeur à Coeur
	Astronomie (b. 1932)	Asterus	Teddy / Astrella
		Likka	Sardanapale / Diane Mallory
COREJADA (b. 1947)	Pharis II (br. 1936)	Pharos	Phalaris / Scapa Flow
		Carissima	Clarissimus / Casquetts
	Tourzima (b. 1939)	Tourbillon	Ksar / Durban
		Djezima	Asterus / Heldifann

45   ARCTIC STORM 2 (br.c., March 31, 1959)

Bred by Mrs. E. M. Carroll.

Won 4 races, placed 5, £27,937, in Ireland and England, at 2 and 3 years, incl. Irish 2,000 Guineas, Champion Stakes; 2nd Irish Derby, Anglesey Stakes, Phoenix Stakes (dead-heat); 3rd King George VI and Queen Elizabeth Stakes.

ARCTIC STAR (br. 1942)	Nearco (br. 1935)	Pharos	Phalaris / Scapa Flow
		Nogara	Havresac II / Catnip
	Serena (b. 1929)	Winalot	Son-in-Law / Gallenza
		Charmione	Captivation / Pearl of the Loch
RABINA (b. or br. 1939)	Blanding (br. 1931)	Blandford	Swynford / Blanche
		Flying home	Flying Orb or Barcadaile / Eryholme
	Rahab (b. 1929)	Passer	Spearmint / Lesbia
		Medford	Mediator / Wellford

46   ARCTIC TERN 2 (ch.c., May 11, 1973)

Bred by Keswick Stables, in U.S.A.

Won 4 races, placed 10, 1,147,280 fr., in France and England from 2 to 4 years, incl. Prix Ganay, Prix de Fontainebleau and Prix Thomas Bryon; 2nd Prix Lupin, Prix Niel and Prix Dollar; 3rd Prix d'Harcourt and Eclipse Stakes; 4th Champion Stakes.

SEA BIRD II (ch. 1962)	Dan Cupid (ch. 1956)	Native Dancer	Polynesian / Geisha
		Vixenette	Sickle / Lady Reynard
	Sicalade (b. 1956)	Sicambre	Prince Bio / Sif
		Marmelade	Maurepas / Couleur
BUBBLING BEAUTY (ch. 1961)	Hasty Road (b. 1951)	Roman	Sir Gallahad III / Buckup
		Traffic Court	Discovery / Traffic
	Almahmoud (ch. 1947)	Mahmoud	Blenheim / Mah Mahal
		Arbitrator	Peace Chance / Mother Goose

47   ARCTIC VALE 14 (br.c., March 28, 1959)

Bred by Mrs. J. J. Prendergast.

Won 5 races, placed 6, £13,816, in Ireland, England and France from 2 to 6 years, incl. Irish St. Leger, Ormonde Stakes; 2nd Chester Cup, Ebor Handicap, Doncaster Cup, Yorkshire Cup, Prix Jean Prat.

ARCTIC TIME (b. 1952)	Arctic Star (br. 1942)	Nearco	Pharos / Nogara
		Serena	Winalot / Charmione
	Dancing Time (b. 1938)	Colombo	Manna / Lady Nairne
		Show Girl	Son-in-Law / Comedy Star
MILL BABY (b. 1947)	Mazarin (b. 1938)	Mieuxce	Massine / L'Olivete
		Boiarinia	Viceroy / Vilna
	Irreverence (ch. 1938)	Singapore	Gainsborough / Tetrabbazia
		Reverentia	Grand Parade / Reverence

48   ARDALE 6 (b.c., May 12, 1968)

Bred by Dr. Carlo Vittadini, in Italy.

Won 4 races, placed 1, 57,370,000 L., in Italy, at 3 years, incl. Derby Italiano; 2nd Gran Premio d'Italia.

ACCRALE (b. 1962)	Vandale II (b. 1943)	Plassy	Bosworth / Pladda
		Vanille	La Farina / Vaya
	Accrued (b. 1953)	Umidwar	Blandford / Uganda
		Fair Emma	Solario / Fair Venus
ARANDENA (ch. 1962)	Worden II (ch. 1949)	Wild Risk	Rialto / Wild Violet
		Sans Tares	Sind / Tara
	Aranda (br. 1952)	Vatellor	Vatout / Lady Elinor
		Eyewash	Blue Peter / All Moonshine

49   ARDENT DANCER 1 (b.f., April 28, 1962)

Bred by J. P. Frost.

Won 2 races, £6,291, in Ireland and England, at 2 and 3 years, incl. Irish 1,000 Guineas Stakes.

BUISSON ARDENT (b. 1953)	Relic (bl. 1945)	War Relic	Man o' War / Friar's Carse
		Bridal Colors	Black Toney / Vaila
	Rose o'Lynn (b. 1944)	Pherozshah	Pharos / Mah Mahal
		Rocklyn	Easton / Rock Forrard
JUNE BALL (b. 1946)	Ballyogan (ch. 1939)	Fair Trial	Fairway / Lady Juror
		Serial	Solario / Booktalk
	Gala Water (b. or br. 1933)	Kirk-Alloway	Tracery / Cantrip
		Galaday II	Sir Gallahad III / Sunstep

50   ARGUMENT 12 (b.c., February 7, 1977)

Bred by M. and Mme. P. Ribes, in France.

Won 4 races, placed 6, 2,023,090 fr., in France, Belgium and U.S.A. at 2 and 3 years, incl. Washington D.C. International and Grand Prix Prince Rose, Ostende; 2nd Prix de l'Arc de Triomphe, Prix Lupin, Prix de la Cote Normande and Prix La Rochette; 3rd Poule d'Essai des Poulains.

KAUTOKEINO (b. 1967)	Relko (b. 1960)	Tanerko	Tantieme / La Divine
		Relance III	Relic / Polaire II
	Cranberry (b. 1957)	Aureole	Hyperion / Angelola
		Big Berry	Big Game / Red Briar
ARANTELLE (ch. 1966)	Tapioca (b. 1953)	Vandale II	Plassy / Vanille
		Semoule d'Or	Vatellor / Semoule Fine
	Neptune's Doll (ch. 1960)	Neptune II	Crafty Admiral / Timely Tune
		Dzena	Tornado / Doria

51   ARJON 2 (b.c., June 4, 1963)

Bred by Gestüt Quenhorn, in Germany.

Won 5 races, placed 9, 548,672 DM., in Germany and France from 2 to 5 years, incl. Preis von Europa and Prix Henry Delamarre; 2nd Deutsches Derby, Union-Rennen and Prix Maurice de Nieuil; 3rd Grand Prix de Deauville.

JANITOR (b. 1950)	Pharis II (br. 1936)	Pharos	Phalaris / Scapa Flow
		Carissima	Clarissimus / Casquetts
	Orlamonde (b. 1937)	Asterus	Teddy / Astrella
		Naic	Gainsborough / Only One
ASTRAL II (b. 1948)	Watling Street (b. 1939)	Fairway	Phalaris / Scapa Flow
		Ranai	Rabelais / Dark Sedge
	Stargrass (b. 1942)	Noble Star	Hapsburg / Hesper
		Grass Widow	Son-in-Law / Silver Grass

52   ARMISTICE 9 (b.c., May 5, 1959)

Bred by M. Goudchaux, in France.

Won 2 races, placed 4, 610,301 fr., in France, at 2 and 3 years, incl. Grand Prix de Paris; 2nd Grand Prix du Printemps.

WORDEN II (ch. 1949)	Wild Risk (b. 1940)	Rialto	Rabelais / La Grelee
		Wild Violet	Blandford / Wood Violet
	Sans Tares (ch. 1939)	Sind	Solario / Mirawala
		Tara	Teddy / Jean Gow
COMMEMORATION (b. 1953)	Vandale II (b. 1943)	Plassy	Bosworth / Pladda
		Vanille	La Farina / Vaya
	Anne Comnene (b. 1942)	Fair Copy	Fairway / Composure
		Aziyade	Herbalist / Farizade

53   ARRATOS 9 (b.c., March 23, 1969)

Bred by Gestüt Schlenderhan, in Germany.

Won 10 races, placed 13, 594,720 DM., in Germany from 2 to 5 years, incl. Aral-Pokal, Union-Rennen, Deutsches St. Leger, Grosser Preis von Nordrhein-Westfalen, Grosser Hansa Preis, Grosser Preis von Dusseldorf and Grosser Preis der Stadt Gelsenkirchen; 2nd Grosser Preis von Baden and Grosser Preis von Dusseldorf; 3rd Grosser Preis von Baden; 4th Aral-Pokal.

KRONZEUGE (b. 1961)	Neckar (bl. 1948)	Ticino	Athanasius / Terra
		Nixe	Arjaman / Nanon
	Kaiserkrone (b. 1952)	Nebelwerfer	Magnat / Newa
		Kaiserwurde	Bubbles / Katinka
ARALINA (br. 1964)	Birkhahn (br. 1945)	Alchimist	Herold / Aversion
		Bramouse	Cappiello / Peregrine
	Aralia (br. 1945)	Alchimist	Herold / Aversion
		Aster	Oleander / Arkebuse

54   ARTAIUS 14 (b.c., February 26, 1974)

Bred by Mrs. John W. Hanes, in U.S.A.

Won 3 races, placed 3, £134,013, in England, Ireland and France, at 2 and 3 years, incl. Joe Coral Eclipse Stakes, Sussex Stakes, Sandown Classic Trial Stakes; 2nd Benson and Hedges Gold Cup, Beresford Stakes, Prix du Jockey-Club.

ROUND TABLE (b. 1954)	Princequillo (b. 1940)	Prince Rose	Rose Prince / Indolence
		Cosquilla	Papyrus / Quick Thought
	Knight's Daughter (b. 1941)	Sir Cosmo	The Boss / Ayn Hali
		Feola	Friar Marcus / Aloe
STYLISH PATTERN (b. 1961)	My Babu (b. 1945)	Djebel	Tourbillon / Loika
		Perfume II	Badruddin / Lavendula II
	Sunset Gun (ch. 1955)	Hyperion	Gainsborough / Selene
		Ace of Spades	Atout Maitre / Brave Empress

55   ARTHUR 6 (b.c., April 23, 1967)

Bred by D. A. Hicks.

Won 5 races, placed 10, £23,081, in England, Germany and France from 2 to 5 years, incl. Prince of Wales Stakes, Westbury Stakes; 3rd Prix Exbury, Prix d'Harcourt, Prix du Muguet; 4th Grosser Preis von Nordrhein-Westfalen.

HENRY THE SEVENTH (ch. 1958)	King of the Tudors (ch. 1950)	Tudor Minstrel	Owen Tudor
			Sansonnet
		Glen Line	Blue Peter
			Scotia's Girl
	Vestal Girl (ch. 1948)	Fairy Prince	Fairway
			Cachalot
		Vestalia	Abbots Trace
			Vulpina
VACILLATE (b. 1950)	Verso II (b. 1940)	Pinceau	Alcantara II
			Aquarelle
		Variete	La Farina
			Vaya
	Meditation (ch. 1936)	Caerleon	Phalaris
			Canyon
		Serenissima	Minoru
			Gondolette

56   ARTS AND LETTERS 1 (ch.c., April 1, 1966)

Bred by Paul Mellon, in U.S.A.

Won 11 races, placed 7, $632,404, in U.S.A. from 2 to 4 years, incl. Belmont Stakes, Jockey Club Gold Cup, Metropolitan H., Travers Stakes, Woodward Stakes, Blue Grass Stakes, Everglades Stakes, Jim Dandy Stakes and Grey Lag H.; 2nd Kentucky Derby, Preakness Stakes, Flamingo Stakes, Florida Derby and Fountain of Youth Stakes.

RIBOT (b. 1952)	Tenerani (b. 1944)	Bellini	Cavaliere d'Arpino
			Bella Minna
		Tofanella	Apelle
			Try Try Again
	Romanella (ch. 1943)	El Greco	Pharos
			Gay Gamp
		Barbara Burrini	Papyrus
			Bucolic
ALL BEAUTIFUL (ch. 1959)	Battlefield (ch. 1948)	War Relic	Man o'War
			Friar's Carse
		Dark Display	Display
			Dark Loveliness
	Parlo (ch. 1951)	Heliopolis	Hyperion
			Drift
		Fairy Palace	Pilate
			Star Fairy

57   ART STYLE 10 (br.c., March 29, 1973)

Bred by Mrs. J. J. Prendergast, in Ireland.

Won 2 races, placed 2, 43,618,000 L., in Italy at 3 years, incl. Gran Premio d'Italia (dead-heat) and Premio Ambrosiano; 2nd Gran Premio di Milano.

LE LEVANSTELL (b. 1957)	Le Lavandou (b. 1944)	Djebel	Tourbillon
			Loika
		Lavande	Rustom Pasha
			Livadia
	Stella's Sister (ch. 1950)	Ballyogan	Fair Trial
			Serial
		My Aid	Knight of the Garter
			Flying Aid
ARCTRULLAH (br. 1958)	Great Captain (br. 1949)	War Admiral	Man o'War
			Brushup
		Big Hurry	Black Toney
			La Troienne
	Arctic Rullah (b. 1954)	Nasrullah	Nearco
			Mumtaz Begum
		Arctic Blue	Blue Peter
			Arctic Sun

58   ARYENNE 4 (br.f., April 28, 1977)

Bred by Paul Chedeville, in France.

Won 4 races, placed 2, 1,110,000 fr., in France at 2 and 3 years, incl. Poule d'Essai des Pouliches, Criterium des Pouliches and Prix de la Grotte; 2nd Prix de Diane de Revlon; 4th Prix Saint-Alary.

GREEN DANCER (b. 1972)	Nijinsky (b. 1967)	Northern Dancer	Nearctic
			Natalma
		Flaming Page	Bull Page
			Flaring Top
	Green Valley (b./br. 1967)	Val de Loir	Vieux Manoir
			Vali
		Sly Pola	Spy Song
			Ampola
AMERICAINE (ch. 1968)	Cambremont (br. 1962)	Sicambre	Prince Bio
			Sif
		Djebellica	Djebel
			Nica
	Alora (ch. 1954)	Ballyogan	Fair Trial
			Serial
		Agnès (ex Annamirl)	Biribi
			Anne de Bretagne

59   ASHMORE 8 (b.c., April 29, 1971)

Bred by Daniel Wildenstein, in France.

Won 6 races, placed 9, 1,654,186 fr., in France and England from 2 to 5 years, incl. Grand Prix de Deauville (twice) and Prix Jean de Chaudenay; 2nd Grand Prix de Saint-Cloud (twice) and Coronation Cup; 3rd Prix Royal Oak and Prix Maurice de Nieuil.

LUTHIER (br. 1965)	Klairon (b. 1952)	Clarion III	Djebel
			Columba
		Kalmia	Kantar
			Sweet Lavender
	Flute Enchantee (b. 1950)	Cranach	Coronach
			Reine Isaure
		Montagnana	Brantome
			Mauretania
ALMYRE (b. 1964)	Wild Risk (b. 1940)	Rialto	Rabelais
			La Grelee
		Wild Violet	Blandford
			Wood Violet
	Ad Gloriam (b. 1958)	Alizier	Teleferique
			Alizarine
		Ad Altiora	Labrador
			Ultima Ratio

60   ASTEC 5 (b.c., April 9, 1964)

Bred by Baron de la Rochette, in France.

Won 3 races, placed 6, 1,340,520 fr., in France at 2 and 3 years, incl. Prix du Jockey-Club; 2nd Prix Daru; 3rd Grand Prix de Paris.

PRINCE TAJ (b. 1954)	Prince Bio (b. 1941)	Prince Rose	Rose Prince
			Indolence
		Biologie	Bacteriophage
			Eponge
	Malindi (b. 1947)	Nearco	Pharos
			Nogara
		Mumtaz Begum	Blenheim
			Mumtaz Mahal
RUSH FLOOR (b. 1958)	Guersant (b. 1949)	Bubbles	La Farina
			Spring Cleaning
		Montagnana	Brantome
			Mauretania
	Lorance (br. 1952)	Vatellor	Vatout
			Lady Elinor
		Empress of France	Fair Trial
			Malmaison

61　　　**ASTESE** 1 (ch.c., February 18, 1963)

Bred by Scuderia Mantova, in Italy.

Won 14 races, placed 32, 55,601,351 L., in Italy, France and Germany from 2 to 9 years, incl. Premio Roma and Gran Premio Citta di Napoli; 2nd St. Leger Italiano and Premio Presidente della Repubblica; 4th Grosser Preis von Baden.

BARBA TONI (b. 1953)	Fante (b. 1942)	Nesiotes	Hurry On / Catnip
		Farnesiana	Michelangelo / Flush
	Istriana (ch. 1947)	Arco	Singapore / Archidamia
		Dalmazia	Bozzetto / Talma
MOLECA (ch. 1953)	Traghetto (ch. 1942)	Cavaliere d'Arpino	Havresac II / Chuette
		Talma	Papyrus / Tolbooth
	Loredana (b. 1937)	Onafrasimus	Sardanapale / Miss Bachelor
		Germinate	Sunbright / Dorinda

62　　　**ATHENAGORAS** 9 (br.c., March 17, 1970)

Bred by Gestüt Zoppenbroich, in Germany.

Won 9 races, placed 9, 840,740 DM., in Germany from 2 to 6 years, incl. Deutsches Derby, Aral Pokal (twice), Grosser Preis von Baden, Grosser Preis von Nordrhein-Westfalen and Grosser Hertie-Preis; 2nd Aral Pokal, Spreti-Rennen; 3rd Grosser Preis von Baden, Grosser Preis von Nordrhein-Westfalen and Grosser Hansa-Preis.

NASRAM II (b. 1960)	Nasrullah (b. 1940)	Nearco	Pharos / Nogara
		Mumtaz Begum	Blenheim / Mumtaz Mahal
	La Mirambule (b. 1949)	Coaraze	Tourbillon / Corrida
		La Futaie	Gris Perle / La Futelaye
AVENIDA (b. 1959)	Neckar (bl. 1948)	Ticino	Athanasius / Terra
		Nixe	Arjaman / Nanon
	Angela (b. 1952)	Nebelwerfer	Magnat / Newa
		Asgard	Sturmvogel / Arabella

63　　　**ATHENS WOOD** 19 (b.c., February 29, 1968)

Bred by Kilcarn Stud.

Won 8 races, placed 3, £51,558, in England and Germany from 2 to 4 years, incl. St. Leger Stakes, Great Voltigeur Stakes, Gordon Stakes; 3rd Ladbroke Derby Trial Stakes.

CELTIC ASH (ch.-1957)	Sicambre (br. 1948)	Prince Bio	Prince Rose / Biologie
		Sif	Rialto / Suavita
	Ash Plant (gr. 1948)	Nepenthe	Plassy / Frisky
		Amboyna	Bois Roussel / Aurora
BELLE OF ATHENS (b. 1962)	Acropolis (ch. 1952)	Donatello II	Blenheim / Delleana
		Aurora	Hyperion / Rose Red
	Campanette (b. 1948)	Fair Trial	Fairway / Lady Juror
		Calluna	Hyperion / Campanula

64　　　**ATHERSTONE WOOD** 5 (b.c., April 3, 1964)

Bred by S. O'Flaherty.

Won 4 races, placed 11, £18,072, in England, Ireland and France from 2 to 4 years, incl. Irish 2,000 Guineas Stakes, Gallinule Stakes; 2nd Whitehall Stakes; 3rd Wills Mile, Desmond Stakes, Prix de la Jonchere.

BUISSON ARDENT (b. 1953)	Relic (bl. 1945)	War Relic	Man o'War / Friar's Carse
		Bridal Colors	Black Toney / Vaila
	Rose o'Lynn (b. 1944)	Pherozshah	Pharos / Mah Mahal
		Rocklyn	Easton / Rock Forrard
REINE DES BOIS (b. 1950)	Bois Roussel (br. 1935)	Vatout	Prince Chimay / Vasthi
		Plucky Liege	Spearmint / Concertina
	Queen of Shiraz (b. 1937)	Bahram	Blandford / Friar's Daughter
		Qurrat-al-Ain	Buchan / Harpsichord

65　　　**ATILLA** 1 (ch.c., January 28, 1961)

Bred by A. B. Askew, in England.

Won 6 races, placed 4, £41,447, in England, Italy and Germany at 4 and 5 years, incl. Gran Premio del Jockey Club and Grosser Preis von Baden; 2nd Premio Roma; 3rd Coronation Cup.

ALCIDE (b. 1955)	Alycidon (ch. 1945)	Donatello II	Blenheim / Delleana
		Aurora	Hyperion / Rose Red
	Chenille (br. 1940)	King Salmon	Salmon-Trout / Malva
		Sweet Aloe	Cameronian / Aloe
FESTOON (ch. 1951)	Fair Trial (ch. 1932)	Fairway	Phalaris / Scapa Flow
		Lady Juror	Son-in-Law / Lady Josephine
	Monsoon (b. 1941)	Umidwar	Blandford / Uganda
		Heavenly Wind	Tai-Yang / Godetia

66　　　**ATTICA MELI** 16 (b.f., March 9, 1969)

Bred by Sassoon Studs.

Won 7 races, placed 4, £34,846, in England from 2 to 4 years, incl. Yorkshire Oaks, Park Hill Stakes, Geoffrey Freer Stakes, Doncaster Cup, Princess Royal Stakes; 2nd Coronation Cup, Hardwicke Stakes, St. Simon Stakes; 3rd Fred Darling Stakes.

PRIMERA (b. 1954)	My Babu (b. 1945)	Djebel	Tourbillon / Loika
		Perfume II	Badruddin / Lavendula II
	Pirette (b. 1943)	Deiri	Aethelstan / Desra
		Pimpette	Town Guard / Arpette
COME ON HONEY (ch. 1960)	Never Say Die (ch. 1951)	Nasrullah	Nearco / Mumtaz Begum
		Singing Grass	War Admiral / Boreale
	Honeylight (b. 1953)	Honeyway	Fairway / Honey Buzzard
		Crepuscule	Mieuxce / Red Sunset

67   AUNT EDITH 11 (ch.f., March 18, 1962)

Bred by West Grinstead Stud Ltd.

Won 4 races, placed 1, £66,167, in England and France from 2 to 4 years, incl. King George VI and Queen Elizabeth Stakes, Nassau Stakes, Yorkshire Cup, Prix Vermeille; 2nd Musidora Stakes.

PRIMERA (b. 1954)	My Babu (b. 1945)	Djebel	Tourbillon
			Loika
		Perfume II	Badruddin
			Lavendula II
	Pirette (b. 1943)	Deiri	Aethelstan
			Desra
		Pimpette	Town Guard
			Arpette
FAIR EDITH (b. 1947)	Hyperion (ch. 1930)	Gainsborough	Bayardo
			Rosedrop
		Selene	Chaucer
			Serenissima
	Afterthought (b. 1939)	Obliterate	Tracery
			Damage
		Plack	Hurry On
			Groat

68   AURABELLA 13 (b.f., May 12, 1962)

Bred by Lt.-Col. and Mrs. J. Silcock.

Won 2 races, placed 2, £21,412, in Ireland and England, at 2 and 3 years, incl. Irish Guinness Oaks; 2nd Irish 1,000 Guineas; 4th Yorkshire Oaks.

AUREOLE (ch. 1950)	Hyperion (ch. 1930)	Gainsborough	Bayardo
			Rosedrop
		Selene	Chaucer
			Serenissima
	Angelola (b. 1945)	Donatello II	Blenheim
			Delleana
		Feola	Friar Marcus
			Aloe
MONTEBELLA (b. 1953)	Lacaduv (b. 1947)	Tornado	Tourbillon
			Roseola
		Loet	Pharos
			Alta
	Chloris II (b. 1941)	Chateau Bouscaut	Kircubbin
			Ramondie
		Rosalba	Prince Rose
			Feronia

69   AURELIUS 2 (b.c., February 12, 1958)

Bred by Tally Ho Stud Ltd.

Won 7 races, placed 5, £43,818, in England and Ireland, at 2, 3, 4, 6, 7 and 8 years, incl. St. Leger Stakes, King Edward VII Stakes, Hardwicke Stakes, Craven Stakes; 2nd Great Voltigeur Stakes, King George VI and Queen Elizabeth Stakes, Henry II Stakes; 3rd Ballymoss Stakes. Also ran under N.H. Rules, won 5, placed 4, £4,057, over both hurdles and steeplechases.

AUREOLE (ch. 1950)	Hyperion (ch. 1930)	Gainsborough	Bayardo
			Rosedrop
		Selene	Chaucer
			Serenissima
	Angelola (b. 1945)	Donatello II	Blenheim
			Delleana
		Feola	Friar Marcus
			Aloe
NIOBE II (b. 1948)	Sir Gallahad III (b. 1920)	Teddy	Ajax
			Rondeau
		Plucky Liege	Spearmint
			Concertina
	Humility (ch. 1938)	Hyperion	Gainsborough
			Selene
		Priscilla Carter	Omar Khayyam
			The Reef

70   AUTHI 14 (b.c., March 14, 1970)

Bred by Tally Ho Stud Co. Ltd., in Ireland.

Won 4 races, placed 10, 1,192,200 fr., in France and Italy from 2 to 4 years, incl. Gran Premio del Jockey Club and Grand Prix de Vichy; 2nd Grand Prix de Paris and Prix Royal Oak; 3rd Prix du Cadran, Grand Prix de Deauville (twice) and Prix de l'Esperance; 4th Ascot Gold Cup.

AUREOLE (ch. 1950)	Hyperion (ch. 1930)	Gainsborough	Bayardo
			Rosedrop
		Selene	Chaucer
			Serenissima
	Angelola (b. 1945)	Donatello II	Blenheim
			Delleana
		Feola	Friar Marcus
			Aloe
VIRTUOUS (b. 1962)	Above Suspicion (b. 1956)	Court Martial	Fair Trial
			Instantaneous
		Above Board	Straight Deal
			Feola
	Rose of India (b. 1955)	Tulyar	Tehran
			Neocracy
		Eastern Grandeur	Gold Bridge
			China Maiden

71   AUTOBIOGRAPHY 1 (ch.c., March 9, 1968)

Bred by Wheatley Stable, in U.S.A.

Won 10 races, placed 15, $385,909, in U.S.A. from 2 to 5 years, incl. Jockey Club Gold Cup, Discovery H., San Fernando Stakes, Excelsior H. and Westchester H.; 2nd Brooklyn H., Woodward Stakes, Governor Stakes, Hobson H., Gallant Fox H. and Malibu Stakes; 3rd Michigan Mile and One-Eighth H. and San Pasqual H.

SKY HIGH II (b. 1957)	Star Kingdom (ch. 1946)	Stardust	Hyperion
			Sister Stella
		Impromptu	Concerto
			Thoughtless
	Flight's Daughter (b. 1949)	Helios	Hyperion
			Foxy Gal
		Flight	Royal Step
			Lambent
KING'S STORY (ch. 1960)	Bold Ruler (b. 1954)	Nasrullah	Nearco
			Mumtaz Begum
		Miss Disco	Discovery
			Outdone
	Narrative (b. 1952)	War Relic	Man o'War
			Friar's Carse
		Belle Histoire	Blue Larkspur
			La Troienne

72   AVATAR 5 (ch.c., March 10, 1972)

Bred by Arthur A. Seeligson, Jr., in U.S.A.

Won 9 races, placed 9, $464,609, in U.S.A. from 2 to 4 years, incl. Belmont Stakes, Santa Anita Derby and San Luis Rey Stakes; 2nd Kentucky Derby, Hollywood Gold Cup, Del Mar Invitational H. and San Fernando Stakes.

GRAUSTARK (ch. 1963)	Ribot (b. 1952)	Tenerani	Bellini
			Tofanella
		Romanella	El Greco
			Barbara Burrini
	Flower Bowl (b. 1952)	Alibhai	Hyperion
			Teresina
		Flower Bed	Beau Pere
			Boudoir II
BROWN BERRY (b. 1960)	Mount Marcy (ch. 1945)	Mahmoud	Blenheim
			Mah Mahal
		Maud Muller	Pennant
			Truly Rural
	Brown Baby (gr. 1953)	Phalanx	Pilate
			Jacola
		Crawfish	Halcyon
			Crauneen

73   **AVEROF** 16 (br.c., April 5, 1971)

Bred by Captain Marcos D. Lemos.

Won 4 races, placed 3, £24,515, in England, at 2 and 3 years, incl.
  St. James's Palace Stakes, Dee Stakes, Diomed Stakes; 4th Sussex
  Stakes.

SING SING (b. 1957)	Tudor Minstrel (br. 1944)	Owen Tudor	Hyperion / Mary Tudor II
		Sansonnet	Sansovino / Lady Juror
	Agin the Law (b. 1946)	Portlaw	Beresford / Portree
		Revolte	Xandover / Sheba
ARGENTINA (b. or br. 1957)	Nearco (br. 1935)	Pharos	Phalaris / Scapa Flow
		Nogara	Havresac II / Catnip
	Silvery Moon (br. 1943)	Solario	Gainsborough / Sun Worship
		Silver Fox II	Foxhunter / Pearl Maiden

---

74   **AZINCOURT** 3 (b.c., May 4, 1960)

Bred by R. Wattinne, in France.

Won 6 races, placed 9, 423,358 fr., in France, from 2 to 5 years, incl.
  Prix du Cadran and Prix Berteux; 4th Prix du Cadran.

CHINGACGOOK (b. 1952)	Tourment (b. 1944)	Tourbillon	Ksar / Durban
		Fragment	Shred / Pearl Drop
	La Chipotte (b. 1945)	Porphyros	Bishop's Rock / Pointe de Feu
		Chapardeuse	Rustom Pasha / Chara
ALMORA (ch. 1948)	Verso II (b. 1940)	Pinceau	Alcantara II / Aquarelle
		Variete	La Farina / Vaya
	Andrinople (ch. 1933)	Palais Royal	Bruleur / Puntarenas
		Aithe	Sardanapale / Beatitude

---

75   **AZZURRINA** 13 (ch.f., May 10, 1975)

Bred by Scuderia Eleonora, in England.

Won 11 races, placed 10, 142,619,000 L., in Italy, from 2 to 4 years,
  incl. Premio Lydia Tesio, Premio Regina Elena and Premio
  Legnano; 2nd Premio Lydia Tesio; 3rd Derby Italiano, Criterium
  Femminile, Premio Presidente della Repubblica and Premio
  Legnano.

KNIGHTLY MANNER (br. 1961)	Round Table (b. 1954)	Princequillo	Prince Rose / Cosquilla
		Knight's Daughter	Sir Cosmo / Feola
	Courtesy (b. 1952)	Nasrullah	Nearco / Mumtaz Begum
		Highway Code	Hyperion / Book Law
FLORADORA (b. 1963)	French Beige (b. 1953)	Bois Roussel	Vatout / Plucky Liege
		Nivea	Nearco / Deva
	Street Singer (br. 1954)	Kingsway	Fairway / Yenna
		Record Serenade	Straight Deal / Columbia

---

76   **BAALIM** 9 (b.c., April 20, 1958)

Bred by Gestüt Waldfried, in Germany.

Won 7 races, placed 5, 202,500 DM., in Germany, at 2 and 3 years,
  incl. Deutsches Derby, Deutsches St. Leger, Union-Rennen and
  Preis des Winterfavoriten; 2nd Henckel-Rennen and Grosser Preis
  von Baden; 3rd Aral-Pokal.

MANGON (br. 1949)	Gundomar (br. 1942)	Alchimist	Herold / Aversion
		Grossularia	Aurelius / Grollenicht
	Mainkur (b. 1940)	Janus	Buchan / Jane Pierney
		Makrone	Graf Ferry / Makrele
BLAUE ADRIA (b. 1939)	Ladro (b. 1927)	Graf Ferry	Fervor / Grave and Gay
		Ladylove	Fels / Ladylike
	Blaue Blume (b. 1923)	Fels	Hannibal / Festa
		Blaustrumpf	Saphir / St. Alvere

---

77   **BACUCO** 10 (ch.c., May 15, 1966)

Bred by Scuderia Mantova, in Italy.

Won 13 races, placed 10, 149,603,125 L., in Italy and U.S.A., from
  2 to 5 years, incl. Premio Roma (twice), St. Leger Italiano, Gran
  Premio del Jockey Club and Coppa d'Oro di Milano; 2nd Gran
  Premio di Milano and Gran Premio del Jockey Club; 3rd Gran
  Criterium, Washington D.C. International, San Luis Rey H. and
  Premio d'Aprile.

RIO MARIN (ch. 1956)	Traghetto (ch. 1942)	Cavaliere d'Arpino	Havresac II / Chuette
		Talma	Papyrus / Tolbooth
	Cira (ch. 1942)	Cranach	Cannobie / Chuette
		Cilea	Sans Crainte / Calystegia
SIORA MARGARITA (b. 1949)	Bozzetto (ch. 1936)	Pharos	Phalaris / Scapa Flow
		Bunworry	Great Sport / Waffles
	Sbrindola (br. 1940)	Cavaliere d'Arpino	Havresac II / Chuette
		Alesia	Ryan / Queen's Cure

---

78   **BALDRIC II** 13 (b.c., May 16, 1961)

Bred by Bull Run Stud, in U.S.A.

Won 4 races, placed 5, £78,766, in England and France, from 2 to 4
  years, incl. 2,000 Guineas Stakes, Champion Stakes, Prix Perth;
  2nd Eclipse Stakes, Prix de la Salamandre; 3rd Prix Edmond Blanc.

ROUND TABLE (b. 1954)	Princequillo (b. 1940)	Prince Rose	Rose Prince / Indolence
		Cosquilla	Papyrus / Quick Thought
	Knight's Daughter (b. 1940)	Sir Cosmo	The Boss / Ayn Hali
		Feola	Friar Marcus / Aloe
TWO CITIES (b. 1948)	Johnstown (b. 1936)	Jamestown	St. James / Mlle. Dazie
		La France	Sir Gallahad III / Flambette
	Vienna (b. 1941)	Menow	Pharamond / Alcibiades
		Valse	Sir Gallahad III / Valkyr

79   BALIDAR 8 (br.c., April 7, 1966)

Bred by Mrs. A. Hanly, in Ireland.

Won 9 races, placed 5, £27,721, in England and France, from 2 to 4 years, incl. Prix de l'Abbaye de Longchamp, Prix du Gros-Chene and Prix de Meautry; 2nd Cork and Orrery Stakes and Duke of York Stakes; 3rd King's Stand Stakes and Vernons Sprint Cup.

WILL SOMERS (br. 1955)	Tudor Minstrel (br. 1944)	Owen Tudor	Hyperion / Mary Tudor II
		Sansonnet	Sansovino / Lady Juror
	Queen's Jest (br. 1946)	Nearco	Pharos / Nogara
		Mirth	Hurry On / Laughter
VIOLET BANK (b. 1960)	The Phoenix (b. 1940)	Chateau Bouscaut	Kircubbin / Ramondie
		Fille de Poete	Firdaussi / Fille d'Amour
	Leinster (ch. 1954)	Speckled Band	Fair Trial / Speckle
		Garryard	Preciptic / Garryhinch

80   BALLY ACHE 12 (b.c., April 23, 1957)

Bred by Gaines Brothers, in U.S.A.

Won 16 races, placed 13, $758,522, in U.S.A., at 2 and 3 years, incl. Preakness Stakes, Flamingo Stakes, Florida Derby, Jersey Derby and Comely Stakes; 2nd Kentucky Derby, Fountain of Youth Stakes, Arlington Futurity, Washington Park Futurity, Garden State Stakes, Sapling Stakes and World's Playground Stakes; 3rd United Nations H., Champagne Stakes and Cowdin Stakes.

BALLYDAM (ch. 1947)	Ballyogan (ch. 1939)	Fair Trial	Fairway / Lady Juror
		Serial	Solario / Booktalk
	Damians (ch. 1942)	Panorama	Sir Cosmo / Happy Climax
		Thirteen	Bulger / Credenda
CELESTIAL BLUE (b. 1943)	Supremus (b. 1922)	Ultimus	Commando / Running Stream
		Mandy Hamilton	John o'Gaunt / My Sweetheart
	Vanda Cerulea (b./br. 1932)	Blue Larkspur	Black Servant / Blossom Time
		Binnacle	Man o'War / Smoky Lamp

81   BALLYMORE 7 (b.c., March 25, 1969)

Bred by Ardenode Stud Ltd.

Won 2 races, placed 2, £29,490, in Ireland, at 3 and 4 years, incl. Irish 2,000 Guineas, Nijinsky Stakes; 2nd Gallinule Stakes; 3rd Irish Sweeps Derby.

RAGUSA (b. 1960)	Ribot (b. 1952)	Tenerani	Bellini / Tofanella
		Romanella	El Greco / Barbara Burrini
	Fantan II (b. 1952)	Ambiorix II	Tourbillon / Lavendula II
		Red Eye	Petee-Wrack / Charred Keg
PADDY'S SISTER (b. 1957)	Ballyogan (ch. 1939)	Fair Trial	Fairway / Lady Juror
		Serial	Solario / Booktalk
	Birthday Wood (b. 1949)	Bois Roussel	Vatout / Plucky Liege
		Birthday Bouquet	Felicitation / Glycine

82   BALTO 26 (b.c., February 25, 1958)

Bred by Mlle. Fremont-Tousch, in France.

Won 4 races, placed 4, £53,525, in England and France, from 3 to 5 years, incl. Ascot Gold Cup, Grand Prix de Paris; 2nd Prix Royal-Oak, Prix du Cadran; 3rd Goodwood Cup, Prix Jean Prat.

WILD RISK (b. 1940)	Rialto (ch. 1923)	Rabelais	St. Simon / Satirical
		La Grelee	Helicon / Grignouse
	Wild Violet (b. 1935)	Blandford	Swynford / Blanche
		Wood Violet	Ksar / Pervencheres
BOUCLETTE (b. 1948)	Victrix II (b. 1934)	Kantar	Alcantara II / Karabe
		Victory VI	Swynford / Lineage
	Badine (b. 1943)	Finglas	Bruleur / Fair Simone
		Bakou	Blenheim / Voleuse

83   BALY ROCKETTE 1 (ch.c., March 25, 1972)

Bred by Ongar Stud, in Ireland.

Won 9 races, placed 5, 465,578 fr., in France, Italy and Germany, from 2 to 5 years, incl. Premio Emilio Turati, Prix Edmond Blanc, Oettingen-Rennen and Premio Natale di Roma.

CROCKET (ch. 1960)	King of the Tudors (ch. 1950)	Tudor Minstrel	Owen Tudor / Sansonnet
		Glen Line	Blue Peter / Scotia's Glen
	Chandelier (ch. 1955)	Goyama	Goya II / Devineress
		Queen of Light	Borealis / Picture Play
BALETTA (ch. 1966)	Ballymoss (ch. 1954)	Mossborough	Nearco / All Moonshine
		Indian Call	Singapore / Flittemere
	Tanetta (b. 1960)	Tantième	Deux pour Cent / Terka
		Carteretta	Chanteur II / Chart Room

84   BARBARE 2 (b.c., March 12, 1963)

Bred by Comte R. de Chambure, in France.

Won 4 races, placed 8, 638,639 fr., in France, at 2 and 3 years, incl. Prix de la Foret, Prix de Fontainebleau and Prix des Reservoirs; 2nd Poule d'Essai des Poulains, Prix Robert Papin, Prix Lupin and Prix Jean Prat; 3rd Criterium de Maisons-Laffitte and Prix de Seine-et-Oise; 4th Prix du Moulin de Longchamp.

SICAMBRE (br. 1948)	Prince Bio (b. 1941)	Prince Rose	Rose Prince / Indolence
		Biologie	Bacteriophage / Eponge
	Sif (br. 1936)	Rialto	Rabelais / La Grelee
		Suavita	Alcantara II / Shocking
BARBARA (b. 1947)	Fair Trial (ch. 1932)	Fairway	Phalaris / Scapa Flow
		Lady Juror	Son-in-Law / Lady Josephine
	Mistress Ford (b. 1933)	Blandford	Swynford / Blanche
		Polly Flinders II	Teddy / Polloia

85   BARBIERI 1 (ch.c., 1961)

Bred by Baron Guy de Rothschild, in France.

Won 3 races, placed 3, 523,126 fr., in France, at 3 and 4 years, incl. Prix Royal Oak; 2nd Prix Lupin; 3rd Prix Jean Prat.

LA VARENDE (gr. 1949)	Blue Moon (ch. 1936)	Massine	Consols / Mauri
		Halston	Dark Legend / Hurrybelle
	Cappellina (gr. 1940)	Le Capucin	Nimbus / Carmen
		Bellina	Belfonds / Edwina
NAURICA (ch. 1954)	Sicambre (br. 1948)	Prince Bio	Prince Rose / Biologie
		Sif	Rialto / Suavita
	La Grande Mademoiselle (br. 1946)	Mirza II	Blenheim / Mumtaz Mahal
		Paix des Dames	Bubbles / Concorde

86   BASALT 28 (br.c., March 25, 1966)

Bred by Gestüt Bona, in Germany.

Won 7 races, placed 14, 328,430 DM., in Germany, from 3 to 5 years, incl. Aral-Pokal and Deutsches St. Leger; 2nd Union-Rennen, Preis von Europa and Grosser Preis von Nordrhein-Westfalen; 3rd Grosser Preis von Nordrhein-Westfalen, Grosser Preis von Dusseldorf (twice) and Grosser Hansa-Preis.

NECKAR (bl. 1948)	Ticino (b. 1939)	Athanasius	Ferro / Athanasie
		Terra	Aditi / Teufelsrose
	Nixe (b. 1941)	Arjaman	Herold / Aditja
		Nanon	Graf Isolani / Nella da Gubbio
BONA (br. 1954)	Magnat (b. 1938)	Asterus	Teddy / Astrella
		Mafalda	Wallenstein / Madam
	Bereitschaft (b. 1942)	Athanasius	Ferro / Athanasie
		Binse	Prunus / Bunch Grass

87   BATITU 1 (b.c., February 24, 1965)

Bred by J. de Atucha, in France.

Won 5 races, placed 9, 591,585 fr., in France, England and U.S.A., from 2 to 6 years, incl. Prix de la Salamandre and La Coupe de Maisons-Laffitte; 2nd San Bernardino Handicap; 3rd Prix Daphnis; 4th Champion Stakes.

SNOB (b. 1959)	Mourne (ch. 1954)	Vieux Manoir	Brantome / Vieille Maison
		Ballynash	Nasrullah / Ballywellbroke
	Senones (br. 1952)	Prince Bio	Prince Rose / Biologie
		Sif	Rialto / Suavita
QUICK TRICK (b. 1944)	Atout Maitre (br. 1936)	Vatout	Prince Chimay / Vasthi
		Royal Mistress	Teddy / Tout Paris
	Arcola II (br. 1936)	Sandwich	Sansovino / Waffles
		Columba	Colorado / Gay Bird

88   BAY EXPRESS 3 (b.c., April 24, 1971)

Bred by J. M. O'Connor.

Won 6 races, placed 4, £29,048, in England, from 2 to 4 years, incl. King's Stand Stakes, Nunthorpe Stakes, Temple Stakes; 2nd Palace House Stakes; 3rd King George Stakes.

POLYFOTO (br. 1962)	Polic (br. 1953)	Relic	War Relic / Bridal Colors
		Polaire II	Le Volcan / Stella Polaris
	Brabantia (b. or br. 1953)	Honeyway	Fairway / Honey Buzzard
		Porthaven	Portlaw / Peaceful Light
PAL SINNA (ch. 1966)	Palestine (gr. 1947)	Fair Trial	Fairway / Lady Juror
		Una	Tetratema / Uganda
	Sinna (b. 1956)	Birikan	Bahram / Carola
		Inisheer	Devonian / Lady of Aran

89   BEAU CHARMEUR 14 (b.c., April 11, 1968)

Bred by Mme. Jean Blondel, in France.

Won 8 races, placed 10, 809,192 fr., in France and Italy, from 2 to 6 years, incl. Gran Premio di Milano; 2nd Gran Premio Citta di Napoli; 3rd Prix du Cadran and Gran Premio del Jockey Club; 4th Prix du Cadran and Grand Prix de Saint-Cloud.

LE FABULEUX (ch. 1961)	Wild Risk (b. 1940)	Rialto	Rabelais / La Grelee
		Wild Violet	Blandford / Wood Violet
	Anguar (b. 1950)	Verso II	Pinceau / Variete
		La Rochelle	Easton / Sans Tares
CYMBALE (br. 1963)	Soleil Levant (b. 1951)	Sunny Boy III	Jock II / Fille de Soleil
		Sif	Rialto / Suavita
	Blue Kiss (br. 1947)	Pharis II	Pharos / Carissima
		Blue Bear	Blenheim / La Boni

90   BEAUGENCY 7 (b.c., May 4, 1966)

Bred by Alec Head, in France.

Won 5 races, placed 6, 1,013,632 fr., in France, Italy and Germany, from 2 to 4 years, incl. Gran Premio di Milano, Prix Hocquart and Prix Thomas Bryon; 2nd Prix du Jockey-Club, Prix de Guiche and Prix Foy; 3rd Prix Jean de Chaudenay; 4th Grosser Preis von Nordrhein-Westfalen.

VAL DE LOIR (b. 1959)	Vieux Manoir (b. 1947)	Brantome	Blandford / Vitamine
		Vieille Maison	Finglas / Vieille Canaille
	Vali (b. 1954)	Sunny Boy III	Jock II / Fille de Soleil
		Her Slipper	Tetratema / Carpet Slipper
BIOBELLE (b. 1960)	Cernobbio (ch. 1953)	Prince Bio	Prince Rose / Biologie
		Ceruleine	Victrix / Cerulea
	La Beloli (b. 1948)	Domenico Ghirlandaio	Blenheim / Delleana
		Alibranda	Ortello / Nuwara Eliya

91   BEE BEE BEE 9 (b./br.c., April 3, 1969)

Bred by William S. Miller, in U.S.A.

Won 11 races, placed 10, $281,098, in U.S.A., from 2 to 4 years, incl. Preakness Stakes, Hawthorne Juvenile Stakes and Patriot Stakes; 2nd Minuteman H.

BETTER BEE (b. 1954)	Triplicate (ch. 1941)	Reigh Count	Sunreigh / Contessina
		Fairday	Fair Play / Ruthenia
	S. Bee (bl. 1943)	Haste	Maintenant / Miss Malaprop
		Sevres	The Scout / Anna M. Humphrey
PAULA (br. 1953)	Nizami II (b. 1946)	Nearco	Pharos / Nogara
		Mumtaz Begum	Blenheim / Mumtaz Mahal
	Withdrawn (b. 1948)	Haltal	The Porter / False Modesty
		Golden Rose	Sickle / Nipisiquit

92   BE FRIENDLY 5 (ch.c., April 11, 1964)

Bred by W. J. Madden.

Won 11½ races, placed 10, £43,880, in England and France, from 2 to 5 years, incl. King's Stand Stakes, Vernons November Sprint Cup (twice), Palace House Stakes, Prix de l'Abbaye de Longchamp, Prix du Gros-Chene (d-h); 2nd Prix de Saint-Georges, Nunthorpe Stakes, Temple Stakes, Duke of York Stakes, 3rd King's Stand Stakes.

SKYMASTER (ch. 1958)	Golden Cloud (ch. 1941)	Gold Bridge	Swynford or Golden Boss / Flying Diadem
		Rainstorm	Hainault / Stormcloud
	Discipliner (ch. 1948)	Court Martial	Fair Trial / Instantaneous
		Edvina	Figaro / Louise
LADY SLIPTIC (ch. 1954)	Preciptic (ch. 1942)	Precipitation	Hurry On / Double Life
		Artistic	Gainsborough / Ishtar
	Persian Slipper (b. 1939)	Furrokh Siyar	Colorado / Mumtaz Mahal
		Sadowa	Lemberg / After Dark

93   BEHISTOUN 14 (br.c., May 2, 1963)

Bred by Alec Weisweiller, in France.

Won 6 races, placed 6, 1,576,659 fr., in France and U.S.A., from 2 to 4 years, incl. Prix Lupin, Prix Ganay, Prix des Chenes and Washington D.C. International; 2nd Prix Greffulhe; 3rd Prix du Jockey-Club, Grand Prix de Saint-Cloud and Grand Criterium.

O'GRADY (b. 1953)	Relic (bl. 1945)	War Relic	Man o'War / Friar's Carse
		Bridal Colors	Black Toney / Vaila
	Ann's Twin (b. 1939)	Plassy	Bosworth / Pladda
		Slide Along	Alcantara II / Slip Along
BEOTIE (b. 1956)	Worden II (ch. 1949)	Wild Risk	Rialto / Wild Violet
		Sans Tares	Sind / Tara
	Bodicee (b. 1950)	Sayani	Fair Copy / Perfume II
		Bellezza	Solario / Belle Ferronnière

94   BEL BOLIDE 20 (ch.c., February 5, 1978)

Bred by George A. Bolas, in U.S.A.

Won 3 races, placed 3, £56,777, in England, at 2 years, incl. Gimcrack Stakes; 2nd Richmond Stakes, William Hill Middle Park Stakes; 3rd Coventry Stakes.

BOLD BIDDER (b. 1962)	Bold Ruler (b. 1954)	Nasrullah	Nearco / Mumtaz Begum
		Miss Disco	Discovery / Outdone
	High Bid (b. 1956)	To Market	Market Wise / Pretty Does
		Stepping Stone	Princequillo / Step Across
LADY GRAUSTARK (ch. 1969)	Graustark (ch. 1963)	Ribot	Tenerani / Romanella
		Flower Bowl	Alibhai / Flower Bed
	Inyala (ch. 1963)	My Babu	Djebel / Perfume II
		Roman Ronda	The Rhymer / Roman Matron

95   BELDALE FLUTTER 1 (b.c., April 4, 1978)

Bred by Warner L. Jones, Jr., in U.S.A.

Won 3 races, placed 2, £55,358, in England and Belgium, at 2 years, incl. William Hill Futurity Stakes, Grand Criterium International d'Ostende.

ACCIPITER (b. 1971)	Damascus (b. 1964)	Sword Dancer	Sunglow / Highland Fling
		Kerala	My Babu / Blade of Time
	Kingsland (b. or br. 1965)	Bold Ruler	Nasrullah / Miss Disco
		Landmark	Revoked / Oasis
'FLITTER FLUTTER (b. or br. 1966)	Cohoes (b. 1954)	Mahmoud	Blenheim / Mah Mahal
		Belle of Troy	Blue Larkspur / La Troienne
	Ellerslie (br. 1954)	Nasrullah	Nearco / Mumtaz Begum
		Effie B.	Bull Dog / Misleading

96   BELGIO 16 (b.c., March 24, 1977)

Bred by Adolphe Boccara, in France.

Won 2 races, placed 5, 727,000 fr., in France at 2 and 3 years, incl. Prix Lupin; 2nd Criterium de Saint-Cloud; 3rd Prix Thomas Bryon and Prix Hocquart.

DJAKAO (b. 1966)	Tanerko (br. 1953)	Tantieme	Deux pour Cent / Terka
		La Divine	Fair Copy / La Diva
	Diagonale (ch. 1959)	Ribot	Tenerani / Romanella
		Barley Corn	Hyperion / Schiaparelli
TOSTA (ch. 1971)	Timour (b. 1964)	Dan Cupid	Native Dancer / Vixenette
		Cerisoles	Tourment / Paix d'Ecosse
	Frontera (ch. 1964)	Alizier	Teleferique / Alizarine
		Feliza	Escamillo / Farceuse

97   BELLE FERRONNIERE 22 (b.f., February 13, 1960)

Bred by Mme. H. Herbaux, in France.

Won 3 races, placed 6, 518,463 fr., in France, at 2 and 3 years, incl. Prix de Diane; 3rd Prix Chloe and Prix de la Nonette.

COSMOS (b. 1949)	Nosca (b. 1939)	Abjer	Asterus / Zariba
		Capella	Tourbillon / Gracilite
	Chorea (b. 1938)	Caligula	Town Guard / Catherine Swynford
		Choisya	Kircubbin / La Choisille
AMIJA (b. 1952)	Breughel (br. 1939)	Brantome	Blandford / Vitamine
		Buchanite	Son-in-Law / Buchaness
	Bohemienne (ch. 1937)	Monarch	Tracery / Teofani
		Prague	Grand Guignol / La Padon

98   BELLE SICAMBRE 8 (b.f., January 25, 1961)

Bred by Mme. L. Volterra, in France.

Won 4 races, placed 6, 857,963 fr., in France and U.S.A., incl. Prix de Diane, Prix Saint-Alary and Prix Eclipse; 2nd Prix de la Grotte; 4th Poule d'Essai des Pouliches and Prix Vermeille.

SICAMBRE (br. 1948)	Prince Bio (b. 1941)	Prince Rose	Rose Prince / Indolence
		Biologie	Bacteriophage / Eponge
	Sif (br. 1936)	Rialto	Rabelais / La Grelee
		Suavita	Alcantara II / Shocking
LA PERIE (b. 1951)	Hyperion (ch. 1930)	Gainsborough	Bayardo / Rosedrop
		Selene	Chaucer / Serenissima
	Philippa (br. 1943)	Vatellor	Vatout / Lady Elinor
		Philippa of Hainaut	Teddy / Pride of Hainault

99   BE MY GUEST 8 (ch.c., April 12, 1974)

Bred by Walter Haefner, in U.S.A.

Won 4 races, placed 1, £28,814, in Ireland and England, at 2 and 3 years, incl. Ladbroke Blue Riband Trial Stakes, Desmond Stakes and Waterford Crystal Mile; 2nd Nijinsky Stakes.

NORTHERN DANCER (b. 1961)	Nearctic (br. 1954)	Nearco	Pharos / Nogara
		Lady Angela	Hyperion / Sister Sarah
	Natalma (b. 1957)	Native Dancer	Polynesian / Geisha
		Almahmoud	Mahmoud / Arbitrator
WHAT A TREAT (b. 1962)	Tudor Minstrel (br. 1944)	Owen Tudor	Hyperion / Mary Tudor II
		Sansonnet	Sansovino / Lady Juror
	Rare Treat (ch. 1952)	Stymie	Equestrian / Stopwatch
		Rare Perfume	Eight Thirty / Fragrance

100   BEN MARSHALL 2 (b.c., 1962)

Bred by Razza Dormello-Olgiata, in Italy.

Won 10 races, placed 5, 35,946,000 L., in Italy, from 2 to 4 years, incl. Premio Presidente della Repubblica, Premio Principe Amedeo and St. Leger Italiano; 2nd Derby Italiano and Premio Ambrosiano; 4th Gran Premio d'Italia and Gran Premio di Milano.

BOTTICELLI (b. 1951)	Blue Peter (ch. 1936)	Fairway	Phalaris / Scapa Flow
		Fancy Free	Stefan the Great / Celiba
	Buonamica (b. 1943)	Niccolo Dell'Arca	Coronach / Nogara
		Bernina	Pharos / Bunworry
BELLADONNA (b. 1952)	Donatello II (ch. 1934)	Blenheim	Blandford / Malva
		Delleana	Clarissimus / Duccia di Buoninsegna
	Hypericum (b. 1943)	Hyperion	Gainsborough / Selene
		Feola	Friar Marcus / Aloe

101   BIG SPRUCE 9 (dk.b./br.c., April 5, 1969)

Bred by Elmendorf Farm, in U.S.A.

Won 9 races, placed 16, $673,117, in U.S.A and Canada, from 3 to 5 years, incl. Marlboro Cup, San Luis Rey Stakes, Governor Stakes, Lexington H. and Gallant Fox H. (twice); 2nd Canadian International Championship (twice), Washington D.C. International, San Juan Capistrano Invitational H., Charles H. Strub Stakes, Manhattan H., San Luis Rey Stakes and San Marcos H.; 3rd Man o'War Stakes, San Antonio Stakes, Brighton Beach H., Santa Anita H. and San Juan Capistrano Invitational H.

HERBAGER (b. 1956)	Vandale II (b. 1943)	Plassy	Bosworth / Pladda
		Vanille	La Farina / Vaya
	Flagette (ch. 1951)	Escamillo	Firdaussi / Estoril
		Fidgette	Firdaussi / Boxeuse
SILVER SARI (b. 1961)	Prince John (ch. 1953)	Princequillo	Prince Rose / Cosquilla
		Not Afraid	Count Fleet / Banish Fear
	Golden Sari (b. 1956)	Ambiorix II	Tourbillon / Lavendula II
		Banta	Some Chance / Bourtai

102   BIREME 11 (ch.f., May 2, 1977)

Bred by R. D. Hollingsworth.

Won 3 races, placed 1, £89,030, in England, at 2 and 3 years, incl. Oaks Stakes, Musidora Stakes.

GRUNDY (ch. 1972)	Great Nephew (b. 1963)	Honeyway	Fairway / Honey Buzzard
		Sybil's Niece	Admiral's Walk / Sybil's Sister
	Word from Lundy (b. 1966)	Worden II	Wild Risk / Sans Tares
		Lundy Princess	Princely Gift / Lundy Parrot
RIPECK (br. 1959)	Ribot (b. 1952)	Tenerani	Bellini / Tofanella
		Romanella	El Greco / Barbara Burrini
	Kyak (bl./br. 1953)	Big Game	Bahram / Myrobella
		Felucca	Nearco / Felsetta

103   BISCAYNE 1 (b.c., April 6, 1961)

Bred by Mrs. B. Yorke-Reid.

Won 5 races, placed 6, £13,598, in Ireland and U.S.A., from 2 to 4 years, incl. Irish St. Leger, Blandford Stakes, Hennessy Bi-Centenary Handicap; 2nd Desmond Stakes, Whitehall Stakes; 4th Washington D.C. International.

			Pharos
		Nearco	Nogara
	Krakatao		Solario
	(b. 1946)	Life Hill	Lady of the Snows
TALGO			Asterus
(b. 1953)		Jock II	Naic
	Miss France		Abjer
	(b. 1946)	Nafah	Flower
			Blandford
		Windsor Lad	Resplendent
	Windsor Slipper		Phalaris
	(b. 1939)	Carpet Slipper	Simon's Shoes
MARJORIE CASTLE			Solario
(ch. 1947)		Orpen	Harpy
	Salecraft		Apelle
	(br. 1938)	Good Deal	Weeds

104   BLABLA 1 (ch.f., March 23, 1962)

Bred by Baron de Nexon, in France.

Won 3 races, placed 4, 702,156 fr., in France, at 2 and 3 years, incl. Prix de Diane; 2nd Prix Vanteaux and Criterium de Maisons-Laffitte; 3rd Prix de la Nonette.

			Alcantara II
		Pinceau	Aquarelle
	Verso II		La Farina
	(b. 1940)	Variete	Vaya
LAVANDIN			Son-in-Law
(b. 1953)		Rustom Pasha	Cos
	Lavande		Epinard
	(br. 1936)	Livadia	Lady Kroon
			Badajoz
		Epinard	Epine Blanche
	Balthazar		Amant de Coeur
	(ch. 1937)	Biltzalia	Bicarra
BARINA			Town Guard
(ch. 1951)		Caligula	Catherine Swynford
	Balaklava		Badajoz
	(ch. 1936)	Badalona	Canalette

105   BLACK SATIN 42 (br.f., March 24, 1967)

Bred by Mrs. J. Bourke.

Won 4 races, placed 6, £17,891, in Ireland and England, at 2 and 3 years, incl. Irish 1,000 Guineas Stakes; 2nd Coronation Stakes; 3rd 1,000 Guineas Stakes, Cheveley Park Stakes.

			Gainsborough
		Hyperion	Selene
	Rockefella		Felstead
	(br. 1941)	Rockfel	Rockliffe
LINACRE			Sir Cosmo
(bl. 1960)		Panorama	Happy Climax
	True Picture		Chrysler II
	(bl. 1955)	Verity	Fortunedale
			Windsor Slipper
		Solar Slipper	Solar Flower
	Panaslipper		Panorama
	(ch. 1952)	Panastrid	Astrid
PANAVIEW			Vatout
(b. 1960)		Atout Maitre	Royal Mistress
	April View		Panorama
	(b. 1949)	Distant View	Maid of the Heath

106   BLAKENEY 20 (b.c., March 28, 1966)

Bred by Park Farm Stud.

Won 3 races, placed 5, £83,655, in England and Ireland, from 2 to 4 years, incl. Derby Stakes, Ormonde Stakes; 2nd Lingfield Derby Trial Stakes, Gold Cup, King George VI and Queen Elizabeth Stakes; 4th Irish Sweeps Derby.

			Tourbillon
		Djebel	Loika
	Hugh Lupus		Goya II
	(b. 1952)	Sakountala	Samos
HETHERSETT			Bahram
(b. 1959)		Big Game	Myrobella
	Bride Elect		Nearco
	(b. 1952)	Netherton Maid	Phase
			Gainsborough
		Hyperion	Selene
	Hornbeam		Nasrullah
	(ch. 1953)	Thicket	Thorn Wood
WINDMILL GIRL			Chateau Bouscaut
(b. 1961)		Chanteur II	La Diva
	Chorus Beauty		Nearco
	(b. 1952)	Neberna	Springtime

107   BLEEP-BLEEP 1 (b.c., May 15, 1956)

Bred by Southdown Stud Co.

Won 7 races, placed 12, £9,250, in England, from 2 to 5 years, incl. Nunthorpe Stakes, King George Stakes; 2nd Richmond Stakes; 3rd King George Stakes.

			Pharos
		Pharis II	Carissima
	Ardan		Asterus
	(b. 1941)	Adargatis	Helene de Troie
HARD SAUCE			Sir Cosmo
(br. 1948)		Bellacose	Orbella
	Saucy Bella		Mr. Jinks
	(gr. 1941)	Marmite	Gentlemen's Relish
			Broomstick
		Whisk Broom II	Audience
	Diavolo		Peter Pan
	(ch. 1925)	Vexatious	Contrary
CURTSEY			Teddy
(ch. 1937)		Sir Gallahad III	Plucky Liege
	King's Idyll		Fair Play
	(b. 1928)	Etoile Filante	Chit Chat

108   BLUE CASHMERE 16 (br.c., April 17, 1970)

Bred by Cleaboy Farms Company.

Won 7 races, placed 4, £32,733, in England, from 2 to 5 years, incl. Nunthorpe Stakes, Temple Stakes; 3rd Challenge Stakes, Duke of York Stakes.

			Owen Tudor
		Tudor Minstrel	Sansonnet
	Tudor Melody		Dante
	(br. 1956)	Matelda	Fairly Hot
KASHMIR II			Blue Peter
(b. or br. 1963)		Blue Train	Sun Chariot
	Queen of Speed		His Grace
	(b. 1950)	Bishopscourt	Jurisdiction
			Nearco
		Mossborough	All Moonshine
	Ballymoss		Singapore
	(ch. 1954)	Indian Call	Flittemere
BLESSED AGAIN			Nearco
(b. 1965)		Narrator	Phase
	No Saint		Tourbillon
	(b. 1959)	Vellada	Tsianina

109   **BLUE TOM** 1 (br.c., March 19, 1964)

Bred by Mrs. P. A. B. Widener, in U.S.A.

Won 5 races, placed 6, 744,398 fr., in France at 2 and 3 years, incl. Poule d'Essai des Poulains, Prix de la Salamandre and Prix Daphnis; 2nd Prix Morny, Prix de la Foret and Prix de Fontainebleau; 3rd Prix du Rond-Point.

TOMPION (br. 1957)	Tom Fool (b. 1949)	Menow	Pharamond / Alcibiades
		Gaga	Bull Dog / Alpoise
	Sunlight (b. 1952)	Count Fleet	Reigh Count / Quickly
		Halcyon Days	Halcyon / Jabot
PINK SILK (ch. 1957)	Spy Song (br. 1943)	Balladier	Black Toney / Blue Warbler
		Mata Hari	Peter Hastings / War Woman
	Bayrose (b. 1949)	Sir Gallahad III	Teddy / Plucky Liege
		Artistic Rose	Challenger / Dogana

110   **BLUSHING GROOM** 22 (ch.c., April 8, 1974)

Bred by J. McNamee Sullivan, in Ireland.

Won 7 races, placed 3, 1,877,892 fr., in France and England, at 2 and 3 years, incl. Prix Robert Papin, Prix Morny, Prix de la Salamandre, Grand Criterium, Poule d'Essai des Poulains and Prix de Fontainebleau; 2nd Prix Jacques le Marois; 3rd Derby Stakes.

RED GOD (ch. 1954)	Nasrullah (b. 1940)	Nearco	Pharos / Nogara
		Mumtaz Begum	Blenheim / Mumtaz Mahal
	Spring Run (b. 1948)	Menow	Pharamond / Alcibiades
		Boola Brook	Bull Dog / Brookdale
RUNAWAY BRIDE (b. 1962)	Wild Risk (b. 1940)	Rialto	Rabelais / La Grelee
		Wild Violet	Blandford / Wood Violet
	Aimee (b. 1957)	Tudor Minstrel	Owen Tudor / Sansonnet
		Emali	Umidwar / Eclair

111   **BOLD BIDDER** 3 (b.c., March 22, 1962)

Bred by Wheatley Stable, in U.S.A.

Won 13 races, placed 7, $478,021, in U.S.A., from 3 to 5 years, incl. Charles H. Strub Stakes, Hawthorne Gold Cup, Monmouth H., Washington Park H. and Jerome H.; 3rd Roamer H., San Antonio H. and San Fernando Stakes.

BOLD RULER (b. 1954)	Nasrullah (b. 1940)	Nearco	Pharos / Nogara
		Mumtaz Begum	Blenheim / Mumtaz Mahal
	Miss Disco (b. 1944)	Discovery	Display / Ariadne
		Outdone	Pompey / Sweep Out
HIGH BID (b. 1956)	To Market (ch. 1948)	Market Wise	Brokers Tip / On Hand
		Pretty Does	Johnstown / Creese
	Stepping Stone (b. 1950)	Princequillo	Prince Rose / Cosquilla
		Step Across	Balladier / Drawbridge

112   **BOLDBOY** 8 (b.g., March 2, 1970)

Bred by Mrs. T. V. Ryan.

Won 14 races, placed 27, £132,800, in England and France, from 2 to 9 years, incl. Clerical Medical Greenham Stakes, Diadem Stakes, Challenge Stakes (twice), Prix de la Porte Maillot, F.N.F.C. Lockinge Stakes, Duke of York Stakes and Vernons Sprint Cup; 2nd Blue Riband Trial Stakes, Prix Quincey, Prix Messidor and Waterford Crystal Mile; 3rd Diadem Stakes, Queen Anne Stakes (twice), Challenge Stakes, Duke of York Stakes and Hungerford Stakes (twice); 4th Middle Park Stakes and Prix Jacques le Marois.

BOLD LAD (IRE) (b. 1964)	Bold Ruler (b. 1954)	Nasrullah	Nearco / Mumtaz Begum
		Miss Disco	Discovery / Outdone
	Barn Pride (ch. 1957)	Democratic	Denturius / Light Fantasy
		Fair Alycia	Alycidon / Fair Edwine
SOLAR ECHO (b. 1957)	Solar Slipper (b. 1945)	Windsor Slipper	Windsor Lad / Carpet Slipper
		Solar Flower	Solario / Serena
	Eastern Echo (b. 1938)	Colombo	Manna / Lady Nairne
		Singapore's Sister	Gainsborough / Tetrabbazia

113   **BOLD FASCINATOR** 17 (gr.f., May 6, 1968)

Bred by Warner L. Jones, Jr., in U.S.A.

Won 3 races, placed 6, 581,492 fr., in France at 2 and 3 years, incl. Poule d'Essai des Pouliches and Prix de la Grotte; 2nd Prix de la Foret; 3rd Criterium des Pouliches and Prix du Rond-Point.

BOLD LAD (USA) (ch. 1962)	Bold Ruler (b. 1954)	Nasrullah	Nearco / Mumtaz Begum
		Miss Disco	Discovery / Outdone
	Misty Morn (b. 1952)	Princequillo	Prince Rose / Cosquilla
		Grey Flight	Mahmoud / Planetoid
LYSISTRATA (gr. 1954)	Palestinian (ch. 1946)	Sun Again	Sun Teddy / Hug Again
		Dolly Whisk	Whiskaway / Dolly Seth
	Jaconda (gr. 1941)	Belfonds	Isard II / La Buire
		Jacola	Jacopo / La France

114   **BOLD FORBES** 9 (b.c., March 31, 1973)

Bred by Eaton Farms Inc. and Red Bull Stable, in U.S.A.

Won 13 races, placed 5, $546,536, in U.S.A. and Puerto Rico, at 2 and 3 years, incl. Kentucky Derby, Belmont Stakes, Wood Memorial Stakes, Bay Shore Stakes, San Jacinto Stakes, Saratoga Special and Clasico Dia de los Padres; 3rd Preakness Stakes, San Vicente Stakes and Vosburgh H.

IRISH CASTLE (b. 1967)	Bold Ruler (b. 1954)	Nasrullah	Nearco / Mumtaz Begum
		Miss Disco	Discovery / Outdone
	Castle Forbes (b. 1961)	Tulyar	Tehran / Neocracy
		Longford	Menow / Bold Irish
COMELY NELL (b. 1962)	Commodore M. (b. 1951)	Bull Lea	Bull Dog / Rose Leaves
		Early Autumn	Jamestown / Equinoctial
	Nellie L. (b. 1940)	Blenheim	Blandford / Malva
		Nellie Flag	American Flag / Nellie Morse

115   BOLD LAD (IRE) 2 (b.c., March 29, 1964)

Bred by Beatrice, Countess of Granard.

Won 5 races, placed 3, £24,790, in Ireland and England, at 2 and 3 years incl. Coventry Stakes, Champagne Stakes, Middle Park Stakes, Tetrarch Stakes; 2nd Lockinge Stakes; 3rd St. James's Palace Stakes; 4th 2,000 Guineas Stakes.

BOLD RULER (b. 1954)	Nasrullah (b. 1940)	Nearco	Pharos / Nogara
		Mumtaz Begum	Blenheim / Mumtaz Mahal
	Miss Disco (b. 1944)	Discovery	Display / Ariadne
		Outdone	Pompey / Sweep Out
BARN PRIDE (ch. 1957)	Democratic (ch. 1952)	Denturius	Gold Bridge / La Solfatara
		Light Fantasy	Signal Light / Last Act
	Fair Alycia (ch. 1952)	Alycidon	Donatello II / Aurora
		Fair Edwine	Fair Trial / Edvina

116   BOLD 'N DETERMINED 6 (b.f., March 22, 1977)

Bred by Dr. Gordon E. Layton, in U.S.A.

Won 13 races, placed 2, $751,543, in U.S.A., at 2 and 3 years, incl. Coaching Club American Oaks, Kentucky Oaks, Acorn Stakes, Spinster Stakes, Fantasy Stakes, Santa Susana Stakes, Oak Leaf Stakes and Maskette Stakes; 2nd Mother Goose Stakes; 4th Yellow Ribbon Stakes.

BOLD AND BRAVE (b. or br. 1963)	Bold Ruler (b. 1954)	Nasrullah	Nearco / Mumtaz Begum
		Miss Disco	Discovery / Outdone
	Bases Full (b. 1957)	Ambiorix II	Tourbillon / Lavendula II
		Striking	War Admiral / Baby League
PIDI (ch. 1969)	Determine (gr. 1951)	Alibhai	Hyperion / Teresina
		Koubis	Mahmoud / Brown Biscuit
	Perillante (ch. 1951)	Nigromante	Embrujo / Nigua
		Perilla	Alan Breck / Parragana

117   BOLD REASON 19 (b.c., April 8, 1968)

Bred by Capt. Harry F. Guggenheim, in U.S.A.

Won 7 races, placed 6, $304,082, in U.S.A., at 2 and 3 years, incl. Hollywood Derby, American Derby, Travers Stakes and Lexington H.; 3rd Kentucky Derby and Belmont Stakes.

HAIL TO REASON (br. 1958)	Turn-to (b. 1951)	Royal Charger	Nearco / Sun Princess
		Source Sucree	Admiral Drake / Lavendula II
	Nothirdchance (b. 1948)	Blue Swords	Blue Larkspur / Flaming Swords
		Galla Colors	Sir Gallahad III / Rouge et Noir
LALUN (b. 1952)	Djeddah (ch. 1945)	Djebel	Tourbillon / Loika
		Djezima	Asterus / Heldifann
	Be Faithful (br. 1942)	Bimelech	Black Toney / La Troienne
		Bloodroot	Blue Larkspur / Knockaney Bridge

118   BOLKONSKI 19 (ch.c., March 15, 1972)

Bred by Woodpark Ltd.

Won 5 races, placed 3, £77,188, in England and Italy, at 2 and 3 years, incl. 2,000 Guineas Stakes, St. James's Palace Stakes, Sussex Stakes, Premio Tevere; 2nd Ladbroke Craven Stakes.

BALIDAR (br. 1966)	Will Somers (br. 1955)	Tudor Minstrel	Owen Tudor / Sansonnet
		Queen's Jest	Nearco / Mirth
	Violet Bank (b. 1960)	The Phoenix	Chateau Bouscaut / Fille de Poete
		Leinster	Speckled Band / Garryard
PERENNIAL (ch. 1955)	Dante (br. 1942)	Nearco	Pharos / Nogara
		Rosy Legend	Dark Legend / Rosy Cheeks
	Cyphia (ch. 1949)	Watling Street	Fairway / Ranai
		Calluna	Hyperion / Campanula

119   BONCONTE DI MONTEFELTRO 2 (b.c., March 30, 1966)

Bred by Razza Spineta, in Italy.

Won 6 races, placed 2, 105,928,302 L., in Italy and France, at 3 and 4 years, incl. Derby Italiano, Gran Premio d'Italia, Premio Parioli and Premio Ellington; 4th Prix Royal Oak and Coppa d'Oro di Milano.

CHARLOTTESVILLE (b. 1957)	Prince Chevalier (b. 1943)	Prince Rose	Rose Prince / Indolence
		Chevalerie	Abbot's Speed / Kassala
	Noorani (ch. 1950)	Nearco	Pharos / Nogara
		Empire Glory	Singapore / Skyglory
BUONTALENTA (ch. 1949)	Zuccarello (ch. 1938)	Ortello	Teddy / Hollebeck
		Flumigela	Michelangelo / Flush
	Bayuk (ch. 1927)	Clarissimus	Radium / Quintessence
		L'Enigme	Verwood / Clef d'Or

120   BON MOT III 1 (ch.c., March 12, 1963)

Bred by F. W. Burmann, in France.

Won 4 races, placed 8, 1,940,770 fr., in France, at 3 and 4 years, incl. Prix de l'Arc de Triomphe and Prix de Lutece; 2nd Prix du Jockey-Club and Prix Royal Oak; 3rd Grand Prix de Paris, Prix Hocquart and Prix Ganay.

WORDEN II (ch. 1949)	Wild Risk (b. 1940)	Rialto	Rabelais / La Grêlée
		Wild Violet	Blandford / Wood Violet
	Sans Tares (ch. 1939)	Sind	Solario / Mirawala
		Tara	Teddy / Jean Gow
DJEBEL IDRA (b. 1957)	Phil Drake (b. 1952)	Admiral Drake	Craig an Eran / Plucky Liege
		Philippa	Vatellor / Philippa of Hainaut
	Djebellica (ch. 1948)	Djebel	Tourbillon / Loika
		Nica	Nino / Canalette

121　　BONNARD 22 (b.c., February 16, 1958)

Bred by Razza Dormello-Olgiata, in Italy.

Won 5 races, placed 1, £4,561, in Italy and England, from 2 to 5 years, incl. Doncaster Cup.

TENERANI (b. 1944)	Bellini (b. 1937)	Cavaliere d'Arpino	Havresac II / Chuette
		Bella Minna	Bachelor's Double / Santa Minna
	Tofanella (ch. 1931)	Apelle	Sardanapale / Angelina
		Try Try Again	Cylgad / Perseverance II
BUONAMICA (b. 1943)	Niccolo Dell'Arca (b. 1938)	Coronach	Hurry On / Wet Kiss
		Nogara	Havresac II / Catnip
	Bernina (b. 1931)	Pharos	Phalaris / Scapa Flow
		Bunworry	Great Sport / Waffles

122　　BOUCHER 1 (ch.c., April 7, 1969)

Bred by Ogden Phipps, in U.S.A.

Won 6 races, placed 2, £50,468, in England and Ireland, at 2 and 3 years, incl. St. Leger Stakes, Beresford Stakes, Desmond Stakes, Nijinsky Stakes; 4th Observer Gold Cup.

RIBOT (b. 1952)	Tenerani (b. 1944)	Bellini	Cavaliere d'Arpino / Bella Minna
		Tofanella	Apelle / Try Try Again
	Romanella (ch. 1943)	El Greco	Pharos / Gay Gamp
		Barbara Burrini	Papyrus / Bucolic
GLAMOUR (b. 1953)	Nasrullah (b. 1940)	Nearco	Pharos / Nogara
		Mumtaz Begum	Blenheim / Mumtaz Mahal
	Striking (b. 1947)	War Admiral	Man o'War / Brushup
		Baby League	Bubbling Over / La Troienne

123　　BOUNTEOUS 14 (b.c., March 4, 1958)

Bred by Mrs. H. Leggat.

Won 7 races, placed 6, £36,119, in England and France, from 2 to 4 years, incl. Dewhurst Stakes, Prix Kergorlay, Grand Prix de Deauville; 2nd St. Leger, Prix de Barbeville; 3rd Chester Vase, Prix Henry Delamarre.

ROCKEFELLA (br. 1941)	Hyperion (ch. 1930)	Gainsborough	Bayardo / Rosedrop
		Selene	Chaucer / Serenissima
	Rockfel (br. 1935)	Felstead	Spion Kop / Felkington
		Rockliffe	Santorb / Sweet Rocket
MARIE ELIZABETH (ch. 1948)	Mazarin (b. 1938)	Mieuxce	Massine / L'Olivete
		Boiarinia	Viceroy / Vilna
	Miss Honor (ch. 1932)	Mr. Jinks	Tetratema / False Piety
		Bayora	Bayardo / Honora

124　　BOURBON 7 (b.c., January 30, 1968)

Bred by Alec Head, in France.

Won 4 races, placed 3, 819,701 fr., in France and England, from 2 to 4 years, incl. Prix Royal Oak and Prix Hocquart; 2nd Prix de Guiche; 3rd Prix Maurice de Nieuil; 4th Observer Gold Cup.

LE FABULEUX (ch. 1961)	Wild Risk (b. 1940)	Rialto	Rabelais / La Grêlée
		Wild Violet	Blandford / Wood Violet
	Anguar (b. 1950)	Verso II	Pinceau / Variété
		La Rochelle	Easton / Sans Tares
BIOBELLE (b. 1960)	Cernobbio (ch. 1953)	Prince Bio	Prince Rose / Biologie
		Ceruleine	Victrix / Cerulea
	La Beloli (b. 1948)	Domenico Ghirlandaio	Blenheim / Delleana
		Alibranda	Ortello / Nuwara Eliya

125　　BOWL GAME 26 (b.g., April 20, 1974)

Bred by Greentree Stud Inc., in U.S.A.

Won 11 races, placed 11, $907,083, in U.S.A., from 3 to 6 years, incl. Washington D.C. International, Turf Classic, Man o'War Stakes, Gulfstream Park H., Pan American H., Arlington H., Dixie H. and Hialeah Turf Cup; 2nd Hollywood Invitational H., Brooklyn H. and Tidal H.; 3rd Bowling Green H. (twice).

TOM ROLFE (b. 1962)	Ribot (b. 1952)	Tenerani	Bellini / Tofanella
		Romanella	El Greco / Barbara Burrini
	Pocahontas (br. 1955)	Roman	Sir Gallahad III / Buckup
		How	Princequillo / The Squaw
AROUND THE ROSES (br. 1963)	Round Table (b. 1954)	Princequillo	Prince Rose / Cosquilla
		Knight's Daughter	Sir Cosmo / Feola
	Rose Coral (br. 1950)	Rockefella	Hyperion / Rockfel
		Lady Mary Rose	Nearco / Rosemain

126　　BRACCIO DA MONTONE 2 (b.c., 1960)

Bred by Razza Spineta, in Italy.

Won 3 races, 22,800,000 L., in Italy, at 3 years, incl. Derby Italiano and Premio Lazio.

VANDALE II (b. 1943)	Plassy (b. 1932)	Bosworth	Son-in-Law / Serenissima
		Pladda	Phalaris / Rothesay Bay
	Vanille (b. 1929)	La Farina	Sans Souci II / Malatesta
		Vaya	Beppo / Waterhen
BUONTALENTA (ch. 1949)	Zuccarello (ch. 1938)	Ortello	Teddy / Hollebeck
		Flumigela	Michelangelo / Flush
	Bayuk (ch. 1927)	Clarissimus	Radium / Quintessence
		L'Enigme	Verwood / Clef d'Or

127   BRACEY BRIDGE 1 (b.f., April 3, 1962)

Bred by William Hill Studs.

Won 3 races, placed 2, £17,852, in England and Ireland, at 3 years, incl. Ribblesdale Stakes, Park Hill Stakes, Princess Royal Stakes; 3rd Irish Guinness Oaks, Yorkshire Oaks.

CHANTEUR II (br. 1942)	Chateau Bouscaut (b. 1927)	Kircubbin	Captivation / Avon Hack
		Ramondie	Neil Gow / La Rille
	La Diva (br. 1937)	Blue Skies	Blandford / Blue Pill
		La Traviata	Alcantara II / Tregaron
RUTHERFORD BRIDGE (b. 1955)	Sayajirao (br. 1944)	Nearco	Pharos / Nogara
		Rosy Legend	Dark Legend / Rosy Cheeks
	Rustic Bridge (b. 1949)	Bois Roussel	Vatout / Plucky Liege
		Wyn	Winalot / Bon Mot

128   BRAVE JOHNNY 5 (gr.c., April 1, 1975)

Bred by M. and V. Bertella, in France.

Won 4 races, placed 2, 507,200 fr., in France, at 2 and 3 years, incl. Prix Royal Oak and Prix de l'Esperance.

DANCING LAD (gr. 1966)	Sicambre (br. 1948)	Prince Bio	Prince Rose / Biologie
		Sif	Rialto / Suavita
	Hula Dancer (gr. 1960)	Native Dancer	Polynesian / Geisha
		Flash On	Ambrose Light / Generosity
BRAVE HENRIETTE (b./br. 1967)	Abdos (br. 1959)	Arbar	Djebel / Astronomie
		Pretty Lady	Umidwar / La Moqueuse
	La Gamma (br. 1962)	Herbager	Vandale II / Flagette
		Corteira	Goya II / Semiramide

129   BRETON 4 (b.c., April 4, 1967)

Bred by Dr. J. A. Burkhardt, in Ireland.

Won 5 races, placed 2, 924,842 fr., in France, at 2 and 3 years, incl. Grand Criterium, Prix de la Salamandre and Prix de Fontainebleau; 2nd Poule d'Essai des Poulains and Prix Morny.

RELKO (b. 1960)	Tanerko (br. 1953)	Tantieme	Deux pour Cent / Terka
		La Divine	Fair Copy / La Diva
	Relance III (ch. 1952)	Relic	War Relic / Bridal Colors
		Polaire II	Le Volcan / Stella Polaris
LA MELBA (br. 1957)	Chanteur II (b. 1942)	Chateau Bouscaut	Kircubbin / Ramondie
		La Diva	Blue Skies / La Traviata
	Mary Tavy (b./br. 1945)	Chulmleigh	Singapore / Rose of England
		Henriette Maria	Bosworth / Her Majesty II

130   BRIGADIER GERARD 14 (b.c., March 4, 1968)

Bred by Mr. and Mrs. J. L. Hislop.

Won 17 races, placed 1, £253,026, in England, from 2 to 4 years, incl. Middle Park Stakes, 2,000 Guineas Stakes, Sussex Stakes, Champion Stakes (twice), Eclipse Stakes, King George VI and Queen Elizabeth Stakes, St. James's Palace Stakes, Queen Elizabeth II Stakes (twice), Lockinge Stakes, Prince of Wales Stakes, Goodwood Mile, Westbury Stakes; 2nd Benson and Hedges Gold Cup.

QUEEN'S HUSSAR (b. 1960)	March Past (br. 1950)	Petition	Fair Trial / Art Paper
		Marcelette	William of Valence / Permavon
	Jojo (gr. 1950)	Vilmorin	Gold Bridge / Queen of the Meadows
		Fairy Jane	Fair Trial / Light Tackle
LA PAIVA (ch. 1956)	Prince Chevalier (b. 1943)	Prince Rose	Rose Prince / Indolence
		Chevalerie	Abbot's Speed / Kassala
	Brazen Molly (b. 1940)	Horus	Papyrus / Lady Peregrine
		Molly Adare	Phalaris / Molly Desmond

131   BRINGLEY 1 (ch.f., March 9, 1965)

Bred by J. W. Orbell.

Won 5 races, placed 4, £11,860, in England, from 2 to 4 years, incl. Park Hill Stakes, Lancashire Oaks; 3rd Hardwicke Stakes, John Porter Stakes.

POACHING (b. 1952)	Owen Tudor (br. 1938)	Hyperion	Gainsborough / Selene
		Mary Tudor II	Pharos / Anna Bolena
	Game Book (ch. 1947)	Big Game	Bahram / Myrobella
		Justice	Fair Trial / Pelerine
GONDOLETTE II (b. 1960)	Tanerko (br. 1953)	Tantieme	Deux pour Cent / Terka
		La Divine	Fair Copy / La Diva
	Ghaziya (ch. 1954)	Bozzetto	Pharos / Bunworry
		Gambara	Chateau Bouscaut / Golden Calf

132   BROADWAY DANCER 12 (b.f., February 16, 1972)

Bred by Nuckols Brothers, in U.S.A.

Won 2 races, placed 2, 432,535 fr., in France, at 2 and 3 years, incl. Prix Morny; 2nd Prix Robert Papin; 3rd Poule d'Essai des Pouliches.

NORTHERN DANCER (b. 1961)	Nearctic (br. 1954)	Nearco	Pharos / Nogara
		Lady Angela	Hyperion / Sister Sarah
	Natalma (b. 1957)	Native Dancer	Polynesian / Geisha
		Almahmoud	Mahmoud / Arbitrator
BROADWAY MELODY (br. 1964)	Tudor Melody (br. 1956)	Tudor Minstrel	Owen Tudor / Sansonnet
		Matelda	Dante / Fairly Hot
	Goldwyn Girl (ch. 1953)	Court Martial	Fair Trial / Instantaneous
		Zolotaia	Gold Bridge / Thamar

133   **BROOK** 1 (gr.c., March 8, 1970)

Bred by T. Stack.

Won 12 races, placed 4, £44,351, in Italy, England and France, from 2 to 4 years incl. Hungerford Stakes, Premio Emilio Turati, Premio Chiusura and Queen Anne Stakes; 2nd Gran Criterium and Prix de la Porte Maillot.

BIRDBROOK (gr. 1961)	Mossborough (ch. 1947)	Nearco	Pharos / Nogara
		All Moonshine	Bobsleigh / Selene
	Game Bird (gr. 1955)	Big Game	Bahram / Myrobella
		Sweet Pepper	Nasrullah / Saucy Bella
BEAN FEAST (ch. 1965)	Hornbeam (ch. 1953)	Hyperion	Gainsborough / Selene
		Thicket	Nasrullah / Thorn Wood
	Relish (ch. 1959)	Prince Chevalier	Prince Rose / Chevalerie
		Sugar Bun	Mahmoud / Galatea II

134   **BRUNI** 22 (gr.c., May 3, 1972)

Bred by Barrettstown Estates.

Won 5 races, placed 9, £108,148, in England and U.S.A., from 2 to 5 years, incl. St. Leger Stakes, Cumberland Lodge Stakes, Yorkshire Cup, 2nd King George VI and Queen Elizabeth Diamond Stakes, Hardwicke Stakes, Henry II Stakes (won, but disq.), Goodwood Cup; 4th Ascot Gold Cup.

SEA HAWK II (gr. 1963)	Herbager (b. 1956)	Vandale II	Plassy / Vanille
		Flagette	Escamillo / Fidgette
	Sea Nymph (gr. 1957)	Free Man	Norseman / Fantine
		Sea Spray	Ocean Swell / Pontoon
BOMBAZINE (b. 1963)	Shantung (b. 1956)	Sicambre	Prince Bio / Sif
		Barley Corn	Hyperion / Schiaparelli
	Whimsical (br. 1958)	Nearula	Nasrullah / Respite
		Whimbrel	The Phoenix / Lindus

135   **BUCKPASSER** 1 (b.c., April 28, 1963)

Bred by Ogden Phipps, in U.S.A.

Won 25 races, placed 5, $1,462,014, in U.S.A., from 2 to 4 years, incl. Jockey Club Gold Cup, American Derby, Arlington Classic, Brooklyn H., Metropolitan H., Suburban H., San Fernando Stakes, Chicagoan Stakes, Flamingo Stakes, Woodward Stakes, Travers Stakes, Lawrence Realization Stakes, Leonard Richards Stakes, Everglades Stakes, Malibu Stakes, Champagne Stakes, Hopeful Stakes and Sapling Stakes; 2nd Futurity Stakes, Brooklyn H. and Woodward Stakes; 3rd Bowling Green H.

TOM FOOL (b. 1949)	Menow (b. 1935)	Pharamond	Phalaris / Selene
		Alcibiades	Supremus / Regal Roman
	Gaga (b. 1942)	Bull Dog	Teddy / Plucky Liege
		Alpoise	Equipoise / Laughing Queen
BUSANDA (bl. 1947)	War Admiral (br. 1934)	Man o'War	Fair Play / Mahubah
		Brushup	Sweep / Annette K.
	Businesslike (br. 1939)	Blue Larkspur	Black Servant / Blossom Time
		La Troienne	Teddy / Helene de Troie

136   **BUCKSKIN** 3 (b.c., April 1, 1973)

Bred by Dayton Limited, in France.

Won 10 races, placed 7, £185,444, in France, England and Germany, from 3 to 6 years, incl. Prix du Cadran (twice), Doncaster Cup, Jockey Club Cup, Henry II Stakes, Prix Jean Prat and Prix de Barbeville; 2nd Ascot Gold Cup (twice); 3rd Preis von Europa and Prix Gladiateur; 4th Ascot Gold Cup and Grosser Preis von Berlin.

YELAPA (b. 1966)	Mossborough (ch. 1947)	Nearco	Pharos / Nogara
		All Moonshine	Bobsleigh / Selene
	Your Point (br. 1955)	Nirgal	Goya / Castillane
		Your Game	Beau Pere / Winkle II
BETE A BON DIEU (b. 1964)	Herbager (b. 1956)	Vandale II	Plassy / Vanille
		Flagette	Escamillo / Fidgette,
	Caralline (b. 1956)	Wild Risk	Rialto / Wild Violet
		Coral	Colorado Kid / Bon Marche

137   **BUOY** 11 (ch.c., April 7, 1970)

Bred by R. D. Hollingsworth.

Won 6 races, placed 5, £61,306, in England and Ireland, at 3 and 4 years incl. Coronation Cup, Great Voltigeur Stakes, Yorkshire Cup, Princess of Wales's Stakes; 2nd St. Leger, Jockey Club Stakes, Hardwicke Stakes; 3rd Irish Sweeps Derby; 4th King George VI and Queen Elizabeth Stakes.

AUREOLE (ch. 1950)	Hyperion (ch. 1930)	Gainsborough	Bayardo / Rosedrop
		Selene	Chaucer / Serenissima
	Angelola (b. 1945)	Donatello II	Blenheim / Delleana
		Feola	Friar Marcus / Aloe
RIPECK (br. 1959)	Ribot (b. 1952)	Tenerani	Bellini / Tofanella
		Romanella	El Greco / Barbara Burrini
	Kyak (bl. or br. 1953)	Big Game	Bahram / Myrobella
		Felucca	Nearco / Felsetta

138   **BUSACA** 21 (b.f., March 8, 1974)

Bred by Dollanstown Stud Establishment, in France.

Won 5 races, placed 2, £47,948, in England and France, at 3 years, incl. Yorkshire Oaks, Lancashire Oaks; 2nd Ribblesdale Stakes; 4th Prix Vermeille.

BUSTED (b. 1963)	Crepello (ch. 1954)	Donatello II	Blenheim / Delleana
		Crepuscule	Mieuxce / Red Sunset
	Sans le Sou (b. 1957)	Vimy	Wild Risk / Mimi
		Martial Loan	Court Martial / Loan
SARACA (b. 1966)	Shantung (b. 1956)	Sicambre	Prince Bio / Sif
		Barley Corn	Hyperion / Schiaparelli
	Hevea (b. 1961)	Herbager	Vandale II / Flagette
		Princesse Reine	Prince Chevalier / Kingscavil

139   **BUSIRIS** 19 (b.c., April 18, 1971)

Bred by Nelson Bunker Hunt, in U.S.A.

Won 3 races, placed 3, 696,503 fr., in France and England, from 2 to 4 years, incl. Prix Royal Oak; 2nd Prix du Cadran; 4th Prix Ganay and Observer Gold Cup.

RIDAN (b. 1959)	Nantallah (b. 1953)	Nasrullah	Nearco / Mumtaz Begum
		Shimmer	Flares / Broad Ripple
	Rough Shod (b. 1944)	Gold Bridge	Swynford or Golden Boss / Flying Diadem
		Dalmary	Blandford / Simon's Shoes
LILY PONS (b. 1957)	Licencioso (b. 1941)	L'Oriflamme	Madrigal II / Outarde
		Arimathea	Courtisan / Ariege
	Carusa (b. 1951)	Treble Crown	King Salmon / Private Entree
		Urca	Corn Belt / Ufa

140   **BUSTED** 2 (b.c., May 6, 1963)

Bred by Snailwell Stud Co. Ltd.

Won 5 races, placed 3, £59,515, in England, Ireland and France, from 2 to 4 years, incl. King George VI and Queen Elizabeth Stakes, Eclipse Stakes, Gallinule Stakes, Coronation Stakes (Sandown Park), Prix Henri Foy; 2nd Desmond Stakes.

CREPELLO (ch. 1954)	Donatello II (ch. 1934)	Blenheim	Blandford / Malva
		Delleana	Clarissimus / Duccia di Buoninsegna
	Crepuscule (ch. 1948)	Mieuxce	Massine / L'Olivete
		Red Sunset	Solario / Dulce II
SANS LE SOU (b. 1957)	Vimy (b. 1952)	Wild Risk	Rialto / Wild Violet
		Mimi	Black Devil / Mignon
	Martial Loan (gr. 1950)	Court Martial	Fair Trial / Instantaneous
		Loan	Portlaw / Borrow

141   **BUSTINO** 1 (b.c., April 14, 1971)

Bred by E. Cooper Bland.

Won 5 races, placed 4, £145,858, in England and France, from 2 to 4 years, incl. St. Leger, Coronation Cup, Great Voltigeur Stakes, Ladbroke Derby Trial Stakes, Sandown Classic Trial Stakes; 2nd Grand Prix de Paris, King George VI and Queen Elizabeth Diamond Stakes; 4th Derby Stakes.

BUSTED (b. 1963)	Crepello (ch. 1954)	Donatello II	Blenheim / Delleana
		Crepuscule	Mieuxce / Red Sunset
	Sans le Sou (b. 1957)	Vimy	Wild Risk / Mimi
		Martial Loan	Court Martial / Loan
SHIP YARD (ch. 1963)	Doutelle (ch. 1954)	Prince Chevalier	Prince Rose / Chevalerie
		Above Board	Straight Deal / Feola
	Paving Stone (b. 1946)	Fairway	Phalaris / Scapa Flow
		Rosetta	Kantar / Rose Red

142   **CABHURST** 5 (b.c., March 22, 1965)

Bred by Mme. A. Mariotti de Forest, in France.

Won 3 races, placed 7, 414,735 fr., in France, from 2 to 4 years, incl. Prix de la Foret and Prix Eclipse; 2nd Criterium de Maisons-Laffitte and Prix de Seine-et-Oise; 3rd Prix Maurice de Gheest; 4th Poule d'Essai des Poulains.

PENHURST (ch. 1958)	Court Martial (ch. 1942)	Fair Trial	Fairway / Lady Juror
		Instantaneous	Hurry On / Picture
	La Rochelle (br. 1945)	Easton	Dark Legend / Phaona
		Sans Tares	Sind / Tara
CABRELLA (b. 1957)	Caldarium (br. 1939)	Brantome	Blandford / Vitamine
		Chaudiere	Massine / Bouillotte
	Eppine d'Or (b. 1950)	Tourbillon	Ksar / Durban
		Eppe Sauvage	Firdaussi / Esterelle

143   **CAERGWRLE** 7 (ch.f., February 14, 1965)

Bred by Lady Murless.

Won 3 races, placed 3, £22,615, in England, at 2 and 3 years, incl. 1,000 Guineas Stakes.

CREPELLO (ch. 1954)	Donatello II (ch. 1934)	Blenheim	Blandford / Malva
		Delleana	Clarissimus / Duccia di Buoninsegna
	Crepuscule (ch. 1948)	Mieuxce	Massine / L'Olivete
		Red Sunset	Solario / Dulce II
CAERPHILLY (ch. 1959)	Abernant (gr. 1946)	Owen Tudor	Hyperion / Mary Tudor II
		Rustom Mahal	Rustom Pasha / Mumtaz Mahal
	Cheetah (ch. 1954)	Big Game	Bahram / Myrobella
		Malapert	Portlaw / Malatesta

144   **CAIRN ROUGE** 1 (b.f., March 9, 1977)

Bred by Mrs. Janet Brady.

Won 6 races, placed 1, £172,907, in Ireland and England, at 2 and 3 years, incl. Goffs Irish 1,000 Guineas, Champion Stakes, Coronation Stakes, Mulcahy Stakes; 2nd Benson and Hedges Gold Cup.

PITCAIRN (b. 1971)	Petingo (b. 1965)	Petition	Fair Trial / Art Paper
		Alcazar	Alycidon / Quarterdeck
	Border Bounty (b. 1965)	Bounteous	Rockefella / Marie Elizabeth
		B. Flat	Chanteur II / Ardeen
LITTLE HILLS (b. br. 1971)	Candy Cane (b. 1965)	Crepello	Donatello II / Crepuscule
		Candy Gift	Princely Gift / Kandy Sauce
	Ballyogan Queen (br. 1956)	Ballyogan	Fair Trial / Serial
		Stone Crop	Kingstone / Salvia

145 **CALDARELLO** 3 (b.c., March 15, 1962)

Bred by M. Fabiani and E. Speelman, in France.

Won 8 races, placed 8, 763,254 fr., in France, from 2 to 5 years, incl. Prix d'Ispahan and Prix Gontaut-Biron; 3rd Prix du Moulin de Longchamp and Prix Dollar.

KLAIRON (b. 1952)	Clarion III (b. 1944)	Djebel	Tourbillon / Loika
		Columba	Colorado / Gay Bird
	Kalmia (b. 1931)	Kantar	Alcantara II / Karabe
		Sweet Lavender	Swynford / Marchetta
CARALLINE (b. 1956)	Wild Risk (b. 1940)	Rialto	Rabelais / La Grelee
		Wild Violet	Blandford / Wood Violet
	Coral (b. 1943)	Colorado Kid	Colorado / Baby Polly
		Bon Marché	Palais Royal / Lickmolassy

146 **CALIBAN** 13 (b.c., March 13, 1966)

Bred by Snailwell Stud Co. Ltd.

Won 3 races, placed 1, £29,317, in England and France, from 2 to 4 years, incl. Coronation Cup, Blue Riband Trial Stakes; 2nd Prix Lupin.

RAGUSA (b. 1960)	Ribot (b. 1952)	Tenerani	Bellini / Tofanella
		Romanella	El Greco / Barbara Burrini
	Fantan II (b. 1952)	Ambiorix II	Tourbillon / Lavendula II
		Red Eye	Petee-Wrack / Charred Keg
ISLAND LORE (ch. 1959)	Court Martial (ch. 1942)	Fair Trial	Fairway / Lady Juror
		Instantaneous	Hurry On / Picture
	Aleutian (ch. 1952)	Alycidon	Donatello II / Aurora
		Rona	Epigram / Fara

147 **CALVE** 8 (b.f., April 14, 1969)

Bred by Beatrice, Countess of Granard.

Won 2 races, placed 2, £11,812, in Ireland and England, at 2 and 3 years, incl. Coronation Stakes.

BOLD RULER (b. 1954)	Nasrullah (b. 1940)	Nearco	Pharos / Nogara
		Mumtaz Begum	Blenheim / Mumtaz Mahal
	Miss Disco (b. 1944)	Discovery	Display / Ariadne
		Outdone	Pompey / Sweep Out
PATTI (b. 1961)	Chanteur II (b. 1942)	Chateau Bouscaut	Kircubbin / Ràmondie
		La Diva	Blue Skies / La Traviata
	Eastern Fairy (ch. 1947)	Persian Gulf	Bahram / Double Life
		Sea Fairy	Fair Trial / Portree

148 **CANDY SPOTS** 2 (ch.c., April 14, 1960)

Bred by Rex C. Ellsworth, in U.S.A.

Won 12 races, placed 6, $824,718, in U.S.A., from 2 to 5 years, incl. Preakness Stakes, American Derby, Arlington Classic, Florida Derby, Jersey Derby, Santa Anita Derby, Arlington-Washington Futurity and San Pasqual H.; 2nd Belmont Stakes, Chicagoan Stakes, Santa Anita H., San Carlos H. and San Antonio H.; 3rd Kentucky Derby.

NIGROMANTE (ch. 1944)	Embrujo (ch. 1936)	Congreve	Copyright / Per Noi
		Encore	Your Majesty / Efilet
	Nigua (ch. 1936)	Songe	Sundari / Salamanca
		Nitouche	Saint Wolf / Nenette
CANDY DISH (b. 1953)	Khaled (b. 1943)	Hyperion	Gainsborough / Selene
		Eclair	Ethnarch / Black Ray
	Feather Time (b. 1945)	Beau Pere	Son-in-Law / Cinna
		Heather Time	Time Maker / Heatherland

149 **CANISBAY** 12 (ch.c., March 29, 1961)

Bred by H.M. The Queen.

Won 2 races, placed 3, £30,981, in England, at 3 and 4 years, incl. Eclipse Stakes.

DOUTELLE (ch. 1954)	Prince Chevalier (b. 1943)	Prince Rose	Rose Prince / Indolence
		Chevalerie	Abbot's Speed / Kassala
	Above Board (b. 1947)	Straight Deal	Solario / Good Deal
		Feola	Friar Marcus / Aloe
STROMA (ch. 1955)	Luminary (ch. 1946)	Fair Trial	Fairway / Lady Juror
		Luciebella	Rodosto / Lula
	Whoa Emma (b. 1950)	Prince Chevalier	Prince Rose / Chevalerie
		Ready	Signal Light / Judy

150 **CANNONADE** 2 (b.c., May 12, 1971)

Bred by John M. Olin, in U.S.A.

Won 7 races, placed 9, $501,164, in U.S.A., at 2 and 3 years, incl. Kentucky Derby and Kentucky Jockey Club Stakes; 2nd Florida Derby; 3rd Preakness Stakes, Belmont Stakes, Heritage Stakes and Champagne Stakes.

BOLD BIDDER (b. 1962)	Bold Ruler (b. 1954)	Nasrullah	Nearco / Mumtaz Begum
		Miss Disco	Discovery / Outdone
	High Bid (b. 1956)	To Market	Market Wise / Pretty Does
		Stepping Stone	Princequillo / Step Across
QUEEN SUCREE (b. 1966)	Ribot (b. 1952)	Tenerani	Bellini / Tofanella
		Romanella	El Greco / Barbara Burrini
	Cosmah (b. 1953)	Cosmic Bomb	Pharamond / Banish Fear
		Almahmoud	Mahmoud / Arbitrator

151   CANONERO II 4 (b.c., April 24, 1968)

Bred by Edward B. Benjamin, in U.S.A.

Won 9 races, placed 7, $360,980, in U.S.A. and Venezuela, from 2 to 4 years, incl. Kentucky Derby, Preakness Stakes and Stymie H.; 2nd Carter H.; 4th Belmont Stakes.

PRETENDRE (ch. 1963)	Doutelle (ch. 1954)	Prince Chevalier	Prince Rose / Chevalerie
		Above Board	Straight Deal / Feola
	Limicola (ch. 1948)	Verso II	Pinceau / Variété
		Uccello	Donatello II / Great Tit
DIXIELAND II (b. 1961)	Nantallah (b. 1953)	Nasrullah	Nearco / Mumtaz Begum
		Shimmer	Flares / Broad Ripple
	Ragtime Band (b. 1945)	Johnstown	Jamestown / La France
		Martial Air	Man o'War / Baton

152   CAPO BON 11 (b.c., April 12, 1974)

Bred by Razza di Vedano, in England.

Won 10 races, placed 8, 207,280,000 L., in Italy, from 2 to 4 years, incl. Premio Presidente della Repubblica, Premio Parioli, Premio Emilio Turati, Premio Pisa, Premio Besnate (twice), Premio Natale di Roma and Premio Ribot; 2nd Derby Italiano, Criterium Nazionale and Premio Emilio Turati; 3rd Premio Presidente della Repubblica, Gran Criterium and Premio Federico Tesio.

BALLYMOSS (ch. 1954)	Mossborough (ch. 1947)	Nearco	Pharos / Nogara
		All Moonshine	Bobsleigh / Selene
	Indian Call (ch. 1936)	Singapore	Gainsborough / Tetrabbazia
		Flittemere	Buchan / Keysoe
CRIMEA (br. 1964)	Above Suspicion (b. 1956)	Court Martial	Fair Trial / Instantaneous
		Above Board	Straight Deal / Feola
	Chaddleworth (ch. 1954)	Tudor Minstrel	Owen Tudor / Sansonnet
		Quickwood	Precipitation / Cherry Wood

153   CARABELLA 4 (ch.f.; April 15, 1964)

Bred by Beatrice, Countess of Granard, in France.

Won 4 races, placed 2, 253,091 fr., in France, at 2 and 3 years, incl. Prix Jacques le Marois and Prix d'Astarté.

PRINCE TAJ (b. 1954)	Prince Bio (b. 1941)	Prince Rose	Rose Prince / Indolence
		Biologie	Bacteriophage / Eponge
	Malindi (br. 1947)	Nearco	Pharos / Nogara
		Mumtaz Begum	Blenheim / Mumtaz Mahal
LA CARAVELLE (b. 1959)	Worden II (ch. 1949)	Wild Risk	Rialto / Wild Violet
		Sans Tares	Sind / Tara
	Barquerolle (b. 1951)	Turmoil	Tourbillon / Blue Iras
		La Capitane	Admiral Drake / Herlinde

154   CARACOL 4 (b.c., March 7, 1969)

Bred by Gestüt Fährhof, in France.

Won 10 races, placed 6, 402,340 DM., in Germany, from 2 to 5 years, incl. Grosser Preis von Baden, Henckel-Rennen, Furstenberg-Rennen, Grosser Hansa Preis and Grosser Preis der Stadt Gelsenkirchen; 2nd Grosser Preis von Dortmund; 3rd Union-Rennen.

TANERKO (br. 1953)	Tantieme (b. 1947)	Deux pour Cent	Deiri / Dix pour Cent
		Terka	Indus / La Furka
	La Divine (br. 1943)	Fair Copy	Fairway / Composure
		La Diva	Blue Skies / La Traviata
CRAPE BAND (ch. 1960)	Crepello (ch. 1954)	Donatello II	Blenheim / Delleana
		Crepuscule	Mieuxce / Red Sunset
	Band Practice (ch. 1953)	Fair Trial	Fairway / Lady Juror
		Syncopation Rhythm	Mieuxce / Astaire

155   CARACOLERO 4 (ch.c., May 20, 1971)

Bred by Leslie Combs II, in U.S.A.

Won 4 races, placed 2, 1,475,380 fr., in France, at 2 and 3 years, incl. Prix du Jockey-Club.

GRAUSTARK (ch. 1963)	Ribot (b. 1952)	Tenerani	Bellini / Tofanella
		Romanella	El Greco / Barbara Burrini
	Flower Bowl (b. 1952)	Alibhai	Hyperion / Teresina
		Flower Bed	Beau Pere / Boudoir II
BETTY LORAINE (ch. 1965)	Prince John (ch. 1953)	Princequillo	Prince Rose / Cosquilla
		Not Afraid	Count Fleet / Banish Fear
	Gay Hostess (ch. 1957)	Royal Charger	Nearco / Sun Princess
		Your Hostess	Alibhai / Boudoir II

156   CARD KING 17 (br.c., March 26, 1968)

Bred by A. Phipps, in U.S.A.

Won 5 races, placed 19, 2,538,791 fr., in France, Italy, England, Germany and U.S.A., from 2 to 7 years, incl. Grand Prix de Deauville and Prix d'Harcourt; 2nd Prix Ganay, Gran Premio d'Italia, Gran Premio di Milano, Grosser Preis von Baden, Benson and Hedges Gold Cup, Prix du Conseil Municipal, Prix d'Harcourt and La Coupe; 3rd Gran Premio d'Italia and Grosser Preis von Baden; 4th Prix de l'Arc de Triomphe, Prix Ganay, Grand Prix de Saint-Cloud, Gran Premio di Milano and Washington D.C. International.

CARDINGTON KING (b. 1952)	Borealis (ch. 1941)	Brumeux	Teddy / La Brume
		Aurora	Hyperion / Rose Red
	Temple Bar (br. 1945)	Fairway	Phalaris / Scapa Flow
		Jury	Hurry On / Trustful
NANTUA (bl. 1960)	Again II (b. 1948)	Foxhunter	Foxlaw / Trimestral
		Encore Mieuxce	Mieuxce / Cora Deans
	Chtiglia (br. 1950)	Bahram	Blandford / Friar's Daughter
		Kiglia	Biribi / Kill Lady

157   **CARLOS PRIMERO** 5 (b.c., April 25, 1964)

Bred by Allevamento Alpe Ravetta, in Italy.

Won 9 races, placed 11, 58,435,000 L., in Italy, from 2 to 4 years, incl. Premio Roma, St. Leger Italiano and Premio Principe Amedeo; 2nd Gran Premio de: Jockey Club and Gran Premio di Milano; 4th Gran Premio d'Italia.

JANITOR (br. 1950)	Pharis II (br. 1936)	Pharos	Phalaris / Scapa Flow
		Carissima	Clarissimus / Casquetts
	Orlamonde (b. 1937)	Asterus	Teddy / Astrella
		Naic	Gainsborough / Only One
CHARLOTTE (b. 1960)	Antonio Canale (ch. 1946)	Torbido	Ortello / Tempesta
		Acquaforte	Blenheim / Althea
	Cantora (b. 1954)	Tourbillon	Ksar / Durban
		Polaris	Pharis II / Pompeia

158   **CARMARTHEN** 14 (ch.c., April 1, 1964)

Bred by Mme. R. B. Strassburger, in France.

Won 7 races, placed 6, 1,110,089 fr., in France and U.S.A., from 2 to 5 years, incl. Prix Ganay, Prix Daru, Prix du Prince d'Orange, Prix d'Harcourt and Prix Exbury; 2nd Prix des Chenes and Prix du Prince d'Orange; 3rd Prix de l'Arc de Triomphe and Prix Hocquart; 4th Washington D.C. International.

DEVON (ch. 1958)	Worden II (ch. 1949)	Wild Risk	Rialto / Wild Violet
		Sans Tares	Sind / Tara
	Sees (b. 1953)	Court Martial	Fair Trial / Instantaneous
		Carrere	Le Pacha / Lady Penn
KUWAIT (ch. 1956)	Persian Gulf (b. 1940)	Bahram	Blandford / Friar's Daughter
		Double Life	Bachelor's Double / Saint Joan
	Sol d'Or (ch. 1937)	Solario	Gainsborough / Sun Worship
		Fair Flame	Bruleur / Fair Simone

159   **CARNAUBA** 16 (br.f., April 25, 1972)

Bred by Nelson Bunker Hunt, in U.S.A.

Won 8 races, placed 4, 61,406,241 L., in Italy and England, at 2 and 3 years, incl. Oaks d'Italia, Fred Darling Stakes, Premio Chiusura and Criterium di Roma; 3rd Premio Pisa; 4th Premio Lydia Tesio.

NOHOLME II (ch. 1956)	Star Kingdom (ch. 1946)	Stardust	Hyperion / Sister Stella
		Impromptu	Concerto / Thoughtless
	Oceana (b. 1947)	Colombo	Manna / Lady Nairne
		Orama	Diophon / Cantelupe
CARNIVAL QUEEN (br. 1962)	Amerigo (ch. 1955)	Nearco	Pharos / Nogara
		Sanlinea	Precipitation / Sun Helmet
	Circus Ring (br. 1941)	Bull Dog	Teddy / Plucky Liege
		Arena	St. James / Oval

160   **CARO** 3 (gr.c., April 11, 1967)

Bred by Countess Margit Batthyany, in Ireland.

Won 6 races, placed 10, 2,066,755 fr., in France and England, from 2 to 4 years, incl. Poule d'Essai des Poulains, Prix d'Ispahan, Prix Ganay, Prix d'Harcourt and Prix Dollar; 2nd Eclipse Stakes, Prix Foy, Prix Eugene Adam, Prix d'Arenberg, Prix Eclipse and Prix de Ris-Orangis; 3rd Prix du Jockey-Club; 4th Prix de l'Arc de Triomphe, Prix Lupin and Prix Robert Papin.

FORTINO II (gr. 1959)	Grey Sovereign (gr. 1948)	Nasrullah	Nearco / Mumtaz Begum
		Kong	Baytown / Clang
	Ranavalo III (b. 1954)	Relic	War Relic / Bridal Colors
		Navarra II	Orsenigo / Nervesa
CHAMBORD (ch. 1955)	Chamossaire (ch. 1942)	Precipitation	Hurry On / Double Life
		Snowberry	Cameronian / Myrobella
	Life Hill (b. 1940)	Solario	Gainsborough / Sun Worship
		Lady of the Snows	Manna / Arctic Night

161   **CARRY BACK** 24 (br.c., April 16, 1958)

Bred by J. A. Price, in U.S.A.

Won 21 races, placed 22, $1,241,165, in U.S.A., from 2 to 5 years, incl. Kentucky Derby, Preakness Stakes, Florida Derby, Flamingo Stakes, Trenton H. (twice), Jerome H., Everglades Stakes, Whitney Stakes, Metropolitan H., Monmouth H., Garden State Stakes, Cowdin Stakes and Rensen Stakes; 2nd Wood Memorial, Widener H., Grey Lag H., Trenton H., Seminole H., Palm Beach H.; 3rd Sapling Stakes, Woodward Stakes, Lawrence Realization, Fountain of Youth Stakes, Washington D.C. International, Gulfstream Park H., New Orleans H. and United Nations H.

SAGGY (ch. 1945)	Swing and Sway (br. 1938)	Equipoise	Pennant / Swinging
		Nedana	Negofol / Adana
	Chantress (ch. 1939)	Hyperion	Gainsborough / Selene
		Surbine	Bachelor's Double / Datine
JOPPY (br. 1949)	Star Blen (b. 1940)	Blenheim	Blandford / Malva
		Starweed	Phalaris / Versatile
	Miss Fairfax (br. 1943)	Teddy Beau	Teddy / Beautiful Lady
		Bellicent	Sir Gallahad III / Whizz Bang

162   **CARWHITE** 1 (gr.c., April 17, 1974)

Bred by Moyglare Stud, in Ireland.

Won 4 races, placed 4, 1,005,000 fr., in France, from 2 to 4 years, incl. Prix d'Ispahan, Prix Daru and Prix du Prince d'Orange; 2nd Prix Eugene Adam and Prix Dollar; 3rd Prix d'Harcourt; 4th Prix Lupin.

CARO (gr. 1967)	Fortino II (gr. 1959)	Grey Sovereign	Nasrullah / Kong
		Ranavalo III	Relic / Navarra II
	Chambord (ch. 1955)	Chamossaire	Precipitation / Snowberry
		Life Hill	Solario / Lady of the Snows
WHITE PAPER (ch. 1965)	Honeyway (br. 1941)	Fairway	Phalaris / Scapa Flow
		Honey Buzzard	Papyrus / Lady Peregrine
	Alba Nox (b. 1951)	Coaraze	Tourbillon / Corrida
		La Dame Blanche (ex-Ninive)	Biribi / Nymphe Dicte

49

163   **CASAQUE GRISE** 5 (gr.f., March 15, 1964)

Bred by Mme. F. Dupré, in France.

Won 4 races, placed 6, 838,395 fr., in France and U.S.A., at 2 and 3 years, incl. Prix Vermeille, Prix Vanteaux and Prix de Royaumont; 2nd Prix de la Nonette and Prix de Malleret; 3rd Criterium de Saint-Cloud.

SAINT CRESPIN III (ch. 1956)	Aureole (ch. 1950)	Hyperion	Gainsborough / Selene
		Angelola	Donatello II / Feola
	Neocracy (br. 1944)	Nearco	Pharos / Nogara
		Harina	Blandford / Athasi
TOQUE ROSE (gr. 1952)	Count Fleet (br. 1940)	Reigh Count	Sunreigh / Contessina
		Quickly	Haste / Stephanie
	New Pin (gr. 1932)	Royal Minstrel	Tetratema / Harpsichord
		Trig	Chicle / Untidy

164   **CASPOGGIO** 22 (ch.c., January 27, 1965)

Bred by Lt.-Col. and Mrs. M. F. J. Palmer, in Ireland.

Won 14 races, placed 6, 60,780,000 L., in Italy, from 2 to 4 years, incl. Premio Presidente della Repubblica, Gran Criterium and Premio Besnate (twice); 2nd Gran Premio Città di Torino; 3rd Premio Emilio Turati and Coppa d'Oro di Milano.

KINGS TROOP (b. 1957)	Princely Gift (b. 1951)	Nasrullah	Nearco / Mumtaz Begum
		Blue Gem	Blue Peter / Sparkle
	Equiria (b. 1946)	Atout Maitre	Vatout / Royal Mistress
		Epona	Portlaw / Jury
PENDLEHILL (b. 1955)	The Phoenix (b. 1940)	Chateau Bouscaut	Kircubbin / Ramondie
		Fille de Poete	Firdaussi / Fille d'Amour
	Snowdonia (ch. 1941)	Bobsleigh	Gainsborough / Toboggan
		Nestoi	Yutoi / Nesta

165   **CATALPA** 16 (b.f., April 24, 1973)

Bred by Lord Howard de Walden.

Won 2 races, placed 4, £15,389, in England, at 2 and 3 years, incl. Ribblesdale Stakes; 2nd Lancashire Oaks.

REFORM (b. 1964)	Pall Mall (ch. 1955)	Palestine	Fair Trial / Una
		Malapert	Portlaw / Malatesta
	Country House (br. 1955)	Vieux Manoir	Brantome / Vieille Maison
		Miss Coventry	Mieuxce / Coventry Belle
OSTRYA (b. 1960)	Hornbeam (ch. 1953)	Hyperion	Gainsborough / Selene
		Thicket	Nasrullah / Thorn Wood
	Malcolmia (b. 1952)	Sayani	Fair Copy / Perfume II
		Silvery Moon	Solario / Silver Fox II

166   **CATERINA** 15 (gr.f., May 14, 1963)

Bred by Woodpark Ltd.

Won 4 races, placed 3, £8,117, in England, at 2 and 3 years, incl. Nunthorpe Stakes; 2nd Nunthorpe Stakes, King George Stakes.

PRINCELY GIFT (b. 1951)	Nasrullah (b. 1940)	Nearco	Pharos / Nogara
		Mumtaz Begum	Blenheim / Mumtaz Mahal
	Blue Gem (b. 1943)	Blue Peter	Fairway / Fancy Free
		Sparkle	Blandford / Gleam
RADIOPYE (gr. 1954)	Bright News (br. 1943)	Stardust	Hyperion / Sister Stella
		Inkling	Son-in-Law / Gleam
	Silversol (gr. 1940)	Solenoid	Soldennis / Shannon Jug
		Silver Lady	Old Rowley / Elland

167   **CATHERINE WHEEL** 14 (b.f., January 18, 1968)

Bred by Dunchurch Lodge Stud Co.

Won 5 races, placed 6, £16,515, in England and France, at 2 and 3 years, incl. Nassau Stakes, Musidora Stakes; 2nd Lancashire Oaks; 3rd 1,000 Guineas Stakes.

ROAN ROCKET (gr. 1961)	Buisson Ardent (b. 1953)	Relic	War Relic / Bridal Colors
		Rose o'Lynn	Pherozshah / Rocklyn
	Farandole II (gr. 1947)	Deux pour Cent	Deiri / Dix pour Cent
		Faramoude	Mahmoud / Faraude
QUEEN OF ARISAI (b. 1961)	Persian Gulf (b. 1940)	Bahram	Blandford / Friar's Daughter
		Double Life	Bachelor's Double / Saint Joan
	Trial Ground (b. 1944)	Fair Trial	Fairway / Lady Juror
		Tip the Wink	Tetratema / Golden Silence

168   **CAUCASUS** 5 (b.c., May 14, 1972)

Bred by Cragwood Estates Ltd., in U.S.A.

Won 9 races, placed 7, £238,379, in Ireland, England and U.S.A., from 3 to 5 years, incl. Irish St. Leger, Sunset H., Manhattan H., San Luis Rey Stakes, Arcadia H.; 2nd Hollywood Invitational H. (twice); 3rd Hollywood Gold Cup H., San Juan Capistrano H., American H.

NIJINSKY (b. 1967)	Northern Dancer (b. 1961)	Nearctic	Nearco / Lady Angela
		Natalma	Native Dancer / Almahmoud
	Flaming Page (b. 1959)	Bull Page	Bull Lea / Our Page
		Flaring Top	Menow / Flaming Top
QUILL (ch. 1956)	Princequillo (b. 1940)	Prince Rose	Rose Prince / Indolence
		Cosquilla	Papyrus / Quick Thought
	Quick Touch (ch. 1946)	Count Fleet	Reigh Count / Quickly
		Alms	St. Brideaux / Bonus

169   **CAWSTON'S CLOWN** 4 (b.c., March 2, 1974)

Bred by L. B. Hall.

Won 3 races, £17,400, in England, at 2 and 3 years, incl. Coventry Stakes.

	COMEDY STAR (b. 1968)	Tom Fool (b. 1949)	Menow	Pharamond
				Alcibiades
			Gaga	Bull Dog
				Alpoise
		Latin Walk (br. 1960)	Roman Tread	Roman
				Stepwisely
			Stall Walker	Bimelech
				Pansy Walker
CAWSTON'S PRIDE (ch. 1968)	Con Brio (ch. 1961)	Ribot	Tenerani
				Romanella
			Petronella	Petition
				Danse d'Espoir
		Cawston Tower (gr. 1956)	Maharaj Kumar	Stardust
				Pancha
			Silver Ribbon	The Satrap
				Salmonella

170   **CELINA** 9 (b.f., April 23, 1965)

Bred by J. R. Hindley.

Won 2 races, placed 3, £23,204, in England and Ireland, at 2 and 3 years, incl. Irish Guinness Oaks; 2nd Fred Darling Stakes; 3rd Ribblesdale Stakes.

CREPELLO (ch. 1954)	Donatello II (ch. 1934)	Blenheim	Blandford
			Malva
		Delleana	Clarissimus
			Duccia di Buoninsegna
	Crepuscule (ch. 1948)	Mieuxce	Massine
			L'Olivete
		Red Sunset	Solario
			Dulce II
ROSE OF MEDINA (b. 1956)	Never Say Die (ch. 1951)	Nasrullah	Nearco
			Mumtaz Begum
		Singing Grass	War Admiral
			Boreale
	Minaret (br. 1948)	Umidwar	Blandford
			Uganda
		Neolight	Nearco
			Sansonnet

171   **CELLINI** 5 (b.c., April 10, 1971)

Bred by Claiborne Farm, in U.S.A.

Won 6 races, placed 3, £45,407, in England, Ireland and U.S.A., at 2, 3 and 5 years, incl. William Hill Dewhurst Stakes, National Stakes (Curragh), Tetrarch Stakes, Vauxhall Trial Stakes; 2nd St. James's Palace Stakes; 3rd Irish 2,000 Guineas.

ROUND TABLE (b. 1954)	Princequillo (b. 1940)	Prince Rose	Rose Prince
			Indolence
		Cosquilla	Papyrus
			Quick Thought
	Knight's Daughter (b. 1941)	Sir Cosmo	The Boss
			Ayn Hali
		Feola	Friar Marcus
			Aloe
GAMELY (b. 1964)	Bold Ruler (b. 1954)	Nasrullah	Nearco
			Mumtaz Begum
		Miss Disco	Discovery
			Outdone
	Gambetta (b. 1952)	My Babu	Djebel
			Perfume II
		Rough Shod	Gold Bridge
			Dalmary

172   **CELTIC ASH** 1 (ch.c., March 23, 1957)

Bred by Dooneen Stud, in Ireland.

Won 3 races, placed 4, $103,860, in U.S.A., at 2 and 3 years, incl. Belmont Stakes; 3rd Preakness Stakes and Jersey Derby.

SICAMBRE (br. 1948)	Prince Bio (b. 1941)	Prince Rose	Rose Prince
			Indolence
		Biologie	Bacteriophage
			Eponge
	Sif (br. 1936)	Rialto	Rabelais
			La Grelee
		Suavita	Alcantara II
			Shocking
ASH PLANT (gr. 1948)	Nepenthe (gr. 1938)	Plassy	Bosworth
			Pladda
		Frisky	Isard II
			Vierge Blonde
	Amboyna (b. 1943)	Bois Roussel	Vatout
			Plucky Liege
		Aurora	Hyperion
			Rose Red

173   **CERRETO** 1 (ch.c., April 24, 1970)

Bred by Scuderia Alpina, in Italy

Won 6 races, placed 2, 58,000,000 L., in Italy, from 2 to 4 years, incl. Derby Italiano and Premio Lazio; 2nd St. Leger Italiano.

CLAUDE (b. 1964)	Hornbeam (ch. 1953)	Hyperion	Gainsborough
			Selene
		Thicket	Nasrullah
			Thorn Wood
	Aigue Vive (b. 1952)	Vatellor	Vatout
			Lady Elinor
		Vice-Versa II	Verso II
			Nica
CRENELLE (b. 1960)	Crepello (ch. 1954)	Donatello II	Blenheim
			Delleana
		Crepuscule	Mieuxce
			Red Sunset
	Mulberry Harbour (b. 1954)	Sicambre	Prince Bio
			Sif
		Open Warfare	Umidwar
			Frankly

174   **CHAMOUR** 10 (ch.c., April 8, 1957)

Bred by Ballykisteen Stud.

Won 2 races, £8,254, in Ireland, at 2 and 3 years, incl. Irish Derby, Gallinule Stakes.

CHAMIER (ch. 1950)	Chamossaire (ch. 1942)	Precipitation	Hurry On
			Double Life
		Snowberry	Cameronian
			Myrobella
	Therapia (b. 1944)	Panorama	Sir Cosmo
			Happy Climax
		Silvonessa	Royal Dancer
			Silvonah
CRACKNEL (b. 1934)	Manna (b. 1922)	Phalaris	Polymelus
			Bromus
		Waffles	Buckwheat
			Lady Mischief
	Anadyomene (ch. 1919)	Diadumenos	Orby
			Donnetta
		Rosella	St. Frusquin
			Widgeon

51

175   CHAPARRAL 1 (b.c., June 1, 1966)

Bred by Mme. G. Weisweiller, in France.

Won 3 races, placed 4, 1,193,284 fr., in France at 3 and 4 years, incl. Grand Prix de Paris and Prix Berteux; 2nd Prix du Cadran, La Coupe and Prix Jean Prat; 3rd Prix Royal Oak.

VAL DE LOIR (b. 1959)	Vieux Manoir (b. 1947)	Brantome	Blandford
			Vitamine
		Vieille Maison	Finglas
			Vieille Canaille
	Vali (br. 1954)	Sunny Boy III	Jock II
			Fille de Soleil
		Her Slipper	Tetratema
			Carpet Slipper
NICCOLINA (ch. 1950)	Niccolo Dell'Arca (b. 1938)	Coronach	Hurry On
			Wet Kiss
		Nogara	Havresac II
			Catnip
	Light Sentence (ch. 1934)	Pharos	Phalaris
			Scapa Flow
		Book Law	Buchan
			Popingaol

176   CHARLIE BUBBLES 1 (b.c., May 19, 1971)

Bred by R. W. Hall-Dare.

Won 4 races, placed 2, £19,447, in England, from 2 to 4 years, incl. Hardwicke Stakes.

WOLVER HOLLOW (b. 1964)	Sovereign Path (gr. 1956)	Grey Sovereign	Nasrullah
			Kong
		Mountain Path	Bobsleigh
			Path of Peace
	Cygnet (b. 1950)	Caracalla II	Tourbillon
			Astronomie
		Mrs. Swan Song	Sir Walter Raleigh
			Donati's Comet
SIXANDAHALF (b. 1964)	Thirteen of Diamonds (ch. 1949)	Mustang	Mieuxce
			Buzz Fuzz
		Florrie	Pharian
			Cloudless
	Betwixt (br. 1956)	Le Sage	Chamossaire
			Miss Know All
		Foolishness	Furrokh Siyar
			Nun's Folly

177   CHARLOTTESVILLE 14 (b.c., 1957)

Bred by H.H. Aga Khan and Prince Aly Khan, in Ireland.

Won 6 races, 1,020,749 fr., in France at 2 and 3 years, incl. Prix du Jockey-Club, Grand Prix de Paris, Prix Lupin and Prix du Prince d'Orange.

PRINCE CHEVALIER (b. 1943)	Prince Rose (b. 1928)	Rose Prince	Prince Palatine
			Eglantine
		Indolence	Gay Crusader
			Barrier
	Chevalerie (b. 1933)	Abbot's Speed	Abbots Trace
			Mary Gaunt
		Kassala	Cylgad
			Farizade
NOORANI (ch. 1950)	Nearco (br. 1935)	Pharos	Phalaris
			Scapa Flow
		Nogara	Havresac II
			Catnip
	Empire Glory (b. 1933)	Singapore	Gainsborough
			Tetrabbazia
		Skyglory	Sky-rocket
			Simone

178   CHARLOTTOWN 2 (b.c., April 6, 1963)

Bred by Someries Stud.

Won 7 races, placed 3, £116,863, in England and Ireland, from 2 to 4 years, incl. Derby Stakes, Horris Hill Stakes, John Porter Stakes, Coronation Cup; 2nd Irish Sweeps Derby, St. Leger Stakes, Carreras Piccadilly Derby Trial Stakes.

CHARLOTTESVILLE (b. 1957)	Prince Chevalier (b. 1943)	Prince Rose	Rose Prince
			Indolence
		Chevalerie	Abbot's Speed
			Kassala
	Noorani (ch. 1950)	Nearco	Pharos
			Nogara
		Empire Glory	Singapore
			Skyglory
MELD (b. 1952)	Alycidon (ch. 1945)	Donatello II	Blenheim
			Delleana
		Aurora	Hyperion
			Rose Red
	Daily Double (b. 1943)	Fair Trial	Fairway
			Lady Juror
		Doubleton	Bahram
			Double Life

179   CHATEAUGAY 16 (ch.c., February 29, 1960)

Bred by John W. Galbreath, in U.S.A.

Won 11 races, placed 6, $360,722, in U.S.A., from 2 to 5 years, incl. Kentucky Derby, Belmont Stakes, Blue Grass Stakes and Jerome H.; 2nd Preakness Stakes and Roseben H.; 3rd Dwyer H. and Travers Stakes.

SWAPS (ch. 1952)	Khaled (b. 1943)	Hyperion	Gainsborough
			Selene
		Eclair	Ethnarch
			Black Ray
	Iron Reward (b. 1946)	Beau Pere	Son-in-Law
			Cinna
		Iron Maiden	War Admiral
			Betty Derr
BANQUET BELL (ch. 1951)	Polynesian (br. 1942)	Unbreakable	Sickle
			Blue Glass
		Black Polly	Polymelian
			Black Queen
	Dinner Horn (ch. 1937)	Pot au Feu	Bruleur
			Polly Peachum
		Tophorn	Bull Dog
			Leghorn

180   CHEVELEY PRINCESS 8 (ch.f., February 25, 1970)

Bred by White Lodge Stud Ltd.

Won 3 races, placed 3, £17,843, in England, at 2 and 3 years, incl. Nassau Stakes, Sun Chariot Stakes, Ascot 1,000 Guineas Trial Stakes; 3rd Yorkshire Oaks.

BUSTED (b. 1963)	Crepello (ch. 1954)	Donatello II	Blenheim
			Delleana
		Crepuscule	Mieuxce
			Red Sunset
	Sans le Sou (b. 1957)	Vimy	Wild Risk
			Mimi
		Martial Loan	Court Martial
			Loan
FEATHER BED (ch. 1961)	Gratitude (ch. 1953)	Golden Cloud	Gold Bridge
			Rainstorm
		Verdura	Court Martial
			Bura
	Sweet Cygnet (b. or br. 1942)	Hyperion	Gainsborough
			Selene
		Sweet Swan	Cygnus
			Swietenia

181 CHICAGO 4 (b.c., March 20, 1964)

Bred by Citadel Stud Establishment, in Ireland.

Won 9 races, placed 6, £49,845, in England, Italy and Germany, from 2 to 5 years, incl. Henry II Stakes (twice), Cumberland Lodge Stakes, Gran Premio del Jockey Club and Premio Roma; 2nd Hardwicke Stakes and Grosser Preis von Baden.

FIDALGO (b. 1956)	Arctic Star (br. 1942)	Nearco	Pharos / Nogara
		Serena	Winalot / Charmione
	Miss France (b. 1946)	Jock II	Asterus / Naic
		Nafah	Abjer / Flower
GRISCHUNA (b. 1959)	Ratification (b. 1953)	Court Martial	Fair Trial / Instantaneous
		Solesa	Solario / Mesa
	Mountain Path (b. 1948)	Bobsleigh	Gainsborough / Toboggan
		Path of Peace	Winalot / Grand Peace

182 CHOUCRI 22 (dk.b. or br.c., February 23, 1977)

Bred by G. C. Frostad, in Canada.

Won 4 races, placed 6, 706,294 fr., in France, England and Italy, at 2 and 3 years, incl. Prix Robert Papin; 2nd Premio Tevere, Prix de la Salamandre and William Hill Futurity; 4th Grand Criterium.

UP SPIRITS (b. 1961)	Turn-to (b. 1951)	Royal Charger	Nearco / Sun Princess
		Source Sucree	Admiral Drake / Lavendula II
	Spring Run (b. 1948)	Menow	Pharamond / Alcibiades
		Boola Brook	Bull Dog / Brookdale
FITZ'S FANCY (dk.b. or br. 1962)	Billings (ch. 1945)	Mahmoud	Blenheim / Mah Mahal
		Native Gal	Sir Gallahad III / Native Wit
	Jo Ayres (br. 1943)	Halcyon	Broomstick / Prudery
		Agnes Ayres	King James / Sweet Mary

183 CHRIS EVERT 23 (ch.f., February 14, 1971)

Bred by Echo Valley Horse Farm, in U.S.A.

Won 10 races, placed 4, $679,475, in U.S.A., from 2 to 4 years, incl. Coaching Club American Oaks, Mother Goose Stakes, Acorn Stakes, Hollywood Special Stakes, La Canada Stakes, Demoiselle Stakes and Golden Rod Stakes; 2nd Frizette Stakes and Alabama Stakes; 3rd Travers Stakes and Comely Stakes.

SWOON'S SON (b. 1953)	The Doge (br. 1942)	Bull Dog	Teddy / Plucky Liege
		My Auntie	Busy American / Babe K
	Swoon (ch. 1942)	Sweep Like	Sweep / Lady Braxted
		Sadie Greenock	Greenock / Silk Lady
MISS CARMIE (b. 1966)	T.V. Lark (b. 1957)	Indian Hemp	Nasrullah / Sabzy
		Miss Larksfly	Heelfly / Larksnest
	Twice Over (b. 1956)	Ponder	Pensive / Miss Rushin
		Twosy	Bull Lea / Two Bob

184 CHRISTMAS ISLAND 5 (ch.c., March 28, 1960)

Bred by F. F. Tuthill.

Won 6 races, placed 3, £12,692, in Ireland, England and U.S.A., from 2 to 4 years, incl. Irish St. Leger, Gladness Stakes, Chester Vase; 2nd Oxfordshire Stakes.

COURT HARWELL (br. 1954)	Prince Chevalier (b. 1943)	Prince Rose	Rose Prince / Indolence
		Chevalerie	Abbot's Speed / Kassala
	Neutron (ch. 1948)	Hyperion	Gainsborough / Selene
		Participation	Precipitation / Arabella
TAHITI (b. 1948)	Ocean Swell (b. 1941)	Blue Peter	Fairway / Fancy Free
		Jiffy	Hurry On / Juniata
	Jennydang (b. 1938)	Colombo	Manna / Lady Nairne
		Dalmary	Blandford / Simon's Shoes

185 CICADA 9 (b.f., May 7, 1959)

Bred by Meadow Stud, Inc., in U.S.A.

Won 23 races, placed 14, $783,674, in U.S.A., from 2 to 5 years, incl. Beldame Stakes, Mother Goose Stakes, Acorn Stakes, Kentucky Oaks, Gardenia Stakes, Frizette Stakes, Matron Stakes, Spinaway Stakes, Astarita Stakes, Schuylerville Stakes, Jersey Belle Stakes, Columbiana H., Sheepshead Bay H., Distaff H. and Vagrancy H.; 2nd Coaching Club American Oaks, Florida Derby, Delaware H. (twice) and Columbiana H.; 3rd Alabama Stakes, Delaware Oaks and Top Flight H.

BRYAN G. (ch. 1947)	Blenheim (br. 1927)	Blandford	Swynford / Blanche
		Malva	Charles O'Malley / Wild Arum
	Anthemion (ch. 1940)	Pompey	Sun Briar / Cleopatra
		Sicklefeather	Sickle / Fairness
SATSUMA (b. 1949)	Bossuet (b. 1940)	Boswell	Bosworth / Flying Gal
		Vibration	Sir Cosmo / Ciliata
	Hildene (b. 1938)	Bubbling Over	North Star III / Beaming Beauty
		Fancy Racket	Wrack / Ultimate Fancy

186 CISTUS 12 (b.f., May 4, 1975)

Bred by Ballymacoll Stud Farm Ltd.

Won 6 races, placed 3, £90,551, in England and France, at 2 and 3 years, incl. Nassau Stakes, Child Stakes, Prix de l'Opera; 2nd Prix de Diane de Revlon, Criterium des Pouliches.

SUN PRINCE (ch. 1969)	Princely Gift (b. 1951)	Nasrullah	Nearco / Mumtaz Begum
		Blue Gem	Blue Peter / Sparkle
	Costa Sola (ch. 1963)	Worden II	Wild Risk / Sans Tares
		Sunny Cove	Nearco / Sunny Gulf
ROSALIE II (b. 1965)	Molvedo (br. 1958)	Ribot	Tenerani / Romanella
		Maggiolina	Nakamuro / Murcia
	Lovely Rose III (b. 1956)	Owen Tudor	Hyperion / Mary Tudor II
		Galatina	Galène / Phebe

53

187 CLAIRE VALENTINE 16 (ch.f., February 1, 1973)

Bred by Swettenham Stud, in England.

Won 5 races, placed 1, 47,385,284 L., in Italy and France, from 2 to 4 years, incl. Oaks d'Italia.

SEA HAWK II (gr. 1963)	Herbager (b. 1956)	Vandale II	Plassy
			Vanille
		Flagette	Escamillo
			Fidgette
	Sea Nymph (gr. 1957)	Free Man	Norseman
			Fantine
		Sea Spray	Ocean Swell
			Pontoon
VENANTE (ch. 1961)	Chanteur II (b. 1942)	Chateau Bouscaut	Kircubbin
			Ramondie
		La Diva	Blue Skies
			La Traviata
	Court Venture (b. 1955)	Court Martial	Fair Trial
			Instantaneous
		Vertencia	Deiri
			Advertencia

188 CLASSIC EXAMPLE 1 (ch.c., April 26, 1974)

Bred by Col. and Mrs. F. R. Hue-Williams.

Won 4 races, placed 5, £52,451, in England and Ireland, from 2 to 4 years, incl. King Edward VII Stakes, Jockey Club Stakes; 2nd Great Voltigeur Stakes; 3rd Irish Sweeps Derby, St. Leger Stakes.

RUN THE GANTLET (b. 1968)	Tom Rolfe (b. 1962)	Ribot	Tenerani
			Romanella
		Pocahontas	Roman
			How
	First Feather (ch. 1963)	First Landing	Turn-to
			Hildene
		Quill	Princequillo
			Quick Touch
ROYAL SAINT (ch. 1964)	Saint Crespin III (ch. 1956)	Aureole	Hyperion
			Angelola
		Neocracy	Nearco
			Harina
	Bleu Azur (ch. 1959)	Crepello	Donatello II
			Crepuscule
		Blue Prelude	Blue Peter
			Keyboard

189 CLOONAGH 10 (b.f., April 26, 1970)

Bred by Tally Ho Stud Co. Ltd.

Won 3 races, placed 2, £20,744, in Ireland and England, at 2 and 3 years, incl. Irish 1,000 Guineas.

HIGH HAT (ch. 1957)	Hyperion (ch. 1930)	Gainsborough	Bayardo
			Rosedrop
		Selene	Chaucer
			Serenissima
	Madonna (ch. 1945)	Donatello II	Blenheim
			Delleana
		Women's Legion	Coronach
			Victress
ZOOM (b. 1957)	Zucchero (br. 1948)	Nasrullah	Nearco
			Mumtaz Begum
		Castagnola	Bois Roussel
			Queen of Scots
	Martia (b. 1949)	Court Martial	Fair Trial
			Instantaneous
		Serenoa	Solario
			Serena

190 COASTAL 9 (ch.c., April 6, 1976)

Bred by Claiborne Farm, in U.S.A.

Won 8 races, placed 4, $493,929, in U.S.A., at 2 and 3 years, incl. Belmont Stakes, Monmouth Invitational H., Dwyer Stakes and Peter Pan Stakes; 2nd Woodward Stakes; 3rd Jockey Club Gold Cup and Marlboro Cup.

MAJESTIC PRINCE (ch. 1966)	Raise a Native (ch. 1961)	Native Dancer	Polynesian
			Geisha
		Raise You	Case Ace
			Lady Glory
	Gay Hostess (ch. 1957)	Royal Charger	Nearco
			Sun Princess
		Your Hostess	Alibhai
			Boudoir II
ALLUVIAL (ch. 1969)	Buckpasser (b. 1963)	Tom Fool	Menow
			Gaga
		Busanda	War Admiral
			Businesslike
	Bayou (ch. 1954)	Hill Prince	Princequillo
			Hildene
		Bourtai	Stimulus
			Escutcheon

191 CODEX 9 (ch.c., February 28, 1977)

Bred by Tartan Farms, in U.S.A.

Won 6 races, placed 3, $534,576, in U.S.A., at 2 and 3 years, incl. Preakness Stakes, Hollywood Derby and Santa Anita Derby.

ARTS AND LETTERS (ch. 1966)	Ribot (b. 1952)	Tenerani	Bellini
			Tofanella
		Romanella	El Greco
			Barbara Burrini
	All Beautiful (ch. 1959)	Battlefield	War Relic
			Dark Display
		Parlo	Heliopolis
			Fairy Palace
ROUNDUP ROSE (b. 1971)	Minnesota Mac (b. 1964)	Rough 'n Tumble	Free for All
			Roused
		Cow Girl	Mustang
			Ate
	Minnetonka (b. 1967)	Chieftain	Bold Ruler
			Pocahontas
		Heliolight	Helioscope
			Real Delight

192 COMTESSE DE LOIR 20 (b.f., March 18, 1971)

Bred by S. Vanian, in France.

Won 3 races, placed 11, 2,365,850 fr., in France, England, U.S.A. and Canada, from 2 to 4 years, incl. Prix Saint-Alary; 2nd Prix de l'Arc de Triomphe, Prix de Diane, Prix Vermeille, Criterium des Pouliches, Washington D.C. International, and Canadian International Championship; 3rd Prix de l'Arc de Triomphe, Prix Ganay and Prix Chloe; 4th Coronation Cup and Grand Prix de Saint-Cloud.

VAL DE LOIR (b. 1959)	Vieux Manoir (b. 1947)	Brantome	Blandford
			Vitamine
		Vieille Maison	Finglas
			Vieille Canaille
	Vali (br. 1954)	Sunny Boy III	Jock II
			Fille de Soleil
		Her Slipper	Tetratema
			Carpet Slipper
NERIAD (ch. 1964)	Princequillo (b. 1940)	Prince Rose	Rose Prince
			Indolence
		Cosquilla	Papyrus
			Quick Thought
	Sea-Change (b. 1956)	Count Fleet	Reigh Count
			Quickly
		Now What	Chance Play
			That's That

193   CONNAUGHT 4 (b.c., April 28, 1965)

Bred by H. J. Joel.

Won 7 races, placed 5, £69,212, in England, from 2 to 5 years, incl. Eclipse Stakes, King Edward VII Stakes, Great Voltigeur Stakes, Prince of Wales Stakes (twice), Coronation Stakes (Sandown Park), Westbury Stakes; 2nd Derby Stakes, Queen Elizabeth II Stakes, Chester Vase; 3rd Coronation Cup.

ST. PADDY (b. 1957)	Aureole (ch. 1950)	Hyperion	Gainsborough / Selene
		Angelola	Donatello II / Feola
	Edie Kelly (br. 1950)	Bois Roussel	Vatout / Plucky Liege
		Caerlissa	Caerleon / Sister Sarah
NAGAIKA (ch. 1954)	Goyama (ch. 1943)	Goya II	Tourbillon / Zariba
		Devineress	Finglas / Devachon
	Naim (ch. 1946)	Amfortas	Ksar / Persephone
		Nacelle	Cerfeuil / Neomenie

194   CONNAUGHT BRIDGE 1 (ch.f., May 2, 1976)

Bred by Burton Agnes Stud Co. Ltd.

Won 5 races, placed 4, £58,097, in England, at 2 and 3 years, incl. Yorkshire Oaks, Nassau Stakes.

CONNAUGHT (b. 1965)	St. Paddy (b. 1957)	Aureole	Hyperion / Angelola
		Edie Kelly	Bois Roussel / Caerlissa
	Nagaika (ch. 1954)	Goyama	Goya II / Devineress
		Naim	Amfortas / Nacelle
FISHERMAN'S BRIDGE (b. 1970)	Crepello (ch. 1954)	Donatello II	Blenheim / Delleana
		Crepuscule	Mieuxce / Red Sunset
	Riva (b. 1964)	Relic	War Relic / Bridal Colors
		Canvas	Botticelli / Rustic Bridge

195   CONOR PASS 8 (br.c., March 26, 1970)

Bred by Ashleigh Stud.

Won 7 races, placed 13, £26,241, in Ireland and England, from 2 to 5 years, incl. Irish St. Leger, Player-Wills Stakes; 2nd Blandford Stakes; 3rd Desmond Stakes, Railway Stakes.

TIEPOLO II (br. 1964)	Tiepoletto (br. 1956)	Tornado	Tourbillon / Roseola
		Scarlet Skies	Blue Skies / Scarlet Quill
	Jacine (ch. 1957)	Owen Tudor	Hyperion / Mary Tudor II
		Weighbridge	Portlaw / Golden Way
WINDFIELD LILY (b. 1962)	Hard Tack (b. 1955)	Hard Sauce	Ardan / Saucy Bella
		Cowes	Blue Peter / Lighthearted
	Another Marvel (br. 1954)	His Slipper	Stardust / Her Slipper
		Matura	Rhodes Scholar / Isolda

196   CORTEZ 1 (b.c., February 27, 1965)

Bred by Gestüt Zoppenbroich, in Germany

Won 10 races, placed 21, 667,980 DM., in Germany and France, from 2 to 6 years, incl. Preis von Europa, Grosser Preis von Nordrhein-Westfalen, Grosser Preis von Baden and Grosser Preis von Dortmund; 2nd Preis von Europa (twice), Grosser Preis von Baden (twice), Grosser Preis von Dortmund (twice), Aral Pokal, Spreti-Rennen and Grosser Preis von Dusseldorf.

ORSINI (br. 1954)	Ticino (b. 1939)	Athanasius	Ferro / Athanasie
		Terra	Aditi / Teufelsrose
	Oranien (b. 1949)	Nuvolari	Oleander / Nereide
		Omladina	Athanasius / Oblate
COSTA BRAVA (b. 1956)	Nebelwerfer (br. 1944)	Magnat	Asterus / Mafalda
		Newa	Arjaman / Numa
	Campanula (b. 1949)	Ansitz	Aventin / Austria
		Cyclame	Arjaman / Cabalistique

197   COUGAR II 7 (b./br.c., October 16, 1966)

Bred by Haras General Cruz, in Chile.

Won 20 races, placed 24, $1,162,725, in U.S.A. and Chile, from 2 to 7 years, incl. Californian Stakes (twice), Oak Tree Invitational (twice), Century H. (twice), Santa Anita H., San Juan Capistrano Invitational H., Sunset H., Carleton F. Burke H., Ford Pinto Invitational Turf H., San Marcos H. and San Gabriel H.; 2nd Santa Anita H. (twice), Sunset H., San Juan Capistrano Invitational H., San Luis Obispo H., San Pasqual H., and Del Mar H.; 3rd Woodward Stakes (twice), Hollywood Gold Cup, Marlboro Cup, Hollywood Invitational H. (twice), San Juan Capistrano Invitational H., San Luis Rey Stakes, San Antonio Stakes, Century H. and Manhattan H.

TALE OF TWO CITIES (b. 1951)	Tehran (b. 1941)	Bois Roussel	Vatout / Plucky Liege
		Stafaralla	Solario / Mirawala
	Merida II (b. 1944)	Jock II	Asterus / Naic
		Torissima	Tourbillon / Carissima
CINDY LOU II (ch. 1955)	Madara (b. 1949)	Nearco	Pharos / Nogara
		Sun Princess	Solario / Mumtaz Begum
	Maria Bonita (b. 1945)	Afghan II	Mahmoud / Coronal
		Las Palmas	Picacero / La Tentacion

198   COUP DE FEU 21 (b.c., April 7, 1969)

Bred by Lt.-Colonel W. E. Behrens.

Won 6 races, placed 14, £61,492, in England and France, from 2 to 5 years, incl. Benson and Hedges Eclipse Stakes; 2nd Cumberland Lodge Stakes, Westbury Stakes; 3rd Prix Jacques le Marois, Dante Stakes, Brigadier Gerard Stakes, John Porter Stakes, Queen Anne Stakes.

WHITE FIRE III (b. 1962)	Petition (br. 1944)	Fair Trial	Fairway / Lady Juror
		Art Paper	Artist's Proof / Quire
	Danira (br. 1953)	Dante	Nearco / Rosy Legend
		Mah Iran	Bahram / Mah Mahal
WINNING BID (b. 1958)	Great Captain (br. 1949)	War Admiral	Man o' War / Brushup
		Big Hurry	Black Toney / La Troienne
	Straight Bid (b. 1954)	Solonaway	Solferino / Anyway
		Straight Offer	Straight Deal / Olifa

199 CRACKER 8 (ch.f., May 12, 1961)

Bred by F. F. Tuthill.

Won 4 races, placed 2, £4,854, in England, at 3 years, incl. Nassau Stakes.

COURT HARWELL (br. 1954)	Prince Chevalier (b. 1943)	Prince Rose	Rose Prince
			Indolence
		Chevalerie	Abbot's Speed
			Kassala
	Neutron (ch. 1948)	Hyperion	Gainsborough
			Selene
		Participation	Precipitation
			Arabella
ISETTA (b. 1943)	Morland (b. 1934)	Gainsborough	Bayardo
			Rosedrop
		Lichen	Manna
			Loweswater
	Isolda (b. 1933)	Rustom Pasha	Son-in-Law
			Cos
		Yveline	Gardefeu
			Photime

200 CRAIGHOUSE 1 (b.c., February 11, 1962)

Bred by Astor Studs.

Won 3 races, placed 1, £10,442, in England and Ireland, at 3 and 4 years, incl. Irish St. Leger; 3rd Great Voltigeur Stakes.

MOSSBOROUGH (ch. 1947)	Nearco (br. 1935)	Pharos	Phalaris
			Scapa Flow
		Nogara	Havresac II
			Catnip
	All Moonshine (ch. 1941)	Bobsleigh	Gainsborough
			Toboggan
		Selene	Chaucer
			Serenissima
TARBERT BAY (br. 1954)	Persian Gulf (b. 1940)	Bahram	Blandford
			Friar's Daughter
		Double Life	Bachelor's Double
			Saint Joan
	Thicket (b. 1947)	Nasrullah	Nearco
			Mumtaz Begum
		Thorn Wood	Bois Roussel
			Point Duty

201 CREPELLANA 9 (ch.f., May 16, 1966)

Bred by Marcel Boussac, in France.

Won 2 races, placed 5, 1,148,201 fr., in France and England, from 2 to 4 years, incl. Prix de Diane; 2nd Prix Vermeille and Prix d'Ispahan; 3rd King George VI and Queen Elizabeth Stakes.

CREPELLO (ch. 1954)	Donatello II (ch. 1934)	Blenheim	Blandford
			Malva
		Delleana	Clarissimus
			Duccia di Buoninsegna
	Crepuscule (ch. 1948)	Mieuxce	Massine
			L'Olivete
		Red Sunset	Solario
			Dulce II
ASTANA (b. 1956)	Arbar (b. 1944)	Djebel	Tourbillon
			Loika
		Astronomie	Asterus
			Likka
	Theano (b. 1940)	Tourbillon	Ksar
			Durban
		Souryva	Gainsborough
			L'Esperance

202 CRESPINALL 6 (ch.f., April 10, 1969)

Bred by J. Davis.

Won 2 races, placed 1, £9,490, in England, at 2 and 3 years, incl. Nassau Stakes, Princess Elizabeth Stakes.

SAINT CRESPIN III (ch. 1956)	Aureole (ch. 1950)	Hyperion	Gainsborough
			Selene
		Angelola	Donatello II
			Feola
	Neocracy (b. 1944)	Nearco	Pharos
			Nogara
		Harina	Blandford
			Athasi
PINALL (gr. or ro. 1958)	Pinza (b. 1950)	Chanteur II	Chateau Bouscaut
			La Diva
		Pasqua	Donatello II
			Pasca
	Riccal (gr. 1953)	Abernant	Owen Tudor
			Rustom Mahal
		Congo	Bellacose
			Kong

203 CRIMEA II 14 (ch.f, April 8, 1961)

Bred by Mrs. J. W. Hanes, in U.S.A.

Won 2 races, placed 1, £9,302, in England, at 2 and 3 years, incl. Cheveley Park Stakes, Molecomb Stakes; 2nd King George Stakes.

PRINCEQUILLO (b. 1940)	Prince Rose (b. 1928)	Rose Prince	Prince Palatine
			Eglantine
		Indolence	Gay Crusader
			Barrier
	Cosquilla (b. 1933)	Papyrus	Tracery
			Miss Matty
		Quick Thought	White Eagle
			Mindful
VICTORIA CROSS (ch. 1953)	Court Martial (ch. 1942)	Fair Trial	Fairway
			Lady Juror
		Instantaneous	Hurry On
			Picture
	Ladycross (b. 1944)	Mieuxce	Massine
			L'Olivete
		Eleanor Cross	Hyperion
			Queen Christina

204 CRIMSON BEAU 16 (ch.c., March 15, 1975)

Bred by H. T. Spearing, in England.

Won 4 races, placed 9, £96,694, in England, France and Belgium, from 2 to 4 years, incl. Prince of Wales's Stakes and Prix de la Cote Normande; 2nd Coral Eclipse Stakes, Benson and Hedges Gold Cup and Diomed Stakes; 3rd Grand Prix Prince Rose, Ostende.

HIGH LINE (ch. 1966)	High Hat (ch. 1957)	Hyperion	Gainsborough
			Selene
		Madonna	Donatello II
			Women's Legion
	Time Call (b. 1955)	Chanteur II	Chateau Bouscaut
			La Diva
		Aleria	Djebel
			Canidia
CRIMSON BELLE (ch. 1962)	Red God (ch. 1954)	Nasrullah	Nearco
			Mumtaz Begum
		Spring Run	Menow
			Boola Brook
	Signal Belle (ch. 1955)	Signal Box	Signal Light
			Mashaq
		Tide Time	Samphire
			Silver Mystery

205   CRIMSON SATAN 26 (ch.c., May 4, 1959)

Bred by Crimson King Farm, in U.S.A.

Won 18 races, placed 18, $796,077, in U.S.A., from 2 to 5 years, incl. Garden State Stakes, Pimlico Futurity. Hawthorne Juvenile Stakes, Clark H., Charles H. Strub Stakes, Washington Park H., Massachusetts H., Michigan Mile-and-One-Sixteenth H. and San Fernando Stakes; 2nd Aqueduct Stakes, Santa Anita H., John B. Campbell H., Grey Lag H., San Antonio H. and Arlington H.; 3rd Belmont Stakes, Jersey Derby and Woodward Stakes.

SPY SONG (br. 1943)	Balladier (bl. 1932)	Black Toney	Peter Pan / Belgravia
		Blue Warbler	North Star III / May Bird
	Mata Hari (br. 1931)	Peter Hastings	Peter Pan / Nettie Hastings
		War Woman	Man o'War / Topaz
PAPILA (ch. 1943)	Requiebro (b. 1930)	Re-echo	Neil Gow / Corrie Rae
		Trepadora	Tracery / Vis a Vis
	Papalona (gr. 1927)	Papanatas	Pippermint / Kouba
		Tarumba	Val d'Or / Eglantine II

206   CROCKET 1 (ch.c., March 22, 1960)

Bred by Lord Harrington.

Won 7 races, £19,321, in England, at 2 and 3 years, incl. Coventry Stakes, Gimcrack Stakes, Middle Park Stakes, Craven Stakes, St. James's Palace Stakes.

KING OF THE TUDORS (ch. 1950)	Tudor Minstrel (br. 1944)	Owen Tudor	Hyperion / Mary Tudor II
		Sansonnet	Sansovino / Lady Juror
	Glen Line (b. 1942)	Blue Peter	Fairway / Fancy Free
		Scotia's Glen	Beresford / Queen Scotia
CHANDELIER (ch. 1955)	Goyama (ch. 1943)	Goya II	Tourbillon / Zariba
		Devineress	Finglas / Devachon
	Queen of Light (b. 1949)	Borealis	Brumeux / Aurora
		Picture Play	Donatello II / Amuse

207   CROW 3 (ch.c., February 23, 1973)

Bred by Dayton Ltd., in France.

Won 5 races, placed 7, £210,135, in France, England and U.S.A., from 3 to 5 years, incl. St. Leger Stakes, Coronation Cup, Prix Eugene Adam, Ormonde Stakes; 2nd Prix de l'Arc de Triomphe, Benson and Hedges Gold Cup; 3rd Turf Classic Invitational H.

EXBURY (ch. 1959)	Le Haar (ch. 1954)	Vieux Manoir	Brantome / Vieille Maison
		Mince Pie	Teleferique / Cannelle
	Greensward (b. 1953)	Mossborough	Nearco / All Moonshine
		Stargrass	Noble Star / Grass Widow
CARMOSINA (ch. 1963)	Right of Way (ch. 1957)	Honeyway	Fairway / Honey Buzzard
		Magnificent	Migoli / Isle of Capri
	Sixtina (ch. 1956)	Aristophanes	Hyperion / Commotion
		La Dogana	Advocate / Veneta

208   CROWNED PRINCE 4 (ch.c., January 31, 1969)

Bred by Leslie Combs II and F. M. McMahon, in U.S.A.

Won 2 races, £15,823, in England, at 2 years, incl. Dewhurst Stakes, Champagne Stakes.

RAISE A NATIVE (ch. 1961)	Native Dancer (gr. 1950)	Polynesian	Unbreakable / Black Polly
		Geisha	Discovery / Miyako
	Raise You (ch. 1946)	Case Ace	Teddy / Sweetheart
		Lady Glory	American Flag / Beloved
GAY HOSTESS (ch. 1957)	Royal Charger (ch. 1942)	Nearco	Pharos / Nogara
		Sun Princess	Solario / Mumtaz Begum
	Your Hostess (ch. 1949)	Alibhai	Hyperion / Teresina
		Boudoir	Mahmoud / Kampala

209   CRY OF TRUTH 2 (gr.f., March 12, 1972)

Bred by Miss Pearl Lawson-Johnston.

Won 5 races, placed 1, £36,036, in England, at 2 and 3 years, incl. William Hill Cheveley Park Stakes, Lowther Stakes.

TOWN CRIER (gr. 1965)	Sovereign Path (gr. 1956)	Grey Sovereign	Nasrullah / Kong
		Mountain Path	Bobsleigh / Path of Peace
	Corsley Bell (b. 1959)	Owen Tudor	Hyperion / Mary Tudor II
		Dented Bell	Denturius / Boscabell
FALSE EVIDENCE (b. or br. 1963)	Counsel (b. 1952)	Court Martial	Fair Trial / Instantaneous
		Wheedler	Umidwar / Miss Minx
	Idolatry (br. 1948)	Umidwar	Blandford / Uganda
		Katmandu	Concerto / Gold Leaf II

210   CRYSTAL PALACE (FR) 10 (gr.c., March 25, 1974)

Bred by Baron Guy de Rothschild, in France.

Won 4 races, placed 5, 1,629,974 fr., in France and England, at 2 and 3 years, incl. Prix du Jockey Club and Prix Niel; 2nd Prix Lupin; 3rd Prix de l'Arc de Triomphe; 4th King George VI and Queen Elizabeth Diamond Stakes.

CARO (gr. 1967)	Fortino II (gr. 1959)	Grey Sovereign	Nasrullah / Kong
		Ranavalo III	Relic / Navarra II
	Chambord (ch. 1955)	Chamossaire	Precipitation / Snowberry
		Life Hill	Solario / Lady of the Snows
HERMIERES (ch. 1958)	Sicambre (br. 1948)	Prince Bio	Prince Rose / Biologie
		Sif	Rialto / Suavita
	Vieille Pierre (b. 1951)	Blue Peter	Fairway / Fancy Free
		Vieille Maison	Finglas / Vieille Canaille

211   CRYSTAL WATER 14 (b.c., March 11, 1973)

Bred by Mrs. Connie M. Ring, in U.S.A.

Won 9 races, placed 6, $845,072, in U.S.A., from 2 to 5 years, incl. Hollywood Derby, Hollywood Gold Cup, Santa Anita H., Californian Stakes, Oak Tree Invitational and San Felipe H.; 2nd Swaps Stakes and El Dorado H.; 3rd Marlboro Cup and San Fernando Stakes.

WINDY SANDS (br. 1957)	Your Host (ch. 1947)	Alibhai	Hyperion / Teresina
		Boudoir	Mahmoud / Kampala
	Samoa Winds (b. 1950)	Polynesian	Unbreakable / Black Polly
		Windmill	Quatre Bras / Flying Wind
SOFT SNOW (ch. 1967)	T.V. Lark (b. 1957)	Indian Hemp	Nasrullah / Sabzy
		Miss Larksfly	Heelfly / Larksnest
	Winter Snow (ch. 1956)	Alibhai	Hyperion / Teresina
		Fleet Rings	Count Fleet / Banish Fear

212   CURSORIAL 21 (b.f., April 3, 1961)

Bred by Major L. B. Holliday.

Won 2 races, placed 3, £5,465, in England, at 2 and 3 years, incl. Park Hill Stakes; 2nd Carreras Piccadilly Oaks Trial Stakes.

CREPELLO (ch. 1954)	Donatello II (ch. 1934)	Blenheim	Blandford / Malva
		Delleana	Clarissimus / Duccia di Buoninsegna
	Crepuscule (ch. 1948)	Mieuxce	Massine / L'Olivete
		Red Sunset	Solario / Dulce II
NONE NICER (b. 1955)	Nearco (br. 1935)	Pharos	Phalaris / Scapa Flow
		Nogara	Havresac II / Catnip
	Phase (b. 1939)	Windsor Lad	Blandford / Resplendent
		Lost Soul	Solario / Orlass

213   DACTYLOGRAPHER 19 (b.c., April 21, 1975)

Bred by Stavros Niarchos, in U.S.A.

Won 3 races, placed 3, £51,878, in England, at 2 and 3 years, incl. William Hill Futurity Stakes; 3rd Ladbroke Derby Trial Stakes.

SECRETARIAT (ch. 1970)	Bold Ruler (b. 1954)	Nasrullah	Nearco / Mumtaz Begum
		Miss Disco	Discovery / Outdone
	Somethingroyal (b. 1952)	Princequillo	Prince Rose / Cosquilla
		Imperatrice	Caruso / Cinquepace
ARTISTS PROOF (b. 1967)	Ribot (b. 1952)	Tenerani	Bellini / Tofanella
		Romanella	El Greco / Barbara Burrini
	Be Ambitious (br. 1958)	Ambiorix II	Tourbillon / Lavendula II
		Be Faithful	Bimelech / Bloodroot

214   DAHLIA 13 (ch.f., March 25, 1970)

Bred by Nelson Bunker Hunt, in U.S.A.

Won 15 races, placed 15, £653,338, in England, Ireland, France, U.S.A. and Canada, from 2 to 6 years, incl. King George VI and Queen Elizabeth Stakes (twice), Benson and Hedges Gold Cup (twice), Irish Guinness Oaks, Grand Prix de Saint-Cloud, Prix Saint-Alary, Prix de la Grotte, Prix Niel, Washington D.C. International, Man o'War Stakes, Hollywood Invitational H., Canadian International Championship; 2nd Prix de Diane, Grand Prix de Deauville, Prix des Reservoirs; 3rd King George VI and Queen Elizabeth Diamond Stakes, Coronation Cup, Poule d'Essai des Pouliches, Prix du Prince d'Orange (twice), Washington D.C. International, Century H.; 4th Hollywood Gold Cup, Canadian International Championship.

VAGUELY NOBLE (b. 1965)	Vienna (ch. 1957)	Aureole	Hyperion / Angelola
		Turkish Blood	Turkhan / Rusk
	Noble Lassie (b. 1956)	Nearco	Pharos / Nogara
		Belle Sauvage	Big Game / Tropical Sun
CHARMING ALIBI (ch. 1963)	Honeys Alibi (b. 1952)	Alibhai	Hyperion / Teresina
		Honeymoon	Beau Pere / Panoramic
	Adorada II (ch. 1947)	Hierocles	Abjer / Loika
		Gilded Wave	Gallant Fox / Ondulation

215   DAMASCUS 8 (b.c., April 14, 1964)

Bred by Mrs. Edith W. Bancroft, in U.S.A.

Won 21 races, placed 10, $1,176,781, in U.S.A., from 2 to 4 years, incl. Preakness Stakes, Belmont Stakes, American Derby, Jockey Club Gold Cup, Woodward Stakes, Aqueduct Stakes (twice), Wood Memorial Stakes, Travers Stakes, Dwyer H., Leonard Richards Stakes, Bay Shore Stakes, Brooklyn H., Malibu Stakes, San Fernando Stakes, William Dupont Jr. H. and Remsen Stakes; 2nd Woodward Stakes, Washington D.C. International, Charles H. Strub Stakes, Michigan Mile H., Gotham Stakes and William Dupont Jr. H.; 3rd Kentucky Derby, Amory L. Haskell H. and Suburban H.

SWORD DANCER (USA) (ch. 1956)	Sunglow (ch. 1947)	Sun Again	Sun Teddy / Hug Again
		Rosern	Mad Hatter / Rosedrop
	Highland Fling (br. 1950)	By Jimminy	Pharamond / Buginarug
		Swing Time	Royal Minstrel / Speed Boat
KERALA (b. 1958)	My Babu (b. 1945)	Djebel	Tourbillon / Loika
		Perfume II	Badruddin / Lavendula II
	Blade of Time (br. 1938)	Sickle	Phalaris / Selene
		Bar Nothing	Blue Larkspur / Beaming Beauty

216   DANCER'S IMAGE 4 (gr.c., April 10, 1965)

Bred by Peter Fuller, in U.S.A.

Won 12 races, placed 6, $236,636, in U.S.A., at 2 and 3 years, incl. Governor's Gold Cup and Wood Memorial Stakes; also won Kentucky Derby, but disqualified; 2nd Marylander Stakes.

NATIVE DANCER (gr. 1950)	Polynesian (br. 1942)	Unbreakable	Sickle / Blue Glass
		Black Polly	Polymelian / Black Queen
	Geisha (ro. 1943)	Discovery	Display / Ariadne
		Miyako	John P. Grier / La Chica
NOORS IMAGE (b. 1953)	Noor (br. 1945)	Nasrullah	Nearco / Mumtaz Begum
		Queen of Baghdad	Bahram / Queen of Scots
	Little Sphinx (ch. 1943)	Challenger	Swynford / Sword Play
		Khara	Kai-Sang / Decree

58

217   DANCING MAID 14 (b.f., April 29, 1975)

Bred by Jacques Wertheimer, in France.

Won 5 races, placed 3, 1,555,048 fr., in France and England, at 2 and 3 years, incl. Poule d'Essai des Pouliches, Prix Vermeille, Prix Vanteaux and Prix Chloe; 2nd Oaks Stakes; 3rd Prix de l'Arc de Triomphe.

LYPHARD (b. 1969)	Northern Dancer (b. 1961)	Nearctic	Nearco / Lady Angela
		Natalma	Native Dancer / Almahmoud
	Goofed (ch. 1960)	Court Martial	Fair Trial / Instantaneous
		Barra	Formor / La Favorite
MORANA (b. 1968)	Val de Loir (b. 1959)	Vieux Manoir	Brantome / Vieille Maison
		Vali	Sunny Boy III / Her Slipper
	Moira II (b. 1959)	Sicambre	Prince Bio / Sif
		Madrilene	Goya II / Miraflore

---

218   DAN KANO 1 (ch.c., May 18, 1964)

Bred by Merevale Stud.

Won 3 races, placed 5, £19,934, in Ireland, France and England, from 2 to 5 years, incl. Irish St. Leger, Grand Prix de Vichy; 3rd Coronation Cup.

DICTA DRAKE (b. 1958)	Phil Drake (b. 1952)	Admiral Drake	Craig an Eran / Plucky Liege
		Philippa	Vatellor / Philippa of Hainaut
	Dictature (b. 1950)	Transtevere	Bubbles / Farnese
		Nymphe Dicte	Diolite / Nanaia
GILLYLEES (b. 1955)	The Bug (ch. 1943)	Signal Light	Pharos / Ensoleillee
		Flying Meteor	Flying Orb / Reformation
	Chanting Hill (br. 1950)	Nearco	Pharos / Nogara
		Running Wild	His Grace / Wild Lavender II

---

219   DANKARO 14 (ch.c., May 8, 1971)

Bred by Marcel Boussac, in France.

Won 4 races, placed 3, 1,808,090 fr., in France and England, at 2 and 3 years, incl. Prix Lupin, Prix Greffulhe and Prix Daru; 2nd Prix du Jockey-Club; 3rd King George VI and Queen Elizabeth Stakes.

DAN CUPID (ch. 1956)	Native Dancer (gr. 1950)	Polynesian	Unbreakable / Black Polly
		Geisha	Discovery / Miyako
	Vixenette (ch. 1944)	Sickle	Phalaris / Selene
		Lady Reynard	Gallant Fox / Nerva
TAKAROA (b. 1962)	Prince Bio (b. 1941)	Prince Rose	Rose Prince / Indolence
		Biologie	Bacteriophage / Eponge
	Arbencia (b. 1954)	Arbar	Djebel / Astronomie
		Palencia	Pharis II / Hestia

---

220   DANSEUR 8 (b.c., May 23, 1963)

Bred by Francois Dupré, in France.

Won 7 races, placed 9, 1,472,107 fr., in France and England, from 2 to 4 years, incl. Grand Prix de Paris, Prix du Cadran, Prix du Lys and Prix Jean Prat; 2nd Criterium de Maisons-Laffitte; 3rd Ascot Gold Cup.

TANTIEME (b. 1947)	Deux pour Cent (b. 1941)	Deiri	Aethelstan / Desra
		Dix pour Cent	Feridoon / La Chansonnerie
	Terka (br. 1942)	Indus	Alcantara II / Himalaya
		La Furka	Blandford / Brenta
LA DANSE (b. 1951)	Menetrier (br. 1944)	Fair Copy	Fairway / Composure
		La Melodie	Gold Bridge / La Sourcière
	Makada (b. 1936)	Rustom Pasha	Son-in-Law / Cos
		Rayonnante II	Sans le Sou / La Sémillante

---

221   DARING DISPLAY 14 (b.c., April 9, 1969)

Bred by Beatrice, Countess of Granard, in U.S.A.

Won 5 races, placed 3, 627,932 fr., in France, at 2 and 3 years, incl. Prix Morny, Prix de la Jonchere and Prix du Rond-Point; 3rd Poule d'Essai des Poulains, Prix du Moulin de Longchamp and Prix Eugene Adam.

BOLD LAD (IRE) (b. 1964)	Bold Ruler (b. 1954)	Nasrullah	Nearco / Mumtaz Begum
		Miss Disco	Discovery / Outdone
	Barn Pride (ch. 1957)	Democratic	Denturius / Light Fantasy
		Fair Alycia	Alycidon / Fair Edwine
ROYAL DISPLAY (ch. 1963)	Right Royal V (br. 1958)	Owen Tudor	Hyperion / Mary Tudor II
		Bastia	Tornado or Victrix II / Barberybush
	Short Sentence (ch. 1956)	Court Martial	Fair Trial / Instantaneous
		Three Weeks	Big Game / Eleanor Cross

---

222   DARK BABY 4 (b.f., March 25, 1969)

Bred by M. Fournier, in France.

Won 4 races, placed 8, 418,950 fr., in France, from 2 to 4 years, incl. Criterium des Pouliches; 2nd Prix Vanteaux and Prix du Prince d'Orange.

DARK TIGER (b. 1959)	Nasrullah (b. 1940)	Nearco	Pharos / Nogara
		Mumtaz Begum	Blenheim / Mumtaz Mahal
	Spotted Beauty (ro. 1941)	Man o'War	Fair Play / Mahubah
		Silver Beauty	Stefan the Great / Jeanne Bowdre
MAISON DE POUPEE (ch. 1956)	Fontenay (b. 1946)	Tornado	Tourbillon / Roseola
		Flying Colours	Massine / Red Flame
	Doll House (b. 1950)	Cranach	Coronach / Reine Isaure
		Poupee du Roi	Bubbles / Royal Camp

223   DARK MIRAGE 9 (b. or br.f., April 7, 1965)

Bred by Duval A. Headley, in U.S.A.

Won 12 races, placed 5, $362,788, in U.S.A., from 2 to 4 years, incl. Coaching Club American Oaks, Mother Goose Stakes, Acorn Stakes, Kentucky Oaks, Delaware Oaks, Monmouth Oaks and Santa Maria H.

PERSIAN ROAD (ch. 1955)	Persian Gulf (b. 1940)	Bahram	Blandford / Friar's Daughter
		Double Life	Bachelor's Double / Saint Joan
	One For The Road (ch. 1947)	Watling Street	Fairway / Ranai
		Sundae	Hyperion / Bachelor's Fare
HOME BY DARK (ro. 1959)	Hill Prince (b. 1947)	Princequillo	Prince Rose / Cosquilla
		Hildene	Bubbling Over / Fancy Racket
	Sunday Evening (ro. 1947)	Eight Thirty	Pilate / Dinner Time
		Drowsy	Royal Minstrel / Lazy Susan

224   DART BOARD 21 (ch.c., January 29, 1964)

Bred by Ballymacoll Stud Farm Ltd.

Won 4 races, placed 4, £31,298, in England and Ireland, at 2 and 3 years, incl. Dewhurst Stakes; 3rd Derby Stakes, Irish Sweeps Derby; 4th St. Leger Stakes.

DARIUS (b. 1951)	Dante (br. 1942)	Nearco	Pharos / Nogara
		Rosy Legend	Dark Legend / Rosy Cheeks
	Yasna (b. 1936)	Dastur	Solario / Friar's Daughter
		Ariadne	Arion / Security
SHRUBSWOOD (b. 1958)	Straight Deal (b. 1940)	Solario	Gainsborough / Sun Worship
		Good Deal	Apelle / Weeds
	Oleandra (ch. 1951)	Nearco	Pharos / Nogara
		Lady Olivia	Donatello II / Olifa

225   DAVONA DALE 3 (b.f., May 14, 1976)

Bred by Calumet Farm, in U.S.A.

Won 11 races, placed 3, $641,612, in U.S.A., from 2 to 4 years, incl. Coaching Club American Oaks, Mother Goose Stakes, Acorn Stakes, Kentucky Oaks, Fantasy Stakes and Black-Eyed Susan Stakes; 2nd Alabama Stakes.

BEST TURN (br. 1966)	Turn-to (b. 1951)	Royal Charger	Nearco / Sun Princess
		Source Sucree	Admiral Drake / Lavendula II
	Sweet Clementine (b. 1960)	Swaps	Khaled / Iron Reward
		Miz Clementine	Bull Lea / Two Bob
ROYAL ENTRANCE (b. 1965)	Tim Tam (b. 1955)	Tom Fool	Menow / Gaga
		Two Lea	Bull Lea / Two Bob
	Prince's Gate (b. 1957)	Sun Again	Sun Teddy / Hug Again
		Siena Way	Bull Lea / Hydroplane

226   DAYS AT SEA 11 (b.c., May 18, 1971)

Bred by L. J. Tutt, in U.S.A.

Won 3 races, placed 8, 723,702 fr., in France and Germany, at 2 and 3 years, incl. Preis von Europa; 3rd Prix Caracalla.

BLUE PRINCE II (b. 1951)	Princequillo (b. 1940)	Prince Rose	Rose Prince / Indolence
		Cosquilla	Papyrus / Quick Thought
	Blue Denim (b. 1940)	Blue Larkspur	Black Servant / Blossom Time
		Judy O'Grady	Man o' War / Bel Agnes
JENTRA (b. 1962)	Traffic Judge (ch. 1952)	Alibhai	Hyperion / Teresina
		Traffic Court	Discovery / Traffic
	Jenjay (b. 1951)	Brookfield	Bimelech / Knockaney Bridge
		Genevra M.	Percentage / Homebody

227   DEAUVILLE 14 (ch.c., February 10, 1977)

Bred by Scuderia Cieffedi, in England.

Won 4 races, placed 2, 47,490,000 L., in Italy, at 2 and 3 years, incl. Premio Presidente della Repubblica.

RELKO (b. 1960)	Tanerko (br. 1953)	Tantieme	Deux pour Cent / Terka
		La Divine	Fair Copy / La Diva
	Relance III (ch. 1952)	Relic	War Relic / Bridal Colors
		Polaire II	Le Volcan / Stella Polaris
DOBROWA (ch. 1966)	Mossborough (ch. 1947)	Nearco	Pharos / Nogara
		All Moonshine	Bobsleigh / Selene
	Doride II (ch. 1958)	Norseman	Umidwar / Tara
		Donata Veneziana	Tenerani / Domiziana

228   DECIDEDLY 17 (gr.c., March 3, 1959)

Bred by George A. Pope, Jr., in U.S.A.

Won 11 races, placed 13, $318,989, in U.S.A. and Canada, from 2 to 5 years, incl. Kentucky Derby, Monmouth H., Dominion Day H. and Ben Ali H.; 2nd Blue Grass Stakes, Everglades Stakes and Michigan Mile-and-One-Sixteenth H.; 3rd Grey Lag H.; 4th Belmont Stakes.

DETERMINE (gr. 1951)	Alibhai (ch. 1938)	Hyperion	Gainsborough / Selene
		Teresina	Tracery / Blue Tit
	Koubis (gr. 1946)	Mahmoud	Blenheim / Mah Mahal
		Brown Biscuit	Sir Andrew / Swing On
GLOIRE FILLE (b. 1949)	War Glory (ch. 1930)	Man o' War	Fair Play / Mahubah
		Annette K.	Harry of Hereford / Bathing Girl
	Belle Femme (b. 1944)	Beau Pere	Son-in-Law / Cinna
		French Vamp	Stimulus / La France

229 DECIES 7 (b.c., March 9, 1967)

Bred by J. Flahavan.

Won 7 races, placed 12, £43,043, in Ireland, England, France, Italy and U.S.A., from 2 to 6 years, incl. Irish 2,000 Guineas, National Stakes (Curragh), Blue Riband Trial Stakes; 2nd Beresford Stakes, Railway Stakes, Gran Premio d'Italia, Premio U.N.I.R.E.; 3rd Jockey Club Stakes.

PARDAL (b. 1947)	Pharis II (br. 1936)	Pharos	Phalaris / Scapa Flow
		Carissima	Clarissimus / Casquetts
	Adargatis (b. 1931)	Asterus	Teddy / Astrella
		Helene de Troie	Helicon / Lady of Pedigree
RECIPROCATE (b. 1956)	Valerullah (ch. 1951)	Nasrullah	Nearco / Mumtaz Begum
		Painted Vale	Gainsborough / Abbot's Glen
	Coup de Maitre (b. 1939)	Coup de Lyon	Winalot / Sundry
		War Plume	Happy Warrior / War Duck

230 DEEP DIVER 13 (ch.c., May 4, 1969)

Bred by G. A. Harris.

Won 9 races, placed 6, £43,924, in England and France, at 2 and 3 years, incl. Nunthorpe Stakes, July Stakes, Cornwallis Stakes, Prix de l'Abbaye de Longchamp, Prix d'Arenberg, Prix du Petit Couvert; 2nd Norfolk Stakes, Prix Robert Papin, Palace House Stakes, King George Stakes; 3rd New Stakes; 4th Prix Morny.

GULF PEARL (ch. 1962)	Persian Gulf (b. 1940)	Bahram	Blandford / Friar's Daughter
		Double Life	Bachelor's Double / Saint Joan
	Nan (ch. 1955)	Nearco	Pharos / Nogara
		Marsyaka	Marsyas II / Nokka
MISS STEPHEN (ch. 1955)	Stephen Paul (br. 1948)	Panorama	Sir Cosmo / Happy Climax
		Paradise	Dastur / Wandsworth
	Bright Set (ch. 1950)	Denturius	Gold Bridge / La Solfatara
		Firelight	Signal Light / Four Fires

231 DELMORA 4 (br.f., February 11, 1972)

Bred by Cragwood Estates Inc., in U.S.A.

Won 4 races, placed 5, 847,831 fr., in France and England, at 2 and 3 years, incl. Prix de la Salamandre, Prix du Moulin de Longchamp and Prix du Rond-Point; 2nd Cheveley Park Stakes and Prix Maurice de Gheest; 3rd Prix Jacques le Marois.

SIR GAYLORD (b. 1959)	Turn-to (b. 1951)	Royal Charger	Nearco / Sun Princess
		Source Sucree	Admiral Drake / Lavendula II
	Somethingroyal (b. 1952)	Princequillo	Prince Rose / Cosquilla
		Imperatrice	Caruso / Cinquepace
PENITENCE (b. 1961)	Petition (br. 1944)	Fair Trial	Fairway / Lady Juror
		Art Paper	Artist's Proof / Quire
	Bootless (b. 1951)	The Cobbler	Windsor Slipper / Overture
		Careless Nora	Panorama / Careless

232 DEMOCRATIE 4 (b.f., June 14, 1966)

Bred by Commander P. FitzGerald, in Ireland.

Won 4 races, placed 3, 455,130 fr., in France, at 3 years, incl. Prix de la Foret, Prix de la Porte Maillot and Prix de Seine-et-Oise; 4th Poule d'Essai des Pouliches.

IMMORTALITY (b. 1956)	Never Say Die (ch. 1951)	Nasrullah	Nearco / Mumtaz Begum
		Singing Grass	War Admiral / Boreale
	Belle of Troy (br. 1947)	Blue Larkspur	Black Servant / Blossom Time
		La Troienne	Teddy / Helene de Troie
REVIEW (ch. 1951)	Panorama (ch. 1936)	Sir Cosmo	The Boss / Ayn Hali
		Happy Climax	Happy Warrior / Clio
	Pin Up Girl (b. 1943)	Coup de Lyon	Winalot / Sundry
		Careless	Caerleon / Traverse

233 DERRING-DO 21 (b.c., March 25, 1961)

Bred by Burton Agnes Stud Co. Ltd.

Won 6 races, placed 5, £21,079, in England and France, from 2 to 4 years, incl. Queen Elizabeth II Stakes, Hungerford Stakes, Cornwallis Stakes; 2nd National Stakes, Sussex Stakes, Queen Elizabeth II Stakes; 3rd Lockinge Stakes (dead-heat), Prix Quincey.

DARIUS (b. 1951)	Dante (br. 1942)	Nearco	Pharos / Nogara
		Rosy Legend	Dark Legend / Rosy Cheeks
	Yasna (b. 1936)	Dastur	Solario / Friar's Daughter
		Ariadne	Arion / Security
SIPSEY BRIDGE (b. or br. 1954)	Abernant (gr. 1946)	Owen Tudor	Hyperion / Mary Tudor II
		Rustom Mahal	Rustom Pasha / Mumtaz Mahal
	Claudette (br. 1949)	Chanteur II	Chateau Bouscaut / La Diva
		Nearly	Nearco / Lost Soul

234 DESERT BEAUTY 1 (b. or br.f., January 25, 1957)

Bred by Miss D. Paget.

Won 3 races, placed 4, £4,021, in England, at 2 and 3 years, incl. Nassau Stakes; 2nd Princess Royal Stakes; 3rd Fred Darling Stakes.

DANTE (br. 1942)	Nearco (br. 1935)	Pharos	Phalaris / Scapa Flow
		Nogara	Havresac II / Catnip
	Rosy Legend (br. 1931)	Dark Legend	Dark Ronald / Golden Legend
		Rosy Cheeks	St. Just / Purity
DESERT GIRL (b. 1950)	Straight Deal (b. 1940)	Solario	Gainsborough / Sun Worship
		Good Deal	Apelle / Weeds
	Yashmak (b. 1941)	Easton	Dark Legend / Phaona
		Zelina	Blandford / Zoza

235   DESERT VIXEN 2 (dk.b./br.f., April 19, 1970)

Bred by Mrs. Vanderbilt Adams, in U.S.A.

Won 13 races, placed 9, $421,538, in U.S.A., from 2 to 5 years, incl. Beldame Stakes (twice), Alabama Stakes, Delaware Oaks, Monmouth Oaks, Gazelle H., Post-Deb Stakes, Test Stakes and Matchmaker Stakes; 2nd Washington D.C. International and Spinster Stakes.

IN REALITY (b. 1964)	Intentionally (bl. 1956)	Intent	War Relic / Liz F
		My Recipe	Discovery / Perlette
	My Dear Girl (ch. 1957)	Rough'n Tumble	Free for All / Roused
		Iltis	War Relic / We Hail
DESERT TRIAL (ch. 1963)	Moslem Chief (b. 1957)	Alibhai	Hyperion / Teresina
		Up the Hill	Jacopo / Gentle Tryst
	Scotch Verdict (ch. 1960)	Alsab	Good Goods / Winds Chant
		Glen Arvis	Attention / Helen Gleason

236   DETROIT 16 (b.f., February 24, 1977)

Bred by Société Aland, in France.

Won 5 races, placed 1, 1,775,000 fr., in France, at 3 years, incl. Prix de l'Arc de Triomphe, Prix Fille de l'Air, Prix Chloe and Prix de la Nonette; 3rd Prix Vermeille.

RIVERMAN (b. 1969)	Never Bend (br. 1960)	Nasrullah	Nearco / Mumtaz Begum
		Lalun	Djeddah / Be Faithful
	River Lady (b. 1963)	Prince John	Princequillo / Not Afraid
		Nile Lily	Roman / Azalea
DERNA II (b. 1961)	Sunny Boy III (b. 1944)	Jock II	Asterus / Naic
		Fille de Soleil	Solario / Fille de Salut
	Miss Barberie (b. 1950)	Norseman	Umidwar / Tara
		Vaneuse	Vatellor / Diseuse

237   DEVON DITTY 1 (ch.f., May 8, 1976)

Bred by Littleton Stud.

Won 11 races, placed 8, £145,299, in England, Germany and U.S.A., from 2 to 4 years, incl. Flying Childers Stakes, William Hill Cheveley Park Stakes, Cherry Hinton Stakes, Lowther Stakes, Brown Jade Stakes; 2nd Ladbrokes Nell Gwyn Stakes, Goldene Peitsche, Hawthorne H.; 3rd Vernons Sprint Cup, King George Stakes, Queen Mary Stakes, Palomar H.; 4th William Hill July Cup.

SONG (b. 1966)	Sing Sing (b. 1957)	Tudor Minstrel	Owen Tudor / Sansonnet
		Agin the Law	Portlaw / Revolte
	Intent (gr. 1952)	Vilmorin	Gold Bridge / Queen of the Meadows
		Under Canvas	Winterhalter / Shelton
DEVON NIGHT (ch. 1966)	Midsummer Night II (ch. 1957)	Djeddah	Djebel / Djezima
		Night Sound	Mahmoud / Gala Flight
	Devon Violet (b. 1953)	Devonian	Hyperion / Glorious Devon
		Elgin	Donatello II / Nairn

238   DHAUDEVI 2 (b.c., March 19, 1965)

Bred by Mme. G. Courtois, in France.

Won 4 races, placed 3, 1,420,200 fr., in France, at 2 and 3 years, incl. Grand Prix de Paris, Prix Royal Oak and Prix Berteux.

DHAULAGIRI (b. 1956)	High Peak (ch. 1942)	Hyperion	Gainsborough / Selene
		Leger Day	Winalot / Optima
	Solar Circle (b. 1941)	Solar Bear	Solario / Lair
		Trendel	Parenthesis / Moulinet
DEVIVOR (b. 1958)	Worden II (ch. 1949)	Wild Risk	Rialto / Wild Violet
		Sans Tares	Sind / Tara
	Devinette (b. 1949)	Eble	Davout / Even Scales
		Dvina	Sirtam / Devineress

239   DIACONO 4 (br.c., 1961)

Bred by Conte Neni Da Zara, in Ireland.

Won 6 races, placed 9, 34,204,000 L., in Italy, from 2 to 5 years, incl. Derby Italiano; 2nd St. Leger Italiano and Premio Roma.

JADDO (b. 1951)	Djebel (b. 1937)	Tourbillon	Ksar / Durban
		Loika	Gay Crusader / Coeur a Coeur
	Jalapa (b. 1946)	Jock II	Asterus / Naic
		Thoas	Tourbillon / Carissima
DAMIGELLA (br. 1954)	Petition (br. 1944)	Fair Trial	Fairway / Lady Juror
		Art Paper	Artist's Proof / Quire
	Doreuse (b. 1945)	Winterhalter	Gainsborough / Perce-neige
		D'Oraine	Haine / Mots d'Or

240   DIATOME (late Diat) 12 (br.c., 1962)

Bred by Baron Guy de Rothschild, in France.

Won 6 races, placed 6, 1,643,013 fr., in France and U.S.A., from 2 to 4 years, incl. Prix Ganay, Prix Noailles, Prix du Prince d'Orange and Washington D.C. International; 2nd Prix du Jockey-Club, Grand Prix de Paris, Prix Lupin, Grand Prix de Saint-Cloud and Prix Dollar; 3rd Prix de l'Arc de Triomphe.

SICAMBRE (br. 1948)	Prince Bio (b. 1941)	Prince Rose	Rose Prince / Indolence
		Biologie	Bacteriophage / Eponge
	Sif (br. 1936)	Rialto	Rabelais / La Grelee
		Suavita	Alcantara II / Shocking
DICTAWAY (br. 1952)	Honeyway (br. 1941)	Fairway	Phalaris / Scapa Flow
		Honey Buzzard	Papyrus / Lady Peregrine
	Nymphe Dicte (b. 1935)	Diolite	Diophon / Needle Rock
		Nanaia	Kircubbin / Lanette

241   DIBIDALE 19 (ch.f., April 6, 1971)

Bred by Swettenham Stud.

Won 3 races, placed 4, £44,447, in England and Ireland, from 2 to 4 years, incl. Irish Guinness Oaks, Yorkshire Oaks, Cheshire Oaks; 3rd Hardwicke Stakes, Jockey Club Stakes, Oaks Stakes (but disq.).

AGGRESSOR (b. 1955)	Combat (b. 1944)	Big Game	Bahram
			Myrobella
		Commotion	Mieuxce
			Riot
	Phaetonia (ch. 1945)	Nearco	Pharos
			Nogara
		Phaetusa	Hyperion
			Saddle Tor
PRIDDY MAID (ch. 1961)	Acropolis (ch. 1952)	Donatello II	Blenheim
			Delleana
		Aurora	Hyperion
			Rose Red
	Priddy Fair (b. 1956)	Preciptic	Precipitation
			Artistic
		Campanette	Fair Trial
			Calluna

242   DICKENS HILL 11 (ch.c., January 25, 1976)

Bred by Frank Flannery.

Won 5 races, placed 7, £200,012, in Ireland, England and U.S.A., from 2 to 4 years, incl. Airlie/Coolmore Irish 2,000 Guineas, Coral Eclipse Stakes, Sean Graham Ballymoss Stakes, Anglesey Stakes; 2nd Derby Stakes, Irish Sweeps Derby, National Stakes, Curragh, McCairns Vauxhall Trial Stakes; 3rd Canadian Turf H.

MOUNT HAGEN (ch. 1971)	Bold Bidder (b. 1962)	Bold Ruler	Nasrullah
			Miss Disco
		High Bid	To Market
			Stepping Stone
	Moonmadness (ch. 1963)	Tom Fool	Menow
			Gaga
		Sunset	Hyperion
			Fair Ranger
LONDON LIFE (ch. 1961)	Panaslipper (ch. 1952)	Solar Slipper	Windsor Slipper
			Solar Flower
		Panastrid	Panorama
			Astrid
	Court Circular (ch. 1949)	Court Martial	Fair Trial
			Instantaneous
		Queanladdie	Motrico
			Gladiatrix

243   DICTA DRAKE 12 (b.c., May 20, 1958)

Bred by Mme. L. Volterra, in France.

Won 4 races, placed 4, £53,256, in France and England, at 3 and 4 years, incl. Grand Prix de Saint-Cloud, Grand Prix du Printemps, Coronation Cup; 2nd Derby Stakes; 3rd Prix Juigné, St. Leger Stakes.

PHIL DRAKE (b. 1952)	Admiral Drake (br. 1931)	Craig an Eran	Sunstar
			Maid of the Mist
		Plucky Liege	Spearmint
			Concertina
	Philippa (br. 1943)	Vatellor	Vatout
			Lady Elinor
		Philippa of Hainaut	Teddy
			Pride of Hainault
DICTATURE (b. 1950)	Transtevere (ch. 1936)	Bubbles	La Farina
			Spring Cleaning
		Farnese	Mime
			Francoise
	Nymphe Dicte (b. 1935)	Diolite	Diophon
			Needle Rock
		Nanaia	Kircubbin
			Lanette

244   DICTUS 16 (ch.c., April 11, 1967)

Bred by Rene Wattinne, in France.

Won 6 races, placed 8, 631,569 fr., in France and England, from 2 to 4 years, incl. Prix Jacques le Marois and Prix d'Evry; 2nd Queen Elizabeth II Stakes, Prix de Messidor and Prix de la Cote Normande; 4th Champion Stakes.

SANCTUS II (b. 1960)	Fine Top (br. 1949)	Fine Art	Artist's Proof
			Finnoise
		Toupie	Vatellor
			Tarentella
	Sanelta (b. 1954)	Tourment	Tourbillon
			Fragment
		Satanella	Mahmoud
			Avella
DORONIC (ch. 1960)	Worden II (ch. 1949)	Wild Risk	Rialto
			Wild Violet
		Sans Tares	Sind
			Tara
	Dulzetta (ch. 1954)	Bozzetto	Pharos
			Bunworry
		Dulcimer	Donatello II
			Dulce II

245   DIE HARD 1 (ch.c., February 1, 1957)

Bred by Burton Agnes Stud Co.

Won 4 races, placed 5, £17,129, in England, Ireland and Italy, at 3 and 4 years, incl. Players' Navy Cut Stakes, Gold Flake Trigo Stakes, Ebor Handicap; 2nd St. Leger Stakes; 3rd Blandford Stakes, Hardwicke Stakes, Premio Roma.

NEVER SAY DIE (ch. 1951)	Nasrullah (b. 1940)	Nearco	Pharos
			Nogara
		Mumtaz Begum	Blenheim
			Mumtaz Mahal
	Singing Grass (ch. 1944)	War Admiral	Man o' War
			Brushup
		Boreale	Vatout
			Galaday II
MIXED BLESSING (ch. 1946)	Brumeux (b. 1925)	Teddy	Ajax
			Rondeau
		La Brume	Alcantara II
			Aquarelle
	Pot-pourri (ch. 1928)	Rose Prince	Prince Palatine
			Eglantine
		Sweet Lavender	Swynford
			Marchetta

246   DILETTANTE II 19 (b.c., April 2, 1961)

Bred by R. Muller, in France.

Won 1 race, placed 3, £5,551, in England and Ireland, at 3 and 4 years, incl. Warren Stakes; 3rd Derby Stakes, Great Voltigeur Sweepstakes.

SICAMBRE (br. 1948)	Prince Bio (b. 1941)	Prince Rose	Rose Prince
			Indolence
		Biologie	Bacteriophage
			Eponge
	Sif (br. 1936)	Rialto	Rabelais
			La Grelee
		Suavita	Alcantara II
			Shocking
BARBIZONNETTE (b. 1949)	Le Paillon (b. 1942)	Fastnet	Pharos
			Tatoule
		Blue Bear	Blenheim
			La Boni
	Sica (b. 1944)	Meridien	Tourbillon
			Meriem
		Sylla II	Amant de Coeur
			Syrie II

247   DISPLAY 4 (ch.f., April 12, 1959)

Bred by Commander P. J. FitzGerald

Won 5 races, placed 3, £18,368, in Ireland, England and France, at 2 and 3 years, incl. National Stakes (Sandown), Cheveley Park Stakes, Coronation Stakes; 2nd 1,000 Guineas Stakes, Greenlands Stakes; 3rd Prix Morny.

RUSTAM (b. or br. 1953)	Persian Gulf (b. 1940)	Bahram	Blandford
			Friar's Daughter
		Double Life	Bachelor's Double
			Saint Joan
	Samovar (ch. 1940)	Caerleon	Phalaris
			Canyon
		Carolina	Embargo
			Georgia
REVIEW (ch. 1951)	Panorama (ch. 1936)	Sir Cosmo	The Boss
			Ayn Hali
		Happy Climax	Happy Warrior
			Clio
	Pin Up Girl (b. 1943)	Coup de Lyon	Winalot
			Sundry
		Careless	Caerleon
			Traverse

248   DJAKAO 8 (b.c., March 16, 1966)

Bred by Baron Guy de Rothschild, in France.

Won 3 races, placed 5, 823,158 fr., in France at 2 and 3 years, incl. Grand Prix de Deauville; 2nd Grand Prix de Paris and Prix Hocquart; 3rd Prix du Jockey-Club and Prix Saint-Roman.

TANERKO (br. 1953)	Tantième (b. 1947)	Deux pour Cent	Deiri
			Dix pour Cent
		Terka	Indus
			La Furka
	La Divine (br. 1943)	Fair Copy	Fairway
			Composure
		La Diva	Blue Skies
			La Traviata
DIAGONALE (ch. 1959)	Ribot (br. 1952)	Tenerani	Bellini
			Tofanella
		Romanella	El Greco
			Barbara Burrini
	Barley Corn (b. 1950)	Hyperion	Gainsborough
			Selene
		Schiaparelli	Schiavoni
			Aileen

249   DOLESWOOD 1 (ch.c., May 7, 1971)

Bred by Fort Union Stud Farm Ltd.

Won 2 races, placed 3, £8,927, in England, from 2 to 4 years, incl. Coventry Stakes.

DOUBLE JUMP (ch. 1962)	Rustam (b. or br. 1953)	Persian Gulf	Bahram
			Double Life
		Samovar	Caerleon
			Carolina
	Fair Bid (b. 1952)	My Babu	Djebel
			Perfume II
		Market Fair	Fair Trial
			Mrs. Pumpkin
ALLEY CAT (ch. 1962)	Alycidon (ch. 1945)	Donatello II	Blenheim
			Delleana
		Aurora	Hyperion
			Rose Red
	Mistress Ann (ch. 1945)	Nearco	Pharos
			Nogara
		Cheerful Anne	Bahram
			Anne of Brittany

250   DON 4 (ch.c., March 15, 1974)

Bred by W. Vischer.

Won 4 races, placed 8, £52,206, in England, from 2 to 5 years, incl. St. James's Palace Stakes, Lockinge Stakes; 2nd Waterford Crystal Mile; 4th Sussex Stakes.

YELLOW GOD (ch. 1967)	Red God (ch. 1954)	Nasrullah	Nearco
			Mumtaz Begum
		Spring Run	Menow
			Boola Brook
	Sally Deans (ch. 1947)	Fun Fair	Fair Trial
			Humoresque
		Cora Deans	Coronach
			Jennie Deans
DOGANA (b. 1968)	Zank (b. 1961)	Neckar	Ticino
			Nixe
		Zacateca	Zuccarello
			Katherine Roet
	Dominante (br. 1962)	Chief III	Nearco
			Nikellora
		Dekagram	Vatellor
			Programme

251   DON II 14 (gr.c., May 3, 1966)

Bred by Scuderia Alpina, in Italy.

Won 4 races, placed 6, 523,365 fr., in France at 2 and 3 years, incl. Poule d'Essai des Poulains and Prix d'Arenberg; 2nd Prix de la Foret; 4th Prix Morny and Prix d'Ispahan.

GREY SOVEREIGN (gr. 1948)	Nasrullah (b. 1940)	Nearco	Pharos
			Nogara
		Mumtaz Begum	Blenheim
			Mumtaz Mahal
	Kong (gr. 1933)	Baytown	Achtoi
			Princess Herodias
		Clang	Hainault
			Vibration
DIVIANA II (b. 1957)	Toulouse Lautrec (ch. 1950)	Dante	Nearco
			Rosy Legend
		Tokamura	Navarro
			Tofanella
	Desublea (b. 1948)	Niccolo Dell'Arca	Coronach
			Nogara
		Durera	Brantome
			Dossa Dossi

252   DON GIOVANNI 6 (b.c., April 2, 1966)

Bred by Gestüt Schlenderhan, in Germany.

Won 4 races, placed 6, 168,700 DM., in Germany, at 2 and 3 years, incl. Deutsches Derby; 2nd Consul Bayeff-Rennen.

ORSINI (br. 1954)	Ticino (b. 1939)	Athanasius	Ferro
			Athanasie
		Terra	Aditi
			Teufelsrose
	Oranien (b. 1949)	Nuvolari	Oleander
			Nereide
		Omladina	Athanasius
			Oblate
DONNA DIANA (br. 1956)	Neckar (bl. 1948)	Ticino	Athanasius
			Terra
		Nixe	Arjaman
			Nanon
	Donatella (b. 1950)	Allgau	Ortello
			Arabella
		Blaue Donau	Ferro
			An der Wien

253   DOUBLE FORM 14 (b.c., February 14, 1975)

Bred by Baroness H. von Thyssen-Bornemisza.

Won 7 races, placed 9, £127, 852, in England and France, from 2 to 4 years, incl. King's Stand Stakes, Prix de l'Abbaye de Longchamp, Vernons Sprint Cup, Temple Stakes; 2nd Cork and Orrery Stakes, Palace House Stakes; 3rd William Hill July Cup, Prix de l'Abbaye de Longchamp, William Hill Sprint Championship, Clerical Medical Greenham Stakes.

HABITAT (b. 1966)	Sir Gaylord (b. 1959)	Turn-to	Royal Charger / Source Sucree
		Somethingroyal	Princequillo / Imperatrice
	Little Hut (b. 1952)	Occupy	Bull Dog / Miss Bunting
		Savage Beauty	Challenger / Khara
FANGHORN (ch. 1966)	Crocket (ch. 1960)	King of the Tudors	Tudor Minstrel / Glen Line
		Chandelier	Goyama / Queen of Light
	Honeymoon House (ch. 1955)	Honeyway	Fairway / Honey Buzzard
		Primavera	Chamossaire / Gadabout

254   DOUBLE JUMP 6 (ch.c., May 2, 1962)

Bred by A. P. Harris.

Won 5 races, £25,699, in England and France, at 2 years, incl. National Stakes (Sandown), Gimcrack Stakes, Prix Robert Papin.

RUSTAM (b. or br. 1953)	Persian Gulf (b. 1940)	Bahram	Blandford / Friar's Daughter
		Double Life	Bachelor's Double / Saint Joan
	Samovar (ch. 1940)	Caerleon	Phalaris / Canyon
		Carolina	Embargo / Georgia
FAIR BID (b. 1952)	My Babu (b. 1945)	Djebel	Tourbillon / Loika
		Perfume II	Badruddin / Lavendula II
	Market Fair (b. 1944)	Fair Trial	Fairway / Lady Juror
		Mrs. Pumpkin	Royal Lancer / Fairy Godmother

255   DRAGON 2 (gr.c., February 18, 1977)

Bred by Hervé de la Héronnière, in France.

Won 3 races, placed 5, 700,500 fr., in France, at 2 and 3 years, incl. Grand Criterium; 3rd Prix Eclipse.

PHAETON (gr. 1964)	Sicambre (br. 1948)	Prince Bio	Prince Rose / Biologie
		Sif	Rialto / Suavita
	Pasquinade II (gr. 1957)	Vandale II	Plassy / Vanille
		Mademoiselle Paganini	Loliondo / Mademoiselle Petitpas
DROGUE (b. 1971)	Dan Cupid (ch. 1956)	Native Dancer	Polynesian / Geisha
		Vixenette	Sickle / Lady Reynard
	Declaration (b. 1962)	Fine Top	Fine Art / Toupie
		Dalaba	Owen Tudor / Camargue II

256   DR. FAGER 1 (b.c., April 6, 1964)

Bred by Tartan Farm, in U.S.A.

Won 18 races, placed 3, $1,002,642, in U.S.A., from 2 to 4 years, incl. Arlington Classic, New Hampshire Sweepstakes Classic, Hawthorne Gold Cup, Rockingham Special, Gotham Stakes, Withers Stakes, Vosburgh H. (twice), Californian Stakes, Suburban H., United Nations H., Washington Park H., Roseben H., Whitney Stakes, Cowdin Stakes and World's Playground Stakes; also won Jersey Derby, but disqualified; 2nd Champagne Stakes and Brooklyn H.; 3rd Woodward Stakes.

ROUGH'N TUMBLE (b. 1948)	Free for All (br. 1942)	Questionnaire	Sting / Miss Puzzle
		Panay	Chicle / Panasette
	Roused (b. 1943)	Bull Dog	Teddy / Plucky Liege
		Rude Awakening	Upset / Cushion
ASPIDISTRA (b. 1954)	Better Self (b. 1945)	Bimelech	Black Toney / La Troienne
		Bee Mac	War Admiral / Baba Kenny
	Tilly Rose (br. 1948)	Bull Brier	Bull Dog / Rose Eternal
		Tilly Kate	Draymont / Teak

257   DROLL ROLE 21 (br.c., May 11, 1968)

Bred by John M. Schiff, in U.S.A.

Won 10 races, placed 14, $545,497, in U.S.A. and Canada, from 2 to 4 years, incl. Washington D.C. International, Hawthorne Gold Cup, Massachusetts H., Canadian International Championship, Grey Lag H. and Tidal H.; 2nd Hollywood Gold Cup, Gotham Stakes, Bay Shore Stakes, Swift Stakes and Manhattan H.; 3rd Man o'War Stakes and Pimlico-Laurel Futurity.

TOM ROLFE (b. 1962)	Ribot (b. 1952)	Tenerani	Bellini / Tofanella
		Romanella	El Greco / Barbara Burrini
	Pocahontas (br. 1955)	Roman	Sir Gallahad III / Buckup
		How	Princequillo / The Squaw
PRADELLA (b. 1955)	Preciptic (ch. 1942)	Precipitation	Hurry On / Double Life
		Artistic	Gainsborough / Ishtar
	Nearly (b. 1940)	Nearco	Pharos / Nogara
		Lost Soul	Solario / Orlass

258   DUKE OF MARMALADE 4 (b.c., February 11, 1971)

Bred by Mr. and Mrs. T. Whitney, in U.S.A.

Won 7½ races, placed 14, 131,623,427 L., in Italy, England and France, from 3 to 5 years, incl. Premio Roma (twice) and Premio Ellington (twice); 2nd Gran Premio di Milano, Coppa d'Oro di Milano and Prix Foy; 3rd Gran Premio del Jockey Club (twice), Gran Premio di Milano, Premio Presidente della Repubblica, Grand Prix de Deauville, Prix Maurice de Nieuil and Prix Gontaut-Biron.

VAGUELY NOBLE (b. 1965)	Vienna (ch. 1957)	Aureole	Hyperion / Angelola
		Turkish Blood	Turkhan / Rusk
	Noble Lassie (b. 1956)	Nearco	Pharos / Nogara
		Belle Sauvage	Big Game / Tropical Sun
MOCK ORANGE (b. 1959)	Dedicate (b. 1952)	Princequillo	Prince Rose / Cosquilla
		Dini	John P. Grier / Quivira
	Alablue (b. 1945)	Blue Larkspur	Black Servant / Blossom Time
		Double Time	Sir Gallahad III / Virginia L.

65

259 **DUMKA** 21 (b./br.f., March 31, 1971)

Bred by Haras de Saint-Laurent, in France.

Won 2 races, placed 1, 483,445 fr., in France at 2 and 3 years, incl. Poule d'Essai des Pouliches; 2nd Prix des Reservoirs.

KASHMIR II (b./br. 1963)			
Tudor Melody (br. 1956)	Tudor Minstrel	Owen Tudor	
		Sansonnet	
	Matelda	Dante	
		Fairly Hot	
Queen of Speed (b. 1950)	Blue Train	Blue Peter	
		Sun Chariot	
	Bishopscourt	His Grace	
		Jurisdiction	

FAIZEBAD (b./br. 1962)			
Prince Taj (b. 1954)	Prince Bio	Prince Rose	
		Biologie	
	Malindi	Nearco	
		Mumtaz Begum	
Floralie (b. 1954)	Pot O'Luck	Chance Play	
		Potheen	
	Divel	William of Valence	
		Nearly	

---

260 **DUNETTE** 26 (b.f., March 30, 1976)

Bred by SNC M. de Brignac et Cie., in France.

Won 5 races, placed 4, 1,626,796 fr., in France and England, from 2 to 4 years, incl. Prix de Diane de Revlon, Grand Prix de Saint-Cloud (dead-heat), Prix du Prince d'Orange and Prix d'Aumale; 2nd Prix Vanteaux; 3rd Grand Prix d'Evry; 4th Prix Vermeille and King George VI and Queen Elizabeth Diamond Stakes.

HARD TO BEAT (b. 1969)			
Hardicanute (br. 1962)	Hard Ridden	Hard Sauce	
		Toute Belle II	
	Harvest Maid	Umidwar	
		Hay Fell	
Virtuous (b. 1962)	Above Suspicion	Court Martial	
		Above Board	
	Rose of India	Tulyar	
		Eastern Grandeur	

PRAM (br. 1969)			
Fine Top (br. 1949)	Fine Art	Artist's Proof	
		Finnoise	
	Toupie	Vatellor	
		Tarentella	
Gourabe (b. 1950)	Admiral Drake	Craig an Eran	
		Plucky Liege	
	Godille	Godiche	
		Captain's Fancy	

---

261 **DUNFERMLINE** 12 (b.f., April 15, 1974)

Bred by H.M. The Queen.

Won 3 races, placed 8, £139,055, in England and France, from 2 to 4 years, incl. Oaks Stakes, St. Leger Stakes; 2nd Argos Star Fillies' Mile, Hardwicke Stakes; 3rd Yorkshire Oaks, Prix Royal-Oak; 4th Prix de l'Arc de Triomphe.

ROYAL PALACE (b. 1964)			
Ballymoss (ch. 1954)	Mossborough	Nearco	
		All Moonshine	
	Indian Call	Singapore	
		Flittemere	
Crystal Palace (b. 1956)	Solar Slipper	Windsor Slipper	
		Solar Flower	
	Queen of Light	Borealis	
		Picture Play	

STRATHCONA (b. 1967)			
St. Paddy (b. 1957)	Aureole	Hyperion	
		Angelola	
	Edie Kelly	Bois Roussel	
		Caerlissa	
Stroma (ch. 1955)	Luminary	Fair Trial	
		Luciebella	
	Whoa Emma	Prince Chevalier	
		Ready	

---

262 **D'URBERVILLE** 9 (b.c., May 27, 1965)

Bred by D. E. Hely-Hutchinson.

Won 10 races, placed 7, £30,940, in England and France, at 2, 3, 7 and 8 years, incl. King's Stand Stakes, Norfolk Stakes, Temple Stakes, Prix du Petit Couvert; 2nd Dewhurst Stakes, Prix Robert Papin. Also ran in France over hurdles, at 7 and 8 years, placed 2, £559.

KLAIRON (b. 1952)			
Clarion III (b. 1944)	Djebel	Tourbillon	
		Loika	
	Columba	Colorado	
		Gay Bird	
Kalmia (b. 1931)	Kantar	Alcantara II	
		Karabe	
	Sweet Lavender	Swynford	
		Marchetta	

COURTESSA (b. 1955)			
Supreme Court (br. 1948)	Persian Gulf or Precipitation	Hurry On	
		Double Life	
	Forecourt	Fair Trial	
		Overture	
Tessa Gillian (b. 1950)	Nearco	Pharos	
		Nogara	
	Sun Princess	Solario	
		Mumtaz Begum	

---

263 **DURTAL** 16 (b.f., April 9, 1974)

Bred by Société Aland.

Won 4 races, placed 4, £61,364, in England and France, at 2 and 3 years, incl. William Hill Cheveley Park Stakes, Fred Darling Stakes; 2nd Poule d'Essai des Pouliches (dead-heat), Laurent Perrier Champagne Stakes, Lowther Stakes.

LYPHARD (b. 1969)			
Northern Dancer (b. 1961)	Nearctic	Nearco	
		Lady Angela	
	Natalma	Native Dancer	
		Almahmoud	
Goofed (ch. 1960)	Court Martial	Fair Trial	
		Instantaneous	
	Barra	Formor	
		La Favorite	

DERNA II (b. 1961)			
Sunny Boy III (b. 1944)	Jock II	Asterus	
		Naic	
	Fille de Soleil	Solario	
		Fille de Salut	
Miss Barberie (b. 1950)	Norseman	Umidwar	
		Tara	
	Vaneuse	Vatellor	
		Diseuse	

---

264 **DUST COMMANDER** 3 (ch.c., February 8, 1967)

Bred by Pullen Brothers, in U.S.A.

Won 8 races, placed 9, $215,012, in U.S.A., from 2 to 4 years, incl. Kentucky Derby and Blue Grass Stakes; 2nd Fayette H.; 3rd Monmouth Invitational and Clark H.

BOLD COMMANDER (b. 1960)			
Bold Ruler (b. 1954)	Nasrullah	Nearco	
		Mumtaz Begum	
	Miss Disco	Discovery	
		Outdone	
High Voltage (gr. 1952)	Ambiorix II	Tourbillon	
		Lavendula II	
	Dynamo	Menow	
		Bransome	

DUST STORM (ch. 1956)			
Windy City (ch. 1949)	Wyndham	Blenheim	
		Bossover	
	Staunton	The Satrap	
		Crotanstown	
Challure (ch. 1948)	Challedon	Challenger	
		Laura Gal	
	Captivation	Stimulus	
		Laughing Queen	

265   EBANO 19 (br.c., April 1, 1973)

Bred by Gestut Fährhof, in England.

Won 13 races, placed 11, 534,334 DM., in Germany and Holland, from 2 to 6 years, incl. Preis von Europa, Spreti-Rennen and Grosser Preis der Stadt Gelsenkirchen; 2nd Grosser Preis von Dusseldorf; 4th Aral-Pokal.

TANERKO (br. 1953)
- Tantieme (b. 1947)
  - Deux pour Cent — Deiri / Dix pour Cent
  - Terka — Indus / La Furka
- La Divine (br. 1943)
  - Fair Copy — Fairway / Composure
  - La Diva — Blue Skies / La Traviata

ELEKTRA (br. 1962)
- Orsini (br. 1954)
  - Ticino — Athanasius / Terra
  - Oranien — Nuvolari / Omladina
- Egina (ch. 1956)
  - Alycidon — Donatello II / Aurora
  - Rough Justice — Atout Maitre / Justice

266   ELA-MANA-MOU 3 (b.c., February 28, 1976)

Bred by Patrick Clarke.

Won 10 races, placed 5, £373,464, in England and France, from 2 to 4 years, incl. King George VI and Queen Elizabeth Diamond Stakes, Coral Eclipse Stakes, King Edward VII Stakes, Royal Lodge Stakes, Prince of Wales's Stakes, Earl of Sefton Stakes; 2nd Grand Prix de Saint-Cloud; 3rd King George VI and Queen Elizabeth Diamond Stakes, Prix de l'Arc de Triomphe; 4th Derby Stakes.

PITCAIRN (b. 1971)
- Petingo (b. 1965)
  - Petition — Fair Trial / Art Paper
  - Alcazar — Alycidon / Quarterdeck
- Border Bounty (b. 1965)
  - Bounteous — Rockefella / Marie Elizabeth
  - B. Flat — Chanteur II / Ardeen

ROSE BERTIN (ch. 1970)
- High Hat (ch. 1957)
  - Hyperion — Gainsborough / Selene
  - Madonna — Donatello II / Women's Legion
- Wide Awake (b. 1964)
  - Major Portion — Court Martial / Better Half
  - Wake Island — Relic / Alor Star

267   EL BADR 4 (b.c., March 30, 1975)

Bred by Ballymaglassan Stud Farm, in Ireland.

Won 4 races, placed 2, 636,000 fr., in France, from 2 to 4 years, incl. Prix du Cadran and Prix de Barbeville; 2nd Prix Jean Prat.

WEAVERS' HALL (b. 1970)
- Busted (b. 1963)
  - Crepello — Donatello II / Crepuscule
  - Sans le Sou — Vimy / Martial Loan
- Marians (ch. 1963)
  - Macherio — Ortello / Mannozza
  - Damians — Panorama / Thirteen

INDIAN MAID (br. 1969)
- Astec (b. 1964)
  - Prince Taj — Prince Bio / Malindi
  - Rush Floor — Guersant / Lorance
- Currarevagh (b. 1957)
  - Hill Gail — Bull Lea / Jane Gail
  - Dunure — Umidwar / Carrick Shore

268   ELGAY 5 (ch.c., May 21, 1975)

Bred by Razza Ascagnano, in Italy.

Won 6 races, placed 7, 101,268,831 L., in Italy, France and Belgium, from 3 to 5 years, incl. Derby Italiano; 2nd Gran Premio d'Italia; 4th Grand Prix Prince Rose.

GAY LUSSAC (ch. 1969)
- Faberge II (b. 1961)
  - Princely Gift — Nasrullah / Blue Gem
  - Spring Offensive — Legend of France / Batika
- Green as Grass (b. 1963)
  - Red God — Nasrullah / Spring Run
  - Greensward II — Count Turf / Valse Folle

GOLD REEF (b. 1968)
- Reliance II (b. 1962)
  - Tantieme — Deux pour Cent / Terka
  - Relance III — Relic / Polaire II
- Riches (ch. 1962)
  - Rockefella — Hyperion / Rockfel
  - Chambiges — Majano / Chanterelle

269   EL MULETA 4 (b.c., March 28, 1975)

Bred by Milford Stud, in Ireland.

Won 7 races, placed 5, 154,679,096 L., in Italy and France, from 2 to 4 years, incl. Gran Criterium, Prix de Ris-Orangis and Prix de la Porte Maillot; 2nd Prix du Chemin de Fer du Nord; 3rd Premio Emilio Turati; 4th Prix Robert Papin, Prix Morny and Prix Jacques le Marois.

WINDJAMMER (b. 1969)
- Restless Wind (ch. 1956)
  - Windy City — Wyndham / Staunton
  - Lump Sugar — Bull Lea / Sugar Run
- Crowding In (b. 1959)
  - Mister Gus — Nasrullah / Fichu
  - Pin Oak — Endeavour II / Little Acorn

TOBLERONE (br. 1960)
- Honeyway (br. 1941)
  - Fairway — Phalaris / Scapa Flow
  - Honey Buzzard — Papyrus / Lady Peregrine
- Noisette (b. 1949)
  - Prince Bio — Prince Rose / Biologie
  - Nandine — Vatellor / Nantua

270   ELOCUTIONIST 2 (b.c., March 4, 1973)

Bred by Pin Oak Stud Inc., in U.S.A.

Won 9 races, placed 3, $343,150, in U.S.A., at 2 and 3 years, incl. Preakness Stakes, Arkansas Derby and Hawthorne Juvenile Stakes; 3rd Kentucky Derby.

GALLANT ROMEO (b. 1961)
- Gallant Man (b. 1954)
  - Migoli — Bois Roussel / Mah Iran
  - Majideh — Mahmoud / Qurrat-al-Ain
- Juliet's Nurse (br. 1948)
  - Count Fleet — Reigh Count / Quickly
  - Nursemaid — Luke McLuke / Wonderful One

STRICTLY SPEAKING (b. 1967)
- Fleet Nasrullah (b. 1955)
  - Nasrullah — Nearco / Mumtaz Begum
  - Happy Go Fleet — Count Fleet / Draeh
- Believe Me (b. 1954)
  - Alibhai — Hyperion / Teresina
  - Up The Hill — Jacopo / Gentle Tryst

271   **ELVIRO** 19 (b.c., February 10, 1965)

Bred by Gestüt Waldfried, in Germany

Won 6 races, placed 12, 212,148 DM., in Germany and Belgium, from 2 to 5 years, incl. Deutsches Derby and Concentra-Pokal; 2nd Union-Rennen; 3rd Furstenberg-Rennen, Grosser Hansa Preis and Grosser Preis von Dortmund.

ORSINI (br. 1954)	Ticino (b. 1939)	Athanasius	Ferro / Athanasie
		Terra	Aditi / Teufelsrose
	Oranien (b. 1949)	Nuvolari	Oleander / Nereide
		Omladina	Athanasius / Oblate
EGINA (ch. 1956)	Alycidon (ch. 1945)	Donatello II	Blenheim / Delleana
		Aurora	Hyperion / Rose Red
	Rough Justice (b. 1944)	Atout Maitre	Vatout / Royal Mistress
		Justice	Fair Trial / Pelerine

272   **EMPERY** 2 (b.c., March 23, 1973)

Bred by Nelson Bunker Hunt, in U.S.A.

Won 2 races, placed 4, £152,377, in England, Ireland and France, at 2 and 3 years, incl., Derby Stakes; 2nd Irish Sweeps Derby; 3rd Prix Lupin, Prix Thomas Bryon; 4th Poule d'Essai des Poulains.

VAGUELY NOBLE (b. 1965)	Vienna (ch. 1957)	Aureole	Hyperion / Angelola
		Turkish Blood	Turkhan / Rusk
	Noble Lassie (b. 1956)	Nearco	Pharos / Nogara
		Belle Sauvage	Big Game / Tropical Sun
PAMPLONA II (b. 1956)	Postin (ch. 1940)	Hunter's Moon	Hurry On / Selene
		Quintà	Codihue / En Guardia
	Society's Way (b. 1950)	Kingsway	Fairway / Yenna
		Society's Vote	Wyndham / Conversation Piece

273   **ENGLISH PRINCE** 1 (b.c., May 8, 1971)

Bred by Mrs. V. Hue-Williams.

Won 4 races, placed 2, £93,287, in Ireland and England at 3 years, incl. Irish Sweeps Derby, King Edward VII Stakes, White Rose Stakes; 2nd Great Voltigeur Stakes.

PETINGO (b. 1965)	Petition (br. 1944)	Fair Trial	Fairway / Lady Juror
		Art Paper	Artist's Proof / Quire
	Alcazar (ch. 1957)	Alycidon	Donatello II / Aurora
		Quarterdeck	Nearco / Poker Chip
ENGLISH MISS (b. 1955)	Bois Roussel (br. 1935)	Vatout	Prince Chimay / Vasthi
		Plucky Liege	Spearmint / Concertina
	Virelle (gr. 1942)	Casterari	Fiterari / Castleline
		Perfume II	Badruddin / Lavendula II

274   **ENSTONE SPARK** 1 (b.f., June 6, 1975)

Bred by William Hill Studs.

Won 5 races, placed 3, £54,681, in England, at 2 and 3 years, incl. 1,000 Guineas Stakes, Lowther Stakes.

SPARKLER (b. 1968)	Hard Tack (b. 1955)	Hard Sauce	Ardan / Saucy Bella
		Cowes	Blue Peter / Lighthearted
	Diamond Spur (ch. 1961)	Preciptic	Precipitation / Artistic
		Diamond Princess	His Highness / Hatton
LAXMI (ch. 1966)	Palestine (gr. 1947)	Fair Trial	Fairway / Lady Juror
		Una	Tetratema / Uganda
	Courting (gr. 1961)	Quorum	Vilmorin / Akimbo
		Open Court	Court Martial / Tropical Sun

275   **EPIDENDRUM** 6 (ch.c., March 4, 1964)

Bred by Mrs. J. R. H. Thouron, in U.S.A.

Won 6 races, placed 8, £24,604, in England and Italy, from 3 to 5 years, incl. Gran Premio di Milano.

RIBOT (b. 1952)	Tenerani (b. 1944)	Bellini	Cavaliere d'Arpino / Bella Minna
		Tofanella	Apelle / Try Try Again
	Romanella (ch. 1943)	El Greco	Pharos / Gay Gamp
		Barbara Burrini	Papyrus / Bucolic
PARTHENOPE (br. 1948)	Nearco (br. 1935)	Pharos	Phalaris / Scapa Flow
		Nogara	Havresac II / Catnip
	All Moonshine (ch. 1941)	Bobsleigh	Gainsborough / Toboggan
		Selene	Chaucer / Serenissima

276   **ERIMO HAWK** 9 (gr.c., May 20, 1968)

Bred by Kilcarn Stud Ltd.

Won 7 races, placed 5, £30,204, in England, from 2 to 4 years, incl. Ascot Gold Cup, Goodwood Cup.

SEA HAWK II (gr. 1963)	Herbager (b. 1956)	Vandale II	Plassy / Vanille
		Flagette	Escamillo / Fidgette
	Sea Nymph (gr. 1957)	Free Man	Norseman / Fantine
		Sea Spray	Ocean Swell / Pontoon
NICK OF TIME (b. or br. 1955)	Nicolaus (b. 1939)	Solario	Gainsborough / Sun Worship
		Nogara	Havresac II / Catnip
	Queen of Speed (b. 1950)	Blue Train	Blue Peter / Sun Chariot
		Bishopscourt	His Grace / Jurisdiction

277   ESCORT 16 (ch.c., April 2, 1959)

Bred by Astor Studs.

Won 5 races, placed 7, £9,981, in England and South Africa, from 2 to 4 years, incl. Royal Lodge Stakes; 2nd Timeform Gold Cup, Thirsk Classic Trial Stakes, King Edward VII Stakes; 3rd Yorkshire Cup, Henry II Stakes.

PALESTINE (gr. 1947)	Fair Trial (ch. 1932)	Fairway	Phalaris / Scapa Flow
		Lady Juror	Son-in-Law / Lady Josephine
	Una (gr. 1930)	Tetratema	The Tetrarch / Scotch Gift
		Uganda	Bridaine / Hush
WARNING (ch. 1950)	Chanteur II (br. 1942)	Chateau Bouscaut	Kircubbin / Ramondie
		La Diva	Blue Skies / La Traviata
	Vertencia (b. 1945)	Deiri	Aethelstan / Desra
		Advertencia	Ksar / Ad Gloriam II

278   EXAMPLE 1 (ch.f., March 10, 1968)

Bred by H.M. The Queen.

Won 4 races, placed 5, £36,653, in England and France, from 2 to 4 years, incl. Park Hill Stakes, Prix de Royallieu, Prix Jean de Chaudenay; 2nd Lingfield Oaks Trial Stakes; 3rd Geoffrey Freer Stakes, John Porter Stakes, Prix de Pomone.

EXBURY (ch. 1959)	Le Haar (ch. 1954)	Vieux Manoir	Brantome / Vieille Maison
		Mince Pie	Teleferique / Cannelle
	Greensward (b. 1953)	Mossborough	Nearco / All Moonshine
		Stargrass	Noble Star / Grass Widow
AMICABLE (ch. 1960)	Doutelle (ch. 1954)	Prince Chevalier	Prince Rose / Chevalerie
		Above Board	Straight Deal / Feola
	Amy Leigh (ch. 1948)	Bobsleigh	Gainsborough / Toboggan
		Lady Amy	Maltravers / The Matriarch

279   EXAR 22 (br.c., March 22, 1956)

Bred by Tally Ho Stud Ltd.

Won 9 races, placed 10, £25,037, in England and Italy, at 3 and 4 years, incl. Goodwood Cup, Doncaster Cup, Gran Premio d'Italia, Gran Premio di Milano, Premio Ambrosiano; 2nd Yorkshire Cup, Ascot Gold Cup, Jockey Club Stakes, Gran Premio del Jockey Club; 4th Premio Roma.

ARCTIC PRINCE (br. 1948)	Prince Chevalier (b. 1943)	Prince Rose	Rose Prince / Indolence
		Chevalerie	Abbot's Speed / Kassala
	Arctic Sun (br. 1941)	Nearco	Pharos / Nogara
		Solar Flower	Solario / Serena
EXCELSA (ch. 1949)	Owen Tudor (br. 1938)	Hyperion	Gainsborough / Selene
		Mary Tudor II	Pharos / Anna Bolena
	Infra Red (gr. 1936)	Ethnarch	The Tetrarch / Karenza
		Black Ray	Black Jester / Lady Brilliant

280   EXBURY 2 (ch.c., May 5, 1959)

Bred by Baron Guy de Rothschild, in France.

Won 8 races, placed 6, £167,445, in France and England, from 2 to 4 years, incl. Prix Daru, Prix Henri Foy, Prix Boiard, Prix Ganay, Grand Prix de Saint-Cloud, Prix de l'Arc de Triomphe and Coronation Cup; 2nd Grand Prix de Saint-Cloud; 3rd Prix du Jockey-Club, Prix des Chenes.

LE HAAR (ch. 1954)	Vieux Manoir (b. 1947)	Brantome	Blandford / Vitamine
		Vieille Maison	Finglas / Vieille Canaille
	Mince Pie (b. 1949)	Teleferique	Bacteriophage / Beaute de Neige
		Cannelle	Biribi / Armoise
GREENSWARD (b. 1953)	Mossborough (ch. 1947)	Nearco	Pharos / Nogara
		All Moonshine	Bobsleigh / Selene
	Stargrass (b. 1942)	Noble Star	Hapsburg / Hesper
		Grass Widow	Son-in-Law / Silver Grass

281   EXCELLER 21 (b.c., May 12, 1973)

Bred by Mrs. Charles W. Engelhard, in U.S.A.

Won 15 races, placed 9, £844,850, in France, England, Canada and U.S.A., from 2 to 5 years, incl. Prix Royal-Oak, Grand Prix de Paris, Grand Prix de Saint-Cloud, Prix du Lys, Coronation Cup, Canadian International Championship, Hollywood Gold Cup, Hollywood Invitational Turf H., San Juan Capistrano Invitational H., Sunset H., Oak Tree Invitational Stakes, Jockey Club Gold Cup, Arcadia H.; 2nd Prix Ganay, Man o'War Stakes, Woodward Stakes; 3rd Prix de Conde, King George VI and Queen Elizabeth Diamond Stakes, Washington D.C. International.

VAGUELY NOBLE (b. 1965)	Vienna (ch. 1957)	Aureole	Hyperion / Angelola
		Turkish Blood	Turkhan / Rusk
	Noble Lassie (b. 1956)	Nearco	Pharos / Nogara
		Belle Sauvage	Big Game / Tropical Sun
TOO BALD (b./br. 1964)	Bald Eagle (b. 1955)	Nasrullah	Nearco / Mumtaz Begum
		Siama	Tiger / China Face
	Hidden Talent (b. 1956)	Dark Star	Royal Gem II / Isolde
		Dangerous Dame	Nasrullah / Lady Kells

282   EXCHANGE 8 (ch.f., May 14, 1965)

Bred by Hunsdon Stud.

Won 3 races, placed 5, £9,518, in England, at 2 and 3 years, incl. Yorkshire Oaks, Musidora Stakes; 2nd Ribblesdale Stakes.

TUDOR JINKS (gr. 1952)	Owen Tudor (br. 1938)	Hyperion	Gainsborough / Selene
		Mary Tudor II	Pharos / Anna Bolena
	The Poult (gr. 1945)	Mr. Jinks	Tetratema / False Piety
		Golden Pheasant	Gold Bridge / Bonnie Birdie
NYKE (b. 1957)	Niccolo Dell'Arca (b. 1938)	Coronach	Hurry On / Wet Kiss
		Nogara	Havresac II / Catnip
	La Madelon (b. 1947)	Hierocles	Abjer / Loika
		Barsine	Admiral Drake / Black Domino

69

283　　　　**EXPANSIVE** 1 (ch.f., March 14, 1976)

Bred by H.M. The Queen.

Won 1 race, placed 2, £20,085, in England, at 2 and 3 years, incl. Ribblesdale Stakes.

EXBURY (ch. 1959)	Le Haar (ch. 1954)	Vieux Manoir	Brantome / Vieille Maison
		Mince Pie	Teleferique / Cannelle
	Greensward (b. 1953)	Mossborough	Nearco / All Moonshine
		Stargrass	Noble Star / Grass Widow
AMICABLE (ch. 1960)	Doutelle (ch. 1954)	Prince Chevalier	Prince Rose / Chevalerie
		Above Board	Straight Deal / Feola
	Amy Leigh (ch. 1948)	Bobsleigh	Gainsborough / Toboggan
		Lady Amy	Maltravers / The Matriarch

284　　　　**FAIR SALINIA** 16 (b.f., March 18, 1975)

Bred by Oldtown Stud.

Won 4 races, placed 3, £139,354, in England and Ireland, at 2 and 3 years, incl. Oaks Stakes, Yorkshire Oaks, Irish Guinness Oaks; 2nd William Hill Cheveley Park Stakes, 1,000 Guineas Stakes.

PETINGO (b. 1965)	Petition (br. 1944)	Fair Trial	Fairway / Lady Juror
		Art Paper	Artist's Proof / Quire
	Alcazar (ch. 1957)	Alycidon	Donatello II / Aurora
		Quarterdeck	Nearco / Poker Chip
FAIR ARABELLA (br. 1968)	Chateaugay (ch. 1960)	Swaps	Khaled / Iron Reward
		Banquet Bell	Polynesian / Dinner Horn
	Locust Time (br. 1955)	Spy Song	Balladier / Mata Hari
		Snow Goose	Mahmoud / Judy O'Grady

285　　　　**FAIR WINTER** 4 (ch.f., March 27, 1964)

Bred by W. and R. Barnett Ltd.

Won 7 races, placed 3, £5,494, in England, from 2 to 4 years, incl. Nassau Stakes; 2nd Westbury Stakes.

SET FAIR (ch. 1949)	Denturius (ch. 1937)	Gold Bridge	Swynford or Golden Boss / Flying Diadem
		La Solfatara	Lemberg / Ayesha
	Ria Geno (b. 1942)	Pappageno II	Prince Rose / Kassala
		Talaria	Singapore / Grand Step
WINTER GLEAM (ch. 1959)	Aureole (ch. 1950)	Hyperion	Gainsborough / Selene
		Angelola	Donatello II / Feola
	Red Winter (ch. 1951)	My Babu	Djebel / Perfume II
		Bold Maid	Sandwich / Undaunted II

286　　　　**FANFAR** 9 (b.c., May 6, 1960)

Bred by Countess Margit Batthyany, in Germany.

Won 5 races, placed 14, 202,905 DM., in Germany and France, from 2 to 6 years, incl. Deutsches Derby and Grosser Hansa Preis; 3rd Union-Rennen.

SUNNY BOY III (b. 1944)	Jock II (br. 1936)	Asterus	Teddy / Astrella
		Naic	Gainsborough / Only One
	Fille de Soleil (ch. 1935)	Solario	Gainsborough / Sun Worship
		Fille de Salut	Sansovino / Friar's Daughter
FRIEDRICHSDORF (b. 1945)	Athanasius (br. 1931)	Ferro	Landgraf / Frauenlob
		Athanasie	Laland / Athene
	Florida (b. 1936)	Graf Isolani	Graf Ferry / Isabella
		Forsythia	Ferro / Formosa

287　　　　**FANTOMAS** 16 (b.c., April 6, 1961)

Bred by A. Weisweiller, in France.

Won 8 races, placed 15, 916,381 fr., in France and Italy, from 2 to 5 years, incl. Prix du Cadran, La Coupe and Prix Gladiateur; 2nd Grand Prix de Deauville, Prix Kergorlay and Prix Gladiateur; 3rd Prix du Cadran, Gran Premio di Milano and Prix Kergorlay.

FRIC (br. 1952)	Vandale II (b. 1943)	Plassy	Bosworth / Pladda
		Vanille	La Farina / Vaya
	Fripe (gr. 1945)	Mehemet Ali	Felicitation / Firouze Mahal
		Friponne	Priori / Fofolle
HYPRIS (b. 1949)	Prince Bio (b. 1941)	Prince Rose	Rose Prince / Indolence
		Biologie	Bacteriophage / Eponge
	Hysope (b. 1940)	Plassy	Bosworth / Pladda
		Hardiesse	Hurstwood / Hope

288　　　　**FARAWAY SON** 16 (b.c., March 30, 1967)

Bred by Walter M. Jeffords, Jr., in U.S.A.

Won 7 races, placed 8, 1,245,070 fr., in France and England, from 2 to 4 years, incl. Prix du Moulin de Longchamp, Prix de la Foret, Prix de la Porte Maillot, Prix du Rond-Point, Prix de la Jonchere and Criterium de Maisons-Laffitte; also won Poule d'Essai des Poulains, but disqualified and placed 3rd; 2nd Sussex Stakes, Prix de la Foret, Prix d'Evry, Prix du Moulin de Longchamp and Prix de Fontainebleau; 3rd Grand Criterium.

AMBIOPOISE (b. 1958)	Ambiorix II (b. 1946)	Tourbillon	Ksar / Durban
		Lavendula II	Pharos / Sweet Lavender
	Bullpoise (b. 1948)	Bull Lea	Bull Dog / Rose Leaves
		Alpoise	Equipoise / Laughing Queen
LOCUST TIME (br. 1955)	Spy Song (br. 1943)	Balladier	Black Toney / Blue Warbler
		Mata Hari	Peter Hastings / War Woman
	Snow Goose (gr. 1944)	Mahmoud	Blenheim / Mah Mahal
		Judy O'Grady	Man o'War / Bel Agnes

289　　　**FARHANA** 3 (gr.f., 1964)

Bred by H.H. Aga Khan, in Ireland.

Won 4 races, placed 4, 332,955 fr., in France, at 2 and 3 years, incl. Prix de l'Abbaye de Longchamp, Prix d'Arenberg and Prix du Gros-Chene; 2nd Prix de la Grotte; 3rd Prix de Meautry.

ABERNANT (gr. 1946)	Owen Tudor (br. 1938)	Hyperion	Gainsborough / Selene
		Mary Tudor II	Pharos / Anna Bolena
	Rustom Mahal (gr. 1934)	Rustom Pasha	Son-in-Law / Cos
		Mumtaz Mahal	The Tetrarch / Lady Josephine
SICZARIA (ch. 1957)	Sicambre (br. 1948)	Prince Bio	Prince Rose / Biologie
		Sif	Rialto / Suavita
	Nizaria (br. 1947)	Nearco	Pharos / Nogara
		Sonibai	Solario / Udaipur

290　　　**FATUSAEL** 5 (b.c., March 21, 1975)

Bred by Giuseppina Crotti, in Italy.

Won 13 races, placed 13, 202,107,205 L., in Italy and France, from 2 to 5 years, incl. Premio Emilio Turati, Premio Parioli, Premio Ambrosiano and Premio d'Aprile; 2nd Premio Presidente della Repubblica, Prix d'Harcourt and Premio Ribot; 3rd Premio Besnate, Premio Vittorio di Capua and Premio U.N.I.R.E.; 4th Prix du Moulin de Longchamp.

CORFINIO (b. 1961)	Tissot (b. 1953)	Tenerani	Bellini / Tofanella
		Tiepoletta	Niccolo Dell'Arca / Tempesta
	Cesaproba (b. 1956)	Scai	Arco / Plestinia
		Cantata	Zliten / Capuana
SABEFATU (ch. 1968)	Credo (ch. 1960)	Crepello	Donatello II / Crepuscule
		Marsyaka	Marsyas II / Nokka
	Great Joy (b. 1964)	Kythnos	Nearula / Capital Issue
		Merry Xmas	Chamossaire / Merry Perrin

291　　　**FAVOLETTA** 3 (b. or br.f., March 16, 1968)

Bred by White Lodge Stud Ltd.

Won 4 races, placed 5, £17,764, in England and Ireland, at 2 and 3 years, incl. Irish 1,000 Guineas, Falmouth Stakes, Ascot 1,000 Guineas Trial Stakes; 3rd Coronation Stakes, Sun Chariot Stakes.

BALDRIC II (b. 1961)	Round Table (b. 1954)	Princequillo	Prince Rose / Cosquilla
		Knight's Daughter	Sir Cosmo / Feola
	Two Cities (b. 1948)	Johnstown	Jamestown / La France
		Vienna	Menow / Valse
VIOLETTA III (b. 1958)	Pinza (b. 1950)	Chanteur II	Chateau Bouscaut / La Diva
		Pasqua	Donatello II / Pasca
	Urshalim (b. 1951)	Nasrullah	Nearco / Mumtaz Begum
		Horama	Panorama / Lady of Aran

292　　　**FELICIO** 14 (b. or br.c., April 25, 1965)

Bred by Daniel Wildenstein, in France.

Won 3 races, placed 8, 1,306,002 fr., in France and England, from 2 to 4 years, incl. Grand Prix de Saint-Cloud and Prix Jean de Chaudenay; 2nd King George VI and Queen Elizabeth Stakes, Prix Lupin, Prix Foy and Prix de Fontainebleau; 3rd Prix de la Cote Normande; 4th King George VI and Queen Elizabeth Stakes.

SHANTUNG (b. 1956)	Sicambre (br. 1948)	Prince Bio	Prince Rose / Biologie
		Sif	Rialto / Suavita
	Barley Corn (b. 1950)	Hyperion	Gainsborough / Selene
		Schiaparelli	Schiavoni / Aileen
FIGHTING EDIE (b. 1956)	Guersant (b. 1949)	Bubbles	La Farina / Spring Cleaning
		Montagnana	Brantome / Mauretania
	Edie Kelly (br. 1950)	Bois Roussel	Vatout / Plucky Liege
		Caerlissa	Caerleon / Sister Sarah

293　　　**FIDYI** 10 (b.c., April 3, 1967)

Bred by Ettore Tagliabue, in Italy.

Won 9 races, placed 18, 66,090,000 L., in Italy, from 2 to 5 years, incl. Premio Roma and Gran Premio Citta di Napoli; 2nd Premio Presidente della Repubblica, Coppa d'Oro di Milano and Premio Principe Amedeo; 3rd Premio d'Aprile; 4th Gran Premio di Milano.

VERONESE (ch. 1960)	Le Haar (ch. 1954)	Vieux Manoir	Brantome / Vieille Maison
		Mince Pie	Teleferique / Cannelle
	Pointe Seche (ch. 1949)	Bozzetto	Pharos / Bunworry
		Spinella	Ortello / Santaria
FUPLUNA (b. 1956)	Tourment (b. 1944)	Tourbillon	Ksar / Durban
		Fragment	Shred / Pearl Drop
	Flicka de Saint-Cyr (b. 1951)	Sayani	Fair Copy / Perfume II
		Folastra	Astrophel / Pure Folie

294　　　**FIGHTING CHARLIE** 10 (b.c., April 20, 1961)

Bred by Lady Mairi Bury.

Won 8 races, placed 9, £28,114, in England, from 2 to 5 years, incl. Ascot Gold Cup (twice), Henry II Stakes; 2nd Great Voltigeur Stakes, Henry II Stakes, Yorkshire Cup.

TENERANI (b. 1944)	Bellini (b. 1937)	Cavaliere d'Arpino	Havresac II / Chuette
		Bella Minna	Bachelor's Double / Santa Minna
	Tofanella (ch. 1931)	Apelle	Sardanapale / Angelina
		Try Try Again	Cylgad / Perseverance II
FLIGHT OF THE HERON (b. 1941)	Cameronian (b. 1928)	Pharos	Phalaris / Scapa Flow
		Una Cameron	Gainsborough / Cherimoya
	First Flight (b. 1934)	Felstead	Spion Kop / Felkington
		Pick of the Bunch	Picton / Tendril

295   **FIGHTING SHIP** 1 (ch.c., January 29, 1960)

Bred by Lord Rosebery.

Won 4 races, placed 3, £10,031, in England, from 2 to 4 years, incl. Greenham Stakes, Jockey Club Stakes, Henry II Stakes; 2nd Chester Vase; 3rd St. Leger Stakes, King Edward VII Stakes.

DOUTELLE (ch. 1954)	Prince Chevalier (b. 1943)	Prince Rose	Rose Prince / Indolence
		Chevalerie	Abbot's Speed / Kassala
	Above Board (b. 1947)	Straight Deal	Solario / Good Deal
		Feola	Friar Marcus / Aloe
JANE (b. 1951)	Alycidon (ch. 1945)	Donatello II	Blenheim / Delleana
		Aurora	Hyperion / Rose Red
	Speedy (b. 1938)	Fairway	Phalaris / Scapa Flow
		Jiffy	Hurry On / Juniata

296   **FIGONERO** 10 (ch.c., August 23, 1965)

Bred by Haras Argentino, in Argentina.

Won 11 races, placed 25, $483,707, in Argentina and U.S.A., from 2 to 8 years, incl. Gran Premio San Isidro, Hollywood Gold Cup, Del Mar H. and American H.; 2nd Premio Eduardo Casey, Californian Stakes, Michigan Mile-and-One-Eighth H. (twice), Tanforan H. (twice) and Lakeside H.; 3rd Michigan Mile-and-One-Eighth H., San Bernardino H., Golden Gate H., American H., San Pasqual H., Carleton F. Burke H. and San Carlos H.

IDLE HOUR (b. 1959)	Persian Gulf (b. 1940)	Bahram	Blandford / Friar's Daughter
		Double Life	Bachelor's Double / Saint Joan
	Dilettante (b. 1953)	Dante	Nearco / Rosy Legend
		Herringbone	King Salmon / Schiaparelli
FINE FEATHERS II (ch. 1956)	Pardal (b. 1947)	Pharis II	Pharos / Carissima
		Adargatis	Asterus / Helene de Troie
	Eastern Glamour (b. 1951)	Sayajirao	Nearco / Rosy Legend
		Hillhampton	Hyperion / Sparkling Gem

297   **FILIBERTO** 4 (b.c., March 18, 1970)

Bred by Newstead Farm, in U.S.A.

Won 2 races, 292,690 fr., in France, at 2 years, incl. Prix Morny.

RIBOT (b. 1952)	Tenerani (b. 1944)	Bellini	Cavaliere d'Arpino / Bella Minna
		Tofanella	Apelle / Try Try Again
	Romanella (ch. 1943)	El Greco	Pharos / Gay Gamp
		Barbara Burrini	Papyrus / Bucolic
FAST LINE (b. 1958)	Mr. Busher (ch. 1946)	War Admiral	Man o' War / Brushup
		Baby League	Bubbling Over / La Troienne
	Throttle Wide (b. 1936)	Flying Heels	Flying Ebony / Heeltaps
		Let Her Fly	Pataud / Mary King

298   **FILS D'EVE** 8 (b.c., March 17, 1957)

Bred by Ettore Tagliabue, in France.

Won 3 races, placed 6, 14,695,000 L., in Italy, from 2 to 4 years, incl Derby Italiano; 4th Gran Premio di Milano.

WILD RISK (b. 1940)	Rialto (ch. 1923)	Rabelais	St. Simon / Satirical
		La Grelee	Helicon / Grignouse
	Wild Violet (b. 1935)	Blandford	Swynford / Blanche
		Wood Violet	Ksar / Pervencheres
FILLE DES CHAUMES (ch. 1948)	Prince Bio (b. 1941)	Prince Rose	Rose Prince / Indolence
		Biologie	Bacteriophage / Eponge
	Fille du Vent II (b. 1941)	Banstar	Sunstar / Durban
		Arroche	Epinard / Radieuse II

299   **FINAL STRAW** 16 (ch.c., March 4, 1977)

Bred by James Wigan.

Won 5 races, placed 6, £116,708, in England, Ireland and France, at 2 and 3 years, incl. July Stakes, Seaton Delaval Stakes, Laurent Perrier Champagne Stakes and Clerical Medical Greenham Stakes; 2nd St. James's Palace Stakes, Sussex Stakes and Prix Jacques le Marois; 3rd Coventry Stakes and Airlie/Coolmore. Irish 2,000 Guineas.

THATCH (b. 1970)	Forli (ch. 1963)	Aristophanes	Hyperion / Commotion
		Trevisa	Advocate / Veneta
	Thong (b. 1964)	Nantallah	Nasrullah / Shimmer
		Rough Shod	Gold Bridge / Dalmary
LAST CALL (b. 1964)	Klairon (b. 1952)	Clarion III	Djebel / Columba
		Kalmia	Kantar / Sweet Lavender
	Stage Fright (ch. 1954)	Big Game	Bahram / Myrobella
		Bashful	Precipitation / Saucy Sarah

300   **FIN BON** 17 (br.c., March 14, 1964)

Bred by E. Masurel, in France.

Won 3 races, placed 9, 487,363 fr., in France, from 2 to 4 years, incl. Prix Robert Papin; 3rd Prix de la Salamandre, Prix Lupin, Prix du Prince d'Orange and Prix Henry Delamarre; 4th Grand Criterium and Prix Ganay.

FINE TOP (br. 1949)	Fine Art (b. 1939)	Artist's Proof	Gainsborough / Clear Evidence
		Finnoise	Finglas / Unfortunate
	Toupie (br. 1943)	Vatellor	Vatout / Lady Elinor
		Tarentella	Blenheim / Andalusia
BOSNIA (br. 1952)	Bozzetto (ch. 1936)	Pharos	Phalaris / Scapa Flow
		Bunworry	Great Sport / Waffles
	Mieux Née (br. 1943)	Mieuxce	Massine / L'Olivete
		Arachné	Rialto / Argentée

301 FINE PEARL 16 (br.f., April 25, 1963)

Bred by Baron G. de Waldner, in France.

Won 4 races, placed 2, 858,800 fr., in France, at 2 and 3 years, incl. Prix de Diane; 3rd Prix Vermeille.

FINE TOP (br. 1949)	Fine Art (b. 1939)	Artist's Proof	Gainsborough / Clear Evidence
		Finnoise	Finglas / Unfortunate
	Toupie (br. 1943)	Vatellor	Vatout / Lady Elinor
		Tarentella	Blenheim / Andalusia
SEED PEARL (br. 1950)	Tourment (b. 1944)	Tourbillon	Ksar / Durban
		Fragment	Shred / Pearl Drop
	Pearl Cap (b. 1928)	La Capucin	Nimbus / Carmen
		Pearl Maiden	Phaleron / Seashell

302 FIRST LORD 16 (b.c., April 13, 1975)

Bred by H. Liesenfeld, in Germany.

Won 2 races, placed 7, 316,163 DM., in Germany, at 2 and 3 years, incl. Grosser Preis von Berlin; 2nd Deutsches Derby, Henckel-Rennen, Union-Rennen and Preis des Winterfavoriten; 4th Aral Pokal.

KRONZEUGE (br. 1961)	Neckar (bl. 1948)	Ticino	Athanasius / Terra
		Nixe	Arjaman / Nanon
	Kaiserkrone (bl. 1952)	Nebelwerfer	Magnat / Newa
		Kaiserwurde	Bubbles / Katinka
FAIBLESSE (b. 1961)	Caran D'Ache (ch. 1949)	Zliten	Pilade / Severa
		Circignana	Donatello II / Carpaccia
	Faustoper (br. 1954)	Goody	Admiral Drake / Good Bess
		Faustsage	Gundomar / Faustitas

303 FLEET 4 (b.f., April 2, 1964)

Bred by Commander P. J. FitzGerald.

Won 5 races, placed 3, £47,284, in England, at 2 and 3 years, incl. 1,000 Guineas Stakes, Coronation Stakes, Cheveley Park Stakes; 4th Oaks Stakes, Eclipse Stakes.

IMMORTALITY (b. 1956)	Never Say Die (ch. 1951)	Nasrullah	Nearco / Mumtaz Begum
		Singing Grass	War Admiral / Boreale
	Belle of Troy (br. 1947)	Blue Larkspur	Black Servant / Blossom Time
		La Troienne	Teddy / Helene de Troie
REVIEW (ch. 1951)	Panorama (ch. 1936)	Sir Cosmo	The Boss / Ayn Hali
		Happy Climax	Happy Warrior / Clio
	Pin Up Girl (b. 1943)	Coup de Lyon	Winalot / Sundry
		Careless	Caerleon / Traverse

304 FLEET WAHINE 13 (b.f., April 29, 1968)

Bred by Mereworth Farm, in U.S.A.

Won 4 races, placed 4, £18,100, in England and France, at 2 and 3 years, incl. Yorkshire Oaks, Ribblesdale Stakes; 2nd Princess Royal Stakes; 3rd Princess Elizabeth Stakes.

FLEET NASRULLAH (b. 1955)	Nasrullah (b. 1940)	Nearco	Pharos / Nogara
		Mumtaz Begum	Blenheim / Mumtaz Mahal
	Happy Go Fleet (b. 1950)	Count Fleet	Reigh Count / Quickly
		Draeh	Bull Dog / Miss Bunting
FIJI (ch. 1960)	Acropolis (ch. 1952)	Donatello II	Blenheim / Delleana
		Aurora	Hyperion / Rose Red
	Rififi (ch. 1954)	Mossborough	Nearco / All Moonshine
		Khanum	Turkhan / Fair Terms

305 FLIRTING AROUND 2 (b.c., February 5, 1971)

Bred by John W. Winnett Jr., in U.S.A.

Won 7 races, placed 3, £50,918, in France and England, from 2 to 4 years, incl. King's Stand Stakes, Prix du Gros-Chene, Prix de Meautry, Prix de Saint-Georges; 3rd Criterium de Maisons-Laffitte, Prix du Palais Royal, Prix de Seine-et-Oise.

ROUND TABLE (b. 1954)	Princequillo (b. 1940)	Prince Rose	Rose Prince / Indolence
		Cosquilla	Papyrus / Quick Thought
	Knight's Daughter (b. 1941)	Sir Cosmo	The Boss / Ayn Hali
		Feola	Friar Marcus / Aloe
HAPPY FLIRT (b./br. 1958)	Johns Joy (b. 1946)	Bull Dog	Teddy / Plucky Liege
		My Auntie	Busy American / Babe K.
	Saracen Flirt (b. 1945)	Pilate	Friar Rock / Herodias
		Knights Gal	Bright Knight / Ethel Gray

306 FLORIBUNDA 1 (b.c., March 13, 1958)

Bred by Mrs. J. R. Mullion.

Won 5 races, placed 2, £7,176, in Ireland and England, at 2 and 3 years, incl. New Stakes, King George Stakes, Nunthorpe Stakes; 2nd King's Stand Stakes; 3rd Gimcrack Stakes.

PRINCELY GIFT (b. 1951)	Nasrullah (b. 1940)	Nearco	Pharos / Nogara
		Mumtaz Begum	Blenheim / Mumtaz Mahal
	Blue Gem (b. 1943)	Blue Peter	Fairway / Fancy Free
		Sparkle	Blandford / Gleam
ASTRENTIA (ch. 1953)	Denturius (ch. 1937)	Gold Bridge	Swynford or Golden Boss / Flying Diadem
		La Solfatara	Lemberg / Ayesha
	Aherlow Valley (b. or br. 1945)	His Highness	Hyperion / Moti Ranee
		Glen of Aherlow	Young Lover / Diana Bula

307   FLOSSY 21 (b.f., February 12, 1966)

Bred by W. Clout and Mrs. O. Nicol, in France.

Won 4 races, placed 3, £44,400, in France and England, from 2 to 4 years, incl. Champion Stakes, Prix La Rochette; 2nd Prix Eugene Adam.

```
                                               { Bull Dog
                           { Bull Lea          { Rose Leaves
          { Mark-Ye-Well   {
          { (b. 1949)      { Mar-Kell          { Blenheim
SPY WELL  {                                    { Nellie Flag
(b. 1960) {
          { Miss Spy       { Spy Song          { Balladier
          { (b. 1951)      {                   { Mata Hari
                           { Generosity        { Castel Fusano
                                               { Heralder

                                               { Fair Play
                           { Chance Play       { Quelle Chance
          { Pot O'Luck     {
          { (b. 1942)      { Potheen           { Wildair
FLORALIE  {                                    { Rosie O'Grady
(b. 1954) {
          { Divel          { William of Valence{ Vatout
          { (b. 1945)      {                   { Queen Iseult
                           { Nearly            { Nearco
                                               { Lost Soul
```

308   FLYING PASTER 22 (b.c., February 24, 1976)

Bred by B. J. Ridder, in U.S.A.

Won 10 races, placed 9, $907,060, in U.S.A., from 2 to 4 years, incl. Hollywood Derby, Santa Anita Derby, Norfolk Stakes, Del Mar Futurity, California Breeders' Champion Stakes, Sunny Slope Stakes, San Vicente Stakes; 2nd Santa Anita H., Charles H. Strub H., San Fernando Stakes, Malibu Stakes, Hollywood Juvenile Championship Stakes; 3rd San Felipe H., Native Diver H.

```
                                               { Nearco
                           { Nasrullah         { Mumtaz Begum
          { Fleet Nasrullah{
          { (b. 1955)      { Happy Go Fleet    { Count Fleet
GUMMO     {                                    { Draeh
(b. 1962) {
          { Alabama Gal    { Determine         { Alibhai
          { (b. 1957)      {                   { Koubis
                           { Trojan Lass       { Priam
                                               { Rompers

                                               { Take Away
                           { Hillsdale         { Johann
          { Acroterion     {
          { (br. 1962)     { Stage Fright      { Native Dancer
PROCNE    {                                    { Petrify
(b. 1969) {
          { Philomela      { Tudor Minstrel    { Owen Tudor
          { (ch. 1954)     {                   { Sansonnet
                           { Petrovna          { Blue Peter
                                               { Straight Sequence
```

309   FLYING WATER 14 (ch.f., April 8, 1973)

Bred by Dayton Ltd., in France.

Won 7 races, £135,945, in England, France and U.S.A., from 2 to 5 years, incl. 1,000 Guineas Stakes, Ladbroke Nell Gwyn Stakes, Champion Stakes, Prix Jacques le Marois, Prix Maurice de Gheest.

```
                                               { Royal Charger
                           { Turn-to           { Source Sucree
          { Sir Gaylord    {
          { (b. 1959)      { Somethingroyal    { Princequillo
HABITAT   {                                    { Imperatrice
(b. 1966) {
          { Little Hut     { Occupy            { Bull Dog
          { (b. 1952)      {                   { Miss Bunting
                           { Savage Beauty     { Challenger
                                               { Khara

                                               { Bellini
                           { Tenerani          { Tofanella
          { Ribot          {
          { (b. 1952)      { Romanella         { El Greco
FORMENTERA{                                    { Barbara Burrini
(ch. 1968){
          { Fighting Edie  { Guersant          { Bubbles
          { (b. 1956)      {                   { Montagnana
                           { Edie Kelly        { Bois Roussel
                                               { Caerlissa
```

310   FOLLE ROUSSE 3 (ch.f., April 4, 1966)

Bred by P. Burns, in Ireland.

Won 15 races, placed 5, £51,816, in England, France and U.S.A., from 2 to 5 years, incl. Prix Robert Papin; 2nd Prix d'Arenberg; 3rd Sheridan H.

```
                                               { Pharos
                           { Nearco            { Nogara
          { Nasrullah      {
          { (b. 1940)      { Mumtaz Begum      { Blenheim
RED GOD   {                                    { Mumtaz Mahal
(ch. 1954){
          { Spring Run     { Menow             { Pharamond
          { (b. 1948)      {                   { Alcibiades
                           { Boola Brook       { Bull Dog
                                               { Brookdale

                                               { Fairway
                           { Fair Trial        { Lady Juror
          { Luminary       {
          { (ch. 1946)     { Luciebella        { Rodosto
BALLYMISS {                                    { Lula
(b. 1955) {
          { Maiden Tower   { Lighthouse II     { Pharos
          { (b./br. 1949)  {                   { Pyramid
                           { Grey Light        { Taj Ud Din
                                               { Live Spark
```

311   FONTANUS 16 (br.c., February 24, 1961)

Bred by Gestüt Waldfried, in Germany.

Won 8½ races, placed 18, 172,700 DM., in Germany, from 2 to 5 years, incl. Aral-Pokal and Spreti-Rennen; 2nd Grosser Preis von Nordrhein-Westfalen, Grosser Hansa Preis and Grosser Preis von Dusseldorf.

```
                                               { Herold
                           { Arjaman           { Aditja
          { Olymp          {
          { (b. 1942)      { Olympiade         { Oleander
MASETTO   {                                    { Osterfreude
(b. 1952) {
          { Mimosa         { Indus             { Alcantara II
          { (b. 1945)      {                   { Himalaya
                           { Marliese          { Graf Ferry
                                               { Marie-Louise

                                               { Herold
                           { Alchimist         { Aversion
          { Gundomar       {
          { (br. 1942)     { Grossularia       { Aurelius
FARGO     {                                    { Grolle nicht
(br. 1950){
          { Faustitas      { Aurelius or Ladro { Graf Ferry
          { (b. 1935)      {                   { Ladylove
                           { Faustina          { Fervor
                                               { Favilla
```

312   FOOLISH PLEASURE 14 (b.c., March 23, 1972)

Bred by Waldemar Farms Inc., in U.S.A.

Won 16 races, placed 7, $1,216,705, in U.S.A., from 2 to 4 years, incl. Kentucky Derby, Flamingo Stakes, Wood Memorial Stakes, Arlington Golden Invitational H., Suburban H., Donn H., Champagne Stakes, Hopeful Stakes, Cowdin Stakes and Sapling Stakes; 2nd Belmont Stakes, Preakness Stakes and Governor Stakes; 3rd Florida Derby, Brooklyn H. and Bel Air H.

```
                                               { Nearco
                           { Nasrullah         { Mumtaz Begum
          { Bold Ruler     {
          { (b. 1954)      { Miss Disco        { Discovery
WHAT A    {                                    { Outdone
PLEASURE  {
(ch. 1965){ Grey Flight    { Mahmoud           { Blenheim
          { (gr. 1945)     {                   { Mah Mahal
                           { Planetoid         { Ariel
                                               { La Chica

                                               { Pharamond
                           { Menow             { Alcibiades
          { Tom Fool       {
          { (b. 1949)      { Gaga              { Bull Dog
FOOL-ME-NOT{                                   { Alpoise
(b. 1958) {
          { Cuadrilla      { Tourbillon        { Ksar
          { (ch. 1943)     {                   { Durban
                           { Bouillabaisse     { Blenheim
                                               { Becti
```

313   FORDHAM 4 (b.c., March 30, 1975)

Bred by Lyonstown Stud Ltd., in U.S.A.

Won 4 races, placed 2, £31,110, in Ireland and England, at 3 and 4 years, incl. Joe McGrath Memorial Stakes, Cumberland Lodge Stakes.

		Hyperion	Gainsborough
	Aristophanes		Selene
	(ch. 1948)	Commotion	Mieuxce
FORLI			Riot
(ch. 1963)		Advocate	Fair Trial
	Trevisa		Guiding Star
	(ch. 1951)	Veneta	Foxglove
			Dogaresa
		Nasrullah	Nearco
	Bold Ruler		Mumtaz Begum
	(b. 1954)	Miss Disco	Discovery
BOLD ENCHANTRESS			Outdone
(b. 1970)		Princequillo	Prince Rose
	Princessnesian		Cosquilla
	(b. 1964)	Alanesian	Polynesian
			Alablue

314   FOREGO 9 (b.g., April 30, 1970)

Bred by Lazy F Ranch, in U.S.A.

Won 34 races, placed 16, $1,938,957, in U.S.A., from 3 to 8 years, incl. Woodward Stakes (4 times), Jockey Club Gold Cup, Metropolitan H. (twice), Marlboro Cup, Brooklyn H. (3 times), Suburban H., Wildener H. (twice), Carter H. (twice), Gulfstream Park H., Nassau County H. (twice), Vosburgh H., Donn H., Seminole H., Discovery H. and Roamer H.: 2nd Florida Derby, Marlboro Cup, Suburban H. (twice), Brooklyn H., Metropolitan H., Nassau County H. and Jerome H.; 3rd Marlboro Cup, Metropolitan H., Suburban H., Amory L. Haskell H. and Withers Stakes; 4th Kentucky Derby.

		Hyperion	Gainsborough
	Aristophanes		Selene
	(ch. 1948)	Commotion	Mieuxce
FORLI			Riot
(ch. 1963)		Advocate	Fair Trial
	Trevisa		Guiding Star
	(ch. 1951)	Veneta	Foxglove
			Dogaresa
		Roman	Sir Gallahad III
	Hasty Road		Buckup
	(b. 1951)	Traffic Court	Discovery
LADY GOLCONDA			Traffic
(br. 1958)		Bull Lea	Bull Dog
	Girlea		Rose Leaves
	(b. 1951)	Whirling Girl	Whirlaway
			Nellie Flag

315   FORLORN RIVER 8 (br.c., February 16, 1962)

Bred by B. J. Fagan.

Won 11 races, placed 10, £14,226, in England, from 2 to 5 years, incl. July Cup, Nunthorpe Stakes, Challenge Stakes; 3rd Vernons November Sprint Cup.

		Sir Gallahad III	Teddy
	Fighting Fox		Plucky Liege
	(b. 1935)	Marguerite	Celt
FIGHTING DON			Fairy Ray
(b. 1942)		Mad Hatter	Fair Play
	Bird Nest		Madcap
	(b. 1929)	Tree Top	Ultimus
			Thirty-third
		Black Devil	Sir Gallahad III
	Black Rock		La Palina
	(br. 1942)	Council Rock	Son-in-Law
STARFLIGHT			Tuscar Rock
(br. 1950)		Sir Walter Raleigh	Prince Galahad
	Brave Array		Smoke Lass
	(b. 1941)	Bold Front	Forerunner
			Bold Lily

316   FORMIDABLE 7 (b.c., April 8, 1975)

Bred by Ralph C. Wilson, Jr., in U.S.A.

Won 8 races, placed 9, £97,010, in England, from 2 to 4 years, incl. William Hill Middle Park Stakes, Mill Reef Stakes; 2nd Waterford Crystal Mile; 3rd Sussex Stakes, Lockinge Stakes, St. James's Palace Stakes.

		Hyperion	Gainsborough
	Aristophanes		Selene
	(ch. 1948)	Commotion	Mieuxce
FORLI			Riot
(ch. 1963)		Advocate	Fair Trial
	Trevisa		Guiding Star
	(ch. 1951)	Veneta	Foxglove
			Dogaresa
		Native Dancer	Polynesian
	Raise a Native		Geisha
	(ch. 1961)	Raise You	Case Ace
NATIVE PARTNER			Lady Glory
(b. 1966)		Tom Fool	Menow
	Dinner Partner		Gaga
	(b. 1959)	Bluehaze	Blue Larkspur
			Flaming Swords

317   FORT MARCY 2 (b.g., April 2, 1964)

Bred by Paul Mellon, in U.S.A.

Won 21 races, placed 32, $1,109,791, in U.S.A., from 2 to 7 years, incl. Washington D.C. International (twice), Man o'War Stakes, United Nations H., Bowling Green H., Dixie H., Hollywood Park Invitational Turf H., Bougainvillea H., Sunset H., Tidal H. (twice), Kelly-Olympic H., Stars and Stripes H., Bernard Baruch H. and Long Branch Stakes; 2nd Man o'War Stakes (twice), Grey Lag H., Kelly-Olympic H. (twice), Nassau County Stakes, San Juan Capistrano Invitational H., Hollywood Park Invitational Turf H., Century H., Bowling Green H., Bougainvillea H. and Ford Pinto Invitational Turf H.; 3rd Washington D.C. International, United Nations H. (3 times), Man o'War Stakes, Edgemere H., San Juan Capistrano Invitational H., Hialeah Turf Cup and Kelly-Olympic H.

		Pharos	Phalaris
	Nearco		Scapa Flow
	(br. 1935)	Nogara	Havresac II
AMERIGO			Catnip
(ch. 1955)		Precipitation	Hurry On
	Sanlinea		Double Life
	(ch. 1947)	Sun Helmet	Hyperion
			Point Duty
		Prince Rose	Rose Prince
	Princequillo		Indolence
	(b. 1940)	Cosquilla	Papyrus
KEY BRIDGE			Quick Thought
(b. 1959)		War Admiral	Man o'War
	Blue Banner		Brushup
	(b. 1952)	Risque Blue	Blue Larkspur
			Risque

318   FORWARD PASS 9 (b.c., March 28, 1965)

Bred by Calumet Farm, in U.S.A.

Won 10 races, placed 6, $580,631, in U.S.A., at 2 and 3 years, incl. Kentucky Derby, Preakness Stakes, American Derby, Florida Derby, Blue Grass Stakes and Everglades Stakes; 2nd Belmont Stakes and Travers Stakes; 3rd Sanford Stakes.

		Nearco	Pharos
	Nasrullah		Nogara
	(b. 1940)	Mumtaz Begum	Blenheim
ON-AND-ON			Mumtaz Mahal
(b. 1956)		Bull Lea	Bull Dog
	Two Lea		Rose Leaves
	(b. 1946)	Two Bob	The Porter
			Blessings
		Hyperion	Gainsborough
	Heliopolis		Selene
	(b. 1936)	Drift	Swynford
PRINCESS TURIA			Santa Cruz
(ch. 1953)		Blue Larkspur	Black Servant
	Blue Delight		Blossom Time
	(br. 1938)	Chicleight	Chicle
			Ruddy Light

75

319   FRENCH CREAM 1 (b.f., February 16, 1959)

Bred by Stenigot Ltd., in France.

Won 2 races, £7,471, in England and Ireland, at 2 and 3 years, incl. Irish Oaks, Lancashire Oaks.

FAUBOURG II (b. 1949)	Vatellor (br. 1933)	Vatout	Prince Chimay / Vasthi
		Lady Elinor	Teddy / Madame Royale
	Fast Lady (b. 1941)	Fastnet	Pharos / Tatoule
		Intrigue	Indus / Needle Eye
NIVEA (b. 1943)	Nearco (br. 1935)	Pharos	Phalaris / Scapa Flow
		Nogara	Havresac II / Catnip
	Deva (b. 1930)	Gainsborough	Bayardo / Rosedrop
		Lake Van	Lemberg / Vanossa

320   FRÈRE BASILE 5 (br.c., March 6, 1975)

Bred by François Mathet, in France.

Won 3 races, placed 8, 1,382,528 fr., in France and England, from 2 to 4 years, incl. Prix Ganay and Prix Hocquart; 2nd Prix du Jockey-Club, Prix Noailles and Coronation Cup; 3rd Prix Niel and Prix d'Harcourt; 4th Prix de l'Arc de Triomphe.

DJAKAO (b. 1966)	Tanerko (br. 1953)	Tantième	Deux pour Cent / Terka
		La Divine	Fair Copy / La Diva
	Diagonale (ch. 1959)	Ribot	Tenerani / Romanella
		Barley Corn	Hyperion / Schiaparelli
POLA (br. 1962)	Hard Sauce (br. 1948)	Ardan	Pharis II / Adargatis
		Saucy Bella	Bellacose / Marmite
	Texana (ch. 1955)	Relic	War Relic / Bridal Colors
		Tosca	Tourbillon / Eroica

321   FRONTIER GODDESS 1 (b.f., May 4, 1966)

Bred by Kilcarn Stud Ltd.

Won 5 races, placed 3, £18,038, in England, at 2 and 3 years, incl. Yorkshire Oaks; 2nd Oaks Stakes.

CROCKET (ch. 1960)	King of the Tudors (ch. 1950)	Tudor Minstrel	Owen Tudor / Sansonnet
		Glen Line	Blue Peter / Scotia's Glen
	Chandelier (ch. 1955)	Goyama	Goya II / Devineress
		Queen of Light	Borealis / Picture Play
KILCARN GODDESS (b. 1958)	Nearco (br. 1935)	Pharos	Phalaris / Scapa Flow
		Nogara	Havresac II / Catnip
	Sun Goddess (b. 1952)	Migoli	Bois Roussel / Mah Iran
		Solar Myth	Hyperion / Keystone

322   FRONT ROW 42 (b.f., April 17, 1965)

Bred by Mrs. J. Bourke.

Won 3 races, placed 2, £10,106, in Ireland and England, at 2 and 3 years, incl. Irish 1,000 Guineas; 2nd Coronation Stakes; 3rd Ascot 1,000 Guineas Trial.

EPAULETTE (ch. 1951)	Court Martial (ch. 1942)	Fair Trial	Fairway / Lady Juror
		Instantaneous	Hurry On / Picture
	Golden Sari (ch. 1944)	Dastur	Solario / Friar's Daughter
		Fortunedale	Loaningdale / Fortunate Lady
PANAVIEW (b. 1960)	Panaslipper (ch. 1952)	Solar Slipper	Windsor Slipper / Solar Flower
		Panastrid	Panorama / Astrid
	April View (b. 1949)	Atout Maitre	Vatout / Royal Mistress
		Distant View	Panorama / Maid of the Heath

323   FULL DRESS II 16 (b.f., April 18, 1966)

Bred by White Lodge Stud Ltd., in France.

Won 3 races, £24,446, in England, at 2 and 3 years, incl. 1,000 Guineas Stakes, Ascot 1,000 Guineas Trial Stakes.

SHANTUNG (b. 1956)	Sicambre (br. 1948)	Prince Bio	Prince Rose / Biologie
		Sif	Rialto / Suavita
	Barley Corn (b. 1950)	Hyperion	Gainsborough / Selene
		Schiaparelli	Schiavoni / Aileen
FUSIL (b. 1961)	Fidalgo (b. 1956)	Arctic Star	Nearco / Serena
		Miss France	Jock II / Nafah
	Mitraille (b. 1953)	Big Game	Bahram / Myrobella
		Mitrailleuse	Mieuxce / French Kin

324   FULL OF HOPE 10 (b.c., March 18, 1970)

Bred by Dalham Stud Farms Ltd., in England.

Won 11 races, placed 13, 1,224,290 fr., in France, from 2 to 7 years, incl. Prix d'Ispahan, Prix Edmond Blanc and Prix du Chemin de Fer du Nord; 2nd Prix Perth, Prix de Ris-Orangis, Prix Edmond Blanc and Prix d'Harcourt; 3rd Prix du Muguet and Prix Gontaut-Biron.

GREAT NEPHEW (b. 1963)	Honeyway (br. 1941)	Fairway	Phalaris / Scapa Flow
		Honey Buzzard	Papyrus / Lady Peregrine
	Sybil's Niece (ch. 1951)	Admiral's Walk	Hyperion / Tabaris
		Sybil's Sister	Nearco / Sister Sarah
ALPINE BLOOM (ch. 1955)	Chamossaire (ch. 1942)	Precipitation	Hurry On / Double Life
		Snowberry	Cameronian / Myrobella
	Fragrant View (ch. 1941)	Panorama	Sir Cosmo / Happy Climax
		Bouquet	Buchan / Hellespont

76

325 **FUNNY HOBBY** 9 (b.c., April 4, 1974)

Bred by K. G. Besson, in Ireland.

Won 2 races, placed 5, 603,000 fr., in France, at 2 and 3 years, incl.
Grand Prix de Paris.

MEADOW MINT (br. 1969)	Herbager (b. 1956)	Vandale II	Plassy / Vanille
		Flagette	Escamillo / Fidgette
	Spring Muse (b. 1956)	Ambiorix II	Tourbillon / Lavendula II
		Spring Run	Menow / Boola Brook
ZAKYNA (ch. 1965)	Charlottesville (b. 1957)	Prince Chevalier	Prince Rose / Chevalerie
		Noorani	Nearco / Empire Glory
	Kakia (b. 1956)	Sunny Boy III	Jock II / Fille de Soleil
		Omelia	Owen Tudor / Dodoma

---

326 **FURRY GLEN** 8 (b.c., February 6, 1971)

Bred by James Geraghty.

Won 5 races, placed 4, £31,757, in Ireland and England, at 2 and
3 years, incl. Irish 2,000 Guineas, Whitehall Stakes; 2nd Gallinule
Stakes, Vauxhall Trial Stakes; 3rd Coventry Stakes, Larkspur
Stakes.

WOLVER HOLLOW (b. 1964)	Sovereign Path (gr. 1956)	Grey Sovereign	Nasrullah / Kong
		Mountain Path	Bobsleigh / Path of Peace
	Cygnet (b. 1950)	Caracalla II	Tourbillon / Astronomie
		Mrs. Swan Song	Sir Walter Raleigh / Donati's Comet
CLEFTESS (br. 1956)	Hill Gail (b. 1949)	Bull Lea	Bull Dog / Rose Leaves
		Jane Gail	Blenheim / Lady Higloss
	Cleft (br. 1946)	Lighthouse II	Pharos / Pyramid
		Rift	Solario / Pilgrim's Rest

---

327 **GAIA** 11 (b.f., April 11, 1966)

Bred by Romerhof Stud.

Won 2 races, placed 2, £22,120, in Ireland, at 3 years, incl. Irish Guinness Oaks; 2nd Blandford Stakes.

CHARLOTTESVILLE (b. 1957)	Prince Chevalier (b. 1943)	Prince Rose	Rose Prince / Indolence
		Chevalerie	Abbot's Speed / Kassala
	Noorani (ch. 1950)	Nearco	Pharos / Nogara
		Empire Glory	Singapore / Skyglory
GHANA II (b. 1959)	Botticelli (b. 1951)	Blue Peter	Fairway / Fancy Free
		Buonamica	Niccolo Dell'Arca / Bernina
	Grolldochnicht (br. 1952)	Ticino	Athanasius / Terra
		Grolledoch	Alchimist / Grolleja

---

328 **GAILY** 11 (b.f., April 23, 1971)

Bred by Warner L. Jones, in U.S.A.

Won 2 races, placed 4, £37,142, in England, Ireland and France, at
2 and 3 years, incl. Irish 1,000 Guineas; 2nd Irish Guinness Oaks;
3rd Prix Vermeille.

SIR GAYLORD (b. 1959)	Turn-to (b. 1951)	Royal Charger	Nearco / Sun Princess
		Source Sucree	Admiral Drake / Lavendula II
	Somethingroyal (b. 1952)	Princequillo	Prince Rose / Cosquilla
		Imperatrice	Caruso / Cinquepace
SPEARFISH (b. or br. 1963)	Fleet Nasrullah (b. 1955)	Nasrullah	Nearco / Mumtaz Begum
		Happy Go Fleet	Count Fleet / Draeh
	Alabama Gal (b. 1957)	Determine	Alibhai / Koubis
		Trojan Lass	Priam II / Rompers

---

329 **GALIANI** 9 (br.c., February 23, 1975)

Bred by M. Henochsberg, M. Lagasse and R. Romanet, in Ireland.

Won 2 races, placed 6, 509,000 fr., in France, at 2 and 3 years, incl.
Grand Prix de Paris.

LUTHIER (br. 1965)	Klairon (b. 1952)	Clarion III	Djebel / Columba
		Kalmia	Kantar / Sweet Lavender
	Flute Enchantee (b. 1950)	Cranach	Coronach / Reine Isaure
		Montagnana	Brantome / Mauretania
ON THE WING (b. 1970)	Tanerko (br. 1953)	Tantieme	Deux pour Cent / Terka
		La Divine	Fair Copy / La Diva
	Nellie Fleet (b. 1956)	Count Fleet	Reigh Count / Quickly
		Sunshine Nell	Sun Again / Nellie Flag

---

330 **GALIVANTER** 4 (br.c., March 19, 1956)

Bred by Major L. B. Holliday.

Won 9 races, placed 8, £12,797, in England, at 2, 3 and 5 years, incl.
July Cup, Palace House Stakes; 2nd New Stakes, Nunthorpe Stakes;
3rd July Stakes, Diadem Stakes.

GOLDEN CLOUD (ch. 1941)	Gold Bridge (ch. 1929)	Swynford or Golden Boss	The Boss / Golden Hen
		Flying Diadem	Diadumenos / Flying Bridge
	Rainstorm (b. 1924)	Hainault	Swynford / Bromus
		Stormcloud	The Tetrarch / Lancaster Lady
LYCIA (b. 1944)	Nearco (br. 1935)	Pharos	Phalaris / Scapa Flow
		Nogara	Havresac II / Catnip
	Cleres (b. 1931)	Ksar	Bruleur / Kizil Kourgan
		Katuja	Cannobie / Kouba

331 **GALLINA** 4 (ch.f., March 11, 1972)

Bred by Leslie Combs II and Mrs. B. W. Martin, in U.S.A.

Won 2 races, placed 2, £11,975, in Ireland and England, at 2 and 3 years, incl. Ribblesdale Stakes; 3rd Athasi Stakes, Pretty Polly Stakes (Curragh).

RAISE A NATIVE (ch. 1961)	Native Dancer (gr. 1950)	Polynesian	Unbreakable / Black Polly
		Geisha	Discovery / Miyako
	Raise You (ch. 1946)	Case Ace	Teddy / Sweetheart
		Lady Glory	American Flag / Beloved
GALLATIA (ch. 1961)	Gallant Man (b. 1954)	Migoli	Bois Roussel / Mah Iran
		Majideh	Mahmoud / Qurrat-al-Ain
	Your Hostess (ch. 1949)	Alibhai	Hyperion / Teresina
		Boudoir	Mahmoud / Kampala

332 **GALWAY BAY** 3 (b.c., April 12, 1973)

Bred by Ardenode Stud Ltd., in France.

Won 6 races, placed 15, £85,830, in England and Australia, from 2 to 5 years, incl. Coventry Stakes, Craven 'A' Stakes, George Adams H.; 2nd Stradbroke H., Rothmans 'Hundred Thousand' H., Marlboro '50,000'; 3rd C. and G. Gimcrack Stakes; 4th Marlboro Cup, Freeway Stakes.

SASSAFRAS (b. 1967)	Sheshoon (ch. 1956)	Precipitation	Hurry On / Double Life
		Noorani	Nearco / Empire Glory
	Ruta (b. 1960)	Ratification	Court Martial / Solesa
		Dame d'Atour	Cranach / Barley Corn
WINDJAMMER (b. 1962)	Hard Tack (b. 1955)	Hard Sauce	Ardan / Saucy Bella
		Cowes	Blue Peter / Lighthearted
	Arctic Villa (b. 1956)	Arctic Star	Nearco / Serena
		Villainy	Valerian / South Sea Bubble

333 **GAMELY** 5 (b.f., February 10, 1964)

Bred by Claiborne Farm, in U.S.A.

Won 16 races, placed 15, $574,961, in U.S.A., from 3 to 5 years, incl. Alabama Stakes, Beldame Stakes (twice), Princess Stakes, Test Stakes, Wilshire H. (twice), Santa Margarita H., Vanity H., Santa Maria H., Santa Monica H. and Diana H.; 2nd Hollywood Oaks, Railbird Stakes, Santa Anita H., Californian Stakes, Santa Barbara H., Diana H., Vanity H. and Matchmaker Stakes; 3rd Beldame Stakes, Matchmaker Stakes, Vineland H., San Bernardino H., Santa Monica H. and Santa Barbara H.

BOLD RULER (b. 1954)	Nasrullah (b. 1940)	Nearco	Pharos / Nogara
		Mumtaz Begum	Blenheim / Mumtaz Mahal
	Miss Disco (b. 1944)	Discovery	Display / Ariadne
		Outdone	Pompey / Sweep Out
GAMBETTA (b. 1952)	My Babu (b. 1945)	Djebel	Tourbillon / Loika
		Perfume II	Badruddin / Lavendula II
	Rough Shod (b. 1944)	Gold Bridge	Swynford or Golden Boss / Flying Diadem
		Dalmary	Blandford / Simon's Shoes

334 **GARRIDO** 1 (ch.c., March 9, 1977)

Bred by Razza Dormello-Olgiata, in Italy.

Won 2 races, placed 3, 98,615,174 L., in Italy, France and Ireland, at 2 and 3 years, incl. Derby Italiano; 4th Irish Sweeps Derby.

MANNSFELD (ch. 1971)	Crocket (ch. 1960)	King of the Tudors	Tudor Minstrel / Glen Line
		Chandelier	Goyama / Queen of Light
	Martine Boileau (ch. 1965)	Match III	Tantieme / Relance III
		Marguerite Delaroche	Toulouse Lautrec / Mina da Siena
GABRIELLE LEBAUDY (br. 1972)	Murrayfield (br. 1966)	Match III	Tantieme / Relance III
		Erisca	Doutelle / Bahama
	Gouache II (b. 1960)	Rockefella	Hyperion / Rockfel
		Giambellina	Precipitation / Giralda II

335 **GARVIN** 16 (b.c., March 22, 1967)

Bred by Dr. P. Fossa, in Italy.

Won 15 races, placed 47, 93,108,000 L., in Italy, from 2 to 8 years, incl. Gran Premio di Milano; 2nd Premio Ambrosiano; 3rd Coppa d'Oro di Milano and Premio Federico Tesio.

ANDREA MANTEGNA (b. 1961)	Ribot (b. 1952)	Tenerani	Bellini / Tofanella
		Romanella	El Greco / Barbara Burrini
	Angela Rucellai (b. 1954)	Rockefella	Hyperion / Rockfel
		Aristareta	Niccolo Dell'Arca / Acquaforte
GUELPH (ch. 1963)	Nagami (ch. 1955)	Nimbus	Nearco / Kong
		Jennifer	Hyperion / Avena
	Goccia (b. 1950)	Moroni	Ortello / Maratta Faustina
		Gresia	Cavaliere d'Arpino / Green Forest

336 **GAY LUSSAC** 9 (ch.c., April 4, 1969)

Bred by Az. Agr. Allevamenti Gibi, in Italy.

Won 7 races, 79,510,000 L., in Italy, at 2 and 3 years, incl. Derby Italiano, Premio Emanuele Filiberto, Criterium Nazionale and Gran Criterium.

FABERGE II (b. 1961)	Princely Gift (b. 1951)	Nasrullah	Nearco / Mumtaz Begum
		Blue Gem	Blue Peter / Sparkle
	Spring Offensive (b. 1943)	Legend of France	Dark Legend / Francille
		Batika	Blenheim / Brise Bise
GREEN AS GRASS (b. 1963)	Red God (ch. 1954)	Nasrullah	Nearco / Mumtaz Begum
		Spring Run	Menow / Boola Brook
	Greensward II (b. 1956)	Count Turf	Count Fleet / Delmarie
		Valse Folle	Tourbillon / Listen In

337   GAY MECENE 3 (b.c., May 16, 1975)

Bred by George F. Getty III Enterprises, in U.S.A.

Won 5 races, placed 5, 1,560,948 fr., in France and England, from 2 to 4 years, incl. Grand Prix de Saint-Cloud, Prix Eugene Adam, Prix de Guiche and Prix Niel; 2nd King George VI and Queen Elizabeth Diamond Stakes and Grand Prix d'Evry; 3rd Coronation Cup and Prix Foy; 4th Prix Lupin.

VAGUELY NOBLE (b. 1965)	Vienna (ch. 1957)	Aureole	Hyperion / Angelola
		Turkish Blood	Turkhan / Rusk
	Noble Lassie (b. 1956)	Nearco	Pharos / Nogara
		Belle Sauvage	Big Game / Tropical Sun
GAY MISSILE (b. 1967)	Sir Gaylord (b. 1959)	Turn-to	Royal Charger / Source Sucree
		Somethingroyal	Princequillo / Impératrice
	Missy Baba (b. 1958)	Tulyar or My Babu	Djebel / Perfume II
		Uvira	Umidwar / Lady Lawless

338   GAZALA II 8 (br.f., April 7, 1964)

Bred by Nelson Bunker Hunt, in France.

Won 5 races, placed 4, 1,174,103 fr., in France, from 2 to 4 years, incl. Prix de Diane, Poule d'Essai des Pouliches, Prix de la Grotte and Criterium de Maisons-Laffitte; 3rd Prix de la Foret.

DARK STAR (br. 1950)	Royal Gem II (br. 1942)	Dhoti	Dastur / Tricky Aunt
		French Gem	Beau Fils / Fission
	Isolde (br. 1938)	Bull Dog	Teddy / Plucky Liege
		Fiji	Bostonian / O Girl
BELLE ANGEVINE (br. 1957)	L'Amiral (br. 1947)	Admiral Drake	Craig an Eran / Plucky Liege
		Hurrylor	Vatellor / Hurry Off
	Bella II (br. 1945)	Canot	Nino / Canalette
		Bayan Kara	Dark Legend / Black Domino

339   GAZPACHO 22 (b.f., April 5, 1960)

Bred by Mrs. J. R. Mullion.

Won 2 races, £6,682, in Ireland and England, at 2 and 3 years, incl. Irish 1,000 Guineas, Fred Darling Stakes.

HARD SAUCE (br. 1948)	Ardan (b. 1941)	Pharis II	Pharos / Carissima
		Adargatis	Asterus / Helene de Troie
	Saucy Bella (gr. 1941)	Bellacose	Sir Cosmo / Orbella
		Marmite	Mr. Jinks / Gentlemen's Relish
RED CLOAK (br. 1954)	Big Game (b. 1939)	Bahram	Blandford / Friar's Daughter
		Myrobella	Tetratema / Dolabella
	Manetta (b. 1943)	Nearco	Pharos / Nogara
		Wafer	Sansovino / Waffles

340   GENTILHOMBRE 6 (ch.c., April 2, 1973)

Bred by Mrs. M. Simpson.

Won 8½ races, placed 3, £75,284, in England and France, from 2 to 5 years, incl. Prix de l'Abbaye de Longchamp (twice), July Cup, Diadem Stakes, Cork and Orrery Stakes; 3rd Laurent Perrier Champagne Stakes, Challenge Stakes, Clerical Medical Greenham Stakes.

NO MERCY (gr. 1968)	Fortino II (gr. 1959)	Grey Sovereign	Nasrullah / Kong
		Ranavalo III	Relic / Navarra II
	Crowning Mercy (ch. 1960)	Supreme Court	Persian Gulf or Precipitation / Forecourt
		Mistress Grace	Prince Chevalier / Seraglio
KIRISANA (ch. 1966)	Darius (b. 1951) or Kribi (ch. 1953)	Alycidon	Donatello II / Aurora
		Sweet Marie	Brumeux / Sweet Ceylonese
	Tolosana (ch. 1959)	Botticelli	Blue Peter / Buonamica
		Tokamura	Navarro / Tofanella

341   GENTLE THOUGHTS 3 (ch.f., February 23, 1971)

Bred by George F. Getty II, in U.S.A.

Won 4 races, placed 2, £37,232, in Ireland and England, at 2 and 3 years, incl. Flying Childers Stakes, William Hill Cheveley Park Stakes.

BOLD LAD (USA) (ch. 1962)	Bold Ruler (b. 1954)	Nasrullah	Nearco / Mumtaz Begum
		Miss Disco	Discovery / Outdone
	Misty Morn (b. 1952)	Princequillo	Prince Rose / Cosquilla
		Grey Flight	Mahmoud / Planetoid
SOLID THOUGHT (ch. 1957)	Solidarity (b. 1945)	Alibhai	Hyperion / Teresina
		Jerrybuilt	Empire Builder / Varnish
	Unforgettable (ch. 1951)	Burning Dream	Bimelech / By Mistake
		Cantadora	Case Ace / Comeover

342   GENUINE RISK 1 (ch.f., February 15, 1977)

Bred by Mrs. G. Watts Humphrey Jr., in U.S.A.

Won 8 races, placed 4, $603,987, in U.S.A., at 2 and 3 years, incl. Kentucky Derby, Ruffian H. and Demoiselle Stakes; 2nd Preakness Stakes, Belmont Stakes and Maskette H.; 3rd Wood Memorial Stakes.

EXCLUSIVE NATIVE (ch. 1965)	Raise a Native (ch. 1961)	Native Dancer	Polynesian / Geisha
		Raise You	Case Ace / Lady Glory
	Exclusive (ch. 1953)	Shut Out	Equipoise / Goose Egg
		Good Example	Pilate / Parade Girl
VIRTUOUS (b. 1971)	Gallant Man (b. 1954)	Migoli	Bois Roussel / Mah Iran
		Majideh	Mahmoud / Qurrat-al-Ain
	Due Respect (b. 1958)	Zucchero	Nasrullah / Castagnola
		Auld Alliance	Brantome / Iona

343   **GIACOMETTI** 1 (ch.c., February 19, 1971)

Bred by T. Waters.

Won 4 races, placed 5, £104,093, in England, from 2 to 4 years, incl. Champion Stakes, Gimcrack Stakes, Champagne Stakes; 2nd 2,000 Guineas Stakes, St. Leger Stakes, Brigadier Gerard Stakes; 3rd Derby Stakes, Prince of Wales Stakes.

FABERGE II (b. 1961)	Princely Gift (b. 1951)	Nasrullah	Nearco / Mumtaz Begum
		Blue Gem	Blue Peter / Sparkle
	Spring Offensive (b. 1943)	Legend of France	Dark Legend / Francille
		Batika	Blenheim / Brise Bise
NAUJWAN (ch. 1960)	Ommeyad (b. 1954)	Hyperion	Gainsborough / Selene
		Minaret	Umidwar / Neolight
	Migolette (b. 1955)	Migoli	Bois Roussel / Mah Iran
		Sylko	Nearco / Salecraft

344   **GIFT CARD** 5 (b.c., May 3, 1969)

Bred by Duc d'Audiffret-Pasquier, in France.

Won 7 races, placed 6, £77,588, in France and England, from 2 to 4 years, incl. Prix Dollar, Prince of Wales Stakes, Prix Perth, Prix de Ris-Orangis; 2nd Poule d'Essai des Poulains; 3rd Prix Lupin.

DAN CUPID (ch. 1956)	Native Dancer (gr. 1950)	Polynesian	Unbreakable / Black Polly
		Geisha	Discovery / Miyako
	Vixenette (ch. 1944)	Sickle	Phalaris / Selene
		Lady Reynard	Gallant Fox / Nerva
GRACIOUS GIFT (b. 1958)	Princely Gift (b. 1951)	Nasrullah	Nearco / Mumtaz Begum
		Blue Gem	Blue Peter / Sparkle
	Malmaison (br. 1938)	Sir Gallahad III	Teddy / Plucky Liege
		Malvina B.	Sir John Johnson / Love Story

345   **GINEVRA** 3 (b.f., March 22, 1969)

Bred by Lord Suffolk.

Won 4 races, placed 4, £46,135, in England and France, at 2 and 3 years, incl. Oaks Stakes, Ladbroke Oaks Trial; 3rd Yorkshire Oaks, St. Leger Stakes, Cherry Hinton Stakes; 4th Prix Vermeille.

SHANTUNG (b. 1956)	Sicambre (br. 1948)	Prince Bio	Prince Rose / Biologie
		Sif	Rialto / Suavita
	Barley Corn (b. 1950)	Hyperion	Gainsborough / Selene
		Schiaparelli	Schiavoni / Aileen
ZEST (b. 1961)	Crepello (ch. 1954)	Donatello II	Blenheim / Delleana
		Crepuscule	Mieuxce / Red Sunset
	Mary Brandon (b. 1949)	Owen Tudor	Hyperion / Mary Tudor II
		Nipotina	Felicitation / Figliastra

346   **GIOLLA MEAR** 1 (b.c., April 20, 1965)

Bred by Irish National Stud Co. Ltd.

Won 4 races, placed 1, £17,623, in Ireland, at 3 years, incl. Irish St. Leger, Gallinule Stakes, Desmond Stakes; 2nd Blandford Stakes.

HARD RIDDEN (b. 1955)	Hard Sauce (br. 1948)	Ardan	Pharis II / Adargatis
		Saucy Bella	Bellacose / Marmite
	Toute Belle II (br. 1947)	Admiral Drake	Craig an Eran / Plucky Liege
		Chatelaine	Casterari / Yssel II
IACOBELLA (b. 1955)	Relic (bl. 1945)	War Relic	Man o'War / Friar's Carse
		Bridal Colors	Black Toney / Vaila
	Jacopa Bellini (b. 1945)	Bellini	Cavaliere d'Arpino / Bella Minna
		Incisione	Cranach / Ingoberta

347   **GIUSTIZIA** 10 (b.f., March 14, 1975)

Bred by Mrs. J. Shipway-Pratt, in Italy.

Won 6 races, placed 7, 104,660,000 L., in Italy, at 2 and 3 years, incl. Oaks d'Italia and Premio Lydia Tesio; 2nd Premio Dormello; 3rd Premio Regina Elena.

PENTOTAL (b. 1970)	Will Somers (br. 1955)	Tudor Minstrel	Owen Tudor / Sansonnet
		Queen's Jest	Nearco / Mirth
	Pendlemist (b. 1955)	The Phoenix	Château Bouscaut / Fille de Poete
		Snowdonia	Bobsleigh / Nestoi
GRAPPA (b. 1959)	Granet (b. 1947)	Orsenigo	Oleander / Ostana
		Ghirlandina	Ettore Tito / Galeazza
	Aparella (b. 1950)	Royal Charger	Nearco / Sun Princess
		Aprilia	Apron / Jonah's Trace

348   **GLAD RAGS** 13 (ch.f., March 14, 1963)

Bred by Captain D. Rogers.

Won 3 races, placed 2, £28,250, in Ireland and England, at 2 and 3 years, incl. 1,000 Guineas Stakes, Railway Stakes; 3rd Coronation Stakes, Royal Lodge Stakes.

HIGH HAT (ch. 1957)	Hyperion (ch. 1930)	Gainsborough	Bayardo / Rosedrop
		Selene	Chaucer / Serenissima
	Madonna (ch. 1945)	Donatello II	Blenheim / Delleana
		Women's Legion	Coronach / Victress
DRYAD (ch. 1950)	Panorama (ch. 1936)	Sir Cosmo	The Boss / Ayn Hali
		Happy Climax	Happy Warrior / Clio
	Woodside (b. 1937)	Furrokh Siyar	Colorado / Mumtaz Mahal
		Princess Argosy	Argosy / Eminent Lady

349   GLANEUSE 22 (b.f., April 9, 1966)

Bred by Mme. P. Wertheimer, in France.

Won 4 races, placed 4, 719,635 fr., in France and Italy, at 2 and 3 years, incl. Gran Premio del Jockey Club, Prix de Malleret and Prix Chloe; 2nd Prix de la Nonette; 3rd Prix de Diane and Criterium de Maisons-Laffitte; 4th Prix Vermeille.

SNOB (b. 1959)	Mourne (ch. 1954)	Vieux Manoir	Brantome / Vieille Maison
		Ballynash	Nasrullah / Ballywellbroke
	Senones (br. 1952)	Prince Bio	Prince Rose / Biologie
		Sif	Rialto / Suavita
GLAMOUR (br. 1960)	Djebe (gr. 1945)	Djebel	Tourbillon / Loika
		Catherine	Tiberius / Catherinette
	Tudor Gleam (br. 1952)	Owen Tudor	Hyperion / Mary Tudor II
		Riding Rays	Nearco / Infra Red

350   GLINT OF GOLD 21 (b.c., April 5, 1978)

Bred by Paul Mellon, in England.

Won 2 races, placed 1, £23,342, in England and Italy, at 2 years, incl. Gran Criterium.

MILL REEF (b. 1968)	Never Bend (b. 1960)	Nasrullah	Nearco / Mumtaz Begum
		Lalun	Djeddah / Be Faithful
	Milan Mill (b. 1962)	Princequillo	Prince Rose / Cosquilla
		Virginia Water	Count Fleet / Red Ray
CROWN TREASURE (b. 1973)	Graustark (ch. 1963)	Ribot	Tenerani / Romanella
		Flower Bowl	Alibhai / Flower Bed
	Treasure Chest (b. 1962)	Rough'n Tumble	Free for All / Roused
		Iltis	War Relic / We Hail

351   GODETIA 6 (ch.f., April 14, 1976)

Bred by Whitney Stone, in U.S.A.

Won 5 races, placed 1, £95,929, in Ireland, at 2 and 3 years, incl. Goff's Irish 1,000 Guineas, Irish Guinness Oaks, Pretty Polly Stakes, Athasi Stakes.

SIR IVOR (b. 1965)	Sir Gaylord (b. 1959)	Turn-to	Royal Charger / Source Sucree
		Somethingroyal	Princequillo / Imperatrice
	Attica (ch. 1953)	Mr. Trouble	Mahmoud / Motto
		Athenia	Pharamond / Salaminia
NATIVE GLITTER (b. 1966)	Native Dancer (gr. 1950)	Polynesian	Unbreakable / Black Polly
		Geisha	Discovery / Miyako
	Shimmer (b. 1945)	Flares	Gallant Fox / Flambino
		Broad Ripple	Stimulus / Hocus Pocus

352   GODSWALK 2 (gr.c., February 9, 1974)

Bred by Peter Fuller in U.S.A.

Won 8 races, placed 3, £54,406, in Ireland and England, at 2 and 3 years, incl. King's Stand Stakes, Ballyogan Stakes, Norfolk Stakes; 2nd Phoenix Stakes, William Hill Sprint Championship.

DANCER'S IMAGE (gr. 1965)	Native Dancer (gr. 1950)	Polynesian	Unbreakable / Black Polly
		Geisha	Discovery / Miyako
	Noor's Image (b. 1953)	Noor	Nasrullah / Queen of Baghdad
		Little Sphinx	Challenger / Khara
KATE'S INTENT (b. 1964)	Intentionally (bl. 1956)	Intent	War Relic / Liz F.
		My Recipe	Discovery / Perlette
	Julie Kate (b. 1957)	Hill Prince	Princequillo / Hildene
		Doggin' It	Bull Dog / Passerine

353   GOLDEN ACT 3 (ch.c., March 6, 1976)

Bred by W. H. Oldknow and R. W. Phipps, in U.S.A.

Won 8 races, placed 15, $916,268, in U.S.A. and Canada, from 2 to 4 years, incl. Canadian International Championship, Arkansas Derby, Louisiana Derby, Secretariat Stakes, El Camino Real Stakes, Lawrence Realization; 2nd Belmont Stakes, Preakness Stakes, California Derby, Norfolk Stakes, Turf Classic; 3rd Kentucky Derby, Round Table H., Man o'War Stakes, Century H.

GUMMO (b. 1962)	Fleet Nasrullah (b. 1955)	Nasrullah	Nearco / Mumtaz Begum
		Happy Go Fleet	Count Fleet / Draeh
	Alabama Gal (b. 1957)	Determine	Alibhai / Koubis
		Trojan Lass	Priam / Rompers
GOLDEN SHORE (ch. 1971)	Windy Sands (br. 1957)	Your Host	Alibhai / Boudoir II
		Samoa Winds	Polynesian / Windmill
	Retsinato (ch. 1966)	Ridan	Nantallah / Rough Shod
		Silver Song	Royal Note / Beadah

354   GOLDEN HORUS 3 (br.c., April 13, 1964)

Bred by T. J. Ronan.

Won 5 races, placed 9, £17,729, in England and U.S.A., from 2 to 4 years, incl. Gimcrack Stakes, July Stakes; 2nd Middle Park Stakes, Richmond Stakes.

TUDOR MELODY (br. 1956)	Tudor Minstrel (br. 1944)	Owen Tudor	Hyperion / Mary Tudor II
		Sansonnet	Sansovino / Lady Juror
	Matelda (br. 1947)	Dante	Nearco / Rosy Legend
		Fairly Hot	Solario / Fair Cop
PERSIAN UNION (b. 1952)	Persian Gulf (b. 1940)	Bahram	Blandford / Friar's Daughter
		Double Life	Bachelor's Double / Saint Joan
	Reconcile (ch. 1945)	Scottish Union	Cameronian / Trustful
		Discord	Trigo / Amorelle

355   **GOLD RIVER** 22 (ch.f., January 11, 1977)

Bred by Jacques Wertheimer, in France.

Won 4 races, placed 4, 749,000 fr., in France at 3 years, incl. Prix Royal Oak and Prix de Pomone; 2nd Prix Fille de l'Air and Prix de Royallieu; 3rd Prix de Minerve; 4th Prix Vermeille.

RIVERMAN (b. 1969)	Never Bend (br. 1960)	Nasrullah	Nearco / Mumtaz Begum
		Lalun	Djeddah / Be Faithful
	River Lady (b. 1963)	Prince John	Princequillo / Not Afraid
		Nile Lily	Roman / Azalea
GLANEUSE (b. 1966)	Snob (b. 1959)	Mourne	Vieux Manoir / Ballynash
		Senones	Prince Bio / Sif
	Glamour (br. 1960)	Djébé	Djebel / Catherine
		Tudor Gleam	Owen Tudor / Riding Rays

356   **GOLD ROD** 12 (b.c., April 9, 1967)

Bred by Mrs. C. A. Dickson, in England.

Won 7 races, placed 26, £85,925, in England and France, from 2 to 5 years, incl. Prix du Moulin de Longchamp, Prix de la Cote Normande, La Coupe de Maisons-Laffitte and Greenham Stakes; 2nd Eclipse Stakes, Sussex Stakes, Queen Elizabeth II Stakes, Prix du Moulin de Longchamp, Prix Perth, Prix Gontaut-Biron, St. James's Palace Stakes, Craven Stakes, 2,000 Guineas Trial Stakes and Goodwood Mile; 3rd Dante Stakes, Coronation Stakes (Sandown) (twice), Queen Anne Stakes, Goodwood Mile, Benson and Hedges Gold Cup, Lockinge Stakes, Prix Jean Prat and Prix du Rond-Point; 4th Champion Stakes and Prix Ganay.

SONGEDOR (ch. 1959)	Matador (ch. 1953)	Golden Cloud	Gold Bridge / Rainstorm
		Spanish Galantry	Mazarin / Courtship
	Fazeley (ch. 1950)	Watling Street	Fairway / Ranai
		Dinorama	Taj Ud Din / Orama
BANTAM (b. 1962)	Combat (br. 1944)	Big Game	Bahram / Myrobella
		Commotion	Mieuxce / Riot
	Blini (b. 1954)	Linklater	Fleeting Memory / Maugre
		Belinda Blue Eyes	Taj Ud Din / Belinda

357   **GONZALES** 8 (b.c., January 27, 1977)

Bred by Nelson Bunker Hunt, in U.S.A.

Won 4 races, £37,153, in Ireland, at 3 years, incl. Irish St. Leger, Blandford Stakes, Gallinule Stakes.

VAGUELY NOBLE (b. 1965)	Vienna (ch. 1957)	Aureole	Hyperion / Angelola
		Turkish Blood	Turkhan / Rusk
	Noble Lassie (b. 1956)	Nearco	Pharos / Nogara
		Belle Sauvage	Big Game / Tropical Sun
GAZALA II (b. 1964)	Dark Star (br. 1950)	Royal Gem II	Dhoti / French Gem
		Isolde	Bull Dog / Fiji
	Belle Angevine (br. 1957)	L'Amiral	Admiral Drake / Hurrylor
		Bella II	Canot / Bayan Kara

358   **GOODLY** 7 (b.c., April 28, 1966)

Bred by Marcel Labouré, in France.

Won 4 races, placed 3, 1,595,895 fr., in France, at 2 and 3 years, incl. Prix du Jockey-Club, Prix Noailles and Prix du Prince d'Orange; 2nd Grand Prix de Saint-Cloud and Prix Greffulhe.

SNOB (b. 1959)	Mourne (ch. 1954)	Vieux Manoir	Brantôme / Vieille Maison
		Ballynash	Nasrullah / Ballywellbroke
	Senones (br. 1952)	Prince Bio	Prince Rose / Biologie
		Sif	Rialto / Suavita
ALIZETTA (b. 1960)	Alizier (b. 1947)	Teleferique	Bactériophage / Beauté de Neige
		Alizarine	Coronach / Armoise
	Bella Zetta (b. 1951)	Bozzetto	Pharos / Bunworry
		Riva Bella	Rialto / Alathea

359   **GO WEST YOUNG MAN** 20 (gr.c., April 22, 1975)

Bred by Danada Farm, in U.S.A.

Won 8 races, placed 4, $642,245, in U.S.A., from 2 to 5 years, incl. Hollywood Gold Cup, Century H., Del Mar Futurity, Del Mar Invitational H. and Eddie Read H.; 3rd Hollywood Invitational H.

ADVOCATOR (b. 1963)	Round Table (b. 1954)	Princequillo	Prince Rose / Cosquilla
		Knight's Daughter	Sir Cosmo / Feola
	Delta Queen (b. 1946)	Bull Lea	Bull Dog / Rose Leaves
		Bleebok	Blue Larkspur / Forteresse
LADY FORTUNE (gr. 1967)	Lucky Debonair (b. 1962)	Vertex	The Rhymer / Kanace
		Fresh as Fresh	Count Fleet / Airy
	Smoothly (gr. 1956)	Mahmoud	Blenheim / Mah Mahal
		Camelina	Bull Dog / Princess Camelia

360   **GRANDIER** 1 (b.c., March 7, 1964)

Bred by F. Lieux, in France.

Won 7 races, placed 13, 1,944,727 fr., in France, from 2 to 6 years, incl. Prix Ganay, Prix d'Ispahan, Prix Dollar, Prix d'Harcourt, Prix Gontaut-Biron and Prix de Guiche; 2nd Grand Prix de Saint-Cloud, Prix Ganay, Prix Noailles, Prix du Prince d'Orange and Prix Henri Foy; 3rd Prix de l'Arc de Triomphe, Prix Gontaut-Biron and Prix Dollar.

TAPIOCA (b. 1953)	Vandale II (b. 1943)	Plassy	Bosworth / Pladda
		Vanille	La Farina / Vaya
	Semoule d'Or (b. 1945)	Vatellor	Vatout / Lady Elinor
		Semoule Fine	Firdaussi / Semoule
GIRGA (b. 1960)	Fine Top (br. 1949)	Fine Art	Artist's Proof / Finnoise
		Toupie	Vatellor / Tarentella
	Gerboise (b. 1945)	Rodosto	Epinard / Ramondie
		La Galerna	The MacNab / Becassine

361 **GRAUSTARK** 4 (ch.c., April 7, 1963)

Bred by Mr. and Mrs. John W. Galbreath, in U.S.A.

Won 7 races, placed 1, $75,904, in U.S.A., at 2 and 3 years, incl. Arch Ward Stakes and Bahamas Stakes; 2nd Blue Grass Stakes.

RIBOT (b. 1952)	Tenerani (b. 1944)	Bellini	Cavaliere d'Arpino / Bella Minna
		Tofanella	Apelle / Try Try Again
	Romanella (ch. 1943)	El Greco	Pharos / Gay Gamp
		Barbara Burrini	Papyrus / Bucolic
FLOWER BOWL (b. 1952)	Alibhai (ch. 1938)	Hyperion	Gainsborough / Selene
		Teresina	Tracery / Blue Tit
	Flower Bed (b. 1946)	Beau Pere	Son-in-Law / Cinna
		Boudoir	Mahmoud / Kampala

362 **GRAVELINES** 3 (gr.c., March 12, 1972)

Bred by Dayton Ltd., in France.

Won 10 races, placed 5, 1,534,945 fr., in France and U.S.A., from 3 to 5 years, incl. Prix du Moulin de Longchamp, Prix Jacques le Marois, Prix du Palais Royal, Pan American H. and Canadian Turf H.; 2nd Prix du Chemin de Fer du Nord and Bougainvillea H.; 3rd Prix Messidor.

CADMUS (b. 1963)	Supreme Court (br. 1948)	Persian Gulf or Precipitation	Hurry On / Double Life
		Forecourt	Fair Trial / Overture
	Covert Side (gr. 1958)	Abernant	Owen Tudor / Rustom Mahal
		Cub Hunt	Foxhunter / Knight's Daughter
GRAY DOVE (gr. 1966)	T.V. Lark (b. 1957)	Indian Hemp	Nasrullah / Sabzy
		Miss Larksfly	Heelfly / Larksnest
	Ruwenzori (gr. 1956)	Oil Capitol	Mahmoud / Never Again II
		Ruanda	Alibhai / Foxy Tetra

363 **GREAT CONTRACTOR** 10 (ch.c., April 1, 1973)

Bred by Howard P. Wilson, in U.S.A.

Won 8 races, placed 12, $628,559, in U.S.A., from 2 to 6 years, incl. Jockey Club Gold Cup, Lawrence Realization Stakes and Brooklyn H.; 2nd Florida Derby and Jockey Club Gold Cup; 3rd Belmont Stakes, Tropical Park Derby, Woodward H., Jockey Club Gold Cup, Brooklyn H. and Suburban H.

SELARI (b. 1962)	Prince John (ch. 1953)	Princequillo	Prince Rose / Cosquilla
		Not Afraid	Count Fleet / Banish Fear
	Golden Sari (b. 1956)	Ambiorix II	Tourbillon / Lavendula II
		Banta	Some Chance / Bourtai
OH ANNIE (ch. 1965)	Oh Johnny (b. 1953)	John's Joy	Bull Dog / My Auntie
		Saracen Flirt	Pilate / Knights Gal
	Cirene (ch. 1950)	Rolando	Tresiete / Persefona
		Cilly	Copyright / Mila II

364 **GREAT HOST** 12 (ch.c., April 4, 1964)

Bred by R. More O'Ferrall and Lord Elveden.

Won 3 races, £7,131, in Ireland and England, at 2 and 3 years, incl. Great Voltigeur Stakes, Chester Vase.

SICAMBRE (br. 1948)	Prince Bio (b. 1941)	Prince Rose	Rose Prince / Indolence
		Biologie	Bacteriophage / Eponge
	Sif (br. 1936)	Rialto	Rabelais / La Grelee
		Suavita	Alcantara II / Shocking
ABERMAID (gr. 1959)	Abernant (gr. 1946)	Owen Tudor	Hyperion / Mary Tudor II
		Rustom Mahal	Rustom Pasha / Mumtaz Mahal
	Dairymaid (ch. 1947)	Denturius	Gold Bridge / La Solfatara
		Laitron	Soldennis / Chardon

365 **GREAT NEPHEW** 14 (b.c., April 25, 1963)

Bred by Hon. J. P. Philipps, in England.

Won 5 races, placed 11, £65,861, in England and France, from 2 to 4 years, incl. Prix du Moulin de Longchamp and Prix Dollar; 2nd 2,000 Guineas, Prix Ganay, Prix du Moulin de Longchamp, Eclipse Stakes and Lockinge Stakes; 3rd Queen Anne Stakes; 4th Prix de la Foret.

HONEYWAY (br. 1941)	Fairway (b. 1925)	Phalaris	Polymelus / Bromus
		Scapa Flow	Chaucer / Anchora
	Honey Buzzard (ch. 1931)	Papyrus	Tracery / Miss Matty
		Lady Peregrine	White Eagle / Lisma
SYBIL'S NIECE (ch. 1951)	Admiral's Walk (ch. 1936)	Hyperion	Gainsborough / Selene
		Tabaris	Roi Herode / Tip-toe
	Sybil's Sister (b. 1943)	Nearco	Pharos / Nogara
		Sister Sarah	Abbots Trace / Sarita

366 **GREAT WALL** 1 (b.c., April 6, 1967)

Bred by E. N. Hall.

Won 1 race, placed 4, £8,323, in England, from 2 to 4 years, incl. King Edward VII Stakes; 2nd Cumberland Lodge Stakes; 3rd Ascot 2,000 Guineas Trial Stakes; 4th Derby Stakes.

CREPELLO (ch. 1954)	Donatello II (ch. 1934)	Blenheim	Blandford / Malva
		Delleana	Clarissimus / Duccia di Buoninsegna
	Crepuscule (ch. 1948)	Mieuxce	Massine / L'Olivete
		Red Sunset	Solario / Dulce II
TRIP TO THE MOON (br. 1956)	Sicambre (br. 1948)	Prince Bio	Prince Rose / Biologie
		Sif	Rialto / Suavita
	Solar Myth (b. or br. 1946)	Hyperion	Gainsborough / Selene
		Keystone	Umidwar / Rosetta

367   **GREEK MONEY** 1 (ch.c., April 5, 1959)

Bred by Renappi Corp., in U.S.A.

Won 10 races, placed 8, $239,433, in U.S.A., from 2 to 5 years, incl. Preakness Stakes and Excelsior H.; 3rd Michigan Mile-and-One-Sixteenth H.

GREEK SONG (ch. 1947)	Heliopolis (b. 1936)	Hyperion	Gainsborough / Selene
		Drift	Swynford / Santa Cruz
	Sylvan Song (b. 1932)	Royal Minstrel	Tetratema / Harpsichord
		Glade	Touch Me Not / Idle Dell
LUCY LUFTON (ch. 1952)	Nimbus (b. 1946)	Nearco	Pharos / Nogara
		Kong	Baytown / Clang
	Barchester (b. 1944)	Umidwar	Blandford / Uganda
		Belbroughton	King Salmon / Doublure

368   **GREEN BANNER** 5 (gr.c., April 1, 1962)

Bred by J. Lynch.

Won 5 races, placed 4, £13,097, in Ireland and U.S.A., at 2 and 3 years, incl. Irish 2,000 Guineas, Anglesey Stakes; 2nd Tetrarch Stakes.

PALESTINE (gr. 1947)	Fair Trial (ch. 1932)	Fairway	Phalaris / Scapa Flow
		Lady Juror	Son-in-Law / Lady Josephine
	Una (gr. 1930)	Tetratema	The Tetrarch / Scotch Gift
		Uganda	Bridaine / Hush
FAINNE OIR (br. 1950)	Golden Cloud (ch. 1941)	Gold Bridge	Swynford or Golden Boss / Flying Diadem
		Rainstorm	Hainault / Stormcloud
	Rondelet (b. 1940)	Rondo	Bolingbroke / Sardana
		Glassite	Glasgerion / Extravaganza

369   **GREEN DANCER** 16 (b.c., April 14, 1972)

Bred by Mrs. Pierre Wertheimer, in U.S.A.

Won 4 races, placed 2, £148,206, in France and England, at 2 and 3 years, incl. Observer Gold Cup, Poule d'Essai des Poulains, Prix Lupin; 2nd Prix des Chenes, Prix Niel.

NIJINSKY (b. 1967)	Northern Dancer (b. 1961)	Nearctic	Nearco / Lady Angela
		Natalma	Native Dancer / Almahmoud
	Flaming Page (b. 1959)	Bull Page	Bull Lea / Our Page
		Flaring Top	Menow / Flaming Top
GREEN VALLEY (br. 1967)	Val de Loir (b. 1959)	Vieux Manoir	Brantome / Vieille Maison
		Vali	Sunny Boy III / Her Slipper
	Sly Pola (ch. 1957)	Spy Song	Balladier / Mata Hari
		Ampola	Pavot / Blue Denim

370   **GREGORIAN** 13 (b.c., April 25, 1976)

Bred by Harry T. Mangurian, Jr., in U.S.A.

Won 4 races, placed 4, £85,986, in Ireland and England, from 2 to 4 years, incl. Joe McGrath Memorial Stakes, Brigadier Gerard Stakes, Westbury Stakes; 3rd Coral Eclipse Stakes, King George VI and Queen Elizabeth Diamond Stakes, Sean Graham Ballymoss Stakes, Royal Whip Stakes.

GRAUSTARK (ch. 1963)	Ribot (b. 1952)	Tenerani	Bellini / Tofanella
		Romanella	El Greco / Barbara Burrini
	Flower Bowl (b. 1952)	Alibhai	Hyperion / Teresina
		Flower Bed	Beau Pere / Boudoir
NATASHKA (b./br. 1963)	Dedicate (b. 1952)	Princequillo	Prince Rose / Cosquilla
		Dini	John P. Grier / Quivira
	Natasha (b. 1952)	Nasrullah	Nearco / Mumtaz Begum
		Vagrancy	Sir Gallahad III / Valkyr

371   **GREY OF FALLODEN** 16 (ch.g., April 3, 1959)

Bred by Astor Studs.

Won 13 races, placed 23, £28,891, in England, from 2 to 10 years, incl. Doncaster Cup, Queen Alexandra Stakes, Cesarewitch Stakes, Queen's Prize; 2nd Northumberland Plate; 3rd Chester Cup, Yorkshire Cup, Queen Alexandra Stakes. Also raced under N.H. Rules, winning 1 race, placed 2, £561, over hurdles.

ALYCIDON (ch. 1945)	Donatello II (ch. 1934)	Blenheim	Blandford / Malva
		Delleana	Clarissimus / Duccia di Buoninsegna
	Aurora (ch. 1936)	Hyperion	Gainsborough / Selene
		Rose Red	Swynford / Marchetta
SISTER GREY (ch. 1952)	Dante (br. 1942)	Nearco	Pharos / Nogara
		Rosy Legend	Dark Legend / Rosy Cheeks
	Ash Blonde (b. 1945)	The Phoenix	Chateau Bouscaut / Fille de Poete
		Miss Minx	Mr. Jinks / Gerrard's Cross

372   **GRIS VITESSE** 21 (gr.f., March 2, 1966)

Bred by Nelson Bunker Hunt, in U.S.A.

Won 2 races, placed 1, 223,005 fr., in France, at 2 and 3 years, incl. Prix Jacques le Marois.

AMERIGO (ch. 1955)	Nearco (br. 1935)	Pharos	Phalaris / Scapa Flow
		Nogara	Havresac II / Catnip
	Sanlinea (ch. 1947)	Precipitation	Hurry On / Double Life
		Sun Helmet	Hyperion / Point Duty
MATCHICHE II (gr. 1956)	Mat de Cocagne (br. 1948)	Birikil	Biribi / Kill Lady
		Fascine II	Fastnet / Mistigrise
	Chimere Fabuleuse (gr. 1951)	Coaraze	Tourbillon / Corrida
		Nine II	Nino / Iordane

373   GROUP PLAN 19 (b.g., May 6, 1970)

Bred by Eaton Farms, Red Bull Stable and Mrs. George Proskauer, in U.S.A.

Won 9 races, placed 16, $446,236, in U.S.A., from 3 to 6 years, incl. Jockey Club Gold Cup, Hawthorne Gold Cup and Stymie H.; 2nd Massachusetts H., Whitney Stakes, Display H., Gallant Fox H., Seneca H. and Washington Park H.; 3rd Woodward Stakes (twice), Jockey Club Gold Cup, Hawthorne Gold Cup, Queen's County H. and Brighton Beach H.

INTENTIONALLY (bl. 1956)	Intent (ch. 1948)	War Relic	Man o'War / Friar's Carse
		Liz F.	Bubbling Over / Weno
	My Recipe (b. 1947)	Discovery	Display / Ariadne
		Perlette	Percentage / Escarpolette
NANTICIOUS (b. 1965)	Nantallah (b. 1953)	Nasrullah	Nearco / Mumtaz Begum
		Shimmer	Flares / Broad Ripple
	Be Ambitious (br. 1958)	Ambiorix II	Tourbillon / Lavendula II
		Be Faithful	Bimelech / Bloodroot

374   GRUNDY 8 (ch.c., April 3, 1972)

Bred by Overbury Stud.

Won 8 races, placed 3, £326,421, in England and Ireland, at 2 and 3 years, incl. Derby Stakes, Irish Sweeps Derby, Irish 2,000 Guineas, King George VI and Queen Elizabeth Diamond Stakes, William Hill Dewhurst Stakes, Champagne Stakes; 2nd 2,000 Guineas Stakes, Clerical Medical Greenham Stakes; 4th Benson and Hedges Gold Cup.

GREAT NEPHEW (b. 1963)	Honeyway (br. 1941)	Fairway	Phalaris / Scapa Flow
		Honey Buzzard	Papyrus / Lady Peregrine
	Sybil's Niece (ch. 1951)	Admiral's Walk	Hyperion / Tabaris
		Sybil's Sister	Nearco / Sister Sarah
WORD FROM LUNDY (b. 1966)	Worden II (ch. 1949)	Wild Risk	Rialto / Wild Violet
		Sans Tares	Sind / Tara
	Lundy Princess (b. 1960)	Princely Gift	Nasrullah / Blue Gem
		Lundy Parrot	Flamingo / Waterval

375   GUADANINI 16 (ch.c., March 26, 1974)

Bred by R. Vecchione and M. Fabiani, in France.

Won 6 races, placed 5, 1,310,000 fr., in France, from 2 to 4 years, incl. Grand Prix de Saint-Cloud, Grand Prix de Vichy, La Coupe and Prix Jean de Chaudenay; 2nd Prix Hocquart.

LUTHIER (br. 1965)	Klairon (b. 1952)	Clarion III	Djebel / Columba
		Kalmia	Kantar / Sweet Lavender
	Flute Enchantee (b. 1950)	Cranach	Coronach / Reine Isaure
		Montagnana	Brantome / Mauretania
ILREM (ch. 1966)	Prudent II (ch. 1959)	My Babu	Djebel / Perfume II
		Providence	Easton / War Kilt
	Persepolis (ch. 1956)	Caracalla II	Tourbillon / Astronomie
		Fille de Soleil	Solario / Fille de Salut

376   GUN BOW 1 (b.c., March 21, 1960)

Bred by Maine Chance Farm, in U.S.A.

Won 17 races, placed 12, $798,722, in U.S.A., from 3 to 5 years, incl. Woodward Stakes, Brooklyn H., Metropolitan H., Charles H. Strub Stakes, San Antonio H. (twice), Gulfstream Park H., Whitney Stakes, Washington H., San Fernando Stakes and Donn H.; 2nd Washington D.C. International, Aqueduct Stakes, Man o'War Stakes, John B. Campbell H. and Massachusetts H.; 3rd Monmouth H., Carter H. and Gulfstream Park H.

GUN SHOT (ch. 1953)	Hyperion (ch. 1930)	Gainsborough	Bayardo / Rosedrop
		Selene	Chaucer / Serenissima
	Silence (b. 1942)	Bosworth	Son-in-Law / Serenissima
		Surbine	Bachelor's Double / Datine
RIBBONS AND BOWS (b. 1955)	War Admiral (br. 1934)	Man o'War	Fair Play / Mahubah
		Brushup	Sweep / Annette K
	Evening Thrill (b. 1947)	Bull Lea	Bull Dog / Rose Leaves
		Decolte	St. Germans / Humming Bird

377   GUNNER B 3 (ch.c., March 8, 1973)

Bred by T. Barratt.

Won 15 races, placed 14, £159,111, in England, from 2 to 5 years, incl. Joe Coral Eclipse Stakes, Prince of Wales Stakes, Diomed Stakes, Brigadier Gerard Stakes, Earl of Sefton Stakes; 2nd Benson and Hedges Gold Cup, Mecca-Dante Stakes, Dee Stakes (dead-heat); 3rd Champion Stakes, Westbury Stakes, Ormonde Stakes.

ROYAL GUNNER (ch. 1962)	Royal Charger (ch. 1942)	Nearco	Pharos / Nogara
		Sun Princess	Solario / Mumtaz Begum
	Levee (ch. 1953)	Hill Prince	Princequillo / Hildene
		Bourtai	Stimulus / Escutcheon
SWEET COUNCILLOR (b. 1968)	Privy Councillor (ch. 1959)	Counsel	Court Martial / Wheedler
		High Number	His Highness / Lady Luck
	Sugarstick (b. 1956)	Zucchero	Nasrullah / Castagnola
		York Gala	His Grace / Princess Galahad

378   GUSTAV 1 (gr.c., April 2, 1959)

Bred by F. F. Tuthill.

Won 3 races, placed 1, £6,783, in England, at 2 and 3 years, incl. Middle Park Stakes.

GREY SOVEREIGN (gr. 1948)	Nasrullah (b. 1940)	Nearco	Pharos / Nogara
		Mumtaz Begum	Blenheim / Mumtaz Mahal
	Kong (gr. 1933)	Baytown	Achtoi / Princess Herodias
		Clang	Hainault / Vibration
GAMESMISTRESS (ch. 1945)	Big Game (b. 1939)	Bahram	Blandford / Friar's Daughter
		Myrobella	Tetratema / Dolabella
	Taslon (b. 1925)	Hurry On	Marcovil / Tout Suite
		Taslett	William the Third / Burgonet

379 **GYR** 3 (ch.c., April 22, 1967)

Bred by Mr. and Mrs. Winston F. C. Guest, in U.S.A.

Won 4 races, placed 3, 1,557,797 fr., in France and England, at 2 and 3 years, incl. Grand Prix de Saint-Cloud, Prix Daru and Prix Hocquart; 2nd Derby Stakes; 4th Prix de l'Arc de Triomphe and Grand Criterium.

SEA BIRD II (ch. 1962)	Dan Cupid (ch. 1956)	Native Dancer	Polynesian / Geisha
		Vixenette	Sickle / Lady Reynard
	Sicalade (b. 1956)	Sicambre	Prince Bio / Sif
		Marmelade	Maurepas / Couleur
FERIA (b. 1956)	Toulouse Lautrec (ch. 1950)	Dante	Nearco / Rosy Legend
		Tokamura	Navarro / Tofanella
	Feira de Rio (b. 1951)	Way In	Fairway / Instantaneous
		Una Felina	Vezzano / Ulrika Eleonora

380 **HABAT** 9 (gr.c., January 25, 1971)

Bred by Marston Stud.

Won 5 races, placed 2, £49,636, in England, at 2 and 3 years, incl. William Hill Middle Park Stakes, Mill Reef Stakes, Norfolk Stakes, 2,000 Guineas Trial Stakes; 2nd Sussex Stakes.

HABITAT (b. 1966)	Sir Gaylord (b. 1959)	Turn-to	Royal Charger / Source Sucree
		Somethingroyal	Princequillo / Imperatrice
	Little Hut (b. 1952)	Occupy	Bull Dog / Miss Bunting
		Savage Beauty	Challenger / Khara
ATREVIDA (gr. 1958)	Sunny Boy III (b. 1944)	Jock II	Asterus / Naic
		Fille de Soleil	Solario / Fille de Salut
	Palariva (gr. 1953)	Palestine	Fair Trial / Una
		Rivaz	Nearco / Mumtaz Begum

381 **HABITAT** 4 (b.c., May 4, 1966)

Bred by Nuckols Bros., in U.S.A.

Won 5 races, placed 2, £40,840, in England and France, at 3 years, incl. Prix du Moulin de Longchamp, Prix Quincey, Lockinge Stakes and Wills Mile; 2nd St. James's Palace Stakes.

SIR GAYLORD (b. 1959)	Turn-to (b. 1951)	Royal Charger	Nearco / Sun Princess
		Source Sucree	Admiral Drake / Lavendula II
	Somethingroyal (b. 1952)	Princequillo	Prince Rose / Cosquilla
		Imperatrice	Caruso / Cinquepace
LITTLE HUT (b. 1952)	Occupy (b. 1941)	Bull Dog	Teddy / Plucky Liege
		Miss Bunting	Bunting / Mirthful
	Savage Beauty (b. 1943)	Challenger	Swynford / Sword Play
		Khara	Kai-Sang / Decree

382 **HAIL TO ALL** 1 (b.c., May 22, 1962)

Bred by Mrs. Ben Cohen, in U.S.A.

Won 8 races, placed 15, $494,150, in U.S.A., at 2 and 3 years, incl. Belmont Stakes, Jersey Derby and Travers Stakes; 2nd New Hampshire Sweepstakes, Florida Derby, Wood Memorial Stakes, Fountain of Youth Stakes and Pimlico Futurity; 3rd Preakness Stakes, Flamingo Stakes, Garden State Stakes, Dwyer H. and Saranac H.

HAIL TO REASON (br. 1958)	Turn-to (b. 1951)	Royal Charger	Nearco / Sun Princess
		Source Sucree	Admiral Drake / Lavendula II
	Nothirdchance (b. 1948)	Blue Swords	Blue Larkspur / Flaming Swords
		Galla Colors	Sir Gallahad III / Rouge et Noir
ELLEN'S BEST (br. 1952)	War Relic (ch. 1938)	Man o'War	Fair Play / Mahubah
		Friar's Carse	Friar Rock / Problem
	Ellendale (br. 1944)	Bimelech	Black Toney / La Troienne
		The Sward	Sickle / Speed Boat

383 **HAIL TO REASON** 4 (br.c., April 19, 1958)

Bred by Bieber-Jacobs Stable, in U.S.A.

Won 9 races, placed 4, $328,437, in U.S.A., at 2 years, incl. Hopeful Stakes, Sapling Stakes, Sanford Stakes, Saratoga Special and World's Playground Stakes.

TURN-TO (b. 1951)	Royal Charger (ch. 1942)	Nearco	Pharos / Nogara
		Sun Princess	Solario / Mumtaz Begum
	Source Sucree (b. 1940)	Admiral Drake	Craig an Eran / Plucky Liege
		Lavendula II	Pharos / Sweet Lavender
NOTHIRDCHANCE (b. 1948)	Blue Swords (b. 1940)	Blue Larkspur	Black Servant / Blossom Time
		Flaming Swords	Man o'War / Exalted
	Galla Colors (b. 1943)	Sir Gallahad III	Teddy / Plucky Liege
		Rouge et Noir	St. Germans / Baton Rouge

384 **HALTILALA** 1 (ch.f., 1963)

Bred by Baron Guy de Rothschild, in France.

Won 3 races, placed 2, 712,057 fr., in France, at 3 years, incl. Prix Vermeille; 4th Prix de Diane and Prix Saint-Alary.

LE HAAR (ch. 1954)	Vieux Manoir (b. 1947)	Brantome	Blandford / Vitamine
		Vieille Maison	Finglas / Vieille Canaille
	Mince Pie (b. 1949)	Teleferique	Bacteriophage / Beaute de Neige
		Cannelle	Biribi / Armoise
SIRRIMA (ch. 1955)	Hyperion (ch. 1930)	Gainsborough	Bayardo / Rosedrop
		Selene	Chaucer / Serenissima
	Mixed Blessing (ch. 1946)	Brumeux	Teddy / La Brume
		Pot-pourri	Rose Prince / Sweet Lavender

385   HAMETUS 6 (ch.c., April 15, 1965)

Bred by Celbridge Estates Ltd.

Won 2 races, placed 1, £9,571, in England, at 2 and 3 years, incl. Dewhurst Stakes; 3rd 2,000 Guineas Trial Stakes.

HIGH HAT (ch. 1957)	Hyperion (ch. 1930)	Gainsborough	Bayardo / Rosedrop
		Selene	Chaucer / Serenissima
	Madonna (ch. 1945)	Donatello II	Blenheim / Delleana
		Women's Legion	Coronach / Victress
VILLA MEDICI (ch. 1950)	Panorama (ch. 1936)	Sir Cosmo	The Boss / Ayn Hali
		Happy Climax	Happy Warrior / Clio
	Miss Bula (gr. 1932)	Stefan the Great	The Tetrarch / Perfect Peach
		Bula	Lemberg / Indian Star

386   HARDICANUTE 3 (br.c., February 9, 1962)

Bred by R. Greene.

Won 3 races, £31,938, in England and Ireland, at 2 and 3 years, incl. Champagne Stakes, Timeform Gold Cup, Ballymoss Stakes.

HARD RIDDEN (b. 1955)	Hard Sauce (br. 1948)	Ardan	Pharis II / Adargatis
		Saucy Bella	Bellacose / Marmite
	Toute Belle II (br. 1947)	Admiral Drake	Craig an Eran / Plucky Liege
		Chatelaine	Casterari / Yssel II
HARVEST MAID (b. 1949)	Umidwar (b. 1931)	Blandford	Swynford / Blanche
		Uganda	Bridaine / Hush
	Hay Fell (b. 1938)	Felstead	Spion Kop / Felkington
		Hay Fever	Hainault / Catch Crop

387   HARD TO BEAT 14 (b.c., February 24, 1969)

Bred by Tally Ho Stud Co. Ltd., in Ireland.

Won 7 races, placed 2, 3,063,157 fr., in France, from 2 to 4 years, incl. Prix du Jockey-Club, Prix Lupin, Grand Criterium, Prix Niel and Prix de Fontainebleau; 3rd Prix de l'Arc de Triomphe and Grand Prix de Saint-Cloud.

HARDICANUTE (br. 1962)	Hard Ridden (b. 1955)	Hard Sauce	Ardan / Saucy Bella
		Toute Belle II	Admiral Drake / Chatelaine
	Harvest Maid (b. 1949)	Umidwar	Blandford / Uganda
		Hay Fell	Felstead / Hay Fever
VIRTUOUS (b. 1962)	Above Suspicion (b. 1956)	Court Martial	Fair Trial / Instantaneous
		Above Board	Straight Deal / Feola
	Rose of India (b. 1955)	Tulyar	Tehran / Neocracy
		Eastern Grandeur	Gold Bridge / China Maiden

388   HARMONY HALL 20 (b.c., April 6, 1966)

Bred by Someries Stud.

Won 5 races, placed 6, £17,647, in England and France, from 2 to 4 years, incl. Great Voltigeur Stakes, Gordon Stakes, Princess of Wales's Stakes; 3rd Craven Stakes; 4th Dewhurst Stakes.

TUDOR MELODY (br. 1956)	Tudor Minstrel (br. 1944)	Owen Tudor	Hyperion / Mary Tudor II
		Sansonnet	Sansovino / Lady Juror
	Matelda (br. 1947)	Dante	Nearco / Rosy Legend
		Fairly Hot	Solario / Fair Cop
TAHIRI (b. 1959)	Persian Gulf (b. 1940)	Bahram	Blandford / Friar's Daughter
		Double Life	Bachelor's Double / Saint Joan
	Dickneos (b. 1949)	Nearco	Pharos / Nogara
		Miss Pecksniff	Dastur / Florence Dombey

389   HAVEROID 8 (b.c., April 13, 1974)

Bred by T. W. Newton.

Won 6 races, placed 7, £38,577, in England and France, from 2 to 4 years, incl. William Hill Sprint Championship; 3rd King's Stand Stakes, Prix de l'Abbaye de Longchamp; 4th King's Stand Stakes.

TYCOON II (b. 1962)	Tamerlane (br. 1952)	Persian Gulf	Bahram / Double Life
		Eastern Empress	Nearco / Cheveley Lady
	Djebel Idra (b. 1957)	Phil Drake	Admiral Drake / Philippa
		Djebellica	Djebel / Nica
MARTON LADY (b. 1966)	March Past (br. 1950)	Petition	Fair Trial / Art Paper
		Marcelette	William of Valence / Permavon
	Maid of Kintail (ch. 1960)	Atlas	Djebel / Young Entry
		Icewater	Bobsleigh / Early Rivers

390   HAWAII 1 (b.c., September 5, 1964)

Bred by A. L. Dell, in South Africa.

Won 21 races, placed 6, $372,790, in U.S.A. and South Africa, from 2 to 5 years, incl. United Nations H., Man o'War Stakes, Stars and Stripes H., Sunrise H., Bernard Baruch H., South African Guineas, Mellow-wood Guineas, Clairwood Winter H. and Transvaal Spring Champion Stakes; 2nd Washington D.C. International and Champion Stakes; 3rd Tidal H. and Kelly-Olympic H.; 4th Rothmans July H.

UTRILLO II (ch. 1958)	Toulouse Lautrec (ch. 1950)	Dante	Nearco / Rosy Legend
		Tokamura	Navarro / Tofanella
	Urbinella (b. 1953)	Alycidon	Donatello II / Aurora
		Isle of Capri	Fair Trial / Caprifolia
ETHANE (br. 1947)	Mehrali (b. 1939)	Mahmoud	Blenheim / Mah Mahal
		Una	Tetratema / Uganda
	Ethyl (b. 1936)	Clustine	Captain Cuttle / La Mauri
		Armond	Lomond / Arcola

391   HAWAIIAN SOUND 2 (b.c., April 7, 1975)

Bred by A. B. Hancock III, in U.S.A.

Won 5 races, placed 8, £176,024, in England and Ireland, from 2 to 4 years, incl. Benson and Hedges Gold Cup, Earl of Sefton Stakes; 2nd Derby Stakes, King George VI and Queen Elizabeth Diamond Stakes, Champion Stakes, Chester Vase; 3rd Irish Sweeps Derby, Royal Lodge Stakes.

HAWAII (b. 1964)	Utrillo II (ch. 1958)	Toulouse Lautrec	Dante / Tokamura
		Urbinella	Alycidon / Isle of Capri
	Ethane (br. 1947)	Mehrali	Mahmoud / Una
		Ethyl	Clustine / Armond
SOUND OF SUCCESS (ch. 1969)	Successor (b. 1964)	Bold Ruler	Nasrullah / Miss Disco
		Misty Morn	Princequillo / Grey Flight
	Belle Musique (b. 1963)	Tudor Minstrel	Owen Tudor / Sansonnet
		Bellesoeur	Beau Pere / Donatrice

392   HAWKBERRY 5 (b.c., May 6, 1973)

Bred by L. M. Gelb.

Won 3 races, placed 7, £48,326, in England, France and Ireland, from 2 to 5 years, incl. Great Voltigeur Stakes; 2nd Prix Jean Prat; 3rd Ascot Gold Cup, Prix du Cadran, Prix Maurice de Nieuil; 4th Derby Stakes, Irish Sweeps Derby.

SEA HAWK II (gr. 1963)	Herbager (b. 1956)	Vandale II	Plassy / Vanille
		Flagette	Escamillo / Fidgette
	Sea Nymph (br. 1957)	Free Man	Norseman / Fantine
		Sea Spray	Ocean Swell / Pontoon
KHALBERRY (b. 1969)	Khaled (br. 1943)	Hyperion	Gainsborough / Selene
		Eclair	Ethnarch / Black Ray
	Brown Berry (b. 1960)	Mount Marcy	Mahmoud / Maud Miller
		Brown Baby	Phalanx / Crawfish

393   HAYMAKING 6 (br.f., March 21, 1963)

Bred by Limestone Stud.

Won 6 races, placed 5, £11,844, in England, from 2 to 4 years, incl. Nassau Stakes, Coronation Stakes (Ascot); 2nd Coronation Stakes (Sandown); 3rd Westbury Stakes.

GALIVANTER (br. 1956)	Golden Cloud (ch. 1941)	Gold Bridge	Swynford or Golden Boss / Flying Diadem
		Rainstorm	Hainault / Stormcloud
	Lycia (b. 1944)	Nearco	Pharos / Nogara
		Cleres	Ksar / Katuja
HAYTIME (br. 1958)	Alycidon (ch. 1945)	Donatello II	Blenheim / Delleana
		Aurora	Hyperion / Rose Red
	Hazy Moon (b. 1953)	Umidwar	Blandford / Uganda
		New Moon	Solfo / Selene

394   HELLO GORGEOUS 13 (ch.c., March 11, 1977)

Bred by Paul Denes, in U.S.A.

Won 4 races, placed 3, £129,647, in England, at 2 and 3 years, incl. William Hill Futurity Stakes, Royal Lodge Stakes, Mecca-Dante Stakes; 2nd Coral Eclipse Stakes.

MR. PROSPECTOR (b. 1970)	Raise a Native (ch. 1961)	Native Dancer	Polynesian / Geisha
		Raise You	Case Ace / Lady Glory
	Gold Digger (b. 1962)	Nashua	Nasrullah / Segula
		Sequence	Count Fleet / Miss Dogwood
BONNY JET (b. 1959)	Jet Jewel (b. 1949)	Jet Pilot	Blenheim / Black Wave
		Crepe Myrtle	Equipoise / Myrtlewood
	Bonny Bush (ch. 1953)	Mr. Busher	War Admiral / Baby League
		San Bonita	Sansovino / California

395   HENBIT 3 (b.c., March 28, 1977)

Bred by Mrs. J. G. Jones, in U.S.A.

Won 4 races, placed 2, £192,305, in England, at 2 and 3 years, incl. Derby Stakes, Chester Vase, Classic Trial Stakes; 4th William Hill Dewhurst Stakes.

HAWAII (b. 1964)	Utrillo II (ch. 1958)	Toulouse Lautrec	Dante / Tokamura
		Urbinella	Alycidon / Isle of Capri
	Ethane (br. 1947)	Mehrali	Mahmoud / Una
		Ethyl	Clustine / Armond
CHATEAUCREEK (ch. 1970)	Chateaugay (ch. 1960)	Swaps	Khaled / Iron Reward
		Banquet Bell	Polynesian / Dinner Horn
	Mooncreek (ch. 1963)	Sailor	Eight Thirty / Flota
		Ouija	Heliopolis / Psychist

396   HENRI LE BALAFRÉ 4 (b.c., March 10, 1972)

Bred by C. Puerari, in France.

Won 4½ races, placed 3, 873,460 fr., in France and Italy, at 2 and 3 years, incl. Prix Royal Oak and Premio Roma (dead-heat); 2nd Prix de Fontainebleau.

SASSAFRAS (b. 1967)	Sheshoon (ch. 1956)	Precipitation	Hurry On / Double Life
		Noorani	Nearco / Empire Glory
	Ruta (b. 1960)	Ratification	Court Martial / Solesa
		Dame d'Atour	Cranach / Barley Corn
GALOUBINKA (b. 1967)	Tamerlane (br. 1952)	Persian Gulf	Bahram / Double Life
		Eastern Empress	Nearco / Cheveley Lady
	Rhenane (br. 1961)	Tanerko	Tantieme / La Divine
		Rhea II	Gundomar / Regina IV

397   HENRY THE SEVENTH 12 (ch.c., March 12, 1958)

Bred by Miss O. E. Hoole.

Won 6½ races, placed 4, £26,732, in England, from 2 to 4 years, incl. Zetland Gold Cup, Rous Memorial Stakes, Eclipse Stakes, Cambridgeshire Handicap (dead-heat); 2nd Champagne Stakes.

KING OF THE TUDORS (ch. 1950)	Tudor Minstrel (br. 1944)	Owen Tudor	Hyperion / Mary Tudor II
		Sansonnet	Sansovino / Lady Juror
	Glen Line (b. 1942)	Blue Peter	Fairway / Fancy Free
		Scotia's Glen	Beresford / Queen Scotia
VESTAL GIRL (ch. 1948)	Fairy Prince (ch. 1938)	Fairway	Phalaris / Scapa Flow
		Cachalot	Hurry On / Harpoon
	Vestalia (ch. 1926)	Abbots Trace	Tracery / Abbot's Anne
		Vulpina	St. Victrix / Cistus

398   HERERO 19 (ch.c., February 12, 1959)

Bred by Gestüt Römerhof, in Germany.

Won 3 races, placed 2, 121,600 DM., in Germany, at 2 and 3 years, incl. Deutsches Derby and Henckel-Rennen; 3rd Union-Rennen.

BOREALIS (ch. 1941)	Brumeux (b. 1925)	Teddy	Ajax / Rondeau
		La Brume	Alcantara II / Aquarelle
	Aurora (ch. 1936)	Hyperion	Gainsborough / Selene
		Rose Red	Swynford / Marchetta
HORATIA (ch. 1948)	Rockefella (br. 1941)	Hyperion	Gainsborough / Selene
		Rockfel	Felstead / Rockliffe
	Fair Emma (ch. 1943)	Solario	Gainsborough / Sun Worship
		Fair Venus	Fairway / Wings of Love

399   HERMES 11 (b.c., April 20, 1963)

Bred by R. D. Hollingsworth.

Won 5 races, placed 11, £23,946, in England and France, from 2 to 5 years, incl. Great Voltigeur Stakes, Dante Stakes, Jockey Club Cup; 2nd Doncaster Cup, John Porter Stakes, Jockey Club Stakes; 3rd John Porter Stakes, Prix Kergorlay, Prix Gladiateur; 4th Ascot Gold Cup (twice).

AUREOLE (ch. 1950)	Hyperion (ch. 1930)	Gainsborough	Bayardo / Rosedrop
		Selene	Chaucer / Serenissima
	Angelola (b. 1945)	Donatello II	Blenheim / Delleana
		Feola	Friar Marcus / Aloe
ARK ROYAL (bl. or br. 1952)	Straight Deal (b. 1940)	Solario	Gainsborough / Sun Worship
		Good Deal	Apelle / Weeds
	Felucca (b. 1941)	Nearco	Pharos / Nogara
		Felsetta	Felstead / Ka-Lu-A

400   HERMIERES 10 (ch.f., April 10, 1958)

Bred by Baron Guy de Rothschild, in France.

Won 4 races, placed 2, 407,962 fr., in France, at 2 and 3 years, incl. Prix de Diane and Prix Penelope; 2nd Prix Saint-Alary.

SICAMBRE (br. 1948)	Prince Bio (b. 1941)	Prince Rose	Rose Prince / Indolence
		Biologie	Bacteriophage / Eponge
	Sif (br. 1936)	Rialto	Rabelais / La Grelee
		Suavita	Alcantara II / Shocking
VIEILLE PIERRE (b. 1951)	Blue Peter (ch. 1936)	Fairway	Phalaris / Scapa Flow
		Fancy Free	Stefan the Great / Celiba
	Vieille Maison (b. 1936)	Finglas	Bruleur / Fair Simone
		Vieille Canaille	Zionist / Ficelle

401   HETHERSETT 21 (b.c., May 4, 1959)

Bred by Major L. B. Holliday.

Won 4 races, placed 3, £44,240, in England, from 2 to 4 years, incl. St. Leger Stakes, Great Voltigeur Stakes; 2nd Champion Stakes, Jockey Club Stakes, Coronation Cup.

HUGH LUPUS (b. 1952)	Djebel (b. 1937)	Tourbillon	Ksar / Durban
		Loika	Gay Crusader / Coeur à Coeur
	Sakountala (b. 1942)	Goya II	Tourbillon / Zariba
		Samos	Bruleur / Samya
BRIDE ELECT (b. 1952)	Big Game (b. 1939)	Bahram	Blandford / Friar's Daughter
		Myrobella	Tetratema / Dolabella
	Netherton Maid (b. 1944)	Nearco	Pharos / Nogara
		Phase	Windsor Lad / Lost Soul

402   HIBERNIA III 19 (b.f., January 28, 1960)

Bred by Gestüt Romerhof, in Germany.

Won 3 races, placed 5, £8,843, in Ireland, at 2 and 3 years, incl. Irish Guinness Oaks, Pretty Polly Stakes (Curragh); 2nd Irish 1,000 Guineas Stakes, Athasi Stakes.

MASETTO (b. 1952)	Olymp (b. 1942)	Arjaman	Herold / Aditja
		Olympiade	Oleander / Osterfreude
	Mimosa (b. 1945)	Indus	Alcantara II / Himalaya
		Marliese	Graf Ferry / Marie Louise
HORATIA (ch. 1948)	Rockefella (br. 1941)	Hyperion	Gainsborough / Selene
		Rockfel	Felstead / Rockliffe
	Fair Emma (ch. 1943)	Solario	Gainsborough / Sun Worship
		Fair Venus	Fairway / Wings of Love

403 **HIGHCLERE** 2 (b.f., April 9, 1971)

Bred by H.M. The Queen.

Won 3 races, placed 3, £155,255, in England and France, at 2 and 3 years, incl. 1,000 Guineas Stakes, Prix de Diane; 2nd King George VI and Queen Elizabeth Stakes.

QUEEN'S HUSSAR (b. 1960)	March Past (br. 1950)	Petition	Fair Trial / Art Paper
		Marcelette	William of Valence / Permavon
	Jojo (gr. 1950)	Vilmorin	Gold Bridge / Queen of the Meadows
		Fairy Jane	Fair Trial / Light Tackle
HIGHLIGHT (b. 1958)	Borealis (ch. 1941)	Brumeux	Teddy / La Brume
		Aurora	Hyperion / Rose Red
	Hypericum (b. 1943)	Hyperion	Gainsborough / Selene
		Feola	Friar Marcus / Aloe

404 **HIGH ECHELON** 2 (ro.c., March 22, 1967)

Bred by Bieber-Jacobs Stable, in U.S.A.

Won 4 races, placed 9, $383,895, in U.S.A., at 2 and 3 years, incl. Belmont Stakes, Futurity Stakes and Pimlico-Laurel Futurity; 2nd Sanford Stakes; 3rd Kentucky Derby and Saratoga Special.

NATIVE CHARGER (gr. 1962)	Native Dancer (gr. 1950)	Polynesian	Unbreakable / Black Polly
		Geisha	Discovery / Miyako
	Greek Blond (ch. 1946)	Heliopolis	Hyperion / Drift
		Peroxide	High Quest / Blonde Belle
LUQUILLO (b. 1961)	Princequillo (b. 1940)	Prince Rose	Rose Prince / Indolence
		Cosquilla	Papyrus / Quick Thought
	Lulalu (ch. 1950)	Fair Trial	Fairway / Lady Juror
		Luciebella	Rodosto / Lula

405 **HIGHEST HOPES** 14 (b.f., May 13, 1967)

Bred by Exors. of late Major L. B. Holliday, in Ireland.

Won 5 races, placed 2, £90,657, in England and France, at 2 and 3 years, incl. Prix Vermeille, Prix Eugene Adam, Fred Darling Stakes and Ascot 1,000 Guineas Trial Stakes; 2nd Prix de Diane and Yorkshire Oaks.

HETHERSETT (b. 1959)	Hugh Lupus (b. 1952)	Djebel	Tourbillon / Loika
		Sakountala	Goya II / Samos
	Bride Elect (b. 1952)	Big Game	Bahram / Myrobella
		Netherton Maid	Nearco / Phase
VERDURA (ch. 1948)	Court Martial (ch. 1942)	Fair Trial	Fairway / Lady Juror
		Instantaneous	Hurry On / Picture
	Bura (b. 1938)	Bahram	Blandford / Friar's Daughter
		Becti	Salmon-Trout / Mirawala

406 **HIGH LINE** 5 (ch.c., February 6, 1966)

Bred by W. and R. Barnett Ltd.

Won 9 races, placed 8, £24,800, in England, from 2 to 5 years, incl. Jockey Club Cup (3 times) and Geoffrey Freer Stakes (twice); 2nd Princess of Wales's Stakes, Paradise Stakes and John Porter Stakes; 3rd Cumberland Lodge Stakes (twice) and Yorkshire Cup.

HIGH HAT (ch. 1957)	Hyperion (ch. 1930)	Gainsborough	Bayardo / Rosedrop
		Selene	Chaucer / Serenissima
	Madonna (ch. 1945)	Donatello II	Blenheim / Delleana
		Women's Legion	Coronach / Victress
TIME CALL (b. 1955)	Chanteur II (b. 1942)	Chateau Bouscaut	Kircubbin / Ramondie
		La Diva	Blue Skies / La Traviata
	Aleria (ch. 1949)	Djebel	Tourbillon / Loika
		Canidia	Pharis II / Callisto

407 **HIGH TOP** 11 (b.c., February 3, 1969)

Bred by R. J. McCreery.

Won 5 races, placed 4, £62,930, in England and France, at 2 and 3 years, incl. 2,000 Guineas Stakes, Observer Gold Cup; 2nd Sussex Stakes, Prix Jacques le Marois; 4th Prix du Moulin de Longchamp.

DERRING-DO (b. 1961)	Darius (b. 1951)	Dante	Nearco / Rosy Legend
		Yasna	Dastur / Ariadne
	Sipsey Bridge (b. 1954)	Abernant	Owen Tudor / Rustom Mahal
		Claudette	Chanteur II / Nearly
CAMENAE (b. 1961)	Vimy (b. 1952)	Wild Risk	Rialto / Wild Violet
		Mimi	Black Devil / Mignon
	Madrilene (ch. 1951)	Court Martial	Fair Trial / Instantaneous
		Marmite	Mr. Jinks / Gentlemen's Relish

408 **HILL SHADE** 3 (br.f., February 14, 1965)

Bred by George A. Pope, Jr., in U.S.A.

Won 3 races, placed 4, £14,048, in England and France, at 2 and 3 years, incl. Nassau Stakes, Sun Chariot Stakes; 2nd Princess Elizabeth Stakes, Prix de la Nonette.

HILLARY (br. 1952)	Khaled (b. 1943)	Hyperion	Gainsborough / Selene
		Eclair	Ethnarch / Black Ray
	Snow Bunny (b. 1944)	Boswell	Bosworth / Flying Gal II
		La Rose	Jacopo / La Rambla
PENUMBRA (b. 1955)	Imperium (b. 1946)	Piping Rock	Fairway / Eclair
		Imperatrice	Caruso / Cinquepace
	Moonrise (ch. 1947)	Moonlight Run	Bobsleigh / Selene
		Seventh Heaven	Hustle On / Alinka

409 **HIPPODAMIA** 4 (b.f., April 29, 1971)

Bred by Tom Gentry, in U.S.A.

Won 2 races, placed 6, 637,720 fr., in France, at 2 and 3 years, incl. Criterium des Pouliches; 2nd Poule d'Essai des Pouliches, Prix Saint-Alary, Prix de la Grotte and Prix des Chenes; 3rd Prix Robert Papin.

HAIL TO REASON (br. 1958)	Turn-to (b. 1951)	Royal Charger	Nearco / Sun Princess
		Source Sucree	Admiral Drake / Lavendula II
	Nothirdchance (b. 1948)	Blue Swords	Blue Larkspur / Flaming Swords
		Galla Colors	Sir Gallahad III / Rouge et Noir
WHITE LIE (br. 1964)	Bald Eagle (b. 1955)	Nasrullah	Nearco / Mumtaz Begum
		Siama	Tiger / China Face
	Etiquette (ch. 1954)	Bernborough	Emborough / Bern Maid
		Your Hostess	Alibhai / Boudoir

410 **HITCHCOCK** 8 (b.c., February 23, 1966)

Bred by Gestüt Fohlenhof, in Germany.

Won 12 races, placed 19, 1,572,289 DM., in Germany, France and U.S.A., from 2 to 6 years, incl. Henckel-Rennen, Prix Eugene Adam, Consul Bayeff Rennen, Suburban H., Gallant Fox H. (twice) and Display H.; 2nd Amory L. Haskell H., Bougainvillea H., San Luis Rey H. and Massachusetts H., 3rd Deutsches Derby, Grosser Preis von Baden, Preis von Europa, Preis des Winterfavoriten, Union-Rennen, Suburban H., Bowling Green H., Display H., Governor Stakes and Hawthorne Gold Cup; 4th Washington D.C. International.

WAIDMANNSHEIL (br. 1957)	Asterios (br. 1947)	Oleander	Prunus / Orchidée II
		Astarte	Janitor / Arabeske
	Waldrun (br. 1943)	Alchimist	Herold / Aversion
		Walburga	Aurelius / Wally
HUMORADA (br. 1950)	Fante (b. 1942)	Nesiotes	Hurry On / Catnip
		Farnesiana	Michelangelo / Flush
	Huesca (br. 1942)	Pilade	Captain Cuttle / Piera
		Huanguelen	Blenheim / Pommade Divine

411 **HITTITE GLORY** 21 (b.c., April 18, 1973)

Bred by Cleaboy Farms Co.

Won 3 races, placed 1, £33,940, in England, at 2 and 3 years, incl. Flying Childers Stakes, William Hill Middle Park Stakes; 3rd King's Stand Stakes.

HABITAT (b. 1966)	Sir Gaylord (b. 1959)	Turn-to	Royal Charger / Source Sucree
		Somethingroyal	Princequillo / Imperatrice
	Little Hut (b. 1952)	Occupy	Bull Dog / Miss Bunting
		Savage Beauty	Challenger / Khara
HAZY IDEA (b. 1967)	Hethersett (b. 1959)	Hugh Lupus	Djebel / Sakountala
		Bride Elect	Big Game / Netherton Maid
	Won't Linger (ch. 1961)	Worden II	Wild Risk / Sans Tares
		Cherished	Chanteur II / Netherton Maid

412 **HOCHE** 1 (ch.c., April 27, 1968)

Bred by T. G. Johnson, in England.

Won 19 races, placed 16, 70,555,000 L., in Italy, from 2 to 5 years, incl. Premio Presidente della Repubblica, Gran Premio Citta di Torino, Premio Natale di Roma and Premio Ribot; 2nd Premio Roma Vecchia, Premio Umbria and Premio Natale di Roma; 3rd Premio Umbria; 4th Premio Presidente della Repubblica.

CELTIC ASH (ch. 1957)	Sicambre (br. 1948)	Prince Bio	Prince Rose / Biologie
		Sif	Rialto / Suavita
	Ash Plant (gr. 1948)	Nepenthe	Plassy / Frisky
		Amboyna	Bois Roussel / Aurora
HI-BABY (ch. 1961)	High Treason (ch. 1951)	Court Martial	Fair Trial / Instantaneous
		Eastern Grandeur	Gold Bridge / China Maiden
	Babucon (ch. 1956)	My Babu	Djebel / Perfume II
		Conkers	Challenge / Minion

413 **HOGARTH** 1 (b.c., April 7, 1965)

Bred by Razza Dormello-Olgiata, in Italy.

Won 11 races, placed 13, 120,815,500 L., in Italy and England, from 2 to 5 years, incl. Derby Italiano and Premio Presidente della Repubblica; 2nd Gran Premio d'Italia, St. Leger Italiano, Gran Premio di Milano, Premio d'Aprile and Coppa d'Oro di Milano; 3rd Gran Premio di Milano (twice), Eclipse Stakes and King George VI and Queen Elizabeth Stakes; 4th Gran Premio del Jockey Club and Champion Stakes.

NECKAR (bl. 1948)	Ticino (b. 1939)	Athanasius	Ferro / Athanasie
		Terra	Aditi / Teufelsrose
	Nixe (b. 1941)	Arjaman	Herold / Aditja
		Nanon	Graf Isolani / Nella da Gubbio
HOPEFUL DUCHESS (ch. 1948)	Hyperion (ch. 1930)	Gainsborough	Bayardo / Rosedrop
		Selene	Chaucer / Serenissima
	Fair Dame (b. 1937)	Fairway	Phalaris / Scapa Flow
		Daumont	Diligence / Tillywhim

414 **HOIST THE FLAG** 5 (b.c., March 31, 1968)

Bred by John M. Schiff, in U.S.A.

Won 5 races, $78,145, in U.S.A., at 2 and 3 years, incl. Cowdin Stakes and Bay Shore Stakes; also won Champagne Stakes, but disqualified; champion 2-year-old of 1970.

TOM ROLFE (b. 1962)	Ribot (b. 1952)	Tenerani	Bellini / Tofanella
		Romanella	El Greco / Barbara Burrini
	Pocahontas (br. 1955)	Roman	Sir Gallahad III / Buckup
		How	Princequillo / The Squaw II
WAVY NAVY (b. 1954)	War Admiral (br. 1934)	Man o'War	Fair Play / Mahubah
		Brushup	Sweep / Annette K.
	Triomphe (b. 1947)	Tourbillon	Ksar / Durban
		Melibee	Firdaussi / Metairie

415   HOME GUARD 4 (br.c., March 5, 1969)

Bred by Mrs. Richard C. du Pont, in U.S.A.

Won 7 races, placed 6, £30,357, in Ireland, England and France from 2 to 4 years, incl. Tetrarch Stakes, Hungerford Stakes and Diadem Stakes; 2nd Royal Lodge Stakes, St. James's Palace Stakes and Prix de l'Abbaye de Longchamp; 3rd Eclipse Stakes; 4th Irish 2,000 Guineas.

FORLI (ch. 1963)	Aristophanes (ch. 1948)	Hyperion	Gainsborough / Selene
		Commotion	Mieuxce / Riot
	Trevisa (ch. 1951)	Advocate	Fair Trial / Guiding Star
		Veneta	Foxglove / Dogaresa
STAY AT HOME (br. 1961)	Bold Ruler (b. 1954)	Nasrullah	Nearco / Mumtaz Begum
		Miss Disco	Discovery / Outdone
	Alanesian (b. 1954)	Polynesian	Unbreakable / Black Polly
		Alablue	Blue Larkspur / Double Time

416   HOMEWARD BOUND 3 (ch.f., March 21, 1961)

Bred by Sir Foster Robinson.

Won 3 races, placed 2, £42,243, in England, from 2 to 4 years, incl. Oaks Stakes, Yorkshire Oaks, Princess Elizabeth Stakes; 2nd Doncaster Cup; 3rd Coronation Cup.

ALYCIDON (ch. 1945)	Donatello II (ch. 1934)	Blenheim	Blandford / Malva
		Delleana	Clarissimus / Duccia di Buoninsegna
	Aurora (ch. 1936)	Hyperion	Gainsborough / Selene
		Rose Red	Swynford / Marchetta
SABIE RIVER (ch. 1949)	Signal Light (ch. 1936)	Pharos	Phalaris / Scapa Flow
		Ensoleillee	Sunstar / Laughter
	Amorcille (bl. or br. 1941)	Columcille	Foxlaw / Movilla
		Amorelle	Volta / Amanthe

417   HOMING 1 (b.c., March 25, 1975)

Bred by Lord Rotherwick.

Won 6 races, placed 4, £57,674, in England and France, at 2 and 3 years, incl. Prix du Rond-Point and Queen Elizabeth II Stakes; 2nd Prix du Moulin de Longchamp.

HABITAT (b. 1966)	Sir Gaylord (b. 1959)	Turn-to	Royal Charger / Source Sucree
		Somethingroyal	Princequillo / Imperatrice
	Little Hut (b. 1952)	Occupy	Bull Dog / Miss Bunting
		Savage Beauty	Challenger / Khara
HEAVENLY THOUGHT (b. 1967)	St. Paddy (b. 1957)	Aureole	Hyperion / Angelola
		Edie Kelly	Bois Roussel / Caerlissa
	Wishful Thinking (ch. 1960)	Petition	Fair Trial / Art Paper
		Musidora	Nasrullah / Painted Vale

418   HONEST PLEASURE 11 (b./br.c., March 28, 1973)

Bred by Waldemar Farms, in U.S.A.

Won 12 races, placed 8, $839,997, in U.S.A., from 2 to 4 years, incl. Florida Derby, Blue Grass Stakes, Flamingo Stakes, Travers Stakes, Champagne Stakes, Arlington-Washington Futurity, Laurel Futurity, Cowdin Stakes and Ben Ali H.; 2nd Kentucky Derby and Marlboro Cup; 3rd Woodward H. and Monmouth Invitational H.

WHAT A PLEASURE (ch. 1965)	Bold Ruler (b. 1954)	Nasrullah	Nearco / Mumtaz Begum
		Miss Disco	Discovery / Outdone
	Grey Flight (gr. 1945)	Mahmoud	Blenheim / Mah Mahal
		Planetoid	Ariel / La Chica
TULARIA (b. 1955)	Tulyar (br. 1949)	Tehran	Bois Roussel / Stafaralla
		Neocracy	Nearco / Harina
	Suntop (ch. 1940)	Dastur	Solario / Friar's Daughter
		Sunny Mountain	Abbots Trace / Lysandra

419   HOPEFUL VENTURE 6 (b.c., April 21, 1964)

Bred by The National Stud.

Won 7 races, placed 3, £81,597, in England and France, at 3 and 4 years, incl. Hardwicke Stakes, Ormonde Stakes, Princess of Wales's Stakes, Grand Prix de Saint-Cloud; 2nd King Edward VII Stakes, St. Leger Stakes, Prix Henry Delamarre.

AUREOLE (ch. 1950)	Hyperion (ch. 1930)	Gainsborough	Bayardo / Rosedrop
		Selene	Chaucer / Serenissima
	Angelola (b. 1945)	Donatello II	Blenheim / Delleana
		Feola	Friar Marcus / Aloe
WHITE HOUSE (b. 1956)	Supreme Court (br. 1948)	Persian Gulf or Precipitation	Hurry On / Double Life
		Forecourt	Fair Trial / Overture
	Snowberry (br. 1937)	Cameronian	Pharos / Una Cameron
		Myrobella	Tetratema / Dolabella

420   HOT GROVE 12 (b.c., January 16, 1974)

Bred by Lord Leverhulme.

Won 6 races, placed 8, £77,892, in England and France, from 2 to 4 years, incl. Chester Vase, St. Simon Stakes and Westbury Stakes; 2nd Derby Stakes, Ormonde Stakes and Grand Prix d'Evry; 3rd Royal Lodge Stakes, Cumberland Lodge Stakes, and Princess of Wales's Stakes.

HOTFOOT (br. 1966)	Firestreak (br. 1956)	Pardal	Pharis II / Adargatis
		Hot Spell	Umidwar / Haymaker
	Pitter Patter (br. 1953)	Kingstone	King Salmon / Feola
		Rain	Fair Trial / Monsoon
ORANGE GROVE (b. 1967)	Aggressor (b. 1955)	Combat	Big Game / Commotion
		Phaetonia	Nearco / Phaetusa
	Orange Girl (b. 1962)	Grey Sovereign	Nasrullah / Kong
		Mistress Gwynne	Chanteur II / Daring Miss

421   HOT SPARK 1 (ch.c., February 22, 1972)

Bred by Mrs. W. F. Davison.

Won 3 races, placed 2, £20,068, in England and Ireland, at 2 and 3 years, incl. Flying Childers Stakes, Palace House Stakes; 2nd King's Stand Stakes, King George Stakes.

HABITAT (b. 1966)	Sir Gaylord (b. 1959)	Turn-to	Royal Charger
			Source Sucree
		Somethingroyal	Princequillo
			Imperatrice
	Little Hut (b. 1952)	Occupy	Bull Dog
			Miss Bunting
		Savage Beauty	Challenger
			Khara
GARVEY GIRL (ch. 1960)	Princely Gift (b. 1951)	Nasrullah	Nearco
			Mumtaz Begum
		Blue Gem	Blue Peter
			Sparkle
	Tekka (b. 1953)	Ridge Wood	Bois Roussel
			Hanging Fall
		Chart Room	Blue Peter
			Book Debt

422   HULA DANCER 3 (gr.f., May 5, 1960)

Bred by Mrs. P. A. B. Widener, in U.S.A.

Won 8 races, £105,160, in England and France, at 2 and 3 years, incl. 1,000 Guineas Stakes, Champion Stakes, Prix Jacques le Marois, Grand Criterium, Prix du Moulin de Longchamp, Prix de la Salamandre.

NATIVE DANCER (gr. 1950)	Polynesian (br. 1942)	Unbreakable	Sickle
			Blue Glass
		Black Polly	Polymelian
			Black Queen
	Geisha (ro. 1943)	Discovery	Display
			Ariadne
		Miyako	John P. Grier
			La Chica
FLASH ON (b. 1950)	Ambrose Light (ch. 1933)	Pharos	Phalaris
			Scapa Flow
		La Roseraie	Niceas
			Eblouissante
	Generosity (b. 1940)	Castel Fusano	Ksar
			Red Flame
		Heralder	Sir Gallahad III
			Herade

423   HUMBLE DUTY 21 (gr.f., April 28, 1967)

Bred by F. F. Tuthill.

Won 8 races, placed 3, £63,696, in England, at 2 and 3 years, incl. 1,000 Guineas Stakes, Coronation Stakes, Sussex Stakes, Cheveley Park Stakes, Lowther Stakes, Wills Mile; 2nd Fred Darling Stakes; 3rd Queen Mary Stakes.

SOVEREIGN PATH (gr. 1956)	Grey Sovereign (gr. 1948)	Nasrullah	Nearco
			Mumtaz Begum
		Kong	Baytown
			Clang
	Mountain Path (b. 1948)	Bobsleigh	Gainsborough
			Toboggan
		Path of Peace	Winalot
			Grand Peace
FLATTERING (br. 1961)	Abernant (gr. 1946)	Owen Tudor	Hyperion
			Mary Tudor II
		Rustom Mahal	Rustom Pasha
			Mumtaz Mahal
	Flatter (ch. 1947)	Rockefella	Hyperion
			Rockfel
		Daring Miss	Felicitation
			Venturesome

424   HUNTERCOMBE 14 (b.c., January 23, 1967)

Bred by H. H. Renshaw.

Won 6 races, placed 5, £39,452, in England and France, at 2 and 3 years, incl. Middle Park Stakes, July Cup, Nunthorpe Stakes, July Stakes, Cornwallis Stakes, Prix de Seine-et-Oise; 2nd Prix de l'Abbaye de Longchamp, King's Stand Stakes, Gimcrack Stakes, Ascot 2,000 Guineas Trial Stakes.

DERRING-DO (b. 1961)	Darius (b. 1951)	Dante	Nearco
			Rosy Legend
		Yasna	Dastur
			Ariadne
	Sipsey Bridge (b. 1954)	Abernant	Owen Tudor
			Rustom Mahal
		Claudette	Chanteur II
			Nearly
ERGINA (br. 1957)	Fair Trial (ch. 1932)	Fairway	Phalaris
			Scapa Flow
		Lady Juror	Son-in-Law
			Lady Josephine
	Ballechin (br. 1949)	Straight Deal	Solario
			Good Deal
		Gilded	Golden Eagle
			Overture

425   HURRY HARRIET 2 (b.f., March 23, 1970)

Bred by Malcolm D. Thorp.

Won 7 races, placed 13, £75,315, in Ireland, England and France, from 2 to 5 years, incl. Champion Stakes, Pretty Polly Stakes (Curragh), Ballymoss Stakes, Whitehall Stakes; 2nd Blandford Stakes (twice), Desmond Stakes, Royal Whip Stakes, Prix Vermeille; 3rd Irish Guinness Oaks, Player-Wills Stakes.

YRRAH JR. (b. 1964)	Ribot (b. 1952)	Tenerani	Bellini
			Tofanella
		Romanella	El Greco
			Barbara Burrini
	Ola III (b. 1949)	Nakamuro	Cameronian
			Nogara
		Evviva	Navarro
			Sabla
SOMNAMBULA (b. 1961)	Chanteur II (b. 1942)	Chateau Bouscaut	Kircubbin
			Ramondie
		La Diva	Blue Skies
			La Traviata
	Sleeping Beauty II (b. 1951)	Bois Roussel	Vatout
			Plucky Liege
		Fast Beauty	Fastnet
			Dame de Beaute

426   IDLE WATERS 14 (b.f., May 19, 1975)

Bred by R. E. Crutchley.

Won 3 races, placed 9, £28,493, in England, at 2 and 3 years, incl. Park Hill Stakes; 2nd Cumberland Lodge Stakes; 3rd Princess Royal Stakes.

MILL REEF (b. 1968)	Never Bend (b. 1960)	Nasrullah	Nearco
			Mumtaz Begum
		Lalun	Djeddah
			Be Faithful
	Milan Mill (b. 1962)	Princequillo	Prince Rose
			Cosquilla
		Virginia Water	Count Fleet
			Red Ray
MIDSUMMERTIME (b. 1970)	Midsummer Night II (ch. 1957)	Djeddah	Djebel
			Djezima
		Night Sound	Mahmoud
			Gala Flight
	Lifetime (b. 1964)	Darius	Dante
			Yasna
		Life Sentence	Court Martial
			Borobella

427   **ILE DE BOURBON** 4 (br.c., May 23, 1975)

Bred by Mrs. Charles W. Engelhard, in U.S.A.

Won 5 races, placed 4, £175,173, in England, from 2 to 4 years, incl. King George VI and Queen Elizabeth Diamond Stakes, Coronation Cup, King Edward VII Stakes, Geoffrey Freer Stakes.

NIJINSKY (b. 1967)	Northern Dancer (b. 1961)	Nearctic	Nearco
			Lady Angela
		Natalma	Native Dancer
			Almahmoud
	Flaming Page (b. 1959)	Bull Page	Bull Lea
			Our Page
		Flaring Top	Menow
			Flaming Top
ROSELIERE (b. 1965)	Misti IV (b. 1958)	Medium	Meridien
			Melodie
		Mist	Tornado
			La Touche
	Peace Rose (gr. 1959)	Fastnet Rock	Ocean Swell
			Stone of Fortune
		La Paix	Seven Seas
			Anne de Bretagne

428   **ILIX** 14 (br.c., March 9, 1963)

Bred by Stall Wolkenstein, in Germany.

Won 7 races, placed 8, 230,788 DM., in Germany, from 2 to 5 years, incl. Deutsches Derby and Union-Rennen; 4th Preis von Europa.

ORSINI (br. 1954)	Ticino (b. 1939)	Athanasius	Ferro
			Athanasie
		Terra	Aditi
			Teufelsrose
	Oranien (b. 1949)	Nuvolari	Oleander
			Nereide
		Omladina	Athanasius
			Oblate
IVRESSE (br. 1955)	Nuccio (b. 1948)	Traghetto	Cavaliere d'Arpino
			Talma
		Nuvoletta	Muzio
			Neve
	Blue Kiss (br. 1947)	Pharis II	Pharos
			Carissima
		Blue Bear	Blenheim
			La Boni

429   **IMBERLINE** 8 (ch.f., April 7, 1957)

Bred by Baron Guy de Rothschild, in France.

Won 2 races, placed 3, £3,660, in France and England, at 2 and 3 years, incl. Prix Edgard de la Charme; 2nd Prix Vanteaux; 3rd Oaks Stakes.

OCARINA (ch. 1947)	Bubbles (ch. 1925)	La Farina	Sans Souci II
			Malatesta
		Spring Cleaning	Neil Gow
			Spring Night
	Montagnana (b. 1937)	Brantome	Blandford
			Vitamine
		Mauretania	Tetratema
			Lady Maureen
BARLEY CORN (b. 1950)	Hyperion (ch. 1930)	Gainsborough	Bayardo
			Rosedrop
		Selene	Chaucer
			Serenissima
	Schiaparelli (b. 1935)	Schiavoni	Swynford
			Serenissima
		Aileen	Nimbus
			Yveline

430   **INDIANA** 2 (b.c., May 4, 1961)

Bred by F. F. Tuthill.

Won 4 races, placed 6, £72,059, in England and France, from 2 to 4 years, incl. St. Leger Stakes, Great Voltigeur Stakes, Chester Vase, Ormonde Stakes; 2nd Derby Stakes, Yorkshire Cup, Grand Prix de Paris.

SAYAJIRAO (br. 1944)	Nearco (br. 1935)	Pharos	Phalaris
			Scapa Flow
		Nogara	Havresac II
			Catnip
	Rosy Legend (br. 1931)	Dark Legend	Dark Ronald
			Golden Legend
		Rosy Cheeks	St. Just
			Purity
WILLOW ANN (ch. 1942)	Solario (b. 1922)	Gainsborough	Bayardo
			Rosedrop
		Sun Worship	Sundridge
			Doctrine
	Court of Appeal (gr. 1931)	Apelle	Sardanapale
			Angelina
		Brown Princess	Tetratema
			Swagger Cane

431   **IN FIJAR** 4 (b.c., April 1, 1977)

Bred by Ted Waite, Jr., in U.S.A.

Won 3 races, placed 5, 758,000 fr., in France at 2 and 3 years, incl. Poule d'Essai des Poulains and Prix des Chenes; 3rd Prix Lupin and Prix d'Ispahan.

BOLD COMMANDER (b. 1960)	Bold Ruler (b. 1954)	Nasrullah	Nearco
			Mumtaz Begum
		Miss Disco	Discovery
			Outdone
	High Voltage (gr. 1952)	Ambiorix II	Tourbillon
			Lavendula II
		Dynamo	Menow
			Bransome
APACHE QUEEN (b. 1961)	Marshal at Arms (ch. 1950)	Court Martial	Fair Trial
			Instantaneous
		Sea Pride II	Admiral Drake
			Pride of Hainault
	Apache Love (b. 1951)	Apache	Alcazar
			Flying Song
		Love	Count Fleet
			First Love

432   **INFRA GREEN** 3 (ch.f., April 1, 1972)

Bred by Dooneen and Greenmount Studs, in Ireland.

Won 6 races, placed 7, 1,316,120 fr., in France, Italy and Ireland, from 2 to 5 years, incl. Prix Ganay, Gran Premio del Jockey Club, Prix Chloe, Prix de Malleret and Prix d'Astarté; 2nd Gran Premio di Milano, Prix de Sandringham and Prix de la Nonette; 3rd Prix Ganay and Prix d'Harcourt.

LASER LIGHT (ch. 1966)	Aureole (ch. 1950)	Hyperion	Gainsborough
			Selene
		Angelola	Donatello II
			Feola
	Ruby Laser (ch. 1961)	Red God	Nasrullah
			Spring Run
		Dilly Dilly	Windy City
			Lavender Walk
GREENBACK II (b. 1967)	Fric (br. 1952)	Vandale II	Plassy
			Vanille
		Fripe	Mehemet Ali
			Friponne
	Mrs. Green (b. 1960)	Honeyway	Fairway
			Honey Buzzard
		Brilliant Green	Niccolo Dell'Arca
			Faggot

433   **INKERMAN** 14 (b.c., April 4, 1975)

Bred by Mrs. John W. Hanes, in U.S.A.

Won 5 races, placed 9, £92,202, in Ireland, England and U.S.A., from 3 to 5 years, incl. Joe McGrath Memorial Stakes, Gallinule Stakes, Sunset H.; 2nd American H.; 3rd Blandford Stakes, Sunset H., American H.; 4th Irish Sweeps Derby.

VAGUELY NOBLE (b. 1965)	Vienna (ch. 1957)	Aureole	Hyperion / Angelola
		Turkish Blood	Turkhan / Rusk
	Noble Lassie (b. 1956)	Nearco	Pharos / Nogara
		Belle Sauvage	Big Game / Tropical Sun
CRIMEA II (ch. 1961)	Princequillo (b. 1940)	Prince Rose	Rose Prince / Indolence
		Cosquilla	Papyrus / Quick Thought
	Victoria Cross (ch. 1953)	Court Martial	Fair Trial / Instantaneous
		Ladycross	Mieuxce / Eleanor Cross

---

434   **IN REALITY** 21 (b.c., March 1, 1964)

Bred by Mrs. Frances A. Genter Stable, in U.S.A.

Won 14 races, placed 11, $795,824, in U.S.A., from 2 to 4 years, incl. Florida Derby, Jersey Derby, Pimlico Futurity, Fountain of Youth Stakes, John B. Campbell H., Metropolitan H. and Carter H.; 2nd Preakness Stakes, American Derby, New Hampshire Sweepstakes Classic, Cowdin Stakes, Sapling Stakes, Flamingo Stakes and Jerome H.; 3rd Seminole H. and Royal Palm H.

INTENTIONALLY (bl. 1956)	Intent (ch. 1948)	War Relic	Man o'War / Friar's Carse
		Liz F	Bubbling Over / Weno
	My Recipe (b. 1947)	Discovery	Display / Ariadne
		Perlette	Percentage / Escarpolette
MY DEAR GIRL (ch. 1957)	Rough'n Tumble (b. 1948)	Free for All	Questionnaire / Panay
		Roused	Bull Dog / Rude Awakening
	Iltis (b. 1947)	War Relic	Man o'War / Friar's Carse
		We Hail	Balladier / Clonaslee

---

435   **INTERMEZZO** 13 (b.c., February 3, 1966)

Bred by Citadel Stud Establishment.

Won 3 races, placed 6, £49,647, in England, from 2 to 4 years, incl. St. Leger Stakes; 2nd Observer Gold Cup, Hardwicke Stakes; 3rd Geoffrey Freer Stakes.

HORNBEAM (ch. 1953)	Hyperion (ch. 1930)	Gainsborough	Bayardo / Rosedrop
		Selene	Chaucer / Serenissima
	Thicket (b. 1947)	Nasrullah	Nearco / Mumtaz Begum
		Thorn Wood	Bois Roussel / Point Duty
PLAZA (b. 1958)	Persian Gulf (b. 1940)	Bahram	Blandford / Friar's Daughter
		Double Life	Bachelor's Double / Saint Joan
	Wild Success (b. 1949)	Niccolo Dell'Arca	Coronach / Nogara
		Lavinia	Bosworth / Ann Hathaway

---

436   **IRISH BALL** 8 (b.c., April 11, 1968)

Bred by E. Cruz-Valer and E. Coupey, in France.

Won 3 races, placed 7, £116,757, in England, Ireland, France and U.S.A., at 2 and 3 years, incl. Irish Sweeps Derby, Prix Daru; 2nd Washington D.C. International, Prix des Chenes; 3rd Derby Stakes, Prix Lupin.

BALDRIC II (b. 1961)	Round Table (b. 1954)	Princequillo	Prince Rose / Cosquilla
		Knight's Daughter	Sir Cosmo / Feola
	Two Cities (b. 1948)	Johnstown	Jamestown / La France
		Vienna	Menow / Valse
IRISH LASS II (b. 1962)	Sayajirao (br. 1944)	Nearco	Pharos / Nogara
		Rosy Legend	Dark Legend / Rosy Cheeks
	Scollata (b. 1952)	Niccolo Dell'Arca	Coronach / Nogara
		Cutaway	Fairway / Schiaparelli

---

437   **IRISH PLAYBOY** 2 (br.c., March 26, 1978)

Bred by R. A. Kingwell, in U.S.A.

Won 2 races, 249,000 fr., in France, at 2 years, incl. Prix Robert Papin.

IRISH CASTLE (b. 1967)	Bold Ruler (b. 1954)	Nasrullah	Nearco / Mumtaz Begum
		Miss Disco	Discovery / Outdone
	Castle Forbes (b. 1961)	Tulyar	Tehran / Neocracy
		Longford	Menow / Bold Irish
GLOBETROTTER (b. 1968)	Globemaster (b. 1958)	Heliopolis	Hyperion / Drift
		No Strings	Occupation / Irvana
	Anadem (b. 1954)	My Babu	Djebel / Perfume II
		Anne of Essex	Panorama / Queen of Essex

---

438   **IRISH RIVER** 1 (ch.c., April 2, 1976)

Bred by Mme. Raymond Adès, in France.

Won 10 races, placed 2, 2,705,000 fr., in France, at 2 and 3 years, incl. Prix Morny, Prix de la Salamandre, Grand Criterium, Poule d'Essai des Poulains, Prix d'Ispahan, Prix Jacques le Marois, Prix du Moulin de Longchamp and Prix de Fontainebleau; 3rd Prix Lupin; 4th Prix Robert Papin.

RIVERMAN (b. 1969)	Never Bend (br. 1960)	Nasrullah	Nearco / Mumtaz Begum
		Lalun	Djeddah / Be Faithful
	River Lady (b. 1963)	Prince John	Princequillo / Not Afraid
		Nile Lily	Roman / Azalea
IRISH STAR (b. 1960)	Klairon (b. 1952)	Clarion III	Djebel / Columba
		Kalmia	Kantar / Sweet Lavender
	Botany Bay (b. 1954)	East Side	Orwell / Vlasta
		Black Brook	Black Devil / Source Sucree

439   **IRVINE** 9 (gr.c., March 19, 1968)

Bred by Brigadier and Mrs. C. M. Stewart, in Ireland.

Won 12 races, placed 9, £40,515, in England, Italy, Norway and Germany, from 3 to 7 years, incl. Premio Roma, Jockey Club Cup and Oslo Cup; 2nd Jockey Club Stakes; 3rd Ascot Gold Cup, Premio Roma and Grosser Hansa Preis.

SEA HAWK II (gr. 1963)	Herbager (b. 1956)	Vandale II	Plassy / Vanille
		Flagette	Escamillo / Fidgette
	Sea Nymph (gr. 1957)	Free Man	Norseman / Fantine
		Sea Spray	Ocean Swell / Pontoon
ETOILE DE FRANCE (b. 1957)	Arctic Star (br. 1942)	Nearco	Pharos / Nogara
		Serena	Winalot / Charmione
	Miss France (b. 1946)	Jock II	Asterus / Naic
		Nafah	Abjer / Flower

440   **I SAY** 8 (br.c., May 23, 1962)

Bred by F. F. Tuthill.

Won 5 races, placed 2, £23,827, in England, at 3 and 4 years, incl. Coronation Cup, White Rose Stakes; 3rd Derby Stakes, Hardwicke Stakes.

SAYAJIRAO (br. 1944)	Nearco (br. 1935)	Pharos	Phalaris / Scapa Flow
		Nogara	Havresac II / Catnip
	Rosy Legend (br. 1931)	Dark Legend	Dark Ronald / Golden Legend
		Rosy Cheeks	St. Just / Purity
ISETTA (b. 1943)	Morland (b. 1934)	Gainsborough	Bayardo / Rosedrop
		Lichen	Manna / Loweswater
	Isolda (b. 1933)	Rustom Pasha	Son-in-Law / Cos
		Yveline	Gardefeu / Photime

441   **ISOPACH** 23 (b.c., April 1, 1977)

Bred by Nelson Bunker Hunt, in U.S.A.

Won 9 races, placed 6, 168,730,000 L., in Italy, at 2 and 3 years, incl. Premio Emilio Turati, Premio Pisa, Premio Natale di Roma, Premio Nearco and Premio Vittorio di Capua; 2nd Gran Criterium, Premio Chiusura and Premio Ribot; 3rd Premio Chiusura.

REVIEWER (b. 1966)	Bold Ruler (b. 1954)	Nasrullah	Nearco / Mumtaz Begum
		Miss Disco	Discovery / Outdone
	Broadway (b. 1959)	Hasty Road	Roman / Traffic Court
		Flitabout	Challedon / Bird Flower
KLEPTO (ch. 1970)	No Robbery (b. 1960)	Swaps	Khaled / Iron Reward
		Bimlette	Bimelech / Bloodroot
	Blue Blur (b. 1960)	Beau Gar	Count Fleet / Bellesoeur
		Blue Grouse	Vezzano / L'Oiseau Bleu

442   **IT'S IN THE AIR** 4 (b.f., February 10, 1976)

Bred by Happy Valley Farm, in U.S.A.

Won 12 races, placed 14, $818,671, in U.S.A., from 2 to 4 years, incl. Alabama Stakes, Delaware Oaks, Vanity H. (twice), Ruffian H., Oak Leaf Stakes, Arlington-Washington Lassie Stakes and El Encino Stakes; 2nd Hollywood Oaks, Frizette Stakes, Maskette H. and Milady H. (twice); 3rd Santa Susana Stakes, La Canada Stakes, Beldame Stakes, Ruffian H. and Santa Ynez Stakes.

MR. PROSPECTOR (b. 1970)	Raise a Native (ch. 1961)	Native Dancer	Polynesian / Geisha
		Raise You	Case Ace / Lady Glory
	Gold Digger (b. 1962)	Nashua	Nasrullah / Segula
		Sequence	Count Fleet / Miss Dogwood
A WIND IS RISING (b. 1969)	Francis S (ch. 1957)	Royal Charger	Nearco / Sun Princess
		Blue Eyed Momo	War Admiral / Big Event
	Queen Nasra (b. 1952)	Nasrullah	Nearco / Mumtaz Begum
		Bayborough	Stimulus / Scarborough

443   **IVANJICA** 12 (b.f., May 3, 1972)

Bred by Claiborne Farm, in U.S.A.

Won 6 races, placed 4, 2,798,332 fr., in France and U.S.A., from 2 to 4 years, incl. Prix de l'Arc de Triomphe, Poule d'Essai des Pouliches, Prix Vermeille, Prix du Prince d'Orange and Prix de la Nonette; 2nd Prix d'Ispahan; 3rd Prix Ganay, Prix Vanteaux and Washington D.C. International.

SIR IVOR (b. 1965)	Sir Gaylord (b. 1959)	Turn-to	Royal Charger / Source Sucree
		Somethingroyal	Princequillo / Imperatrice
	Attica (ch. 1953)	Mr. Trouble	Mahmoud / Motto
		Athenia	Pharamond / Salaminia
ASTUCE (b. 1964)	Vieux Manoir (b. 1947)	Brantome	Blandford / Vitamine
		Vieille Maison	Finglas / Vieille Canaille
	Ashleen (b. 1956)	Alizier	Teleferique / Alizarine
		Asheratt	Sunny Trace / Fee Esterel

444   **JAAZEIRO** 14 (b.c., March 30, 1975)

Bred by Carelaine Stable, in U.S.A.

Won 5 races, placed 3, £109,956, in England, France and Ireland, at 2 and 3 years, incl. Irish 2,000 Guineas, Sussex Stakes, St. James's Palace Stakes, Prix des Chenes; 3rd Waterford Crystal Mile; 4th Grand Criterium.

SHAM (b. 1970)	Pretense (br. 1963)	Endeavour II	British Empire / Himalaya
		Imitation	Hyperion / Flattery
	Sequoia (b. 1955)	Princequillo	Prince Rose / Cosquilla
		The Squaw II	Sickle / Minnewaska
RULE FORMI (ch. 1969)	Forli (ch. 1963)	Aristophanes	Hyperion / Commotion
		Trevisa	Advocate / Veneta
	Miss Nasrullah (ch. 1958)	Nasrullah	Nearco / Mumtaz Begum
		Not Afraid	Count Fleet / Banish Fear

445   JACINTH 21 (b.f., April 23, 1970)

Bred by William Hill Studs.

Won 5 races, placed 2, £44,062, in England, at 2 and 3 years, incl. Cheveley Park Stakes, Coronation Stakes, Falmouth Stakes, Goodwood Mile; 2nd 1,000 Guineas Stakes, Sussex Stakes.

RED GOD (ch. 1954)	Nasrullah (b. 1940)	Nearco	Pharos
			Nogara
		Mumtaz Begum	Blenheim
			Mumtaz Mahal
	Spring Run (b. 1948)	Menow	Pharamond
			Alcibiades
		Boola Brook	Bull Dog
			Brookdale
JAFFA (b. 1965)	Right Royal V (br. 1958)	Owen Tudor	Hyperion
			Mary Tudor II
		Bastia	Tornado or Victrix II
			Barberybush
	Mistress Gwynne (ch. 1955)	Chanteur II	Chateau Bouscaut
			La Diva
		Daring Miss	Felicitation
			Venturesome

446   JAIPUR 8 (b.c., April 8, 1959)

Bred by Erdenheim Farms Co., in U.S.A.

Won 10 races, placed 6, $618,926, in U.S.A., from 2 to 4 years, incl. Belmont Stakes, Jersey Derby, Travers Stakes, Gotham Stakes, Withers Stakes, Hopeful Stakes and Cowdin Stakes; 2nd Champagne Stakes, Futurity Stakes, Saratoga Special, Woodward Stakes, Roamer H. and Palm Beach H.

NASRULLAH (b. 1940)	Nearco (br. 1935)	Pharos	Phalaris
			Scapa Flow
		Nogara	Havresac II
			Catnip
	Mumtaz Begum (b. 1932)	Blenheim	Blandford
			Malva
		Mumtaz Mahal	The Tetrarch
			Lady Josephine
RARE PERFUME (b. 1947)	Eight Thirty (ch. 1936)	Pilate	Friar Rock
			Herodias
		Dinner Time	High Time
			Seaplane
	Fragrance (b. 1942)	Sir Gallahad III	Teddy
			Plucky Liege
		Rosebloom	Chicle
			Rowes Bud

447   JAVELOT 16 (b.c., January 31, 1956)

Bred by Baron G. de Waldner, in France.

Won 7 races, placed 11, £40,211, in France and England, from 2 to 5 years, incl. Prix Ganay, Prix de Fontainebleau, Prix Dollar, Prix d'Ispahan, Eclipse Stakes; 2nd Prix Lupin, Prix d'Harcourt, Eclipse Stakes; 3rd Prix d'Ispahan, Champion Stakes, Prix Edmond Blanc; 4th Prix du Jockey Club.

FAST FOX (br. 1947)	Fastnet (b. or br. 1933)	Pharos	Phalaris
			Scapa Flow
		Tatoule	Alcantara II
			Titanite
	Foxcraft (b. 1940)	Foxhunter	Foxlaw
			Trimestral
		Philomene	Phalaris
			Hythe
DJAINA (br. 1944)	Djebel (b. 1937)	Tourbillon	Ksar
			Durban
		Loika	Gay Crusader
			Coeur à Coeur
	Fille d'Amour (br. 1932)	Asterus	Teddy
			Astrella
		Amourette IX	Dominion
			Whiba

448   JIMMY REPPIN 7 (ch.c., March 16, 1965)

Bred by S. H. J. Bates

Won 9 races, placed 7, £49,034, in England and France, from 2 to 4 years, incl. Sussex Stakes, Queen Elizabeth II Stakes, Hungerford Stakes (twice), Wills Mile, Prix Perth; 2nd Lockinge Stakes, Coronation Stakes, Queen Anne Stakes; 3rd 2,000 Guineas Stakes, Wills Mile.

MIDSUMMER NIGHT II (ch. 1957)	Djeddah (ch. 1945)	Djebel	Tourbillon
			Loika
		Djezima	Asterus
			Heldifann
	Night Sound (b. 1946)	Mahmoud	Blenheim
			Mah Mahal
		Gala Flight	Sir Gallahad III
			Starflight
SWEET MOLLY (ch. 1958)	Chamier (ch. 1950)	Chamossaire	Precipitation
			Snowberry
		Therapia	Panorama
			Silvonessa
	Cockles and Mussels (ch. 1950)	Owenstown or Walvis Bay	Fairway
			Cachalot
		Mulligatawny	Hot Night
			Multijuga

449   JOHN DE COOMBE 4 (gr.c., February 25, 1975)

Bred by Windwhistle Stud, in England.

Won 3 races, placed 3, £45,761, in England and France at 2 and 3 years, incl. Prix de la Salamandre.

MOULTON (b. 1969)	Pardao (ch. 1958)	Pardal	Pharis II
			Adargatis
		Three Weeks	Big Game
			Eleanor Cross
	Close Up (br. 1958)	Nearula	Nasrullah
			Respite
		Horama	Panorama
			Lady of Aran
MADAM CLARE (gr. 1965)	Ennis (b. 1954)	Golden Cloud	Gold Bridge
			Rainstorm
		First House	Link Boy
			Early Doors
	Madame De (gr. 1953)	Vilmorin	Gold Bridge
			Queen of the Meadows
		Spun Silk	Coup de Lyon
			Ozora

450   JOHN HENRY 8 (b.g., March 9, 1975)

Bred by Golden Chance Farm, Inc., in U.S.A.

Won 21 races, placed 18, $1,224,780, in U.S.A., from 2 to 5 years, incl. San Juan Capistrano Invitational H., Oak Tree Invitational H., San Luis Rey Stakes, Hollywood Invitational H., Hialeah Turf Cup, Brighton Beach H., San Marcos H., San Gabriel H. and Round Table H.; 2nd Jockey Club Gold Cup, Bowling Green H., Carleton F. Burke H. and Lexington H.; 3rd Turf Classic, Volante H. and Lamplighter H.

OLE BOB BOWERS (b. 1963)	Prince Blessed (b. 1957)	Princequillo	Prince Rose
			Cosquilla
		Dog Blessed	Bull Dog
			Blessed Again
	Blue Jeans (b. 1950)	Bull Lea	Bull Dog
			Rose Leaves
		Blue Grass	Blue Larkspur
			Camelot
ONCE DOUBLE (b. or br. 1967)	Double Jay (br. 1944)	Balladier	Black Toney
			Blue Warbler
		Broomshot	Whisk Broom II
			Centre Shot
	Intent One (ch. 1955)	Intent	War Relic
			Liz F
		Dusty Legs	Mahmoud
			Dustemall

451   **JOHNNY D** 9 (b.c., February 28, 1974)

Bred by Miss Peggy Augustus, in U.S.A.

Won 7 races, placed 8, $371,256, in U.S.A. and Canada, at 2 and 3 years, incl. Washington D.C. International, Turf Classic and Lexington H.; 3rd Canadian International Championship, Man o'War Stakes and Lawrence Realization Stakes.

STAGE DOOR JOHNNY (ch. 1965)	Prince John (ch. 1953)	Princequillo	Prince Rose / Cosquilla
		Not Afraid	Count Fleet / Banish Fear
	Peroxide Blonde (ch. 1960)	Ballymoss	Mossborough / Indian Call
		Folie Douce	Caldarium / Folle Nuit
DUSK (b. 1968)	Olden Times (b. 1958)	Relic	War Relic / Bridal Colors
		Djenne	Djebel / Teza
	Tropic Star (ch. 1959)	Tropique	Fontenay / Aurore Boreale
		Patricia's Star	Prince Chevalier / Noah's Ark

---

452   **J. O. TOBIN** 3 (br.c., March 28, 1974)

Bred by George A. Pope, Jr., in U.S.A.

Won 12 races, placed 4, $659,555, in England, France and U.S.A., from 2 to 4 years, incl. Richmond Stakes, Laurent Perrier Champagne Stakes, Swaps Stakes, Californian Stakes, San Bernardino H., Los Angeles H. and Malibu Stakes; 2nd San Fernando Stakes; 3rd Grand Criterium and Charles H. Strub Stakes.

NEVER BEND (b. 1960)	Nasrullah (b. 1940)	Nearco	Pharos / Nogara
		Mumtaz Begum	Blenheim / Mumtaz Mahal
	Lalun (b. 1952)	Djeddah	Djebel / Djezima
		Be Faithful	Bimelech / Bloodroot
HILL SHADE (br. 1965)	Hillary (br. 1952)	Khaled	Hyperion / Eclair
		Snow Bunny	Boswell / La Rose
	Penumbra (b. 1955)	Imperium	Piping Rock / Imperatrice
		Moonrise	Moonlight Run / Seventh Heaven

---

453   **JULIETTE MARNY** 6 (b.f., March 20, 1972)

Bred by Fonthill Stud.

Won 3 races, placed 2, £74,460, in England and Ireland, at 2 and 3 years, incl. Oaks Stakes, Irish Guinness Oaks, Ladbroke Oaks Trial Stakes; 3rd Yorkshire Oaks. Also won Princess Elizabeth Stakes but disqualified.

BLAKENEY (b. 1966)	Hethersett (b. 1959)	Hugh Lupus	Djebel / Sakountala
		Bride Elect	Big Game / Netherton Maid
	Windmill Girl (b. 1961)	Hornbeam	Hyperion / Thicket
		Chorus Beauty	Chanteur II / Neberna
SET FREE (b. 1964)	Worden II (ch. 1949)	Wild Risk	Rialto / Wild Violet
		Sans Tares	Sind / Tara
	Emancipation (b. 1954)	Le Sage	Chamossaire / Miss Know All
		Fair Freedom	Fair Trial / Democratie

---

454   **JULIO MARINER** 6 (b.c., January 24, 1975)

Bred by Fonthill Stud.

Won 3 races, placed 4, £75,090, in England, at 2 and 3 years, incl. St. Leger Stakes; 2nd William Hill Futurity Stakes, Mecca-Dante Stakes.

BLAKENEY (b. 1966)	Hethersett (b. 1959)	Hugh Lupus	Djebel / Sakountala
		Bride Elect	Big Game / Netherton Maid
	Windmill Girl (b. 1961)	Hornbeam	Hyperion / Thicket
		Chorus Beauty	Chanteur II / Neberna
SET FREE (b. 1964)	Worden II (ch. 1949)	Wild Risk	Rialto / Wild Violet
		Sans Tares	Sind / Tara
	Emancipation (b. 1954)	Le Sage	Chamossaire / Miss Know All
		Fair Freedom	Fair Trial / Democratie

---

455   **JUNIUS** 3 (br.c., March 15, 1976)

Bred by Warner L. Jones, Jr., in U.S.A.

Won 3 races, placed 1, £32,863, in Ireland and England, at 2 years, incl. William Hill Middle Park Stakes.

RAJA BABA (b. 1968)	Bold Ruler (b. 1954)	Nasrullah	Nearco / Mumtaz Begum
		Miss Disco	Discovery / Outdone
	Missy Baba (b. 1958)	Tulyar or My Babu	Djebel / Perfume II
		Uvira	Umidwar / Lady Lawless
SOLID THOUGHT (ch. 1957)	Solidarity (b. 1945)	Alibhai	Hyperion / Teresina
		Jerrybuilt	Empire Builder / Varnish
	Unforgettable (ch. 1951)	Burning Dream	Bimelech / By Mistake
		Cantadora	Case Ace / Comeover

---

456   **KALAMOUN** 9 (gr.c., April 30, 1970)

Bred by H.H. Aga Khan, in England.

Won 4 races, placed 5, 1,564,777 fr., in France and England, at 2 and 3 years, incl. Poule d'Essai des Poulains, Prix Lupin and Prix Jacques le Marois; 2nd Prix du Moulin de Longchamp, Prix de Fontainebleau and Prix Thomas Bryon; 4th Observer Gold Cup.

ZEDDAAN (gr. 1965)	Grey Sovereign (gr. 1948)	Nasrullah	Nearco / Mumtaz Begum
		Kong	Baytown / Clang
	Vareta (gr. 1953)	Vilmorin	Gold Bridge / Queen of the Meadows
		Veronique II	Mon Talisman / Volubilis
KHAIRUNISSA (gr. 1960)	Prince Bio (b. 1941)	Prince Rose	Rose Prince / Indolence
		Biologie	Bacteriophage / Eponge
	Palariva (gr. 1953)	Palestine	Fair Trial / Una
		Rivaz	Nearco / Mumtaz Begum

457   KAMICIA 9 (b.f., April 22, 1974)

Bred by Mme. H. Rabatel, in France.

Won 4 races, placed 5, 1,071,000 fr., in France, from 2 to 4 years, incl. Prix Vermeille, Criterium des Pouliches and Prix de la Nonette; 2nd Prix de la Grotte; 3rd Prix de Malleret and Prix Exbury.

KASHMIR II (b./br. 1963)	Tudor Melody (br. 1956)	Tudor Minstrel	Owen Tudor
			Sansonnet
		Matelda	Dante
			Fairly Hot
	Queen of Speed (b. 1950)	Blue Train	Blue Peter
			Sun Chariot
		Bishopscourt	His Grace
			Jurisdiction
MICIA (ch. 1967)	Mincio (br. 1957)	Relic	War Relic
			Bridal Colors
		Merise	Le Pacha
			Miraflore
	Furka (b. 1954)	Tantieme	Deux pour Cent
			Terka
		Francia	Jock II
			Sameya

458   KANDIA 5 (b.f., February 23, 1972)

Bred by Frau I. Bscher and Prinzessin Oettingen-Wallerstein, in Germany.

Won 5 races, placed 13, 334,200 DM., in Germany, from 2 to 4 years, incl. Aral Pokal and Ludwig Goebels Erinnerungsrennen; 2nd Grosser Preis von Nordrhein-Westfalen, Grosser Hansa Preis, Grosser Preis der Stadt Gelsenkirchen and Deutscher Stutenpreis; 3rd Aral Pokal and Grosser Preis von Dusseldorf; 4th Grosser Preis von Baden.

LUCIANO (br. 1964)	Henry the Seventh (ch. 1958)	King of the Tudors	Tudor Minstrel
			Glen Line
		Vestal Girl	Fairy Prince
			Vestalia
	Light Arctic (br. 1954)	Arctic Prince	Prince Chevalier
			Arctic Sun
		Incandescent	Pont l'Eveque
			Invisible
KRONUNGSGABE (bl. 1963)	Orsini (br. 1954)	Ticino	Athanasius
			Terra
		Oranien	Nuvolari
			Omladina
	Kronung (b. 1957)	Olymp	Arjaman
			Olympiade
		Kaiserkrone	Nebelwerfer
			Kaiserwurde

459   KARABAS 10 (b.c., April 4, 1965)

Bred by Collinstown Stud.

Won 11 races, placed 6, £103,387, in Ireland, England, France and U.S.A., from 2 to 5 years, incl. Hardwicke Stakes, Prix du Conseil Municipal, La Coupe de Maisons-Laffitte, Washington D.C. International; 2nd Eclipse Stakes, Prix Dollar; 3rd King Edward VII Stakes; 4th King George VI and Queen Elizabeth Stakes.

WORDEN II (ch. 1949)	Wild Risk (b. 1940)	Rialto	Rabelais
			La Grelee
		Wild Violet	Blandford
			Wood Violet
	Sans Tares (ch. 1939)	Sind	Solario
			Mirawala
		Tara	Teddy
			Jean Gow
FAIR SHARE (b. 1957)	Tantieme (b. 1947)	Deux pour Cent	Deiri
			Dix pour Cent
		Terka	Indus
			La Furka
	Fair Linda (ch. 1946)	Fair Trial	Fairway
			Lady Juror
		Ortlinde	Hyperion
			Brunhild

460   KASHMIR II 9 (b. or br.c., April 27, 1963)

Bred by Mrs. A. Levins Moore.

Won 5 races, placed 4, £53,441, in France and England, at 2 and 3 years, incl. Prix Robert Papin, 2,000 Guineas Stakes; 2nd Prix La Rochette, Prix de la Foret; 3rd Prix Jean Prat, Prix Morny.

TUDOR MELODY (br. 1956)	Tudor Minstrel (br. 1944)	Owen Tudor	Hyperion
			Mary Tudor II
		Sansonnet	Sansovino
			Lady Juror
	Matelda (br. 1947)	Dante	Nearco
			Rosy Legend
		Fairly Hot	Solario
			Fair Cop
QUEEN OF SPEED (b. 1950)	Blue Train (ch. 1944)	Blue Peter	Fairway
			Fancy Free
		Sun Chariot	Hyperion
			Clarence
	Bishopscourt (br. 1945)	His Grace	Blandford
			Malva
		Jurisdiction	Abbots Trace
			Lady Juror

461   KAUAI KING A4 (br.c., April 3, 1963)

Bred by Dr. Frank A. O'Keefe, in U.S.A.

Won 9 races, placed 3, $381,397, in U.S.A., at 2 and 3 years, incl. Kentucky Derby, Preakness Stakes, Governor's Gold Cup and Fountain of Youth Stakes; 4th Belmont Stakes.

NATIVE DANCER (gr. 1950)	Polynesian (br. 1942)	Unbreakable	Sickle
			Blue Glass
		Black Polly	Polymelian
			Black Queen
	Geisha (ro. 1943)	Discovery	Display
			Ariadne
		Miyako	John P. Grier
			La Chica
SWEEP IN (b. 1942)	Blenheim (br. 1927)	Blandford	Swynford
			Blanche
		Malva	Charles O'Malley
			Wild Arum
	Sweepesta (b. 1925)	Sweep	Ben Brush
			Pink Domino
		Celesta	Sempronius
			Rezia

462   KEBAH 4 (b.c., 1966)

Bred by Mme. Leon Volterra, in Ireland.

Won 6 races, placed 11, 640,895 fr., in France, from 2 to 5 years, incl. Prix de la Salamandre; 2nd La Coupe de Maisons-Laffitte; 3rd Prix Robert Papin and Prix Henry Delamarre. Also won 1 race, placed 1, 19,000 fr., over hurdles in France, at 4 and 5 years.

BEL BARAKA (ch. 1955)	Worden II (ch. 1949)	Wild Risk	Rialto
			Wild Violet
		Sans Tares	Sind
			Tara
	Fleur des Neiges (ch. 1947)	Norseman	Umidwar
			Tara
		Avila	Astrophel
			Sevilla
KLAINIA (b. 1960)	Klairon (b. 1952)	Clarion III	Djebel
			Columba
		Kalmia	Kantar
			Sweet Lavender
	Kalitka (b. 1954)	Tourment	Tourbillon
			Fragment
		Princesse d'Amour	Prince Bio
			Vers l'Amour

463　　　　**KELSO** 20 (br.g., April 4, 1957)

Bred by Mrs. Richard C. du Pont, in U.S.A.

Won 39 races, placed 14, $1,977,896, in U.S.A., from 2 to 9 years, incl. Jockey Club Gold Cup (5 times), Woodward Stakes (3 times), Washington D.C. International, Whitney Stakes (3 times), Aqueduct Stakes (twice), Suburban H. (twice), Brooklyn H., Metropolitan H., Stymie H. (twice), Hawthorne Gold Cup, Lawrence Realization, Discovery H., Jerome H., Gulfstream Park H., John B. Campbell H., Seminole H. and Nassau County H.; 2nd Washington D.C. International (3 times), Woodward Stakes, Suburban H. (twice), Monmouth H. (twice), Man o'War Stakes and Widener H.; 3rd Brooklyn H.

YOUR HOST (ch. 1947)	Alibhai (ch. 1938)	Hyperion	Gainsborough / Selene
		Teresina	Tracery / Blue Tit
	Boudoir (gr. 1938)	Mahmoud	Blenheim / Mah Mahal
		Kampala	Clarissimus / La Soupe II
MAID OF FLIGHT (br. 1951)	Count Fleet (br. 1940)	Reigh Count	Sunreigh / Contessina
		Quickly	Haste / Stephanie
	Maidoduntreath (br. 1939)	Man o'War	Fair Play / Mahubah
		Mid Victorian	Victorian / Black Betty

464　　　　**KENMARE** 1 (gr.c., May 5, 1975)

Bred by Baron Guy de Rothschild, in France.

Won 6 races, placed 2, 675,000 fr., in France, at 2 and 3 years, incl. Prix Jacques le Marois, Prix Thomas Bryon and Prix de Fontainebleau; 3rd Prix de la Salamandre; 4th Poule d'Essai des Poulains.

KALAMOUN (gr. 1970)	Zeddaan (gr. 1965)	Grey Sovereign	Nasrullah / Kong
		Vareta	Vilmorin / Veronique II
	Khairunissa (gr. 1960)	Prince Bio	Prince Rose / Biologie
		Palariva	Palestine / Rivaz
BELLE OF IRELAND (ch. 1964)	Milesian (b. 1953)	My Babu	Djebel / Perfume II
		Oatflake	Coup de Lyon / Avena
	Belle of the Ball (br. 1958)	Nearula	Nasrullah / Respite
		Geifang Belle	Big Game / Foxtrot

465　　　　**KENNEDY ROAD** 9 (b.c., April 18, 1968)

Bred by Angus Glen Farm, in Canada.

Won 17 races, placed 15, $481,007, in Canada and U.S.A., from 2 to 5 years, incl. Hollywood Gold Cup, Queen's Plate, Cup and Saucer Stakes, Grey H., Dominion Day H. and San Antonio Stakes; 2nd Coronation Futurity, Marine Stakes, Canadian Maturity Stakes, Californian Stakes, Santa Anita H., San Carlos H. and San Pasqual H.; 3rd Prince of Wales Stakes and Lakeside H.

VICTORIA PARK (b. 1957)	Chop Chop (b. 1940)	Flares	Gallant Fox / Flambino
		Sceptical	Buchan / Clodagh
	Victoriana (b. 1952)	Windfields	Bunty Lawless / Nandi
		Iribelle	Osiris II / Belmona
NEARIS (ch. 1964)	Nearctic (br. 1954)	Nearco	Pharos / Nogara
		Lady Angela	Hyperion / Sister Sarah
	Bolaris (br. 1946)	Fairaris	Fair Trial / Nunnery
		Bold Fay	Bull Dog / Busy Fairy

466　　　　**KESAR QUEEN** 11 (b.f., March 19, 1973)

Bred by Shawnee Farm, in U.S.A.

Won 4 races, placed 7, £44,060, in England, France and U.S.A., from 2 to 4 years, incl. Coronation Stakes; 2nd Prix de la Grotte, Prix de Sandringham; 3rd 1,000 Guineas Stakes, Prix de l'Opera.

NASHUA (b. 1952)	Nasrullah (b. 1940)	Nearco	Pharos / Nogara
		Mumtaz Begum	Blenheim / Mumtaz Mahal
	Segula (b. 1942)	Johnstown	Jamestown / La France
		Sekhmet	Sardanapale / Prosopopee
MEADOW SAFFRON (b. 1964)	High Perch (ch. 1956)	Alycidon	Donatello II / Aurora
		Phaetonia	Nearco / Phaetusa
	Meadow Music (b. 1956)	Tom Fool	Menow / Gaga
		Miss Grillo	Rolando / Cedulilla

467　　　　**KEY TO THE MINT** 2 (b.c., March 9, 1969)

Bred by Paul Mellon, in U.S.A.

Won 14 races, placed 7, $576,015, in U.S.A., from 2 to 4 years, incl. Woodward Stakes, Brooklyn H., Suburban H., Travers Stakes, Whitney Stakes, Withers Stakes, Excelsior H. and Remsen Stakes; 2nd Jockey Club Gold Cup, Metropolitan H. and Cowdin Stakes; 3rd Preakness Stakes and Garden State Stakes; 4th Belmont Stakes.

GRAUSTARK (ch. 1963)	Ribot (b. 1952)	Tenerani	Bellini / Tofanella
		Romanella	El Greco / Barbara Burrini
	Flower Bowl (b. 1952)	Alibhai	Hyperion / Teresina
		Flower Bed	Beau Pere / Boudoir
KEY BRIDGE (b. 1959)	Princequillo (b. 1940)	Prince Rose	Rose Prince / Indolence
		Cosquilla	Papyrus / Quick Thought
	Blue Banner (b. 1952)	War Admiral	Man o'War / Brushup
		Risque Blue	Blue Larkspur / Risque

468　　　　**KHALKIS** 5 (b.c., March 30, 1960)

Bred by S. Macey.

Won 3 races, placed 2, £22,634, in England and Ireland, from 2 to 4 years, incl. Eclipse Stakes, Gladness Stakes, Wills Gold Flake Stakes; 2nd Coronation Cup; 3rd Coronation Stakes.

VIMY (b. 1952)	Wild Risk (b. 1940)	Rialto	Rabelais / La Grelee
		Wild Violet	Blandford / Wood Violet
	Mimi (b. 1943)	Black Devil	Sir Gallahad III / La Palina
		Mignon	Epinard / Mammee
MERRY XMAS (ch. 1951)	Chamossaire (ch. 1942)	Precipitation	Hurry On / Double Life
		Snowberry	Cameronian / Myrobella
	Merry Perrin (b. 1942)	Hyperion	Gainsborough / Selene
		Merry Vixen	Sir Gallahad III / Medora II

469 KILIJARO 11 (b.f., February 8, 1976)

Bred by Irish National Stud Co. Ltd., in Ireland.

Won 8 races, placed 10, £224,821, in Ireland, England, France and U.S.A., from 2 to 4 years, incl. Prix du Moulin de Longchamp, Prix Quincey, Prix de Meautry, Prix de Seine-et-Oise, Patrick S. Gallagher Phoenix Stakes and Yellow Ribbon Stakes; 2nd Queen Mary Stakes, William Hill Cheveley Park Stakes, Prix de l'Abbaye de Longchamp, Prix de la Foret and Prix Mercedes; 3rd Prix de la Foret and Prix Maurice de Gheest.

AFRICAN SKY (b. 1970)	Sing Sing (b. 1957)	Tudor Minstrel	Owen Tudor / Sansonnet
		Agin the Law	Portlaw / Revolte
	Sweet Caroline (b. 1954)	Nimbus	Nearco / Kong
		Lackaday	Bobsleigh / Lackadaisy
MANFILIA (b. 1968)	Mandamus (br. 1960)	Petition	Fair Trial / Art Paper
		Great Fun	Big Game / Merry Devon
	Spare Filly (b. 1961)	Beau Sabreur	His Highness / Mashaq
		La Pucelle	Prince Chevalier / Dainty Miss

470 KING PELLINORE 5 (b.c., May 3, 1972)

Bred by A. B. Hancock, Jr., in U.S.A.

Won 11 races, placed 6, $625,157, in U.S.A., Ireland and England, from 2 to 5 years, incl. Gallinule Stakes, Blandford Stakes, Champions Invitational H., Oak Tree Invitational Stakes, American H. and Carleton F. Burke H.; 2nd St. Leger Stakes, Irish Sweeps Derby, Sunset H. and San Luis Rey Stakes; 3rd Santa Anita H.

ROUND TABLE (b. 1954)	Princequillo (b. 1940)	Prince Rose	Rose Prince / Indolence
		Cosquilla	Papyrus / Quick Thought
	Knight's Daughter (b. 1941)	Sir Cosmo	The Boss / Ayn Hali
		Feola	Friar Marcus / Aloe
THONG (b. 1964)	Nantallah (br. 1953)	Nasrullah	Nearco / Mumtaz Begum
		Shimmer	Flares / Broad Ripple
	Rough Shod (b. 1944)	Gold Bridge	Swynford or Golden Boss / Flying Diadem
		Dalmary	Blandford / Simon's Shoes

471 KING'S COMPANY 13 (ch.c., March 24, 1968)

Bred by G. A. Harris.

Won 5 races, placed 3, £22,132, in Ireland and England, at 2 and 3 years, incl. Irish 2,000 Guineas, National Stakes (Curragh), Cork and Orrery Stakes; 2nd Tetrarch Stakes.

KING'S TROOP (b. 1957)	Princely Gift (b. 1951)	Nasrullah	Nearco / Mumtaz Begum
		Blue Gem	Blue Peter / Sparkle
	Equiria (b. 1946)	Atout Maitre	Vatout / Royal Mistress
		Epona	Portlaw / Jury
MISS STEPHEN (ch. 1955)	Stephen Paul (br. 1948)	Panorama	Sir Cosmo / Happy Climax
		Paradise	Dastur / Wandsworth
	Bright Set (ch. 1950)	Denturius	Gold Bridge / La Solfatara
		Firelight	Signal Light / Four Fires

472 KLAIRVIMY 3 (ch.c., April 30, 1970)

Bred by A. G. Allen (Ireland) Ltd.

Won 12 races, placed 8, £47,304, in Ireland, England, Italy, Switzerland and Germany, from 2 to 5 years, incl. King Edward VII Stakes, Royal Whip Stakes, Grosser Preis von St. Moritz; 2nd Gran Premio Città di Napoli; 3rd Player-Wills Stakes, Hardwicke Stakes, Preis von Europa, Premio Roma; 4th Irish 2,000 Guineas Stakes.

KLAIRON (b. 1952)	Clarion III (b. 1944)	Djebel	Tourbillon / Loika
		Columba	Colorado / Gay Bird
	Kalmia (b. 1931)	Kantar	Alcantara II / Karabe
		Sweet Lavender	Swynford / Marchetta
VIMY LINE (b. 1963)	Vimy (b. 1952)	Wild Risk	Rialto / Wild Violet
		Mimi	Black Devil / Mignon
	Fair Line (b. 1951)	Prince Chevalier	Prince Rose / Chevalerie
		So Fair	Fair Trial / Soria

473 KNOWN FACT 2 (b.c., March 15, 1977)

Bred by Dr. Wm. O. Reed, in U.S.A.

Won 6 races, placed 3, £133,895, in England, at 2 and 3 years, incl. William Hill Middle Park Stakes, 2,000 Guineas Stakes, Waterford Crystal Mile, Queen Elizabeth II Stakes; 3rd Mill Reef Stakes.

IN REALITY (b. 1964)	Intentionally (bl. 1956)	Intent	War Relic / Liz F.
		My Recipe	Discovery / Perlette
	My Dear Girl (ch. 1957)	Rough 'n Tumble	Free for All / Roused
		Iltis	War Relic / We Hail
TAMERETT (b. or br. 1962)	Tim Tam (b. 1955)	Tom Fool	Menow / Gaga
		Two Lea	Bull Lea / Two Bob
	Mixed Marriage (b. 1952)	Tudor Minstrel	Owen Tudor / Sansonnet
		Persian Maid	Tehran / Aroma

474 KOBLENZA 1 (br.f., February 9, 1966)

Bred by Mme. F. Dupré, in France.

Won 4 races, placed 3, 522,330 fr., in France, at 2 and 3 years, incl. Poule d'Essai des Pouliches and Prix de la Grotte; 2nd Prix Saint-Alary.

HUGH LUPUS (b. 1952)	Djebel (b. 1937)	Tourbillon	Ksar / Durban
		Loika	Gay Crusader / Coeur a Coeur
	Sakountala (b. 1942)	Goya II	Tourbillon / Zariba
		Samos	Bruleur / Samya
KALIMARA (b. 1960)	Norseman (b. 1940)	Umidwar	Blandford / Uganda
		Tara	Teddy / Jean Gow
	Montana (b. 1943)	Mirko	Figaro / Miss Teddy
		Indiara	Indus / Rima

475   **KONIGSSEE** 4 (ch.c., January 20, 1972)

Bred by Gestüt Hohe Weide, in Germany.

Won 4 races, placed 4, 259,000 DM., in Germany, at 2 and 3 years, incl. Deutsches Derby and Consul Bayeff Erinnerungsrennen.

SODERINI (b. 1961)	Crepello (ch. 1954)	Donatello II	Blenheim / Delleana
		Crepuscule	Mieuxce / Red Sunset
	Matuta (b. 1955)	Tantieme	Deux pour Cent / Terka
		Maitrise	Atout Maitre / Mabama
KONIGSBIRKE (ch. 1962)	Birkhahn (br. 1945)	Alchimist	Herold / Aversion
		Bramouse	Cappiello / Peregrine
	Konigstreue (b. 1949)	Ticino	Athanasius / Terra
		Konigswiese	Wahnfried / Contessa Oleanda

476   **KONIGSSTUHL** 5 (br.c., May 17, 1976)

Bred by Gestüt Zoppenbroich, in Germany.

Won 8 races, placed 6, 653,525 DM., in Germany, from 2 to 4 years, incl. Deutsches Derby, Aral-Pokal, Henckel-Rennen, Grosser Thier-Preis Deutsches St. Leger and Grosser Preis der Stadt Gelsenkirchen; 2nd Union-Rennen, Grosser Preis von Baden and Grosser Preis von Dusseldorf.

DSCHINGIS KHAN (br. 1961)	Tamerlane (b. 1952)	Persian Gulf	Bahram / Double Life
		Eastern Empress	Nearco / Cheveley Lady
	Donna Diana (br. 1956)	Neckar	Ticino / Nixe
		Donatella IV	Allgau / Blaue Donau
KONIGSKRONUNG (br. 1965)	Tiepoletto (b. 1956)	Tornado	Tourbillon / Roseola
		Scarlet Skies	Blue Skies / Scarlet Quill
	Kronung (b. 1957)	Olymp	Arjaman / Olympiade
		Kaiserkrone	Nebelwerfer / Kaiserwurde

477   **KRIS** 2 (ch.c., March 23, 1976)

Bred by Lord Howard de Walden.

Won 14 races, placed 2, £195,401, in England, from 2 to 4 years, incl. Sussex Stakes, St, James's Palace Stakes, Waterford Crystal Mile, Queen Elizabeth II Stakes, Tote Lockinge Stakes, Horris Hill Stakes, Bisquit Cognac Challenge Stakes, Clerical Medical Greenham Stakes; 2nd 2,000 Guineas Stakes, Queen Elizabeth II Stakes.

SHARPEN UP (ch. 1969)	Atan (ch. 1961)	Native Dancer	Polynesian / Geisha
		Mixed Marriage	Tudor Minstrel / Persian Maid
	Rocchetta (ch. 1961)	Rockefella	Hyperion / Rockfel
		Chambiges	Majano / Chanterelle
DOUBLY SURE (b. 1971)	Reliance II (b. 1962)	Tantieme	Deux pour Cent / Terka
		Relance III	Relic / Polaire II
	Soft Angels (ch. 1963)	Crepello	Donatello II / Crepuscule
		Sweet Angel	Honeyway / No Angel

478   **KRONENKRANICH** 5 (bl.c., April 29, 1972)

Bred by Gestüt Zoppenbroich, in Germany.

Won 12 races, placed 11, 550,490 DM., in Germany, France and Italy, from 2 to 5 years, incl. Henckel-Rennen, Premio Emilio Turati, Zukunftsrennen, Goldene Peitsche, Grosser Kaufhof Preis and Grosser Preis der Badischen Wirtschaft; 2nd Grosser Preis von Dortmund, Goldene Peitsche and Grosser Kaufhof Preis; 3rd Prix de Ris-Orangis; 4th Prix de la Foret.

STUPENDOUS (b./br. 1963)	Bold Ruler (b. 1954)	Nasrullah	Nearco / Mumtaz Begum
		Miss Disco	Discovery / Outdone
	Magneto (br. 1953)	Ambiorix II	Tourbillon / Lavendula II
		Dynamo	Menow / Bransome
KRONPRINZESSIN (br. 1964)	Orsini (br. 1954)	Ticino	Athanasius / Terra
		Oranien	Nuvolari / Omladina
	Kaiserkrone (b. 1952)	Nebelwerfer	Magnat / Newa
		Kaiserwurde	Bubbles / Katinka

479   **KRONZEUGE** 5 (br.c., March 14, 1961)

Bred by Gestüt Zoppenbroich, in Germany.

Won 7½ races, placed 12, 328,850 DM., in Germany, from 2 to 5 years, incl. Grosser Preis von Nordrhein-Westfalen and Aral-Pokal; 2nd Deutsches Derby, Preis von Europa and Grosser Preis von Baden; 3rd Grosser Preis von Baden (twice), Union-Rennen, Furstenberg-Rennen and Spreti-Rennen.

NECKAR (bl. 1948)	Ticino (b. 1939)	Athanasius	Ferro / Athanasie
		Terra	Aditi / Teufelsrose
	Nixe (b. 1941)	Arjaman	Herold / Aditja
		Nanon	Graf Isolani / Nella da Gubbio
KAISERKRONE (b. 1952)	Nebelwerfer (br. 1944)	Magnat	Asterus / Mafalda
		Newa	Arjaman / Numa
	Kaiserwurde (bl. 1945)	Bubbles	La Farina / Spring Cleaning
		Katinka	Biribi / Killeen

480   **KSAR** 26 (ch.c., March 31, 1970)

Bred by Northmore Stud Farm Ltd.

Won 7 races, placed 4, £75,332, in England, France and Italy, from 2 to 4 years, incl. Ladbroke Classic Trial Stakes, Ladbroke Derby Trial Stakes, Prix de la Cote Normande, Brigadier Gerard Stakes, Prix Gontaut-Biron and Premio del Sempione; 2nd Observer Gold Cup, Prix d'Harcourt and Eclipse Stakes; 4th Derby Stakes.

KALYDON (b. 1956)	Alycidon (ch. 1945)	Donatello II	Blenheim / Delleana
		Aurora	Hyperion / Rose Red
	Lackaday (b. 1947)	Bobsleigh	Gainsborough / Toboggan
		Lackadaisy	Felstead / Complacent
CASTLE MONA (ch. 1962)	Sound Track (ch. 1957)	Whistler	Panorama / Farthing Damages
		Bridle Way	Mustang / Straight Path
	Peggy West (ch. 1956)	Premonition	Precipitation / Trial Ground
		Oola Hills	Denturius / Chikoo

481   KYTHNOS 1 (b.c., May 18, 1957)

Bred by T. Lilley.

Won 2 races, placed 2, £7,867, in Ireland and England, at 3 years, viz. Tetrarch Stakes, Irish 2,000 Guineas; 3rd Derby Stakes, King George VI and Queen Elizabeth Stakes.

NEARULA (b. 1950)	Nasrullah (b. 1940)	Nearco	Pharos / Nogara
		Mumtaz Begum	Blenheim / Mumtaz Mahal
	Respite (b. 1941)	Flag of Truce	Truculent / Concordia
		Orama	Diophon / Cantelupe
CAPITAL ISSUE (b. 1947)	Straight Deal (b. 1940)	Solario	Gainsborough / Sun Worship
		Good Deal	Apelle / Weeds
	Pilch (b. 1938)	Windsor Lad	Blandford / Resplendent
		Pillion	Chaucer / Double Back

482   LA BAMBA 1 (br.f., February 1, 1961)

Bred by Baron Guy de Rothschild, in France.

Won 4 races, placed 5, £33,467, in France and England, at 2 and 3 years, incl. Prix Jacques le Marois, Prix de la Cote Normande; 2nd Grand Criterium, Prix Penelope; 3rd Oaks Stakes, Prix Vermeille, Prix de l'Arc de Triomphe.

SHANTUNG (b. 1956)	Sicambre (br. 1948)	Prince Bio	Prince Rose / Biologie
		Sif	Rialto / Suavita
	Barley Corn (b. 1950)	Hyperion	Gainsborough / Selene
		Schiaparelli	Schiavoni / Aileen
FRONTIER SONG (b. 1939)	Dastur (b. 1929)	Solario	Gainsborough / Sun Worship
		Friar's Daughter	Friar Marcus / Garron Lass
	Song of the Marches (ch. 1932)	Warden of the Marches	Phalaris / Mary Mona
		Cradle Song	Hurry On / Verve

483   LACQUER 3 (b.f., March 3, 1964)

Bred by White Lodge Stud Ltd.

Won 5 races, placed 5, £16,240, in England and Ireland, at 2 and 3 years, incl. Irish 1,000 Guineas Stakes, Cambridgeshire Stakes, 3rd 1,000 Guineas Stakes.

SHANTUNG (b. 1956)	Sicambre (br. 1948)	Prince Bio	Prince Rose / Biologie
		Sif	Rialto / Suavita
	Barley Corn (b. 1950)	Hyperion	Gainsborough / Selene
		Schiaparelli	Schiavoni / Aileen
URSHALIM (b. 1951)	Nasrullah (b. 1940)	Nearco	Pharos / Nogara
		Mumtaz Begum	Blenheim / Mumtaz Mahal
	Horama (b. 1943)	Panorama	Sir Cosmo / Happy Climax
		Lady of Aran	Orpen / Queen of the Nore

484   LADY BERRY 14 (ch.f., April 3, 1970)

Bred by Baron Guy de Rothschild, in France.

Won 6 races, 756,470 fr., in France, at 2 and 3 years, incl. Prix Royal Oak and Prix de Pomone.

VIOLON D'INGRES (b. 1959)	Tourment (b. 1944)	Tourbillon	Ksar / Durban
		Fragment	Shred / Pearl Drop
	Flute Enchantee (b. 1950)	Cranach	Coronach / Reine Isaure
		Montagnana	Brantome / Mauretania
MOSS ROSE (ch. 1963)	Mossborough (ch. 1947)	Nearco	Pharos / Nogara
		All Moonshine	Bobsleigh / Selene
	Damasi (ch. 1953)	Djebel	Tourbillon / Loika
		Monrovia	Pharis II / Geranium

485   LADY CAPULET 1 (ro.f., April 3, 1974)

Bred by Claiborne Farm, in U.S.A.

Won 1 race, placed 2, £37,459, in Ireland and England, at 3 years, viz. Irish 1,000 Guineas; 2nd Coronation Stakes; 3rd Pretty Polly Stakes.

SIR IVOR (b. 1965)	Sir Gaylord (b. 1959)	Turn-to	Royal Charger / Source Sucree
		Somethingroyal	Princequillo / Imperatrice
	Attica (ch. 1953)	Mr. Trouble	Mahmoud / Motto
		Athenia	Pharamond / Salaminia
CAP AND BELLS (gr. 1958)	Tom Fool (b. 1949)	Menow	Pharamond / Alcibiades
		Gaga	Bull Dog / Alpoise
	Ghazni (gr. 1942)	Mahmoud	Blenheim / Mah Mahal
		Sun Miss	Sun Briar / Missinaibi

486   LADY PITT 20 (ch.f., May 10, 1963)

Bred by John W. Greathouse, in U.S.A.

Won 10 races, placed 19, $413,382, in U.S.A., from 2 to 5 years, incl. Coaching Club American Oaks, Mother Goose Stakes, Delaware Oaks, Vineland H. and Astarita Stakes; 2nd Kentucky Oaks, Alabama Stakes, Gazelle H., Orchid Stakes, Frizette Stakes, Gardenia Stakes, Demoiselle Stakes and Schuylerville Stakes; 3rd Beldame Stakes, Maskette H. and Santa Barbara H.

SWORD DANCER (ch. 1956)	Sunglow (ch. 1947)	Sun Again	Sun Teddy / Hug Again
		Rosern	Mad Hatter / Rosedrop
	Highland Fling (br. 1950)	By Jimminy	Pharamond / Buginarug
		Swing Time	Royal Minstrel / Speed Boat
ROCK DRILL (ch. 1951)	Whirlaway (ch. 1938)	Blenheim	Blandford / Malva
		Dustwhirl	Sweep / Ormonda
	Flyaway Home (br. 1937)	Display	Fair Play / Cicuta
		Canfli	Campfire / Flivver

487   LADY SENATOR 13 (b. or br.f., March 2, 1958)

Bred by G. A. Harris.

Won 3 races, placed 7, £5,276, in Ireland and England, at 2 and 3 years, incl. Irish 1,000 Guineas; 3rd Sussex Stakes.

THE PHOENIX (b. 1940)	Chateau Bouscaut (b. 1927)	Kircubbin	Captivation / Avon Hack
		Ramondie	Neil Gow / La Rille
	Fille de Poete (ch. 1935)	Firdaussi	Pharos / Brownhylda
		Fille d'Amour	Hurry On / Friar's Daughter
PEACE TERMS (b. 1946)	Flag of Truce (b. 1934)	Truculent	Teddy / Saucy Sue
		Concordia	Son-in-Law / Ciceronetta
	Fairholme (b. 1939)	Fair Trial	Fairway / Lady Juror
		Safe Return	Stratford / Flying home

488   LAGUNETTE 7 (b.f., April 17, 1973)

Bred by H. Berlin, in France.

Won 4 races, placed 2, £124,814, in France and Ireland, from 2 to 4 years, incl. Irish Guinness Oaks, Prix Vermeille; 3rd Prix de Diane.

VAL DE LOIR (b. 1959)	Vieux Manoir (b. 1947)	Brantome	Blandford / Vitamine
		Vieille Maison	Finglas / Vieille Canaille
	Vali (br. 1954)	Sunny Boy III	Jock II / Fille de Soleil
		Her Slipper	Tetratema / Carpet Slipper
LANDERINETTE (ch. 1953)	Sicambre (br. 1948)	Prince Bio	Prince Rose / Biologie
		Sif	Rialto / Suavita
	Lais (ch. 1940)	Fantastic	Aethelstan / Fanatic
		Lady Chatterley	Rialto / Shameless

489   LAKE CITY 2 (ch.c., May 15, 1976)

Bred by William D. Fishback, in U.S.A.

Won 2 races, placed 5, £29,506, in England, at 2 and 3 years, incl. Coventry Stakes, Salisbury 2,000 Guineas Trial; 3rd Mecca-Dante Stakes. Ran once unplaced in U.S.A., at 4 years.

ANNIHILATE 'EM (ch. 1970)	Hempen (ch. 1962)	Indian Hemp	Nasrullah / Sabzy
		Serry	Spy Song / Santa Roseanna
	Spots to Spare (ro. 1962)	Star Rover	Flushing II / Miss Moonbeam
		Fast Cat	Tiger / Head Smart
SASSY JUTTA (ch. 1966)	Nadir (b. 1955)	Nasrullah	Nearco / Mumtaz Begum
		Gallita	Challenger / Gallette
	Nell's Joy (b. 1958)	Johns Joy	Bull Dog / My Auntie
		Nell K	Crowfoot / Sea Elf

490   LAKEVILLE MISS 9 (dk.b./br.f., March 27, 1975)

Bred by Randolph Weinsier, in U.S.A.

Won 7 races, placed 5, $371,582, in U.S.A., at 2 and 3 years, incl. Coaching Club American Oaks, Frizette Stakes, Selima Stakes, Matron Stakes and Astarita Stakes; 2nd Mother Goose Stakes, Acorn Stakes and Demoiselle Stakes; 3rd Schuylerville Stakes.

RAINY LAKE (ch. 1959)	Royal Charger (ch. 1942)	Nearco	Pharos / Nogara
		Sun Princess	Solario / Mumtaz Begum
	Portage (b. 1952)	War Admiral	Man o'War / Brushup
		Carillon	Case Ace / Sunfeathers
HEW (b. 1959)	Blue Prince II (b. 1951)	Princequillo	Prince Rose / Cosquilla
		Blue Denim	Blue Larkspur / Judy O'Grady
	Jitsa (b. 1944)	Questionnaire	Sting / Miss Puzzle
		Fair Perdita	Eternal / Lady Wave

491   LA LAGUNE 7 (b.f., March 29, 1965)

Bred by Marquis du Vivier, in France.

Won 4 races, placed 2, £51,046, in England, France and U.S.A., at 2 and 3 years, incl. Oaks Stakes, Prix Vanteaux, Prix de Conde; 3rd Prix Vermeille.

VAL DE LOIR (b. 1959)	Vieux Manoir (b. 1947)	Brantome	Blandford / Vitamine
		Vieille Maison	Finglas / Vieille Canaille
	Vali (br. 1954)	Sunny Boy III	Jock II / Fille de Soleil
		Her Slipper	Tetratema / Carpet Slipper
LANDERINETTE (ch. 1953)	Sicambre (br. 1948)	Prince Bio	Prince Rose / Biologie
		Sif	Rialto / Suavita
	Lais (ch. 1940)	Fantastic	Aethelstan / Fanatic
		Lady Chatterley	Rialto / Shameless

492   LALIBELA 8 (ch.f., February 10, 1965)

Bred by Dalham Stud Farms Ltd.

Won 2 races, placed 4, £9,567, in England, Ireland and France, at 2 and 3 years, incl. Cheveley Park Stakes.

HONEYWAY (br. 1941)	Fairway (b. 1925)	Phalaris	Polymelus / Bromus
		Scapa Flow	Chaucer / Anchora
	Honey Buzzard (ch. 1931)	Papyrus	Tracery / Miss Matty
		Lady Peregrine	White Eagle / Lisma
BLUE MARK (ch. 1949)	Blue Train (ch. 1944)	Blue Peter	Fairway / Fancy Free
		Sun Chariot	Hyperion / Clarence
	Pecked (ch. 1937)	Flamingo	Flamboyant / Lady Peregrine
		Little Mark	Friar Marcus / Lilaline

493   LALIKA 5 (ch.f., April 22, 1967)

Bred by Mme. Pierre Wertheimer, in France.

Won 2 races, 435,215 fr., at 3 years, incl. Prix Saint-Alary.

LE FABULEUX (ch. 1961)	Wild Risk (b. 1940)	Rialto	Rabelais / La Grelee
		Wild Violet	Blandford / Wood Violet
	Anguar (b. 1950)	Verso II	Pinceau / Variete
		La Rochelle	Easton / Sans Tares
KALILA (b. 1961)	Beau Prince II (ch. 1952)	Prince Chevalier	Prince Rose / Chevalerie
		Isabelle Brand	Black Devil / Isabelle d'Este
	Vali (br. 1954)	Sunny Boy III	Jock II / Fille de Soleil
		Her Slipper	Tetratema / Carpet Slipper

494   LAOMEDONTE 2 (ch.c., April 4, 1972)

Bred by Mrs. G. Proskauer, in U.S.A.

Won 6 races, placed 8, 103,326,285 L., in Italy and England, from 2 to 5 years, incl. Gran Premio d'Italia, Gran Premio del Jockey Club, St. Leger Italiano and Premio Ambrosiano; 3rd Premio Tevere and Premio Emanuele Filiberto; 4th Gran Premio di Milano and Coronation Cup.

RAISE A NATIVE (ch. 1961)	Native Dancer (gr. 1950)	Polynesian	Unbreakable / Black Polly
		Geisha	Discovery / Miyako
	Raise You (ch. 1946)	Case Ace	Teddy / Sweetheart
		Lady Glory	American Flag / Beloved
LOST MESSAGE (ch. 1962)	Toulouse Lautrec (ch. 1950)	Dante	Nearco / Rosy Legend
		Tokamura	Navarro / Tofanella
	Khaling U (b. 1950)	Khaled	Hyperion / Eclair
		U Time	Beau Pere / Heather Time

495   LARKSPUR 1 (ch.c., January 31, 1959)

Bred by Philip A. Love Ltd.

Won 3 races, placed 3, £38,587, in Ireland and England, at 2 and 3 years, incl. Derby Stakes, Wills' Gold Flake Stakes; 2nd Blandford Stakes; 3rd National Stakes (Curragh); 4th Irish Sweeps Derby.

NEVER SAY DIE (ch. 1951)	Nasrullah (b. 1940)	Nearco	Pharos / Nogara
		Mumtaz Begum	Blenheim / Mumtaz Mahal
	Singing Grass (ch. 1944)	War Admiral	Man o'War / Brushup
		Boreale	Vatout / Galaday II
SKYLARKING (ch. 1950)	Precipitation (ch. 1933)	Hurry On	Marcovil / Tout Suite
		Double Life	Bachelor's Double / Saint Joan
	Woodlark (b. 1944)	Bois Roussel	Vatout / Plucky Liege
		Aurora	Hyperion / Rose Red

496   LA SEGA 8 (br.f., April 20, 1959)

Bred by Francois Dupré, in France.

Won 9 races, placed 5, 944,500 fr., in France, at 2 and 3 years, incl. Prix de Diane, Poule d'Essai des Pouliches, Prix Saint-Alary, Prix d'Ispahan, Prix de la Grotte, Prix du Petit Couvert and Prix La Rochette; 2nd Prix de l'Abbaye de Longchamp, Prix Robert Papin and Prix d'Arenberg; 4th Prix Morny.

TANTIEME (b. 1947)	Deux pour Cent (b. 1941)	Deiri	Aethelstan / Desra
		Dix pour Cent	Feridoon / La Chansonnerie
	Terka (br. 1942)	Indus	Alcantara II / Himalaya
		La Furka	Blandford / Brenta
LA DANSE (b. 1951)	Menetrier (br. 1944)	Fair Copy	Fairway / Composure
		La Melodie	Gold Bridge / La Souriciere
	Makada (b. 1936)	Rustom Pasha	Son-in-Law / Cos
		Rayonnante II	Sans le Sou / La Semillante

497   LASSALLE 2 (b.c., February 28, 1969)

Bred by L. Champion, in France.

Won 6 races, placed 9, £105,437, in France and England, from 2 to 5 years, incl. Ascot Gold Cup, Prix du Cadran, Prix Gladiateur, Prix de l'Esperance, Prix Berteux; 2nd Prix du Cadran, Prix Jean Prat; 3rd Ascot Gold Cup, Prix Royal-Oak, Prix Greffulhe, Prix Hocquart, Prix de Conde, Criterium de Saint-Cloud.

BON MOT III (ch. 1963)	Worden II (ch. 1949)	Wild Risk	Rialto / Wild Violet
		Sans Tares	Sind / Tara
	Djebel Idra (b. 1957)	Phil Drake	Admiral Drake / Philippa
		Djebellica	Djebel / Nica
WINDY CLIFF (br. 1955)	Hard Sauce (br. 1948)	Ardan	Pharis II / Adargatis
		Saucy Bella	Bellacose / Marmite
	Foretaste (b. 1938)	Umidwar	Blandford / Uganda
		Feola	Friar Marcus / Aloe

498   LA TENDRESSE 8 (b.f., March 21, 1959)

Bred by F. F. Tuthill.

Won 6 races, placed 3, £10,797, in Ireland and England, at 2 and 3 years, incl. Seaton Delaval Stakes, Molecomb Stakes, Lowther Stakes, King George Stakes; 2nd King's Stand Stakes.

GREY SOVEREIGN (gr. 1948)	Nasrullah (b. 1940)	Nearco	Pharos / Nogara
		Mumtaz Begum	Blenheim / Mumtaz Mahal
	Kong (gr. 1933)	Baytown	Achtoi / Princess Herodias
		Clang	Hainault / Vibration
ISETTA (b. 1943)	Morland (b. 1934)	Gainsborough	Bayardo / Rosedrop
		Lichen	Manna / Loweswater
	Isolda (b. 1933)	Rustom Pasha	Son-in-Law / Cos
		Yveline	Gardefeu / Photime

499   LA TROUBLERIE 10 (ch.f., April 5, 1969)

Bred by G. A. Harris, in Ireland.

Won 7 races, placed 6, 761,416 fr., in France, from 2 to 4 years, incl. Prix d'Ispahan, Prix Edmond Blanc, Prix Chloe and Prix de la Cote Normande; 2nd Prix Penelope and Prix de Royaumont.

WILL SOMERS (br. 1955)	Tudor Minstrel (br. 1944)	Owen Tudor	Hyperion
			Mary Tudor II
		Sansonnet	Sansovino
			Lady Juror
	Queen's Jest (br. 1946)	Nearco	Pharos
			Nogara
		Mirth	Hurry On
			Laughter
MISS CRACKNEL (ch. 1959)	Cagire II (b. 1947)	Tourbillon	Ksar
			Durban
		Source Sucree	Admiral Drake
			Lavendula II
	My Margaret (b. 1951)	The Phoenix	Chateau Bouscaut
			Fille de Poete
		Cracknel	Manna
			Anadyomene

500   LAUSCHER 7 (b.c., March 4, 1968)

Bred by Gestüt Rösler, in Germany.

Won 2 races, placed 9, 180,480 DM., in Germany, at 2 and 3 years, incl. Deutsches Derby; 4th Grosser Preis von Baden.

PANTHEON (b. 1958)	Borealis (ch. 1941)	Brumeux	Teddy
			La Brume
		Aurora	Hyperion
			Rose Red
	Palazzo (br. 1950)	Dante	Nearco
			Rosy Legend
		Edifice	Monument
			Phalconia
LIPOMA (b. 1963)	Birkhahn (br. 1945)	Alchimist	Herold
			Aversion
		Bramouse	Cappiello
			Peregrine
	Liebeslied (b. 1953)	Ticino	Athanasius
			Terra
		Liebesgottin	Tourbillon
			Legation

501   LAUSO 16 (b.c., February 28, 1958)

Bred by Razza del Soldo, in France.

Won 4 races, placed 3, 16,140,000 L., in Italy, from 2 to 5 years, incl. Derby Italiano.

OCARINA (ch. 1947)	Bubbles (ch. 1925)	La Farina	Sans Souci II
			Malatesta
		Spring Cleaning	Neil Gow
			Spring Night
	Montagnana (b. 1937)	Brantome	Blandford
			Vitamine
		Mauretania	Tetratema
			Lady Maureen
LA CANEA (b. 1953)	Vatellor (br. 1933)	Vatout	Prince Chimay
			Vasthi
		Lady Elinor	Teddy
			Madame Royale
	La Cadette (ch. 1947)	Le Pacha	Biribi
			Advertencia
		Fidgette	Firdaussi
			Boxeuse

502   LE BAVARD 3 (ch.c., May 8, 1971)

Bred by Henri Aubert, in France.

Won 5 races, placed 10, 972,368 fr., in France and England, from 2 to 4 years, incl. Prix du Cadran, Prix Berteux and Prix Jean Prat; 2nd Ascot Gold Cup and Prix Kergorlay; 4th Grand Prix de Paris and Prix Royal Oak.

DEVON (ch. 1958)	Worden II (ch. 1949)	Wild Risk	Rialto
			Wild Violet
		Sans Tares	Sind
			Tara
	Sees (b. 1953)	Court Martial	Fair Trial
			Instantaneous
		Carrere	Le Pacha
			Lady Penn
LUEUR DOREE (ch. 1964)	Le Haar (ch. 1954)	Vieux Manoir	Brantome
			Vieille Maison
		Mince Pie	Teleferique
			Cannelle
	Lueur d'Espoir (ch. 1948)	Escamillo	Firdaussi
			Estoril
		Light of Morning	Hurry On
			Silvretta

503   LE CANTILIEN 8 (b.c., March 2, 1959)

Bred by Mme. L. Volterra, in France.

Won 3 races, placed 8, £8,553, in France and England, from 3 to 5 years, incl. 2nd Prix Lupin; 3rd Derby Stakes.

NORSEMAN (b. 1940)	Umidwar (b. 1931)	Blandford	Swynford
			Blanche
		Uganda	Bridaine
			Hush
	Tara (ch. 1932)	Teddy	Ajax
			Rondeau
		Jean Gow	Neil Gow
			Jane Shore
LA PERIE (b. 1951)	Hyperion (ch. 1930)	Gainsborough	Bayardo
			Rosedrop
		Selene	Chaucer
			Serenissima
	Philippa (br. 1943)	Vatellor	Vatout
			Lady Elinor
		Philippa of Hainaut	Teddy
			Pride of Hainault

504   LE CHOUAN 5 (b.c., April 5, 1966)

Bred by F. de Linares, in France.

Won 5 races, placed 16, 1,152,715 fr., in France, England and U.S.A., from 2 to 6 years, incl. Prix Royal Oak and Prix du Cadran; 2nd Doncaster Cup, Brighton Beach Handicap and Prix Berteux; 3rd Prix du Cadran, La Coupe and Prix Gladiateur; 4th Ascot Gold Cup.

LE TYROL (b. 1948)	Verso II (b. 1940)	Pinceau	Alcantara II
			Aquarelle
		Variete	La Farina
			Vaya
	Princesse Lointaine II (ch. 1941)	Prince Rose	Rose Prince
			Indolence
		Madam Barcarolle	Loch Lomond
			Carmenmelis
FOSSINETTE (ch. 1948)	Magister (ch. 1939)	Bubbles	La Farina
			Spring Cleaning
		Murcie	Passebreul
			Mayotte
	Fossette (b. 1941)	Hutton	Fiterari
			Hudson
		Miss Florida	Radis Rose
			Floride

505   **LE CONQUERANT** 1 (b.c., April 8, 1964)

Bred by M. Lemaigre-Dubreuil, in France.

Won 5 races, placed 23, 480,730 fr., in France, from 2 to 7 years, incl. Prix Morny; 3rd Prix Robert Papin.

CÔTE D'OR II (b. 1951)	Blue Tzar (b. 1939)	Blue Skies	Blandford / Blue Pill
		Deauville	Clarissimus / Dagora
	Côte de Melon (b. 1939)	Le Gosse	Massine / La Gasse
		Courgette	Fiterari / Sheen
FLY HIGH (b. 1950)	Coastal Traffic (br. 1941)	Hyperion	Gainsborough / Selene
		Rose of England	Teddy / Perce-Neige
	Fairy's Love (ch. 1939)	Fair Trial	Fairway / Lady Juror
		Lovescape	Gainsborough / Hasty Love

506   **LE FABULEUX** 13 (ch.c., February 12, 1961)

Bred by Mme. G. Weisweiller, in France.

Won 8 races, placed 1, 1,441,192 fr., in France, from 2 to 4 years, incl. Prix du Jockey-Club, Prix Lupin, Prix Noailles, Prix du Prince d'Orange, Prix de Condé and Criterium de Saint-Cloud; 2nd Prix Greffulhe.

WILD RISK (b. 1940)	Rialto (ch. 1923)	Rabelais	St. Simon / Satirical
		La Grelee	Helicon / Grignouse
	Wild Violet (b. 1935)	Blandford	Swynford / Blanche
		Wood Violet	Ksar / Pervencheres
ANGUAR (b. 1950)	Verso II (b. 1940)	Pinceau	Alcantara II / Aquarelle
		Variete	La Farina / Vaya
	La Rochelle (br. 1945)	Easton	Dark Legend / Phaona
		Sans Tares	Sind / Tara

507   **LE LOUP GAROU** 17 (b.c., March 28, 1956)

Bred by Mme. Jean Blondel, in France.

Won 7 races, placed 11, 332,614 fr., in France and England, from 2 to 4 years, incl. Prix du Cadran and Criterium de Saint-Cloud; 2nd Grand Prix de Paris, Prix Greffulhe, Prix Noailles and Prix Jean Prat; 3rd Prix de l'Arc de Triomphe and Ascot Gold Cup; 4th Prix Royal Oak.

PRINCE BIO (b. 1941)	Prince Rose (b. 1928)	Rose Prince	Prince Palatine / Eglantine
		Indolence	Gay Crusader / Barrier
	Biologie (ch. 1935)	Bacteriophage	Tetratema / Pharmacie
		Eponge	Cadum / Sea Moss
ROXELANE (ch. 1940)	Foxhunter (ch. 1929)	Foxlaw	Son-in-Law / Alope
		Trimestral	William the Third / Mistrella
	La Favorite (b. 1934)	Biribi	Rabelais / La Bidouze
		La Pompadour	La Farina / Fly Away

508   **LE MARMOT** 16 (b.c., May 14, 1976)

Bred by Marquis Rene de Talhouet-Roy, in France.

Won 7 races, placed 4, 2,362,334 fr., in France and U.S.A., from 2 to 4 years, incl. Prix Ganay, Prix Foy, Prix Greffulhe, Prix Hocquart, Prix Niel and Prix La Rochette; 2nd Prix du Jockey-Club and Prix de l'Arc de Triomphe; 3rd Washington D.C. International and Prix d'Harcourt.

AMARKO (b. 1965)	Tanerko (br. 1953)	Tantieme	Deux pour Cent / Terka
		La Divine	Fair Copy / La Diva
	Thamar (ch. 1958)	Mat de Cocagne	Birikil / Fascine II
		Ines	Admiral Drake / Ann's Twin
MOLINKA (b. 1967)	Molvedo (br. 1958)	Ribot	Tenerani / Romanella
		Maggiolina	Nakamuro / Murcia
	Telstar (ch. 1962)	Cambremer	Chamossaire / Tomorrow
		Sanelta	Tourment / Satanella

509   **LE MOSS** 1 (ch.c., April 3, 1975)

Bred by McGrath Trust Co.

Won 11 races, placed 2, £173,438, in England and France, from 2 to 5 years, incl. Ascot Gold Cup (twice), Goodwood Cup (twice), Doncaster Cup (twice), Queen's Vase; 2nd St. Leger Stakes, Prix Gladiateur.

LE LEVANSTELL (b. 1957)	Le Lavandou (b. 1944)	Djebel	Tourbillon / Loika
		Lavande	Rustom Pasha / Livadia
	Stella's Sister (ch. 1950)	Ballyogan	Fair Trial / Serial
		My Aid	Knight of the Garter / Flying Aid
FEEMOSS (b. 1960)	Ballymoss (ch. 1954)	Mossborough	Nearco / All Moonshine
		Indian Call	Singapore / Flittemere
	Feevagh (b. 1951)	Solar Slipper	Windsor Slipper / Solar Flower
		Astrid Wood	Bois Roussel / Astrid

510   **LEVMOSS** 1 (b.c., May 16, 1965)

Bred by McGrath Trust Co.

Won 8 races, placed 2, £142,226, in Ireland, England and France, from 2 to 4 years, incl. Ascot Gold Cup, Prix du Cadran, Prix de l'Arc de Triomphe; 3rd Prix Royal-Oak, Prix Jean Prat.

LE LEVANSTELL (b. 1957)	Le Lavandou (b. 1944)	Djebel	Tourbillon / Loika
		Lavande	Rustom Pasha / Livadia
	Stella's Sister (ch. 1950)	Ballyogan	Fair Trial / Serial
		My Aid	Knight of the Garter / Flying Aid
FEEMOSS (b. 1960)	Ballymoss (ch. 1954)	Mossborough	Nearco / All Moonshine
		Indian Call	Singapore / Flittemere
	Feevagh (b. 1951)	Solar Slipper	Windsor Slipper / Solar Flower
		Astrid Wood	Bois Roussel / Astrid

511 LIANGA 22 (bl.f., February 1, 1971)

Bred by Mrs. B. M. Donaldson, in U.S.A.

Won 11 races, placed 7, £123,961, in France and England, from 2 to 4 years, incl. Prix Robert Papin, Prix Jacques le Marois, Prix Maurice de Gheest, Prix de l'Abbaye de Longchamp, July Cup, Vernons Sprint Cup; 2nd Prix du Rond-Point, Prix de la Porte Maillot; 3rd Prix du Moulin de Longchamp, Prix du Rond-Point, Sussex Stakes; 4th Prix Morny, Prix du Moulin de Longchamp.

DANCER'S IMAGE (gr. 1965)	Native Dancer (gr. 1950)	Polynesian	Unbreakable / Black Polly
		Geisha	Discovery / Miyako
	Noors Image (b. 1953)	Noor	Nasrullah / Queen of Baghdad
		Little Sphinx	Challenger / Khara
LEVEN ONES (ch. 1961)	Sailor (ch. 1952)	Eight Thirty	Pilate / Dinner Time
		Flota	Jack High / Armada
	Olympia Dell (ch. 1953)	Olympia	Heliopolis / Miss Dolphin
		Star Student	Rhodes Scholar / Delmarie

512 LIGHT CAVALRY 1 (b.c., February 7, 1977)

Bred by H. J. Joel.

Won 4 races, placed 3, £111,063, in England, at 2 and 3 years, incl. St. Leger Stakes, King Edward VII Stakes; 2nd Great Voltigeur Stakes; 3rd Chester Vase, Gordon Stakes.

BRIGADIER GERARD (b. 1968)	Queen's Hussar (b. 1960)	March Past	Petition / Marcelette
		Jojo	Vilmorin / Fairy Jane
	La Paiva (ch. 1956)	Prince Chevalier	Prince Rose / Chevalerie
		Brazen Molly	Horus / Molly Adare
GLASS SLIPPER (b./br. 1969)	Relko (b. 1960)	Tanerko	Tantieme / La Divine
		Relance III	Relic / Polaire II
	Crystal Palace (b. 1956)	Solar Slipper	Windsor Slipper / Solar Flower
		Queen of Light	Borealis / Picture Play

513 LIGHTNING 22 (b.c., March 31, 1974)

Bred by Baron Guy de Rothschild, in France.

Won 5 races, 705,000 fr., in France, at 2 and 3 years, incl. Prix d'Ispahan, Prix Jean Prat and Prix de la Jonchere.

KASHMIR II (b./br. 1963)	Tudor Melody (br. 1956)	Tudor Minstrel	Owen Tudor / Sansonnet
		Matelda	Dante / Fairly Hot
	Queen of Speed (b. 1950)	Blue Train	Blue Peter / Sun Chariot
		Bishopscourt	His Grace / Jurisdiction
FIDRA (ch. 1961)	Sicambre (br. 1948)	Prince Bio	Prince Rose / Biologie
		Sif	Rialto / Suavita
	Aurore Polaire (b. 1955)	Alizier	Teleferique / Alizarine
		Aurore Boreale (ex-Vorderrisserin)	Brantome / Voute Celeste

514 LIGHT WIND 3 (b.c., March 11, 1965)

Bred by R. and N. Seabra, in France.

Won 6 races, placed 9, 399,035 fr., in France and Italy, from 2 to 5 years incl. Premio Presidente della Repubblica; 3rd Prix de Fontainebleau.

ROMULUS (b. 1959)	Ribot (b. 1952)	Tenerani	Bellini / Tofanella
		Romanella	El Greco / Barbara Burrini
	Arietta (br. 1953)	Tudor Minstrel	Owen Tudor / Sansonnet
		Anne of Essex	Panorama / Queen of Essex
LIGHT FANTASTIC (ch. 1955)	Denturius (ch. 1937)	Gold Bridge	Swynford or Golden Boss / Flying Diadem
		La Solfatara	Lemberg / Ayesha
	Light Fantasy (ch. 1945)	Signal Light	Pharos / Ensoleillee
		Last Act	Call Boy / Mafia

515 LIGHT YEAR 5 (ch.c., March 24, 1958)

Bred by Exors. of J. A. McEnery.

Won 3 races, placed 4, £5,972, in Ireland, from 2 to 4 years, incl. Irish 2,000 Guineas; 2nd Tetrarch Stakes, Whitehall Stakes; 3rd National Stakes (Curragh).

CHAMIER (ch. 1950)	Chamossaire (ch. 1942)	Precipitation	Hurry On / Double Life
		Snowberry	Cameronian / Myrobella
	Therapia (b. 1944)	Panorama	Sir Cosmo / Happy Climax
		Silvonessa	Royal Dancer / Silvonah
SPRING LIGHT (b. 1949)	Signal Light (ch. 1936)	Pharos	Phalaris / Scapa Flow
		Ensoleillee	Sunstar / Laughter
	Gold Mary (b. 1939)	Solario	Gainsborough / Sun Worship
		Dalmary	Blandford / Simon's Shoes

516 LINACRE 15 (bl.c., March 20, 1960)

Bred by Lord Ennisdale.

Won 6 races, placed 6, £29,600, in France, Ireland and England, from 2 to 4 years, incl. Irish 2,000 Guineas, Queen Elizabeth II Stakes, Whitehall Stakes, Prix de la Porte Maillot; 2nd Sussex Stakes, Champion Stakes (twice), Prix Jacques le Marois, Prix Gontaut-Biron.

ROCKEFELLA (br. 1941)	Hyperion (ch. 1930)	Gainsborough	Bayardo / Rosedrop
		Selene	Chaucer / Serenissima
	Rockfel (br. 1935)	Felstead	Spion Kop / Felkington
		Rockliffe	Santorb / Sweet Rocket
TRUE PICTURE (bl. 1955)	Panorama (ch. 1936)	Sir Cosmo	The Boss / Ayn Hali
		Happy Climax	Happy Warrior / Clio
	Verity (b. 1941)	Chrysler II	Teddy / Quick Change
		Fortunedale	Loaningdale / Fortunate Lady

517   LINDEN TREE 12 (ch.c., April 26, 1968)

Bred by Mrs. D. McCalmont, in France.

Won 3 races, placed 1, £42,554, in England, at 2 and 3 years, incl. Observer Gold Cup, Chester Vase; 2nd Derby Stakes.

CREPELLO (ch. 1954)	Donatello II (ch. 1934)	Blenheim	Blandford / Malva
		Delleana	Clarissimus / Duccia di Buoninsegna
	Crepuscule (ch. 1948)	Mieuxce	Massine / L'Olivete
		Red Sunset	Solario / Dulce II
VERBENA (b. 1958)	Vimy (b. 1952)	Wild Risk	Rialto / Wild Violet
		Mimi	Black Devil / Mignon
	Val d'Assa (br. 1947)	Dante	Nearco / Rosy Legend
		Lapel	Apelle / Lampeto

518   LISADELL 5 (b.f., April 9, 1971)

Bred by Claiborne Farm, in U.S.A.

Won 2 races, placed 1, £13,132, in England and Ireland, at 2 and 3 years, incl. Coronation Stakes, Athasi Stakes; 2nd Mulcahy Stakes.

FORLI (ch. 1963)	Aristophanes (ch. 1948)	Hyperion	Gainsborough / Selene
		Commotion	Mieuxce / Riot
	Trevisa (ch. 1951)	Advocate	Fair Trial / Guiding Star
		Veneta	Foxglove / Dogaresa
THONG (b. 1964)	Nantallah (br. 1953)	Nasrullah	Nearco / Mumtaz Begum
		Shimmer	Flares / Broad Ripple
	Rough Shod (b. 1944)	Gold Bridge	Swynford or Golden Boss / Flying Diadem
		Dalmary	Blandford / Simon's Shoes

519   LITTLE CURRENT 16 (ch.c., April 5, 1971)

Bred by John W. Galbreath, in U.S.A.

Won 4 races, placed 4, $354,704, in U.S.A., at 2 and 3 years, incl. Preakness Stakes, Belmont Stakes and Everglades Stakes; 2nd Monmouth Invitational H. and Travers Stakes.

SEA BIRD II (ch. 1962)	Dan Cupid (ch. 1956)	Native Dancer	Polynesian / Geisha
		Vixenette	Sickle / Lady Reynard
	Sicalade (b. 1956)	Sicambre	Prince Bio / Sif
		Marmelade	Maurepas / Couleur
LUIANA (ch. 1963)	My Babu (b. 1945)	Djebel	Tourbillon / Loika
		Perfume II	Badruddin / Lavendula II
	Banquet Bell (ch. 1951)	Polynesian	Unbreakable / Black Polly
		Dinner Horn	Pot au Feu / Tophorn

520   LOCHNAGER 20 (br.c., March 4, 1972)

Bred by E. A. Dandy.

Won 9 races, placed 3, £69,542, in England, from 2 to 4 years, incl. King's Stand Stakes, July Cup, William Hill Sprint Championship, Temple Stakes.

DUMBARNIE (br. 1949)	Dante (br. 1942)	Nearco	Pharos / Nogara
		Rosy Legend	Dark Legend / Rosy Cheeks
	Lost Soul (b. 1931)	Solario	Gainsborough / Sun Worship
		Orlass	Orby / Simon Lass
MISS BARBARA (br. 1961)	Le Dieu d'Or (br. 1952)	Petition	Fair Trial / Art Paper
		Gilded Bee	Gold Bridge / Lady Buzzer
	Barbarona (br. 1947)	Punt Gun	Roar / Lily Willy
		Bessarona	Thyestes / Obscure

521   LOMBARD 1 (ch.c., January 31, 1967)

Bred by Gestüt Schlenderhan, in Germany.

Won 20 races, placed 6, 1,157,063 DM., in Germany and France, from 2 to 6 years, incl. Grosser Preis von Nordrhein-Westfalen (twice), Preis von Europa, Grosser Preis von Dusseldorf (3 times), Grosser Hansa Preis, Spreti-Rennen, Henckel-Rennen, Deutsches St. Leger, Furstenberg-Rennen and Preis des Winterfavoriten; 2nd Deutsches Derby, Union-Rennen and Prix Exbury; 3rd Preis von Europa.

AGIO (br. 1955)	Tantieme (b. 1947)	Deux pour Cent	Deiri / Dix pour Cent
		Terka	Indus / La Furka
	Aralia (br. 1945)	Alchimist	Herold / Aversion
		Aster	Oleander / Arkebuse
PROMISED LADY (ch. 1961)	Prince Chevalier (b. 1943)	Prince Rose	Rose Prince / Indolence
		Chevalerie	Abbot's Speed / Kassala
	Belle Sauvage (ch. 1949)	Big Game	Bahram / Myrobella
		Tropical Sun	Hyperion / Brulette

522   LONG LOOK 16 (b.f., March 23, 1962)

Bred by J. C. Brady, in U.S.A.

Won 2 races, placed 2, £38,093, in England, Ireland and France, at 2 and 3 years, incl. Oaks Stakes; 2nd Irish Guinness Oaks; 3rd Prix Vermeille.

RIBOT (b. 1952)	Tenerani (b. 1944)	Bellini	Cavaliere d'Arpino / Bella Minna
		Tofanella	Apelle / Try Try Again
	Romanella (ch. 1943)	El Greco	Pharos / Gay Gamp
		Barbara Burrini	Papyrus / Bucolic
SANTORIN (ch. 1956)	Greek Song (ch. 1947)	Heliopolis	Hyperion / Drift
		Sylvan Song	Royal Minstrel / Glade
	Secret Meeting (ch. 1950)	Alibhai	Hyperion / Teresina
		Burgoo Maid	Burgoo King / Miss Kid

523 LORD NELSON 20 (br.c., February 26, 1969)

Bred by J. R. Hine, in France.

Won 1 race, placed 2, £6,807, in England, from 2 to 5 years, incl. King Edward VII Stakes.

NELCIUS (br. 1963)		
Tenareze (ch. 1953)	Goyama	Goya II
		Devineress
	La Taglioni	Colombo
		La Truite II
Namagua (br. 1954)	Fontenay	Tornado
		Flying Colours
	Namesake	Fearless Fox
		Concordia
EXPERIENCE II (ch. 1950)		
Rienzo (gr. 1931)	Rialto	Rabelais
		La Grelee
	L'Avalanche	Isard II
		Beattie
Giralda (ch. 1943)	Majano	Deiri
		Madgi Moto
	Ginevra	Ortello
		Giovanna Dupre

524 LORD UDO 7 (ch.c., March 25, 1971)

Bred by Gestüt Röttgen, in Germany.

Won 6 races, placed 7, 616,900 DM., in Germany, from 2 to 4 years, incl. Aral Pokal, Grosser Preis von Dusseldorf, Henckel-Rennen and Zukunftsrennen; 2nd Deutsches Derby, Union-Rennen, Preis von Europa, Grosser Preis von Nordrhein-Westfalen and Grosser Preis von Baden; 3rd Furstenberg-Rennen; 4th Aral Pokal.

UTRILLO (br. 1954)		
Orator (b. 1938)	Athanasius	Ferro
		Athanasie
	Osmunda	Augias
		Orla
Unterwegs (ch. 1942)	Wahnfried	Flamboyant
		Winnica
	Unverzagt	Le Voleur
		Unschuld
LADY WINDERMERE (br. 1965)		
Waldcanter (ch. 1956)	Caran D'Ache	Zliten
		Circignana
	Wappenau	Abendfrieden
		Waffenart
Liatris (br. 1961)	Orsini	Ticino
		Oranien
	Liebesgottin	Tourbillon
		Legation

525 LORENZACCIO 5 (ch.c., February 1, 1965)

Bred by T. Rogers.

Won 7 races, placed 15, £87,041, in England, France and U.S.A., from 2 to 5 years, incl. July Stakes, Champion Stakes, Prix Jean Prat, Prix Quincey, Prix Foy; 2nd Prix Morny, Champagne Stakes, La Coupe de Maisons-Laffitte; 3rd Prix Robert Papin, Queen Elizabeth II Stakes, Champion Stakes; 4th Observer Gold Cup, Prix d'Ispahan.

KLAIRON (b. 1952)		
Clarion III (b. 1944)	Djebel	Tourbillon
		Loika
	Columba	Colorado
		Gay Bird
Kalmia (b. 1931)	Kantar	Alcantara II
		Karabe
	Sweet Lavender	Swynford
		Marchetta
PHOENISSA (b. 1951)		
The Phoenix (b. 1940)	Chateau Bouscaut	Kircubbin
		Ramondie
	Fille de Poete	Firdaussi
		Fille d'Amour
Erica Fragrans (b. 1946)	Big Game	Bahram
		Myrobella
	Jennydang	Colombo
		Dalmary

526 LUCASLAND B3 (b.f., April 26, 1962)

Bred by Crimbourne Stud.

Won 8 races, placed 13, £17,976, in England, from 2 to 5 years, incl. July Cup, Diadem Stakes; 2nd Nunthorpe Stakes.

LUCERO (br. 1953)		
Solonaway (b. 1946)	Solferino	Fairway
		Sol Speranza
	Anyway	Grand Glacier
		The Widow Murphy
Cuguan (ch. 1942)	Fair Trial	Fairway
		Lady Juror
	Tracemond	Abbots Trace
		Icemond
LAVANT (b. 1955)		
Le Lavandou (b. 1944)	Djebel	Tourbillon
		Loika
	Lavande	Rustom Pasha
		Livadia
Firle (br. 1938)	Noble Star	Hapsburg
		Hesper
	Versicle	Sickle
		Verdict

527 LUCIANO 7 (b.c., May 7, 1964)

Bred by Mrs. L. Scott, in England.

Won 10 races, placed 3, 595,800 DM., in Germany, at 3 and 4 years, incl. Deutsches Derby, Aral-Pokal (twice), Grosser Preis von Nordrhein-Westfalen, Grosser Preis von Baden, Grosser Hansa Preis, Union-Rennen and Deutsches St. Leger; 2nd Preis von Europa (twice) and Grosser Preis von Baden.

HENRY THE SEVENTH (ch. 1958)		
King of the Tudors (ch. 1950)	Tudor Minstrel	Owen Tudor
		Sansonnet
	Glen Line	Blue Peter
		Scotia's Glen
Vestal Girl (ch. 1948)	Fairy Prince	Fairway
		Cachalot
	Vestalia	Abbots Trace
		Vulpina
LIGHT ARCTIC (br. 1954)		
Arctic Prince (br. 1948)	Prince Chevalier	Prince Rose
		Chevalerie
	Arctic Sun	Nearco
		Solar Flower
Incandescent (b. 1942)	Pont l'Eveque	Barneveldt
		Ponteba
	Invisible	Asterus
		Will o' the Wisp

528 LUCKY DEBONAIR 3 (b.c., May 2, 1962)

Bred by Mrs. Ada L. Rice, in U.S.A.

Won 9 races, placed 3, $370,960, in U.S.A., at 3 and 4 years, incl. Kentucky Derby, Santa Anita Derby, Blue Grass Stakes, Santa Anita H. and San Vicente H.; 2nd San Felipe H.

VERTEX (ch. 1954)		
The Rhymer (ch. 1938)	St. Germans	Swynford
		Hamoaze
	Rhythmic	Royal Minstrel
		Rinkey
Kanace (gr. 1945)	Case Ace	Teddy
		Sweetheart
	Kanlast	Kantar
		Last Light
FRESH AS FRESH (b. 1957)		
Count Fleet (br. 1940)	Reigh Count	Sunreigh
		Contessina
	Quickly	Haste
		Stephanie
Airy (b. 1945)	Bull Lea	Bull Dog
		Rose Leaves
	Proud One	Blenheim
		Some Pomp

529   LUCKY WEDNESDAY 1 (b./br.c., May 31, 1973)

Bred by Mrs. B. Alexander.

Won 6 races, placed 6, £46,392, in Ireland and England, from 2 to 4 years, incl. Prince of Wales Stakes, Westbury Stakes, Vauxhall Trial Stakes; 2nd Joe Coral Eclipse Stakes; 3rd Irish 2,000 Guineas, Earl of Sefton Stakes.

ROI SOLEIL (ch. 1967)	Skymaster (ch. 1958)	Golden Cloud	Gold Bridge / Rainstorm
		Discipliner	Court Martial / Edvina
	Kessall (br. 1957)	Stephen Paul	Panorama / Paradise
		Kess	Dark Legend / Dolores
PAVLOVA (br. 1962)	Fidalgo (b. 1956)	Arctic Star	Nearco / Serena
		Miss France	Jock II / Nafah
	Time and Chance (b. 1957)	Supreme Court	Persian Gulf or Precipitation / Forecourt
		Foxtrot	Foxhunter / Premiere Danseuse

530   LUCYROWE 14 (b.f., April 10, 1966)

Bred by Burton Agnes Stud Co. Ltd.

Won 6 races, placed 2, £22,202, in England, at 2 and 3 years, incl. Coronation Stakes, Nassau Stakes, Sun Chariot Stakes; 2nd Cheveley Park Stakes, Wills Mile.

CREPELLO (ch. 1954)	Donatello II (ch. 1934)	Blenheim	Blandford / Malva
		Delleana	Clarissimus / Duccia di Buoninsegna
	Crepuscule (ch. 1948)	Mieuxce	Massine / L'Olivete
		Red Sunset	Solario / Dulce II
ESQUIRE GIRL (b. 1952)	My Babu (b. 1945)	Djebel	Tourbillon / Loika
		Perfume II	Badruddin / Lavendula II
	Lady Sybil (b. 1940)	Nearco	Pharos / Nogara
		Sister Sarah	Abbots Trace / Sarita

531   LUNCHTIME 7 (ch.c., April 9, 1970)

Bred by Lt.-Col. R. D. Poole.

Won 3 races, placed 1, £16,984, in England, at 2 and 3 years, incl. Dewhurst Stakes; 2nd Clerical Medical Greenham Stakes.

SILLY SEASON (b. 1962)	Tom Fool (b. 1949)	Menow	Pharamond / Alcibiades
		Gaga	Bull Dog / Alpoise
	Double Deal (b. 1946)	Straight Deal	Solario / Good Deal
		Nonats	King Salmon / Whitebait
GREAT OCCASION (ch. 1965)	Hornbeam (ch. 1953)	Hyperion	Gainsborough / Selene
		Thicket	Nasrullah / Thorn Wood
	Golden Wedding (br. 1959)	Sunny Brae	Torbido / Sun Petal
		Flighty Falls	Falls of Clyde / Swarm

532   LUPE 1 (b.f., February 23, 1967)

Bred by Snailwell Stud Co. Ltd.

Won 6 races, £53,764, in England, from 2 to 4 years, incl. Oaks Stakes, Cheshire Oaks, Yorkshire Oaks, Coronation Cup and Princess of Wales's Stakes.

PRIMERA (b. 1954)	My Babu (b. 1945)	Djebel	Tourbillon / Loika
		Perfume II	Badruddin / Lavendula II
	Pirette (b. 1943)	Deiri	Aethelstan / Desra
		Pimpette	Town Guard / Arpette
ALCOA (ch. 1957)	Alycidon (ch. 1945)	Donatello II	Blenheim / Delleana
		Aurora	Hyperion / Rose Red
	Phyllis Court (ch. 1948)	Court Martial	Fair Trial / Instantaneous
		Lady Grand	Solario / Begum

533   LUTHIER 14 (br.c., March 22, 1965)

Bred by Baron Guy de Rothschild, in France.

Won 4 races, placed 2, 953,285 fr., in France, from 2 to 4 years, incl. Prix Lupin, Prix Jacques le Marois and Prix Noailles; 4th Grand Criterium and Prix Ganay.

KLAIRON (b. 1952)	Clarion III (b. 1944)	Djebel	Tourbillon / Loika
		Columba	Colorado / Gay Bird
	Kalmia (b. 1931)	Kantar	Alcantara II / Karabe
		Sweet Lavender	Swynford / Marchetta
FLUTE ENCHANTEE (b. 1950)	Cranach (b. 1938)	Coronach	Hurry On / Wet Kiss
		Reine Isaure	Blandford / Oriane
	Montagnana (b. 1937)	Brantome	Blandford / Vitamine
		Mauretania	Tetratema / Lady Maureen

534   LYNCHRIS 8 (b.f., March 20, 1957)

Bred by Baroda Stud.

Won 6 races, placed 2, £15,960, in Ireland and England, from 2 to 4 years, incl. Irish Oaks, Irish St. Leger, Yorkshire Oaks, Wills' Gold Flake Stakes, Beresford Stakes; 4th Irish 1,000 Guineas.

SAYAJIRAO (br. 1944)	Nearco (br. 1935)	Pharos	Phalaris / Scapa Flow
		Nogara	Havresac II / Catnip
	Rosy Legend (br. 1931)	Dark Legend	Dark Ronald / Golden Legend
		Rosy Cheeks	St. Just / Purity
SCOLLATA (b. 1952)	Niccolo Dell'Arca (b. 1938)	Coronach	Hurry On / Wet Kiss
		Nogara	Havresac II / Catnip
	Cutaway (b. 1943)	Fairway	Phalaris / Scapa Flow
		Schiaparelli	Schiavoni / Aileen

111

535 LYPHARD 17 (b.c., May 10, 1969)

Bred by Mrs. J. O. Burgwin, in U.S.A.

Won 6 races, placed 3, 1,020,239 fr., in France, at 2 and 3 years, incl. Prix Jacques le Marois, Prix de la Foret and Prix Daru; 2nd Prix du Moulin de Longchamp; 4th Prix Lupin.

NORTHERN DANCER (b. 1961)	Nearctic (br. 1954)	Nearco	Pharos / Nogara
		Lady Angela	Hyperion / Sister Sarah
	Natalma (b. 1957)	Native Dancer	Polynesian / Geisha
		Almahmoud	Mahmoud / Arbitrator
GOOFED (ch. 1960)	Court Martial (ch. 1942)	Fair Trial	Fairway / Lady Juror
		Instantaneous	Hurry On / Picture
	Bárra (ch. 1950)	Formor	Ksar / Formose
		La Favorite	Biribi / La Pompadour

536 MABEL 15 (br.f., April 26, 1962)

Bred by G. P. Williams.

Won 5 races, placed 4, £11,953, in England, at 2 and 3 years, incl. Yorkshire Oaks; 2nd Oaks Stakes, Park Hill Stakes; 3rd 1,000 Guineas Stakes.

FRENCH BEIGE (b. 1953)	Bois Roussel (br. 1935)	Vatout	Prince Chimay / Vasthi
		Plucky Liege	Spearmint / Concertina
	Nivea (b. 1943)	Nearco	Pharos / Nogara
		Deva	Gainsborough / Lake Van
AUNT MAY (gr. 1955)	Grey Sovereign (gr. 1948)	Nasrullah	Nearco / Mumtaz Begum
		Kong	Baytown / Clang
	Mrs. Mops (b. 1941)	Colombo	Manna / Lady Nairne
		Charwoman	Apron / Lady Earn

537 MAC DIARMIDA 1 (dk.b./br.c., April 13, 1975)

Bred by J. H. Hartigan, in U.S.A.

Won 12 races, placed 2, $503,184, in U.S.A. and Canada, at 2 and 3 years, incl. Washington D.C. International, Canadian International Championship, Secretariat Stakes, Lawrence Realization Stakes, Lexington H., Long Branch Stakes and Leonard Richards Stakes; 3rd Man o'War Stakes.

MINNESOTA MAC (b. 1964)	Rough'n Tumble (b. 1948)	Free for All	Questionnaire / Panay
		Roused	Bull Dog / Rude Awakening
	Cow Girl (b. 1949)	Mustang	Mieuxce / Buzz Fuzz
		Ate	Phideas / Messe
FLYING TAMMIE (b. 1970)	Tim Tam (b. 1955)	Tom Fool	Menow / Gaga
		Two Lea	Bull Lea / Two Bob
	Compact (b. 1953)	Rush Act	Jacopo / Gotta Gonow
		Compassion	Flying Scot / Humane

538 MADELIA 1 (ch.f., April 20, 1974)

Bred by Dayton Ltd., in France.

Won 4 races, 1,385,000 fr., in France, at 3 years, incl. Prix de Diane, Poule d'Essai des Pouliches and Prix Saint-Alary.

CARO (gr. 1967)	Fortino II (gr. 1959)	Grey Sovereign	Nasrullah / Kong
		Ranavalo III	Relic / Navarra II
	Chambord (ch. 1955)	Chamossaire	Precipitation / Snowberry
		Life Hill	Solario / Lady of the Snows
MOONMADNESS (ch. 1963)	Tom Fool (b. 1949)	Menow	Pharamond / Alcibiades
		Gaga	Bull Dog / Alpoise
	Sunset (ch. 1950)	Hyperion	Gainsborough / Selene
		Fair Ranger	Bois Roussel / Point Duty

539 MADINA 14 (b.f., February 17, 1965)

Bred by Baron Guy de Rothschild, in France.

Won 1 race, placed 2, 291,950 fr., in France, at 2 years, incl. Prix Morny; 2nd Prix de la Salamandre.

BEAU PRINCE II (ch. 1952)	Prince Chevalier (b. 1943)	Prince Rose	Rose Prince / Indolence
		Chevalerie	Abbot's Speed / Kassala
	Isabelle Brand (b. 1943)	Black Devil	Sir Gallahad III / La Palina
		Isabelle d'Este	Godiche / Farnèse
GRANADA (br. 1957)	Auriban (br. 1949)	Pharis II	Pharos / Carissima
		Arriba	Tourbillon / Orlanda
	Callais (b. 1943)	Tourbillon	Ksar / Durban
		Aralia	Asterus / Naic

540 MAESTRALE 14 (b.c., March 18, 1966)

Bred by Razza di Mezzaluna, in U.S.A.

Won 14 races, placed 5, 57,500,000 L., in Italy, from 3 to 6 years, incl. Premio Presidente della Repubblica, Premio Ellington and Premio U.N.I.R.E.; 3rd Gran Premio di Milano.

MOLVEDO (br. 1958)	Ribot (b. 1952)	Tenerani	Bellini / Tofanella
		Romanella	El Greco / Barbara Burrini
	Maggiolina (br. 1946)	Nakamuro	Cameronian / Nogara
		Murcia	Pilade / Muci
MARIELLA (b./br. 1960)	Rustam (b./br. 1953)	Persian Gulf	Bahram / Double Life
		Samovar	Caerleon / Carolina
	Mary Ellard (b. 1951)	Tudor Minstrel	Owen Tudor / Sansonnet
		Anacapri	Tiberius / Travos

541   MAGAZINE 4 (b.f., April 10, 1970)

Bred by Elmendorf Farm, in U.S.A.

Won 4 races, placed 4, $99,887, in U.S.A., at 3 and 4 years, incl. Coaching Club American Oaks; 3rd Brighton Beach H.

PRINCE JOHN (ch. 1953)	Princequillo (b. 1940)	Prince Rose	Rose Prince / Indolence
		Cosquilla	Papyrus / Quick Thought
	Not Afraid (b. 1948)	Count Fleet	Reigh Count / Quickly
		Banish Fear	Blue Larkspur / Herodiade
DAY LINE (b./br. 1963)	Day Court (br. 1955)	Petition	Fair Trial / Art Paper
		Joyce Grove	Bois Roussel / Samovar
	Fast Line (b. 1958)	Mr. Busher	War Admiral / Baby League
		Throttle Wide	Flying Heels / Let Her Fly

542   MAGIC FLUTE 14 (br.f., April 19, 1968)

Bred by Lord Howard de Walden.

Won 5 races, placed 3, £21,827, in England, at 2 and 3 years, incl. Cheveley Park Stakes, Coronation Stakes; 4th 1,000 Guineas Stakes.

TUDOR MELODY (br. 1956)	Tudor Minstrel (br. 1944)	Owen Tudor	Hyperion / Mary Tudor II
		Sansonnet	Sansovino / Lady Juror
	Matelda (br. 1947)	Dante	Nearco / Rosy Legend
		Fairly Hot	Solario / Fair Cop
FILIGRANA (br. 1953)	Niccolo Dell'Arca (b. 1938)	Coronach	Hurry On / Wet Kiss
		Nogara	Havresac II / Catnip
	Gamble in Gold (b. or br. 1948)	Big Game	Bahram / Myrobella
		Gold Rush	Gold Bridge / Gold Race

543   MAJESTIC PRINCE 4 (ch.c., March 19, 1966)

Bred by Leslie Combs II, in U.S.A.

Won 9 races, placed 1, $414,200, in U.S.A., at 2 and 3 years, incl. Kentucky Derby, Preakness Stakes, Santa Anita Derby, San Vicente Stakes and San Jacinto Stakes; 2nd Belmont Stakes.

RAISE A NATIVE (ch. 1961)	Native Dancer (gr. 1950)	Polynesian	Unbreakable / Black Polly
		Geisha	Discovery / Miyako
	Raise You (ch. 1946)	Case Ace	Teddy / Sweetheart
		Lady Glory	American Flag / Beloved
GAY HOSTESS (ch. 1957)	Royal Charger (ch. 1942)	Nearco	Pharos / Nogara
		Sun Princess	Solario / Mumtaz Begum
	Your Hostess (ch. 1949)	Alibhai	Hyperion / Teresina
		Boudoir	Mahmoud / Kampala

544   MAJORITY BLUE 10 (ch.c., April 6, 1961)

Bred by Irish National Stud Co. Ltd.

Won 9 races, placed 6, £8,877, in Ireland and England, from 2 to 4 years, incl. Tetrarch Stakes, Diadem Stakes, Cork and Orrery Stakes.

MAJOR PORTION (ch. 1955)	Court Martial (ch. 1942)	Fair Trial	Fairway / Lady Juror
		Instantaneous	Hurry On / Picture
	Better Half (b. 1946)	Mieuxce	Massine / L'Olivete
		Malay Bride	Colombo / Singapore's Sister
GORM ABU (b. 1954)	My Babu (b. 1945)	Djebel	Tourbillon / Loika
		Perfume II	Badruddin / Lavendula II
	Cnoc Gorm (ch. 1947)	Blue Peter	Fairway / Fancy Free
		Hillhampton	Hyperion / Sparkling Gem

545   MALACATE 20 (b.c., April 18, 1973)

Bred by Thomas C. Sturgill, in U.S.A.

Won 8 races, placed 3, £161,217, in France, Ireland and England, from 2 to 4 years, incl. Irish Sweeps Derby, Joe McGrath Memorial Stakes, Prix La Force, Prix Foy; 3rd Prix du Jockey-Club, Prix Niel; 4th Champion Stakes.

LUCKY DEBONAIR (b. 1962)	Vertex (ch. 1954)	The Rhymer	St. Germans / Rhythmic
		Kanace	Case Ace / Kanlast
	Fresh as Fresh (b. 1957)	Count Fleet	Reigh Count / Quickly
		Airy	Bull Lea / Proud One
EYESHADOW (b. 1959)	My Babu (b. 1945)	Djebel	Tourbillon / Loika
		Perfume II	Badruddin / Lavendula II
	Pretty One (b. 1947)	Bull Dog	Teddy / Plucky Liege
		Irvana	Blue Larkspur / Princess Camelia

546   MALHOA 6 (b.c., 1955)

Bred by Razza Dormello-Olgiata, in England.

Won 13 races, placed 15, 32,357,000 L., in Italy, from 2 to 5 years, incl. Gran Premio di Milano, Premio Emilio Turati and Gran Premio Citta di Napoli; 2nd Premio Roma, Premio Ambrosiano, St. Leger Italiano, Gran Premio Citta di Napoli and Premio d'Aprile; 3rd Gran Premio di Milano and Gran Premio del Jockey Club.

TENERANI (b. 1944)	Bellini (b. 1937)	Cavaliere d'Arpino	Havresac II / Chuette
		Bella Minna	Bachelor's Double / Santa Minna
	Tofanella (ch. 1931)	Apelle	Sardanapale / Angelina
		Try Try Again	Cylgad / Perseverance II
MACCHIETTA (br. 1946)	Niccolo Dell'Arca (b. 1938)	Coronach	Hurry On / Wet Kiss
		Nogara	Havresac II / Catnip
	Milldoria (br. 1932)	Milton	Marcovil / Misfit
		Doria	Symington / Depeche

547   MANADO 3 (b.c., February 26, 1973)

Bred by J. R. S. Coggan, in Ireland.

Won 3 races, placed 6, 1,021,735 fr., in France, at 2 and 3 years, incl. Grand Criterium and Prix de la Salamandre; 3rd Prix du Moulin de Longchamp, Prix de la Foret and Prix du Rond-Point; 4th Prix Jacques le Marois.

CAPTAIN'S GIG (b./br. 1965)	Turn-to (b. 1951)	Royal Charger	Nearco / Sun Princess
		Source Sucree	Admiral Drake / Lavendula II
	Make Sail (br. 1957)	Ambiorix II	Tourbillon / Lavendula II
		Anchors Aweigh	Devil Diver / True Bearing
SLIPSTREAM (gr. 1967)	Sing Sing (b. 1957)	Tudor Minstrel	Owen Tudor / Sansonnet
		Agin the Law	Portlaw / Revolte
	Palestream (gr. 1959)	Palestine	Fair Trial / Una
		Millstream	Mieuxce / Millrock

548   MANDRAKE MAJOR 21 (b.c., March 23, 1974)

Bred by F. F. Tuthill and Mrs. A. W. F. Whitehead.

Won 3 races, placed 5, £32,749, in England, at 2 and 3 years, incl. Flying Childers Stakes; 3rd William Hill Middle Park Stakes, July Cup, King George Stakes, Diadem Stakes.

ON YOUR MARK (ch. 1964)	Restless Wind (ch. 1956)	Windy City	Wyndham / Staunton
		Lump Sugar	Bull Lea / Sugar Run
	Super Scope (ch. 1958)	Swaps	Khaled / Iron Reward
		Weeber	Panorama / Amy Leigh
FLATTERED (br. 1960)	Zarathustra (bl. 1951)	Persian Gulf	Bahram / Double Life
		Salvia	Sansovino / Love in the Mist
	Flatter (ch. 1947)	Rockefella	Hyperion / Rockfel
		Daring Miss	Felicitation / Venturesome

549   MANNSFELD 6 (ch.c., January 19, 1971)

Bred by Razza Dormello-Olgiata, in Italy.

Won 8 races, placed 2, 106,940,856 L., in Italy, England and France, from 2 to 4 years, incl. Premio Presidente della Repubblica (twice), Premio Parioli and Prix Eugene Adam; 4th Prix Jacques le Marois.

CROCKET (ch. 1960)	King of the Tudors (ch. 1950)	Tudor Minstrel	Owen Tudor / Sansonnet
		Glen Line	Blue Peter / Scotia's Glen
	Chandelier (ch. 1955)	Goyama	Goya II / Devineress
		Queen of Light	Borealis / Picture Play
MARTINE BOILEAU (ch. 1965)	Match III (b. 1958)	Tantieme	Deux pour Cent / Terka
		Relance III	Relic / Polaire II
	Marguerite Delaroche (ch. 1956)	Toulouse Lautrec	Dante / Tokamura
		Mina da Siena	Cavaliere d'Arpino / Milldoria

550   MARBLE ARCH 9 (ch.f., February 7, 1970)

Bred by Warner L. Jones, Jr., in U.S.A.

Won 3 races, placed 3, £15,984, in England and Ireland, at 2 and 3 years, incl. Norfolk Stakes, Phoenix Stakes; 2nd King's Stand Stakes; 3rd Cheveley Park Stakes, Cornwallis Stakes.

BOLD LAD (USA) (ch. 1962)	Bold Ruler (b. 1954)	Nasrullah	Nearco / Mumtaz Begum
		Miss Disco	Discovery / Outdone
	Misty Morn (b. 1952)	Princequillo	Prince Rose / Cosquilla
		Grey Flight	Mahmoud / Planetoid
DE CATHY (b. 1961)	Decathlon (b. 1953)	Olympia	Heliopolis / Miss Dolphin
		Dog Blessed	Bull Dog / Blessed Again
	Farce (b. 1957)	Tom Fool	Menow / Gaga
		Whirla Lea	Whirlaway / Ore-the-Lea

551   MARCO VISCONTI 4 (ch.c., February 20, 1962)

Bred by Razza Spineta, in Italy.

Won 9 races, placed 6, 99,820,000 L., in Italy, from 3 to 5 years, incl. Gran Premio di Milano (twice), Gran Premio del Jockey Club, Premio Ambrosiano and Premio Ellington; 2nd Gran Premio di Milano, Premio Presidente della Repubblica (twice) and Premio Roma; 3rd Derby Italiano; 4th Gran Premio del Jockey Club.

ANTONIO CANALE (ch. 1946)	Torbido (br. 1941)	Ortello	Teddy / Hollebeck
		Tempesta	Michelangelo / Turletta
	Acquaforte (ch. 1936)	Blenheim	Blandford / Malva
		Althea	Hurry On / Miss Jean
MAGONZA (ch. 1954)	Traghetto (ch. 1942)	Cavaliere d'Arpino	Havresac II / Chuette
		Talma	Papyrus / Tolbooth
	Maestosa (br. 1943)	Navarro	Michelangelo / Nuvolona
		Maba	The Yellow Dwarf / Arbe

552   MARDUK 19 (b.c., March 15, 1971)

Bred by Gestüt Erlenhof, in Germany.

Won 9 races, placed 10, 775,500 DM., in Germany, from 2 to 5 years, incl. Deutsches Derby, Grosser Preis von Baden (twice), Deutsches St. Leger and Spreti-Rennen; 2nd Aral Pokal; 3rd Preis von Europa, Aral Pokal, Grosser Preis von Dusseldorf and Grosser Preis der Stadt Gelsenkirchen; 4th Preis von Europa.

ORSINI (br. 1954)	Ticino (b. 1939)	Athanasius	Ferro / Athanasie
		Terra	Aditi / Teufelsrose
	Oranien (b. 1949)	Nuvolari	Oleander / Nereide
		Omladina	Athanasius / Oblate
MARLIA (b. 1962)	Crepello (ch. 1954)	Donatello II	Blenheim / Delleana
		Crepuscule	Mieuxce / Red Sunset
	Mirnaya (b. 1956)	Nearco	Pharos / Nogara
		Solar System	Hyperion / Jury

553   MARGUERITE VERNAUT 14 (ch.f., March 21, 1957)

Bred by Razza Dormello-Olgiata, in Italy

Won 9 races, placed 1, £21,880, in Italy and England, at 2 and 3 years, incl. Gran Premio d'Italia, Premio Emanuele Filiberto, Gran Criterium, Criterium Nazionale, Premio Primi Passi, Champion Stakes; 2nd Premio Bimbi.

TOULOUSE LAUTREC (ch. 1950)	Dante (br. 1942)	Nearco	Pharos / Nogara
		Rosy Legend	Dark Legend / Rosy Cheeks
	Tokamura (ch. 1940)	Navarro	Michelangelo / Nuvolona
		Tofanella	Apelle / Try Try Again
MARIEBELLE (ch. 1948)	Mieuxce (b. 1933)	Massine	Consols / Mauri
		L'Olivete	Opott / Jonicole
	Myrtle Green (ch. 1937)	Trigo	Blandford / Athasi
		Simone Vergnes	Diadumenos / Incense

554   MARIACCI 9 (b.c., April 13, 1972)

Bred by Baron Guy de Rothschild, in France.

Won 4 races, placed 3, 1,406,625 fr., in France, at 2 and 3 years, incl. Grand Criterium, Prix Greffulhe and Prix des Chenes; 2nd Prix Lupin and Prix d'Ispahan; 3rd Prix du Jockey-Club.

DJAKAO (b. 1966)	Tanerko (br. 1953)	Tantieme	Deux pour Cent / Terka
		La Divine	Fair Copy / La Diva
	Diagonale (ch. 1959)	Ribot	Tenerani / Romanella
		Barley Corn	Hyperion / Schiaparelli
MARBRISA (b. 1966)	Exbury (ch. 1959)	Le Haar	Vieux Manoir / Mince Pie
		Greensward	Mossborough / Stargrass
	Supremora (b. 1958)	Supreme Court	Persian Gulf or Precipitation / Forecourt
		Temora	Tourbillon / Pharyva

555   MARIA WALESKA 2 (ch.f., January 21, 1976)

Bred by Soc. Agr. All. National, in Ireland.

Won 6 races, placed 4, 119,990,000 L., in Italy, at 2 and 3 years, incl. Oaks d'Italia, Gran Premio d'Italia and Criterium Femminile; 2nd Premio Regina Elena and Premio Dormello.

FILIBERTO (b. 1970)	Ribot (br. 1952)	Tenerani	Bellini / Tofanella
		Romanella	El Greco / Barbara Burrini
	Fast Line (ch. 1958)	Mr. Busher	War Admiral / Baby League
		Throttle Wide	Flying Heels / Let Her Fly
MISS PROTEGE (ch. 1970)	Successor (b. 1964)	Bold Ruler	Nasrullah / Miss Disco
		Misty Morn	Princequillo / Grey Flight
	Belle Musique (b. 1963)	Tudor Minstrel	Owen Tudor / Sansonnet
		Bellesoeur	Beau Pere / Donatrice

556   MARIELLA 4 (b.f., April 21, 1977)

Bred by Citadel Stud Establishment, in England.

Won 3 races, placed 2, 518,100 fr., in France and Italy, at 2 and 3 years, incl. Premio Roma and Prix de Royallieu; 2nd Prix de Pomone.

SIR GAYLORD (b. 1959)	Turn-to (b. 1951)	Royal Charger	Nearco / Sun Princess
		Source Sucree	Admiral Drake / Lavendula II
	Somethingroyal (b. 1952)	Princequillo	Prince Rose / Cosquilla
		Imperatrice	Caruso / Cinquepace
ZAMBARA (b. 1966)	Mossborough (ch. 1947)	Nearco	Pharos / Nogara
		All Moonshine	Bobsleigh / Selene
	Grischuna (b. 1959)	Ratification	Court Martial / Solesa
		Mountain Path	Bobsleigh / Path of Peace

557   MARINER 11 (b.c., March 4, 1964)

Bred by R. D. Hollingsworth.

Won 4 races, placed 4, £10,135, in England, from 2 to 4 years, incl. King Edward VII Stakes; 2nd Jockey Club Cup; 3rd Great Voltigeur Stakes.

ACROPOLIS (ch. 1952)	Donatello II (ch. 1934)	Blenheim	Blandford / Malva
		Delleana	Clarissimus / Duccia di Buoninsegna
	Aurora (ch. 1936)	Hyperion	Gainsborough / Selene
		Rose Red	Swynford / Marchetta
KYAK (bl. or br. 1953)	Big Game (b. 1939)	Bahram	Blandford / Friar's Daughter
		Myrobella	Tetratema / Dolabella
	Felucca (b. 1941)	Nearco	Pharos / Nogara
		Felsetta	Felstead / Ka-Lu-A

558   MARK ROYAL 22 (b.c., March 19, 1965)

Bred by J. S. M. Cosgrove.

Won 5 races, placed 5, £9,541, in Ireland and England, from 2 to 4 years incl. Coventry Stakes; 2nd Richmond Stakes.

MONET (ch. 1957)	Whistler (ch. 1950)	Panorama	Sir Cosmo / Happy Climax
		Farthing Damages	Fair Trial / Futility
	Gold Proof (ch. 1950)	Court Martial	Fair Trial / Instantaneous
		Gold-craft	Gold Bridge / Witchford Lady
ROYAL STRAIGHT (b. 1955)	Straight Deal (b. 1940)	Solario	Gainsborough / Sun Worship
		Good Deal	Apelle / Weeds
	Archduchess (br. 1951)	Nearco	Pharos / Nogara
		Queenpot	Big Game / Poker Chip

559   **MARMOLADA** 13 (br.f., April 20, 1977)

Bred by Scuderia Alpina, in Ireland.

Won 9 races, placed 3, 169,300,000 L., in Italy, at 2 and 3 years, incl. Oaks d'Italia, Premio Lydia Tesio and Premio Federico Tesio; 3rd Gran Premio di Milano, Gran Premio del Jockey Club and Premio Dormello.

SASSAFRAS (b. 1967)	Sheshoon (ch. 1956)	Precipitation	Hurry On / Double Life
		Noorani	Nearco / Empire Glory
	Ruta (b. 1960)	Ratification	Court Martial / Solesa
		Dame d'Atour	Cranach / Barley Corn
MOBOLA (b. 1969)	Mincio (b. 1957)	Relic	War Relic / Bridal Colors
		Merise	Le Pacha / Miraflore
	Waltzing Matilda (ch. 1963)	Sound Track	Whistler / Bridle Way
		Farandole II	Deux pour Cent / Faramoude

560   **MARQUIS DE SADE** 5 (b. or br.c., April 10, 1973)

Bred by Sir Freddie Laker.

Won 4 races, placed 2, £21,395, in England, at 2 and 3 years, incl. King Edward VII Stakes.

QUEEN'S HUSSAR (b. 1960)	March Past (br. 1950)	Petition	Fair Trial / Art Paper
		Marcelette	William of Valence / Permavon
	Jojo (gr. 1950)	Vilmorin	Gold Bridge / Queen of the Meadows
		Fairy Jane	Fair Trial / Light Tackle
SWEET CHARITY (b. 1966)	Javelot (b. 1956)	Fast Fox	Fastnet / Foxcraft
		Djaina	Djebel / Fille d'Amour
	Phoenissa (b. 1951)	The Phoenix	Chateau Bouscaut / Fille de Poete
		Erica Fragrans	Big Game / Jennydang

561   **MARRACCI** 6 (br.c., February 4, 1976)

Bred by Razza Dormello-Olgiata, in England.

Won 3 races, placed 6, 206,977,200 L., in Italy, France and Germany, at 3 and 4 years, incl. Derby Italiano and Gran Premio di Milano: 2nd Premio Presidente della Repubblica and Grosser Preis von Berlin; 3rd Grosser Preis von Baden and Premio Federico Tesio.

SIR GAYLORD (b. 1959)	Turn-to (b. 1951)	Royal Charger	Nearco / Sun Princess
		Source Sucree	Admiral Drake / Lavendula II
	Somethingroyal (b. 1952)	Princequillo	Prince Rose / Cosquilla
		Imperatrice	Caruso / Cinquepace
MARTINE BOILEAU (ch. 1965)	Match III (b. 1958)	Tantieme	Deux pour Cent / Terka
		Relance III	Relic / Polaire II
	Marguerite Delaroche (ch. 1956)	Toulouse Lautrec	Dante / Tokamura
		Mina da Siena	Cavaliere d'Arpino / Milldoria

562   **MARTIAL** 2 (ch.c., April 6, 1957)

Bred by Captain A. D. D. Rogers.

Won 3 races, placed 2, £19,922, in Ireland and England, at 2 and 3 years, incl. 2,000 Guineas Stakes, Coventry Stakes; 2nd Sussex Stakes, Thirsk Classic Trial Stakes.

HILL GAIL (b. 1949)	Bull Lea (br. 1935)	Bull Dog	Teddy / Plucky Liege
		Rose Leaves	Ballot / Colonial
	Jane Gail (ch. 1944)	Blenheim	Blandford / Malva
		Lady Higloss	Ladkin / Hi Gloss
DISCIPLINER (ch. 1948)	Court Martial (ch. 1942)	Fair Trial	Fairway / Lady Juror
		Instantaneous	Hurry On / Picture
	Edvina (ch. 1940)	Figaro	Colorado / Tillywhim
		Louise	Finglas / Devonshire House

563   **MARWELL** 14 (b.f., May 21, 1978)

Bred by E. J. Loder.

Won 5 races, £62,552, in England, at 2 years, incl. William Hill Cheveley Park Stakes, Flying Childers Stakes, Molecomb Stakes.

HABITAT (b. 1966)	Sir Gaylord (b. 1959)	Turn-to	Royal Charger / Source Sucree
		Somethingroyal	Princequillo / Imperatrice
	Little Hut (b. 1952)	Occupy	Bull Dog / Miss Bunting
		Savage Beauty	Challenger / Khara
LADY SEYMOUR (b. 1972)	Tudor Melody (br. 1956)	Tudor Minstrel	Owen Tudor / Sansonnet
		Matelda	Dante / Fairly Hot
	My Game (br. 1957)	My Babu	Djebel / Perfume II
		Flirting	Big Game / Overture

564   **MASTER DERBY** 1 (ch.c., April 24, 1972)

Bred by R. E. Lehmann, in U.S.A.

Won 16 races, placed 12, $698,624, in U.S.A., from 2 to 4 years, incl. Preakness Stakes, Louisiana Derby, Blue Grass Stakes, New Orleans H., Oaklawn H. and Kindergarten Stakes; 2nd Metropolitan H., Trenton H., Breeders' Futurity and Kentucky Jockey Club H.; 3rd Belmont Stakes, Ak-Sar-Ben Omaha Gold Cup and Heritage Stakes; 4th Kentucky Derby.

DUST COMMANDER (ch. 1967)	Bold Commander (b. 1960)	Bold Ruler	Nasrullah / Miss Disco
		High Voltage	Ambiorix II / Dynamo
	Dust Storm (ch. 1956)	Windy City	Wyndham / Staunton
		Challure	Challedon / Captivation
MADAM JERRY (ch. 1961)	Royal Coinage (br. 1952)	Eight Thirty	Pilate / Dinner Time
		Canina	Bull Dog / Coronium
	Our Kretchen (ch. 1955)	Crafty Admiral	Fighting Fox / Admiral's Lady
		Adjournment	Court Martial / Blank Day

565　　MASTER WILLIE 4 (ch.c., April 12, 1977)

Bred by W. and R. Barnett Ltd.

Won 4 races, placed 7, £198,271, in England, at 2 and 3 years, incl. Benson and Hedges Gold Cup; 2nd Derby Stakes, Mecca-Dante Stakes, Champion Stakes.

HIGH LINE (ch. 1966)	High Hat (ch. 1957)	Hyperion	Gainsborough / Selene
		Madonna	Donatello II / Women's Legion
	Time Call (b. 1955)	Chanteur II	Chateau Bouscaut / La Diva
		Aleria	Djebel / Canidia
FAIR WINTER (ch. 1964)	Set Fair (ch. 1949)	Denturius	Gold Bridge / La Solfatara
		Ria Geno	Pappageno II / Talaria
	Winter Gleam (ch. 1959)	Aureole	Hyperion / Angelola
		Red Winter	My Babu / Bold Maid

566　　MATA HARI 19 (br.f., February 10, 1969)

Bred by Countess Margit Batthyany, in Germany.

Won 4 races, placed 6, 612,309 fr., in France, at 2 and 3 years, incl. Poule d'Essai des Pouliches; 2nd Prix de la Grotte; 3rd Criterium de Maisons-Laffitte.

ORSINI (br. 1954)	Ticino (b. 1939)	Athanasius	Ferro / Athanasie
		Terra	Aditi / Teufelsrose
	Oranien (b. 1949)	Nuvolari	Oleander / Nereide
		Omladina	Athanasius / Oblate
MARLIA (b. 1962)	Crepello (ch. 1954)	Donatello II	Blenheim / Delleana
		Crepuscule	Mieuxce / Red Sunset
	Mirnaya (b. 1956)	Nearco	Pharos / Nogara
		Solar System	Hyperion / Jury

567　　MATAHAWK 3 (b./br.c., March 10, 1972)

Bred by J. S. Furno, in Ireland.

Won 1 race, placed 4, 1,311,800 fr., in France at 2 and 3 years, incl. Grand Prix de Paris; 3rd Prix Lupin and Prix Daru.

SEA HAWK II (gr. 1963)	Herbager (b. 1956)	Vandale II	Plassy / Vanille
		Flagette	Escamillo / Fidgette
	Sea Nymph (gr. 1957)	Free Man	Norseman / Fantine
		Sea Spray	Ocean Swell / Pontoon
CARROMATA (b. 1965)	St. Paddy (b. 1957)	Aureole	Hyperion / Angelola
		Edie Kelly	Bois Roussel / Caerlissa
	Carrozza (b./br. 1954)	Dante	Nearco / Rosy Legend
		Calash	Hyperion / Clarence

568　　MATATINA 6 (b.f., March 23, 1960)

Bred by J. Hylton.

Won 5 races, placed 10, £13,342, in England, from 2 to 4 years, incl. Nunthorpe Stakes, King George Stakes; 2nd King's Stand Stakes, July Cup (twice), Nunthorpe Stakes, Cornwallis Stakes, Molecomb Stakes, Palace House Stakes.

GREY SOVEREIGN (gr. 1948)	Nasrullah (b. 1940)	Nearco	Pharos / Nogara
		Mumtaz Begum	Blenheim / Mumtaz Mahal
	Kong (gr. 1933)	Baytown	Achtoi / Princess Herodias
		Clang	Hainault / Vibration
ZANZARA (ch. 1951)	Fairey Fulmar (ch. 1943)	Fair Trial	Fairway / Lady Juror
		First Flight	Felstead / Pick of the Bunch
	Sunright (b. 1940)	Solario	Gainsborough / Sun Worship
		Democratie	Epinard / Queenly

569　　MATCH III 16 (br.c., April 27, 1958)

Bred by F. Dupré, in France.

Won 7 races, placed 4, £126,541, in France, England and U.S.A., at 3 and 4 years, incl. Prix Royal-Oak, Grand Prix de Saint-Cloud, Prix Noailles, King George VI and Queen Elizabeth Stakes, Washington D.C. International; 2nd Grand Prix de Paris, Prix du Jockey-Club, Prix Lupin; 4th Prix Ganay.

TANTIEME (b. 1947)	Deux pour Cent (b. 1941)	Deiri	Aethelstan / Desra
		Dix pour Cent	Feridoon / La Chansonnerie
	Terka (br. 1942)	Indus	Alcantara II / Himalaya
		La Furka	Blandford / Brenta
RELANCE III (ch. 1952)	Relic (bl. 1945)	War Relic	Man o'War / Friar's Carse
		Bridal Colors	Black Toney / Vaila
	Polaire II (br. 1947)	Le Volcan	Tourbillon / Eroica
		Stella Polaris	Papyrus / Crepuscule

570　　MATTABOY 14 (ch.c., March 3, 1978)

Bred by Cheveley Park Stud Ltd.

Won 2 races, placed 3, £46,343, in England, at 2 years, incl. William Hill Middle Park Stakes; 2nd Mill Reef Stakes.

MUSIC BOY (ch. 1973)	Jukebox (b. 1966)	Sing Sing	Tudor Minstrel / Agin the Law
		Bibi Mah	Tehran / Mulier Magnifica
	Veronique (b. 1961)	Matador	Golden Cloud / Spanish Galantry
		Narcisse	Niccolo Dell'Arca / Asphodele
GREEN CHARTREUSE (b. 1970)	French Beige (b. 1953)	Bois Roussel	Vatout / Plucky Liege
		Nivea	Nearco / Deva
	Green Velvet (ch. 1965)	Epaulette	Court Martial / Golden Sari
		Greenheart	Borealis / Greenbridge

571   MAY HILL 15 (b.f., March 13, 1972)

Bred by G. P. Williams.

Won 4 races, placed 8, £43,752, in England and France, from 2 to 4 years, incl. Yorkshire Oaks, Park Hill Stakes; 2nd Fred Darling Stakes, Musidora Stakes; 3rd Prix Vermeille, Jockey Club Cup; 4th Oaks Stakes.

HILL CLOWN (b. 1963)	Hillary (br. 1952)	Khaled	Hyperion
			Eclair
		Snow Bunny	Boswell
			La Rose
	Mary Machree (b. 1951)	Moonlight Run	Bobsleigh
			Selene
		Jessie-O-Doon	Brig o' Doon
			Editrix
MABEL (b. 1962)	French Beige (b. 1953)	Bois Roussel	Vatout
			Plucky Liege
		Nivea	Nearco
			Deva
	Aunt May (gr. 1955)	Grey Sovereign	Nasrullah
			Kong
		Mrs. Mops	Colombo
			Charwoman

572   MEADOW COURT 11 (ch.c., April 3, 1962)

Bred by Mrs. Parker Poe.

Won 3 races, placed 4, £101,668, in England and Ireland, at 2 and 3 years, incl. Irish Sweeps Derby, King George VI and Queen Elizabeth Stakes; 2nd Derby Stakes, St. Leger Stakes, Dante Stakes, Gladness Stakes. Ran unplaced in U.S.A. as an 8 year old.

COURT HARWELL (br. 1954)	Prince Chevalier (b. 1943)	Prince Rose	Rose Prince
			Indolence
		Chevalerie	Abbot's Speed
			Kassala
	Neutron (ch. 1948)	Hyperion	Gainsborough
			Selene
		Participation	Precipitation
			Arabella
MEADOW MUSIC (b. 1956)	Tom Fool (b. 1949)	Menow	Pharamond
			Alcibiades
		Gaga	Bull Dog
			Alpoise
	Miss Grillo (ch. 1942)	Rolando	Tresiete
			Persefona
		Cedulilla	Picacero
			Consulta

573   MEADOWVILLE 1 (ch.c., April 6, 1967)

Bred by P. A. Love.

Won 6 races, placed 11, £52,200, in England, Ireland and France, from 3 to 5 years, incl. Great Voltigeur Stakes, Jockey Club Stakes, John Porter Stakes, Lingfield Derby Trial Stakes; 2nd Irish Sweeps Derby, St. Leger, Irish St. Leger; 3rd St. Simon Stakes, Chester Vase, Doncaster Cup.

CHARLOTTESVILLE (b. 1957)	Prince Chevalier (b. 1943)	Prince Rose	Rose Prince
			Indolence
		Chevalerie	Abbot's Speed
			Kassala
	Noorani (ch. 1950)	Nearco	Pharos
			Nogara
		Empire Glory	Singapore
			Skyglory
MEADOW PIPIT (ch. 1961)	Worden II (ch. 1949)	Wild Risk	Rialto
			Wild Violet
		Sans Tares	Sind
			Tara
	Rising Wings (ch. 1955)	The Phoenix	Chateau Bouscaut
			Fille de Poete
		Skylarking	Precipitation
			Woodlark

574   MEAUTRY 2 (ch.c., May 17, 1970)

Bred by Baron Guy de Rothschild, in France.

Won 5 races, placed 13, 708,918 fr., in France, Germany and Sweden, from 3 to 5 years, incl. Grosser Preis von Baden.

LIONEL (ch. 1963)	Herbager (b. 1956)	Vandale II	Plassy
			Vanille
		Flagette	Escamillo
			Fidgette
	La Strada (b. 1955)	Fervent	Blenheim
			Hug Again
		Coca Cola III	Felstead
			Arcola II
GREENSWARD (b. 1953)	Mossborough (ch. 1947)	Nearco	Pharos
			Nogara
		All Moonshine	Bobsleigh
			Selene
	Stargrass (b. 1942)	Noble Star	Hapsburg
			Hesper
		Grass Widow	Son-in-Law
			Silver Grass

575   MENDIP MAN 3 (b.c., March 10, 1972)

Bred by J. Davis, in England.

Won 3½ races, placed 12, 447,042 fr., in France, England and U.S.A., from 2 to 5 years, incl. Prix de l'Abbaye de Longchamp (dead-heat); 2nd Prix du Palais Royal; 3rd Prix de l'Abbaye de Longchamp and Prix de Seine-et-Oise.

MANACLE (b. 1964)	Sing Sing (b. 1957)	Tudor Minstrel	Owen Tudor
			Sansonnet
		Agin the Law	Portlaw
			Revolte
	Hard and Fast (b. 1957)	Hard Sauce	Ardan
			Saucy Bella
		Boodley	Borealis
			Estrellita
GRANDERA (ch. 1963)	Primera (b. 1954)	My Babu	Djebel
			Perfume II
		Pirette	Deiri
			Pimpette
	Palm Court (ch. 1957)	Royal Palm	Royal Charger
			Pasquinade
		Grande Corniche	Panorama
			Joy-Ride

576   MENEVAL 9 (b.c., March 30, 1973)

Bred by Mrs. G. M. Humphrey, in U.S.A.

Won 5 races, placed 2, £44,005, in Ireland and England, from 2 to 5 years, incl. Irish St. Leger, Gallinule Stakes, Nijinsky Stakes, Hardwicke Stakes; 2nd Cumberland Lodge Stakes.

LE FABULEUX (ch. 1961)	Wild Risk (b. 1940)	Rialto	Rabelais
			La Grelee
		Wild Violet	Blandford
			Wood Violet
	Anguar (b. 1950)	Verso II	Pinceau
			Variete
		La Rochelle	Easton
			Sans Tares
NALEE (b. 1960)	Nashua (b. 1952)	Nasrullah	Nearco
			Mumtaz Begum
		Segula	Johnstown
			Sekhmet
	Levee (ch. 1953)	Hill Prince	Princequillo
			Hildene
		Bourtai	Stimulus
			Escutcheon

577 MERCHANT VENTURER 3 (ch.c., March 12, 1960)

Bred by Sir Foster Robinson.

Won 1 race, placed 8, £7,977, in England, at 2 and 3 years, incl. Dante Stakes; 2nd Derby Stakes, Gordon Stakes, Washington Singer Stakes; 3rd Royal Lodge Stakes, Craven Stakes, Great Voltigeur Stakes; 4th St. Leger Stakes.

HORNBEAM (ch. 1953)	Hyperion (ch. 1930)	Gainsborough	Bayardo / Rosedrop
		Selene	Chaucer / Serenissima
	Thicket (b. 1947)	Nasrullah	Nearco / Mumtaz Begum
		Thorn Wood	Bois Roussel / Point Duty
MARTINHOE (ch. 1947)	Mieuxce (b. 1933)	Massine	Consols / Mauri
		L'Olivete	Opott / Jonicole
	Vocation (b. or br. 1942)	Atout Maitre	Vatout / Royal Mistress
		Maiden's Choice	Mr. Jinks / Nun's Veil

578 MERRY MATE 7 (b.f., April 16, 1963)

Bred by J. McShain.

Won 1 race, £18,599, in Ireland, at 3 years, viz. Irish Guinness Oaks.

BALLYMOSS (ch. 1954)	Mossborough (ch. 1947)	Nearco	Pharos / Nogara
		All Moonshine	Bobsleigh / Selene
	Indian Call (ch. 1936)	Singapore	Gainsborough / Tetrabbazia
		Flittemere	Buchan / Keysoe
GLADNESS (b. or br. 1953)	Sayajirao (br. 1944)	Nearco	Pharos / Nogara
		Rosy Legend	Dark Legend / Rosy Cheeks
	Bright Lady (br. 1938)	April the Fifth	Craig an Eran / Sold Again
		Bright Spot	Solario / Postmark

579 MEXICO 6 (b.c., February 12, 1958)

Bred by Allevamento Gibi, in Italy.

Won 10 races, placed 9, 50,721,000 L., in Italy and Germany, from 2 to 5 years, incl. Gran Premio di Milano (twice) Coppa d'Oro di Milano and Gran Premio Citta di Torino; 2nd Premio Roma, St. Leger Italiano and Grosser Preis von Nordrhein-Westfalen; 3rd Grosser Preis von Baden; 4th Derby Italiano.

TRAGHETTO (ch. 1942)	Cavaliere d'Arpino (b. 1926)	Havresac II	Rabelais / Hors Concours
		Chuette	Cicero / Chute
	Talma (br. 1933)	Papyrus	Tracery / Miss Matty
		Tolbooth	Buchan / Popingaol
MACCHIETTA (br. 1946)	Niccolo Dell'Arca (b. 1938)	Coronach	Hurry On / Wet Kiss
		Nogara	Havresac II / Catnip
	Milldoria (br. 1932)	Milton	Marcovil / Misfit
		Doria	Symington / Depeche

580 MIGE 1 (b.f., April 15, 1966)

Bred by Mme. P. Wertheimer, in France.

Won 3 races, placed 4, £29,148, in France and England, at 2 and 3 years, incl. Cheveley Park Stakes; 2nd Prix Quincey, Prix d'Astarte; 4th Prix de la Foret.

SAINT CRESPIN III (ch. 1956)	Aureole (ch. 1950)	Hyperion	Gainsborough / Selene
		Angelola	Donatello II / Feola
	Neocracy (b. 1944)	Nearco	Pharos / Nogara
		Harina	Blandford / Athasi
MIDGET II (gr. 1953)	Djebe (gr. 1945)	Djebel	Tourbillon / Loika
		Catherine	Tiberius / Catherinette
	Mimi (b. 1943)	Black Devil	Sir Gallahad III / La Palina
		Mignon	Epinard / Mammee

581 MILL REEF 22 (b.c., February 23, 1968)

Bred by Paul Mellon, in U.S.A.

Won 12 races, placed 2, £315,263, in England and France, from 2 to 4 years, incl. Derby Stakes, Eclipse Stakes, King George VI and Queen Elizabeth Stakes, Prix de l'Arc de Triomphe, Prix Ganay, Coronation Cup, Coventry Stakes, Gimcrack Stakes, Dewhurst Stakes, Greenham Stakes; 2nd 2,000 Guineas, Prix Robert Papin.

NEVER BEND (b. 1960)	Nasrullah (b. 1940)	Nearco	Pharos / Nogara
		Mumtaz Begum	Blenheim / Mumtaz Mahal
	Lalun (b. 1952)	Djeddah	Djebel / Djezima
		Be Faithful	Bimelech / Bloodroot
MILAN MILL (b. 1962)	Princequillo (b. 1940)	Prince Rose	Rose Prince / Indolence
		Cosquilla	Papyrus / Quick Thought
	Virginia Water (gr. 1953)	Count Fleet	Reigh Count / Quickly
		Red Ray	Hyperion / Infra Red

582 MIL'S BOMB 2 (ch.f., April 6, 1971)

Bred by Sassoon Studs.

Won 4 races, placed 9, £30,687, in England, from 2 to 4 years, incl. Nassau Stakes, Park Hill Stakes, Lancashire Oaks; 2nd Yorkshire Oaks, Cheshire Oaks; 3rd Coronation Cup, Sun Chariot Stakes (twice), Fred Darling Stakes, St. Simon Stakes.

CREPELLO (ch. 1954)	Donatello II (ch. 1934)	Blenheim	Blandford / Malva
		Delleana	Clarissimus / Duccia di Buoninsegna
	Crepuscule (ch. 1948)	Mieuxce	Massine / L'Olivete
		Red Sunset	Solario / Dulce II
BALLY'S MIL (ch. 1964)	Ballymoss (ch. 1954)	Mossborough	Nearco / All Moonshine
		Indian Call	Singapore / Flittemere
	No Angel (b. 1949)	Nasrullah	Nearco / Mumtaz Begum
		Fair Angela	Fair Trial / Pomme d'Amour

583   MIRALGO 12 (ch.c., April 10, 1959)

Bred by Sir P. Loraine and R. More O'Ferrall.

Won 4 races, placed 8, £36,006, in England, from 2 to 4 years, incl. Timeform Gold Cup, Hardwicke Stakes, Westbury Stakes; 2nd Eclipse Stakes, King George VI and Queen Elizabeth Stakes, Great Voltigeur Stakes, Lingfield Derby Trial Stakes; 3rd St. Leger Stakes, Chester Vase, Gordon Stakes, Gimcrack Stakes.

AUREOLE (ch. 1950)	Hyperion (ch. 1930)	Gainsborough	Bayardo
			Rosedrop
		Selene	Chaucer
			Serenissima
	Angelola (b. 1945)	Donatello II	Blenheim
			Delleana
		Feola	Friar Marcus
			Aloe
NELLA (ch. 1949)	Nearco (br. 1935)	Pharos	Phalaris
			Scapa Flow
		Nogara	Havresac II
			Catnip
	Laitron (ch. 1932)	Soldennis	Tredennis
			Soligena
		Chardon	Aldford
			Thistle

584   MIRALLA 11 (ch.f., April 27, 1972)

Bred by Lady Nugent and Lady Lister Kaye.

Won 3 races, placed 3, £23,908, in Ireland, from 2 to 4 years, incl. Irish 1,000 Guineas Stakes, Athasi Stakes.

ALLANGRANGE (ch. 1967)	Le Levanstell (b. 1957)	Le Lavandou	Djebel
			Lavande
		Stella's Sister	Ballyogan
			My Aid
	Silken Princess (ch. 1956)	Arctic Prince	Prince Chevalier
			Arctic Sun
		Silken Slipper	Bois Roussel
			Carpet Slipper
MIRALIFE (ch. 1967)	Miralgo (ch. 1959)	Aureole	Hyperion
			Angelola
		Nella	Nearco
			Laitron
	London Life (ch. 1961)	Panaslipper	Solar Slipper
			Panastrid
		Court Circular	Court Martial
			Queanladdie

585   MISS DAN 13 (ch.f., April 2, 1967)

Bred by Achille Fould, in France.

Won 4 races, placed 8, 1,294,571 fr., in France, Germany and U.S.A., from 2 to 4 years, incl. Grand Prix de Deauville, Prix Kergorlay and Prix Fille de l'Air; 2nd Prix Vermeille, Washington D.C. International and Prix d'Harcourt; 3rd Prix de l'Arc de Triomphe and Preis von Europa.

DAN CUPID (ch. 1956)	Native Dancer (gr. 1950)	Polynesian	Unbreakable
			Black Polly
		Geisha	Discovery
			Miyako
	Vixenette (ch. 1944)	Sickle	Phalaris
			Selene
		Lady Reynard	Gallant Fox
			Nerva
MIRALOMA (ch. 1954)	Clarion III (b. 1944)	Djebel	Tourbillon
			Loika
		Columba	Colorado
			Gay Bird
	Mormyre (b. 1946)	Atys	Asterus
			Esclarmonde
		Morkande	Ksar
			Mortagne

586   MISSILE BELLE 5 (ch.f., April 10, 1967)

Bred by John A. Morris, in U.S.A.

Won 9 races, placed 5, $213,968, in U.S.A., from 2 to 4 years, incl. Coaching Club American Oaks and Gazelle H.; 2nd Acorn Stakes and Test Stakes; 3rd Mother Goose Stakes.

MISSILE (ch. 1954)	War Relic (ch. 1938)	Man o'War	Fair Play
			Mahubah
		Friar's Carse	Friar Rock
			Problem
	Inajiffy (ch. 1948)	Heliopolis	Hyperion
			Drift
		Lull	Bull Dog
			Luscinia
RIVER PRINCESS (b. 1959)	Princequillo (b. 1940)	Prince Rose	Rose Prince
			Indolence
		Cosquilla	Papyrus
			Quick Thought
	Crevasse (br. 1945)	Johnstown	Jamestown
			La France
		Predestined	Stimulus
			Destiny Bay

587   MISSISSIPIAN 8 (b.c., May 16, 1971)

Bred by Nelson Bunker Hunt, in U.S.A.

Won 3 races, placed 6, 1,263,301 fr., in France, England and Ireland, at 2 and 3 years, incl. Grand Criterium and Prix Niel; 2nd Observer Gold Cup, Poule d'Essai des Poulains and Prix Lupin; 4th Prix du Jockey-Club and Irish Sweeps Derby.

VAGUELY NOBLE (b. 1965)	Vienna (ch. 1957)	Aureole	Hyperion
			Angelola
		Turkish Blood	Turkhan
			Rusk
	Noble Lassie (b. 1956)	Nearco	Pharos
			Nogara
		Belle Sauvage	Big Game
			Tropical Sun
GAZALA II (b. 1964)	Dark Star (br. 1950)	Royal Gem II	Dhoti
			French Gem
		Isolde	Bull Dog
			Fiji
	Belle Angevine (br. 1957)	L'Amiral	Admiral Drake
			Hurrylor
		Bella II	Canot
			Bayan Kara

588   MISS PETARD 1 (ch.f., April 22, 1970)

Bred by Mrs. G. Marcow.

Won 3 races, placed 3, £10,650, in England, at 2 and 3 years, incl. Ribblesdale Stakes; 3rd Nassau Stakes.

PETINGO (b. 1965)	Petition (br. 1944)	Fair Trial	Fairway
			Lady Juror
		Art Paper	Artist's Proof
			Quire
	Alcazar (ch. 1957)	Alycidon	Donatello II
			Aurora
		Quarterdeck	Nearco
			Poker Chip
MISS UPWARD (b. 1964)	Alcide (b. 1955)	Alycidon	Donatello II
			Aurora
		Chenille	King Salmon
			Sweet Aloe
	Aiming High (gr. 1958)	Djebe	Djebel
			Catherine
		Annie Oakley	Big Game
			Annetta

589   **MISTER SIC TOP** 3 (br.c., March 25, 1967)

Bred by L. Deshayes, in France.

Won 9 races, placed 18, 1,277,277 fr., in France, from 2 to 7 years, incl. Prix d'Ispahan, Prix Exbury (twice) and Prix du Prince d'Orange; 2nd Prix Dollar, Prix Foy and Prix d'Harcourt; 3rd Prix Ganay, Prix d'Harcourt (twice) and Prix Gontaut-Biron; 4th Prix d'Ispahan.

TIFFAUGES (b. 1958)	Fine Top (br. 1949)	Fine Art	Artist's Proof / Finnoise
		Toupie	Vatellor / Tarentella
	La Lorie (ch. 1950)	Coastal Traffic	Hyperion / Rose of England
		Ann's Twin	Plassy / Slide Along
MADAME DAURADE (br. 1953)	Sicambre (br. 1948)	Prince Bio	Prince Rose / Biologie
		Sif	Rialto / Suavita
	Dugazon (ch. 1936)	Rialto	Rabelais / La Grelee
		Drachma	Corcyra / Penny Forfeit

590   **MISTIGO** 14 (ch.c., April 16, 1965)

Bred by B. J. Fagan.

Won 3 races, placed 4, £13,009, in Ireland, at 2 and 3 years, incl. Irish 2,000 Guineas Stakes; 2nd Larkspur Stakes.

MIRALGO (ch. 1959)	Aureole (ch. 1950)	Hyperion	Gainsborough / Selene
		Angelola	Donatello II / Feola
	Nella (ch. 1949)	Nearco	Pharos / Nogara
		Laitron	Soldennis / Chardon
FLOWING LAVA (b. 1955)	Krakatao (b. 1946)	Nearco	Pharos / Nogara
		Life Hill	Solario / Lady of the Snows
	Rorke's Drift (br. 1938)	Spion Kop	Spearmint / Hammerkop
		Bridgemount	Bridge of Earn / Mountain Mint

591   **MISTIGRI** 22 (b.c., May 26, 1971)

Bred by Dollanstown Stud Establishment.

Won 5 races, placed 13, £53,258, in Ireland, England and France, from 2 to 7 years, incl. Irish St. Leger, Desmond Stakes; 2nd Dee Stakes, Desmond Stakes, Prix Jean Prat, Prix de Barbeville; 3rd Blandford Stakes; 4th Ascot Gold Cup, Prix du Cadran (twice). Also won 2 races, placed 1, £27,284, over jumps in France at 6 years.

MISTI IV (b. or br. 1958)	Medium (b. 1946)	Meridien	Tourbillon / Meriem
		Melodie	Monarch / Mitidja II
	Mist (gr. 1953)	Tornado	Tourbillon / Roseola
		La Touche	Rienzo / La Rasina
NYANGA (b. 1963)	Never Say Die (ch. 1951)	Nasrullah	Nearco / Mumtaz Begum
		Singing Grass	War Admiral / Boreale
	Picaresque (br. 1954)	Cranach	Coronach / Reine Isaure
		Laura	Dante / Avena

592   **MISWAKI** 16 (ch.c., February 22, 1978)

Bred by Bruce Campbell and Early Bird Stud, in U.S.A.

Won 2 races, placed 2, 504,964 fr., in France and England, at 2 years, incl. Prix de la Salamandre; 2nd Prix Morny; 3rd William Hill Dewhurst Stakes.

MR. PROSPECTOR (b. 1970)	Raise a Native (ch. 1961)	Native Dancer	Polynesian / Geisha
		Raise You	Case Ace / Lady Glory
	Gold Digger (b. 1962)	Nashua	Nasrullah / Segula
		Sequence	Count Fleet / Miss Dogwood
HOPESPRINGSETERNAL (ch. 1971)	Buckpasser (b. 1963)	Tom Fool	Menow / Gaga
		Busanda	War Admiral / Businesslike
	Rose Bower (ch. 1958)	Princequillo	Prince Rose / Cosquilla
		Lea Lane	Nasrullah / Lea Lark

593   **M-LOLSHAN** 19 (br.c., May 22, 1975)

Bred by Yeomanstown Stud.

Won 6 races, placed 15, £143,929, in England, Ireland and Germany, from 2 to 5 years, incl. Irish St. Leger, Grosser Preis von Baden; 2nd Princess of Wales's Stakes, Geoffrey Freer Stakes; 3rd St. Leger Stakes, Geoffrey Freer Stakes, Preis von Europa; 4th Coronation Cup, King George VI and Queen Elizabeth Diamond Stakes.

LEVMOSS (b. 1965)	Le Levanstell (b. 1957)	Le Lavandou	Djebel / Lavande
		Stella's Sister	Ballyogan / My Aid
	Feemoss (b. 1960)	Ballymoss	Mossborough / Indian Call
		Feevagh	Solar Slipper / Astrid Wood
SUPREME LADY (b. 1965)	Grey Sovereign (gr. 1948)	Nasrullah	Nearco / Mumtaz Begum
		Kong	Baytown / Clang
	Ulupi's Sister (b. 1955)	Combat	Big Game / Commotion
		Puff Adder	Easton / Madder

594   **MOLVEDO** 16 (br.c., April 25, 1958)

Bred by Razza Ticino, in Italy.

Won 7 races, placed 1, 131,135,230 L., in Italy and France, at 2 and 3 years, incl. Prix de l'Arc de Triomphe, Grand Prix de Deauville, Gran Premio del Jockey Club, Premio d'Estate and Gran Criterium; 3rd Criterium Nazionale.

RIBOT (b. 1952)	Tenerani (b. 1944)	Bellini	Cavaliere d'Arpino / Bella Minna
		Tofanella	Apelle / Try Try Again
	Romanella (ch. 1943)	El Greco	Pharos / Gay Gamp
		Barbara Burrini	Papyrus / Bucolic
MAGGIOLINA (br. 1946)	Nakamuro (b. 1940)	Cameronian	Pharos / Una Cameron
		Nogara	Havresac II / Catnip
	Murcia (ch. 1940)	Pilade	Captain Cuttle / Piera
		Muci	Tetrameter / Pearl Maiden

595   **MONADE** 13 (br.f., May 16, 1959)

Bred by A. Fould, in France.

Won 9 races, placed 11, £85,478, in France and England, from 2 to 5 years, incl. Prix Vermeille, Prix Penelope, La Coupe de Maisons-Laffitte, Prix de Pomone, Oaks Stakes; 2nd Prix de l'Arc de Triomphe, Prix Ganay, Prix Yacowlef, Prix d'Ispahan, Prix Jacques le Marois; 3rd Prix Jacques le Marois, Prix Messidor.

KLAIRON (b. 1952)	Clarion III (b. 1944)	Djebel	Tourbillon / Loika
		Columba	Colorado / Gay Bird
	Kalmia (b. 1931)	Kantar	Alcantara II / Karabe
		Sweet Lavender	Swynford / Marchetta
MORMYRE (b. 1946)	Atys (b. 1934)	Asterus	Teddy / Astrella
		Esclarmonde	Sunstar / Desmond Lassie
	Morkande (ch. 1934)	Ksar	Bruleur / Kizil Kourgan
		Mortagne	Prince Eugene / Marmara II

---

596   **MON FILS** 1 (br.c., May 1, 1970)

Bred by J. Davis.

Won 3 races, placed 3, £40,305, in England, at 2 and 3 years, incl. 2,000 Guineas Stakes, Mill Reef Stakes; 3rd Clerical Medical Greenham Stakes.

SHESHOON (ch. 1956)	Precipitation (ch. 1933)	Hurry On	Marcovil / Tout Suite
		Double Life	Bachelor's Double / Saint Joan
	Noorani (ch. 1950)	Nearco	Pharos / Nogara
		Empire Glory	Singapore / Skyglory
NOW WHAT (b. 1956)	Premonition (b. 1950)	Precipitation	Hurry On / Double Life
		Trial Ground	Fair Trial / Tip the Wink
	Orange Flash (b. 1951)	Court Martial	Fair Trial / Instantaneous
		Nonats	King Salmon / Whitebait

---

597   **MONGO** 21 (ch.c., March 28, 1959)

Bred by Mrs. Marion Dupont Scott, in U.S.A.

Won 22 races, placed 14, $820,766, in U.S.A., from 2 to 5 years, incl. Washington D.C. International, United Nations H. (twice), Trenton H. (twice), Monmouth H., Widener H., Lexington H., Ventnor Turf H., Kelly-Olympic H. and John B. Campbell H.; 2nd Monmouth H., Trenton H., Salvator Mile, Grey Lag H., Whitney Stakes and Knickerbocker H.

ROYAL CHARGER (ch. 1942)	Nearco (br. 1935)	Pharos	Phalaris / Scapa Flow
		Nogara	Havresac II / Catnip
	Sun Princess (b. 1937)	Solario	Gainsborough / Sun Worship
		Mumtaz Begum	Blenheim / Mumtaz Mahal
ACCRA (ch. 1941)	Annapolis (br. 1926)	Man o'War	Fair Play / Mahubah
		Panoply	Peter Pan / Inaugural
	Ladala (ch. 1927)	Ladkin	Fair Play / Lading
		Tonala	Broomstick / Polly Flinders

---

598   **MONTCONTOUR** 1 (b. or br.c., April 10, 1974)

Bred by A. Head, in France.

Won 3 races, placed 3, £70,380, in France, England and Germany, from 2 to 4 years, incl. Prix Hocquart, Hardwicke Stakes; 3rd King George VI and Queen Elizabeth Diamond Stakes; 4th Grosser Preis von Baden.

LUTHIER (b./br. 1965)	Klairon (b. 1952)	Clarion III	Djebel / Columba
		Kalmia	Kantar / Sweet Lavender
	Flute Enchantée (b. 1950)	Cranach	Coronach / Reine Isaure
		Montagnana	Brantome / Mauretania
MOSKVITCHKA (gr. 1967)	Mossborough (ch. 1947)	Nearco	Pharos / Nogara
		All Moonshine	Bobsleigh / Selene
	Tout Sweet Twenty (gr. 1961)	Abernant	Owen Tudor / Rustom Mahal
		Stormy Session	Court Martial / Squall

---

599   **MONTERRICO** 2 (ch.c., March 16, 1959)

Bred by Measures Farms Ltd.

Won 2 races, placed 8, £15,982, in England, from 2 to 5 years, incl. 2nd St. Leger Stakes; 3rd Great Voltigeur Stakes, Jockey Club Cup.

ALYCIDON (ch. 1945)	Donatello II (ch. 1934)	Blenheim	Blandford / Malva
		Delleana	Clarissimus / Duccia di Buoninsegna
	Aurora (ch. 1936)	Hyperion	Gainsborough / Selene
		Rose Red	Swynford / Marchetta
TIMID TILLY (ch. 1953)	Rockefella (br. 1941)	Hyperion	Gainsborough / Selene
		Rockfel	Felstead / Rockliffe
	Sarah Madeline (ch. 1948)	Nasrullah	Nearco / Mumtaz Begum
		Marshfield	Tolgus / Marsh Maiden

---

600   **MONTEVERDI** 22 (ch.c., April 10, 1977)

Bred by L. K. McCreery.

Won 4 races, placed 2, £78,145, in Ireland and England, at 2 and 3 years, incl. National Stakes (Curragh), William Hill Dewhurst Stakes, Ashford Castle Stakes; 2nd McCairns Trial Stakes, Clerical Medical Greenham Stakes.

LYPHARD (b. 1969)	Northern Dancer (b. 1961)	Nearctic	Nearco / Lady Angela
		Natalma	Native Dancer / Almahmoud
	Goofed (ch. 1960)	Court Martial	Fair Trial / Instantaneous
		Barra	Formor / La Favorite
JANINA II (br. 1965)	Match III (br. 1958)	Tantieme	Deux pour Cent / Terka
		Relance III	Relic / Polaire II
	Jennifer (b. 1948)	Hyperion	Gainsborough / Selene
		Avena	Blandford / Athasi

601   MONTORSELLI 14 (b.c., May 19, 1974)

Bred by Razza Dormello-Olgiata, in Ireland.

Won 6 races, placed 13, 834,622 fr., in France and Italy, from 3 to 6 years, incl. Premio Roma, Premio Ellington and Prix de l'Esperance; 2nd Prix Berteux; 3rd Prix Kergorlay.

RIBERO (b. 1965)	Ribot (b. 1952)	Tenerani	Bellini
			Tofanella
		Romanella	El Greco
			Barbara Burrini
	Libra (ch. 1956)	Hyperion	Gainsborough
			Selene
		Weighbridge	Portlaw
			Golden Way
MARIE ALLAN (b./br. 1966)	Sicambre (br. 1948)	Prince Bio	Prince Rose
			Biologie
		Sif	Rialto
			Suavita
	Marguerite Vernaut (ch. 1957)	Toulouse Lautrec	Dante
			Tokamura
		Mariebelle	Mieuxce
			Myrtle Green

602   MOORESTYLE 5 (b.c., April 27, 1977)

Bred by John Parker.

Won 9 races, placed 4, £191,086, in England and France, at 2 and 3 years, incl. William Hill July Stakes, Prix de l'Abbaye de Longchamp, Prix de la Foret, Vernons Sprint Cup, Bisquit Cognac Challenge Stakes; 2nd Poule d'Essai des Poulains, Prix Maurice de Gheest.

MANACLE (b. 1964)	Sing Sing (b. 1957)	Tudor Minstrel	Owen Tudor
			Sansonnet
		Agin the Law	Portlaw
			Revolte
	Hard and Fast (b. 1957)	Hard Sauce	Ardan
			Saucy Bella
		Boodley	Borealis
			Estrellita
GUIDING STAR (SWE) (ch. 1969)	Reliance II (b. 1962)	Tantieme	Deux pour Cent
			Terka
		Relance III	Relic
			Polaire II
	Star of Bethlehem (b. 1959)	Arctic Star	Nearco
			Serena
		Merry Xmas	Chamossaire
			Merry Perrin

603   MORE SO 19 (br.f., May 1, 1975)

Bred by G. Spann.

Won 6 races, placed 8, £103,271, in Ireland and U.S.A., from 2 to 5 years, incl. Irish 1,000 Guineas, Desmond Stakes, Palomar Handicap, Children's Hospital Handicap; 2nd Ramona H.; 3rd Beverly Hills H.

BALLYMORE (b. 1969)	Ragusa (b. 1960)	Ribot	Tenerani
			Romanella
		Fantan II	Ambiorix II
			Red Eye
	Paddy's Sister (b. 1957)	Ballyogan	Fair Trial
			Serial
		Birthday Wood	Bois Roussel
			Birthday Bouquet
DEMARE (br. 1967)	Pardao (ch. 1958)	Pardal	Pharis II
			Adargatis
		Three Weeks	Big Game
			Eleanor Cross
	Merdemain (b. 1960)	Tamerlane	Persian Gulf
			Eastern Empress
		Damians	Panorama
			Thirteen

604   MORSTON 20 (ch.c., April 11, 1970)

Bred by Park Farm Stud, in France.

Won 2 races, £67,039, in England, at 3 years, incl. Derby Stakes.

RAGUSA (b. 1960)	Ribot (b. 1952)	Tenerani	Bellini
			Tofanella
		Romanella	El Greco
			Barbara Burrini
	Fantan II (b. 1952)	Ambiorix II	Tourbillon
			Lavendula II
		Red Eye	Petee-Wrack
			Charred Keg
WINDMILL GIRL (b. 1961)	Hornbeam (ch. 1953)	Hyperion	Gainsborough
			Selene
		Thicket	Nasrullah
			Thorn Wood
	Chorus Beauty (b. 1952)	Chanteur II	Chateau Bouscaut
			La Diva
		Neberna	Nearco
			Springtime

605   MOSS BANK 1 (ch.g., March 16, 1956)

Bred by F. F. Tuthill.

Won 4 races, placed 7, £3,714, in Ireland and England, from 2 to 6 years, incl. Queen Alexandra Stakes; 3rd Desmond Stakes, Queen Alexandra Stakes. Also ran over hurdles at 5 and 6 years, won 4, placed 2, £1,893, incl. 2nd Champion Hurdle Challenge Cup.

MOSSBOROUGH (ch. 1947)	Nearco (br. 1935)	Pharos	Phalaris
			Scapa Flow
		Nogara	Havresac II
			Catnip
	All Moonshine (ch. 1941)	Bobsleigh	Gainsborough
			Toboggan
		Selene	Chaucer
			Serenissima
GAMESMISTRESS (ch. 1945)	Big Game (b. 1939)	Bahram	Blandford
			Friar's Daughter
		Myrobella	Tetratema
			Dolabella
	Taslon (b. 1925)	Hurry On	Marcovil
			Tout Suite
		Taslett	William the Third
			Burgonet

606   MOUBARIZ 9 (br.c., April 25, 1971)

Bred by H.H. Aga Khan, in Ireland.

Won 7 races, placed 5, 524,205 fr., in France, at 2 and 3 years, incl. Prix de l'Abbaye de Longchamp and Prix du Petit Couvert; 2nd Prix du Gros-Chene and Prix du Petit Couvert; 3rd Prix de Saint-Georges; 4th Prix de l'Abbaye de Longchamp.

SING SING (b. 1957)	Tudor Minstrel (br. 1944)	Owen Tudor	Hyperion
			Mary Tudor II
		Sansonnet	Sansovino
			Lady Juror
	Agin the Law (b. 1946)	Portlaw	Beresford
			Portree
		Revolte	Xandover
			Sheba
MUSAKA (b. 1964)	Guard's Tie (b. 1954)	Alizier	Teleferique
			Alizarine
		Noria	Mirza II
			Niloufer
	Artemisa (br. 1958)	Fair Trial	Fairway
			Lady Juror
		Escasida	Pharis II
			Nerissa

607 **MOULINES** 2 (b.c., January 29, 1971)

Bred by F. de Linares, G. Nezan and Mme. H. Ogier-Denys de Collors, in France.

Won 4 races, placed 10, 815,995 fr., in France, from 2 to 4 years, incl. Poule d'Essai des Poulains; 3rd Prix Lupin, Prix de la Salamandre, Prix Eclipse, Prix Edmond Blanc and Prix La Rochette; 4th Prix de la Foret.

KASHMIR II (b./br. 1963)	Tudor Melody (br. 1956)	Tudor Minstrel	Owen Tudor / Sansonnet
		Matelda	Dante / Fairly Hot
	Queen of Speed (b. 1950)	Blue Train	Blue Peter / Sun Chariot
		Bishopscourt	His Grace / Jurisdiction
GOLDEN GLORY (ch. 1956)	Never Say Die (ch. 1951)	Nasrullah	Nearco / Mumtaz Begum
		Singing Grass	War Admiral / Boreale
	Golden Twilight (b. 1946)	Gold Bridge	Swynford or Golden Boss / Flying Diadem
		Decameron Nights	Cameronian / Devachon

608 **MOULTON** 3 (b.c., April 23, 1969)

Bred by White Lodge Stud Ltd.

Won 6 races, placed 5, £94,724, in England, France and Italy, from 2 to 4 years, incl. Benson and Hedges Gold Cup, Premio Presidente della Repubblica, Prix Henry Delamarre, White Rose Stakes; 2nd Eclipse Stakes, Dante Stakes, Prix du Prince d'Orange; 3rd Prix d'Ispahan; 4th Champion Stakes.

PARDAO (ch. 1958)	Pardal (b. 1947)	Pharis II	Pharos / Carissima
		Adargatis	Asterus / Helene de Troie
	Three Weeks (ch. 1946)	Big Game	Bahram / Myrobella
		Eleanor Cross	Hyperion / Queen Christina
CLOSE UP (br. 1958)	Nearula (b. 1950)	Nasrullah	Nearco / Mumtaz Begum
		Respite	Flag of Truce / Orama
	Horama (b. 1943)	Panorama	Sir Cosmo / Happy Climax
		Lady of Aran	Orpen / Queen of the Nore

609 **MOUNT HAGEN** 1 (ch.c., March 4, 1971)

Bred by Daniel Wildenstein, in France.

Won 4 races, placed 6, 719,949 fr., in France and England, at 2 and 3 years, incl. Prix du Moulin de Longchamp and Prix de Fontainebleau; 2nd Prix Niel; 3rd Grand Criterium, Benson and Hedges Eclipse Stakes and Sussex Stakes; 4th Poule d'Essai des Poulains.

BOLD BIDDER (b. 1962)	Bold Ruler (b. 1954)	Nasrullah	Nearco / Mumtaz Begum
		Miss Disco	Discovery / Outdone
	High Bid (b. 1956)	To Market	Market Wise / Pretty Does
		Stepping Stone	Princequillo / Step Across
MOONMADNESS (ch. 1963)	Tom Fool (b. 1949)	Menow	Pharamond / Alcibiades
		Gaga	Bull Dog / Alpoise
	Sunset (ch. 1950)	Hyperion	Gainsborough / Selene
		Fair Ranger	Bois Roussel / Point Duty

610 **MR. RIGHT** 3 (b.c., May 21, 1963)

Bred by George Zauderer, in U.S.A.

Won 17 races, placed 23, $667,193, in U.S.A., from 2 to 6 years, incl. Woodward Stakes, Santa Anita H., Suburban H., Trenton H. (3 times), Queen's County H., Dwyer H. and Roamer H.; 2nd Stuyvesant H., Boardwalk H., Amory L. Haskell H., San Pasqual H., Stymie H. and Michigan Mile-and-One-Eighth H. (twice); 3rd Brooklyn H. (twice), Arcadia H. and Queen's County H.

AUDITING (br. 1948)	Count Fleet (br. 1940)	Reigh Count	Sunreigh / Contessina
		Quickly	Haste / Stephanie
	Businesslike (br. 1939)	Blue Larkspur	Black Servant / Blossom Time
		La Troienne	Teddy / Helene de Troie
LA GRECQUE (ch. 1956)	Tehran (b. 1941)	Bois Roussel	Vatout / Plucky Liege
		Stafaralla	Solario / Mirawala
	Gay Grecque (b. 1949)	Heliopolis	Hyperion / Drift
		Dark Tower	Blenheim / Brunoro

611 **MRS. McARDY** 14 (b.f., March 10, 1974)

Bred by Lord Grimthorpe.

Won 8 races, placed 4, £61,376, in England and U.S.A., from 2 to 4 years, incl. 1,000 Guineas Stakes.

TRIBAL CHIEF (b. 1967)	Princely Gift (b. 1951)	Nasrullah	Nearco / Mumtaz Begum
		Blue Gem	Blue Peter / Sparkle
	Mwanza (b. 1961)	Petition	Fair Trial / Art Paper
		Lake Tanganyika	Ujiji / Blue Girl
HANINA (b. 1965)	Darling Boy (ch. 1958)	Darius	Dante / Yasna
		Sugar Bun	Mahmoud / Galatea II
	Blue Sash (gr. 1958)	Djebe	Djebel / Catherine
		Star of India	Court Martial / Eastern Grandeur

612 **MRS. PENNY** 25 (ch.f., March 22, 1977)

Bred by Derry Meeting Farm, in U.S.A.

Won 5 races, placed 8, £276,149, in England and France, at 2 and 3 years, incl. William Hill Cheveley Park Stakes, Prix de Diane de Revlon, Prix Vermeille, Cherry Hinton Stakes, Lowther Stakes; 2nd King George VI and Queen Elizabeth Diamond Stakes, Fred Darling Stakes; 3rd 1,000 Guineas Stakes, Goffs Irish 1,000 Guineas; 4th Benson and Hedges Gold Cup.

GREAT NEPHEW (b. 1963)	Honeyway (br. 1941)	Fairway	Phalaris / Scapa Flow
		Honey Buzzard	Papyrus / Lady Peregrine
	Sybil's Niece (ch. 1951)	Admiral's Walk	Hyperion / Tabaris
		Sybil's Sister	Nearco / Sister Sarah
TANANARIVE (b. 1970)	Le Fabuleux (ch. 1961)	Wild Risk	Rialto / Wild Violet
		Anguar	Verso II / La Rochelle
	Ten Double (b. 1961)	Decathlon	Olympia / Dog Blessed
		Roodles	Princequillo / Ace Card

124

613 MUMMY'S PET 1 (b.c., April 27, 1968)

Bred by Overbury Stud.

Won 6 races, placed 3, £17,165, in England, at 2 and 3 years, incl. Norfolk Stakes, Temple Stakes; 2nd Middle Park Stakes, Cornwallis Stakes, King's Stand Stakes.

SING SING (b. 1957)	Tudor Minstrel (br. 1944)	Owen Tudor	Hyperion / Mary Tudor II
		Sansonnet	Sansovino / Lady Juror
	Agin the Law (b. 1946)	Portlaw	Beresford / Portree
		Revolte	Xandover / Sheba
MONEY FOR NOTHING (br. 1962)	Grey Sovereign (gr. 1948)	Nasrullah	Nearco / Mumtaz Begum
		Kong	Baytown / Clang
	Sweet Nothings (ch. 1952)	Honeyway	Fairway / Honey Buzzard
		Farthing Damages	Fair Trial / Futility

614 MURRAYFIELD 16 (bl. or br.c., February 6, 1966)

Bred by Mrs. P. R. H. Hastings.

Won 9 races, placed 11, £25,546, in England and Italy, from 2 to 4 years, incl. Coventry Stakes, Premio Roma Vecchia; 3rd Dewhurst Stakes, Royal Lodge Stakes, St. James's Palace Stakes, Sussex Stakes, Gran Premio Citta di Napoli, Premio Ribot; 4th 2,000 Guineas Stakes, Premio Emilio Turati.

MATCH III (b. 1958)	Tantieme (b. 1947)	Deux pour Cent	Deiri / Dix pour Cent
		Terka	Indus / La Furka
	Relance III (ch. 1952)	Relic	War Relic / Bridal Colors
		Polaire II	Le Volcan / Stella Polaris
ERISCA (ch. 1960)	Doutelle (ch. 1954)	Prince Chevalier	Prince Rose / Chevalerie
		Above Board	Straight Deal / Feola
	Bahama (ch. 1954)	Persian Gulf	Bahram / Double Life
		Nassau	Nasrullah / Meraline

615 MUSIC BOY 5 (ch.c., January 28, 1973)

Bred by Mrs. R. G. Cookson.

Won 6 races, placed 2, £37,716, in England, at 2 and 3 years, incl. C. and G. Gimcrack Stakes, King George Stakes; 2nd Flying Childers Stakes.

JUKEBOX (b. 1966)	Sing Sing (b. 1957)	Tudor Minstrel	Owen Tudor / Sansonnet
		Agin the Law	Portlaw / Revolte
	Bibi Mah (b. 1955)	Tehran	Bois Roussel / Stafaralla
		Mulier Magnifica	Mieuxce / Swell Dame
VERONIQUE (b. 1961)	Matador (ch. 1953)	Golden Cloud	Gold Bridge / Rainstorm
		Spanish Galantry	Mazarin / Courtship
	Narcisse (b. 1949)	Niccolo Dell'Arca	Coronach / Nogara
		Asphodele	Quai d'Orsay / Halston

616 MUSIC MAESTRO 3 (b.c., May 15, 1975)

Bred by J. R. Mitchell.

Won 5 races, placed 3, £38,786, in England, at 2 and 3 years, incl. Flying Childers Stakes, King George Stakes; 3rd King's Stand Stakes, Palace House Stakes.

SONG (b. 1966)	Sing Sing (b. 1957)	Tudor Minstrel	Owen Tudor / Sansonnet
		Agin the Law	Portlaw / Revolte
	Intent (gr. 1952)	Vilmorin	Gold Bridge / Queen of the Meadows
		Under Canvas	Winterhalter / Shelton
SAULISA (br. 1963)	Hard Sauce (br. 1948)	Ardan	Pharis II / Adargatis
		Saucy Bella	Bellacose / Marmite
	L.S.D. (b. 1946)	Lighthouse II	Pharos / Pyramid
		Styrian Dye	Diophon / Styrian Steel

617 MY GOODNESS ME 9 (b.f., April 20, 1960)

Bred by David Robinson.

Won 5 races, placed 3, £9,059, in England, at 2 and 3 years, incl. Cheveley Park Stakes; 3rd King's Stand Stakes.

ABERNANT (gr. 1946)	Owen Tudor (br. 1938)	Hyperion	Gainsborough / Selene
		Mary Tudor II	Pharos / Anna Bolena
	Rustom Mahal (gr. 1934)	Rustom Pasha	Son-in-Law / Cos
		Mumtaz Mahal	The Tetrarch / Lady Josephine
PERSIAN DISH (ch. 1951)	Persian Gulf (b. 1940)	Bahram	Blandford / Friar's Daughter
		Double Life	Bachelor's Double / Saint Joan
	Kettle of Fish (ch. 1936)	King Salmon	Salmon-Trout / Malva
		Riot	Colorado / Lady Juror

618 MYSTERIOUS 3 (ch.f., April 11, 1970)

Bred by G. A. Pope (Jnr.).

Won 5 races, placed 2, £84,967, in England and Ireland, at 2 and 3 years, incl. Oaks Stakes, 1,000 Guineas Stakes, Yorkshire Oaks, Cherry Hinton Stakes, Fred Darling Stakes; 2nd Irish Guinness Oaks, Sun Chariot Stakes.

CREPELLO (ch. 1954)	Donatello II (ch. 1934)	Blenheim	Blandford / Malva
		Delleana	Clarissimus / Duccia di Buoninsegna
	Crepuscule (ch. 1948)	Mieuxce	Massine / L'Olivete
		Red Sunset	Solario / Dulce II
HILL SHADE (br. 1965)	Hillary (br. 1952)	Khaled	Hyperion / Eclair
		Snow Bunny	Boswell / La Rose
	Penumbra (b. 1955)	Imperium	Piping Rock / Imperatrice
		Moonrise	Moonlight Run / Seventh Heaven

619   MY SWALLOW 2 (b.c., February 22, 1968)

Bred by M. A. Walshe, in Ireland.

Won 8 races, placed 3, £98,235, in England and France, at 2 and 3 years, incl. Prix Robert Papin, Prix Morny, Prix de la Salamandre and Grand Criterium; 2nd Prix de la Porte Maillot and July Cup; 3rd 2,000 Guineas.

LE LEVANSTELL (b. 1957)	Le Lavandou (b. 1944)	Djebel	Tourbillon / Loika
		Lavande	Rustom Pasha / Livadia
	Stella's Sister (ch. 1950)	Ballyogan	Fair Trial / Serial
		My Aid	Knight of the Garter / Flying Aid
DARRIGLE (b. 1960)	Vilmoray (ch. 1950)	Vilmorin	Gold Bridge / Queen of the Meadows
		Iverley Way	Apron / Smoke Alley
	Dollar Help (b. 1952)	Falls of Clyde	Fair Trial / Hyndford Bridge
		Dollar Crisis	Pink Flower / Silver Loan

620   NADJAR 4 (gr.c., February 20, 1976)

Bred by Pierre Dubois, in France.

Won 5 races, placed 7, 1,357,053 fr., in France and England, from 2 to 4 years, incl. Prix d'Ispahan, Prix Jacques le Marois and Prix de Ris-Orangis; 2nd Prix du Moulin de Longchamp and Prix de Fontainebleau; 3rd Poule d'Essai des Poulains, Prix de la Salamandre and Champion Stakes.

ZEDDAAN (gr. 1965)	Grey Sovereign (gr. 1948)	Nasrullah	Nearco / Mumtaz Begum
		Kong	Baytown / Clang
	Vareta (gr. 1953)	Vilmorin	Gold Bridge / Queen of the Meadows
		Veronique II	Mon Talisman / Volubilis
NUCLEA (br. 1961)	Orsini (br. 1954)	Ticino	Athanasius / Terra
		Oranien	Nuvolari / Omladina
	Nixe (b. 1941)	Arjaman	Herold / Aditja
		Nanon	Graf Isolani / Nella da Gubbio

621   NANTICIOUS 21 (ch.f., March 25, 1974)

Bred by Mrs. M. E. Farrell.

Won 6 races, placed 4, £48,574, in Ireland, England and U.S.A., from 2 to 4 years, incl. Ribblesdale Stakes, Silken Glider Stakes; 3rd Irish Guinness Oaks, Gallorette H.; 4th Irish 1,000 Guineas.

NORTHFIELDS (ch. 1968)	Northern Dancer (b. 1961)	Nearctic	Nearco / Lady Angela
		Natalma	Native Dancer / Almahmoud
	Little Hut (b. 1952)	Occupy	Bull Dog / Miss Bunting
		Savage Beauty	Challenger / Khara
NANETTE (b. 1961)	Worden II (ch. 1949)	Wild Risk	Rialto / Wild Violet
		Sans Tares	Sind / Tara
	Claudette (br. 1949)	Chanteur II	Chateau Bouscaut / La Diva
		Nearly	Nearco / Lost Soul

622   NASRAM II 11 (b.c., May 4, 1960)

Bred by Bull Run Stud, in U.S.A.

Won 3 races, placed 6, £48,517, in England and France, at 3 and 4 years, incl. King George VI and Queen Elizabeth Stakes, Prix du Lys; 2nd Prix Dollar, Prix du Prince d'Orange; 3rd Prix Ganay, Grand Prix de Saint-Cloud; 4th Grand Prix de Saint-Cloud.

NASRULLAH (b. 1940)	Nearco (br. 1935)	Pharos	Phalaris / Scapa Flow
		Nogara	Havresac II / Catnip
	Mumtaz Begum (b. 1932)	Blenheim	Blandford / Malva
		Mumtaz Mahal	The Tetrarch / Lady Josephine
LA MIRAMBULE (b. 1949)	Coaraze (b. 1942)	Tourbillon	Ksar / Durban
		Corrida	Coronach / Zariba
	La Futaie (b. 1937)	Gris Perle	Brabant / Mauve
		La Futelaye	Collaborator / La Francaise

623   NATIVE DIVER 2 (br.g., April 16, 1959)

Bred by Mr. and Mrs. L. K. Shapiro, in U.S.A.

Won 37 races, placed 19, $1,026,500, in U.S.A., from 2 to 8 years, incl. Hollywood Gold Cup (3 times), Los Angeles H. (twice), American H., Malibu Stakes, San Carlos H. (twice), San Pasqùal H., San Bernardino H., Del Mar H. and Golden Gate H.; 2nd Santa Anita H., American H. (twice), San Pasqual H. and San Fernando Stakes; 3rd Hollywood Gold Cup, Santa Anita H., San Carlos H. (twice), San Antonio H. and San Pasqual H.

IMBROS (ch. 1950)	Polynesian (br. 1942)	Unbreakable	Sickle / Blue Glass
		Black Polly	Polymelian / Black Queen
	Fire Falls (b. 1942)	Bull Dog	Teddy / Plucky Liege
		Stricken	Pennant / Moody Mary
FLEET DIVER (b. 1950)	Devil Diver (b. 1939)	St. Germans	Swynford / Hamoaze
		Dabchick	Royal Minstrel / Ruddy Duck
	Our Fleet (ch. 1946)	Count Fleet	Reigh Count / Quickly
		Duchess Anita	Count Gallahad / French Duchess

624   NAVARINO 1 (b.c., April 5, 1977)

Bred by H. Einschutz, in Germany.

Won 4 races, placed 3, 276,300 DM., in Germany, at 2 and 3 years, incl. Deutsches Derby and Union-Rennen; 2nd Grosser Thier-Preis Deutsches St. Leger.

MADRUZZO (br. 1968)	Kaiseradler (br. 1957)	Nebelwerfer	Magnat / Newa
		Kaiserwurde	Bubbles / Katinka
	Madonnina (b. 1960)	Stani	Nuvolari / Stammesart
		Madonna	Birikil / Manita
NACHTVIOLE (b. 1961)	Altrek (ch. 1952)	Antonio Canale	Torbido / Acquaforte
		Altea	Navarro / Arpisanda
	Nonnea (b. 1953)	Magnat	Asterus / Mafalda
		Norne	Der Mohr / Numa

625   NEBBIOLO 19 (ch.c., February 2, 1974)

Bred by Niels Schibbye.

Won 6 races, placed 4, £91,513, in England and Ireland, at 2 and 3 years incl. 2,000 Guineas Stakes, Gimcrack Stakes, Curragh Stakes; 2nd William Hill Middle Park Stakes, Vauxhall Trial Stakes; 3rd Irish 2,000 Guineas.

YELLOW GOD (ch. 1967)	Red God (ch. 1954)	Nasrullah	Nearco
			Mumtaz Begum
		Spring Run	Menow
			Boola Brook
	Sally Deans (ch. 1947)	Fun Fair	Fair Trial
			Humoresque
		Cora Deans	Coronach
			Jennie Deans
NOVARA (b. 1965)	Birkhahn (br. 1945)	Alchimist	Herold
			Aversion
		Bramouse	Cappiello
			Peregrine
	Norbelle (b. 1957)	Norman	Norseman
			Macreuse
		Mirabelle	Sind
			Mitidja II

626   NEBOS 4 (b.c., March 30, 1976)

Bred by Countess Margit Batthyany, in Germany.

Won 12 races, placed 5, 1,265,955 DM., in Germany, from 2 to 4 years, incl. Grosser Preis von Berlin (twice), Preis von Europa, Grosser Preis von Baden, Union-Rennen, Grosser Preis von Dusseldorf, Grosser Preis von Dortmund and Zukunfts-Rennen; 2nd Deutsches Derby, Aral-Pokal (twice) and Preis des Winterfavoriten; 3rd Preis von Europa.

CARO (gr. 1967)	Fortino II (gr. 1959)	Grey Sovereign	Nasrullah
			Kong
		Ranavalo III	Relic
			Navarra II
	Chambord (ch. 1955)	Chamossaire	Precipitation
			Snowberry
		Life Hill	Solario
			Lady of the Snows
NOSTRANA (br. 1960)	Botticelli (b. 1951)	Blue Peter	Fairway
			Fancy Free
		Buonamica	Niccolo Dell'Arca
			Bernina
	Naxos (br. 1950)	Ticino	Athanasius
			Terra
		Nixe	Arjaman
			Nanon

627   NELCIUS 10 (br.c., March 18, 1963)

Bred by P. and R. Duboscq, in France.

Won 6 races, placed 7, 1,462,681 fr., in France and England, from 2 to 4 years, incl. Prix du Jockey-Club and Prix de Chantilly; 2nd Coronation Cup, Grand Prix de Saint-Cloud, Prix de Guiche, Prix Noailles and La Coupe de Maisons-Laffitte.

TENAREZE (ch. 1953)	Goyama (ch. 1943)	Goya II	Tourbillon
			Zariba
		Devineress	Finglas
			Devachon
	La Taglioni (b. 1948)	Colombo	Manna
			Lady Nairne
		La Truite II	Salmon-Trout
			Quince
NAMAGUA (br. 1954)	Fontenay (b. 1946)	Tornado	Tourbillon
			Roseola
		Flying Colours	Massine
			Red Flame
	Namesake (b. 1944)	Fearless Fox	Foxlaw
			Molly Adare
		Concordia	Son-in-Law
			Ciceronnetta

628   NEVER BEND 19 (b.c., March 15, 1960)

Bred by Capt. Harry F. Guggenheim, in U.S.A.

Won 13 races, placed 8, $641,524, in U.S.A., at 2 and 3 years, incl. Flamingo Stakes, Champagne Stakes, Futurity Stakes and Cowdin Stakes; 2nd Kentucky Derby, Woodward Stakes, Arlington-Washington Futurity and United Nations H.; 3rd Preakness Stakes, Garden State Stakes, Sapling Stakes and Long Island H.

NASRULLAH (b. 1940)	Nearco (br. 1935)	Pharos	Phalaris
			Scapa Flow
		Nogara	Havresac II
			Catnip
	Mumtaz Begum (b. 1932)	Blenheim	Blandford
			Malva
		Mumtaz Mahal	The Tetrarch
			Lady Josephine
LALUN (b. 1952)	Djeddah (ch. 1945)	Djebel	Tourbillon
			Loika
		Djezima	Asterus
			Heldifann
	Be Faithful (br. 1942)	Bimelech	Black Toney
			La Troienne
		Bloodroot	Blue Larkspur
			Knockaney Bridge

629   NEVER SAY 16 (ch.f., April 3, 1958)

Bred by Astor Studs.

Won 2 races, placed 4, £5,585, in England, at 3 and 4 years, incl. Park Hill Stakes.

NEVER SAY DIE (ch. 1951)	Nasrullah (b. 1940)	Nearco	Pharos
			Nogara
		Mumtaz Begum	Blenheim
			Mumtaz Mahal
	Singing Grass (ch. 1944)	War Admiral	Man o'War
			Brushup
		Boreale	Vatout
			Galaday II
ALISCIA (ch. 1951)	Alycidon (ch. 1945)	Donatello II	Blenheim
			Delleana
		Aurora	Hyperion
			Rose Red
	Miss Minx (ch. 1936)	Mr. Jinks	Tetratema
			False Piety
		Gerrard's Cross	Teddy
			Never Cross

630   NEVER TOO LATE II 4 (ch.f., March 10, 1957)

Bred by Bull Run Stud, in U.S.A.

Won 5 races, placed 2, £37,992, in England and France, at 2 and 3 years, incl. 1,000 Guineas Stakes, Oaks Stakes, Prix de la Salamandre; 2nd Champion Stakes, Grand Criterium.

NEVER SAY DIE (ch. 1951)	Nasrullah (b. 1940)	Nearco	Pharos
			Nogara
		Mumtaz Begum	Blenheim
			Mumtaz Mahal
	Singing Grass (ch. 1944)	War Admiral	Man o'War
			Brushup
		Boreale	Vatout
			Galaday II
GLORIA NICKY (ch. 1952)	Alycidon (ch. 1945)	Donatello II	Blenheim
			Delleana
		Aurora	Hyperion
			Rose Red
	Weighbridge (ch. 1945)	Portlaw	Beresford
			Portree
		Golden Way	Gold Bridge
			Adria II

631 **NIGHT OFF** 16 (b.f., March 11, 1962)

Bred by Major L. B. Holliday.

Won 2 races, placed 1, £27,954, in England, at 2 and 3 years, incl. 1,000 Guineas Stakes, Cheveley Park Stakes; 2nd Coronation Stakes.

NARRATOR (b. 1951)	Nearco (br. 1935)	Pharos	Phalaris / Scapa Flow
		Nogara	Havresac II / Catnip
	Phase (b. 1939)	Windsor Lad	Blandford / Resplendent
		Lost Soul	Solario / Orlass
PERSUADER (b. 1954)	Petition (br. 1944)	Fair Trial	Fairway / Lady Juror
		Art Paper	Artist's Proof / Quire
	Palma Rosa (gr. 1941)	Mahmoud	Blenheim / Mah Mahal
		Tsianina	Asterus / Merry Girl

632 **NIJINSKY** 8 (b.c., February 21, 1967)

Bred by E. P. Taylor, in Canada.

Won 11 races, placed 2, £282,359, in England, Ireland and France, at 2 and 3 years, incl. Derby Stakes, 2,000 Guineas Stakes, St. Leger Stakes, King George VI and Queen Elizabeth Stakes, Irish Sweeps Derby, Dewhurst Stakes, Beresford Stakes, Anglesey Stakes, Railway Stakes, Gladness Stakes; 2nd Champion Stakes, Prix de l'Arc de Triomphe.

NORTHERN DANCER (b. 1961)	Nearctic (br. 1954)	Nearco	Pharos / Nogara
		Lady Angela	Hyperion / Sister Sarah
	Natalma (b. 1957)	Native Dancer	Polynesian / Geisha
		Almahmoud	Mahmoud / Arbitrator
FLAMING PAGE (b. 1959)	Bull Page (b. 1947)	Bull Lea	Bull Dog / Rose Leaves
		Our Page	Blue Larkspur / Occult
	Flaring Top (ch. 1947)	Menow	Pharamond / Alcibiades
		Flaming Top	Omaha / Firetop

633 **NIKOLI** 1 (b.c., March 8, 1977)

Bred by McGrath Trust Co.

Won 3 races, £88,525, in Ireland, at 2 and 3 years, incl. Airlie/Coolmore Irish 2,000 Guineas, McCairns Trial Stakes.

GREAT NEPHEW (b. 1963)	Honeyway (br. 1941)	Fairway	Phalaris / Scapa Flow
		Honey Buzzard	Papyrus / Lady Peregrine
	Sybil's Niece (ch. 1951)	Admiral's Walk	Hyperion / Tabaris
		Sybil's Sister	Nearco / Sister Sarah
ALICEVA (b. 1966)	Alcide (b. 1955)	Alycidon	Donatello II / Aurora
		Chenille	King Salmon / Sweet Aloe
	Feevagh (b. 1951)	Solar Slipper	Windsor Slipper / Solar Flower
		Astrid Wood	Bois Roussel / Astrid

634 **NIKSAR** 7 (ch.c., May 1, 1962)

Bred by Marquis de Nicolay, in France.

Won 2 races, placed 2, £33,335, in England, at 2 and 3 years, incl. 2,000 Guineas Stakes; 3rd Champion Stakes.

LE HAAR (ch. 1954)	Vieux Manoir (b. 1947)	Brantome	Blandford / Vitamine
		Vieille Maison	Finglas / Vieille Canaille
	Mince Pie (b. 1949)	Teleferique	Bacteriophage / Beaute de Neige
		Cannelle	Biribi / Armoise
NISKAMPE (ch. 1955)	Shikampur (ch. 1950)	Tehran	Bois Roussel / Stafaralla
		Mehmany	Mieuxce / Dulce II
	Nise (ch. 1944)	Nino	Clarissimus / Azalee
		Frileuse	Mousson / Gallia III

635 **NINISKI** 16 (b.c., February 15, 1976)

Bred by Caper Hill Farm Inc., in U.S.A.

Won 6 races, placed 4, £138,637, in England, Ireland and France, from 2 to 4 years, incl. Irish St. Leger, Prix Royal-Oak, Geoffrey Freer Stakes, John Porter Stakes, Ormonde Stakes; 2nd Coronation Cup, Gordon Stakes; 3rd St. Leger Stakes.

NIJINSKY (b. 1967)	Northern Dancer (b. 1961)	Nearctic	Nearco / Lady Angela
		Natalma	Native Dancer / Almahmoud
	Flaming Page (b. 1959)	Bull Page	Bull Lea / Our Page
		Flaring Top	Menow / Flaring Top
VIRGINIA HILLS (b. 1971)	Tom Rolfe (b. 1962)	Ribot	Tenerani / Romanella
		Pocahontas	Roman / How
	Ridin' Easy (ch. 1967)	Ridan	Nantallah / Rough Shod
		Easy Eight	Eight Thirty / Your Game

636 **NISHAPOUR** 9 (gr.c., February 17, 1975)

Bred by H.H. Aga Khan, in France.

Won 2 races, placed 6, 533,000 fr., in France, at 2 and 3 years, incl. Poule d'Essai des Poulains; 2nd Prix La Rochette and Prix de Fontainebleau; 3rd Prix du Moulin de Longchamp.

ZEDDAAN (gr. 1965)	Grey Sovereign (gr. 1948)	Nasrullah	Nearco / Mumtaz Begum
		Kong	Baytown / Clang
	Vareta (gr. 1953)	Vilmorin	Gold Bridge / Queen of the Meadows
		Veronique II	Mon Talisman / Volubilis
ALAMA (b. 1969)	Aureole (ch. 1950)	Hyperion	Gainsborough / Selene
		Angelola	Donatello II / Feola
	Nucciolina (b. 1957)	Nuccio	Traghetto / Nuvoletta
		Mah Behar	Bois Roussel / Mah Iran

128

637 **NIZON** 1 (ch.c., February 21, 1975)

Bred by R. E. Sangster, in U.S.A.

Won 5 races, placed 3, 581,639 fr., in France and Italy, at 2 and 3 years, incl. Premio Roma, Prix de Lutece and Prix du Lys; 4th Grand Prix de Paris and Prix Royal Oak.

NIJINSKY (b. 1967)	Northern Dancer (b. 1961)	Nearctic	Nearco / Lady Angela
		Natalma	Native Dancer / Almahmoud
	Flaming Page (b. 1959)	Bull Page	Bull Lea / Our Page
		Flaring Top	Menow / Flaming Top
EXIT SMILING (ch. 1970)	Stage Door Johnny (ch. 1965)	Prince John	Princequillo / Not Afraid
		Peroxide Blonde	Ballymoss / Folie Douce
	Chandelier (ch. 1955)	Goyama	Goya II / Devineress
		Queen of Light	Borealis / Picture Play

---

638 **NOBILIARY** 17 (ch.f., February 14, 1972)

Bred by Nelson Bunker Hunt, in U.S.A.

Won 4 races, placed 6, 1,807,204 fr., in France, England, Ireland and U.S.A., at 2 and 3 years, incl. Prix Saint-Alary, Washington D.C. International and Prix de la Grotte; 2nd Derby Stakes, Poule d'Essai des Pouliches and Prix Vermeille; 3rd Irish Guinness Oaks and Prix des Reservoirs.

VAGUELY NOBLE (b. 1965)	Vienna (ch. 1957)	Aureole	Hyperion / Angelola
		Turkish Blood	Turkhan / Rusk
	Noble Lassie (b. 1956)	Nearco	Pharos / Nogara
		Belle Sauvage	Big Game / Tropical Sun
GOOFED (ch. 1960)	Court Martial (ch. 1942)	Fair Trial	Fairway / Lady Juror
		Instantaneous	Hurry On / Picture
	Barra (ch. 1950)	Formor	Ksar / Formose
		La Favorite	Biribi / La Pompadour

---

639 **NOBLE DANCER** 2 (b.c., April 30, 1972)

Bred by I. Werry, in England.

Won 22 races, placed 8, $945,893, in Norway, England, France and U.S.A., from 2 to 7 years, incl. Oslo Cup (twice), Norsk St. Leger, Bergen Bank Aerespremie, San Luis Rey Stakes, United Nations H., Bougainvillea H., Pan American H., Tidal H., Canadian Turf H. and Hialeah Turf Cup; 2nd Norsk Derby, Norsk 2,000 Guineas and San Juan Capistrano H.; 3rd Hollywood Invitational Turf H., Bowling Green H. and Edgemere H.; 4th Prix de l'Arc de Triomphe and Washington D.C. International.

PRINCE DE GALLES (b./br. 1966)	Welsh Abbot (b./br. 1955)	Abernant	Owen Tudor / Rustom Mahal
		Sister Sarah	Abbots Trace / Sarita
	Vauchellor (b. 1959)	Honeyway	Fairway / Honey Buzzard
		Niobe	Caracalla II / Phaetusa
HELEN TRAUBEL (b. 1962)	Sing Sing (b. 1957)	Tudor Minstrel	Owen Tudor / Sansonnet
		Agin the Law	Portlaw / Revolte
	Rose Petal (br. 1954)	Flocon	Fastnet / Fragment
		Rose Bay Willow	Fairhaven / Willow Ann

---

640 **NOBLE DECREE** 16 (b.c., March 6, 1970)

Bred by Kinsman Stud Farms, in U.S.A.

Won 3 races, placed 3, £37,167, in England, at 2 and 3 years, incl. Observer Gold Cup; 2nd 2,000 Guineas Stakes, Royal Lodge Stakes.

VAGUELY NOBLE (b. 1965)	Vienna (ch. 1957)	Aureole	Hyperion / Angelola
		Turkish Blood	Turkhan / Rusk
	Noble Lassie (b. 1956)	Nearco	Pharos / Nogara
		Belle Sauvage	Big Game / Tropical Sun
HIDDEN SECRET (b. 1963)	Promulgation (b. 1955)	Court Martial	Fair Trial / Instantaneous
		Picture Play	Donatello II / Amuse
	Secret Session (b. 1954)	Your Host	Alibhai / Boudoir
		Bravely Go	Challenger / Chessel

---

641 **NOBLE SAINT** 9 (b.c., March 31, 1976)

Bred by Raymond R. Guest, in U.S.A.

Won 4 races, placed 3, £68,301, in England and Italy, from 2 to 4 years, incl. Premio Roma, Great Voltigeur Stakes, Yorkshire Cup.

VAGUELY NOBLE (b. 1965)	Vienna (ch. 1957)	Aureole	Hyperion / Angelola
		Turkish Blood	Turkhan / Rusk
	Noble Lassie (b. 1956)	Nearco	Pharos / Nogara
		Belle Sauvage	Big Game / Tropical Sun
SANTA PAULA (b. 1967)	Santa Claus (br. 1961)	Chamossaire	Precipitation / Snowberry
		Aunt Clara	Arctic Prince / Sister Clara
	Pocahontas (br. 1955)	Roman	Sir Gallahad III / Buckup
		How	Princequillo / The Squaw II

---

642 **NOBLESSE** 14 (ch.f., January 24, 1960)

Bred by Mrs. P. G. Margetts.

Won 4 races, placed 1, £47,534, in England and France, at 2 and 3 years, incl. Oaks Stakes, Timeform Gold Cup, Musidora Stakes, Blue Seal Stakes; 4th Prix Vermeille.

MOSSBOROUGH (ch. 1947)	Nearco (br. 1935)	Pharos	Phalaris / Scapa Flow
		Nogara	Havresac II / Catnip
	All Moonshine (ch. 1941)	Bobsleigh	Gainsborough / Toboggan
		Selene	Chaucer / Serenissima
DUKE'S DELIGHT (ch. 1946)	His Grace (b. 1933)	Blandford	Swynford / Blanche
		Malva	Charles O'Malley / Wild Arum
	Early Light (b. 1938)	Easton	Dark Legend / Phaona
		Sun Mist	Soldennis / Silver Mist

643   NOCTURNAL SPREE 1 (gr.f., March 8, 1972)

Bred by J. Dillon.

Won 2 races, placed 2, £29,771, in Ireland and England, at 2 and 3 years, incl. 1,000 Guineas Stakes; 4th Irish 1,000 Guineas Stakes.

SUPREME SOVEREIGN (gr. 1964)	Sovereign Path (gr. 1956)	Grey Sovereign	Nasrullah / Kong
		Mountain Path	Bobsleigh / Path of Peace
	Valtellina (b. 1953)	Vatellor	Vatout / Lady Elinor
		Asti Spumante	Dante / Blanco
NIGHT ATTIRE (ch. 1966)	Shantung (b. 1956)	Sicambre	Prince Bio / Sif
		Barley Corn	Hyperion / Schiaparelli
	Twilight Hour (gr. 1950)	Nearco	Pharos / Nogara
		Moonstone	Mahmoud / Rosetta

644   NODOUBLE A1 (ch.c., March 4, 1965)

Bred by Verna Lea Farm, in U.S.A.

Won 13 races, placed 16, $846,749, in U.S.A., from 2 to 5 years, incl. Santa Anita H., Hawthorne Gold Cup (twice), Brooklyn H., Metropolitan H., Michigan Mile H., Arkansas Derby, Californian Stakes and San Pasqual H.; 2nd American Derby, Hollywood Gold Cup, Charles H. Strub Stakes, Jockey Club Gold Cup, Woodward Stakes, Metropolitan H. and Gulfstream Park H.; 3rd Preakness Stakes and Californian Stakes.

NOHOLME II (ch. 1956)	Star Kingdom (ch. 1946)	Stardust	Hyperion / Sister Stella
		Impromptu	Concerto / Thoughtless
	Oceana (b. 1947)	Colombo	Manna / Lady Nairne
		Orama	Diophon / Cantelupe
ABLA-JAY (b. 1955)	Double Jay (br. 1944)	Balladier	Black Toney / Blue Warbler
		Broomshot	Whisk Broom II / Centre Shot
	Ablamucha (ch. 1947)	Don Bingo	Serio / Lirica
		Sweet Betty	Challenger / Betty Dalme

645   NONOALCO 2 (b.c., April 6, 1971)

Bred by Forrest E. Mars, in U.S.A.

Won 7 races, placed 1, £148,255, in England and France, at 2 and 3 years, incl. 2,000 Guineas, Prix Morny, Prix de la Salamandre, Prix Jacques le Marois, Prix du Rond-Point; 2nd Grand Criterium.

NEARCTIC (b. 1954)	Nearco (br. 1935)	Pharos	Phalaris / Scapa Flow
		Nogara	Havresac II / Catnip
	Lady Angela (ch. 1944)	Hyperion	Gainsborough / Selene
		Sister Sarah	Abbots Trace / Sarita
SEXIMEE (ch. 1966)	Hasty Road (b. 1951)	Roman	Sir Gallahad III / Buckup
		Traffic Court	Discovery / Traffic
	Jambo (ch. 1959)	Crafty Admiral	Fighting Fox / Admiral's Lady
		Bank Account	Shut Out / Balla Tryst

646   NORFOLK 1 (b.c., April 12, 1964)

Bred by H. Pferdmenges, in Germany.

Won 8 races, placed 12, 259,200 DM., in Germany, from 2 to 6 years, incl. Grosser Preis von Nordrhein-Westfalen, Grosser Preis von Dusseldorf and Spreti-Rennen; 2nd Deutsches Derby, Deutsches St. Leger and Grosser Preis von Nordrhein-Westfalen; 3rd Grosser Hansa Preis; 4th Aral-Pokal.

MASETTO (b. 1952)	Olymp (b. 1942)	Arjaman	Herold / Aditja
		Olympiade	Oleander / Osterfreude
	Mimosa (b. 1945)	Indus	Alcantara II / Himalaya
		Marliese	Graf Ferry / Marie Louise
NAMEDY (br. 1954)	Ticino (b. 1939)	Athanasius	Ferro / Athanasie
		Terra	Aditi / Teufelsrose
	Nuance (br. 1949)	Magnat	Asterus / Mafalda
		Nanette	Arjaman / Numa

647   NORTHERN BABY 17 (b.c., April 1, 1976)

Bred by Kinghaven Farms, in Canada.

Won 5 races, placed 7, £165,715, in France and England, from 2 to 4 years, incl. Champion Stakes, Prix Dollar, Prix de la Cote Normande; 2nd Prix La Force; 3rd Derby Stakes, Coral Eclipse Stakes, Prix Ganay, Prix du Prince d'Orange (twice).

NORTHERN DANCER (b. 1961)	Nearctic (br. 1954)	Nearco	Pharos / Nogara
		Lady Angela	Hyperion / Sister Sarah
	Natalma (b. 1957)	Native Dancer	Polynesian / Geisha
		Almahmoud	Mahmoud / Arbitrator
TWO RINGS (b. 1970)	Round Table (b. 1954)	Princequillo	Prince Rose / Cosquilla
		Knight's Daughter	Sir Cosmo / Feola
	Allofthem (ch. 1964)	Bagdad	Double Jay / Bazura
		Gal I Love	Nasrullah / Gallita

648   NORTHERN DANCER 2 (b.c., May 27, 1961)

Bred by E. P. Taylor, in Canada.

Won 14 races, placed 4, $580,647, in Canada and U.S.A., at 2 and 3 years, incl. Kentucky Derby, Preakness Stakes, Flamingo Stakes, Florida Derby, Queen's Plate, Blue Grass Stakes, Remsen Stakes, Coronation Futurity and Summer Stakes; 2nd Cup and Saucer Stakes; 3rd Belmont Stakes.

NEARCTIC (br. 1954)	Nearco (br. 1935)	Pharos	Phalaris / Scapa Flow
		Nogara	Havresac II / Catnip
	Lady Angela (ch. 1944)	Hyperion	Gainsborough / Selene
		Sister Sarah	Abbots Trace / Sarita
NATALMA (b. 1957)	Native Dancer (gr. 1950)	Polynesian	Unbreakable / Black Polly
		Geisha	Discovery / Miyako
	Almahmoud (ch. 1947)	Mahmoud	Blenheim / Mah Mahal
		Arbitrator	Peace Chance / Mother Goose

649   NORTHERN PRINCESS 19 (b.f., March 4, 1971)

Bred by Mrs. A. Harries.

Won 3 races, placed 1, £12,418, in England, at 2 and 3 years, incl. Ribblesdale Stakes.

SIR IVOR (b. 1965)	Sir Gaylord (b. 1959)	Turn-to	Royal Charger
			Source Sucree
		Somethingroyal	Princequillo
			Imperatrice
	Attica (ch. 1953)	Mr. Trouble	Mahmoud
			Motto
		Athenia	Pharamond
			Salaminia
CARAMEL (ch. 1964)	Crepello (ch. 1954)	Donatello II	Blenheim
			Delleana
		Crepuscule	Mieuxce
			Red Sunset
	Maple Leaf (ch. 1953)	Big Game	Bahram
			Myrobella
		Northern Hope	Borealis
			Esperance

650   NORTHERN TASTE 14 (ch.c., March 13, 1971)

Bred by E. P. Taylor, in Canada.

Won 5 races, placed 9, 777,262 fr., in France and England, from 2 to 4 years, incl. Prix de la Foret, Prix Eclipse and Prix Thomas Bryon; 2nd Prix du Moulin de Longchamp; 3rd Prix Eugene Adam and Prix de Ris-Orangis; 4th 2,000 Guineas.

NORTHERN DANCER (b. 1961)	Nearctic (br. 1954)	Nearco	Pharos
			Nogara
		Lady Angela	Hyperion
			Sister Sarah
	Natalma (b. 1957)	Native Dancer	Polynesian
			Geisha
		Almahmoud	Mahmoud
			Arbitrator
LADY VICTORIA (br. 1962)	Victoria Park (b. 1957)	Chop Chop	Flares
			Sceptical
		Victoriana	Windfields
			Iribelle
	Lady Angela (ch. 1944)	Hyperion	Gainsborough
			Selene
		Sister Sarah	Abbots Trace
			Sarita

651   NORTHERN TREASURE 9 (ch.c., February 18, 1973)

Bred by T. Rogers and C. Gaisford-St. Lawrence.

Won 4 races, placed 14, £55,544, in Ireland and England, at 2 and 3 years, incl. Irish 2,000 Guineas, Blandford Stakes; 3rd Irish Sweeps Derby, Champion Stakes; 4th Joe McGrath Memorial Stakes.

NORTHFIELDS (ch. 1968)	Northern Dancer (b. 1961)	Nearctic	Nearco
			Lady Angela
		Natalma	Native Dancer
			Almahmoud
	Little Hut (b. 1952)	Occupy	Bull Dog
			Miss Bunting
		Savage Beauty	Challenger
			Khara
PLACE D'ETOILE (b. 1967)	Kythnos (b. 1957)	Nearula	Nasrullah
			Respite
		Capital Issue	Straight Deal
			Pilch
	Etoile de France (b. 1957)	Arctic Star	Nearco
			Serena
		Miss France	Jock II
			Nafah

652   NORTH STOKE 5 (ch.c., April 4, 1974)

Bred by Ongar Stud.

Won 8 races, placed 2, £63,877, in England, Ireland, Germany and Belgium, at 2 and 3 years, incl. Joe McGrath Memorial Stakes, Furstenberg-Rennen, Grand Prix de Bruxelles; 3rd Champion Stakes.

NORTHFIELDS (ch. 1968)	Northern Dancer (b. 1961)	Nearctic	Nearco
			Lady Angela
		Natalma	Native Dancer
			Almahmoud
	Little Hut (b. 1952)	Occupy	Bull Dog
			Miss Bunting
		Savage Beauty	Challenger
			Khara
MOTHER (b. 1963)	Whistler (ch. 1950)	Panorama	Sir Cosmo
			Happy Climax
		Farthing Damages	Fair Trial
			Futility
	Esmeralda (br. 1956)	Tulyar	Tehran
			Neocracy
		Mahallat	Nearco
			Majideh

653   NORTIA 5 (b.f., February 19, 1959)

Bred by Major L. B. Holliday.

Won 4 races, placed 6, £9,452, in England, from 2 to 4 years, incl. Nassau Stakes, Lingfield Oaks Trial Stakes; 3rd Yorkshire Oaks.

NARRATOR (b. 1951)	Nearco (br. 1935)	Pharos	Phalaris
			Scapa Flow
		Nogara	Havresac II
			Catnip
	Phase (b. 1939)	Windsor Lad	Blandford
			Resplendent
		Lost Soul	Solario
			Orlass
MAITRISE (b. 1948)	Atout Maitre (br. 1936)	Vatout	Prince Chimay
			Vasthi
		Royal Mistress	Teddy
			Tout Paris
	Mabama (b. 1938)	Mahmoud	Blenheim
			Mah Mahal
		Qurrat-al-Ain	Buchan
			Harpsichord

654   OAK HILL 8 (b.f., February 16, 1972)

Bred by S. Houyvet, in England.

Won 3 races, placed 2, 323,980 fr., in France, at 2 and 3 years, incl. Criterium des Pouliches; 4th Prix Saint-Alary.

SHESHOON (ch. 1956)	Precipitation (ch. 1933)	Hurry On	Marcovil
			Tout Suite
		Double Life	Bachelor's Double
			Saint Joan
	Noorani (ch. 1950)	Nearco	Pharos
			Nogara
		Empire Glory	Singapore
			Skyglory
TYPHA (b. 1965)	Tantieme (b. 1947)	Deux pour Cent	Deiri
			Dix pour Cent
		Terka	Indus
			La Furka
	Ruta (b. 1960)	Ratification	Court Martial
			Solesa
		Dame d'Atour	Cranach
			Barley Corn

655 — OBRAZTSOVY 1 (b.c., February 25, 1975)

Bred by John M. Olin, in U.S.A.

Won 8 races, placed 11, £119,607, in England, Germany and U.S.A., from 2 to 5 years, incl. Hardwicke Stakes, St. Simon Stakes, Jockey Club Stakes; 2nd Grosser Preis von Berlin, Yorkshire Cup; 3rd King Edward VII Stakes, John Porter Stakes, Cumberland Lodge Stakes and Sunset H.; 4th St. Leger Stakes.

HIS MAJESTY (b. 1968)	Ribot (b. 1952)	Tenerani	Bellini / Tofanella
		Romanella	El Greco / Barbara Burrini
	Flower Bowl (b. 1952)	Alibhai	Hyperion / Teresina
		Flower Bed	Beau Pere / Boudoir
AZEEZ (b. 1963)	Nashua (b. 1952)	Nasrullah	Nearco / Mumtaz Begum
		Segula	Johnstown / Sekhmet
	La Dauphine (b. 1957)	Princequillo	Prince Rose / Cosquilla
		Baby League	Bubbling Over / La Troienne

656 — OLWYN 9 (b.f., January 27, 1974)

Bred by Dollanstown Stud Establishment.

Won 1 race, placed 5, £47,861, in Ireland and England, at 2 and 3 years, incl. Irish Guinness Oaks; 2nd Lancashire Oaks.

RELKO (b. 1960)	Tanerko (br. 1953)	Tantieme	Deux pour Cent / Terka
		La Divine	Fair Copy / La Diva
	Relance III (ch. 1952)	Relic	War Relic / Bridal Colors
		Polaire II	Le Volcan / Stella Polaris
NANTAHALA (br. 1967)	Nantallah (b. 1953)	Nasrullah	Nearco / Mumtaz Begum
		Shimmer	Flares / Broad Ripple
	Second Edition (ch. 1958)	Alibhai	Hyperion / Teresina
		Pocket Edition	Roman / Never Again II

657 — ONCIDIUM 16 (b.c., April 14, 1961)

Bred by Lord Howard de Walden.

Won 5 races, placed 5, £29,984, in England, from 2 to 4 years, incl. Coronation Cup, Jockey Club Cup, Carreras Piccadilly Derby Trial; 3rd King George VI and Queen Elizabeth Stakes, Royal Lodge Stakes.

ALCIDE (b. 1955)	Alycidon (ch. 1945)	Donatello II	Blenheim / Delleana
		Aurora	Hyperion / Rose Red
	Chenille (br. 1940)	King Salmon	Salmon-Trout / Malva
		Sweet Aloe	Cameronian / Aloe
MALCOLMIA (b. 1952)	Savaji (b. 1943)	Fair Copy	Fairway / Composure
		Perfume II	Badruddin / Lavendula II
	Silvery Moon (b. 1943)	Solario	Gainsborough / Sun Worship
		Silver Fox II	Foxhunter / Pearl Maiden

658 — ONE IN A MILLION 16 (b.f., April 25, 1976)

Bred by Mount Coote Waverton Stud.

Won 5 races, £79,784, in England, at 2 and 3 years, incl. 1,000 Guineas Stakes, Coronation Stakes, Ladbrokes Nell Gwyn Stakes.

RARITY (b. 1967)	Hethersett (b. 1959)	Hugh Lupus	Djebel / Sakountala
		Bride Elect	Big Game / Netherton Maid
	Who Can Tell (ch. 1958)	Worden II	Wild Risk / Sans Tares
		Javotte	Whirlaway / Galatea II
SINGE (b. 1972)	Tudor Music (br. 1966)	Tudor Melody	Tudor Minstrel / Matelda
		Fran	Acropolis / Madrilene
	Trial by Fire (ch. 1958)	Court Martial	Fair Trial / Instantaneous
		Mitrailleuse	Mieuxce / French Kin

659 — ONLY FOR LIFE 14 (b.c., April 17, 1960)

Bred by Hanstead Stud.

Won 3 races, placed 4, £36,666, in England, from 2 to 4 years, incl. 2,000 Guineas Stakes, King Edward VII Stakes; 2nd Great Voltigeur Stakes, John Porter Stakes; 3rd Greenham Stakes.

CHANTEUR II (br. 1942)	Chateau Bouscaut (b. 1927)	Kircubbin	Captivation / Avon Hack
		Ramondie	Neil Gow / La Rille
	La Diva (br. 1937)	Blue Skies	Blandford / Blue Pill
		La Traviata	Alcantara II / Tregaron
LIFE SENTENCE (br. 1949)	Court Martial (ch. 1942)	Fair Trial	Fairway / Lady Juror
		Instantaneous	Hurry On / Picture
	Borobella (br. 1942)	Bois Roussel	Vatout / Plucky Liege
		Annabel	Blandford / Arabella

660 — ON THE SLY 4 (br.c., April 10, 1973)

Bred by Shoshone Farm, in U.S.A.

Won 14 races, placed 15, $667,293, in U.S.A., from 3 to 5 years, incl. Jockey Club Gold Cup, Hawthorne Gold Cup, Grey Lag H. and Donald P. Ross H.; 2nd Wood Memorial Stakes, Gallant Fox H. and Marylander H.; 3rd Michigan Mile-and-One-Eighth H. and Grey Lag H.

ROI DAGOBERT (b. 1964)	Sicambre (br. 1948)	Prince Bio	Prince Rose / Biologie
		Sif	Rialto / Suavita
	Dame d'Atour (b. 1955)	Cranach	Coronach / Reine Isaure
		Barley Corn	Hyperion / Schiaparelli
TRICK CHICK (ch. 1966)	Prince John (ch. 1953)	Princequillo	Prince Rose / Cosquilla
		Not Afraid	Count Fleet / Banish Fear
	Fast Line (ch. 1958)	Mr. Busher	War Admiral / Baby League
		Throttle Wide	Flying Heels / Let Her Fly

661 OPALINE II 3 (ch.f., April 30, 1958)

Bred by Prince Aly Khan.

Won 5 races, placed 3, £11,498, in England and France, at 2 and 3 years, incl. Cheveley Park Stakes, Prix de Seine-et-Oise, Prix Yacowlef; 2nd Coronation Stakes, Prix de Meautry.

HYPERION (ch. 1930)	Gainsborough (b. 1915)	Bayardo	Bay Ronald / Galicia
		Rosedrop	St. Frusquin / Rosaline
	Selene (b. 1919)	Chaucer	St. Simon / Canterbury Pilgrim
		Serenissima	Minoru / Gondolette
MARTINE (b. 1952)	Palestine (gr. 1947)	Fair Trial	Fairway / Lady Juror
		Una	Tetratema / Uganda
	Pale Ale (b. 1936)	Mannamead	Manna / Pinprick
		Compromise	White Eagle / Jean's Folly

662 ORANGE BAY 16 (b.c., March 28, 1972)

Bred by Dr. C. Vittadini.

Won 9 races, placed 9, £135,551, in Italy and England, from 2 to 5 years, incl. Derby Italiano, Premio Emanuele Filiberto, Hardwicke Stakes, Jockey Club Stakes, Cumberland Lodge Stakes; 2nd Gran Criterium, Gran Premio d'Italia, King George VI and Queen Elizabeth Diamond Stakes; 3rd Gran Premio di Milano, King George VI and Queen Elizabeth Diamond Stakes, Earl of Sefton Stakes, Benson and Hedges Gold Cup.

CANISBAY (ch. 1961)	Doutelle (ch. 1954)	Prince Chevalier	Prince Rose / Chevalerie
		Above Board	Straight Deal / Feola
	Stroma (ch. 1955)	Luminary	Fair Trial / Luciebella
		Whoa Emma	Prince Chevalier / Ready
ORANGE TRIUMPH (b. 1965)	Molvedo (br. 1958)	Ribot	Tenerani / Romanella
		Maggiolina	Nakamuro / Murcia
	Orange (br. 1954)	Dante	Nearco / Rosy Legend
		Fior d'Orchidea	Apelle / Osa

663 ORCHESTRA 1 (ch.c., April 12, 1974)

Bred by Lord Donoughmore.

Won 7 races, placed 14, £62,320, in Ireland and England, from 2 to 5 years, incl. Beresford Stakes, Nijinsky Stakes, John Porter Stakes and Whitehall Stakes; 2nd Gallinule Stakes, Ballymoss Stakes (twice), Irish St. Leger and Blandford Stakes; 3rd William Hill Futurity Stakes, Jockey Club Stakes, Joe McGrath Memorial Stakes, Gladness Stakes and Royal Whip; 4th Irish Sweeps Derby and Joe McGrath Memorial Stakes.

TUDOR MUSIC (br. 1966)	Tudor Melody (br. 1956)	Tudor Minstrel	Owen Tudor / Sansonnet
		Matelda	Dante / Fairly Hot
	Fran (ch. 1959)	Acropolis	Donatello II / Aurora
		Madrilene	Court Martial / Marmite
GOLDEN MOSS (ch. 1965)	Sheshoon (ch. 1956)	Precipitation	Hurry On / Double Life
		Noorani	Nearco / Empire Glory
	Muscosa (b. 1956)	Mossborough	Nearco / All Moonshine
		Sylvan	Torbido / Woodlark

664 ORCHESTRATION 5 (b.f., April 28, 1974)

Bred by Major V. McCalmont.

Won 4 races, £20,280, in Ireland and England, at 2 and 3 years, incl. Athasi Stakes, Coronation Stakes.

WELSH PAGEANT (b. 1966)	Tudor Melody (br. 1956)	Tudor Minstrel	Owen Tudor / Sansonnet
		Matelda	Dante / Fairly Hot
	Picture Light (b. 1954)	Court Martial	Fair Trial / Instantaneous
		Queen of Light	Borealis / Picture Play
TRINITY TERM (b. 1968)	Primera (b. 1954)	My Babu	Djebel / Perfume II
		Pirette	Deiri / Pimpette
	Hilary Term (b. 1962)	Supreme Court	Persian Gulf or Precipitation / Forecourt
		Spring Running	Nearula / Bagheera

665 ORSA MAGGIORE 16 (br.f., February 17, 1970)

Bred by Scuderia Metauro, in Ireland.

Won 9 races, placed 4, 138,650,000 L., in Italy, from 2 to 4 years, incl. Oaks d'Italia, Gran Premio di Milano, Premio Ellington, Premio Roma, Premio Lydia Tesio and Premio Legnano; 2nd Gran Premio del Jockey Club and Premio Lydia Tesio.

RUYSDAEL (b. 1964)	Right Royal V (br. 1958)	Owen Tudor	Hyperion / Mary Tudor II
		Bastia	Tornado or Victrix II / Barberybush
	Rossellina (b. 1957)	Tenerani	Bellini / Tofanella
		Romanella	El Greco / Barbara Burrini
OLIVEIRA (br. 1963)	Herbager (b. 1956)	Vandale II	Plassy / Vanille
		Flagette	Escamillo / Fidgette
	Orange (br. 1954)	Dante	Nearco / Rosy Legend
		Fior d'Orchidea	Apelle / Osa

666 ORTIS 14 (ch.c., February 16, 1967)

Bred by P. Mezzanotte and Dr. C. Vittadini, in Italy.

Won 7 races, placed 7, £98,460, in Italy, England and Ireland, from 2 to 4 years, incl. Derby Italiano, Gran Premio d'Italia, Premio Emanuele Filiberto, Hardwicke Stakes; 2nd Gran Criterium, Gran Premio del Jockey Club, Coronation Stakes, Player-Wills Stakes, King George VI and Queen Elizabeth Stakes.

TISSOT (b. 1953)	Tenerani (b. 1944)	Bellini	Cavaliere d'Arpino / Bella Minna
		Tofanella	Apelle / Try Try Again
	Tiepoletta (br. 1946)	Niccolo Dell'Arca	Coronach / Nogara
		Tempesta	Michelangelo / Turletta
ORIENTALE (ch. 1961)	Nagami (ch. 1955)	Nimbus	Nearco / Kong
		Jennifer	Hyperion / Avena
	Oria (b. 1948)	Arco	Singapore / Archidamia
		Olema	Cappiello / Oderiga da Gubbio

667 **OUR CHERI AMOUR** 4 (b.f., April 28, 1968)

Bred by C. McGhee Baxter, in U.S.A.

Won 7 races, placed 12, $176,839, in U.S.A., from 2 to 5 years, incl. Coaching Club American Oaks, Militia H. and Open Fire Stakes; 2nd Villager Stakes and Gazelle H.

PORTERHOUSE (br. 1951)	Endeavour II (b. 1942)	British Empire	Colombo
			Rose of England
		Himalaya	Hunter's Moon
			Partenope
	Red Stamp (b. 1943)	Bimelech	Black Toney
			La Troienne
		Peggy Porter	The Porter
			Pretty Peggy
FOR LOVE (b. 1964)	Blue Prince II (b. 1951)	Princequillo	Prince Rose
			Cosquilla
		Blue Denim	Blue Larkspur
			Judy O'Grady
	Forfeit (b. 1950)	Count Fleet	Reigh Count
			Quickly
		Everget	Snark
			Memorandum

668 **OUR MIMS** 9 (b.f., March 8, 1974)

Bred by Calumet Farm, in U.S.A.

Won 6 races, placed 7, $368,034, in U.S.A., from 2 to 4 years, incl. Coaching Club American Oaks, Delaware H., Alabama Stakes and Fantasy Stakes; 2nd Kentucky Oaks and Demoiselle Stakes; 3rd Ashland Stakes.

HERBAGER (b. 1956)	Vandale II (b. 1943)	Plassy	Bosworth
			Pladda
		Vanille	La Farina
			Vaya
	Flagette (ch. 1951)	Escamillo	Firdaussi
			Estoril
		Fidgette	Firdaussi
			Boxeuse
SWEET TOOTH (b. 1965)	On-and-On (b. 1956)	Nasrullah	Nearco
			Mumtaz Begum
		Two Lea	Bull Lea
			Two Bob
	Plum Cake (ch. 1958)	Ponder	Pensive
			Miss Rushin
		Real Delight	Bull Lea
			Blue Delight

669 **OUR MIRAGE** 11 (ch.c., May 23, 1969)

Bred by R. J. Donworth.

Won 7 races, placed 6, £63,460, in England, France, Ireland and Germany, from 2 to 4 years, incl. Prix de la Salamandre, Great Voltigeur Stakes, Princess of Wales's Stakes, Dee Stakes, Jockey Club Stakes; 2nd St. Leger Stakes, Irish St. Leger; 3rd King George VI and Queen Elizabeth Stakes; 4th Derby Stakes, Preis von Europa.

MIRALGO (ch. 1959)	Aureole (ch. 1950)	Hyperion	Gainsborough
			Selene
		Angelola	Donatello II
			Feola
	Nella (ch. 1949)	Nearco	Pharos
			Nogara
		Laitron	Soldennis
			Chardon
ARDENT RANGE (b. or br. 1960)	Buisson Ardent (b. 1953)	Relic	War Relic
			Bridal Colors
		Rose o'Lynn	Pherozshah
			Rocklyn
	Blue Range (b. 1951)	Blue Peter	Fairway
			Fancy Free
		Mountain Fastness	Umidwar
			Lennoxlove

670 **OUTCROP** 5 (b.f., April 5, 1960)

Bred by Lambourn Stud Ltd. and Brig. W. W. T. Torr.

Won 7 races, placed 7, £14,137, in England, from 2 to 4 years, incl. Yorkshire Oaks, Park Hill Stakes.

ROCKEFELLA (br. 1941)	Hyperion (ch. 1930)	Gainsborough	Bayardo
			Rosedrop
		Selene	Chaucer
			Serenissima
	Rockfel (br. 1935)	Felstead	Spion Kop
			Felkington
		Rockliffe	Santorb
			Sweet Rocket
CHAMBIGES (b. 1949)	Majano (b. 1937)	Deiri	Aethelstan
			Desra
		Madgi Moto	Ksar
			Groseille à Maquereau
	Chanterelle (ch. 1940)	Gris Perle	Brabant
			Mauve
		Shah Bibi	Pharos
			Hajibibi

671 **OVAC** 16 (b.c., February 9, 1973)

Bred by Scuderia Alpina, in Italy.

Won 11 races, placed 8, £89,338, in Italy and England, from 2 to 5 years, incl. Premio Parioli, Premio Besnate, Premio Ribot, Premio Chiusura, Premio Natale di Roma, Gran Premio Città di Torino and Diomed Stakes; 2nd Premio Emilio Turati and Queen Anne Stakes; 3rd Premio Emilio Turati and Lockinge Stakes; 4th Sussex Stakes.

FURIBONDO (ch. 1966)	Floribunda (b. 1958)	Princely Gift	Nasrullah
			Blue Gem
		Astrentia	Denturius
			Aherlow Valley
	Blue Range (ch. 1951)	Blue Peter	Fairway
			Fancy Free
		Mountain Fastness	Umidwar
			Lennoxlove
ORATCH (b. 1966)	Match III (br. 1958)	Tantieme	Deux pour Cent
			Terka
		Relance III	Relic
			Polaire II
	Orange (br. 1954)	Dante	Nearco
			Rosy Legend
		Fior d'Orchidea	Apelle
			Osa

672 **OVERSKATE** 22 (ch.c., March 23, 1975)

Bred by Stafford Farms, in Canada.

Won 24 races, placed 9, $791,634, in Canada and U.S.A., from 2 to 5 years, incl. Prince of Wales Stakes, Breeders' Stakes, Manitoba Derby, Coronation Futurity, Canadian Maturity, Bowling Green H., Stars and Stripes H., Bernard Baruch H. and Jockey Club Cup H.; 2nd Queen's Plate and Cornhusker H.; 3rd United Nations H. and Stars and Stripes H.

NODOUBLE (ch. 1965)	Noholme II (ch. 1956)	Star Kingdom	Stardust
			Impromptu
		Oceana	Colombo
			Orama
	Abla-Jay (b. 1955)	Double Jay	Balladier
			Broomshot
		Ablamucha	Don Bingo
			Sweet Betty
OVERSTATE (br. 1969)	Speak John (b. 1958)	Prince John	Princequillo
			Not Afraid
		Nuit de Folies	Tornado
			Folle Nuit
	Battle Eve (ch. 1957)	Battlefield	War Relic
			Dark Display
		Evening Out	Shut Out
			Evening Belle

673   **PAIMPONT** 9 (ch.f., March 22, 1957)

Bred by R. B. Strassburger, in France.

Won 2 races, placed 3, £4,158, in France and England, at 2 and 3 years, incl. 2nd Oaks Stakes; 3rd Prix de Conde.

```
                                    ┌ Hurry On        ┌ Marcovil
                    Precipitation  ┤                  └ Tout Suite
                    (ch. 1933)      └ Double Life     ┌ Bachelor's Double
CHAMOSSAIRE                                           └ Saint Joan
(ch. 1942)                          ┌ Cameronian      ┌ Pharos
                    Snowberry      ┤                  └ Una Cameron
                    (br. 1937)      └ Myrobella       ┌ Tetratema
                                                      └ Dolabella

                                    ┌ Nearco          ┌ Pharos
                    Nasrullah      ┤                  └ Nogara
                    (b. 1940)       └ Mumtaz Begum    ┌ Blenheim
BALLYNASH                                            └ Mumtaz Mahal
(b. 1946)                           ┌ Ballyferis      ┌ Apron
                    Ballywellbroke ┤                  └ Gilford
                    (b. or br. 1933)└ The Beggar      ┌ Le Souvenir
                                                      └ Avonbeg
```

674   **PALATCH** 14 (b.f., April 26, 1964)

Bred by Sledmere Stud Co. Ltd.

Won 2 races, placed 5, £6,845, in England, from 2 to 4 years, incl. Yorkshire Oaks, Musidora Stakes; 2nd Yorkshire Cup, Craven Stakes, Jockey Club Stakes; 4th Coronation Cup.

```
                                    ┌ Deux pour Cent  ┌ Deiri
                    Tantieme       ┤                  └ Dix pour Cent
                    (b. 1947)       └ Terka           ┌ Indus
MATCH III                                            └ La Furka
(br. 1958)                          ┌ Relic           ┌ War Relic
                    Relance III    ┤                  └ Bridal Colors
                    (ch. 1952)      └ Polaire II      ┌ Le Volcan
                                                      └ Stella Polaris

                                    ┌ Fair Trial      ┌ Fairway
                    Palestine      ┤                  └ Lady Juror
                    (gr. 1947)      └ Una             ┌ Tetratema
PALAZZOLI                                            └ Uganda
(b. 1954)                           ┌ Solario         ┌ Gainsborough
                    Maintenon      ┤                  └ Sun Worship
                    (b. 1941)       └ Queen Christina ┌ Buchan
                                                      └ Molly Adare
```

675   **PAMPALINA** 8 (br.f., February 26, 1964)

Bred by Mrs. S. J. Parr.

Won 4 races, placed 2, £23,184, in Ireland, at 2 and 3 years, incl. Irish Guinness Oaks; 2nd Pretty Polly Stakes (Curragh).

```
                                    ┌ Pharos          ┌ Phalaris
                    Nearco         ┤                  └ Scapa Flow
                    (br. 1935)      └ Nogara          ┌ Havresac II
BAIRAM II                                            └ Catnip
(b. 1955)                           ┌ Owen Tudor      ┌ Hyperion
                    Bibi Toori     ┤                  └ Mary Tudor II
                    (b. 1949)       └ Bibibeg         ┌ Bahram
                                                      └ Mumtaz Begum

                                    ┌ Umidwar         ┌ Blandford
                    Anwar          ┤                  └ Uganda
                    (b. 1943)       └ Stafaralla      ┌ Solario
PADUS                                                └ Mirawala
(br. 1955)                          ┌ Airway          ┌ Fairway
                    Cherry Way     ┤                  └ Udaipur
                    (b. 1944)       └ Cherry Pie      ┌ Wychwood Abbot
                                                      └ Cherry Brook
```

676   **PAMPAPAUL** 8 (b.c., March 24, 1974)

Bred by Hans Paul.

Won 3 races, placed 5, £62,228, in Ireland and England, at 2 and 3 years, incl. Irish 2,000 Guineas, National Stakes (Curragh); 2nd Royal Lodge Stakes, Railway Stakes.

```
                                    ┌ Nasrullah       ┌ Nearco
                    Red God        ┤                  └ Mumtaz Begum
                    (ch. 1954)      └ Spring Run      ┌ Menow
YELLOW GOD                                           └ Boola Brook
(ch. 1967)                          ┌ Fun Fair        ┌ Fair Trial
                    Sally Deans    ┤                  └ Humoresque
                    (ch. 1947)      └ Cora Deans      ┌ Coronach
                                                      └ Jennie Deans

                                    ┌ Nearco          ┌ Pharos
                    Bairam II      ┤                  └ Nogara
                    (b. 1955)       └ Bibi Toori      ┌ Owen Tudor
PAMPALINA                                            └ Bibibeg
(br. 1964)                          ┌ Anwar           ┌ Umidwar
                    Padus          ┤                  └ Stafaralla
                    (br. 1955)      └ Cherry Way      ┌ Airway
                                                      └ Cherry Pie
```

677   **PAMPERED MISS** 2 (ch.f., April 5, 1967)

Bred by Nelson Bunker Hunt, in U.S.A.

Won 4 races, placed 3, 643,531 fr., in France, at 2 and 3 years, incl. Poule d'Essai des Pouliches and Prix de la Grotte; 3rd Prix de Diane.

```
                                    ┌ Moslem          ┌ Rustom Pasha
                    Petare         ┤                  └ Merrose
                    (b. 1951)       └ Collette        ┌ Diadoque
SADAIR                                               └ Colombine
(b. 1962)                           ┌ Blue Pair       ┌ Pairbypair
                    Blue Missy     ┤                  └ Eva B.
                    (ch. 1946)      └ Miss Champion   ┌ Waygood
                                                      └ Home Product

                                    ┌ Hunter's Moon   ┌ Hurry On
                    Postin         ┤                  └ Selene
                    (ch. 1940)      └ Quinta          ┌ Codihue
PAMPLONA II                                          └ En Guardia
(b. 1956)                           ┌ Kingsway        ┌ Fairway
                    Society's Way  ┤                  └ Yenna
                    (b. 1950)       └ Society's Vote  ┌ Wyndham
                                                      └ Conversation Piece
```

678   **PANDOFELL** 31 (b.c., April 29, 1957)

Bred by H. J. Joel.

Won 8 races, placed 4, £20,482, in England, from 2 to 4 years, incl. Ascot Gold Cup, Yorkshire Cup, Doncaster Cup; 2nd John Porter Stakes.

```
                                    ┌ Windsor Lad     ┌ Blandford
                    Windsor Slipper┤                  └ Resplendent
                    (b. 1939)       └ Carpet Slipper  ┌ Phalaris
SOLAR SLIPPER                                        └ Simon's Shoes
(b. 1945)                           ┌ Solario         ┌ Gainsborough
                    Solar Flower   ┤                  └ Sun Worship
                    (br. 1935)      └ Serena          ┌ Winalot
                                                      └ Charmione

                                    ┌ Abjer           ┌ Asterus
                    Nosca          ┤                  └ Zariba
                    (b. 1939)       └ Capella         ┌ Tourbillon
NADIKA                                               └ Gracilite
(b. 1948)                           ┌ Olibrius        ┌ Pilliwinkie
                    Adoli          ┤                  └ Oriane
                    (gr. 1939)      └ Fraicheur       ┌ Flechois
                                                      └ Mind the Paint
```

679   **PANDORA BAY** 1 (b.f., April 22, 1965)

Bred by Mrs. H. J. Morton.

Won 7 races, placed 6, £36,223, in England and France, from 2 to 4 years, incl. Ribblesdale Stakes, Prix Kergorlay; 3rd Oaks Stakes, Cheshire Oaks, Prix Foy; 4th Yorkshire Oaks.

PANDOFELL (b. 1957)	Solar Slipper (b. 1945)	Windsor Slipper	Windsor Lad / Carpet Slipper
		Solar Flower	Solario / Serena
	Nadika (b. 1948)	Nosca	Abjer / Capella
		Adoli	Olibrius / Fraicheur
FRENCH MOSS (b. 1953)	Mossborough (ch. 1947)	Nearco	Pharos / Nogara
		All Moonshine	Bobsleigh / Selene
	L'Abbesse de Matriarch (br. 1941)	The Black Abbot	Abbots Trace / Lady Juror
		The Matriarch	Cyclonic / Dail

680   **PARANETE** 4 (b.f., May 13, 1977)

Bred by Mme. Jean Couturié, in France.

Won 2 races, placed 4, 625,000 fr., in France, at 2 and 3 years, incl. Prix Saint-Alary; 3rd Prix de Diane de Revlon, Prix Vanteaux and Prix Cleopatre.

KING OF THE CASTLE (b. 1966)	Bold Ruler (b. 1954)	Nasrullah	Nearco / Mumtaz Begum
		Miss Disco	Discovery / Outdone
	Ambulance (b. 1954)	Ambiorix II	Tourbillon / Lavendula II
		Big Hurry	Black Toney / La Troienne
PARTHENIA (b./br. 1969)	Sea Hawk II (gr. 1963)	Herbager	Vandale II / Flagette
		Sea Nymph	Free Man / Sea Spray
	Tiepolina (b. 1963)	Tiepoletto	Tornado / Scarlet Skies
		Jacine	Owen Tudor / Weighbridge

681   **PARBURY** 6 (b.c., March 9, 1963)

Bred by Major H. P. Holt.

Won 5 races, placed 9, £18,494, in England, from 2 to 5 years, incl. Ascot Gold Cup, Henry II Stakes; 2nd Jockey Club Cup, Goodwood Cup; 3rd Craven Stakes, Goodwood Cup, Henry II Stakes.

PARDAL (b. 1947)	Pharis II (br. 1936)	Pharos	Phalaris / Scapa Flow
		Carissima	Clarissimus / Casquetts
	Adargatis (b. 1931)	Asterus	Teddy / Astrella
		Helene de Troie	Helicon / Lady of Pedigree
ALCONBURY (ch. 1954)	Alycidon (ch. 1945)	Donatello II	Blenheim / Delleana
		Aurora	Hyperion / Rose Red
	Chanctonbury (ch. 1937)	Papyrus	Tracery / Miss Matty
		Chincona	Buchan / Chinchilla

682   **PARDALLO II** 8 (b.c., April 13, 1963)

Bred by Mme. L. Volterra, in France.

Won 8 races, placed 7, £64,617, in France and England, from 3 to 6 years, incl. Prix de Barbeville (twice), Prix Jean Prat, Prix Kergorlay, Ascot Gold Cup; 2nd Prix Kergorlay; 4th Prix Lupin. Also won 3 races, placed 1, £8,648, over hurdles in France, 1967.

PARDAL (b. 1947)	Pharis II (br. 1936)	Pharos	Phalaris / Scapa Flow
		Carissima	Clarissimus / Casquetts
	Adargatis (b. 1931)	Asterus	Teddy / Astrella
		Helene de Troie	Helicon / Lady of Pedigree
GREAT SUCCESS II (b. 1954)	Niccolo Dell'Arca (b. 1938)	Coronach	Hurry On / Wet Kiss
		Nogara	Havresac II / Catnip
	L'Orgueilleuse (br. 1947)	Vatellor	Vatout / Lady Elinor
		Philippa of Hainaut	Teddy / Pride of Hainault

683   **PARDAO** 14 (ch.c., February 12, 1958)

Bred by Sledmere Stud Co. Ltd.

Won 6 races, placed 8, £45,810, in England and U.S.A., from 2 to 5 years, incl. Lingfield Derby Trial Stakes, Gordon Stakes, Jockey Club Cup, San Juan Capistrano H. and San Marino H.; 2nd Richmond Stakes, Ormonde Stakes; 3rd Derby Stakes, Great Voltigeur Stakes.

PARDAL (b. 1947)	Pharis II (br. 1936)	Pharos	Phalaris / Scapa Flow
		Carissima	Clarissimus / Casquetts
	Adargatis (b. 1931)	Asterus	Teddy / Astrella
		Helene de Troie	Helicon / Lady of Pedigree
THREE WEEKS (ch. 1946)	Big Game (b. 1939)	Bahram	Blandford / Friar's Daughter
		Myrobella	Tetratema / Dolabella
	Eleanor Cross (ch. 1939)	Hyperion	Gainsborough / Selene
		Queen Christina	Buchan / Molly Adare

684   **PAREO** 16 (ch.c., March 1, 1977)

Bred by Mme. Jean Couturié, in France.

Won 5 races, placed 2, 125,550,000 L., in Italy, at 2 and 3 years, incl. Gran Criterium and Gran Premio d'Italia; 2nd Gran Premio di Milano and Premio Emanuele Filiberto.

ARMOS (ch. 1967)	Mossborough (ch. 1947)	Nearco	Pharos / Nogara
		All Moonshine	Bobsleigh / Selene
	Ardelle (b. 1958)	Supreme Court	Persian Gulf or Precipitation / Forecourt
		Per Ardua	Hyperion / Ad Astra
EL PALOMAR (br. 1971)	Le Mesnil (b. or br. 1960)	Tyrone	Tornado / Statira
		Flying Colours	Massine / Red Flame
	Sly Pola (ch. 1957)	Spy Song	Balladier / Mata Hari
		Ampola	Pavot / Blue Denim

685   PARK TOP 26 (b.f., May 27, 1964)

Bred by Mrs. L. Scott.

Won 13 races, placed 8, £137,572, in England and France, from 3 to 6 years, incl. Ribblesdale Stakes, Coronation Cup, Hardwicke Stakes, King George VI and Queen Elizabeth Stakes, Prix Foy, La Coupe, Cumberland Lodge Stakes; 2nd Ormonde Stakes, Cumberland Lodge Stakes, Eclipse Stakes, Prix de l'Arc de Triomphe, Champion Stakes, Coronation Cup; 3rd Prix de Royallieu (dead-heat).

KALYDON (b. 1956)	Alycidon (ch. 1945)	Donatello II	Blenheim / Delleana
		Aurora	Hyperion / Rose Red
	Lackaday (b. 1947)	Bobsleigh	Gainsborough / Toboggan
		Lackadaisy	Felstead / Complacent
NELLIE PARK (b. 1957)	Arctic Prince (br. 1948)	Prince Chevalier	Prince Rose / Chevalerie
		Arctic Sun	Nearco / Solar Flower
	Oola Hills (br. 1945)	Denturius	Gold Bridge / La Solfatara
		Chikoo	Firdaussi / Chor Bazar

686   PARMELIA 14 (b.f., April 2, 1967)

Bred by Sassoon Studs.

Won 2 races, placed 5, £23,439, in England and France, at 2 and 3 years, incl. Ribblesdale Stakes, Park Hill Stakes, 2nd Irish Guinness Oaks, Musidora Stakes, Princess Royal Stakes; 3rd Prix Vermeille.

BALLYMOSS (ch. 1954)	Mossborough (ch. 1947)	Nearco	Pharos / Nogara
		All Moonshine	Bobsleigh / Selene
	Indian Call (ch. 1936)	Singapore	Gainsborough / Tetrabbazia
		Flittemere	Buchan / Keysoe
EDIE KELLY (br. 1950)	Bois Roussel (br. 1935)	Vatout	Prince Chimay / Vasthi
		Plucky Liege	Spearmint / Concertina
	Caerlissa (b. 1935)	Caerleon	Phalaris / Canyon
		Sister Sarah	Abbots Trace / Sarita

687   PARNELL 12 (ch.c., April 24, 1968)

Bred by R. More O'Ferrall and Earl of Iveagh.

Won 14 races, placed 13, £115,107, in Ireland, England, France, Italy and U.S.A., from 2 to 6 years, incl. Irish St. Leger, Prix Jean Prat (twice), Jockey Club Cup, Queen's Vase; 2nd King George VI and Queen Elizabeth Stakes, Gran Premio del Jockey Club, Washington D.C. International, Prix du Cadran, Prix de Barbeville; 3rd Blandford Stakes, Goodwood Cup, Prix Royal Oak, Prix Gladiateur (won but disqualified); 4th Premio Roma.

ST. PADDY (b. 1957)	Aureole (ch. 1950)	Hyperion	Gainsborough / Selene
		Angelola	Donatello II / Feola
	Edie Kelly (br. 1950)	Bois Roussel	Vatout / Plucky Liege
		Caerlissa	Caerleon / Sister Sarah
NELLA (ch. 1949)	Nearco (br. 1935)	Pharos	Phalaris / Scapa Flow
		Nogara	Havresac II / Catnip
	Laitron (ch. 1932)	Soldennis	Tredennis / Soligena
		Chardon	Aldford / Thistle

688   PARSIMONY 1 (ch.f., May 3, 1969)

Bred by Overbury Stud.

Won 4 races, placed 7, £14,305, in England, at 2 and 3 years, incl. July Cup, Cork and Orrery Stakes; 2nd Diadem Stakes, Vernons Sprint Cup; 3rd Nunthorpe Stakes, Challenge Stakes.

PARTHIA (b. 1956)	Persian Gulf (b. 1940)	Bahram	Blandford / Friar's Daughter
		Double Life	Bachelor's Double / Saint Joan
	Lightning (b. 1950)	Hyperion	Gainsborough / Selene
		Chenille	King Salmon / Sweet Aloe
MONEY FOR NOTHING (br. 1962)	Grey Sovereign (gr. 1948)	Nasrullah	Nearco / Mumtaz Begum
		Kong	Baytown / Clang
	Sweet Nothings (ch. 1952)	Honeyway	Fairway / Honey Buzzard
		Farthing Damages	Fair Trial / Futility

689   PARTHIAN GLANCE 9 (b.f., 1963)

Bred by W. H. D. Riley-Smith.

Won 3 races, placed 5, £19,935, in England and France, at 3 and 4 years, incl. Yorkshire Oaks, Park Hill Stakes, Ribblesdale Stakes; 2nd Carreras Piccadilly Oaks Trial Stakes, Prix de Lutece.

PARTHIA (b. 1956)	Persian Gulf (b. 1940)	Bahram	Blandford / Friar's Daughter
		Double Life	Bachelor's Double / Saint Joan
	Lightning (b. 1950)	Hyperion	Gainsborough / Selene
		Chenille	King Salmon / Sweet Aloe
TENACITY (b. 1958)	Wilwyn (b. 1948)	Pink Flower	Oleander / Plymstock
		Saracen	Donatello II / Lovely Rosa
	Ela Tengam (b. 1950)	Kingsway	Fairway / Yenna
		Trixie from Tad	Flag of Truce / Tad

690   PASS CATCHER 1 (b.c., April 6, 1968)

Bred by October House Farm, in U.S.A.

Won 7 races, placed 11, $268,729, in U.S.A., from 2 to 4 years, incl. Belmont Stakes; 2nd Jersey Derby, Sapling Stakes, Hopeful Stakes and Kindergarten Stakes; 3rd Amory L. Haskell H.

ALL HANDS (b. or br. 1957)	Turn-to (b. 1951)	Royal Charger	Nearco / Sun Princess
		Source Sucree	Admiral Drake / Lavendula II
	Best Risk (b. 1940)	Blenheim	Blandford / Malva
		Risk	Sir Gallahad III / Risky
LA GRUE (ch. 1964)	Flaneur (ch. 1954)	Prince Chevalier	Prince Rose / Chevalerie
		Sun Princess	Solario / Mumtaz Begum
	Glenpavia (br. 1954)	Pavot	Case Ace / Coquelicot
		Gaffery	Fairy Manhurst / Galtown

691 **PASTY** 19 (gr.f., May 1, 1973)

Bred by G. P. Williams.

Won 5 races, placed 1, £28,365, in England, at 2 and 3 years, incl. William Hill Cheveley Park Stakes, Lowther Stakes.

RAFFINGORA (gr. 1965)	Grey Sovereign (gr. 1948)	Nasrullah	Nearco / Mumtaz Begum
		Kong	Baytown / Clang
	Cameo (b. 1955)	Como	Sir Cosmo / Maia
		Record Serenade	Straight Deal / Columbia
MA MARIE (b. 1956)	My Babu (b. 1945)	Djebel	Tourbillon / Loika
		Perfume II	Badruddin / Lavendula II
	Marie d'Ecosse (b. 1947)	Mieuxce	Massine / L'Olivete
		Scotia's Glen	Beresford / Queen Scotia

692 **PATCH** 14 (ch.c., March 21, 1972)

Bred by Dr. C. Vittadini.

Won 3 races, placed 4, £60,154, in England, Italy and France, from 2 to 4 years, incl. Great Voltigeur Stakes, Ladbroke Derby Trial Stakes; 2nd Prix du Jockey Club; 3rd Benson and Hedges Gold Cup.

ST. PADDY (b. 1957)	Aureole (ch. 1950)	Hyperion	Gainsborough / Selene
		Angelola	Donatello II / Feola
	Edie Kelly (br. 1950)	Bois Roussel	Vatout / Plucky Liege
		Caerlissa	Caerleon / Sister Sarah
PALATCH (b. 1964)	Match III (br. 1958)	Tantieme	Deux pour Cent / Terka
		Relance III	Relic / Polaire II
	Palazzoli (b. 1954)	Palestine	Fair Trial / Una
		Maintenon	Solario / Queen Christina

693 **PATTI** 8 (b.f., February 16, 1961)

Bred by Beatrice, Countess of Granard.

Won 1 race, placed 3, £9,241, in Ireland, England and France, at 2 and 3 years, incl. 2nd Irish Guinness Oaks, St. Leger Stakes; 3rd Prix de Malleret.

CHANTEUR II (br. 1942)	Chateau Bouscaut (b. 1927)	Kircubbin	Captivation / Avon Hack
		Ramondie	Neil Gow / La Rille
	La Diva (br. 1937)	Blue Skies	Blandford / Blue Pill
		La Traviata	Alcantara II / Tregaron
EASTERN FAIRY (ch. 1947)	Persian Gulf (b. 1940)	Bahram	Blandford / Friar's Daughter
		Double Life	Bachelor's Double / Saint Joan
	Sea Fairy (ch. 1939)	Fair Trial	Fairway / Lady Juror
		Portree	Stefan the Great / Saddlemark

694 **PAULISTA** 11 (br.f., March 26, 1971)

Bred by Stackallan Stud, in Ireland.

Won 6 races, placed 2, 1,021,630 fr., in France, at 2 and 3 years, incl. Prix Vermeille, Prix de Minerve and Prix de la Nonette; 3rd Prix de Malleret.

SEA HAWK II (gr. 1963)	Herbager (b. 1956)	Vandale II	Plassy / Vanille
		Flagette	Escamillo / Fidgette
	Sea Nymph (gr. 1957)	Free Man	Norseman / Fantine
		Sea Spray	Ocean Swell / Pontoon
PETITE MARMITE (br. 1963)	Babur (b. 1953)	My Babu	Djebel / Perfume II
		Reseda	Cameronian / Rockfoil
	Madrilene (ch. 1951)	Court Martial	Fair Trial / Instantaneous
		Marmite	Mr. Jinks / Gentlemen's Relish

695 **PAVEH** 1 (b.c., January 18, 1963)

Bred by P. A. B. Widener.

Won 6 races, placed 3, £35,510, in Ireland and England, from 2 to 4 years, incl. Irish 2,000 Guineas Stakes, Sussex Stakes; 3rd Irish Sweeps Derby, Beresford Stakes.

TROPIQUE (b. 1952)	Fontenay (b. 1946)	Tornado	Tourbillon / Roseola
		Flying Colours	Massine / Red Flame
	Aurore Boreale (b. 1941)	Brantome	Blandford / Vitamine
		Voute Celeste	Legatee / La Grande Ourse
PERSIAN SHOE (ch. 1952)	Tehran (b. 1941)	Bois Roussel	Vatout / Plucky Liege
		Stafaralla	Solario / Mirawala
	Canvas Shoe (ch. 1944)	Windsor Slipper	Windsor Lad / Carpet Slipper
		Picture	Gainsborough / Plymstock

696 **PAWIMENT** 13 (b.c., March 6, 1974)

Bred by Stud Iwno, in Poland.

Won 16 races, placed 7, £144,761 (excluding Eastern European earnings), in Poland, Czechoslovakia, Germany and Italy, from 2 to 6 years, incl. Preis von Europa, Gran Premio del Jockey Club, Grosser Preis von Dortmund, Polish 2,000 Guineas (Nagroda Rulera), Nagroda Iwna, Wielka Warszawska, Prize of Budapest and Criterium (twice), Warsaw; 2nd Polish Derby.

MEHARI (b. 1963)	Lavandin (b. 1953)	Verso II	Pinceau / Variete
		Lavande	Rustom Pasha / Livadia
	Eos (br. 1946)	Solferino	Fairway / Sol Speranza
		Ormel	Ormenus / Laitron
PYTIA (b. 1965)	De Corte (b. 1951)	San II	Leb w leb / Eloe
		Dossa Dossi	Spike Island / Delleana
	Putnia (br. 1957)	Pink Pearl	Pilade / Rosa Nera
		Presja	Bobsleigh / Pretty Piece

697   PAWNEESE 9 (b.f., April 5, 1973)

Bred by Dayton Ltd.

Won 6 races, placed 2, £239,309, in England and France, at 2 and 3 years, incl. Oaks Stakes, King George VI and Queen Elizabeth Diamond Stakes, Prix de Diane, Prix Cleopatre, Prix Penelope.

CARVIN (b. 1962)	Marino (ch. 1956)	Worden II	Wild Risk / Sans Tares
		Buena Vista	Orwell / Anne de Bretagne
	Coraline (b. 1957)	Fine Top	Fine Art / Toupie
		Copelina	Loliondo / Casserole
PLENCIA (ch. 1968)	Le Haar (ch. 1954)	Vieux Manoir	Brantome / Vieille Maison
		Mince Pie	Teleferique / Cannelle
	Petite Saguenay (ch. 1961)	Nordiste	Norseman / Berthe
		Ballynash	Nasrullah / Ballywellbroke

698   PAYSANNE 8 (ch.f., April 20, 1969)

Bred by Baron Guy de Rothschild, in France.

Won 2½ races, placed 5, 848,960 fr., in France, at 2 and 3 years, incl. Prix Vermeille (dead-heat) and Prix de Minerve; 2nd Criterium des Pouliches; 3rd Prix de Diane, Prix Saint-Alary and Prix de la Nonette.

AUREOLE (ch. 1950)	Hyperion (ch. 1930)	Gainsborough	Bayardo / Rosedrop
		Selene	Chaucer / Serenissima
	Angelola (b. 1945)	Donatello II	Blenheim / Delleana
		Feola	Friar Marcus / Aloe
PERCALE (ch. 1964)	Emerson (b. 1958)	Coaraze	Tourbillon / Corrida
		Empenosa	Full Sail / Ermua
	Imberline (ch. 1957)	Ocarina	Bubbles / Montagnana
		Barley Corn	Hyperion / Schiaparelli

699   PAY TRIBUTE 3 (ch.c., May 21, 1972)

Bred by Elmendorf Farm, in U.S.A.

Won 9 races, placed 10, $463,245, in U.S.A., from 3 to 7 years, incl. Hollywood Gold Cup and Meadowlands Cup; 2nd Californian Stakes, Bel Air H., Arlington Classic Invitational H. and San Marcos H.; 3rd Citation H.

HIGH TRIBUTE (ch. 1964)	Prince John (ch. 1953)	Princequillo	Prince Rose / Cosquilla
		Not Afraid	Count Fleet / Banish Fear
	En Casserole (ch. 1952)	War Relic	Man o'War / Friar's Carse
		Beanie M.	Black Toney / Betty Beall
DRUMMER GIRL (b. 1966)	Tompion (br. 1957)	Tom Fool	Menow / Gaga
		Sunlight	Count Fleet / Halcyon Days
	Twenty-one Plus (ch. 1955)	Supreme Court	Persian Gulf or Precipitation / Forecourt
		Pontresina	Foxhunter / Ponteba

700   PELEID 21 (b.c., March 31, 1970)

Bred by Lt.-Colonel W. E. Behrens.

Won 6 races, placed 10, £60,215, in England, France and Hungary, from 2 to 4 years, incl. St. Leger Stakes, Hungarian Grand Breeders' Prize; 2nd John Porter Stakes; 3rd Jockey Club Stakes.

DERRING-DO (b. 1961)	Darius (b. 1951)	Dante	Nearco / Rosy Legend
		Yasna	Dastur / Ariadne
	Sipsey Bridge (b. 1954)	Abernant	Owen Tudor / Rustom Mahal
		Claudette	Chanteur II / Nearly
WINNING BID (b. 1958)	Great Captain (br. 1949)	War Admiral	Man o'War / Brushup
		Big Hurry	Black Toney / La Troienne
	Straight Bid (b. 1954)	Solonaway	Solferino / Anyway
		Straight Offer	Straight Deal / Olifa

701   PENTATHLON 3 (gr.c., January 25, 1964)

Bred by L. G. Creed, in England.

Won 10 races, placed 11, 305,205 DM., in Germany and France, from 2 to 5 years, incl. Prix de l'Abbaye de Longchamp, Prix du Petit Couvert, Goldene Peitsche (twice); 2nd Henckel-Rennen; 3rd Prix de l'Abbaye de Longchamp and Zukunfts-Rennen.

ENNIS (b. 1954)	Golden Cloud (ch. 1941)	Gold Bridge	Swynford or Golden Boss / Flying Diadem
		Rainstorm	Hainault / Stormcloud
	First House (b. 1939)	Link Boy	Pharos / Market Girl
		Early Doors	Call Boy / Douceur
PALMURAL (gr. 1957)	Palestine (gr. 1947)	Fair Trial	Fairway / Lady Juror
		Una	Tetratema / Uganda
	Fresco (b. 1951)	Torbido	Ortello / Tempesta
		Cornice	Epigram / Cordon

702   PERDU 3 (br.c., February 17, 1970)

Bred by J. Brendon Clarke.

Won 4 races, placed 4, £13,167, in England, from 2 to 4 years, incl. Coventry Stakes, July Stakes; 2nd Challenge Stakes; 3rd Diadem Stakes, Ascot 2,000 Guineas Trial Stakes.

LINACRE (bl. 1960)	Rockefella (br. 1941)	Hyperion	Gainsborough / Selene
		Rockfel	Felstead / Rockliffe
	True Picture (bl. 1955)	Panorama	Sir Cosmo / Happy Climax
		Verity	Chrysler II / Fortunedale
LOVE-IN-THE-MIST (br. 1963)	Aureole (ch. 1950)	Hyperion	Gainsborough / Selene
		Angelola	Donatello II / Feola
	Belle of All (b. 1948)	Nasrullah	Nearco / Mumtaz Begum
		Village Beauty	Winalot / Village Green

703   PERSONALITY 1 (b.c., May 27, 1967)

Bred by Bieber-Jacobs Stable, in U.S.A.

Won 8 races, placed 6, $462,603, in U.S.A., at 3 and 4 years, incl. Preakness Stakes, Jersey Derby, Woodward Stakes, Wood Memorial Stakes and Jim Dandy Stakes; 2nd Excelsior H. and Stymie H.; 3rd Paumonok H.

HAIL TO REASON (br. 1958)	Turn-to (b. 1951)	Royal Charger	Nearco / Sun Princess
		Source Sucree	Admiral Drake / Lavendula II
	Nothirdchance (b. 1948)	Blue Swords	Blue Larkspur / Flaming Swords
		Galla Colors	Sir Gallahad III / Rouge et Noir
AFFECTIONATELY (b. 1960)	Swaps (ch. 1952)	Khaled	Hyperion / Eclair
		Iron Reward	Beau Pere / Iron Maiden
	Searching (b. 1952)	War Admiral	Man o' War / Brushup
		Big Hurry	Black Toney / La Troienne

704   PETINGO 22 (b.c., April 25, 1965)

Bred by E. N. Hall.

Won 6 races, placed 2, £40,480, in England, at 2 and 3 years, incl. Gimcrack Stakes, Middle Park Stakes, Craven Stakes, St. James's Palace Stakes, Sussex Stakes; 2nd 2,000 Guineas Stakes, Wills Mile.

PETITION (br. 1944)	Fair Trial (ch. 1932)	Fairway	Phalaris / Scapa Flow
		Lady Juror	Son-in-Law / Lady Josephine
	Art Paper (br. 1933)	Artist's Proof	Gainsborough / Clear Evidence
		Quire	Fairy King / Queen Carbine
ALCAZAR (ch. 1957)	Alycidon (ch. 1945)	Donatello II	Blenheim / Delleana
		Aurora	Hyperion / Rose Red
	Quarterdeck (b. 1947)	Nearco	Pharos / Nogara
		Poker Chip	The Recorder / Straight Sequence

705   PETITE ETOILE 9 (gr.f., March 14, 1956)

Bred by H.H. Aga and Prince Aly Khan.

Won 14 races, placed 5, £72,626, in England, from 2 to 5 years, incl. 1,000 Guineas Stakes, Oaks Stakes, Sussex Stakes, Yorkshire Oaks, Champion Stakes, Coronation Cup (twice); 2nd King George VI and Queen Elizabeth Stakes, Molecomb Stakes, Queen Elizabeth II Stakes.

PETITION (br. 1944)	Fair Trial (ch. 1932)	Fairway	Phalaris / Scapa Flow
		Lady Juror	Son-in-Law / Lady Josephine
	Art Paper (br. 1933)	Artist's Proof	Gainsborough / Clear Evidence
		Quire	Fairy King / Queen Carbine
STAR OF IRAN (gr. 1949)	Bois Roussel (br. 1935)	Vatout	Prince Chimay / Vasthi
		Plucky Liege	Spearmint / Concertina
	Mah Iran (gr. 1939)	Bahram	Blandford / Friar's Daughter
		Mah Mahal	Gainsborough / Mumtaz Mahal

706   PHAETON 7 (gr.c., 1964)

Bred by Mme. Jean Stern, in Ireland.

Won 2 races, placed 3, 918,337 fr., in France, at 2 and 3 years, incl. Grand Prix de Paris and Prix de Condé; 2nd Prix Greffulhe; 3rd Prix Noailles.

SICAMBRE (br. 1948)	Prince Bio (b. 1941)	Prince Rose	Rose Prince / Indolence
		Biologie	Bacteriophage / Eponge
	Sif (br. 1936)	Rialto	Rabelais / La Grelee
		Suavita	Alcantara II / Shocking
PASQUINADE II (gr. 1957)	Vandale II (b. 1943)	Plassy	Bosworth / Pladda
		Vanille	La Farina / Vaya
	Mlle. Paganini (gr. 1950)	Loliondo	Badruddin / Liebelei
		Mlle. Petitpas	Blue Skies / Mlle. Salle

707   PHARLY 9 (ch.c., April 22, 1974)

Bred by J. P. Van Gysel, in France.

Won 5 races, placed 7, 1,547,500 fr., in France, at 2 and 3 years, incl. Prix Lupin, Prix du Moulin de Longchamp, Prix de la Foret and Prix du Rond-Point; 2nd Poule d'Essai des Poulains, Prix d'Ispahan and Prix de la Foret; 3rd Prix de Fontainebleau.

LYPHARD (b. 1969)	Northern Dancer (b. 1961)	Nearctic	Nearco / Lady Angela
		Natalma	Native Dancer / Almahmoud
	Goofed (ch. 1960)	Court Martial	Fair Trial / Instantaneous
		Barra	Formor / La Favorite
COMELY (ch. 1966)	Boran (ch. 1960)	Mourne	Vieux Manoir / Ballynash
		Bethora	Clarion III / Lady Penn
	Princesse Comnene (ch. 1961)	Beau Prince II	Prince Chevalier / Isabelle Brand
		Commemoration	Vandale II / Anne Comnene

708   PIA 16 (br.f., April 5, 1964)

Bred by Countess Margit Batthyany.

Won 4½ races, placed 4, £36,797, in England, at 2 and 3 years, incl. Oaks Stakes, Park Hill Stakes (dead-heat), Cherry Hinton Stakes, Lowther Stakes; 2nd Cheveley Park Stakes; 3rd Musidora Stakes; 4th Champion Stakes.

DARIUS (b. 1951)	Dante (br. 1942)	Nearco	Pharos / Nogara
		Rosy Legend	Dark Legend / Rosy Cheeks
	Yasna (b. 1936)	Dastur	Solario / Friar's Daughter
		Ariadne	Arion / Security
PESETA II (br. 1957)	Neckar (bl. 1948)	Ticino	Athanasius / Terra
		Nixe	Arjaman / Nanon
	Prompt Payment (br. 1950)	Rockefella	Hyperion / Rockfel
		Satanella	Mahmoud / Avella

709   PIDGET 3 (gr.f., April 22, 1969)

Bred by Kilboy Estates Ltd.

Won 6 races, placed 5, £35,856, in Ireland, from 2 to 4 years, incl. Irish 1,000 Guineas, Irish St. Leger, Pretty Polly Stakes; 2nd Athasi Stakes, Ballymoss Stakes, Desmond Stakes; 3rd Irish Guinness Oaks.

FORTINO II (gr. 1959)	Grey Sovereign (gr. 1948)	Nasrullah	Nearco
			Mumtaz Begum
		Kong	Baytown
			Clang
	Ranavalo III (b. 1954)	Relic	War Relic
			Bridal Colors
		Navarra II	Orsenigo
			Nervesa
PRIMLACE (ch. 1960)	Chamossaire (ch. 1942)	Precipitation	Hurry On
			Double Life
		Snowberry	Cameronian
			Myrobella
	Prim Diana (ch. 1944)	Foxhunter	Foxlaw
			Trimestral
		Necklace II	Lemberg
			Straitlace

710   PIECES OF EIGHT 3 (bl. or br.c., March 24, 1963)

Bred by E. N. Hall.

Won 3 races, placed 6, £57,802, in England and Ireland, from 2 to 4 years, incl. Eclipse Stakes, Champion Stakes; 2nd Ballymoss Stakes, Gallinule Stakes.

RELIC (bl. 1945)	War Relic (ch. 1938)	Man o'War	Fair Play
			Mahubah
		Friar's Carse	Friar Rock
			Problem
	Bridal Colors (bl. 1931)	Black Toney	Peter Pan
			Belgravia
		Vaila	Fariman
			Padilla
BABY DOLL (br. 1956)	Dante (br. 1942)	Nearco	Pharos
			Nogara
		Rosy Legend	Dark Legend
			Rosy Cheeks
	Bebe Grande (ch. 1950)	Niccolo Dell'Arca	Coronach
			Nogara
		Grande Corniche	Panorama
			Joy-Ride

711   PINK GEM 1 (ch.f., April 1, 1964)

Bred by H. J. Joel.

Won 2½ races, placed 1, £4,500, in England, at 2 and 3 years, incl. Park Hill Stakes (dead-heat), Cheshire Oaks; 2nd Musidora Stakes.

CREPELLO (ch. 1954)	Donatello II (ch. 1934)	Blenheim	Blandford
			Malva
		Delleana	Clarissimus
			Duccia di Buoninsegna
	Crepuscule (ch. 1948)	Mieuxce	Massine
			L'Olivete
		Red Sunset	Solario
			Dulce II
TOPAZ (ch. 1954)	Honeyway (br. 1941)	Fairway	Phalaris
			Scapa Flow
		Honey Buzzard	Papyrus
			Lady Peregrine
	Moonstone (gr. 1940)	Mahmoud	Blenheim
			Mah Mahal
		Rosetta	Kantar
			Rose Red

712   PISTOL PACKER 14 (ch.f., May 9, 1968)

Bred by Doe Run Inc., in U.S.A.

Won 7 races, placed 5, 2,939,977 fr., in France, from 2 to 4 years, incl. Prix de Diane, Prix Vermeille, Prix Saint-Alary, Prix Chloe, Prix de la Nonette and Prix d'Harcourt; 2nd Prix de l'Arc de Triomphe and Prix Gontaut-Biron; 3rd Prix Foy.

GUN BOW (b. 1960)	Gun Shot (ch. 1953)	Hyperion	Gainsborough
			Selene
		Silence	Bosworth
			Surbine
	Ribbons and Bows (b. 1955)	War Admiral	Man o'War
			Brushup
		Evening Thrill	Bull Lea
			Decolte
GEORGE'S GIRL (ch. 1959)	Ossian II (br. 1952)	Royal Charger	Nearco
			Sun Princess
		Prudent Polly	Atout Maitre
			Sister Anne
	Dawn Chorus (ch. 1951)	Rising Light	Hyperion
			Bread Card
		Duke's Delight	His Grace
			Early Light

713   PITASIA 14 (b.f., March 8, 1976)

Bred by Collinstown Stud Farm Ltd., in Ireland.

Won 6 races, placed 5, 1,359,000 fr., in France, at 2 and 3 years, incl. Prix Robert Papin, Criterium des Pouliches, Prix de Malleret and Prix de la Nonette; 2nd Prix Morny, Prix Saint Alary and Prix Jean Prat; 3rd Prix Vermeille; 4th Prix de Diane de Revlon.

PITSKELLY (br. 1970)	Petingo (b. 1965)	Petition	Fair Trial
			Art Paper
		Alcazar	Alycidon
			Quarterdeck
	French Bird (b. 1959)	Guersant	Bubbles
			Montagnana
		Golden Pheasant	Gold Bridge
			Bonnie Birdie
ASIAN PRINCESS (b. 1969)	Native Prince (b. 1964)	Native Dancer	Polynesian
			Geisha
		Sungari	Eight Thirty
			Swabia
	Valadier (b. 1962)	Charlottesville	Prince Chevalier
			Noorani
		Palazzoli	Palestine
			Maintenon

714   PITCAIRN 7 (b.c., March 20, 1971)

Bred by Airlie Stud.

Won 5 races, placed 7, £42,481, in England, Ireland and Italy, at 2 and 3 years, incl. Ladbroke Blue Riband Trial Stakes, Hungerford Stakes and Goodwood Mile; 2nd William Hill Middle Park Stakes, William Hill Dewhurst Stakes, Irish 2,000 Guineas and Premio Chiusura; 3rd Champagne Stakes and Champion Stakes.

PETINGO (b. 1965)	Petition (br. 1944)	Fair Trial	Fairway
			Lady Juror
		Art Paper	Artist's Proof
			Quire
	Alcazar (ch. 1957)	Alycidon	Donatello II
			Aurora
		Quarterdeck	Nearco
			Poker Chip
BORDER BOUNTY (b. 1965)	Bounteous (b. 1958)	Rockefella	Hyperion
			Rockfel
		Marie Elizabeth	Mazarin
			Miss Honor
	B. Flat (b. 1958)	Chanteur II	Chateau Bouscaut
			La Diva
		Ardeen	Ardan
			Peradventure

715   PLEASURE SEEKER 8 (b.c., May 13, 1966)

Bred by Mr. and Mrs. H. C. Vandervoort, Jr., in U.S.A.

Won 7 races, placed 5, $211,297, in U.S.A., from 2 to 4 years, incl. Hollywood Gold Cup; 2nd Brooklyn H.; 3rd Michigan Mile-and-One-Eighth H.

AMBIORIX II (b. 1946)	Tourbillon (b. 1928)	Ksar	Bruleur
			Kizil Kourgan
		Durban	Durbar II
			Banshee
	Lavendula II (br. 1930)	Pharos	Phalaris
			Scapa Flow
		Sweet Lavender	Swynford
			Marchetta
TROUBLEPEG (ch. 1960)	Mr. Trouble (ch. 1947)	Mahmoud	Blenheim
			Mah Mahal
		Motto	Sir Gallahad III
			Maxima
	Pellene (b. 1952)	Revoked	Blue Larkspur
			Gala Belle
		Pella	Pharamond
			Salaminia

716   PLEBEN 12 (ch.c., April 30, 1969)

Bred by Limestone Stud, in England.

Won 3 races, placed 3, 1,736,419 fr., in France, at 3 and 4 years, incl. Grand Prix de Paris and Prix Royal Oak; 2nd Prix du Cadran.

SHESHOON (ch. 1956)	Precipitation (ch. 1933)	Hurry On	Marcovil
			Tout Suite
		Double Life	Bachelor's Double
			Saint Joan
	Noorani (ch. 1950)	Nearco	Pharos
			Nogara
		Empire Glory	Singapore
			Skyglory
DEVASTATING (ch. 1960)	Honeyway (br. 1941)	Fairway	Phalaris
			Scapa Flow
		Honey Buzzard	Papyrus
			Lady Peregrine
	Fascinating (ch. 1954)	Big Game	Bahram
			Myrobella
		Neartic	Nearco
			Red Biddy

717   POLA BELLA 4 (b.f., March 27, 1965)

Bred by François Dupré, in France.

Won 6 races, placed 4, 1,415,705 fr., in France, at 2 and 3 years, incl. Poule d'Essai des Pouliches, Prix du Moulin de Longchamp, Prix de la Grotte, Prix de la Nonette and Criterium de Maisons-Laffitte; 2nd Prix de Diane, Prix Vermeille and Grand Criterium.

DARIUS (b. 1951)	Dante (br. 1942)	Nearco	Pharos
			Nogara
		Rosy Legend	Dark Legend
			Rosy Cheeks
	Yasna (b. 1936)	Dastur	Solario
			Friar's Daughter
		Ariadne	Arion
			Security
BELLA PAOLA (br. 1955)	Ticino (b. 1939)	Athanasius	Ferro
			Athanasie
		Terra	Aditi
			Teufelsrose
	Rhea II (b. 1950)	Gundomar	Alchimist
			Grossularia
		Regina IV	Indus
			Reine d'Ouilly

718   POLICEMAN 6 (b.c., April 16, 1977)

Bred by F. E. Tinsley, in France.

Won 3 races, placed 5, 1,149,500 fr., in France, at 3 years, incl. Prix du Jockey-Club; 3rd Grand Prix de Saint-Cloud and Prix de Guiche.

RIVERMAN (b. 1969)	Never Bend (br. 1960)	Nasrullah	Nearco
			Mumtaz Begum
		Lalun	Djeddah
			Be Faithful
	River Lady (b. 1963)	Prince John	Princequillo
			Not Afraid
		Nile Lily	Roman
			Azalea
INDIANAPOLIS (ch. 1969)	Barbare (b. 1963)	Sicambre	Prince Bio
			Sif
		Barbara	Fair Trial
			Mistress Ford
	Iberide (ch. 1962)	Charlottesville	Prince Chevalier
			Noorani
		Candytuft	Mossborough
			Cretan Belle

719   POLYGAMY 4 (b.f., March 16, 1971)

Bred by Cliveden Stud.

Won 5 races, placed 4, £62,250, in England, Ireland and France, at 2 and 3 years, incl. Oaks Stakes, Ascot 1,000 Guineas Trial Stakes; 2nd 1,000 Guineas Stakes; 3rd Irish Guinness Oaks; 4th Criterium des Pouliches.

REFORM (b. 1964)	Pall Mall (ch. 1955)	Palestine	Fair Trial
			Una
		Malapert	Portlaw
			Malatesta
	Country House (br. 1955)	Vieux Manoir	Brantome
			Vieille Maison
		Miss Coventry	Mieuxce
			Coventry Belle
SEVENTH BRIDE (b. 1966)	Royal Record II (b. 1958)	Nasrullah	Nearco
			Mumtaz Begum
		Belle Histoire	Blue Larkspur
			La Troienne
	Little Miss Muffet (b. 1959)	Tourment	Tourbillon
			Fragment
		My Mascot	Deiri
			Favorite

720   POSSE 8 (ch.c., May 15, 1977)

Bred by Ogden Mills Phipps, in U.S.A.

Won 2 races, placed 4, £96,652, in England and Ireland, at 2 and 3 years incl. Sussex Stakes, St. James's Palace Stakes; 2nd 2,000 Guineas Stakes; 3rd Clerical Medical Greenham Stakes; 4th Airlie/Coolmore Irish 2,000 Guineas.

FORLI (ch. 1963)	Aristophanes (ch. 1948)	Hyperion	Gainsborough
			Selene
		Commotion	Mieuxce
			Riot
	Trevisa (ch. 1951)	Advocate	Fair Trial
			Guiding Star
		Veneta	Foxglove
			Dogaresa
IN HOT PURSUIT (b. 1971)	Bold Ruler (b. 1954)	Nasrullah	Nearco
			Mumtaz Begum
		Miss Disco	Discovery
			Outdone
	Lady Be Good (b. 1956)	Better Self	Bimelech
			Bee Mac
		Past Eight	Eight Thirty
			Helvetia

721   POUPONNE 9 (b.f., May 28, 1960)

Bred by W. H. D. Riley Smith.

Won 1 race, placed 4, £1,551, in England, at 2 and 3 years, incl. 3rd Oaks Stakes, Nassau Stakes.

OWEN TUDOR or PRINCE CHEVALIER (b. 1943)	Prince Rose (b. 1928)	Rose Prince	Prince Palatine / Eglantine
		Indolence	Gay Crusader / Barrier
	Chevalerie (b. 1933)	Abbot's Speed	Abbots Trace / Mary Gaunt
		Kassala	Cylgad / Farizade
ELA TENGAM (b. 1950)	Kingsway (b. 1940)	Fairway	Phalaris / Scapa Flow
		Yenna	Ksar / Yane
	Trixie from Tad (b. 1942)	Flag of Truce	Truculent / Concordia
		Tad	Tetrameter / Lemonade

722   POURPARLER 4 (b.f., May 8, 1961)

Bred by Commander P. J. FitzGerald.

Won 3 races, placed 5, £39,344, in England, Ireland and France, at 2 and 3 years, incl. 1,000 Guineas Stakes, National Stakes (Sandown), Lowther Sweepstakes; 3rd Coronation Stakes, Prix Robert Papin.

HUGH LUPUS (b. 1952)	Djebel (b. 1937)	Tourbillon	Ksar / Durban
		Loika	Gay Crusader / Coeur à Coeur
	Sakountala (b. 1942)	Goya II	Tourbillon / Zariba
		Samos	Bruleur / Samya
REVIEW (ch. 1951)	Panorama (ch. 1936)	Sir Cosmo	The Boss / Ayn Hali
		Happy Climax	Happy Warrior / Clio
	Pin Up Girl (b. 1943)	Coup de Lyon	Winalot / Sundry
		Careless	Caerleon / Traverse

723   PRECIPICE WOOD 16 (gr.c., April 4, 1966)

Bred by Mrs. L. Scott.

Won 6 races, placed 7, £26,920, in England and France, from 2 to 4 years, incl. Ascot Gold Cup; 2nd John Porter Stakes, Prix Kergorlay.

LAUSO (b. 1958)	Ocarina (ch. 1947)	Bubbles	La Farina / Spring Cleaning
		Montagnana	Brantome / Mauretania
	La Canea (b. 1953)	Vatellor	Vatout / Lady Elinor
		La Cadette	Le Pacha / Fidgette
GRECIAN GARDEN (gr. 1949)	Kingstone (b. 1942)	King Salmon	Salmon-Trout / Malva
		Feola	Friar Marcus / Aloe
	Academia (gr. 1936)	Plantago	Phalaris / Scarlet Martagon
		Athena	Roi Herode / Eufrosina

724   PREDOMINATE 8 (ch.g., April 11, 1952)

Bred by J. McCutcheon.

Won 14 races, placed 9, £17,030, in England, from 2 to 9 years, incl. Goodwood Cup, Queen Alexandra Stakes, Goodwood Stakes (3 times); 2nd Cesarewitch Stakes, Goodwood Cup; 3rd Cesarewitch Stakes.

PRECIPTIC (ch. 1942)	Precipitation (ch. 1933)	Hurry On	Marcovil / Tout Suite
		Double Life	Bachelor's Double / Saint Joan
	Artistic (ch. 1930)	Gainsborough	Bayardo / Rosedrop
		Ishtar	The Tetrarch / Perfect Peach
GARRYHINCH (ch. 1936)	Great Scot (ch. 1926)	Grand Parade	Orby / Grand Geraldine
		Dalkeith	White Eagle / Quick
	Rose Petal (ch. 1926)	Tetrameter	The Tetrarch / Mandola
		Rosemead	Rossendale / Meadow Rue

725   PRETENDRE 1 (ch.c., January 15, 1963)

Bred by H.R.H. The Princess Royal.

Won 6 races, placed 3, £44,414, in England, at 2 and 3 years, incl. Dewhurst Stakes, Observer Gold Cup, Blue Riband Trial Stakes, King Edward VII Stakes; 2nd Derby Stakes; 3rd Eclipse Stakes.

DOUTELLE (ch. 1954)	Prince Chevalier (b. 1943)	Prince Rose	Rose Prince / Indolence
		Chevalerie	Abbot's Speed / Kassala
	Above Board (b. 1947)	Straight Deal	Solario / Good Deal
		Feola	Friar Marcus / Aloe
LIMICOLA (ch. 1948)	Verso II (b. 1940)	Pinceau	Alcantara II / Aquarelle
		Variete	La Farina / Vaya
	Uccello (ch. 1943)	Donatello II	Blenheim / Delleana
		Great Tit	Stefan the Great / Canary Seed

726   PRIAMOS 6 (br.c., February 13, 1964)

Bred by Gestüt Schlenderhan, in Germany.

Won 14 races, placed 12, 522,681 DM., in Germany and France, from 2 to 6 years, incl. Prix Jacques le Marois, Prix Dollar, Grosser Preis von Dortmund, Grosser Preis von Gelsenkirchen and Zukunfts-Rennen; 2nd Grosser Preis von Nordrhein-Westfalen, Grosser Hansa Preis and Grosser Preis von Dortmund; 4th Preis von Europa (twice), Aral-Pokal and Grosser Preis von Nordrhein-Westfalen.

BIRKHAHN (br. 1945)	Alchimist (br. 1930)	Herold	Dark Ronald / Hornisse
		Aversion	Nuage / Antwort
	Bramouse (b. 1936)	Cappiello	Apelle / Kopje
		Peregrine	Phalaris / Clotho
PALAZZO (br. 1950)	Dante (br. 1942)	Nearco	Pharos / Nogara
		Rosy Legend	Dark Legend / Rosy Cheeks
	Edifice (br. 1941)	Monument	Sansovino / Queen of the Hills
		Phalconia	Diomedes / Princess Charming

727 PRINCE BEE 9 (br.c., April 27, 1977)

Bred by Ballymacoll Stud Farm Ltd.

Won 4 races, placed 3, £102,629, in England, Ireland and France, at 3 years, incl. Great Voltigeur Stakes, Gordon Stakes, Prix Niel; 2nd Irish Sweeps Derby, Dee Stakes.

SUN PRINCE (ch. 1969)	Princely Gift (b. 1951)	Nasrullah	Nearco
			Mumtaz Begum
		Blue Gem	Blue Peter
			Sparkle
	Costa Sola (ch. 1963)	Worden II	Wild Risk
			Sans Tares
		Sunny Cove	Nearco
			Sunny Gulf
HONERKO (b. 1968)	Tanerko (br. 1953)	Tantième	Deux pour Cent
			Terka
		La Divine	Fair Copy
			La Diva
	Be a Honey (b. 1959)	Honey's Alibi	Alibhai
			Honeymoon
		Neola	Nearco
			Sansonnet

728 PRINCE HANSEL 5 (ch.c., April 27, 1961)

Bred by Captain Sir Cecil Boyd-Rochfort.

Won 6 races, placed 8, £9,006, in England, from 2 to 5 years, incl. Doncaster Cup; 2nd Jersey Stakes, Jockey Club Cup. Also ran under N.H. Rules, placed 2, £134, over hurdles.

THE PHOENIX (b. 1940)	Chateau Bouscaut (b. 1927)	Kircubbin	Captivation
			Avon Hack
		Ramondie	Neil Gow
			La Rille
	Fille de Poete (ch. 1935)	Firdaussi	Pharos
			Brownhylda
		Fille d'Amour	Hurry On
			Friar's Daughter
SAUCY WILHELMINA (b. or br. 1949)	William of Valence (br. 1932)	Vatout	Prince Chimay
			Vasthi
		Queen Iseult	Teddy
			Sweet Agnes
	Merry Perrin (b. 1942)	Hyperion	Gainsborough
			Selene
		Merry Vixen	:Sir Gallahad III
			Medora II

729 PRINCE IPPI 1 (br.c., April 9, 1969)

Bred by Gestüt Röttgen, in Germany.

Won 4 races, placed 5, 549,810 DM., in Germany and Italy, from 2 to 4 years, incl. Preis von Europa and Gran Premio d'Italia; 3rd Deutsches Derby and Furstenberg-Rennen; 4th Aral Pokal.

IMPERIAL (ch. 1960)	Imi (b. 1953)	Intermezzo II	Caissot
			Alcyone
		Minci	Mannamead
			Rawena
	Hurry (b. 1952)	Canot	Nino
			Canalette
		Huanguelen	Blenheim
			Pommade Divine
PRINZESS ADDI (gr. 1955)	Agamemnon (b. 1941)	Herold	Dark Ronald
			Hornisse
		Astrologie	Ferro
			Antonia
	Pindarella (gr. 1938)	Indus	Alcantara II
			Himalaya
		La Pitchi Grise	Filibert de Savoie
			Bizkorra III

730 PRINCELINE 12 (b.f., April 27, 1966)

Bred by Pierre Ribes, in France.

Won 4 races, placed 4, 467,642 fr., in France and U.S.A., from 2 to 4 years, incl. Prix Morny; 2nd Poule d'Essai des Pouliches and Prix Jean Prat; 4th Prix de la Salamandre.

PRINCELY GIFT (b. 1951)	Nasrullah (b. 1940)	Nearco	Pharos
			Nogara
		Mumtaz Begum	Blenheim
			Mumtaz Mahal
	Blue Gem (b. 1943)	Blue Peter	Fairway
			Fancy Free
		Sparkle	Blandford
			Gleam
ASHLEEN (b. 1956)	Alizier (b. 1947)	Teleferique	Bacteriophage
			Beaute de Neige
		Alizarine	Coronach
			Armoise
	Asheratt (b. 1935)	Sunny Trace	Abbots Trace
			Sunny Moya
		Fee Esterel	Cadum
			Reine Mab

731 PRINCE REGENT 1 (br.c., March 12, 1966)

Bred by Countess de la Valdene, in France.

Won 6 races, placed 5, £153,283, in France, Ireland and England, from 2 to 4 years, incl. Prix Greffulhe, Prix Lupin, Irish Sweeps Derby, Prix Saint-Roman, Prix d'Evry; 3rd Prix Morny, Prix d'Harcourt, Prix Ganay, Prix Dollar, Derby Stakes.

RIGHT ROYAL V (br. 1958)	Owen Tudor (br. 1938)	Hyperion	Gainsborough
			Selene
		Mary Tudor II	Pharos
			Anna Bolena
	Bastia (b. 1951)	Tornado or Victrix II	Kantar
			Victory
		Barberybush	Ksar
			Pervencheres
NODULEUSE (b. 1954)	Nosca (b. 1939)	Abjer	Asterus
			Zariba
		Capella	Tourbillon
			Gracilite
	Quemandeuse (ch. 1943)	Quai d'Orsay	Town Guard
			Kiss
		Macreuse	Massine
			Empire Crusade

732 PRINCE ROYAL II 3 (b.c., January 30, 1961)

Bred by C. Wacker III, in England.

Won 7 races, placed 4, 165,450,590 L., in Italy and France, at 2 and 3 years, incl. Prix de l'Arc de Triomphe and Gran Premio di Milano; 3rd Gran Criterium; 4th Gran Premio d'Italia.

RIBOT (b. 1952)	Tenerani (b. 1944)	Bellini	Cavaliere d'Arpino
			Bella Minna
		Tofanella	Apelle
			Try Try Again
	Romanella (ch. 1943)	El Greco	Pharos
			Gay Gamp
		Barbara Burrini	Papyrus
			Bucolic
PANGE (ch. 1955)	King's Bench (b. 1949)	Court Martial	Fair Trial
			Instantaneous
		King's Cross	King Salmon
			Doublure
	York Gala (b. 1939)	His Grace	Blandford
			Malva
		Princess Galahad	Prince Galahad
			Penny Flyer

733   **PRINCESSE LIDA** 1 (b.f., February 4, 1977)

Bred by Jacques Wertheimer, in U.S.A.

Won 4 races, placed 3, 900,000 fr., in France, at 2 and 3 years, incl. Prix Morny and Prix de la Salamandre; 2nd Prix de la Grotte; 3rd Grand Criterium and Poule d'Essai des Pouliches.

NIJINSKY (b. 1967)	Northern Dancer (b. 1961)	Nearctic	Nearco / Lady Angela
		Natalma	Native Dancer / Almahmoud
	Flaming Page (b. 1959)	Bull Page	Bull Lea / Our Page
		Flaring Top	Menow / Flaming Top
PRINCESSE LEE (b. 1972)	Habitat (b. 1966)	Sir Gaylord	Turn-to / Somethingroyal
		Little Hut	Occupy / Savage Beauty
	Princesse Tora (b. 1967)	Prince Taj	Prince Bio / Malindi
		Torbella III	Tornado / Djebellica

734   **PRINCESSNESIAN** 4 (b.f., April 28, 1964)

Bred by William Haggin Perry, in U.S.A.

Won 11 races, placed 11, $332,035, in U.S.A., from 3 to 5 years, incl. Hollywood Gold Cup, Santa Margarita Invitational H., Santa Barbara H. and Milady H.; 2nd Santa Margarita H., Santa Maria H. and Vanity H.; 3rd Hollywood Oaks, Firenze H. and New York H.

PRINCEQUILLO (b. 1940)	Prince Rose (b. 1928)	Rose Prince	Prince Palatine / Eglantine
		Indolence	Gay Crusader / Barrier
	Cosquilla (b. 1933)	Papyrus	Tracery / Miss Matty
		Quick Thought	White Eagle / Mindful
ALANESIAN (b. 1954)	Polynesian (br. 1942)	Unbreakable	Sickle / Blue Glass
		Black Polly	Polymelian / Black Queen
	Alablue (b. 1945)	Blue Larkspur	Black Servant / Blossom Time
		Double Time	Sir Gallahad III / Virginia L

735   **PRINCE TENDERFOOT** 8 (b.c., March 20, 1967)

Bred by Shawnee Farm, in U.S.A.

Won 3 races, placed 2, £7,094, in England and Ireland, at 2 and 3 years, incl. Coventry Stakes; 3rd Gladness Stakes.

BLUE PRINCE II (b. 1951)	Princequillo (b. 1940)	Prince Rose	Rose Prince / Indolence
		Cosquilla	Papyrus / Quick Thought
	Blue Denim (b. 1940)	Blue Larkspur	Black Servant / Blossom Time
		Judy O'Grady	Man o'War / Bel Agnes
LA TENDRESSE (b. 1959)	Grey Sovereign (gr. 1948)	Nasrullah	Nearco / Mumtaz Begum
		Kong	Baytown / Clang
	Isetta (b. 1943)	Morland	Gainsborough / Lichen
		Isolda	Rustom Pasha / Yveline

736   **PRIVY COUNCILLOR** 19 (ch.c., February 23, 1959)

Bred by Major G. Glover.

Won 5 races, placed 3, £35,028, in England, at 2 and 3 years, incl. 2,000 Guineas Stakes.

COUNSEL (b. 1952)	Court Martial (ch. 1942)	Fair Trial	Fairway / Lady Juror
		Instantaneous	Hurry On / Picture
	Wheedler (b. 1943)	Umidwar	Blandford / Uganda
		Miss Minx	Mr. Jinks / Gerrard's Cross
HIGH NUMBER (gr. 1947)	His Highness (gr. 1936)	Hyperion	Gainsborough / Selene
		Moti Ranee	Spion Kop / Moti Mahal
	Lady Luck (b. 1941)	Fairway	Phalaris / Scapa Flow
		Thirteen	Bulger / Credenda

737   **PRODICE** 1 (ch.f., February 5, 1969)

Bred by Mme. G. Chandioux, in France.

Won 3 races, placed 5, 955,602 fr., in France, at 2 and 3 years, incl. Prix Saint-Alary; 2nd Prix de Diane; 3rd Grand Criterium.

PROMINER (ch. 1962)	Beau Sabreur (ch. 1945)	His Highness	Hyperion / Moti Ranee
		Mashaq	Massine / Buzz Fuzz
	Snob Hill (ch. 1957)	Rockefella	Hyperion / Rockfel
		Rossenhall	Chamossaire / Grace Abounding
EURIDICE (ch. 1962)	Tabriz (gr. 1947)	Tehran	Bois Roussel / Stafaralla
		La Li	Blenheim / La Boni
	Euroclydon (ch. 1947)	Tourbillon	Ksar / Durban
		Astaria	Asterus / Diamond Star

738   **PRODUCER** 8 (b. or br.f., May 4, 1976)

Bred by Carelaine Stables, in U.S.A.

Won 10 races, placed 7, 1,756,426 fr., in France, Ireland and U.S.A., at 3 and 4 years, incl. Prix de la Foret, Prix du Royaumont, Prix Chloe and Prix de l'Opera; 2nd Irish Guinness Oaks, Prix de Malleret, Chrysanthemum Handicap and Nettie Stakes; 3rd Prix de Diane de Revlon and Prix de la Nonette.

NASHUA (b. 1952)	Nasrullah (b. 1940)	Nearco	Pharos / Nogara
		Mumtaz Begum	Blenheim / Mumtaz Mahal
	Segula (br. 1942)	Johnstown	Jamestown / La France
		Sekhmet	Sardanapale / Prosopopee
MARION (b. or br. 1961)	Tantieme (b. 1947)	Deux pour Cent	Deiri / Dix pour Cent
		Terka	Indus / La Furka
	Magda (br. 1954)	Relic	War Relic / Bridal Colors
		Makada	Rustom Pasha / Rayonnante II

145

739 **PROMINER** 8 (ch.c., 1962)

Bred by K. Prendergast.

Won 4½ races, placed 7, £41,399, in Ireland, England and France, from 2 to 5 years, incl. National Stakes (Curragh), Royal Lodge Stakes, Hardwicke Stakes, La Coupe de Maisons-Laffitte (dead-heat); 2nd Coronation Cup, Prix d'Harcourt, Ormonde Stakes; 3rd King George VI and Queen Elizabeth Stakes.

BEAU SABREUR (ch. 1945)	His Highness (gr. 1936)	Hyperion	Gainsborough / Selene
		Moti Ranee	Spion Kop / Moti Mahal
	Mashaq (ch. 1939)	Massine	Consols / Mauri
		Buzz Fuzz	The Recorder / Lady Buzzer
SNOB HILL (ch. 1957)	Rockefella (br. 1941)	Hyperion	Gainsborough / Selene
		Rockfel	Felstead / Rockliffe
	Rossenhall (b. 1949)	Chamossaire	Precipitation / Snowberry
		Grace Abounding	William of Valence / Grace Dalrymple

740 **PROUD BIRDIE** 1 (b.c., March 3, 1973)

Bred by Diamond C Farm Inc., in U.S.A.

Won 9 races, placed 6, $324,842, in U.S.A., from 2 to 5 years, incl. Marlboro Cup and Everglades Stakes; 2nd Fountain of Youth Stakes; 3rd Florida Derby.

PROUD CLARION (b. 1964)	Hail to Reason (br. 1958)	Turn-to	Royal Charger / Source Sucree
		Nothirdchance	Blue Swords / Galla Colors
	Breath O'Morn (ch. 1952)	Djeddah	Djebel / Djezima
		Darby Dunedin	Blenheim / Ethel Dear
BERNIE BIRD (b./br. 1965)	Bolero (ch. 1946)	Eight Thirty	Pilate / Dinner Time
		Stepwisely	Wise Counsellor / Stephanie
	Great Heart (br. 1953)	Pavot	Case Ace / Coquelicot
		Hasty Kiss	Haste / Kiss

741 **PROUD CLARION** 1 (b.c., May 4, 1964)

Bred by John W. Galbreath, in U.S.A.

Won 6 races, placed 6, $218,730, in U.S.A., from 2 to 4 years, incl. Kentucky Derby and Roamer H.; 2nd Queen's County H. and Blue Grass Stakes; 3rd Preakness Stakes; 4th Belmont Stakes.

HAIL TO REASON (br. 1958)	Turn-to (b. 1951)	Royal Charger	Nearco / Sun Princess
		Source Sucree	Admiral Drake / Lavendula II
	Nothirdchance (b. 1948)	Blue Swords	Blue Larkspur / Flaming Swords
		Galla Colors	Sir Gallahad III / Rouge et Noir
BREATH O'MORN (ch. 1952)	Djeddah (ch. 1945)	Djebel	Tourbillon / Loika
		Djezima	Asterus / Heldifann
	Darby Dunedin (b. 1942)	Blenheim	Blandford / Malva
		Ethel Dear	Peter Pan / Royal Amante

742 **PROVE OUT** 4 (ch.c., March 15, 1969)

Bred by King Ranch, in U.S.A.

Won 9 races, placed 10, $270,426, in U.S.A., from 2 to 5 years, incl. Jockey Club Gold Cup, Woodward Stakes and Grey Lag H.; 2nd Trenton H.; 3rd Westchester H.

GRAUSTARK (ch. 1963)	Ribot (b. 1952)	Tenerani	Bellini / Tofanella
		Romanella	El Greco / Barbara Burrini
	Flower Bowl (b. 1952)	Alibhai	Hyperion / Teresina
		Flower Bed	Beau Pere / Boudoir
EQUAL VENTURE (ch. 1953)	Bold Venture (ch. 1933)	St. Germans	Swynford / Hamoaze
		Possible	Ultimus / Lida Flush
	Igual (ch. 1937)	Equipoise	Pennant / Swinging
		Incandescent	Chicle / Masda

743 **PROVERB** 1 (ch.c., April 29, 1970)

Bred by Lt.-Col. J. Chandos-Pole.

Won 5 races, placed 6, £30,162, in England and France, from 2 to 5 years, incl. Goodwood Cup (twice), Doncaster Cup, Chester Vase; 2nd Ascot Gold Cup; 3rd King Edward VII Stakes, Doncaster Cup, Prix Gladiateur, Henry II Stakes.

RELIANCE II (b. 1962)	Tantieme (b. 1947)	Deux pour Cent	Deiri / Dix pour Cent
		Terka	Indus / La Furka
	Relance III (ch. 1952)	Relic	War Relic / Bridal Colors
		Polaire II	Le Volcan / Stella Polaris
CAUSERIE (b. 1961)	Cagire II (b. 1947)	Tourbillon	Ksar / Durban
		Source Sucree	Admiral Drake / Lavendula II
	Happy Thought (b. 1953)	Happy Landing	Windsor Lad / Happy Morn
		Barley Mow	Brumeux / Gleanings

744 **PROVOKE** 1 (b.c., May 21, 1962)

Bred by Astor Studs.

Won 4 races, placed 1, £45,622, in England, at 2 and 3 years, incl. St. Leger Stakes.

AUREOLE (ch. 1950)	Hyperion (ch. 1930)	Gainsborough	Bayardo / Rosedrop
		Selene	Chaucer / Serenissima
	Angelola (b. 1945)	Donatello II	Blenheim / Delleana
		Feola	Friar Marcus / Aloe
TANTALIZER (b. 1955)	Tantieme (b. 1947)	Deux pour Cent	Deiri / Dix pour Cent
		Terka	Indus / La Furka
	Indian Night (br. 1946)	Umidwar	Blandford / Uganda
		Fairly Hot	Solario / Fair Cop

745   PSIDIUM 14 (ch.c., April 14, 1958)

Bred by Mrs. Arpad Plesch.

Won 2 races, placed 4, £37,968, in England and France, at 2 and 3 years, incl. Derby Stakes; 2nd Horris Hill Stakes, Dewhurst Stakes.

```
                        ┌ Pharos ────────┌ Phalaris
            ┌ Pharis II ┤                └ Scapa Flow
            │ (br. 1936)└ Carissima ─────┌ Clarissimus
PARDAL      │                            └ Casquetts
(b. 1947)   │           ┌ Asterus ───────┌ Teddy
            └ Adargatis ┤                └ Astrella
              (b. 1931) └ Helene de Troie ┌ Helicon
                                         └ Lady of Pedigree

                          ┌ Coronach ─────┌ Hurry On
            ┌ Niccolo Dell'Arca┤           └ Wet Kiss
            │ (b. 1938)    └ Nogara ───────┌ Havresac II
DINARELLA   │                             └ Catnip
(ch. 1947)  │           ┌ Manna ─────────┌ Phalaris
            └ Dagherotipia┤               └ Waffles
              (b. 1936)  └ Dossa Dossi ───┌ Spike Island
                                         └ Delleana
```

746   PUISSANT CHEF 12 (ch.c., April 24, 1957)

Bred by Henry Aubert, in France.

Won 7 races, placed 4, 1,066,354 fr., in France, from 2 to 4 years, incl. Prix de l'Arc de Triomphe, Prix Royal Oak, Prix du Cadran, Prix Jean Prat, Prix La Force and Prix de Chantilly; 2nd Prix Jean Prat; 4th Prix du Jockey-Club.

```
                        ┌ Tourbillon ────┌ Ksar
            ┌ Djebel    ┤                └ Durban
            │ (b. 1937) └ Loika ─────────┌ Gay Crusader
DJEFOU      │                            └ Coeur à Coeur
(b. 1945)   │           ┌ Monarch ───────┌ Tracery
            └ Douce Folie┤               └ Teofani
              (b. 1936) └ Pure Folie ────┌ Pitchoury
                                         └ L'Ile du Reve

                        ┌ Asterus ───────┌ Teddy
            ┌ Astrophel ┤                └ Astrella
            │ (ch. 1931)└ Dorina ────────┌ La Farina
LA SIRENE   │                            └ Dora Agnes
(ch. 1943)  │           ┌ Massine ───────┌ Consols
            └ Melusine  ┤                └ Mauri
              (ch. 1929)└ Sweepward ─────┌ Sweeper
                                         └ Froward
```

747   PULCHRA 4 (b.f., May 15, 1967)

Bred by Cloghran Stud Farm Co.

Won 2 races, £5,853, in England, at 3 years, incl. Nassau Stakes, Lingfield Oaks Trial Stakes.

```
                        ┌ Prince Bio ────┌ Prince Rose
            ┌ Sicambre  ┤                └ Biologie
            │ (br. 1948)└ Sif ───────────┌ Rialto
CELTIC ASH  │                            └ Suavita
(ch. 1957)  │           ┌ Nepenthe ──────┌ Plassy
            └ Ash Plant ┤                └ Frisky
              (gr. 1948)└ Amboyna ───────┌ Bois Roussel
                                         └ Aurora

                        ┌ Nearco ────────┌ Pharos
            ┌ Sayajirao ┤                └ Nogara
            │ (br. 1944)└ Rosy Legend ───┌ Dark Legend
SAY LESS    │                            └ Rosy Cheeks
(b. 1957)   │           ┌ The Cobbler ───┌ Windsor Slipper
            └ Bootless  ┤                └ Overture
              (b. 1951) └ Careless Nora ─┌ Panorama
                                         └ Careless
```

748   PUSHFUL 1 (ch.c., April 17, 1961)

Bred by Major L. B. Holliday.

Won 4 races, placed 10, £28,441, in England, from 2 to 7 years, incl. Timeform Gold Cup; 2nd Carreras Piccadilly Derby Trial Stakes. Also ran over hurdles 1970/71 season, placed 2, £66.

```
                        ┌ Fairway ───────┌ Phalaris
            ┌ Fair Trial┤                └ Scapa Flow
            │ (ch. 1932)└ Lady Juror ────┌ Son-in-Law
PETITION    │                            └ Lady Josephine
(br. 1944)  │           ┌ Artist's Proof ┌ Gainsborough
            └ Art Paper ┤                └ Clear Evidence
              (br. 1933)└ Quire ─────────┌ Fairy King
                                         └ Queen Carbine

                          ┌ Hurry On ────┌ Marcovil
            ┌ Precipitation┤             └ Tout Suite
            │ (ch. 1933)  └ Double Life ─┌ Bachelor's Double
PRESS FORWARD│                           └ Saint Joan
(ch. 1953)  │           ┌ His Grace ─────┌ Blandford
            └ Running Wild┤              └ Malva
              (ch. 1943) └ Wild Lavender II ┌ Mr. Jinks
                                         └ Lavendula II
```

749   QUACK 1 (b.c., February 26, 1969)

Bred by Bwamazon Farm, in U.S.A.

Won 8 races, placed 8, $514,400, in U.S.A., from 3 to 5 years, incl. Hollywood Gold Cup, California Derby, Californian Stakes (twice), Will Rogers Stakes and San Bernardino H.; 2nd Santa Anita Derby, Hollywood Gold Cup, Lakeside H., Cinema H. and San Felipe H.; 3rd San Luis Rey Stakes.

```
                        ┌ Nasrullah ─────┌ Nearco
            ┌ Indian Hemp┤               └ Mumtaz Begum
            │ (ch. 1949)└ Sabzy ─────────┌ Stardust
T.V. LARK   │                            └ Sarita
(b. 1957)   │           ┌ Heelfly ───────┌ Royal Ford
            └ Miss Larksfly┤             └ Canfli
              (br. 1948) └ Larksnest ────┌ Bull Dog
                                         └ Light Lark

                        ┌ Prince Rose ───┌ Rose Prince
            ┌ Princequillo┤              └ Indolence
            │ (b. 1940) └ Cosquilla ─────┌ Papyrus
QUILLON     │                            └ Quick Thought
(ch. 1964)  │           ┌ Court Martial ─┌ Fair Trial
            └ Nato      ┤                └ Instantaneous
              (ch. 1953)└ Safari Moon ───┌ Big Game
                                         └ Moonstone
```

750   QUADRANGLE 2 (b.c., April 16, 1961)

Bred by Paul Mellon, in U.S.A.

Won 10 races, placed 11, $559,386, in U.S.A., from 2 to 4 years, incl. Belmont Stakes, Dwyer H., Travers Stakes, Wood Memorial Stakes, Lawrence Realization and Pimlico Futurity; 2nd Californian Stakes, Metropolitan H. and Jim Dandy Stakes; 3rd Jockey Club Gold Cup, Woodward Stakes, Flamingo Stakes and Jerome H.; 4th Preakness Stakes.

```
                        ┌ Blenheim ──────┌ Blandford
            ┌ Mahmoud   ┤                └ Malva
            │ (gr. 1933)└ Mah Mahal ─────┌ Gainsborough
COHOES      │                            └ Mumtaz Mahal
(b. 1954)   │           ┌ Blue Larkspur ─┌ Black Servant
            └ Belle of Troy┤             └ Blossom Time
              (br. 1947) └ La Troienne ──┌ Teddy
                                         └ Helene de Troie

                        ┌ Bull Dog ──────┌ Teddy
            ┌ Bull Lea  ┤                └ Plucky Liege
            │ (br. 1935)└ Rose Leaves ───┌ Ballot
TAP DAY     │                            └ Colonial
(b. 1947)   │           ┌ Diavolo ───────┌ Whisk Broom II
            └ Scurry    ┤                └ Vexatious
              (b. 1937) └ Slapdash ──────┌ Stimulus
                                         └ Tetrarchy
```

751   QUAY LINE 14 (b.f., February 21, 1976)

Bred by W. and R. Barnett Ltd.

Won 6 races, placed 1, £25,905, in England, at 2 and 3 years, incl. Park Hill Stakes.

HIGH LINE (ch. 1966)	High Hat (ch. 1957)	Hyperion	Gainsborough
			Selene
		Madonna	Donatello II
			Women's Legion
	Time Call (b. 1955)	Chanteur II	Chateau Bouscaut
			La Diva
		Aleria	Djebel
			Canidia
DARK FINALE (b. 1965)	Javelot (b. 1956)	Fast Fox	Fastnet
			Foxcraft
		Djaina	Djebel
			Fille d'Amour
	Peeky (b. 1943)	Epigram	Son-in-Law
			Flying Sally
		Chantage	Epinard
			Blackmail

752   QUICK AS LIGHTNING 5 (b.f., March 17, 1977)

Bred by Ogden Mills Phipps, in U.S.A.

Won 3 races, placed 4, £80,223, in England, at 2 and 3 years, incl. 1,000 Guineas Stakes, Hoover Fillies Mile; 2nd Coronation Stakes; 3rd Fred Darling Stakes; 4th Oaks Stakes.

BUCKPASSER (b. 1963)	Tom Fool (b. 1949)	Menow	Pharamond
			Alcibiades
		Gaga	Bull Dog
			Alpoise
	Busanda (bl. 1947)	War Admiral	Man o'War
			Brushup
		Businesslike	Blue Larkspur
			La Troienne
CLEAR CEILING (b. 1968)	Bold Ruler (b. 1954)	Nasrullah	Nearco
			Mumtaz Begum
		Miss Disco	Discovery
			Outdone
	Grey Flight (gr. 1945)	Mahmoud	Blenheim
			Mah Mahal
		Planetoid	Ariel
			La Chica

753   QUICKEN TREE 5 (ch.g., April 18, 1963)

Bred by Louis Rowan, in U.S.A.

Won 15 races, placed 22, $718,303, in U.S.A., from 3 to 7 years, incl. Jockey Club Gold Cup, Santa Anita H., San Juan Capistrano Invitational H., Display H. (twice), Manhattan H., Del Mar H., San Luis Rey H. and San Luis Obispo H.; 2nd Charles H. Strub Stakes, Gallant Fox H., San Gabriel H., Sunset H., San Antonio Stakes, San Luis Rey H. and Arcadia H.; 3rd Hollywood Gold Cup, Santa Anita H., Del Mar H., San Carlos H., Long Beach H., Gallant Fox H. and San Luis Rey H.

ROYAL ORBIT (ch. 1956)	Royal Charger (ch. 1942)	Nearco	Pharos
			Nogara
		Sun Princess	Solario
			Mumtaz Begum
	Admiral's Belle (b. 1952)	War Admiral	Man o'War
			Brushup
		Belle Cane	Beau Pere
			Duck's Egg
MOTHER WIT (ch. 1954)	Counterpoint (ch. 1948)	Count Fleet	Reigh Count
			Quickly
		Jabot	Sickle
			Frilette
	Recce (ch. 1942)	Mahmoud	Blenheim
			Mah Mahal
		Schwester	Pennant
			Swinging

754   QUIET FLING 1 (b.c., April 3, 1972)

Bred by Beckhampton Ltd., in U.S.A.

Won 5 races, placed 4, £46,064, in England and Ireland, from 2 to 5 years, incl. Coronation Cup, John Porter Stakes; 2nd Irish St. Leger, Coronation Cup; 3rd Hardwicke Stakes.

NIJINSKY (b. 1967)	Northern Dancer (b. 1961)	Nearctic	Nearco
			Lady Angela
		Natalma	Native Dancer
			Almahmoud
	Flaming Page (b. 1959)	Bull Page	Bull Lea
			Our Page
		Flaring Top	Menow
			Flaming Top
PEACE (ch. 1966)	Klairon (b. 1952)	Clarion III	Djebel
			Columba
		Kalmia	Kantar
			Sweet Lavender
	Sun Rose (ch. 1960)	Mossborough	Nearco
			All Moonshine
		Suntime	Precipitation
			Sun Helmet

755   QUILLO QUEEN 3 (b.f., March 21, 1964)

Bred by E. V. Benjamin, Jr., E. V. Benjamin III, S. P. Serio and R. K. Punches, in U.S.A.

Won 4 races, placed 10, $211,692, in U.S.A., from 2 to 4 years, incl. Coaching Club American Oaks and Monmouth Oaks; 2nd Selima Stakes, Mother Goose Stakes and Acorn Stakes.

PRINCEQUILLO (b. 1940)	Prince Rose (b. 1928)	Rose Prince	Prince Palatine
			Eglantine
		Indolence	Gay Crusader
			Barrier
	Cosquilla (b. 1933)	Papyrus	Tracery
			Miss Matty
		Quick Thought	White Eagle
			Mindful
SPAR MAID (b. 1955)	Spartan Valor (br. 1948)	Attention	Equipoise
			Fizzaz
		Arishi	Bull Dog
			Laila Wild
	Nut Brown Maid (b. 1951)	Nasrullah	Nearco
			Mumtaz Begum
		Quincey	Mieuxce
			Queen's Pipe

756   RACHEL 1 (b. or br.f., May 26, 1958)

Bred by E. H. Covell and M. Moss.

Won 5 races, placed 3, £4,631, in England, at 2 and 3 years, incl. Nassau Stakes.

TUDOR MINSTREL (br. 1944)	Owen Tudor (br. 1938)	Hyperion	Gainsborough
			Selene
		Mary Tudor II	Pharos
			Anna Bolena
	Sansonnet (b. 1933)	Sansovino	Swynford
			Gondolette
		Lady Juror	Son-in-Law
			Lady Josephine
PAR AVION (b. 1948)	Phideas (b. 1934)	Pharos	Phalaris
			Scapa Flow
		Imagery	Gainsborough
			Sun Worship
	Acid Flight (ch. 1929)	Lemonora	Lemberg
			Honora
		Scutter	Stornoway
			Scotch Rose

757 RADETZKY A13 (b. or br.c., March 16, 1973)

Bred by M. Berger.

Won 3 races, placed 15, £76,577, in England and France, from 2 to 6 years, incl. St. James's Palace Stakes, Queen Anne Stakes; 2nd Joe Coral Eclipse, Prix Jacques le Marois (dead-heat), Sussex Stakes, Dee Stakes (dead-heat), Hungerford Stakes; 3rd Waterford Crystal Mile, Prince of Wales Stakes, Queen Elizabeth II Stakes, Challenge Stakes, Joe Coral Eclipse Stakes; 4th William Hill Dewhurst Stakes.

HUNTERCOMBE (b. 1967)	Derring-Do (b. 1961)	Darius	Dante
			Yasna
		Sipsey Bridge	Abernant
			Claudette
	Ergina (br. 1957)	Fair Trial	Fairway
			Lady Juror
		Ballechin	Straight Deal
			Gilded
SELINA FAIR (b. 1964)	Hugh Lupus (b. 1952)	Djebel	Tourbillon
			Loika
		Sakountala	Goya II
			Samos
	Raggoty Ann (br. 1954)	Bright News	Stardust
			Inkling
		Costume	Sir Cosmo
			Boscage

758 RAFFINGORA 13 (gr.c., February 11, 1965)

Bred by Eveton Stud.

Won 20 races, placed 12, £26,066, in England and France, from 2 to 5 years, incl. Temple Stakes and King George Stakes; 2nd King George Stakes; 3rd Prix de l'Abbaye de Longchamp, Nunthorpe Stakes and Palace House Stakes; 4th King's Stand Stakes.

GREY SOVEREIGN (gr. 1948)	Nasrullah (b. 1940)	Nearco	Pharos
			Nogara
		Mumtaz Begum	Blenheim
			Mumtaz Mahal
	Kong (gr. 1933)	Baytown	Achtoi
			Princess Herodias
		Clang	Hainault
			Vibration
CAMEO (b. 1955)	Como (b. 1942)	Sir Cosmo	The Boss
			Ayn Hali
		Maia	Prestissimo
			Aerial Flight
	Record Serenade (b. br. 1948)	Straight Deal	Solario
			Good Deal
		Columbia	Colombo
			Islay II

759 RAGSTONE 8 (br.c., March 16, 1970)

Bred by Duke of Norfolk.

Won 7 races, placed 1, £28,588, in England, from 2 to 4 years, incl. Ascot Gold Cup, Henry II Stakes; 3rd Geoffrey Freer Stakes.

RAGUSA (b. 1960)	Ribot (b. 1952)	Tenerani	Bellini
			Tofanella
		Romanella	El Greco
			Barbara Burrini
	Fantan II (b. 1952)	Ambiorix II	Tourbillon
			Lavendula II
		Red Eye	Petee-Wrack
			Charred Keg
FOTHERINGAY (b. 1964)	Right Royal V (br. 1958)	Owen Tudor	Hyperion
			Mary Tudor II
		Bastia	Tornado or Victrix II
			Barberybush
	La Fresnes (ch. 1953)	Court Martial	Fair Trial
			Instantaneous
		Pin Stripe	Hyperion
			Herringbone

760 RAGUSA 9 (b.c., May 26, 1960)

Bred by H. F. Guggenheim.

Won 7 races, placed 3, £148,741, in England and Ireland, from 2 to 4 years, incl. King George VI and Queen Elizabeth Stakes, Irish Sweeps Derby, Great Voltigeur Stakes, St. Leger Stakes, Eclipse Stakes; 3rd Derby Stakes.

RIBOT (b. 1952)	Tenerani (b. 1944)	Bellini	Cavaliere d'Arpino
			Bella Minna
		Tofanella	Apelle
			Try Try Again
	Romanella (ch. 1943)	El Greco	Pharos
			Gay Gamp
		Barbara Burrini	Papyrus
			Bucolic
FANTAN II (b. 1952)	Ambiorix II (b. 1946)	Tourbillon	Ksar
			Durban
		Lavendula II	Pharos
			Sweet Lavender
	Red Eye (ch. 1936)	Petee-Wrack	Wrack
			Marguerite
		Charred Keg	Stimulus
			Jug of Wine

761 RAISE A NATIVE 8 (ch.c., April 18, 1961)

Bred by Happy Hill Farm, in U.S.A.

Won 4 races (unbeaten), $45,955, at 2 years, incl. Juvenile Stakes and Great American Stakes.

NATIVE DANCER (gr. 1950)	Polynesian (br. 1942)	Unbreakable	Sickle
			Blue Glass
		Black Polly	Polymelian
			Black Queen
	Geisha (ro. 1943)	Discovery	Display
			Ariadne
		Miyako	John P. Grier
			La Chica
RAISE YOU (ch. 1946)	Case Ace (b. 1934)	Teddy	Ajax
			Rondeau
		Sweetheart	Ultimus
			Humanity
	Lady Glory (br. 1934)	American Flag	Man o'War
			Lady Comfey
		Beloved	Whisk Broom II
			Bill and Coo

762 RAISE YOU TEN 6 (br.c., 1960)

Bred by P. A. B. Widener.

Won 4 races, placed 4, £12,442, in England, from 2 to 4 years, incl. Yorkshire Cup, Doncaster Cup, Goodwood Cup; 2nd Dante Stakes, Goodwood Cup, Doncaster Cup.

TEHRAN (b. 1941)	Bois Roussel (br. 1935)	Vatout	Prince Chimay
			Vasthi
		Plucky Liege	Spearmint
			Concertina
	Stafaralla (b. 1935)	Solario	Gainsborough
			Sun Worship
		Mirawala	Phalaris
			Miranda
VISOR (br. 1951)	Combat (b. 1944)	Big Game	Bahram
			Myrobella
		Commotion	Mieuxce
			Riot
	Eyewash (ch. 1946)	Blue Peter	Fairway
			Fancy Free
		All Moonshine	Bobsleigh
			Selene

763   **RAMIREZ** 22 (b.c., May 30, 1971)

Bred by Mereworth Farm, in U.S.A.

Won 5 races, placed 12, 910,208 fr., in France and England, from 3 to 5 years, incl. Prix d'Ispahan; 2nd Prix Gontaut-Biron, Prix du Prince d'Orange and Prix d'Harcourt; 3rd Champion Stakes.

T.V. LARK (b. 1957)	Indian Hemp (ch. 1949)	Nasrullah	Nearco / Mumtaz Begum
		Sabzy	Stardust / Sarita
	Miss Larksfly (br. 1948)	Heelfly	Royal Ford / Canfli
		Larksnest	Bull Dog / Light Lark
DANCE FAN (b. br. 1960)	Dedicate (b. 1952)	Princequillo	Prince Rose / Cosquilla
		Dini	John P. Grier / Quivira
	Evening Belle (b. 1945)	Eight Thirty	Pilate / Dinner Time
		Evening	St. James / Crepuscule

764   **RAMSIN** 7 (ch.c., March 31, 1967)

Bred by Baron T. de Zuylen de Nyevelt, in France.

Won 5 races, placed 2, 1,276,271 fr., in France, at 3 and 4 years, incl. Prix du Cadran, Grand Prix de Saint-Cloud, Prix de Barbeville and Prix Maurice de Nieuil; 2nd Prix Jean Prat.

LE HAAR (ch. 1954)	Vieux Manoir (b. 1947)	Brantome	Blandford / Vitamine
		Vieille Maison	Finglas / Vieille Canaille
	Mince Pie (b. 1949)	Teleferique	Bactériophage / Beauté de Neige
		Cannelle	Biribi / Armoise
MARITCHIA (gr. or ro. 1961)	La Varende (gr. 1949)	Blue Moon	Massine / Halston
		Cappellina	Le Capucin / Bellina
	Love Gift (b. 1955)	Amour Drake	Admiral Drake / Vers l'Aurore
		Fancy Girl	Knight of the Garter / Englewood

765   **RANDOM SHOT** 1 (b.c., May 6, 1967)

Bred by Mrs. J. Benskin.

Won 6 races, placed 6, £21,548, in England, from 2 to 5 years, incl. Ascot Gold Cup; 3rd Goodwood Cup.

PIRATE KING (br. 1953)	Prince Chevalier (b. 1943)	Prince Rose	Rose Prince / Indolence
		Chevalerie	Abbot's Speed / Kassala
	Netherton Maid (b. 1944)	Nearco	Pharos / Nogara
		Phase	Windsor Lad / Lost Soul
TIME AND CHANCE (b. 1957)	Supreme Court (br. 1948)	Persian Gulf or Precipitation	Hurry On / Double Life
		Forecourt	Fair Trial / Overture
	Foxtrot (b. 1943)	Foxhunter	Foxlaw / Trimestral
		Premiere Danseuse	Phalaris / Queen of the Ballet

766   **RAPID RIVER** 22 (br.c., May 2, 1970)

Bred by W. A. Richardson.

Won 7 races, placed 7, £29,841, in England, from 2 to 4 years, incl. Gimcrack Stakes, Seaton Delaval Stakes; 2nd Nunthorpe Stakes, Vernons Sprint Cup, Cornwallis Stakes; 3rd King's Stand Stakes; 4th King's Stand Stakes.

FORLORN RIVER (br. 1962)	Fighting Don (b. 1942)	Fighting Fox	Sir Gallahad III / Marguerite
		Bird Nest	Mad Hatter / Tree Top
	Starflight (br. 1950)	Black Rock	Black Devil / Council Rock
		Brave Array	Sir Walter Raleigh / Bold Front
WHO-DONE-IT (b. 1958)	Lucero (br. 1953)	Solonaway	Solferino / Anyway
		Cuguan	Fair Trial / Tracemond
	Ring the Bell (b. 1938)	Umidwar	Blandford / Uganda
		Musician	Soldennis / Magical Music

767   **REALM** 12 (b.c., May 19, 1967)

Bred by Norton Court Stud Farm Ltd.

Won 5 races, placed 6, £17,733, in England, from 2 to 4 years, incl. July Cup, Diadem Stakes, Challenge Stakes; 2nd Lockinge Stakes; July Cup; 3rd King George Stakes, Hungerford Stakes.

PRINCELY GIFT (b. 1951)	Nasrullah (b. 1940)	Nearco	Pharos / Nogara
		Mumtaz Begum	Blenheim / Mumtaz Mahal
	Blue Gem (b. 1943)	Blue Peter	Fairway / Fancy Free
		Sparkle	Blandford / Gleam
QUITA II (b. 1962)	Lavandin (b. 1953)	Verso II	Pinceau / Variete
		Lavande	Rustom Pasha / Livadia
	Eos (br. 1946)	Solferino	Fairway / Sol Speranza
		Ormel	Ormenus / Laitron

768   **RECITATION** 16 (b.c., February 20, 1978)

Bred by Marvin L. Warner, in U.S.A.

Won 3 races, placed 5, £93,299, in England and France, at 2 years, incl Coventry Stakes, Grand Criterium; 2nd Royal Lodge Stakes. July Stakes; 4th William Hill Futurity Stakes.

ELOCUTIONIST (b. 1973)	Gallant Romeo (b. 1961)	Gallant Man	Migoli / Majideh
		Juliets Nurse	Count Fleet / Nursemaid
	Strictly Speaking (b. 1967)	Fleet Nasrullah	Nasrullah / Happy Go Fleet
		Believe Me	Alibhai / Up the Hill
IRISH PARTY (br. 1968)	Irish Lancer (b. 1957)	Royal Charger	Nearco / Sun Princess
		Tige O Myheart	Bull Lea / Unerring
	Party Favor (b. 1960)	Tim Tam	Tom Fool / Two Lea
		Beaukiss	Mahmoud / Gayee

150

769   RECORD RUN 1 (b.c., May 21, 1971)

Bred by F. F. Tuthill and Mrs. A. W. F. Whitehead.

Won 14 races, placed 4, £60,887, in England, Germany, France and Italy, from 2 to 5 years, incl. Prince of Wales Stakes, Grosser Hansa-Preis, Prix Gontaut Biron, Concentra-Pokal des Deutschen Investment-Trust; 2nd Premio Presidente della Repubblica; 3rd Westbury Stakes.

TRACK SPARE (b. 1963)	Sound Track (ch. 1957)	Whistler	Panorama / Farthing Damages
		Bridle Way	Mustang / Straight Path
	Rosy Myth (b. or br. 1958)	Nearco	Pharos / Nogara
		Rosy Dolly	Bois Roussel / Rosy Legend
BENCH GAME (ch. 1960)	King's Bench (b. 1949)	Court Martial	Fair Trial / Instantaneous
		King's Cross	King Salmon / Doublure
	Gamesmistress (ch. 1945)	Big Game	Bahram / Myrobella
		Taslon	Hurry On / Taslett

770   RECUPERE 1 (ch.c., May 8, 1970)

Bred by Burton Agnes Stud Co. Ltd., in England.

Won 9 races, placed 6, 1,685,315 fr., in France and U.S.A., from 3 to 6 years, incl. Prix du Cadran, Prix de Barbeville (twice), Prix Berteux, Prix Henry Delamarre, Prix Jean Prat, Prix du Conseil Municipal, Prix Reiset and Seneca Handicap; 3rd Grosser Preis von Baden; 4th Prix Royal Oak.

RELIANCE II (b. 1962)	Tantième (b. 1947)	Deux pour Cent	Deiri / Dix pour Cent
		Terka	Indus / La Furka
	Relance III (ch. 1952)	Relic	War Relic / Bridal Colors
		Polaire II	Le Volcan / Stella Polaris
NELION (b. 1964)	Grey Sovereign (gr. 1948)	Nasrullah	Nearco / Mumtaz Begum
		Kong	Baytown / Clang
	Maurine (b. br. 1955)	Worden II	Wild Risk / Sans Tares
		Muscida	Barneveldt / Mackwiller

771   RED ARROW 19 (b.c., March 10, 1973)

Bred by Scuderia Diamante, in Italy.

Won 6 races, placed 5, 88,280,000 L., in Italy, at 3 and 4 years, incl. Derby Italiano and Gran Premio d'Italia.

MOLVEDO (b. 1958)	Ribot (b. 1952)	Tenerani	Bellini / Tofanella
		Romanella	El Greco / Barbara Burrini
	Maggiolina (br. 1946)	Nakamuro	Cameronian / Nogara
		Murcia	Pilade / Muci
ROTATION (b. 1962)	Mourne (ch. 1954)	Vieux Manoir	Brantome / Vieille Maison
		Ballynash	Nasrullah / Ballywellbroke
	Roving Girl (b. 1950)	Royal Charger	Nearco / Sun Princess
		Leave Me Alone	Empire Builder / Family Honour

772   RED GIRL 2 (ch.f., March 28, 1971)

Bred by Scuderia El-Vi, in Italy.

Won 3 races, placed 3, 30,090,000 L., in Italy, at 2 and 3 years, incl. Oaks d'Italia; 3rd Premio Regina Elena.

LUTHIER (b. br. 1965)	Klairon (b. 1952)	Clarion III	Djebel / Columba
		Kalmia	Kantar / Sweet Lavender
	Flute Enchantee (b. 1950)	Cranach	Coronach / Reine Isaure
		Montagnana	Brantome / Mauretania
RED DRAGONESS (ch. 1965)	Red God (ch. 1954)	Nasrullah	Nearco / Mumtaz Begum
		Spring Run	Menow / Boola Brook
	Heliosian (b. 1961)	Helioscope	Heliopolis / War Flower
		Persian Maid	Tehran / Aroma

773   RED LORD 11 (b.c., April 7, 1973)

Bred by William Hill Studs, in England.

Won 3 races, placed 3, 440,966 fr., in France, at 2 and 3 years, incl. Poule d'Essai des Poulains; 3rd Prix La Rochette and Criterium de Maisons-Laffitte.

RED GOD (ch. 1954)	Nasrullah (b. 1940)	Nearco	Pharos / Nogara
		Mumtaz Begum	Blenheim / Mumtaz Mahal
	Spring Run (b. 1948)	Menow	Pharamond / Alcibiades
		Boola Brook	Bull Dog / Brookdale
DAME DE GRACE (b. 1968)	Armistice III (b. 1959)	Worden II	Wild Risk / Sans Tares
		Commemoration	Vandale II / Anne Comnene
	Aglae Grace (br. 1947)	Mousson	Rose Prince / Spring Tide
		Agathe	Amfortas / Melanie

774   REFORM 5 (b.c., March 3, 1964)

Bred by Ballymacoll Stud Farm Ltd.

Won 11 races, placed 3, £44,721, in England, at 2 and 3 years, incl. Champion Stakes, Sussex Stakes, St. James's Palace Stakes, Queen Elizabeth II Stakes; 2nd Wills Mile, Greenham Stakes.

PALL MALL (ch. 1955)	Palestine (gr. 1947)	Fair Trial	Fairway / Lady Juror
		Una	Tetratema / Uganda
	Malapert (ch. 1946)	Portlaw	Beresford / Portree
		Malatesta	Sansovino / Tetranella
COUNTRY HOUSE (br. 1955)	Vieux Manoir (b. 1947)	Brantome	Blandford / Vitamine
		Vieille Maison	Finglas / Vieille Canaille
	Miss Coventry (b. or br. 1943)	Mieuxce	Massine / L'Olivete
		Coventry Belle	Hyperion / Carpet Slipper

775   **REGAL EXCEPTION** 16 (b.f., May 22, 1969)

Bred by Robin F. Scully, in U.S.A.

Won 2 races, placed 3, £44,752, in Ireland, England and France, at 2 and 3 years, incl. Irish Guinness Oaks; 2nd Oaks Stakes; 4th Prix de l'Arc de Triomphe.

RIBOT (b. 1952)	Tenerani (b. 1944)	Bellini	Cavaliere d'Arpino / Bella Minna
		Tofanella	Apelle / Try Try Again
	Romanella (ch. 1943)	El Greco	Pharos / Gay Gamp
		Barbara Burrini	Papyrus / Bucolic
RAJPUT PRINCESS (ch. 1961)	Prince Taj (b. 1954)	Prince Bio	Prince Rose / Biologie
		Malindi	Nearco / Mumtaz Begum
	Royal Arrival (ch. 1954)	Vieux Manoir	Brantome / Vieille Maison
		Bellatrix II	Victrix II / Fille de Soleil

776   **REGENT STREET** 12 (b.c., January 16, 1965)

Bred by E. Fernandez-Guerrico, in Argentina.

Won 6 races, placed 14, 779,620 fr., in France, from 2 to 5 years, incl. Prix de la Foret, Prix du Muguet, Prix du Palais-Royal and Prix du Chemin de Fer du Nord; 2nd Prix Messidor and Prix du Rond-Point; 3rd Prix du Palais-Royal and Prix de la Porte Maillot; 4th Prix du Moulin de Longchamp (twice), Prix de la Foret (twice) and Prix Jacques le Marois.

GULF STREAM (br. 1943)	Hyperion (ch. 1930)	Gainsborough	Bayardo / Rosedrop
		Selene	Chaucer / Serenissima
	Tide-way (br. 1933)	Fairway	Phalaris / Scapa Flow
		Drift	Swynford / Santa Cruz
FAIR SPOKEN (b. 1953)	Savani (b. 1943)	Fair Copy	Fairway / Composure
		Perfume II	Badruddin / Lavendula II
	Tudor Fair (ch. 1947)	Owen Tudor	Hyperion / Mary Tudor II
		Fair Ease	Fair Trial / Montez

777   **REINDEER** 5 (b. or br.c., May 11, 1966)

Bred by S. O'Flaherty.

Won 6 races, placed 3, £37,350, in Ireland, France and England, at 3 and 4 years, incl. Irish St. Leger, Desmond Stakes, Royal Whip Stakes, Prix Kergorlay; 3rd Irish Sweeps Derby, Hardwicke Stakes, Jockey Club Stakes.

SANTA CLAUS (br. 1961)	Chamossaire (ch. 1942)	Precipitation	Hurry On / Double Life
		Snowberry	Cameronian / Myrobella
	Aunt Clara (br. 1953)	Arctic Prince	Prince Chevalier / Arctic Sun
		Sister Clara	Scarlet Tiger / Clarence
REINE DES BOIS (b. 1950)	Bois Roussel (br. 1935)	Vatout	Prince Chimay / Vasthi
		Plucky Liege	Spearmint / Concertina
	Queen of Shiraz (b. 1937)	Bahram	Blandford / Friar's Daughter
		Qurrat-al-Ain	Buchan / Harpsichord

778   **REINE DE SABA** 2 (b.f., May 7, 1975)

Bred by Jacques Wertheimer, in France.

Won 5 races, placed 6, 1,327,500 fr., in France and U.S.A., from 2 to 4 years, incl. Prix de Diane de Revlon and Prix Saint-Alary; 4th Yellow Ribbon Stakes.

LYPHARD (b. 1969)	Northern Dancer (b. 1961)	Nearctic	Nearco / Lady Angela
		Natalma	Native Dancer / Almahmoud
	Goofed (ch. 1960)	Court Martial	Fair Trial / Instantaneous
		Barra	Formor / La Favorite
SIRYA (ch. 1967)	Sicambre (br. 1948)	Prince Bio	Prince Rose / Biologie
		Sif	Rialto / Suavita
	Carva (ch. 1955)	Rockefella	Hyperion / Rockfel
		Sarah Madeline	Nasrullah / Marshfield

779   **REINE DU CHANT** 12 (b.f., February 10, 1970)

Bred by P. Tetard, in France.

Won 2 races, placed 1, 261,782 fr., in France, at 2 years, incl. Prix Robert Papin; 4th Prix de la Salamandre.

PREMIER VIOLON (br. 1963)	Klairon (b. 1952)	Clarion III	Djebel / Columba
		Kalmia	Kantar / Sweet Lavender
	Flute Enchantee (b. 1950)	Cranach	Coronach / Reine Isaure
		Montagnana	Brantome / Mauretania
REINE MARTIALE (ch. 1953)	Court Martial (ch. 1942)	Fair Trial	Fairway / Lady Juror
		Instantaneous	Hurry On / Picture
	Reine Shub Ad (ch. 1939)	Brantome	Blandford / Vitamine
		Nanaia	Kircubbin / Lanette

780   **RELAY RACE** 4 (br.c., May 6, 1970)

Bred by Lady Macdonald-Buchanan.

Won 4 races, placed 6, £21,847, in England, from 2 to 5 years, incl. Hardwicke Stakes, Jockey Club Stakes; 2nd Dante Stakes, Doncaster Cup; 3rd John Porter Stakes, Princess of Wales's Stakes.

RELKO (b. 1960)	Tanerko (br. 1953)	Tantieme	Deux pour Cent / Terka
		La Divine	Fair Copy / La Diva
	Relance III (ch. 1952)	Relic	War Relic / Bridal Colors
		Polaire II	Le Volcan / Stella Polaris
ANTONIETTA CORSINI (b. 1962)	Herbager (b. 1956)	Vandale II	Plassy / Vanille
		Flagette	Escamillo / Fidgette
	Angela Rucellai (b. 1954)	Rockefella	Hyperion / Rockfel
		Aristareta	Niccolo Dell'Arca / Acquaforte

781   **RELFO** 20 (br.f., April 22, 1975)

Bred by Establissement Equine Investment.

Won 4 races, placed 3, £53,578, in Ireland, England and France, at 2 and 3 years, incl. Ribblesdale Stakes; 2nd Prix Vermeille, Park Stakes; 3rd Irish Guinness Oaks.

RELKO (b. 1960)	Tanerko (br. 1953)	Tantieme	Deux pour Cent / Terka
		La Divine	Fair Copy / La Diva
	Relance III (ch. 1952)	Relic	War Relic / Bridal Colors
		Polaire II	Le Volcan / Stella Polaris
LUFAR (b. 1970)	Bold Lad (IRE) (b. 1964)	Bold Ruler	Nasrullah / Miss Disco
		Barn Pride	Democratic / Fair Alycia
	Radiance (ch. 1956)	Alycidon	Donatello II / Aurora
		Magnificent	Migoli / Isle of Capri

782   **RELIANCE II** 16 (b.c., April 11, 1962)

Bred by Francois Dupré, in France.

Won 5 races, placed 1, 2,319,696 fr., in France, at 3 years, incl. Prix du Jockey-Club, Grand Prix de Paris, Prix Royal Oak and Prix Hocquart; 2nd Prix de l'Arc de Triomphe.

TANTIEME (b. 1947)	Deux pour Cent (b. 1941)	Deiri	Aethelstan / Desra
		Dix pour Cent	Feridoon / La Chansonnerie
	Terka (br. 1942)	Indus	Alcantara II / Himalaya
		La Furka	Blandford / Brenta
RELANCE III (ch. 1952)	Relic (bl. 1945)	War Relic	Man o'War / Friar's Carse
		Bridal Colors	Black Toney / Vaila
	Polaire II (br. 1947)	Le Volcan	Tourbillon / Eroica
		Stella Polaris	Papyrus / Crepuscule

783   **RELKINO** 13 (b.c., April 21, 1973)

Bred by Cleaboy Farms Co.

Won 4 races, placed 6, £127,556, in England, from 2 to 4 years, incl. Benson and Hedges Gold Cup, Lockinge Stakes, Ascot 2,000 Guineas Trial Stakes; 2nd Derby, Champion Stakes; Westbury Stakes; 3rd Sussex Stakes.

RELKO (b. 1960)	Tanerko (br. 1953)	Tantieme	Deux pour Cent / Terka
		La Divine	Fair Copy / La Diva
	Relance III (ch. 1952)	Relic	War Relic / Bridal Colors
		Polaire II	Le Volcan / Stella Polaris
PUGNACITY (b. 1962)	Pampered King (b. 1954)	Prince Chevalier	Prince Rose / Chevalerie
		Netherton Maid	Nearco / Phase
	Ballynulta (b. 1953)	Djebel	Tourbillon / Loika
		Ballisland	The Phoenix / Aherlow

784   **RELKO** 16 (b.c., 1960)

Bred by Francois Dupré.

Won 9 races, placed 3, £151,787, in England and France, from 2 to 4 years, incl. Derby Stakes, Coronation Cup, Poule d'Essai des Poulains, Prix Royal-Oak, Prix Ganay, Grand Prix de Saint-Cloud, Prix de Guiche; 2nd Criterium de Maisons-Laffitte, Prix Thomas Bryon; 4th Grand Criterium.

TANERKO (br. 1953)	Tantieme (b. 1947)	Deux pour Cent	Deiri / Dix pour Cent
		Terka	Indus / La Furka
	La Divine (br. 1943)	Fair Copy	Fairway / Composure
		La Diva	Blue Skies / La Traviata
RELANCE III (ch. 1952)	Relic (bl. 1945)	War Relic	Man o'War / Friar's Carse
		Bridal Colors	Black Toney / Vaila
	Polaire II (br. 1947)	Le Volcan	Tourbillon / Eroica
		Stella Polaris	Papyrus / Crepuscule

785   **RELOAD** 16 (ch.f., April 2, 1970)

Bred by White Lodge Stud Ltd., in France.

Won 3 races, placed 2, £10,195, in England, at 3 years, incl. Park Hill Stakes; 2nd Cheshire Oaks, Jockey Club Cup.

RELKO (b. 1960)	Tanerko (br. 1953)	Tantieme	Deux pour Cent / Terka
		La Divine	Fair Copy / La Diva
	Relance III (ch. 1952)	Relic	War Relic / Bridal Colors
		Polaire II	Le Volcan / Stella Polaris
FUSIL (b. 1961)	Fidalgo (b. 1956)	Arctic Star	Nearco / Serena
		Miss France	Jock II / Nafah
	Mitraille (b. 1953)	Big Game	Bahram / Myrobella
		Mitrailleuse	Mieuxce / French Kin

786   **RESCOUSSE** 10 (b.f., February 18, 1969)

Bred by C. Guerlain, in France.

Won 4 races, placed 5, 1,807,347 fr., in France, at 2 and 3 years, incl. Prix de Diane, Prix Penelope and Prix de la Nonette; 2nd Prix de l'Arc de Triomphe; 3rd Prix Vanteaux.

EMERSON (b. 1958)	Coaraze (b. 1942)	Tourbillon	Ksar / Durban
		Corrida	Coronach / Zariba
	Empenosa (br. 1945)	Full Sail	Fairway / Fancy Free
		Ermua	Congreve / Guernica
BELLA MOURNE (b. 1962)	Mourne (ch. 1954)	Vieux Manoir	Brantome / Vieille Maison
		Ballynash	Nasrullah / Ballywellbroke
	Cecropia (b. 1955)	Alizier	Teleferique / Alizarine
		Fallaha	Sayani / Madame Patrol

787   REVIDERE 4 (ch.f., March 24, 1973)

Bred by Claiborne Farm, in U.S.A.

Won 8 races, placed 3, $330,019, in U.S.A., at 3 and 4 years, incl. Coaching Club American Oaks, Monmouth Oaks, Ruffian Stakes. Gazelle H. and Cotillion Stakes; 2nd Beldame Stakes; 3rd Jockey Club Gold Cup.

REVIEWER (b. 1966)	Bold Ruler (b. 1954)	Nasrullah	Nearco / Mumtaz Begum
		Miss Disco	Discovery / Outdone
	Broadway (b. 1959)	Hasty Road	Roman / Traffic Court
		Flitabout	Challedon / Bird Flower
QUILLESIAN (ch. 1965)	Princequillo (b. 1940)	Prince Rose	Rose Prince / Indolence
		Cosquilla	Papyrus / Quick Thought
	Alanesian (b. 1954)	Polynesian	Unbreakable / Black Polly
		Alablue	Blue Larkspur / Double Time

788   REX MAGNA 12 (br.c., April 11, 1974)

Bred by Mme. J. Couturié, in France.

Won 4 races, placed 2, 641,159 fr., in France and England, from 2 to 4 years, incl. Prix Royal Oak and Prix Greffulhe; 4th Hardwicke Stakes.

RIGHT ROYAL V (br. 1958)	Owen Tudor (br. 1938)	Hyperion	Gainsborough / Selene
		Mary Tudor II	Pharos / Anna Bolena
	Bastia (b. 1951)	Tornado or Victrix II	Kantar / Victory
		Barberybush	Ksar / Pervencheres
CHAMBRE D'AMOUR (ch. 1967)	Blockhaus (ch. 1953)	Relic	War Relic / Bridal Colors
		Belle Princesse	Prince Rose / Bay Berry
	Fleche d'Amour (ch. 1962)	Dan Cupid	Native Dancer / Vixenette
		Tahiti	Tornado / Gradisca

789   RHEFFIC 4 (b.c., April 6, 1968)

Bred by Mme. Francois Dupŗé, in France.

Won 5 races, placed 1, 2,670,685 fr., in France, at 2 and 3 years, incl. Prix du Jockey-Club, Grand Prix de Paris, Prix Greffulhe and Criterium de Saint-Cloud; 2nd Prix de Condé.

TRAFFIC (ch. 1961)	Traffic Judge (ch. 1952)	Alibhai	Hyperion / Teresina
		Traffic Court	Discovery / Traffic
	Capelet (ch. 1954)	Bolero	Eight Thirty / Stepwisely
		Quick Touch	Count Fleet / Alms
RHENANE (br. 1961)	Tanerko (br. 1953)	Tantieme	Deux pour Cent / Terka
		La Divine	Fair Copy / La Diva
	Rhea II (b. 1950)	Gundomar	Alchimist / Grossularia
		Regina IV	Indus / Reine d'Ouilly

790   RHEINGOLD 10 (b.c., May 11, 1969)

Bred by Dr. James Russell.

Won 9 races, placed 7, £335,290, in England and France, from 2 to 4 years, incl. Dante Stakes, Hardwicke Stakes, John Porter Stakes, Prix de l'Arc de Triomphe, Grand Prix de Saint-Cloud (twice), Prix Ganay; 2nd Champagne Stakes, Dewhurst Stakes, Derby Stakes, King George VI and Queen Elizabeth Stakes; 3rd Benson and Hedges Gold Cup; 4th Benson and Hedges Gold Cup.

FABERGE II (b. 1961)	Princely Gift (b. 1951)	Nasrullah	Nearco / Mumtaz Begum
		Blue Gem	Blue Peter / Sparkle
	Spring Offensive (b. 1943)	Legend of France	Dark Legend / Francille
		Batika	Blenheim / Brise Bise
ATHENE (b. 1960)	Supreme Court (br. 1948)	Persian Gulf or Precipitation	Hurry On / Double Life
		Forecourt	Fair Trial / Overture
	Necelia (b. or br. 1949)	Nearco	Pharos / Nogara
		Cecily	Cecil / Matanilla

791   RIBECOURT 2 (b.c., May 4, 1971)

Bred by Mme. J. Couturié, in France.

Won 4 races, placed 3, 666,415 fr., in France and Italy, at 2 and 3 years, incl. Gran Premio d'Italia, Prix Kergorlay and Criterium de Saint-Cloud; 2nd Gran Premio del Jockey Club and Premio Roma; 3rd Prix de Condé.

RIBERO (b. 1965)	Ribot (b. 1952)	Tenerani	Bellini / Tofanella
		Romanella	El Greco / Barbara Burrini
	Libra (ch. 1956)	Hyperion	Gainsborough / Selene
		Weighbridge	Portlaw / Golden Way
VILLARRICA (b. 1966)	Dan Cupid (ch. 1956)	Native Dancer	Polynesian / Geisha
		Vixenette	Sickle / Lady Reynard
	High Class (b. 1960)	Tyrone	Tornado / Statira
		Distinction	Fair Copy / Ad Astra

792   RIBERO 4 (b.c., March 13, 1965)

Bred by Mrs. Julian G. Rogers, in U.S.A.

Won 3 races, placed 6, £92,343, in England and Ireland, from 2 to 4 years, incl. St. Leger Stakes, Irish Sweeps Derby; 2nd King Edward VII Stakes; 3rd Dante Stakes, Jockey Club Stakes, Westbury Stakes; 4th King George VI and Queen Elizabeth Stakes.

RIBOT (b. 1952)	Tenerani (b. 1944)	Bellini	Cavaliere d'Arpino / Bella Minna
		Tofanella	Apelle / Try Try Again
	Romanella (ch. 1943)	El Greco	Pharos / Gay Gamp
		Barbara Burrini	Papyrus / Bucolic
LIBRA (ch. 1956)	Hyperion (ch. 1930)	Gainsborough	Bayardo / Rosedrop
		Selene	Chaucer / Serenissima
	Weighbridge (ch. 1945)	Portlaw	Beresford / Portree
		Golden Way	Gold Bridge / Adria II

793   **RIBOCCO** 4 (b.c., March 23, 1964)

Bred by Mrs. Julian G. Rogers, in U.S.A.

Won 5 races, placed 6, £155,736, in England, Ireland and France, at 2 and 3 years, incl. Observer Gold Cup, Irish Sweeps Derby, St. Leger Stakes; 2nd Derby Stakes, Champagne Stakes, Dee Stakes; 3rd King George VI and Queen Elizabeth Stakes, Prix de l'Arc de Triomphe.

RIBOT (b. 1952)	Tenerani (b. 1944)	Bellini	Cavaliere d'Arpino / Bella Minna
		Tofanella	Apelle / Try Try Again
	Romanella (ch. 1943)	El Greco	Pharos / Gay Gamp
		Barbara Burrini	Papyrus / Bucolic
LIBRA (ch. 1956)	Hyperion (ch. 1930)	Gainsborough	Bayardo / Rosedrop
		Selene	Chaucer / Serenissima
	Weighbridge (ch. 1945)	Portlaw	Beresford / Portree
		Golden Way	Gold Bridge / Adria II

794   **RIBOFILIO** 7 (b.c., April 6, 1966)

Bred by Mrs. D. P. Barrett, in U.S.A.

Won 7 races, placed 9, £64,095, in England, Ireland and U.S.A., from 2 to 4 years, incl. Dewhurst Stakes, Champagne Stakes, Ascot 2,000 Guineas Trial Stakes, Longfellow Handicap; 2nd Irish Sweeps Derby, St. Leger Stakes, Governor's Cup H.; 3rd Stars & Stripes H.

RIBOT (b. 1952)	Tenerani (b. 1944)	Bellini	Cavaliere d'Arpino / Bella Minna
		Tofanella	Apelle / Try Try Again
	Romanella (ch. 1943)	El Greco	Pharos / Gay Gamp
		Barbara Burrini	Papyrus / Bucolic
ISLAND CREEK (bl. 1960)	Khaled (br. 1943)	Hyperion	Gainsborough / Selene
		Eclair ^	Ethnarch / Black Ray
	Rippling Rythm (b. 1951)	Bull Lea	Bull Dog / Rose Leaves
		Easy Lass	Blenheim / Slow and Easy

795   **RIGHT AWAY** 16 (gr.f., February 10, 1963)

Bred by Mrs. P. A. B. Widener, in France.

Won 2 races, placed 1, 284,371 fr., in France, at 3 years, incl. Poule d'Essai des Pouliches.

RIGHT ROYAL V (br. 1958)	Owen Tudor (br. 1938)	Hyperion	Gainsborough / Selene
		Mary Tudor II	Pharos / Anna Bolena
	Bastia (b. 1951)	Tornado or Victrix II	Kantar / Victory
		Barberybush	Ksar / Pervencheres
POLAMIA (gr. 1955)	Mahmoud (gr. 1933)	Blenheim	Blandford / Malva
		Mah Mahal	Gainsborough / Mumtaz Mahal
	Ampola (ch. 1949)	Pavot	Case Ace / Coquelicot
		Blue Denim	Blue Larkspur / Judy O'Grady

796   **RIGHT ROYAL V** 3 (br.c., March 23, 1958)

Bred by Mme. J. Couturié, in France.

Won 8 races, placed 2, £111,465, in France and England, at 2 and 3 years, incl. Grand Criterium, Prix de la Salamandre, Poule d'Essai des Poulains, Prix Lupin, Prix du Jockey Club, King George VI and Queen Elizabeth Stakes and Prix Henri Foy; 2nd Prix de l'Arc de Triomphe.

OWEN TUDOR (br. 1938)	Hyperion (ch. 1930)	Gainsborough	Bayardo / Rosedrop
		Selene	Chaucer / Serenissima
	Mary Tudor II (b. 1931)	Pharos	Phalaris / Scapa Flow
		Anna Bolena	Teddy / Queen Elizabeth II
BASTIA (b. 1951)	Tornado or Victrix II (b. 1934)	Kantar	Alcantara II / Karabe
		Victory	Swynford / Lineage
	Barberybush (ch. 1934)	Ksar	Bruleur / Kizil Kourgan
		Pervencheres	Maboul / Poet's Star

797   **RIGHT TACK** 10 (b.c., April 13, 1966)

Bred by P. Larkin.

Won 8 races, placed 3, £59,843, in England and Ireland, at 2 and 3 years, incl. 2,000 Guineas Stakes, Irish 2,000 Guineas Stakes, Middle Park Stakes, St. James's Palace Stakes; 2nd Greenham Stakes.

HARD TACK (b. 1955)	Hard Sauce (br. 1948)	Ardan	Pharis II / Adargatis
		Saucy Bella	Bellacose / Marmite
	Cowes (b. 1949)	Blue Peter	Fairway / Fancy Free
		Lighthearted	Hyperion / Merry Devon
POLLY MACAW (b. or br. 1959)	Polly's Jet (ch. 1953)	Polynesian	Unbreakable / Black Polly
		Mary's Dell	Case Ace / Pixey Dell
	Listowel (b. or br. 1953)	Solonaway	Solferino / Anyway
		Lady Fairford	Fairford / Pure Gaiety

798   **RIVA RIDGE** 1 (b.c., April 13, 1969)

Bred by Meadow Stud, in U.S.A.

Won 17 races, placed 4, $1,111,497, in U.S.A., from 2 to 4 years, incl. Kentucky Derby, Belmont Stakes, Hollywood Derby, Blue Grass Stakes, Champagne Stakes, Garden State Stakes, Futurity Stakes, Pimlico-Laurel Futurity, Brooklyn H., Massachusetts H. and Stuyvesant H.; 2nd Marlboro Cup and Stymie H.; 3rd Jockey Club Gold Cup; 4th Preakness Stakes.

FIRST LANDING (b. 1956)	Turn-to (b. 1951)	Royal Charger	Nearco / Sun Princess
		Source Sucree	Admiral Drake / Lavendula II
	Hildene (b. 1938)	Bubbling Over	North Star III / Beaming Beauty
		Fancy Racket	Wrack / Ultimate Fancy
IBERIA (ch. 1954)	Heliopolis (b. 1936)	Hyperion	Gainsborough / Selene
		Drift	Swynford / Santa Cruz
	War East (b. 1947)	Easton	Dark Legend / Phaona
		Warrior Lass	Man o'War / Sweetheart

799   RIVERMAN 10 (b.c., March 22, 1969)

Bred by Capt. H. F. Guggenheim, in U.S.A.

Won 5 races, placed 3, 1,256,175 fr., in France and England, at 2 and 3 years, incl. Poule d'Essai des Poulains, Prix d'Ispahan and Prix Jean Prat; 2nd Champion Stakes and Criterium de Maisons-Laffitte; 3rd King George VI and Queen Elizabeth Stakes.

NEVER BEND (b. 1960)	Nasrullah (b. 1940)	Nearco	Pharos
			Nogara
		Mumtaz Begum	Blenheim
			Mumtaz Mahal
	Lalun (b. 1952)	Djeddah	Djebel
			Djezima
		Be Faithful	Bimelech
			Bloodroot
RIVER LADY (b. 1963)	Prince John (ch. 1953)	Princequillo	Prince Rose
			Cosquilla
		Not Afraid	Count Fleet
			Banish Fear
	Nile Lily (b. 1954)	Roman	Sir Gallahad III
			Buckup
		Azalea	Sun Teddy
			Coquelicot

800   RIVERQUEEN 1 (b.f., January 31, 1973)

Bred by Société Aland, in France.

Won 5 races, placed 1, 1,662,040 fr., in France, at 2 and 3 years, incl. Poule d'Essai des Pouliches, Prix Saint-Alary, Grand Prix de Saint-Cloud and Prix de la Grotte; 2nd Prix de Diane.

LUTHIER (b./br. 1965)	Klairon (b. 1952)	Clarion III	Djebel
			Columba
		Kalmia	Kantar
			Sweet Lavender
	Flute Enchantee (b. 1950)	Cranach	Coronach
			Reine Isaure
		Montagnana	Brantome
			Mauretania
RIVERSIDE (b. 1966)	Sheshoon (ch. 1956)	Precipitation	Hurry On
			Double Life
		Noorani	Nearco
			Empire Glory
	Renounce (b. 1957)	Big Game	Bahram
			Myrobella
		Refreshed	Hyperion
			Monsoon

801   ROAN STAR 16 (ro.c., May 19, 1973)

Bred by Mr. and Mrs. J. H. King, in U.S.A.

Won 8 races, placed 20, 1,204,356 fr., in France and U.S.A., from 2 to 6 years, incl. Prix de la Foret, Prix Eclipse and Canadian Turf H.; 2nd Poule d'Essai des Poulains and Prix de Fontainebleau; 3rd La Coupe de Maisons-Laffitte; 4th Prix Robert Papin and Prix Lupin.

AL HATTAB (ro. 1966)	The Axe II (gr. 1958)	Mahmoud	Blenheim
			Mah Mahal
		Blackball	Shut Out
			Big Event
	Abyssinia (gr. 1953)	Abernant	Owen Tudor
			Rustom Mahal
		Serengeti	Big Game
			Mercy
HAIL A STAR (b. 1967)	Hail to Reason (br. 1958)	Turn-to	Royal Charger
			Source Sucree
		Nothirdchance	Blue Swords
			Galla Colors
	Bornastar (br. 1953)	Alibhai	Hyperion
			Teresina
		Farmerette	Sickle
			Cottage Cheese

802   ROBERTO 12 (b.c., March 16, 1969)

Bred by J. W. Galbreath, in U.S.A.

Won 7 races, placed 4, £131,767, in England, Ireland and France, from 2 to 4 years, incl. Derby Stakes, Benson and Hedges Gold Cup, Coronation Cup, National Stakes (Curragh), Anglesey Stakes, Vauxhall Trial Stakes; 2nd 2,000 Guineas Stakes, Prix Niel, Nijinsky Stakes; 4th Grand Criterium.

HAIL TO REASON (br. 1958)	Turn-to (b. 1951)	Royal Charger	Nearco
			Sun Princess
		Source Sucree	Admiral Drake
			Lavendula II
	Nothirdchance (b. 1948)	Blue Swords	Blue Larkspur
			Flaming Swords
		Galla Colors	Sir Gallahad III
			Rouge et Noir
BRAMALEA (b. or br. 1959)	Nashua (b. 1952)	Nasrullah	Nearco
			Mumtaz Begum
		Segula	Johnstown
			Sekhmet
	Rarelea (b. 1949)	Bull Lea	Bull Dog
			Rose Leaves
		Bleebok	Blue Larkspur
			Forteresse

803   ROCKAVON 2 (b.c., May 11, 1958)

Bred by Biddlesden Park Stud.

Won 5 races, placed 3, £25,462, in England, at 2 and 3 years, incl. 2,000 Guineas Stakes; 3rd King George VI and Queen Elizabeth Stakes.

ROCKEFELLA (br. 1941)	Hyperion (ch. 1930)	Gainsborough	Bayardo
			Rosedrop
		Selene	Chaucer
			Serenissima
	Rockfel (br. 1935)	Felstead	Spion Kop
			Felkington
		Rockliffe	Santorb
			Sweet Rocket
COSMETIC (ch. 1940)	Sir Cosmo (b. 1926)	The Boss	Orby
			Southern Cross II
		Ayn Hali	Desmond
			Lalla Rookh
	Beautiful Girl (b. 1933)	Son-in-Law	Dark Ronald
			Mother in Law
		Ars Divina	Gainsborough
			Eos

804   ROCK ROI 14 (ch.c., April 24, 1967)

Bred by Mrs. V. Hue-Williams, in England.

Won 9 races, placed 9, £60,741, in England and France, from 2 to 5 years, including Gordon Stakes, Goodwood Cup, Doncaster Cup, John Porter Stakes and Prix du Cadran; also first (twice) in Gold Cup, but disqualified each time (placed second in 1972); 2nd Great Voltigeur Sweepstakes and Prix du Cadran; 3rd Craven Stakes and John Porter Stakes.

MOURNE (ch. 1954)	Vieux Manoir (b. 1947)	Brantome	Blandford
			Vitamine
		Vieille Maison	Finglas
			Vieille Canaille
	Ballynash (b. 1946)	Nasrullah	Nearco
			Mumtaz Begum
		Ballywellbroke	Ballyferis
			The Beggar
SECRET SESSION (ch. 1958)	Court Martial (ch. 1942)	Fair Trial	Fairway
			Lady Juror
		Instantaneous	Hurry On
			Picture
	Code Militaire (b. 1948)	Mieuxce	Massine
			L'Olivete
		Battle Law	Portlaw
			Battle Queen

805   ROI DAGOBERT 8 (b.c., February 25, 1964)

Bred by Maurice Hennessy, in France.

Won 4 races, placed 4, 1,208,254 fr., in France, from 2 to 4 years, incl. Prix Lupin, Prix Greffulhe and Prix Noailles; 2nd Grand Criterium, Prix Ganay and Criterium de Maisons-Laffitte; 4th Prix de l'Arc de Triomphe.

SICAMBRE (br. 1948)	Prince Bio (b. 1941)	Prince Rose	Rose Prince / Indolence
		Biologie	Bacteriophage / Eponge
	Sif (br. 1936)	Rialto	Rabelais / La Grelee
		Suavita	Alcantara II / Shocking
DAME D'ATOUR (b. 1955)	Cranach (b. 1938)	Coronach	Hurry On / Wet Kiss
		Reine Isaure	Blandford / Oriane
	Barley Corn (b. 1950)	Hyperion	Gainsborough / Selene
		Schiaparelli	Schiavoni / Aileen

806   ROI LEAR 5 (b.c., May 27, 1970)

Bred by Mme. P. Wertheimer, in France.

Won 3 races, placed 1, 1,654,949 fr., in France, at 2 and 3 years, incl. Prix du Jockey-Club and Prix Greffulhe; 3rd Prix Lupin.

REFORM (b. 1964)	Pall Mall (ch. 1955)	Palestine	Fair Trial / Una
		Malapert	Portlaw / Malatesta
	Country House (br. 1955)	Vieux Manoir	Brantome / Vieille Maison
		Miss Coventry	Mieuxce / Coventry Belle
KALILA (b. 1961)	Beau Prince II (ch. 1952)	Prince Chevalier	Prince Rose / Chevalerie
		Isabelle Brand	Black Devil / Isabelle d'Este
	Vali (br. 1954)	Sunny Boy III	Jock II / Fille de Soleil
		Her Slipper	Tetratema / Carpet Slipper

807   ROLAND GARDENS 19 (b.c., May 9, 1975)

Bred by Mrs. C. A. Ryan.

Won 4 races, placed 5, £72,657, in England and France, from 2 to 4 years, incl. 2,000 Guineas Stakes, Ladbroke Blue Riband Trial Stakes; 3rd Horris Hill Stakes (won but disqualified).

DERRING-DO (b. 1961)	Darius (b. 1951)	Dante	Nearco / Rosy Legend
		Yasna	Dastur / Ariadne
	Sipsey Bridge (b. 1954)	Abernant	Owen Tudor / Rustom Mahal
		Claudette	Chanteur II / Nearly
KATRICIA (ch. 1968)	Skymaster (ch. 1958)	Golden Cloud	Gold Bridge / Rainstorm
		Discipliner	Court Martial / Edvina
	Anxious Call (ch. 1963)	Whistler	Panorama / Farthing Damages
		Julie	Denturius / Justitia

808   ROLLE 19 (ch.c., January 20, 1975)

Bred by Scuderia Alpina, in England.

Won 6 races, placed 15, 158,100,000 L., in Italy, from 2 to 4 years, incl. Premio Presidente della Repubblica; 2nd Gran Premio di Milano, Premio Parioli, Premio Presidente della Repubblica and Premio Pisa; 3rd Gran Premio di Milano, St. Leger Italiano and Premio Tevere; 4th Derby Italiano and Gran Criterium.

LORENZACCIO (ch. 1965)	Klairon (b. 1952)	Clarion III	Djebel / Columba
		Kalmia	Kantar / Sweet Lavender
	Phoenissa (b. 1951)	The Phoenix	Chateau Bouscaut / Fille de Poete
		Erica Fragrans	Big Game / Jennydang
RAYMONDA (ch. 1965)	Primera (b. 1954)	My Babu	Djebel / Perfume II
		Pirette	Deiri / Pimpette
	Pirouette (b. 1950)	Sayajirao	Nearco / Rosy Legend
		Epona	Portlaw / Jury

809   ROLL OF HONOUR 13 (ch.c., April 14, 1967)

Bred by Mrs. C. Weld, in Ireland.

Won 2 races, placed 3, 1,346,138 fr., in France, at 3 years, incl. Grand Prix de Paris; 2nd Prix du Jockey-Club.

MIRALGO (ch. 1959)	Aureole (ch. 1950)	Hyperion	Gainsborough / Selene
		Angelola	Donatello II / Feola
	Nella (ch. 1949)	Nearco	Pharos / Nogara
		Laitron	Soldennis / Chardon
TIME-HONOURED (b. or br. 1958)	Supreme Court (br. 1948)	Persian Gulf or Precipitation	Hurry On / Double Life
		Forecourt	Fair Trial / Overture
	Clockwise (ch. 1946)	Turkhan	Bahram / Theresina
		Hour-Glass	Horus / Castalian

810   ROMAN BROTHER 16 (b.g., May 27, 1961)

Bred by Ocala Stud Farms Inc., in U.S.A.

Won 16 races, placed 15, $943,473, in U.S.A., from 2 to 5 years, incl. Jockey Club Gold Cup, Woodward Stakes, American Derby, Jersey Derby, New Hampshire Sweepstakes, Champagne Stakes, Manhattan H., Discovery H. and Everglades Stakes; 2nd Belmont Stakes, Jockey Club Gold Cup, Garden State Stakes, Brooklyn H., Michigan Mile-and-One-Eighth H., Chicagoan Stakes, Lawrence Realization and Fountain of Youth Stakes; 3rd Washington D.C. International, Aqueduct Stakes, Wood Memorial Stakes and Dwyer H.; 4th Kentucky Derby.

THIRD BROTHER (b. 1953)	Princequillo (b. 1940)	Prince Rose	Rose Prince / Indolence
		Cosquilla	Papyrus / Quick Thought
	Hildene (b. 1938)	Bubbling Over	North Star III / Beaming Beauty
		Fancy Racket	Wrack / Ultimate Fancy
ROMAN ZEPHYR (b. 1947)	Roman (b. 1937)	Sir Gallahad III	Teddy / Plucky Liege
		Buckup	Buchan / Look Up
	Blois (b. 1940)	Man o'War	Fair Play / Mahubah
		Mademoiselle de Valois	Sardanapale / Marguerite de Valois

157

811 ROMULUS 2 (b.c., February 20, 1959)

Bred by Phil Bull.

Won 6 races, placed 4, £25,130, in England and France, from 2 to 4 years, incl. Greenham Stakes, Sussex Stakes, Queen Elizabeth II Stakes, Hungerford Stakes, Prix du Moulin de Longchamp; 2nd 2,000 Guineas, Champagne Stakes; 3rd Lockinge Stakes.

RIBOT (b. 1952)	Tenerani (b. 1944)	Bellini	Cavaliere d'Arpino / Bella Minna
		Tofanella	Apelle / Try Try Again
	Romanella (ch. 1943)	El Greco	Pharos / Gay Gamp
		Barbara Burrini	Papyrus / Bucolic
ARIETTA (br. 1953)	Tudor Minstrel (br. 1944)	Owen Tudor	Hyperion / Mary Tudor II
		Sansonnet	Sansovino / Lady Juror
	Anne of Essex (ch. 1941)	Panorama	Sir Cosmo / Happy Climax
		Queen of Essex	Essexford / Queen Cole

812 ROSE BOWL 4 (b.f., May 24, 1972)

Bred by Cragwood Estates Inc., in U.S.A.

Won 6 races, placed 9, £95,858, in England, France and U.S.A., from 2 to 4 years, incl. Champion Stakes, Queen Elizabeth II Stakes (twice), Ladbroke Nell Gwyn Stakes; 2nd Sussex Stakes, Champion Stakes, Waterford Crystal Mile; 3rd William Hill Cheveley Park Stakes, Prince of Wales Stakes; 4th 1,000 Guineas Stakes, Prix Ganay; 5th Washington D.C. International.

HABITAT (b. 1966)	Sir Gaylord (b. 1959)	Turn-to	Royal Charger / Source Sucree
		Somethingroyal	Princequillo / Imperatrice
	Little Hut (b. 1952)	Occupy	Bull Dog / Miss Bunting
		Savage Beauty	Challenger / Khara
ROSELIERE (b. 1965)	Misti IV (b. 1958)	Medium	Meridien / Melodie
		Mist	Tornado / La Touche
	Peace Rose (gr. 1959)	Fastnet Rock	Ocean Swell / Stone of Fortune
		La Paix	Seven Seas / Anne de Bretagne

813 ROSE DUBARRY 9 (b.f., May 2, 1969)

Bred by Brook Stud Co.

Won 3 races, placed 1, £13,614, in England, at 2 and 3 years, incl. Norfolk Stakes, Lowther Stakes; 3rd 1,000 Guineas Stakes.

KLAIRON (b. 1952)	Clarion III (b. 1944)	Djebel	Tourbillon / Loika
		Columba	Colorado / Gay Bird
	Kalmia (b. 1931)	Kantar	Alcantara II / Karabe
		Sweet Lavender	Swynford / Marchetta
PRISTINA (b. 1962)	Petition (br. 1944)	Fair Trial	Fairway / Lady Juror
		Art Paper	Artist's Proof / Quire
	Tina II (b. 1957)	Tulyar	Tehran / Neocracy
		Bibi Toori	Owen Tudor / Bibibeg

814 ROSELIERE 4 (b.f., May 1, 1965)

Bred by Mme. G. Bridgland and Mme. R. Canivet, in France.

Won 5 races, placed 3, 1,624,825 fr., in France, from 2 to 4 years, incl. Prix de Diane, Prix Vermeille, Prix Penelope and Prix de Pomone; 4th Prix de l'Arc de Triomphe.

MISTI IV (b. 1958)	Medium (b. 1946)	Meridien	Tourbillon / Meriem
		Melodie	Monarch / Mitidja II
	Mist (gr. 1953)	Tornado	Tourbillon / Roseola
		La Touche	Rienzo / La Rasina
PEACE ROSE (gr. 1959)	Fastnet Rock (gr. 1947)	Ocean Swell	Blue Peter / Jiffy
		Stone of Fortune	Mahmoud / Rosetta
	La Paix (b. 1951)	Seven Seas	Hyperion / Drift
		Anne de Bretagne	Teddy / Our Liz

815 ROUGE SANG 1 (b.c., February 14, 1972)

Bred by Elmendorf Farm, in U.S.A.

Won 4 races, placed 3, 507,446 fr., in France, Italy, England and U.S.A., at 3 and 4 years, incl. Gran Premio di Milano; 2nd John Porter Stakes; 3rd Grand Prix d'Evry and Man o'War Stakes.

BOLD BIDDER (b. 1962)	Bold Ruler (b. 1954)	Nasrullah	Nearco / Mumtaz Begum
		Miss Disco	Discovery / Outdone
	High Bid (b. 1956)	To Market	Market Wise / Pretty Does
		Stepping Stone	Princequillo / Step Across
RED DAMASK (ch. 1960)	Jet Action (ch. 1951)	Jet Pilot	Blenheim / Black Wave
		Busher	War Admiral / Baby League
	Nuit de Folies (b. 1947)	Tornado	Tourbillon / Roseola
		Folle Nuit	Astrophel / Folle Passion

816 ROUGHLYN 1 (ch.g., 1961)

Bred by H. Moss.

Won 12 races, placed 8, £10,259, in England, from 2 to 7 years, incl. King's Stand Stakes.

BALLYLINAN (br. 1950)	Denturius (ch. 1937)	Gold Bridge	Swynford or Golden Boss / Flying Diadem
		La Solfatara	Lemberg / Ayesha
	Rose Glen (br. 1941)	Rosewell	Orwell / Bower of Roses
		Glenart	Diligence / Tres Bonne
SUN GARDEN (ch. 1946)	Hyperides (ch. 1939)	Hyperion	Gainsborough / Selene
		Priscilla	Phalaris / Lammermuir
	Passefleur (b. 1940)	Pasch	Blandford / Pasca
		Alwoodley	Chaucer / Tatika

817   ROUSSALKA 9 (b.f., February 20, 1972)

Bred by Dalham Stud Farms Ltd.

Won 7 races, placed 6, £49,675, in England, from 2 to 4 years, incl. Nassau Stakes (twice), Coronation Stakes, Cherry Hinton Stakes; 2nd Child Stakes; 3rd Waterford Crystal Mile; 4th William Hill Cheveley Park Stakes.

HABITAT (b. 1966)	Sir Gaylord (b. 1959)	Turn-to	Royal Charger / Source Sucree
		Somethingroyal	Princequillo / Imperatrice
	Little Hut (b. 1952)	Occupy	Bull Dog / Miss Bunting
		Savage Beauty	Challenger / Khara
OH SO FAIR (b. 1967)	Graustark (ch. 1963)	Ribot	Tenerani / Romanella
		Flower Bowl	Alibhai / Flower Bed
	Chandelle (b. 1959)	Swaps	Khaled / Iron Reward
		Malindi	Nearco / Mumtaz Begum

818   ROYAL DANSEUSE 2 (b.f., May 12, 1961)

Bred by McGrath Trust Co.

Won 3 races, placed 3, £6,622, in Ireland and England, at 2 and 3 years, incl. Irish 1,000 Guineas Stakes, Athasi Stakes; 3rd 1,000 Guineas Stakes (dead-heat), Pretty Polly Stakes (Curragh).

PRINCE CHEVALIER (b. 1943)	Prince Rose (b. 1928)	Rose Prince	Prince Palatine / Eglantine
		Indolence	Gay Crusader / Barrier
	Chevalerie (b. 1933)	Abbot's Speed	Abbots Trace / Mary Gaunt
		Kassala	Cylgad / Farizade
STAR DANCER (br. 1954)	Arctic Star (br. 1942)	Nearco	Pharos / Nogara
		Serena	Winalot / Charmione
	Dancing Time (b. 1938)	Colombo	Manna / Lady Nairne
		Show Girl	Son-in-Law / Comedy Star

819   ROYAL GLINT 1 (b.g., May 8, 1970)

Bred by Claiborne Farm, in U.S.A.

Won 21 races, placed 13, $1,004,816, in U.S.A., from 3 to 6 years, incl. Santa Anita H., Trenton H., Grey Lag H., Razorback H., Salvator Mile, Amory L. Haskell H., Arlington H., United Nations H., Hawthorne Gold Cup, San Bernardino H., Kelly-Olympic H. and Patriot Stakes; 2nd Arlington Park H., National Thoroughbred Championship Invitational Stakes and Oaklawn H.; 3rd Minuteman H.

ROUND TABLE (b. 1954)	Princequillo (b. 1940)	Prince Rose	Rose Prince / Indolence
		Cosquilla	Papyrus / Quick Thought
	Knight's Daughter (br. 1941)	Sir Cosmo	The Boss / Ayn Hali
		Feola	Friar Marcus / Aloe
REGAL GLEAM (b. 'br. 1964)	Hail to Reason (br. 1958)	Turn-to	Royal Charger / Source Sucree
		Nothirdchance	Blue Swords / Galla Colors
	Miz Carol (b. 1953)	Stymie	Equestrian / Stop Watch
		No Fiddling	King Cole / Big Hurry

820   ROYAL HIVE 16 (b.f., February 20, 1974)

Bred by Beech House and Cliveden Studs.

Won 4 races, placed 6, £66,918, in England and France, from 2 to 4 years, incl. Park Hill Stakes; 2nd Yorkshire Oaks, Ascot Gold Cup, Prix Vermeille, Princess Royal Stakes.

ROYAL PALACE (b. 1964)	Ballymoss (ch. 1954)	Mossborough	Nearco / All Moonshine
		Indian Call	Singapore / Flittemere
	Crystal Palace (b. 1956)	Solar Slipper	Windsor Slipper / Solar Flower
		Queen of Light	Borealis / Picture Play
COME ON HONEY (ch. 1960)	Never Say Die (ch. 1951)	Nasrullah	Nearco / Mumtaz Begum
		Singing Grass	War Admiral / Boreale
	Honeylight (b. 1953)	Honeyway	Fairway / Honey Buzzard
		Crepuscule	Mieuxce / Red Sunset

821   ROYAL PALACE 1 (b.c., February 10, 1964)

Bred by H. J. Joel.

Won 9 races, placed 1, £166,063, in England, from 2 to 4 years, incl. Derby Stakes, 2,000 Guineas, King George VI and Queen Elizabeth Stakes, Eclipse Stakes, Coronation Cup, Prince of Wales Stakes, Royal Lodge Stakes, Coronation Stakes (Sandown Park); 3rd Champion Stakes.

BALLYMOSS (ch. 1954)	Mossborough (ch. 1947)	Nearco	Pharos / Nogara
		All Moonshine	Bobsleigh / Selene
	Indian Call (ch. 1936)	Singapore	Gainsborough / Tetrabbazia
		Flittemere	Buchan / Keysoe
CRYSTAL PALACE (b. 1956)	Solar Slipper (b. 1945)	Windsor Slipper	Windsor Lad / Carpet Slipper
		Solar Flower	Solario / Serena
	Queen of Light (b. 1949)	Borealis	Brumeux / Aurora
		Picture Play	Donatello II / Amuse

822   RUBY'S PRINCESS 31 (b.f., February 25, 1962)

Bred by E. A. Holt.

Won 4 races, placed 3, £6,108, in England, at 2 and 3 years, incl. 2nd Cherry Hinton Stakes; 3rd Oaks Stakes.

FIDALGO (b. 1956)	Arctic Star (br. 1942)	Nearco	Pharos / Nogara
		Serena	Winalot / Charmione
	Miss France (b. 1946)	Jock II	Asterus / Naic
		Nafah	Abjer / Flower
PERSIAN RUBY (ch. 1951)	Cambyses (ch. 1943)	Khosro	Sir Cosmo / Straight Sequence
		Mizzenette	Silvern / Orby Lass
	Rubric (ch. 1943)	Canon Law	Colorado / Book Law
		Rose Cygnet	Cygnus / Rose Window

823   **RUFFIAN** 8 (b./br.f., April 17, 1972)

Bred by Mr. and Mrs. Stuart S. Janney, Jr., in U.S.A.

Won 10 races, $313,428, in U.S.A., at 2 and 3 years, incl. Coaching Club American Oaks, Mother Goose Stakes, Acorn Stakes, Comely Stakes, Sorority Stakes and Spinaway Stakes.

REVIEWER (b. 1966)	Bold Ruler (b. 1954)	Nasrullah	Nearco
			Mumtaz Begum
		Miss Disco	Discovery
			Outdone
	Broadway (b. 1959)	Hasty Road	Roman
			Traffic Court
		Flitabout	Challedon
			Bird Flower
SHENANIGANS (gr. 1963)	Native Dancer (gr. 1950)	Polynesian	Unbreakable
			Black Polly
		Geisha	Discovery
			Miyako
	Bold Irish (b. 1948)	Fighting Fox	Sir Gallahad III
			Marguerite
		Erin	Transmute
			Rosie O'Grady

824   **RUN THE GANTLET** 5 (b.c., April 10, 1968)

Bred by Paul Mellon, in U.S.A.

Won 9 races, placed 5, $559,079, in U.S.A., from 2 to 4 years, incl. Washington D.C. International, Garden State Stakes, Man o'War Stakes, United Nations H., Tidal H., Kelly-Olympic H. and Bowling Green H.

TOM ROLFE (b. 1962)	Ribot (b. 1952)	Tenerani	Bellini
			Tofanella
		Romanella	El Greco
			Barbara Burrini
	Pocahontas (br. 1955)	Roman	Sir Gallahad III
			Buckup
		How	Princequillo
			The Squaw
FIRST FEATHER (ch. 1963)	First Landing (b. 1956)	Turn-to	Royal Charger
			Source Sucree
		Hildene	Bubbling Over
			Fancy Racket
	Quill (ch. 1956)	Princequillo	Prince Rose
			Cosquilla
		Quick Touch	Count Fleet
			Alms

825   **RUYSDAEL** 4 (b.c., April 23, 1964)

Bred by Razza Dormello-Olgiata, in England.

Won 8 races, placed 4, 86,743,200 L., in Italy and England, from 2 to 4 years, incl. Derby Italiano, Gran Premio d'Italia and Gran Premio del Jockey Club; 3rd St. Leger and Premio Emanuele Filiberto.

RIGHT ROYAL V (br. 1958)	Owen Tudor (br. 1938)	Hyperion	Gainsborough
			Selene
		Mary Tudor II	Pharos
			Anna Bolena
	Bastia (b. 1951)	Tornado or Victrix II	Kantar
			Victory
		Barberybush	Ksar
			Pervencheres
ROSSELLINA (b. 1957)	Tenerani (b. 1944)	Bellini	Cavaliere d'Arpino
			Bella Minna
		Tofanella	Apelle
			Try Try Again
	Romanella (ch. 1943)	El Greco	Pharos
			Gay Gamp
		Barbara Burrini	Papyrus
			Bucolic

826   **SAGACITY** 2 (b. or br.c., April 15, 1958)

Bred by Tally Ho Stud Co. Ltd.

Won 5 races, placed 9, £12,425, in England, at 3 and 4 years, incl. Yorkshire Cup, Goodwood Cup; 2nd Ascot Gold Cup, Doncaster Cup; 3rd Queen's Vase, Doncaster Cup, Princess of Wales's Stakes.

LE SAGE (b. 1948)	Chamossaire (ch. 1942)	Precipitation	Hurry On
			Double Life
		Snowberry	Cameronian
			Myrobella
	Miss Know All (br. 1940)	Rhodes Scholar	Pharos
			Book Law
		Dalmary	Blandford
			Simon's Shoes
DOUBLE CHARM (b. or br. 1951)	Epigram (br. 1933)	Son-in-Law	Dark Ronald
			Mother in Law
		Flying Sally	Flying Orb
			Salamandra
	Didima (br. 1944)	Nearco	Pharos
			Nogara
		Doubleton	Bahram
			Double Life

827   **SAGARO** 4 (ch.c., March 7, 1971)

Bred by Citadel Stud Establishment.

Won 10 races, placed 11, £270,780, in England and France, from 2 to 6 years, incl. Ascot Gold Cup (3 times), Grand Prix de Paris, Prix du Cadran, Prix de l'Esperance, Prix de Barbeville; 2nd Prix du Cadran, Prix Jean Prat, Prix de Barbeville (twice); 3rd Prix du Cadran, Prix Niel.

ESPRESSO (ch. 1958)	Acropolis (ch. 1952)	Donatello II	Blenheim
			Delleana
		Aurora	Hyperion
			Rose Red
	Babylon (b. 1940)	Bahram	Blandford
			Friar's Daughter
		Clairvoyante III	Clarissimus
			Doddles
ZAMBARA (b. 1966)	Mossborough (ch. 1947)	Nearco	Pharos
			Nogara
		All Moonshine	Bobsleigh
			Selene
	Grischuna (b. 1959)	Ratification	Court Martial
			Solesa
		Mountain Path	Bobsleigh
			Path of Peace

828   **SAINTLY SONG** 14 (b.c., February 21, 1967)

Bred by Eyrefield Stud Co.

Won 4 races, placed 2, £14,983, in England, from 2 to 4 years, incl. St. James's Palace Stakes, Champagne Stakes; 3rd Coventry Stakes, Westbury Stakes.

AUREOLE (ch. 1950)	Hyperion (ch. 1930)	Gainsborough	Bayardo
			Rosedrop
		Selene	Chaucer
			Serenissima
	Angelola (b. 1945)	Donatello II	Blenheim
			Delleana
		Feola	Friar Marcus
			Aloe
PRINCESS CECILIA (br. 1960)	Princely Gift (b. 1951)	Nasrullah	Nearco
			Mumtaz Begum
		Blue Gem	Blue Peter
			Sparkle
	Overture (br. 1937)	Dastur	Solario
			Friar's Daughter
		Overmantle	Apron
			Arabella

829 **SALLUST** 2 (ch.c., March 14, 1969)

Bred by Ballymacoll Stud Farm Ltd.

Won 7 races, placed 1, £57,925, in England and France, at 2 and 3 years, incl. Sussex Stakes, Prix du Moulin de Longchamp, Richmond Stakes, Goodwood Mile, Diomed Stakes, Prix de la Porte Maillot; 2nd National Stakes (Sandown).

PALL MALL (ch. 1955)	Palestine (gr. 1947)	Fair Trial	Fairway / Lady Juror
		Una	Tetratema / Uganda
	Malapert (ch. 1946)	Portlaw	Beresford / Portree
		Malatesta	Sansovino / Tetranella
BANDARILLA (ch. 1960)	Matador (ch. 1953)	Golden Cloud	Gold Bridge / Rainstorm
		Spanish Galantry	Mazarin / Courtship
	Interval (ch. 1948)	Jamaica Inn	King Salmon / Jamaica
		Second Act	The Font / Third Act

830 **SALVO** 16 (ch.c., April 18, 1963)

Bred by John W. Galbreath and Winston Guest, in U.S.A.

Won 6 races, placed 6, £73,677, in England, Germany and France, from 2 to 4 years, incl. Hardwicke Stakes, Yorkshire Cup, Craven Stakes, Grosser Preis von Baden; 2nd King George VI and Queen Elizabeth Stakes, John Porter Stakes, Preis von Europa, Prix de l'Arc de Triomphe; 3rd Dante Stakes.

RIGHT ROYAL V (br. 1958)	Owen Tudor (br. 1938)	Hyperion	Gainsborough / Selene
		Mary Tudor II	Pharos / Anna Bolena
	Bastia (b. 1951)	Tornado or Victrix II	Kantar / Victory
		Barberybush	Ksar / Pervencheres
MANERA (ch. 1957)	Macherio (ch. 1941)	Ortello	Teddy / Hollebeck
		Mannozza	Manna / Moireen Rhue
	Maenza (b. 1952)	Orsenigo	Oleander / Ostana
		Maggiolina	Nakamuro / Murcia

831 **SAMMY DAVIS** 5 (br.c., April 25, 1960)

Bred by Mrs. A. Levins Moore.

Won 5 races, placed 1, £7,439, in England, at 2 and 3 years, incl. Palace House Stakes, Diadem Stakes.

WHISTLER (ch. 1950)	Panorama (ch. 1936)	Sir Cosmo	The Boss / Ayn Hali
		Happy Climax	Happy Warrior / Clio
	Farthing Damages (ch. 1939)	Fair Trial	Fairway / Lady Juror
		Futility	Solario / Hasty Love
SAMARIA (br. 1955)	Migoli (gr. 1944)	Bois Roussel	Vatout / Plucky Liege
		Mah Iran	Bahram / Mah Mahal
	Sarie (b. 1946)	Nearco	Pharos / Nogara
		Gold Mary	Solario / Dalmary

832 **SAMOS III** 16 (ch.c., 1964)

Bred by Countess Margit Batthyany, in Ireland.

Won 7 races, placed 12, 1,544,412 fr., in France, England, Germany and U.S.A., from 3 to 6 years, incl. Prix Royal Oak and Prix Gladiateur; 2nd Ascot Gold Cup and Prix Jean Prat (twice); 3rd Prix du Cadran, Prix Kergorlay (twice) and Prix de Barbeville (twice); 4th Grosser Preis von Baden and Yankee Gold Cup.

SHESHOON (ch. 1956)	Precipitation (ch. 1933)	Hurry On	Marcovil / Tout Suite
		Double Life	Bachelor's Double / Saint Joan
	Noorani (ch. 1950)	Nearco	Pharos / Nogara
		Empire Glory	Singapore / Skyglory
SOLOTANZERIN (b. 1954)	Ticino (b. 1939)	Athanasius	Ferro / Athanasie
		Terra	Aditi / Teufelsrose
	Sansovina (ch. 1947)	Niccolo Dell'Arca	Coronach / Nogara
		Serangela	El Greco / Santaria

833 **SANCTUS II** 16 (b.c., February 28, 1960)

Bred by Jean Ternynck, in France.

Won 6 races, placed 5, 1,503,121 fr., in France, at 2 and 3 years, incl. Prix du Jockey Club and Grand Prix de Paris; 2nd Criterium de Saint-Cloud; 3rd Prix Lupin; 4th Prix Royal Oak.

FINE TOP (br. 1949)	Fine Art (b. 1939)	Artist's Proof	Gainsborough / Clear Evidence
		Finnoise	Finglas / Unfortunate
	Toupie (br. 1943)	Vatellor	Vatout / Lady Elinor
		Tarentella	Blenheim / Andalusia
SANELTA (b. 1954)	Tourment (b. 1944)	Tourbillon	Ksar / Durban
		Fragment	Shred / Pearl Drop
	Satanella (bl. 1941)	Mahmoud	Blenheim / Mah Mahal
		Avella	Epinard / Noor Jahan

834 **SANDFORD LAD** 13 (ch.c., April 27, 1970)

Bred by Mrs. P. Grubb.

Won 7 races, placed 1, £24,648, in England and France, at 2 and 3 years, incl. Prix de l'Abbaye de Longchamp, Nunthorpe Stakes, King George Stakes.

ST. ALPHAGE (ch. 1963)	Red God (ch. 1954)	Nasrullah	Nearco / Mumtaz Begum
		Spring Run	Menow / Boola Brook
	Sally Deans (ch. 1947)	Fun Fair	Fair Trial / Humoresque
		Cora Deans	Coronach / Jennie Deans
HILL QUEEN (b. 1958)	Djebe (gr. 1945)	Djebel	Tourbillon / Loika
		Catherine	Tiberius / Catherinette
	Home Rule (b. 1950)	Norseman	Umidwar / Tara
		Motherland	Gainsborough / Fair Isle

835   **SANDY CREEK** 1 (ch.c., March 21, 1976)

Bred by O. Freaney.

Won 2 races, placed 2, £43,836, in Ireland and England, at 2 years, incl. William Hill Futurity Stakes, Larkspur Stakes; 2nd Beresford Stakes; 3rd National Stakes (Curragh).

PETINGO (b. 1965)	Petition (br. 1944)	Fair Trial	Fairway / Lady Juror
		Art Paper	Artist's Proof / Quire
	Alcazar (ch. 1957)	Alycidon	Donatello II / Aurora
		Quarterdeck	Nearco / Poker Chip
KEEP RIGHT (ch. 1969)	Klairon (b. 1952)	Clarion III	Djebel / Columba
		Kalmia	Kantar / Sweet Lavender
	Narrow Escape (ch. 1960)	Narrator	Nearco / Phase
		Press Forward	Precipitation / Running Wild

---

836   **SANEDTKI** 22 (b.f., April 13, 1974)

Bred by C. J. Powell, in Ireland.

Won 10 races, placed 13, 2,183,331 fr., in France, England and U.S.A., from 2 to 5 years, incl. Prix de la Foret (twice), Prix du Moulin de Longchamp, Ascot 1,000 Guineas Trial Stakes, Prix d'Astarté, Prix de Ris-Orangis, Prix Edmond Blanc and Santa Margarita Invitational H.; 2nd July Cup, Vernons Sprint Cup, Prix Jacques le Marois, Prix des Reservoirs, Prix Quincey, Prix du Rond-Point and Prix du Muguet; 3rd 1,000 Guineas, Prix Saint-Alary, Prix du Moulin de Longchamp and Prix Maurice de Gheest.

SALLUST (ch. 1969)	Pall Mall (ch. 1955)	Palestine	Fair Trial / Una
		Malapert	Portlaw / Malatesta
	Bandarilla (ch. 1960)	Matador	Golden Cloud / Spanish Galantry
		Interval	Jamaica Inn / Second Act
FORTLIN (b. 1966)	Fortino II (gr. 1959)	Grey Sovereign	Nasrullah / Kong
		Ranavalo III	Relic / Navarra II
	Creepy Crawley (br. 1956)	The Bug	Signal Light / Flying Meteor
		Iverley Way	Apron / Smoke Alley

---

837   **SANG BLEU** 23 (b.c., May 11, 1969)

Bred by Mme. Cino Del Duca, in France.

Won 5 races, placed 8, 1,060,750 fr., in France and Italy, from 2 to 5 years, incl. Gran Premio del Jockey Club, Premio Roma and La Coupe; 2nd Gran Premio di Milano, Gran Premio del Jockey Club, Prix Noailles and Prix de Barbeville; 3rd Prix Foy (twice).

RIGHT ROYAL V (br. 1958)	Owen Tudor (br. 1938)	Hyperion	Gainsborough / Selene
		Mary Tudor II	Pharos / Anna Bolena
	Bastia (b. 1951)	Tornado or Victrix II	Kantar / Victory
		Barberybush	Ksar / Pervencheres
ROYAL GIRL (b. 1960)	Norseman (b. 1940)	Umidwar	Blandford / Uganda
		Tara	Teddy / Jean Gow
	Royal Union (b. 1943)	Scottish Union	Cameronian / Trustful
		Joan Drake	Admiral Drake / Joan of Navarre

---

838   **SAN SAN** 7 (b.f., April 9, 1969)

Bred by Capt. H. F. Guggenheim, in U.S.A.

Won 4½ races, placed 9, 2,152,605 fr., in France and U.S.A., at 2 and 3 years, incl. Prix de l'Arc de Triomphe, Prix Vermeille (dead-heat) and Prix de Psyche; 2nd Prix de la Nonette; 4th Washington D.C. International.

BALD EAGLE (b. 1955)	Nasrullah (b. 1940)	Nearco	Pharos / Nogara
		Mumtaz Begum	Blenheim / Mumtaz Mahal
	Siama (b. 1947)	Tiger	Bull Dog / Starless Moment
		China Face	Display / Sweepilla
SAIL NAVY (b. 1958)	Princequillo (b. 1940)	Prince Rose	Rose Prince / Indolence
		Cosquilla	Papyrus / Quick Thought
	Anchors Aweigh (b. 1949)	Devil Diver	St. Germans / Dabchick
		True Bearing	Sir Gallahad III / Dead Reckoning

---

839   **SANTA CLAUS** 3 (b.c., February 12, 1961)

Bred by Dr. F. A. Smorfitt.

Won 4 races, placed 2, £153,714, in England, Ireland and France, at 2 and 3 years, incl. Derby Stakes, Irish 2,000 Guineas, Irish Sweeps Derby, National Stakes (Curragh); 2nd King George VI and Queen Elizabeth Stakes, Prix de l'Arc de Triomphe.

CHAMOSSAIRE (ch. 1942)	Precipitation (ch. 1933)	Hurry On	Marcovil / Tout Suite
		Double Life	Bachelor's Double / Saint Joan
	Snowberry (br. 1937)	Cameronian	Pharos / Una Cameron
		Myrobella	Tetratema / Dolabella
AUNT CLARA (br. 1953)	Arctic Prince (br. 1948)	Prince Chevalier	Prince Rose / Chevalerie
		Arctic Sun	Nearco / Solar Flower
	Sister Clara (b. 1938)	Scarlet Tiger	Colorado / Trilogy
		Clarence	Diligence / Nun's Veil

---

840   **SANTA TINA** 5 (br.f., June 2, 1967)

Bred by S. O'Flaherty.

Won 7 races, placed 1, £49,095, in Ireland, France and U.S.A., at 3 and 4 years, incl. Irish Guinness Oaks, Prix de Royaumont, Prix de Pomone.

SANTA CLAUS (b. 1961)	Chamossaire (ch. 1942)	Precipitation	Hurry On / Double Life
		Snowberry	Cameronian / Myrobella
	Aunt Clara (br. 1953)	Arctic Prince	Prince Chevalier / Arctic Sun
		Sister Clara	Scarlet Tiger / Clarence
REINE DES BOIS (b. 1950)	Bois Roussel (br. 1935)	Vatout	Prince Chimay / Vasthi
		Plucky Liege	Spearmint / Concertina
	Queen of Shiraz (b. 1937)	Bahram	Blandford / Friar's Daughter
		Qurrat-al-Ain	Buchan / Harpsichord

841   SARACA 21 (b.f., 1966)

Bred by Dollanstown Stud Establishment, in Ireland.

Won 5 races, placed 1, 1,360,124 fr., in France, at 2 and 3 years, incl. Prix Vermeille, Prix Saint-Alary, Prix Penelope and Criterium de Saint-Cloud; 2nd Prix de Diane.

SHANTUNG (b. 1956)	Sicambre (br. 1948)	Prince Bio	Prince Rose / Biologie
		Sif	Rialto / Suavita
	Barley Corn (b. 1950)	Hyperion	Gainsborough / Selene
		Schiaparelli	Schiavoni / Aileen
HEVEA (b. 1961)	Herbager (b. 1956)	Vandale II	Plassy / Vanille
		Flagette	Escamillo / Fidgette
	Princesse Reine (b. 1954)	Prince Chevalier	Prince Rose / Chevalerie
		Kingscavil	Fair Trial / Phase

842   SARAH SIDDONS 9 (b.f., May 6, 1973)

Bred by Ardenode Stud Ltd., in France.

Won 3 races, placed 6, £82,967, in Ireland, England and France, from 2 to 4 years, incl. Irish 1,000 Guineas, Yorkshire Oaks; 2nd Irish Guinness Oaks, Prix Vermeille, Athasi Stakes; 3rd Gladness Stakes; 4th Benson and Hedges Gold Cup.

LE LEVANSTELL (b. 1957)	Le Lavandou (b. 1944)	Djebel	Tourbillon / Loika
		Lavande	Rustom Pasha / Livadia
	Stella's Sister (ch. 1950)	Ballyogan	Fair Trial / Serial
		My Aid	Knight of the Garter / Flying Aid
MARIEL (b. 1968)	Relko (b. 1960)	Tanerko	Tantieme / La Divine
		Relance III	Relic / Polaire II
	Ela Marita (ch. 1961)	Red God	Nasrullah / Spring Run
		Fantan II	Ambiorix II / Red Eye

843   SARITAMER 14 (gr.c., March 9, 1971)

Bred by Mrs. Bruce M. Donaldson, in U.S.A.

Won 8 races, placed 4, £27,054, in Ireland and England, at 2 and 3 years, incl. Beresford Stakes, Anglesey Stakes, Cork and Orrery Stakes, July Cup, Diadem Stakes; 3rd Curragh Stakes, Nunthorpe Stakes; 4th William Hill Middle Park Stakes.

DANCER'S IMAGE (gr. 1965)	Native Dancer (gr. 1955)	Polynesian	Unbreakable / Black Polly
		Geisha	Discovery / Miyako
	Noors Image (b. 1953)	Noor	Nasrullah / Queen of Baghdad
		Little Sphinx	Challenger / Khara
IRISH CHORUS (b. 1960)	Ossian II (b. 1952)	Royal Charger	Nearco / Sun Princess
		Prudent Polly	Atout Maitre / Sister Anne
	Dawn Chorus (ch. 1951)	Rising Light	Hyperion / Bread Card
		Duke's Delight	His Grace / Early Light

844   SASSAFRAS 8 (b.c., February 19, 1967)

Bred by Dollanstown Stud Establishment, in France.

Won 6 races, placed 4, 3,306,460 fr., in France, at 2 and 3 years, incl. Prix du Jockey-Club, Prix Royal Oak, Prix de l'Arc de Triomphe and Prix La Force; 3rd Prix Lupin.

SHESHOON (ch. 1956)	Precipitation (ch. 1933)	Hurry On	Marcovil / Tout Suite
		Double Life	Bachelor's Double / Saint Joan
	Noorani (ch. 1950)	Nearco	Pharos / Nogara
		Empire Glory	Singapore / Skyglory
RUTA (b. 1960)	Ratification (b. 1953)	Court Martial	Fair Trial / Instantaneous
		Solesa	Solario / Mesa
	Dame d'Atour (b. 1955)	Cranach	Coronach / Reine Isaure
		Barley Corn	Hyperion / Schiaparelli

845   SATINGO 3 (b.c., March 9, 1970)

Bred by Mme. P. Wertheimer, in Ireland.

Won 4 races, placed 2, 842,159 fr., in France, at 2 and 3 years, incl. Grand Criterium, Prix La Rochette and Prix de la Jonchere; 3rd Poule d'Essai des Poulains and Prix de Fontainebleau.

PETINGO (b. 1965)	Petition (br. 1944)	Fair Trial	Fairway / Lady Juror
		Art Paper	Artist's Proof / Quire
	Alcazar (ch. 1957)	Alycidon	Donatello II / Aurora
		Quarterdeck	Nearco / Poker Chip
SAQUEBUTE (b. 1961)	Klairon (b. 1952)	Clarion III	Djebel / Columba
		Kalmia	Kantar / Sweet Lavender
	Synaldo (b. 1955)	Tantieme	Deux pour Cent / Terka
		Stratonice	Priam II / Step Along

846   SCHÖNBRUNN 16 (b.f., April 6, 1966)

Bred by Gestüt Schlenderhan, in Germany.

Won 6 races, placed 9, 496,675 fr., in Germany and France, from 2 to 4 years, incl. Schwarzgold-Rennen, Preis der Diana and Grand Prix de Deauville; 2nd Prix de Flore; 3rd Prix de la Nonette and Prix Foy.

PANTHEON (b. 1958)	Borealis (ch. 1941)	Brumeux	Teddy / La Brume
		Aurora	Hyperion / Rose Red
	Palazzo (br. 1950)	Dante	Nearco / Rosy Legend
		Edifice	Monument / Phalconia
SCHEHEREZADE (br. 1952)	Ticino (b. 1939)	Athanasius	Ferro / Athanasie
		Terra	Aditi / Teufelsrose
	Schwarzblaurot (br. 1947)	Magnat	Asterus / Mafalda
		Schwarzgold	Alchimist / Schwarzliesel

847   **SCINTILLATE** 6 (b.f., January 24, 1976)

Bred by Fonthill Stud.

Won 2 races, placed 3, £52,027, in England, at 2 and 3 years, incl. Oaks Stakes.

SPARKLER (b. 1968)	Hard Tack (b. 1955)	Hard Sauce	Ardan / Saucy Bella
		Cowes	Blue Peter / Lighthearted
	Diamond Spur (ch. 1961)	Preciptic	Precipitation / Artistic
		Diamond Princess	His Highness / Hatton
SET FREE (b. 1964)	Worden II (ch. 1949)	Wild Risk	Rialto / Wild Violet
		Sans Tares	Sind / Tara
	Emancipation (b. 1954)	Le Sage	Chamossaire / Miss Know All
		Fair Freedom	Fair Trial / Democratie

848   **SCORPIO** 4 (b.c., March 8, 1976)

Bred by G. A. Oldham, in France.

Won 7 races, placed 2, £129,412, in France, Italy, England and Ireland, at 3 and 4 years, incl. Gran Premio del Jockey Club, Grand Prix d'Evry, Hardwicke Stakes; 2nd Prix du Lys; 4th Irish Sweeps Derby.

SIR GAYLORD (b. 1959)	Turn-to (b. 1951)	Royal Charger	Nearco / Sun Princess
		Source Sucree	Admiral Drake / Lavendula
	Somethingroyal (b. 1952)	Princequillo	Prince Rose / Cosquilla
		Imperatrice	Caruso / Cinquepace
ZAMBARA (b. 1966)	Mossborough (ch. 1947)	Nearco	Pharos / Nogara
		All Moonshine	Bobsleigh / Selene
	Grischuna (b. 1959)	Ratification	Court Martial / Solesa
		Mountain Path	Bobsleigh / Path of Peace

849   **SCOTTISH RIFLE** 15 (br.c., April 17, 1969)

Bred by Woodpark Ltd.

Won 10 races, placed 8, £91,822, in England, Ireland and U.S.A., from 2 to 4 years, incl. Eclipse Stakes, Gordon Stakes, Earl of Sefton Stakes, Brigadier Gerard Stakes, Westbury Stakes, Cumberland Lodge Stakes; 2nd Irish Sweeps Derby, Benson and Hedges Gold Cup, Prince of Wales's Stakes, Blue Riband Trial Stakes; 3rd Washington D.C. International.

SUNNY WAY (b. 1957)	Honeyway (br. 1941)	Fairway	Phalaris / Scapa Flow
		Honey Buzzard	Papyrus / Lady Peregrine
	Red Sunset (b. 1941)	Solario	Gainsborough / Sun Worship
		Dulce II	Asterus / Dorina
RADIOPYE (gr. 1954)	Bright News (b. 1943)	Stardust	Hyperion / Sister Stella
		Inkling	Son-in-Law / Gleam
	Silversol (gr. 1940)	Solenoid	Soldennis / Shannon Jug
		Silver Lady	Old Rowley / Elland

850   **SEA ANCHOR** 11 (ch.c., March 21, 1972)

Bred by R. D. Hollingsworth.

Won 5 races, placed 6, £40,857, in England and Ireland, from 2 to 4 years, incl. King Edward VII Stakes, Henry II Stakes, Doncaster Cup; 2nd Great Voltigeur Stakes; 3rd Ascot Gold Cup, Yorkshire Cup; 4th Irish Sweeps Derby.

ALCIDE (b. 1955)	Alycidon (ch. 1945)	Donatello II	Blenheim / Delleana
		Aurora	Hyperion / Rose Red
	Chenille (br. 1940)	King Salmon	Salmon-Trout / Malva
		Sweet Aloe	Cameronian / Aloe
ANCHOR (ch. 1966)	Major Portion (ch. 1955)	Court Martial	Fair Trial / Instantaneous
		Better Half	Mieuxce / Malay Bride
	Ripeck (br. 1959)	Ribot	Tenerani / Romanella
		Kyak	Big Game / Felucca

851   **SEA BIRD II** 2 (ch.c., March 8, 1962)

Bred by J. Ternynck, in France.

Won 7 races, placed 1, £230,174, in France and England, at 2 and 3 years, incl. Prix de l'Arc de Triomphe, Grand Prix de Saint-Cloud, Prix Lupin, Prix Greffulhe, Derby Stakes; 2nd Grand Criterium.

DAN CUPID (ch. 1956)	Native Dancer (gr. 1950)	Polynesian	Unbreakable / Black Polly
		Geisha	Discovery / Miyako
	Vixenette (ch. 1944)	Sickle	Phalaris / Selene
		Lady Reynard	Gallant Fox / Nerva
SICALADE (b. 1956)	Sicambre (br. 1948)	Prince Bio	Prince Rose / Biologie
		Sif	Rialto / Suavita
	Marmelade (b. 1949)	Maurepas	Aethelstan / Broceliande
		Couleur	Biribi / Colour Bar

852   **SEA CHIMES** 13 (ch.c., March 8, 1976)

Bred by Ballykisteen Stud.

Won 8 races, placed 3, £80,717, in England, from 2 to 4 years, incl. Coronation Cup; 4th Coral Eclipse Stakes.

GULF PEARL (ch. 1962)	Persian Gulf (b. 1940)	Bahram	Blandford / Friar's Daughter
		Double Life	Bachelor's Double / Saint Joan
	Nan (ch. 1955)	Nearco	Pharos / Nogara
		Marsyaka	Marsyas II / Nokka
CANTERBURY BELLE (ch. 1971)	St. Alphage (ch. 1963)	Red God	Nasrullah / Spring Run
		Sally Deans	Fun Fair / Cora Deans
	Palamina (ch. 1962)	Pall Mall	Palestine / Malapert
		Miss Stephen	Stephen Paul / Bright Set

853   **SEAFRIEND** 14 (ch.c., March 11, 1968)

Bred by Captain D. Rogers.

Won 4 races, placed 3, £17,663, in Ireland and England, at 2 and 3 years incl. King Edward VII Stakes, Nijinsky Stakes.

SEA HAWK II (gr. 1963)	Herbager (b. 1956)	Vandale II	Plassy / Vanille
		Flagette	Escamillo / Fidgette
	Sea Nymph (gr. 1957)	Free Man	Norseman / Fantine
		Sea Spray	Ocean Swell / Pontoon
CHARA (ch. 1961)	Buisson Ardent (ch. 1953)	Relic	War Relic / Bridal Colors
		Rose o'Lynn	Pherozshah / Rocklyn
	Witness (b. or br. 1955)	Court Martial	Fair Trial / Instantaneous
		Crawley Beauty	Big Game / Overture

854   **SEA HAWK II** 3 (gr.c., March 16, 1963)

Bred by C. Puerari, in France.

Won 3 races, placed 3, 703,279 fr., in France, at 2 and 3 years, incl. Grand Prix de Saint-Cloud and Criterium de Saint-Cloud; 2nd Prix Hocquart.

HERBAGER (b. 1956)	Vandale II (b. 1943)	Plassy	Bosworth / Pladda
		Vanille	La Farina / Vaya
	Flagette (ch. 1951)	Escamillo	Firdaussi / Estoril
		Fidgette	Firdaussi / Boxeuse
SEA NYMPH (gr. 1957)	Free Man (b. 1948)	Norseman	Umidwar / Tara
		Fantine	Fantastic / Sif
	Sea Spray (gr. 1947)	Ocean Swell	Blue Peter / Jiffy
		Pontoon	Mahmoud / Ponteba

855   **SEATTLE SLEW** 13 (br.c., February 15, 1974)

Bred by Ben S. Castleman, in U.S.A.

Won 14 races, placed 2, $1,208,726, in U.S.A., from 2 to 4 years, incl. Kentucky Derby, Preakness Stakes, Belmont Stakes, Wood Memorial Stakes, Flamingo Stakes, Marlboro Cup, Woodward Stakes, Champagne Stakes and Stuyvesant H.; 2nd Jockey Club Gold Cup and Paterson H.

BOLD REASONING (br. 1968)	Boldnesian (b. 1963)	Bold Ruler	Nasrullah / Miss Disco
		Alanesian	Polynesian / Alablue
	Reason to Earn (b. 1963)	Hail to Reason	Turn-to / Nothirdchance
		Sailing Home	Wait A Bit / Marching Home
MY CHARMER (b. 1969)	Poker (b. 1963)	Round Table	Princequillo / Knight's Daughter
		Glamour	Nasrullah / Striking
	Fair Charmer (ch. 1959)	Jet Action	Jet Pilot / Busher
		Myrtle Charm	Alsab / Crepe Myrtle

856   **SECRETARIAT** 2 (ch.c., March 30, 1970)

Bred by Meadow Stud Inc., in U.S.A.

Won 16 races, placed 4, $1,316,808, in U.S.A. and Canada, at 2 and 3 years, incl. Kentucky Derby, Preakness Stakes, Belmont Stakes, Marlboro Cup, Arlington Invitational Stakes, Canadian International Championship, Man o'War Stakes, Gotham Stakes, Bay Shore Stakes, Garden State Stakes, Futurity Stakes, Hopeful Stakes, Laurel Futurity and Sanford Stakes; 2nd Champagne Stakes, Woodward Stakes and Whitney Stakes; 3rd Wood Memorial Stakes.

BOLD RULER (b. 1954)	Nasrullah (b. 1940)	Nearco	Pharos / Nogara
		Mumtaz Begum	Blenheim / Mumtaz Mahal
	Miss Disco (b. 1944)	Discovery	Display / Ariadne
		Outdone	Pompey / Sweep Out
SOMETHINGROYAL (b. 1952)	Princequillo (b. 1940)	Prince Rose	Rose Prince / Indolence
		Cosquilla	Papyrus / Quick Thought
	Imperatrice (b. 1938)	Caruso	Polymelian / Sweet Music
		Cinquepace	Brown Bud / Assignation

857   **SECRET STEP** 2 (gr.f., April 26, 1959)

Bred by P. Mellon, in U.S.A.

Won 6 races, placed 4, £12,122, in England, from 2 to 4 years, incl. July Cup, King George Stakes; 2nd Nunthorpe Stakes, Diadem Stakes.

NATIVE DANCER (gr. 1950)	Polynesian (br. 1942)	Unbreakable	Sickle / Blue Glass
		Black Polly	Polymelian / Black Queen
	Geisha (ro. 1943)	Discovery	Display / Ariadne
		Miyako	John P. Grier / La Chica
TAP DAY (b. 1947)	Bull Lea (br. 1935)	Bull Dog	Teddy / Plucky Liege
		Rose Leaves	Ballot / Colonial
	Scurry (b. 1937)	Diavolo	Whisk Broom II / Vexatious
		Slapdash	Stimulus / Tetrarchy

858   **SELHURST** 1 (b.c., April 26, 1968)

Bred by H. J. Joel.

Won 4 races, placed 7, £21,400, in England, from 2 to 4 years, incl. Hardwicke Stakes, Ormonde Stakes; 2nd King Edward VII Stakes, Gordon Stakes, John Porter Stakes; 3rd Royal Lodge Stakes, Dee Stakes, Doncaster Cup.

CHARLOTTESVILLE (b. 1957)	Prince Chevalier (b. 1943)	Prince Rose	Rose Prince / Indolence
		Chevalerie	Abbot's Speed / Kassala
	Noorani (ch. 1950)	Nearco	Pharos / Nogara
		Empire Glory	Singapore / Skyglory
CRYSTAL PALACE (b. 1956)	Solar Slipper (b. 1945)	Windsor Slipper	Windsor Lad / Carpet Slipper
		Solar Flower	Solario / Serena
	Queen of Light (b. 1949)	Borealis	Brumeux / Aurora
		Picture Play	Donatello II / Amuse

859 SEROV 19 (b.c., April 7, 1963)

Bred by Allevamento Gibi, in Italy.

Won 16 races, placed 21, 37,729,000 L., in Italy, from 2 to 8 years, incl. Gran Premio d'Italia; 3rd Premio Ambrosiano.

BOTTICELLI (b. 1951)	Blue Peter (ch. 1936)	Fairway	Phalaris / Scapa Flow
		Fancy Free	Stefan the Great / Celiba
	Buonamica (b. 1943)	Niccolo Dell'Arca	Coronach / Nogara
		Bernina	Pharos / Bunworry
SERNAGLIA (b. 1946)	Orsenigo (b. 1940)	Oleander	Prunus / Orchidee II
		Ostana	Havresac II / Olba
	Signa (b. 1939)	Ortello	Teddy / Hollebeck
		Superga	Michelangelo / Suna

860 SEXTON BLAKE 9 (gr.c., May 20, 1975)

Bred by C. A. Ryan.

Won 5 races, placed 6, £74,858, in England and Ireland, from 2 to 4 years, incl. Seaton Delaval Stakes, Laurent Perrier Champagne Stakes, Gordon Stakes and Westbury Stakes; 2nd William Hill Dewhurst Stakes, Great Voltigeur Stakes and Joe McGrath Memorial Stakes; 3rd Mecca-Dante Stakes and Brigadier Gerard Stakes.

BLAKENEY (b. 1966)	Hethersett (b. 1959)	Hugh Lupus	Djebel / Sakountala
		Bride Elect	Big Game / Netherton Maid
	Windmill Girl (b. 1961)	Hornbeam	Hyperion / Thicket
		Chorus Beauty	Chanteur II / Neberna
MAYO BLUES (gr. 1964)	Abernant (gr. 1946)	Owen Tudor	Hyperion / Mary Tudor II
		Rustom Mahal	Rustom Pasha / Mumtaz Mahal
	Persian Harp (br./bl. 1951)	Persian Gulf	Bahram / Double Life
		Belle Travers	Mr. Jinks / Futurity

861 SHAFARAZ 11 (b.c., May 5, 1973)

Bred by H.H. Aga Khan, in France.

Won 10 races, placed 12, 1,349,500 fr., in France, from 3 to 7 years, incl. Prix du Cadran, Prix Kergorlay and Prix de Barbeville; 2nd Prix du Cadran; 3rd Grand Prix de Vichy, Prix Kergorlay (twice), Prix Jean Prat and Prix Gladiateur; 4th Prix Royal Oak.

LEVMOSS (b. 1965)	Le Levanstell (b. 1957)	Le Lavandou	Djebel / Lavande
		Stella's Sister	Ballyogan / My Aid
	Feemoss (b. 1960)	Ballymoss	Mossborough / Indian Call
		Feevagh	Solar Slipper / Astrid Wood
ASHARAZ (gr. 1967)	Sicambre (br. 1948)	Prince Bio	Prince Rose / Biologie
		Sif	Rialto / Suavita
	Vareta (gr. 1953)	Vilmorin	Gold Bridge / Queen of the Meadows
		Veronique II	Mon Talisman / Volubilis

862 SHAKAPOUR 3 (gr.c., April 2, 1977)

Bred by H.H. Aga Khan, in Ireland.

Won 2½ races, placed 4, 1,032,000 fr., in France, at 2 and 3 years, incl. Grand Prix de Saint-Cloud (dead-heat) and Prix de Guiche; 2nd Prix du Jockey-Club.

KALAMOUN (gr. 1970)	Zeddaan (gr. 1965)	Grey Sovereign	Nasrullah / Kong
		Vareta	Vilmorin / Veronique II
	Khairunissa (gr. 1960)	Prince Bio	Prince Rose / Biologie
		Palariva	Palestine / Rivaz
SHAMIM (ch. 1968)	Le Haar (ch. 1954)	Vieux Manoir	Brantome / Vieille Maison
		Mince Pie	Teleferique / Cannelle
	Diamond Drop (ch. 1963)	Charlottesville	Prince Chevalier / Noorani
		Martine	Palestine / Pale Ale

863 SHAM 9 (b.c., April 9, 1970)

Bred by Claiborne Farm, in U.S.A.

Won 5 races, placed 6, $204,808, in U.S.A., at 2 and 3 years, incl. Santa Anita Derby; 2nd Kentucky Derby, Preakness Stakes and Wood Memorial Stakes.

PRETENSE (b./br. 1963)	Endeavour II (b. 1942)	British Empire	Colombo / Rose of England
		Himalaya	Hunter's Moon / Partenope
	Imitation (ch. 1951)	Hyperion	Gainsborough / Selene
		Flattery	Winalot / Fickle
SEQUOIA (b. 1955)	Princequillo (b. 1940)	Prince Rose	Rose Prince / Indolence
		Cosquilla	Papyrus / Quick Thought
	The Squaw II (b. 1939)	Sickle	Phalaris / Selene
		Minnewaska	Blandford / Nipisiquit

864 SHAMSAN 31 (ch.c., March 14, 1969)

Bred by Ballydoyle Stud, in Ireland.

Won 13 races, placed 13, 119,665,331 L., in Italy, England and France, from 2 to 7 years, incl. Premio Presidente della Repubblica, Premio Emilio Turati and Premio Roma Vecchia; 3rd Premio Presidente della Repubblica and Premio Chiusura.

FORTINO II (gr. 1959)	Grey Sovereign (gr. 1948)	Nasrullah	Nearco / Mumtaz Begum
		Kong	Baytown / Clang
	Ranavalo III (b. 1954)	Relic	War Relic / Bridal Colors
		Navarra II	Orsenigo / Nervesa
CHAMPAC (ch. 1957)	Chamier (ch. 1950)	Chamossaire	Precipitation / Snowberry
		Therapia	Panorama / Silvonessa
	Greek Train (b. 1951)	Blue Train	Blue Peter / Sun Chariot
		Fair Greek	Fairhaven / Grecian Rose

166

865   SHANDON BELLE 8 (br.f., March 1, 1959)

Bred by W. Davison.

Won 4 races, placed 3, £5,300, in Ireland, at 2 and 3 years, incl. Irish 1,000 Guineas Stakes; 2nd Phoenix Stakes (dead-heat).

HOOK MONEY (ch. 1951)	Bernborough (b. 1939)	Emborough	Gainsborough / Embarras de Richesse
		Bern Maid	Bernard / Bridesmaid
	Besieged (b. 1940)	Balladier	Black Toney / Blue Warbler
		La Troienne	Teddy / Helene de Troie
MERLETTE (b. 1946)	Devonian (ch. 1938)	Hyperion	Gainsborough / Selene
		Glorious Devon	Pommern / Skyglory
	Ballingham Lady (br. 1924)	Honey Bee	Tredennis / April Flower
		Bernera	Stornoway / Cascatel

866   SHANGAMUZO 14 (ch.c., March 13, 1973)

Bred by Lord Fairhaven.

Won 8 races, placed 17, £92,222, in England and France, from 2 to 6 years, incl. Ascot Gold Cup, Doncaster Cup; 2nd Jockey Club Cup (3 times), Yorkshire Cup, Henry II Stakes; 3rd Yorkshire Cup, Goodwood Cup, Doncaster Cup; 4th Prix du Cadran (twice), Ascot Gold Cup.

KLAIRON (b. 1952)	Clarion III (b. 1944)	Djebel	Tourbillon / Loika
		Columba	Colorado / Gay Bird
	Kalmia (b. 1931)	Kantar	Alcantara II / Karabe
		Sweet Lavender	Swynford / Marchetta
FRENCH FERN (ch. 1957)	Mossborough (ch. 1947)	Nearco	Pharos / Nogara
		All Moonshine	Bobsleigh / Selene
	Star of France (ch. 1947)	William of Valence	Vatout / Queen Iseult
		Allied Girl	Bold Archer / French Kiss

867   SHARP EDGE 11 (gr.c., May 3, 1970)

Bred by Sir John Astor.

Won 5 races, placed 3, £51,673, in England, Ireland and France, at 2 and 3 years, incl. Irish 2,000 Guineas, Prix Jean Prat; 3rd 2,000 Guineas Stakes, Champion Stakes, Royal Lodge Stakes.

SILVER SHARK (gr. 1963)	Buisson Ardent (ch. 1953)	Relic	War Relic / Bridal Colors
		Rose o'Lynn	Pherozshah / Rocklyn
	Palsaka (gr. 1954)	Palestine	Fair Trial / Una
		Masaka	Nearco / Majideh
CUTLE (ch. 1963)	Saint Crespin III (ch. 1956)	Aureole	Hyperion / Angelola
		Neocracy	Nearco / Harina
	Cutter (b. 1955)	Donatello II	Blenheim / Delleana
		Felucca	Nearco / Felsetta

868   SHARPEN UP 5 (ch.c., March 17, 1969)

Bred by Mrs. B. van Cutsem.

Won 5 races, placed 2, £19,888, in England, at 2 and 3 years, incl. Middle Park Stakes, Seaton Delaval Stakes; 2nd July Cup, Greenham Stakes.

ATAN (ch. 1961)	Native Dancer (gr. 1950)	Polynesian	Unbreakable / Black Polly
		Geisha	Discovery / Miyako
	Mixed Marriage (b. 1952)	Túdor Minstrel	Owen Tudor / Sansonnet
		Persian Maid	Tehran / Aroma
ROCCHETTA (ch. 1961)	Rockefella (br. 1941)	Hyperion	Gainsborough / Selene
		Rockfel	Felstead / Rockliffe
	Chambiges (b. 1949)	Majano	Deiri / Madgi Moto
		Chanterelle	Gris Perle / Shah Bibi

869   SHARPER 5 (gr.c., April 14, 1973)

Bred by Ballymacoll Stud Farm Ltd., in Ireland.

Won 4 races, placed 6, 504,133 fr., in France and Germany, from 2 to 5 years, incl. Grosser Preis von Baden.

SEA HAWK II (gr. 1963)	Herbager (b. 1956)	Vandale II	Plassy / Vanille
		Flagette	Escamillo / Fidgette
	Sea Nymph (gr. 1957)	Free Man	Norseman / Fantine
		Sea Spray	Ocean Swell / Pontoon
MAGIC THRUST (b. 1968)	Zarathustra (bl. 1951)	Persian Gulf	Bahram / Double Life
		Salvia	Sansovino / Love in the Mist
	Pappagena (b. 1952)	Pappageno II	Prince Rose / Kassala
		Brave City	Big Game / Coventry Belle

870   SHARPO 9 (ch.c., March 17, 1977)

Bred by K. V. Stenborg and R. E. Shingles.

Won 2 races, placed 4, £56,719, in England and France, at 2 and 3 years, incl. William Hill Sprint Championship, Temple Stakes; 2nd Cork and Orrery Stakes, Prix de l'Abbaye de Longchamp; 3rd William Hill July Cup.

SHARPEN UP (ch. 1969)	Atan (ch. 1961)	Native Dancer	Polynesian / Geisha
		Mixed Marriage	Tudor Minstrel / Persian Maid
	Rocchetta (ch. 1961)	Rockefella	Hyperion / Rockfel
		Chambiges	Majano / Chanterelle
MOIETY BIRD (ch. 1971)	Falcon (b. 1964)	Milesian	My Babu / Oatflake
		Pretty Swift	Petition / Fragilite
	Gaska (ch. 1961)	Gilles de Retz	Royal Charger / Ma Soeur Anne
		Sally Deans	Fun Fair / Cora Deans

871   SHERLUCK 3 (b.c., April 20, 1958)

Bred by Mrs. M. E. Lunn, in U.S.A.

Won 6 races, placed 4, $239,176, in U.S.A., from 2 to 4 years, incl. Belmont Stakes, Lawrence Realization, Blue Grass Stakes and Roamer H.; 2nd Everglades Stakes; 3rd Pimlico Futurity.

CORRESPONDENT (b. 1950)	Khaled (b. 1943)	Hyperion	Gainsborough / Selene
		Eclair	Ethnarch / Black Ray
	Heather Time (ch. 1936)	Time Maker	The Porter / Dream of Allah
		Heatherland	Crusader / Highland Mary II
SAMMINIATO (b. 1951)	Dante (br. 1942)	Nearco	Pharos / Nogara
		Rosy Legend	Dark Legend / Rosy Cheeks
	Life Hill (b. 1940)	Solario	Gainsborough / Sun Worship
		Lady of the Snows	Manna / Arctic Night

872   SHESHOON 14 (ch.c., March 17, 1956)

Bred by H.H. Aga Khan and Prince Aly Khan.

Won 7½ races, placed 3, £47,094, in England, France and Germany, at 3 and 4 years, incl. Ascot Gold Cup, Grand Prix de Saint-Cloud, Grosser Preis von Baden, Prix de Barbeville, Prix Gontaut-Biron; 2nd Prix du Cadran, Great Voltigeur Stakes.

PRECIPITATION (ch. 1933)	Hurry On (ch. 1913)	Marcovil	Marco / Lady Villikins
		Tout Suite	Sainfoin / Star
	Double Life (ch. 1926)	Bachelor's Double	Tredennis / Lady Bawn
		Saint Joan	Willbrook / Flo Desmond
NOORANI (ch. 1950)	Nearco (br. 1935)	Pharos	Phalaris / Scapa Flow
		Nogara	Havresac II / Catnip
	Empire Glory (b. 1933)	Singapore	Gainsborough / Tetrabbazia
		Skyglory	Sky-rocket / Simone

873   SHIRLEY HEIGHTS 1 (b.c., March 1, 1975)

Bred by Lord Halifax and Lord Irwin.

Won 6 races, placed 4, £205,711, in England and Ireland, at 2 and 3 years, incl. Derby Stakes, Irish Sweeps Derby, Royal Lodge Stakes, Mecca-Dante Stakes; 3rd Seaton Delaval Stakes.

MILL REEF (b. 1968)	Never Bend (b. 1960)	Nasrullah	Nearco / Mumtaz Begum
		Lalun	Djeddah / Be Faithful
	Milan Mill (b. 1962)	Princequillo	Prince Rose / Cosquilla
		Virginia Water	Count Fleet / Red Ray
HARDIEMMA (b. 1969)	Hardicanute (br. 1962)	Hard Ridden	Hard Sauce / Toute Belle II
		Harvest Maid	Umidwar / Hay Fell
	Grand Cross (br. 1952)	Grandmaster	Atout Maitre / Honorarium
		Blue Cross	Blue Peter / King's Cross

874   SHOOT A LINE 11 (b.f., April 2, 1977)

Bred by R. A. Budgett.

Won 6 races, £137,856, in England and Ireland, at 2 and 3 years, incl. Yorkshire Oaks, Irish Guinness Oaks, Ribblesdale Stakes, Park Hill Stakes, Cheshire Oaks.

HIGH LINE (ch. 1966)	High Hat (ch. 1957)	Hyperion	Gainsborough / Selene
		Madonna	Donatello II / Women's Legion
	Time Call (b. 1955)	Chanteur II	Chateau Bouscaut / La Diva
		Aleria	Djebel / Canidia
DEATH RAY (b. 1959)	Tamerlane (br. 1952)	Persian Gulf	Bahram / Double Life
		Eastern Empress	Nearco / Cheveley Lady
	Luminant (b. 1951)	Nimbus	Nearco / Kong
		Bardia	Colombo / Felsetta

875   SHOWDOWN 6 (ch.c., April 11, 1961)

Bred by Ashleigh Stud.

Won 6 races, placed 4, £25,702, in England, from 2 to 4 years, incl. Coventry Stakes, Middle Park Stakes, Queen Anne Stakes; 2nd Lockinge Stakes; 3rd Sussex Stakes; 4th 2,000 Guineas Stakes.

INFATUATION (br. 1951)	Nearco (br. 1935)	Pharos	Phalaris / Scapa Flow
		Nogara	Havresac II / Catnip
	Allure (ch. 1937)	Sir Cosmo	The Boss / Ayn Hali
		Simonella	Simon Pure / Coronella
ZANZARA (ch. 1951)	Fairey Fulmar (ch. 1943)	Fair Trial	Fairway / Lady Juror
		First Flight	Felstead / Pick of the Bunch
	Sunright (b. 1940)	Solario	Gainsborough / Sun Worship
		Democratie	Epinard / Queenly

876   SHUVEE 9 (ch.f., January 22, 1966)

Bred by Whitney Stone, in U.S.A.

Won 16 races, placed 16, $890,445, in U.S.A., from 2 to 5 years, incl. Coaching Club American Oaks, Mother Goose Stakes, Acorn Stakes, Alabama Stakes, Frizette Stakes, Selima Stakes, Jockey Club Gold Cup (twice), Top Flight H. (twice), Diana H. (twice), Beldame Stakes, Ladies H. and Cotillion H.; 2nd Beldame Stakes, Firenze H., Comely Stakes, Gardenia Stakes, Gallorette H. and Bed o' Roses H.; 3rd Beldame Stakes, Whitney Stakes, Gazelle H. and Astarita Stakes.

NASHUA (b. 1952)	Nasrullah (b. 1940)	Nearco	Pharos / Nogara
		Mumtaz Begum	Blenheim / Mumtaz Mahal
	Segula (b. 1942)	Johnstown	Jamestown / La France
		Sekhmet	Sardanapale / Prosopopee
LEVEE (ch. 1953)	Hill Prince (b. 1947)	Princequillo	Prince Rose / Cosquilla
		Hildene	Bubbling Over / Fancy Racket
	Bourtai (b. 1942)	Stimulus	Ultimus / Hurakan
		Escutcheon	Sir Gallahad III / Affection

168

877   SICILIAN PRINCE 8 (ch.c., February 16, 1959)

Bred by Commander G. Lennox Cotton, in Ireland.

Won 6 races, placed 2, £21,934, in Ireland and France, at 2 and 3 years, incl. Prix Royal Oak, Desmond Stakes and Blandford Stakes; 2nd Wills Gold Flake Stakes.

STRAIGHT DEAL (b. 1940)	Solario (b. 1922)	Gainsborough	Bayardo / Rosedrop
		Sun Worship	Sundridge / Doctrine
	Good Deal (ch. 1932)	Apelle	Sardanapale / Angelina
		Weeds	Arion / Dandelion
SYRACRUSE (b. 1947)	Furrokh Siyar (ch. 1929)	Colorado	Phalaris / Canyon
		Mumtaz Mahal	The Tetrarch / Lady Josephine
	Sycamore (b. 1936)	Singapore	Gainsborough / Tetrabbazia
		Marjolaine	Friar Marcus / Lilaline

878   SIGY 14 (b.f., March 9, 1976)

Bred by Comte Roland de Chambure, in France.

Won 5 races, placed 2, 534,800 fr., in France, at 2 and 3 years, incl. Prix de l'Abbaye de Longchamp, Prix d'Arenberg and Prix du Gros-Chene; 3rd Prix de Saint-Georges.

HABITAT (b. 1966)	Sir Gaylord (b. 1959)	Turn-to	Royal Charger / Source Sucree
		Somethingroyal	Princequillo / Imperatrice
	Little Hut (b. 1952)	Occupy	Bull Dog / Miss Bunting
		Savage Beauty	Challenger / Khara
SATU (b. 1965)	Primera (b. 1954)	My Babu	Djebel / Perfume II
		Pirette	Deiri / Pimpette
	Creation (ch. 1960)	Crepello	Donatello II / Crepuscule
		Cyclorama	Panorama / Gadabout

879   SILLY SEASON 1 (br.c., February 23, 1962)

Bred by Paul Mellon, in U.S.A.

Won 7 races, placed 8, £61,999, in England, from 2 to 4 years, incl. Champion Stakes, Dewhurst Stakes, Coventry Stakes, St. James's Palace Stakes, Lockinge Stakes, Greenham Stakes, Hungerford Stakes; 2nd 2,000 Guineas Stakes, Sussex Stakes, Queen Elizabeth II Stakes.

TOM FOOL (b. 1949)	Menow (b. 1935)	Pharamond	Phalaris / Selene
		Alcibiades	Supremus / Regal Roman
	Gaga (b. 1942)	Bull Dog	Teddy / Plucky Liege
		Alpoise	Equipoise / Laughing Queen
DOUBLE DEAL (b. 1946)	Straight Deal (b. 1940)	Solario	Gainsborough / Sun Worship
		Good Deal	Apelle / Weeds
	Nonats (b. 1937)	King Salmon	Salmon-Trout / Malva
		Whitebait	Sansovino / Blanchisseuse

880   SILVER CLOUD 11 (ch.c., May 4, 1959)

Bred by T. F. Blackwell.

Won 5 races, placed 5, £8,142, in England, from 2 to 5 years, incl. Chester Vase, Princess of Wales's Stakes, Cumberland Lodge Stakes; 2nd Blue Riband Trial Stakes; 3rd King Edward VII Stakes, Princess of Wales's Stakes.

AUREOLE (ch. 1950)	Hyperion (ch. 1930)	Gainsborough	Bayardo / Rosedrop
		Selene	Chaucer / Serenissima
	Angelola (b. 1945)	Donatello II	Blenheim / Delleana
		Feola	Friar Marcus / Aloe
BROLLY (b. 1950)	Precipitation (ch. 1933)	Hurry On	Marcovil / Tout Suite
		Double Life	Bachelor's Double / Saint Joan
	Unfurl (b. 1944)	Blue Peter	Fairway / Fancy Free
		Weathervane	Son-in-Law / Buchaness

881   SILVER CLOUD (FR) 1 (ch.f., February 24, 1964)

Bred by C. and J. Puerari, in France.

Won 3 races, placed 3, 546,344 fr., in France, at 2 and 3 years, incl. Grand Criterium and Prix de la Nonette; 3rd Prix de Diane.

DAN CUPID (ch. 1956)	Native Dancer (gr. 1950)	Polynesian	Unbreakable / Black Polly
		Geisha	Discovery / Miyako
	Vixenette (ch. 1944)	Sickle	Phalaris / Selene
		Lady Reynard	Gallant Fox / Nerva
BEACTIVE (b. 1954)	Johns Joy (br. 1946)	Bull Dog	Teddy / Plucky Liege
		My Auntie	Busy American / Babe K
	Providence (br. 1947)	Easton	Dark Legend / Phaona
		War Kilt	Man o'War / Friar's Carse

882   SILVER SHARK 5 (gr.c., May 12, 1963)

Bred by H.H. Aga Khan, in Ireland.

Won 10 races, placed 4, 1,090,790 fr., in France and U.S.A., at 2 and 3 years, incl. Prix du Moulin de Longchamp, Prix de l'Abbaye de Longchamp, Prix d'Ispahan, Prix La Rochette, Prix du Petit Couvert, Prix Eugene Adam, Prix Daphnis and Prix Jean Prat; 2nd Prix de Fontainebleau.

BUISSON ARDENT (ch. 1953)	Relic (bl. 1945)	War Relic	Man o'War / Friar's Carse
		Bridal Colors	Black Toney / Vaila
	Rose o'Lynn (b. 1944)	Pherozshah	Pharos / Mah Mahal
		Rocklyn	Easton / Rock Forrard
PALSAKA (gr. 1954)	Palestine (gr. 1947)	Fair Trial	Fairway / Lady Juror
		Una	Tatratema / Uganda
	Masaka (b. 1945)	Nearco	Pharos / Nogara
		Majideh	Mahmoud / Qurrat-al-Ain

169

883 SIR GAYLORD 2 (b.c., February 12, 1959)

Bred by Meadow Stud, Inc., in U.S.A.

Won 10 races, placed 4, $237,404, in U.S.A., at 2 and 3 years, incl. Sapling Stakes and Everglades Stakes; 3rd Champagne Stakes, Futurity Stakes, Hopeful Stakes and Cowdin Stakes.

TURN-TO (b. 1951)	Royal Charger (ch. 1942)	Nearco	Pharos / Nogara
		Sun Princess	Solario / Mumtaz Begum
	Source Sucree (b. 1940)	Admiral Drake	Craig an Eran / Plucky Liege
		Lavendula II	Pharos / Sweet Lavender
SOMETHINGROYAL (b. 1952)	Princequillo (b. 1940)	Prince Rose	Rose Prince / Indolence
		Cosquilla	Papyrus / Quick Thought
	Imperatrice (b. 1938)	Caruso	Polymelian / Sweet Music
		Cinquepace	Brown Bud / Assignation

884 SIR IVOR 8 (b.c., May 5, 1965)

Bred by Mrs. Reynolds W. Bell, in U.S.A.

Won 8 races, placed 4, £227,512, in England, Ireland, France and U.S.A., at 2 and 3 years, incl. Derby Stakes, 2,000 Guineas Stakes, Champion Stakes, Grand Criterium, Washington D.C. International, 2,000 Guineas Trial (Ascot), National Stakes (Curragh); 2nd Prix de l'Arc de Triomphe, Prix Henry Delamarre, Irish Sweeps Derby; 3rd Eclipse Stakes.

SIR GAYLORD (b. 1959)	Turn-to (b. 1951)	Royal Charger	Nearco / Sun Princess
		Source Sucree	Admiral Drake / Lavendula II
	Somethingroyal (b. 1952)	Princequillo	Prince Rose / Cosquilla
		Imperatrice	Caruso / Cinquepace
ATTICA (ch. 1953)	Mr. Trouble (ch. 1947)	Mahmoud	Blenheim / Mah Mahal
		Motto	Sir Gallahad III / Maxima
	Athenia (b. 1943)	Pharamond	Phalaris / Selene
		Salaminia	Man o'War / Alcibiades

885 SIRLAD 19 (ch.c., February 24, 1974)

Bred by Razza La Tesa, in Ireland.

Won 11 races, placed 5, 399,775,201 L., in Italy, France and U.S.A., from 2 to 5 years, incl. Derby Italiano, Gran Premio di Milano, Gran Criterium, Criterium Nazionale, Premio Emanuele Filiberto, Bel Air H. and Sunset H.; 2nd Hollywood Gold Cup; 3rd Prix Ganay; 4th Gran Premio di Milano.

BOLD LAD (USA) (ch. 1962)	Bold Ruler (b. 1954)	Nasrullah	Nearco / Mumtaz Begum
		Miss Disco	Discovery / Outdone
	Misty Morn (b. 1952)	Princequillo	Prince Rose / Cosquilla
		Grey Flight	Mahmoud / Planetoid
SORAGNA (b. 1965)	Orvieto (ch. 1951)	Macherio	Ortello / Mannozza
		Fior d'Orchidea	Apelle / Osa
	Savigny (br. 1953)	Mistral	Admiral Drake / La Foux
		Sernaglia	Orsenigo / Signa

886 SKY COMMANDER 16 (b.c., April 2, 1972)

Bred by E. V. Benjamin and E. V. Benjamin III, in U.S.A.

Won 6 races, placed 5, 623,658 fr., in France and U.S.A., from 2 to 5 years, incl. Prix Robert Papin and Prix Maurice de Gheest; 2nd Prix Jacques le Marois; 3rd Prix de la Salamandre; 4th Prix Morny.

LT. STEVENS (b. 1961)	Nantallah (b. 1953)	Nasrullah	Nearco / Mumtaz Begum
		Shimmer	Flares / Broad Ripple
	Rough Shod (b. 1944)	Gold Bridge	Swynford or Golden Boss / Flying Diadem
		Dalmary	Blandford / Simon's Shoes
STAR OF WONDER (b. 1964)	Dark Star (br. 1950)	Royal Gem II	Dhoti / French Gem
		Isolde	Bull Dog / Fiji
	Green Pastures (br. 1956)	Turn-to	Royal Charger / Source Sucree
		Clover	Bull Dog / Farmerette

887 SKYMASTER 2 (ch.c., March 22, 1958)

Bred by Airlie Stud.

Won 7 races, placed 7, £11,452, in England, at 2 and 3 years, incl. Middle Park Stakes; 3rd Diadem Stakes.

GOLDEN CLOUD (ch. 1941)	Gold Bridge (ch. 1929)	Swynford or Golden Boss	The Boss / Golden Hen
		Flying Diadem	Diadumenos / Flying Bridge
	Rainstorm (b. 1924)	Hainault	Swynford / Bromus
		Stormcloud	The Tetrarch / Lancaster Lady
DISCIPLINER (ch. 1948)	Court Martial (ch. 1942)	Fair Trial	Fairway / Lady Juror
		Instantaneous	Hurry On / Picture
	Edvina (ch. 1940)	Figaro	Colorado / Tillywhim
		Louise	Finglas / Devonshire House

888 SLEEPING PARTNER 16 (gr.f., April 3, 1966)

Bred by Lord Rosebery.

Won 4 races, placed 6, £39,245, in England, from 2 to 4 years, incl. Oaks Stakes, Ribblesdale Stakes, Lingfield Oaks Trial; 3rd Yorkshire Oaks.

PARTHIA (br. 1956)	Persian Gulf (b. 1940)	Bahram	Blandford / Friar's Daughter
		Double Life	Bachelor's Double / Saint Joan
	Lightning (b. 1950)	Hyperion	Gainsborough / Selene
		Chenille	King Salmon / Sweet Aloe
OLD DUTCH (gr. 1959)	Fastnet Rock (gr. 1947)	Ocean Swell	Blue Peter / Jiffy
		Stone of Fortune	Mahmoud / Rosetta
	Donah (ch. 1942)	Donatello II	Blenheim / Delleana
		Silver Fox II	Foxhunter / Pearl Maiden

889   SNOW KNIGHT 6 (ch.c., March 23, 1971)

Bred by J. A. C. Lilley.

Won 9 races, placed 7, £223,918, in England, Canada and U.S.A., from 2 to 4 years, incl. Derby Stakes, Canadian International Championship, Man o'War Stakes, Manhattan H., Seneca H., Brighton Beach H.; 2nd Champagne Stakes, Sandown Classic Trial Stakes; 3rd Benson and Hedges Gold Cup, Ladbroke Derby Trial Stakes.

FIRESTREAK (br. 1956)	Pardal (b. 1947)	Pharis II	Pharos / Carissima
		Adargatis	Asterus / Helene de Troie
	Hot Spell (b. 1944)	Umidwar	Blandford / Uganda
		Haymaker	Hyperion / Festuca
SNOW BLOSSOM (b. br. 1957)	Flush Royal (b. 1945)	Majano	Deiri / Madgi Moto
		Altamira	Olibrius / Koenigsmark
	Ariana (br. 1951)	Tehran	Bois Roussel / Stafaralla
		Snowberry	Cameronian / Myrobella

890   SO BLESSED B3 (br.c., April 13, 1965)

Bred by Crimbourne Stud.

Won 6 races, placed 7, £19,616, in England and France, from 2 to 4 years, incl. July Cup, Nunthorpe Stakes, Cornwallis Stakes, King George Stakes; 2nd King's Stand Stakes, Palace House Stakes; 3rd Prix de l'Abbaye de Longchamp, Greenham Stakes; 4th 2,000 Guineas.

PRINCELY GIFT (b. 1951)	Nasrullah (b. 1940)	Nearco	Pharos / Nogara
		Mumtaz Begum	Blenheim / Mumtaz Mahal
	Blue Gem (b. 1943)	Blue Peter	Fairway / Fancy Free
		Sparkle	Blandford / Gleam
LAVANT (b. 1955)	Le Lavandou (b. 1944)	Djebel	Tourbillon / Loika
		Lavande	Rustom Pasha / Livadia
	Firle (br. 1938)	Noble Star	Hapsburg / Hesper
		Versicle	Sickle / Verdict

891   SODERINI 5 (b.c., April 17, 1961)

Bred by L. L. Lawrence.

Won 4 races, placed 6, £28,128, in England, from 2 to 4 years, incl. John Porter Stakes, Hardwicke Stakes; 2nd Dewhurst Stakes, Coronation Cup, King George VI and Queen Elizabeth Stakes, Goodwood Cup; 3rd St. Leger Stakes.

CREPELLO (ch. 1954)	Donatello II (ch. 1934)	Blenheim	Blandford / Malva
		Delleana	Clarissimus / Duccia di Buoninsegna
	Crepuscule (ch. 1948)	Mieuxce	Massine / L'Olivete
		Red Sunset	Solario / Dulce II
MATUTA (b. 1955)	Tantieme (b. 1947)	Deux pour Cent	Deiri / Dix pour Cent
		Terka	Indus / La Furka
	Maitrise (b. 1948)	Atout Maitre	Vatout / Royal Mistress
		Mabama	Mahmoud / Qurrat-al-Ain

892   SODIUM 1 (b.c., April 20, 1963)

Bred by Kilcarn Stud Ltd.

Won 3 races, placed 6, £103,016, in England and Ireland, from 2 to 4 years, incl. Irish Sweeps Derby Stakes, St. Leger Stakes; 2nd King George VI and Queen Elizabeth Stakes, Hardwicke Stakes, Royal Lodge Stakes; 3rd White Rose Stakes; 4th Observer Gold Cup, Derby Stakes.

PSIDIUM (ch. 1958)	Pardal (b. 1947)	Pharis II	Pharos / Carissima
		Adargatis	Asterus / Helene de Troie
	Dinarella (ch. 1947)	Niccolo Dell'Arca	Coronach / Nogara
		Dagherotipia	Manna / Dossa Dossi
GAMBADE (b. 1951)	Big Game (b. 1939)	Bahram	Blandford / Friar's Daughter
		Myrobella	Tetratema / Dolabella
	Amber Flash (b. 1942)	Precipitation	Hurry On / Double Life
		Traffic Light	Solario / Point Duty

893   SOLEIL 22 (b.c., April 15, 1963)

Bred by Baron Guy de Rothschild, in France.

Won 5 races, placed 3, 1,009,547 fr., in France, at 2 and 3 years, incl. Grand Criterium, Prix Morny, Poule d'Essai des Poulains and Prix de la Porte Maillot; 2nd Prix Jacques le Marois; 3rd Prix Robert Papin and Prix Lupin.

MAJOR PORTION (ch. 1955)	Court Martial (ch. 1942)	Fair Trial	Fairway / Lady Juror
		Instantaneous	Hurry On / Picture
	Better Half (b. 1946)	Mieuxce	Massine / L'Olivete
		Malay Bride	Colombo / Singapore's Sister
AURORE POLAIRE (b. 1955)	Alizier (b. 1947)	Teleferique	Bacteriophage / Beaute de Neige
		Alizarine	Coronach / Armoise
	Aurore Boreale (b. 1941)	Brantome	Blandford / Vitamine
		Voute Celeste	Legatee / La Grande Ourse

894   SOLEIL NOIR 22 (gr.c., May 20, 1976)

Bred by Baron Guy de Rothschild, in France.

Won 3 races, placed 9, 994,976 fr., in France and England, from 2 to 4 years, incl. Grand Prix de Paris and Prix de l'Esperance; 2nd St. Leger Stakes; 3rd Coronation Cup and Prix Greffulhe.

EXBURY (ch. 1959)	Le Haar (ch. 1954)	Vieux Manoir	Brantome / Vieille Maison
		Mince Pie	Teleferique / Cannelle
	Greensward (b. 1953)	Mossborough	Nearco / All Moonshine
		Stargrass	Noble Star / Grass Widow
SKELDA (gr. 1968)	La Varende (gr. 1949)	Blue Moon	Massine / Halstone
		Cappellina	Le Capucin / Bellina
	Fidra (ch. 1961)	Sicambre	Prince Bio / Sif
		Aurore Polaire	Alizier / Aurore Boreale

895 SOLINUS 4 (b.c., February 18, 1975)

Bred by L. B. Hall.

Won 8 races, placed 2, £109,215, in England, Ireland and France, at 2 and 3 years, incl. King's Stand Stakes, William Hill July Cup, Coventry Stakes, William Hill Sprint Championship, Anglesey Stakes, Ballyogan Stakes; 2nd Prix de l'Abbaye de Longchamp, Laurent Perrier Champagne Stakes.

COMEDY STAR (b. 1968)	Tom Fool (b. 1949)	Menow	Pharamond / Alcibiades
		Gaga	Bull Dog / Alpoise
	Latin Walk (br. 1960)	Roman Tread	Roman / Stepwisely
		Stall Walker	Bimelech / Pansy Walker
CAWSTON'S PRIDE (ch. 1968)	Con Brio (ch. 1961)	Ribot	Tenerani / Romanella
		Petronella	Petition / Danse d'Espoir
	Cawston Tower (gr. 1956)	Maharaj Kumar	Stardust / Pancha
		Silver Ribbon	The Satrap / Salmonella

896 SOLSTICE 8 (br.c. April 5, 1962)

Bred by Mereworth Farm, in U.S.A.

Won 1 race, placed 3, £10,413, in England, from 2 to 4 years, incl. Carreras Piccadilly Derby Trial Stakes; 3rd St. Leger Stakes, Ormonde Stakes

SOLAR SLIPPER (b. 1945)	Windsor Slipper (b. 1939)	Windsor Lad	Blandford / Resplendent
		Carpet Slipper	Phalaris / Simon's Shoes
	Solar Flower (br. 1935)	Solario	Gainsborough / Sun Worship
		Serena	Winalot / Charmione
THIRTY SCENTS (b. 1949)	Eight Thirty (ch. 1936)	Pilate	Friar Rock / Herodias
		Dinner Time	High Time / Seaplane
	Fragrance (b. 1942)	Sir Gallahad III	Teddy / Plucky Liege
		Rosebloom	Chicle / Rowes Bud

897 SOLTIKOFF 11 (b.c., 1959)

Bred by E. Cruz-Valer, in France.

Won 4 races, placed 10, 1,271,486 fr., in France and Italy, from 3 to 5 years, incl. Prix de l'Arc de Triomphe, Gran Premio del Jockey Club, Prix Henry Delamarre and Prix du Prince d'Orange; 2nd Prix Eugene Adam and Prix d'Harcourt; 3rd Prix Ganay, Prix Lupin and Prix de Chantilly; 4th Prix de l'Arc de Triomphe and Prix Ganay.

PRINCE CHEVALIER (b. 1943)	Prince Rose (b. 1928)	Rose Prince	Prince Palatine / Eglantine
		Indolence	Gay Crusader / Barrier
	Chevalerie (b. 1933)	Abbot's Speed	Abbots Trace / Mary Gaunt
		Kassala	Cylgad / Farizade
AGLAE GRACE (br. 1947)	Mousson (b. 1934)	Rose Prince	Prince Palatine / Eglantine
		Spring Tide	Sans Souci II / Spring Cleaning
	Agathe (b. 1936)	Amfortas	Ksar / Persephone
		Melanie	Brabant / Menthe

898 SONG 5 (b.c., March 31, 1966)

Bred by J. R. Hine.

Won 7 races, placed 3, £18,003, in England, from 2 to 4 years, incl. King's Stand Stakes, Temple Stakes, Diadem Stakes, New Stakes; 2nd Gimcrack Stakes.

SING SING (b. 1957)	Tudor Minstrel (br. 1944)	Owen Tudor	Hyperion / Mary Tudor II
		Sansonnet	Sansovino / Lady Juror
	Agin the Law (b. 1946)	Portlaw	Beresford / Portree
		Revolte	Xandover / Sheba
INTENT (gr. 1952)	Vilmorin (gr. 1943)	Gold Bridge	Swynford or Golden Boss / Flying Diadem
		Queen of the Meadows	Fairway / Queen of the Blues
	Under Canvas (b. 1943)	Winterhalter	Gainsborough / Perce-Neige
		Shelton	Caerleon / Melanite

899 SONNEN GOLD 1 (b.c., February 11, 1977)

Bred by T. M. Madden.

Won 7 races, placed 3, £55,441, in England, at 2 and 3 years, incl. Gimcrack Stakes; 2nd William Hill Middle Park Stakes.

HOME GUARD (br. 1969)	Forli (ch. 1963)	Aristophanes	Hyperion / Commotion
		Trevisa	Advocate / Veneta
	Stay at Home (br. 1961)	Bold Ruler	Nasrullah / Miss Disco
		Alanesian	Polynesian / Alablue
MULATTIN (br. 1969)	Henry the Seventh (ch. 1958)	King of the Tudors	Tudor Minstrel / Glen Line
		Vestal Girl	Fairy Prince / Vestalia
	Mrs. Gail (b. 1960)	Hill Gail	Bull Lea / Jane Gail
		Mrs. Dent	Denturius / Miss Winston

900 SON OF LOVE 5 (ch.c., April 24, 1976)

Bred by Haras du Hoguenet, in France.

Won 3 races, placed 13, £136,844, in France, England and U.S.A., from 2 to 4 years, incl. St. Leger Stakes; 2nd Grand Prix de Paris, Prix Noailles, Prix Maurice de Nieuil, Prix Kergorlay; 3rd Prix Exbury; 4th Washington D.C. International.

JEFFERSON (ch. 1967)	Charlottesville (b. 1957)	Prince Chevalier	Prince Rose / Chevalerie
		Noorani	Nearco / Empire Glory
	Monticella (ch. 1955)	Cranach	Coronach / Reine Isaure
		Montenica	Djebel / Nica
MOT D'AMOUR (ch. 1970)	Bon Mot III (ch. 1963)	Worden II	Wild Risk / Sans Tares
		Djebel Idra	Phil Drake / Djebellica
	Anamour (b. 1961)	Amber X	Zuccarello / Pantomine
		Princesse Niloufer	Tantieme / Malekeh

172

901 **SOOKERA** 11 (b.f., May 15, 1975)

Bred by Swettenham Stud, in U.S.A.

Won 3 races, placed 2, £44,552, in England and Ireland, at 2 years. incl. William Hill Cheveley Park Stakes; 2nd Moyglare Stud Stakes.

ROBERTO (b. 1969)	Hail to Reason (br. 1958)	Turn-to	Royal Charger / Source Sucree
		Nothirdchance	Blue Swords / Galla Colors
	Bramalea (b. or br. 1959)	Nashua	Nasrullah / Segula
		Rarelea	Bull Lea / Bleebok
IRULE (gr. 1968)	Young Emperor (gr. 1963)	Grey Sovereign	Nasrullah / Kong
		Young Empress	Petition / Jennifer
	Iaround (b. 1961)	Round Table	Princequillo / Knight's Daughter
		Itsabet	Heliopolis / Jayjean

902 **SORTINGO** 19 (b.c., February 16, 1975)

Bred by Razza La Tesa, in Ireland.

Won 5 races, placed 6, 130,695,000 L., in Italy, from 2 to 4 years, incl. Gran Premio d'Italia and Gran Premio di Milano; 2nd Derby Italiano.

PETINGO (b. 1965)	Petition (br. 1944)	Fair Trial	Fairway / Lady Juror
		Art Paper	Artist's Proof / Quire
	Alcazar (ch. 1957)	Alycidon	Donatello II / Aurora
		Quarterdeck	Nearco / Poker Chip
SORAGNA (b. 1965)	Orvieto (ch. 1951)	Macherio	Ortello / Mannozza
		Fior d'Orchidea	Apelle / Osa
	Savigny (br. 1953)	Mistral	Admiral Drake / La Foux
		Sernaglia	Orsenigo / Signa

903 **SOVEREIGN** 3 (b.f., March 13, 1965)

Bred by White Lodge Stud Co.

Won 5 races, placed 1, £20,251, in England, at 2 and 3 years, incl. Coronation Stakes, Queen Mary Stakes, National Stakes (Sandown), Lowther Stakes; 3rd 1,000 Guineas Stakes.

PARDAO (ch. 1958)	Pardal (b. 1947)	Pharis II	Pharos / Carissima
		Adargatis	Asterus / Helene de Troie
	Three Weeks (ch. 1946)	Big Game	Bahram / Myrobella
		Eleanor Cross	Hyperion / Queen Christina
URSHALIM (b. 1951)	Nasrullah (b. 1940)	Nearco	Pharos / Nogara
		Mumtaz Begum	Blenheim / Mumtaz Mahal
	Horama (b. 1943)	Panorama	Sir Cosmo / Happy Climax
		Lady of Aran	Orpen / Queen of the Nore

904 **SOVEREIGN LORD** 2 (b.c., March 10, 1959)

Bred by Measures Farms Ltd.

Won 2 races, placed 3, £10,122, in England, at 2 and 3 years, incl. Richmond Stakes, Gimcrack Stakes; 2nd Middle Park Stakes, St. James's Palace Stakes.

GREY SOVEREIGN (gr. 1948)	Nasrullah (b. 1940)	Nearco	Pharos / Nogara
		Mumtaz Begum	Blenheim / Mumtaz Mahal
	Kong (gr. 1933)	Baytown	Achtoi / Princess Herodias
		Clang	Hainault / Vibration
ARDUE (b. 1949)	Admiral's Walk (ch. 1936)	Hyperion	Gainsborough / Selene
		Tabaris	Roi Herode / Tip-toe
	Uags (b. 1933)	Buen Ojo	Chili II or Craganour / View
		Ishtar	The Tetrarch / Perfect Peach

905 **SPANISH EXPRESS** 19 (b.c., March 3, 1962)

Bred by Major J. H. de Burgh.

Won 3 races, placed 3, £22,337, in England, at 2 and 3 years, incl. Middle Park Stakes; 2nd Greenham Stakes.

SOVEREIGN PATH (gr. 1956)	Grey Sovereign (gr. 1948)	Nasrullah	Nearco / Mumtaz Begum
		Kong	Baytown / Clang
	Mountain Path (b. 1948)	Bobsleigh	Gainsborough / Toboggan
		Path of Peace	Winalot / Grand Peace
SAGE FEMME (ch. 1954)	Le Sage (b. 1948)	Chamossaire	Precipitation / Snowberry
		Miss Know All	Rhodes Scholar / Dalmary
	Sylvia's Grove (ch. 1938)	Fairway	Phalaris / Scapa Flow
		Trustful	Bachelor's Double / Credenda

906 **SPARKLER** 2 (b.c., April 8, 1968)

Bred by Donal O'Brien, in Ireland.

Won 13 races, placed 13, £101,000, in England, Ireland, France and Germany, from 2 to 5 years, incl. Diomed Stakes, Prix Quincey (twice), Prix Perth, Queen Anne Stakes, Grosser Preis der Spielbank Bad Wiessee, Lockinge Stakes and Prix du Moulin de Longchamp; 2nd Irish 2,000 Guineas, St. James's Palace Stakes, Prix Jacques le Marois, Queen Elizabeth II Stakes, Prix Perth and Queen Anne Stakes; 3rd Sussex Stakes, Prix de Ris-Orangis and Prix Jacques le Marois.

HARD TACK (b. 1955)	Hard Sauce (br. 1948)	Ardan	Pharis II / Adargatis
		Saucy Bella	Bellacose / Marmite
	Cowes (b. 1949)	Blue Peter	Fairway / Fancy Free
		Lighthearted	Hyperion / Merry Devon
DIAMOND SPUR (ch. 1961)	Preciptic (ch. 1942)	Precipitation	Hurry On / Double Life
		Artistic	Gainsborough / Ishtar
	Diamond Princess (ch. 1944)	His Highness	Hyperion / Moti Ranee
		Hatton	Mr. Jinks / Organic

907   SPECTACULAR BID 2 (gr.c., February 17, 1976)

Bred by Mrs. William M. Jason, in U.S.A.

Won 26 races, placed 3, $2,781,607, in U.S.A., from 2 to 4 years, incl. Kentucky Derby, Preakness Stakes, Marlboro Cup, Santa Anita H., Californian Stakes, Woodward Stakes, Charles H. Strub Stakes, Florida Derby, Flamingo Stakes, Blue Grass Stakes, Champagne Stakes, Laurel Futurity, Amory L. Haskell H., Mervyn Le Roy H., San Fernando Stakes, Malibu Stakes, Meadowlands Cup, Heritage Stakes, World's Playground Stakes, Fountain of Youth Stakes and Washington Park Stakes; 2nd Jockey Club Gold Cup; 3rd Belmont Stakes.

BOLD BIDDER (b. 1962)	Bold Ruler (b. 1954)	Nasrullah	Nearco / Mumtaz Begum
		Miss Disco	Discovery / Outdone
	High Bid (b. 1956)	To Market	Market Wise / Pretty Does
		Stepping Stone	Princequillo / Step Across
SPECTACULAR (ro. 1970)	Promised Land (gr. 1954)	Palestinian	Sun Again / Dolly Whisk
		Mahmoudess	Mahmoud / Forever Yours
	Stop on Red (ch. 1959)	To Market	Market Wise / Pretty Does
		Danger Ahead	Head Play / Lady Beware

908   SPORTING YANKEE 14 (b.c., January 31, 1974)

Bred by Nelson Bunker Hunt, in U.S.A.

Won 3 races, placed 5, £50,420, in England, from 2 to 4 years, incl. William Hill Futurity Stakes; 2nd Geoffrey Freer Stakes, Ladbroke Craven Stakes; 3rd John Porter Stakes.

VAGUELY NOBLE (b. 1965)	Vienna (ch. 1957)	Aureole	Hyperion / Angelola
		Turkish Blood	Turkhan / Rusk
	Noble Lassie (b. 1956)	Nearco	Pharos / Nogara
		Belle Sauvage	Big Game / Tropical Sun
SALE DAY (b. 1965)	To Market (ch. 1948)	Market Wise	Brokers Tip / On Hand
		Pretty Does	Johnstown / Creese
	Hasty Girl (b. 1951)	Princequillo	Prince Rose / Cosquilla
		In Love	Tintagel / Highland Dell

909   SPREE 6 (b. or br.f., April 14, 1960)

Bred by Fonthill Stud.

Won 3 races, placed 6, £6,127, in England, at 2 and 3 years, incl. Nassau Stakes; 2nd 1,000 Guineas Stakes, Oaks Stakes, Fred Darling Stakes, Queen Elizabeth II Stakes.

ROCKEFELLA (br. 1941)	Hyperion (ch. 1930)	Gainsborough	Bayardo / Rosedrop
		Selene	Chaucer / Serenissima
	Rockfel (br. 1935)	Felstead	Spion Kop / Felkington
		Rockliffe	Santorb / Sweet Rocket
EMANCIPATION (b. 1954)	Le Sage (b. 1948)	Chamossaire	Precipitation / Snowberry
		Miss Know All	Rhodes Scholar / Dalmary
	Fair Freedom (b. 1945)	Fair Trial	Fairway / Lady Juror
		Democratie	Epinard / Queenly

910   STAGE DOOR JOHNNY 1 (ch.c., March 11, 1965)

Bred by Greentree Stud, Inc., in U.S.A.

Won 5 races, placed 3, $223,965, in U.S.A., at 2 and 3 years, incl. Belmont Stakes, Dwyer H. and Saranac H.

PRINCE JOHN (ch. 1953)	Princequillo (b. 1940)	Prince Rose	Rose Prince / Indolence
		Cosquilla	Papyrus / Quick Thought
	Not Afraid (b. 1948)	Count Fleet	Reigh Count / Quickly
		Banish Fear	Blue Larkspur / Herodiade
PEROXIDE BLONDE (ch. 1960)	Ballymoss (ch. 1954)	Mossborough	Nearco / All Moonshine
		Indian Call	Singapore / Flittemere
	Folie Douce (b. 1949)	Caldarium	Brantome / Chaudiere
		Folle Nuit	Astrophel / Folle Passion

911   STANFORD 4 (ch.c., March 20, 1976)

Bred by Shanbally House Stud.

Won 2 races, placed 2, £27,057, in England, at 2 and 3 years, incl. Gimcrack Stakes.

RED GOD (ch. 1954)	Nasrullah (b. 1940)	Nearco	Pharos / Nogara
		Mumtaz Begum	Blenheim / Mumtaz Mahal
	Spring Run (b. 1948)	Menow	Pharamond / Alcibiades
		Boola Brook	Bull Dog / Brookdale
SWEET ALMOND (ch. 1970)	Busted (b. 1963)	Crepello	Donatello II / Crepuscule
		Sans Le Sou	Vimy / Martial Loan
	Schonbrunn (b. 1957)	Blue Peter	Fairway / Fancy Free
		Marie Therese	Mieuxce / Mary Tavy

912   STAR APPEAL 5 (b.c., May 12, 1970)

Bred by Gestut Rottgen.

Won 11 races, placed 17, £263,015, in Ireland, Germany, France, England, Italy and U.S.A., from 2 to 5 years, incl. Eclipse Stakes, Prix de l'Arc de Triomphe, Grosser Preis der Badischen Wirtschaft (twice), Gran Premio di Milano, Concentra-Pokal des Deutschen Investment-Trust; 2nd Grosser Preis der Stadt Gelsenkirchen; 3rd Irish St. Leger, Benson and Hedges Gold Cup, Gallinule Stakes; 4th Champion Stakes (twice), Grosser Preis von Baden; 5th Washington D.C. International.

APPIANI II (b. 1963)	Herbager (b. 1956)	Vandale II	Plassy / Vanille
		Flagette	Escamillo / Fidgette
	Angela Rucellai (b. 1954)	Rockefella	Hyperion / Rockfel
		Aristareta	Niccolo Dell'Arca / Acquaforte
STERNA (br. 1960)	Neckar (bl. 1948)	Ticino	Athanasius / Terra
		Nixe	Arjaman / Nanon
	Stammesart (b. 1944)	Alchimist	Herold / Aversion
		Stammesfahne	Flamboyant / Selika

913   STAR MOSS 14 (ch.c., May 8, 1960)

Bred by Major H. R. Broughton.

Won 2 races, placed 3, £9,967, in England, at 2 and 3 years, incl. Royal Lodge Stakes; 2nd St. Leger Stakes; 3rd Timeform Gold Cup.

MOSSBOROUGH (ch. 1947)	Nearco (br. 1935)	Pharos	Phalaris / Scapa Flow
		Nogara	Havresac II / Catnip
	All Moonshine (ch. 1941)	Bobsleigh	Gainsborough / Toboggan
		Selene	Chaucer / Serenissima
STAR OF FRANCE (ch. 1947)	William of Valence (br. 1932)	Vatout	Prince Chimay / Vasthi
		Queen Iseult	Teddy / Sweet Agnes
	Allied Girl (b. 1938)	Bold Archer	Phalaris / Miss Matty
		French Kiss	Somme Kiss / Reprisal

914   STAR SHIP 5 (br.f., February 5, 1969)

Bred by T. G. R. Cook.

Won 4 races, placed 1, £11,759, in England, from 2 to 4 years, incl. Ribblesdale Stakes, Lancashire Oaks.

DICTA DRAKE (b. 1958)	Phil Drake (b. 1952)	Admiral Drake	Craig an Eran / Plucky Liege
		Philippa	Vatellor / Philippa of Hainaut
	Dictature (b. 1950)	Transtevere	Bubbles / Farnese
		Nymphe Dicte	Diolite / Nanaia
STAR TROPHY (b. 1960)	Umberto (b. 1951)	Umidwar	Blandford / Uganda
		Shello	Donatello II / Show Girl
	Star Lady (b. 1946)	Etoile de Lyons	Coup de Lyon / Rose of Jericho
		Roman Spring	Caerleon / Yanwath

915   STATEFF 14 (ch.c., February 25, 1974)

Bred by Stenigot Ltd., in England.

Won 7 races, placed 8, 129,030,000 L., in Italy, from 2 to 4 years, incl. Gran Premio del Jockey Club, Premio d'Aprile, Gran Premio Citta di Torino and Premio Federico Tesio; 2nd Premio Presidente della Repubblica, Premio Emanuele Filiberto and Premio Ambrosiano; 3rd St. Leger Italiano and Premio Ellington; 4th Gran Criterium.

PIECES OF EIGHT (br. 1963)	Relic (bl. 1945)	War Relic	Man o'War / Friar's Carse
		Bridal Colors	Black Toney / Vaila
	Baby Doll (br. 1956)	Dante	Nearco / Rosy Legend
		Bebe Grande	Niccolo dell'Arca / Grande Corniche
GREEN VELVET (ch. 1965)	Epaulette (ch. 1951)	Court Martial	Fair Trial / Instantaneous
		Golden Sari	Dastur / Fortunedale
	Greenheart (ch. 1952)	Borealis	Brumeux / Aurora
		Greenbridge	Fairway / Buckeye

916   STEEL HEART 7 (b.c., March 25, 1972)

Bred by W. F. Davison.

Won 5 races, placed 4, £66,471, in England and Germany, at 2 and 3 years, incl. William Hill Middle Park Stakes, C. and G. Gimcrack Stakes, Duke of York Stakes, Goldene Peitsche; 2nd William Hill Dewhurst Stakes, July Cup.

HABITAT (b. 1966)	Sir Gaylord (b. 1959)	Turn-to	Royal Charger / Source Sucree
		Somethingroyal	Princequillo / Imperatrice
	Little Hut (b. 1952)	Occupy	Bull Dog / Miss Bunting
		Savage Beauty	Challenger / Khara
A.1. (gr. 1963)	Abernant (gr. 1946)	Owen Tudor	Hyperion / Mary Tudor II
		Rustom Mahal	Rustom Pasha / Mumtaz Mahal
	Asti Spumante (ch. 1947)	Dante	Nearco / Rosy Legend
		Blanco	Blandford / Snow Storm

917   STEEL PULSE 1 (br.c., February 28, 1969)

Bred by Southdown Stud Co.

Won 5 races, placed 8, £99,069, in England, Ireland, France and U.S.A., from 2 to 4 years, incl. Irish Sweeps Derby, Criterium de Maisons-Laffitte; 2nd Observer Gold Cup, Craven Stakes, Prince of Wales Stakes, Grand Criterium; 3rd Washington D. C. International; 4th 2,000 Guineas Stakes (dead-heat), King George VI and Queen Elizabeth Stakes.

DIATOME (br. 1962)	Sicambre (br. 1948)	Prince Bio	Prince Rose / Biologie
		Sif	Rialto / Suavita
	Dictaway (br. 1952)	Honeyway	Fairway / Honey Buzzard
		Nymphe Dicte	Diolite / Nanaia
RACHEL (br. 1958)	Tudor Minstrel (br. 1944)	Owen Tudor	Hyperion / Mary Tudor II
		Sansonnet	Sansovino / Lady Juror
	Par Avion (b. 1948)	Phideas	Pharos / Imagery
		Acid Flight	Lemonora / Scutter

918   STINTINO 1 (b.c., February 17, 1967)

Bred by Citadel Stud Establishment, in Ireland.

Won 5 races, placed 5, 1,133,424 fr., in France and England, from 2 to 4 years, incl. Prix Lupin, Prix de Guiche, Prix de Chantilly and Criterium de Saint-Cloud; 2nd Coronation Cup; 3rd Derby Stakes, Prix Ganay and Prix d'Ispahan; 4th King George VI and Queen Elizabeth Stakes.

SHESHOON (ch. 1956)	Precipitation (ch. 1933)	Hurry On	Marcovil / Tout Suite
		Double Life	Bachelor's Double / Saint Joan
	Noorani (ch. 1950)	Nearco	Pharos / Nogara
		Empire Glory	Singapore / Skyglory
CYNARA (gr. 1958)	Grey Sovereign (gr. 1948)	Nasrullah	Nearco / Mumtaz Begum
		Kong	Baytown / Clang
	Ladycroft (gr. 1941)	Portlaw	Beresford / Portree
		Cosmobelle	Sir Cosmo / Kilmeny

919   **STONE** 4 (ch.c., February 2, 1975)

Bred by Banstead Manor Stud, in England.

Won 10 races, placed 8, 189,404,024 L., in Italy and England, from 2 to 4 years, incl. Premio Presidente della Repubblica, Gran Premio del Jockey Club, Premio Pisa, Premio Ambrosiano and Premio Federico Tesio; 2nd Gran Premio di Milano, Premio Emanuele Filiberto and Premio d'Aprile; 4th Gran Premio di Milano and Coral Eclipse Stakes.

MOULTON (b. 1969)	Pardao (ch. 1958)	Pardal	Pharis II / Adargatis
		Three Weeks	Big Game / Eleanor Cross
	Close Up (br. 1958)	Nearula	Nasrullah / Respite
		Horama	Panorama / Lady of Aran
SCALA DI SETA (b. 1969)	Shantung (b. 1956)	Sicambre	Prince Bio / Sif
		Barley Corn	Hyperion / Schiaparelli
	Donata di Formello (b. 1954)	Antonio Canale	Torbido / Acquaforte
		Donnina II	Niccolo dell'Arca / Daniela da Volterra

920   **STORM BIRD** 4 (b.c., April 19, 1978)

Bred by E. P. Taylor, in Canada.

Won 5 races, £72,594, in Ireland and England, at 2 years, incl. William Hill Dewhurst Stakes, National Stakes (Curragh), Anglesey Stakes, Larkspur Stakes.

NORTHERN DANCER (b. 1961)	Nearctic (br. 1954)	Nearco	Pharos / Nogara
		Lady Angela	Hyperion / Sister Sarah
	Natalma (b. 1957)	Native Dancer	Polynesian / Geisha
		Almahmoud	Mahmoud / Arbitrator
SOUTH OCEAN (b. 1967)	New Providence (b. 1956)	Bull Page	Bull Lea / Our Page
		Fair Colleen	Preciptic / Fairvale
	Shining Sun (b. 1962)	Chop Chop	Flares / Sceptical
		Solar Display	Sun Again / Dark Display

921   **STOUCI** 4 (ch.c., January 28, 1976)

Bred by Banstead Manor Stud, in England.

Won 6 races, placed 3, 81,620,000 L., in Italy, at 2 and 3 years, incl. Gran Criterium, Criterium di Roma and Premio Nearco; 2nd Premio Emanuele Filiberto.

UPPER CASE (b. 1969)	Round Table (b. 1954)	Princequillo	Prince Rose / Cosquilla
		Knight's Daughter	Sir Cosmo / Feola
	Bold Experience (ch. 1962)	Bold Ruler	Nasrullah / Miss Disco
		First Flush	Flushing II / Hildene
SCALA DI SETA (b. 1969)	Shantung (b. 1956)	Sicambre	Prince Bio / Sif
		Barley Corn	Hyperion / Schiaparelli
	Donata di Formello (b. 1954)	Antonio Canale	Torbido / Acquaforte
		Donnina II	Niccolo dell'Arca / Daniela da Volterra

922   **ST. PADDY** 14 (b.c., January 18, 1957)

Bred by Eve Stud Ltd.

Won 9 races, placed 3, £101,527, in England, at 2 to 4 years, incl. Derby Stakes, St. Leger Stakes, Eclipse Stakes, Royal Lodge Stakes, Dante Stakes, Great Voltigeur Stakes, Hardwicke Stakes, Jockey Club Stakes; 2nd King George VI and Queen Elizabeth Stakes, Champion Stakes, Gordon Stakes.

AUREOLE (ch. 1950)	Hyperion (ch. 1930)	Gainsborough	Bayardo / Rosedrop
		Selene	Chaucer / Serenissima
	Angelola (b. 1945)	Donatello II	Blenheim / Delleana
		Feola	Friar Marcus / Aloe
EDIE KELLY (br. 1950)	Bois Roussel (br. 1935)	Vatout	Prince Chimay / Vasthi
		Plucky Liege	Spearmint / Concertina
	Caerlissa (b. 1935)	Caerleon	Phalaris / Canyon
		Sister Sarah	Abbots Trace / Sarita

923   **STRAIGHT DEAL** 1 (b.f., June 9, 1962)

Bred by Bieber-Jacobs Stable, in U.S.A.

Won 21 races, placed 30, $733,020, in U.S.A., from 2 to 7 years, incl. Hollywood Oaks, Delaware H., Spinster Stakes, Ladies H., Top Flight H., Firenze H., Santa Margarita H., Sheepshead Bay H., Santa Barbara H., Bed o' Roses H. (twice), Vineland H. and Orchid H.; 2nd Beldame Stakes, Matchmaker Stakes, Diana H. (twice), Gallorette H. (twice), Firenze H., Post-Deb Stakes, Ladies H., Molly Pitcher H. (twice), Maskette H., Santa Maria H., Black Helen H., Excelsior H. and Barbara Fritchie H.; 3rd Beldame Stakes, Aqueduct Stakes, Whitney Stakes, Columbiana H., Top Flight H., Maskette H. and New York H.

HAIL TO REASON (br. 1958)	Turn-to (b. 1951)	Royal Charger	Nearco / Sun Princess
		Source Sucree	Admiral Drake / Lavendula II
	Nothirdchance (b. 1948)	Blue Swords	Blue Larkspur / Flaming Swords
		Galla Colors	Sir Gallahad III / Rouge et Noir
NO FIDDLING (b. 1945)	King Cole (b. 1938)	Pharamond	Phalaris / Selene
		Golden Melody	Mont d'Or II / Ormonda
	Big Hurry (br. 1936)	Black Toney	Peter Pan / Belgravia
		La Troienne	Teddy / Helene de Troie

924   **STRATEGE** 2 (b.c., February 26, 1968)

Bred by Jean Ternynck, in U.S.A.

Won 3 races, placed 2, 311,550 fr., in France, at 2 years, incl. Prix de la Foret and Prix Eclipse.

SANCTUS II (b. 1960)	Fine Top (br. 1949)	Fine Art	Artist's Proof / Finnoise
		Toupie	Vatellor / Tarentella
	Sanelta (b. 1954)	Tourment	Tourbillon / Fragment
		Satanella	Mahmoud / Avella
SINE DIE (br. 1963)	Sing Sing (b. 1957)	Tudor Minstrel	Owen Tudor / Sansonnet
		Agin the Law	Portlaw / Revolte
	Cantata (br. 1957)	Nearula	Nasrullah / Respite
		Organette	Cecil / Organic

925   **STRATFORD** 19 (b.c., May 23, 1964)

Bred by Razza Ticino, in Italy.

Won 12 races, placed 10, 82,719,041 L., in Italy and Germany, from 3 to 6 years, incl. Gran Premio di Milano, Coppa d'Oro di Milano (twice) and Grosser Preis von Baden; 3rd Gran Premio del Jockey Club, Premio Roma and Gran Premio di Milano.

CHARLOTTESVILLE (b. 1957)	Prince Chevalier (b. 1943)	Prince Rose	Rose Prince / Indolence
		Chevalerie	Abbot's Speed / Kassala
	Noorani (ch. 1950)	Nearco	Pharos / Nogara
		Empire Glory	Singapore / Skyglory
STAFFARDA (b. 1953)	Macherio (ch. 1941)	Ortello	Teddy / Hollebeck
		Mannozza	Manna / Moireen Rhue
	Staffa (b. 1948)	Orsenigo	Oleander / Ostana
		Signa	Ortello / Superga

926   **STUYVESANT** 16 (br.c., April 26, 1973)

Bred by Gestüt Schlenderhan, in Germany.

Won 7 races, placed 9, 658,500 DM., in Germany and Italy, from 2 to 5 years, incl. Deutsches Derby, Deutsches St. Leger, Grosser Hansa Preis and Gran Premio di Milano; 2nd Union-Rennen and Grosser Preis von Baden; 3rd Aral Pokal, Grosser Hertie Preis and Grosser Preis von Dortmund.

PRIAMOS (br. 1964)	Birkhahn (br. 1945)	Alchimist	Herold / Aversion
		Bramouse	Cappiello / Peregrine
	Palazzo (br. 1950)	Dante	Nearco / Rosy Legend
		Edifice	Monument / Phalconia
SABERA (b. 1961)	Fast Fox (br. 1947)	Fastnet	Pharos / Tatoule
		Foxcraft	Foxhunter / Philomene
	Suleika (br. 1954)	Ticino	Athanasius / Terra
		Schwarzblaurot	Magnat / Schwarzgold

927   **SUCCESSOR** 5 (b.c., March 27, 1964)

Bred by Wheatley Stable, in U.S.A.

Won 7 races, placed 12, $532,254, in U.S.A., from 2 to 4 years, incl. Champagne Stakes, Garden State Stakes and Lawrence Realization; 2nd Futurity Stakes, Pimlico Futurity, Roamer H. and Discovery H.; 3rd Jockey Club Gold Cup, Queens County H. and Cowdin Stakes.

BOLD RULER (b. 1954)	Nasrullah (b. 1940)	Nearco	Pharos / Nogara
		Mumtaz Begum	Blenheim / Mumtaz Mahal
	Miss Disco (b. 1944)	Discovery	Display / Ariadne
		Outdone	Pompey / Sweep Out
MISTY MORN (b. 1952)	Princequillo (b. 1940)	Prince Rose	Rose Prince / Indolence
		Cosquilla	Papyrus / Quick Thought
	Grey Flight (gr. 1945)	Mahmoud	Blenheim / Mah Mahal
		Planetoid	Ariel / La Chica

928   **SUFFOLK** 7 (ch.c., May 4, 1971)

Bred by Scuderia Aurora, in England.

Won 4 races, placed 6, 59,240,000 L., in Italy, from 2 to 4 years, incl. Derby Italiano; 2nd St. Leger Italiano; 3rd Gran Premio d'Italia.

PRETENDRE (ch. 1963)	Doutelle (ch. 1954)	Prince Chevalier	Prince Rose / Chevalerie
		Above Board	Straight Deal / Feola
	Limicola (ch. 1948)	Verso II	Pinceau / Variete
		Uccello	Donatello II / Great Tit
SAIGON (ch. 1965)	Mossborough (ch. 1947)	Nearco	Pharos / Nogara
		All Moonshine	Bobsleigh / Selene
	Savona II (ch. 1959)	Sky High	Hyperion / Pyramid
		Shooting Star VI	Big Game / Siesta

929   **SUMMER GUEST** 4 (ch.f., March 18, 1969)

Bred by H. B. Phipps, in U.S.A.

Won 13 races, placed 16, $480,760, in U.S.A., from 2 to 5 years, incl. Coaching Club American Oaks, Monmouth Oaks, Alabama Stakes, Spinster Stakes, Black-Eyed Susan Stakes, Hempstead H., Grey Lag H. and Bowling Green H.; 2nd Beldame Stakes, Delaware H., Black Helen H. and Top Flight H.; 3rd Woodward Stakes, Mother Goose Stakes, Delaware H., Diana H., Westchester H. and Bed o' Roses H.

NATIVE CHARGER (gr. 1962)	Native Dancer (gr. 1950)	Polynesian	Unbreakable / Black Polly
		Geisha	Discovery / Miyako
	Greek Blond (ch. 1946)	Heliopolis	Hyperion / Drift
		Peroxide	High Quest / Blonde Belle
CEE ZEE (b. 1956)	Heliopolis (b. 1936)	Hyperion	Gainsborough / Selene
		Drift	Swynford / Santa Cruz
	Sicily (br. 1942)	Reaping Reward	Sickle / Dustwhirl
		Gino Patty	Gino / Suntica

930   **SUNNY COVE** 1 (ch.f., March 13, 1957)

Bred by Miss D. Paget.

Won 4 races, placed 2, £7,574, in England and Ireland, at 2 and 3 years, incl. Park Hill Stakes, Newmarket Oaks; 2nd Irish Oaks.

NEARCO (br. 1935)	Pharos (b. 1920)	Phalaris	Polymelus / Bromus
		Scapa Flow	Chaucer / Anchora
	Nogara (b. 1928)	Havresac II	Rabelais / Hors Concours
		Catnip	Spearmint / Sibola
SUNNY GULF (b. 1951)	Persian Gulf (b. 1940)	Bahram	Blandford / Friar's Daughter
		Double Life	Bachelor's Double / Saint Joan
	Solana (b. 1936)	Solario	Gainsborough / Sun Worship
		Jamaica	Phalaris / Love-oil

931 **SUN PRINCE** 1 (ch.c., April 22, 1969)

Bred by Ballymacoll Stud Farm Ltd.

Won 4 races, placed 7, £47,922, in England and France, from 2 to 4 years, incl. Coventry Stakes, Prix Robert Papin, St. James's Palace Stakes, Queen Anne Stakes; 3rd 2,000 Guineas Stakes, Middle Park Stakes, Lockinge Stakes, Eclipse Stakes, Sussex Stakes.

PRINCELY GIFT (b. 1951)	Nasrullah (b. 1940)	Nearco	Pharos / Nogara
		Mumtaz Begum	Blenheim / Mumtaz Mahal
	Blue Gem (b. 1943)	Blue Peter	Fairway / Fancy Free
		Sparkle	Blandford / Gleam
COSTA SOLA (ch. 1963)	Worden II (ch. 1949)	Wild Risk	Rialto / Wild Violet
		Sans Tares	Sind / Tara
	Sunny Cove (ch. 1957)	Nearco	Pharos / Nogara
		Sunny Gulf	Persian Gulf / Solana

932 **SUPER CONCORDE** 3 (b.c., April 20, 1975)

Bred by Nelson Bunker Hunt, in U.S.A.

Won 4 races, placed 2, 900,000 fr., in France, at 2 and 3 years, incl. Prix Morny and Grand Criterium; 4th Prix de la Salamandre and Prix d'Ispahan.

BOLD REASONING (br. 1968)	Boldnesian (b. 1963)	Bold Ruler	Nasrullah / Miss Disco
		Alanesian	Polynesian / Alablue
	Reason to Earn (b. 1963)	Hail to Reason	Turn-to / Nothirdchance
		Sailing Home	Wait a Bit / Marching Home
PRIME ABORD (br. 1967)	Primera (b. 1954)	My Babu	Djebel / Perfume II
		Pirette	Deiri / Pimpette
	Homeward Bound (ch. 1961)	Alycidon	Donatello II / Aurora
		Sabie River	Signal Light / Amorcille

933 **SURUMU** 19 (ch.c., February 26, 1974)

Bred by Gestüt Fährhof, in Germany.

Won 3 races, placed 4, 376,510 DM., in Germany, at 2 and 3 years, incl. Deutsches Derby and Union-Rennen; 2nd Aral-Pokal.

LITERAT (br. 1965)	Birkhahn (br. 1945)	Alchimist	Herold / Aversion
		Bramouse	Cappiello / Peregrine
	Lis (b. 1960)	Masetto	Olymp / Mimosa
		Liebeslied	Ticino / Liebesgottin
SURAMA (bl. 1970)	Reliance II (b. 1962)	Tantieme	Deux pour Cent / Terka
		Relance III	Relic / Polaire II
	Suncourt (br. 1952)	Hyperion	Gainsborough / Selene
		Inquisition	Dastur / Jury

934 **SUSAN'S GIRL** 7 (b.f., March 23, 1969)

Bred by Fred W. Hooper, Jr., in U.S.A.

Won 29 races, placed 25, $1,251,668, in U.S.A., from 2 to 6 years, incl. Beldame Stakes (twice), Kentucky Oaks, Acorn Stakes, Delaware H. (twice), Spinster Stakes (twice), Matchmaker Stakes, Santa Margarita Invitational H., Santa Barbara H., Cotillion H., Gazelle H., Santa Susana Stakes, Santa Ynez Stakes, Santa Maria H., Susquehanna H., Falls City H., Apple Blossom H., Long Beach H., Signature Stakes and Villager Stakes; 2nd Mother Goose Stakes, Princess Stakes, Frizette Stakes, Gardenia Stakes, Demoiselle Stakes, Santa Monica H. (twice), Milady H., Long Beach H., Santa Margarita Invitational H., Vanity H. and Wilshire H.; 3rd Coaching Club American Oaks, Hollywood Oaks, Beldame Stakes, Matchmaker Stakes, Vanity H., Ladies H., San Pasqual H., Santa Maria H. and Maskette H.

QUADRANGLE (b. 1961)	Cohoes (b. 1954)	Mahmoud	Blenheim / Mah Mahal
		Belle of Troy	Blue Larkspur / La Troienne
	Tap Day (b. 1947)	Bull Lea	Bull Dog / Rose Leaves
		Scurry	Diavolo / Slapdash
QUAZE (ch. 1957)	Quibu (b. 1942)	Meadow	Fairway / Silver Mist
		Querendona	Diadochos / Querella
	Heavenly Sun (ch. 1952)	Olympia	Heliopolis / Miss Dolphin
		Daffy	The Porter / Lady Pike

935 **SUTTON PLACE** 1 (ch.f., May 27, 1975)

Bred by McGrath Trust Co.

Won 1 race, placed 6, £19,953, in England and Ireland, at 2 and 3 years, incl. Coronation Stakes; 2nd Mulcahy Stakes; 4th Irish 1,000 Guineas.

TYRANT (b. 1966)	Bold Ruler (b. 1954)	Nasrullah	Nearco / Mumtaz Begum
		Miss Disco	Discovery / Outdone
	Anadem (b. 1954)	My Babu	Djebel / Perfume II
		Anne of Essex	Panorama / Queen of Essex
ALICEVA (b. 1966)	Alcide (b. 1955)	Alycidon	Donatello II / Aurora
		Chenille	King Salmon / Sweet Aloe
	Feevagh (b. 1951)	Solar Slipper	Windsor Slipper / Solar Flower
		Astrid Wood	Bois Roussel / Astrid

936 **SWAN PRINCESS** 9 (b.f., March 8, 1978)

Bred by A. R. Jones Morgan.

Won 3 races, placed 5, £25,995, in England and Ireland, at 2 years, incl. Gallaghouse Phoenix Stakes; 2nd National Stakes (Sandown Park) and Molecomb Stakes.

SO BLESSED (br. 1965)	Princely Gift (b. 1951)	Nasrullah	Nearco / Mumtaz Begum
		Blue Gem	Blue Peter / Sparkle
	Lavant (b. 1955)	Le Lavandou	Djebel / Lavande
		Firle	Noble Star / Versicle
SWAN ANN (ch. 1971)	My Swanee (gr. 1963)	Petition	Fair Trial / Art Paper
		Grey Rhythm	Grey Sovereign / Metronome
	Anna Barry (ch. 1964)	Falls of Clyde	Fair Trial / Hyndford Bridge
		Anagram	Vilmoray / Matigram

937   **SWEET MIMOSA** 1 (b.f., April 27, 1967)

Bred by McGrath Trust Co., in Ireland.

Won 4 races, placed 2, £76,407, in Ireland and France, at 3 years, incl. Prix de Diane; 3rd Irish Guinness Oaks and Player-Wills Stakes.

LE LEVANSTELL (b. 1957)	Le Lavandou (b. 1944)	Djebel	Tourbillon
			Loika
		Lavande	Rustom Pasha
			Livadia
	Stella's Sister (ch. 1950)	Ballyogan	Fair Trial
			Serial
		My Aid	Knight of the Garter
			Flying Aid
FEEMOSS (b. 1960)	Ballymoss (ch. 1954)	Mossborough	Nearco
			All Moonshine
		Indian Call	Singapore
			Flittemere
	Feevagh (b. 1951)	Solar Slipper	Windsor Slipper
			Solar Flower
		Astrid Wood	Bois Roussel
			Astrid

938   **SWEET REVENGE** 13 (ch.c., April 24, 1967)

Bred by M. Burdett-Coutts.

Won 10 races, placed 10, £40,424, in England and France, from 2 to 5 years, incl. Prix de l'Abbaye de Longchamp, King's Stand Stakes, Prix Maurice de Gheest; 2nd Vernons Sprint Cup; 3rd Diadem Stakes, Prix de Meautry.

COMPENSATION (ch. 1959)	Gratitude (ch. 1953)	Golden Cloud	Gold Bridge
			Rainstorm
		Verdura	Court Martial
			Bura
	Shillelagh (ch. 1952)	Irish Dance	Columcille
			La Scala
		Killorcure	Nothing Venture
			Sovereign Remedy
TOO MUCH HONEY (ch. 1952)	Honeyway (br. 1941)	Fairway	Phalaris
			Scapa Flow
		Honey Buzzard	Papyrus
			Lady Peregrine
	Honey Hill (br. 1944)	Panorama	Sir Cosmo
			Happy Climax
		Calgary	Bosworth
			California

939   **SWEET SOLERA** 11 (ch.f., February 14, 1958)

Bred by Mrs. D. M. Walker.

Won 6 races, placed 2, £40,165, in England, at 2 and 3 years, incl. 1,000 Guineas Stakes, Oaks Stakes, Cherry Hinton Stakes; 3rd Queen Mary Stakes.

SOLONAWAY (b. 1946)	Solferino (b. 1940)	Fairway	Phalaris
			Scapa Flow
		Sol Speranza	Ballyferis
			Sunbridge
	Anyway (b. 1935)	Grand Glacier	Grand Parade
			Glaspia
		The Widow Murphy	Hainault or Pomme-de-terre
			Waterwitch
MISS GAMMON (b. 1947)	Grandmaster (b. 1942)	Atout Maitre	Vatout
			Royal Mistress
		Honorarium	Colorado Kid
			Emolument
	Rasher (ch. 1942)	His Grace	Blandford
			Malva
		Bacona	Call Boy
			Etona

940   **SWING EASY** 4 (b.c., February 20, 1968)

Bred by Mrs. Joseph Walker, Jr., in U.S.A.

Won 7 races, placed 5, £36,164, in England and France, at 2 and 3 years, incl. Nunthorpe Stakes, King's Stand Stakes, New Stakes, July Stakes, Richmond Stakes; 2nd Prix de l'Abbaye de Longchamp; 3rd Middle Park Stakes, Prix de la Salamandre, Greenham Stakes.

DELTA JUDGE (b. or br. 1960)	Traffic Judge (ch. 1952)	Alibhai	Hyperion
			Teresina
		Traffic Court	Discovery
			Traffic
	Beautillion (bl. 1953)	Noor	Nasrullah
			Queen of Baghdad
		Delta Queen	Bull Lea
			Bleebok
FREE FLOWING (b. 1958)	Polynesian (br. 1942)	Unbreakable	Sickle
			Blue Glass
		Black Polly	Polymelian
			Black Queen
	Rytina (br. 1943)	Milkman	Cudgel
			Milkmaid
		Sea Cradle	Toro
			Sea Dream

941   **SWISS MAID** 1 (b.f., February 13, 1975)

Bred by Mrs. J. R. Hine.

Won 5 races, placed 7, £102,109, in England, at 3 and 4 years, incl. Champion Stakes, Sun Chariot Stakes; 2nd Sussex Stakes; 3rd Hardwicke Stakes; 4th Benson and Hedges Gold Cup.

WELSH PAGEANT (b. 1966)	Tudor Melody (br. 1956)	Tudor Minstrel	Owen Tudor
			Sansonnet
		Matelda	Dante
			Fairly Hot
	Picture Light (b. 1954)	Court Martial	Fair Trial
			Instantaneous
		Queen of Light	Borealis
			Picture Play
HORNTON GRANGE (ch. 1967)	Hornbeam (ch. 1953)	Hyperion	Gainsborough
			Selene
		Thicket	Nasrullah
			Thorn Wood
	Grove Hall (ch. 1959)	Hook Money	Bernborough
			Besieged
		Ski Club	Chamossaire
			Private Entree

942   **TACHYPOUS** 3 (b.c., March 13, 1974)

Bred by G. L. Cambanis.

Won 2 races, placed 5, £57,026, in England, at 2 and 3 years, incl. William Hill Middle Park Stakes; 2nd 2,000 Guineas, Clerical Medical Greenham Stakes; 3rd St. James's Palace Stakes, Richmond Stakes.

HOTFOOT (br. 1966)	Firestreak (br. 1956)	Pardal	Pharis II
			Adargatis
		Hot Spell	Umidwar
			Haymaker
	Pitter Patter (br. 1953)	Kingstone	King Salmon
			Feola
		Rain	Fair Trial
			Monsoon
STILVI (b. 1969)	Derring-Do (b. 1961)	Darius	Dante
			Yasna
		Sipsey Bridge	Abernant
			Claudette
	Djerella (ch. 1960)	Guersant	Bubbles
			Montagnana
		Djeretta	Djebel
			Candida

943   TAINE 1 (ch.c., May 3, 1957)

Bred by S. Vagliano, in France.

Won 13 races, placed 10, 871,933 fr., and 1 jumping race, placed 5, 33,050 fr., in France, Italy and England, from 3 to 6 years, incl. Prix du Cadran (twice), Prix Jean Prat, Prix de Barbeville and Prix Gladiateur; also won Premio Roma, but disqualified and placed second; 2nd Prix Jean Prat; 3rd Prix du Cadran, Prix Ganay, Ascot Gold Cup, Grand Prix de Deauville and Prix Jean Prat.

VANDALE II (b. 1943)	Plassy (b. 1932)	Bosworth	Son-in-Law / Serenissima
		Pladda	Phalaris / Rothesay Bay
	Vanille (b. 1929)	La Farina	Sans Souci II / Malatesta
		Vaya	Beppo / Waterhen
TAUCHERE (ch. 1948)	Mustang (b. 1941)	Mieuxce	Massine / L'Olivete
		Buzz Fuzz	The Recorder / Lady Buzzer
	Tabaret (br. 1933)	Son-in-Law	Dark Ronald / Mother in Law
		Tabaris	Roi Herode / Tip-toe

944   TAJ DEWAN 2 (br.c., March 8, 1964)

Bred by Mme. G. Courtois, in France.

Won 4 races, placed 9, 1,129,157 fr., in France and England, from 2 to 4 years, incl. Prix Ganay and Prix de Chantilly; 2nd 2,000 Guineas, Champion Stakes, Eclipse Stakes, Prix Robert Papin and Prix de la Salamandre; 3rd Prix Morny, Grand Criterium, Prix du Jockey-Club and Grand Prix de Saint-Cloud.

PRINCE TAJ (b. 1954)	Prince Bio (b. 1941)	Prince Rose	Rose Prince / Indolence
		Biologie	Bacteriophage / Eponge
	Malindi (br. 1947)	Nearco	Pharos / Nogara
		Mumtaz Begum	Blenheim / Mumtaz Mahal
DEVINETTE (b. 1949)	Eble (br. 1940)	Davout	Parth / Dieuze
		Even Scales	Salmon-Trout / Lady Juror
	Dvina (b. 1941)	Sirtam	Sir Nigel / Tambourine
		Devineress	Finglas / Devachon

945   TAJO 21 (br.c., May 13, 1965)

Bred by Gestüt Ravensberg, in Germany.

Won 10 races, placed 19, 451,750 DM., in Germany, from 2 to 6 years, incl. Preis von Europa, Grosser Hansa Preis, Grosser Preis von Dortmund and Spreti-Rennen; 2nd Spreti-Rennen; 3rd Grosser Preis von Nordrhein-Westfalen and Aral-Pokal; 4th Preis von Europa and Aral-Pokal.

WAIDMANN (bl. 1956)	Neckar (bl. 1948)	Ticino	Athanasius / Terra
		Nixe	Arjaman / Nanon
	Waldrun (b. 1943)	Alchimist	Herold / Aversion
		Walburga	Aurelius / Wally
TREIBERWEHR (b. 1958)	Zuccarello (ch. 1938)	Ortello	Teddy / Hollebeck
		Flumigela	Michelangelo / Flush
	Trophae (b. 1949)	Abendfrieden	Ferro / Antonia
		Treibjagd	Graf Isolani / Teyde

946   TAKE YOUR PLACE 5 (b.c., February 4, 1973)

Bred by J. R. Gaines, Skara Glen Stable and D. R. Lasater, in U.S.A.

Won 3 races, placed 2, £28,878, in England, at 2 and 3 years, incl. Observer Gold Cup; 2nd Sandown Classic Trial Stakes.

ROUND TABLE (b. 1954)	Princequillo (b. 1940)	Prince Rose	Rose Prince / Indolence
		Cosquilla	Papyrus / Quick Thought
	Knight's Daughter (b. 1941)	Sir Cosmo	The Boss / Ayn Hali
		Feola	Friar Marcus / Aloe
ZONAH (b. 1958)	Nasrullah (b. 1940)	Nearco	Pharos / Nogara
		Mumtaz Begum	Blenheim / Mumtaz Mahal
	Gambetta (b. 1952)	My Babu	Djebel / Perfume II
		Rough Shod	Gold Bridge / Dalmary

947   TALAHASSE 14 (ch.c., March 10, 1961)

Bred by Mrs. R. Laye.

Won 6 races, £18,192, in England, at 2 and 3 years, incl. Gimcrack Stakes, Champagne Stakes, Hyperion Stakes.

RUSTAM (b. or br. 1953)	Persian Gulf (b. 1940)	Bahram	Blandford / Friar's Daughter
		Double Life	Bachelor's Double / Saint Joan
	Samovar (ch. 1940)	Caerleon	Phalaris / Canyon
		Carolina	Embargo / Georgia
MARY ELLARD (b. 1951)	Tudor Minstrel (br. 1944)	Owen Tudor	Hyperion / Mary Tudor II
		Sansonnet	Sansovino / Lady Juror
	Anacapri (b. 1939)	Tiberius	Foxlaw / Glenabatrick
		Travos	Salmon-Trout / Davos

948   TAMBOURINE II 11 (b.c., April 25, 1959)

Bred by Bull Run Stud, in U.S.A.

Won 3 races, placed 2, £56,469, in Ireland and France, at 3 years, incl. Irish Sweeps Derby; 4th Prix du Jockey Club.

PRINCEQUILLO (b. 1940)	Prince Rose (b. 1928)	Rose Prince	Prince Palatine / Eglantine
		Indolence	Gay Crusader / Barrier
	Cosquilla (b. 1933)	Papyrus	Tracery / Miss Matty
		Quick Thought	White Eagle / Mindful
LA MIRAMBULE (b. 1949)	Coaraze (b. 1942)	Tourbillon	Ksar / Durban
		Corrida	Coronach / Zariba
	La Futaie (b. 1937)	Gris Perle	Brabant / Mauve
		La Futelaye	Collaborator / La Francaise

949 **TANEB** 1 (b.c., March 24, 1963)

Bred by Ernest Masurel, in France.

Won 9 races, placed 12, 1,757,334 fr., in France, Germany and U.S.A., from 2 to 6 years, incl. Grand Prix de Saint-Cloud, Prix Henri Foy and San Luis Rey H.; 2nd Yankee Gold Cup, Bougainvillea H. and Dixie H.; 3rd Preis von Europa; 4th Grand Prix de Saint-Cloud and Prix Jacques le Marois.

TAPIOCA (b. 1953)	Vandale II (b. 1943)	Plassy	Bosworth / Pladda
		Vanille	La Farina / Vaya
	Semoule d'Or (b. 1945)	Vatellor	Vatout / Lady Elinor
		Semoule Fine	Firdaussi / Semoule
TENEBREUSE (ch. 1949)	Teleferique (ch. 1934)	Bacteriophage	Tetratema / Pharmacie
		Beaute de Neige	Saint Just / Bellezza
	Macreuse (ch. 1938)	Massine	Consols / Mauri
		Empire Crusade	Orpheus / Vervelle

950 **TANNENBERG** 21 (b.c., May 12, 1970)

Bred by Gestüt Ravensberg, in Germany.

Won 4 races, placed 7, 345,765 DM., in Germany, from 2 to 5 years, incl. Grosser Preis von Nordrhein-Westfalen, Deutsches St. Leger and Preis des Winterfavoriten; 2nd Deutsches Derby and Grosser Preis von Dusseldorf; 3rd Aral Pokal.

NECKAR (bl. 1948)	Ticino (b. 1939)	Athanasius	Ferro / Athanasie
		Terra	Aditi / Teufelsrose
	Nixe (b. 1941)	Arjaman	Herold / Aditja
		Nanon	Graf Isolani / Nella da Gubbio
TREIBERWEHR (br. 1958)	Zuccarello (ch. 1938)	Ortello	Teddy / Hollebeck
		Flumigela	Michelangelo / Flush
	Trophae (b. 1949)	Abendfrieden	Ferro / Antonia
		Treibjagd	Graf Isolani / Teyde

951 **TAPALQUE** 12 (b.c., April 25, 1965)

Bred by J. de Atucha, in France.

Won 5 races, placed 3, 1,573,604 fr., in France, from 3 to 5 years, incl. Prix du Jockey-Club; 2nd Grand Prix de Paris; 4th Grand Prix de Saint-Cloud.

ALIZIER (b. 1947)	Teleferique (ch. 1934)	Bacteriophage	Tetratema / Pharmacie
		Beauté de Neige	Saint Just / Bellezza
	Alizarine (b. 1939)	Coronach	Hurry On / Wet Kiss
		Armoise	Blandford / Coriandre
XORA (b. 1949)	Deux pour Cent (b. 1941)	Deiri	Aethelstan / Desra
		Dix pour Cent	Feridoon / La Chansonnerie
	Sikoro (b. 1944)	Maurepas or Vatellor	Vatout / Lady Elinor
		Vanikoro	Friar Marcus / Willowmore

952 **TAP ON WOOD** 14 (ch.c., February 15, 1976)

Bred by Irish National Stud Co. Ltd.

Won 10 races, placed 5, £99,045, in Ireland and England, at 2 and 3 years, incl. 2,000 Guineas Stakes, National Stakes (Curragh).

SALLUST (ch. 1969)	Pall Mall (ch. 1955)	Palestine	Fair Trial / Una
		Malapert	Portlaw / Malatesta
	Bandarilla (ch. 1960)	Matador	Golden Cloud / Spanish Galantry
		Interval	Jamaica Inn / Second Act
CAT O'MOUNTAINE (ch. 1967)	Ragusa (b. 1960)	Ribot	Tenerani / Romanella
		Fantan II	Ambiorix II / Red Eye
	Marie Elizabeth (ch. 1948)	Mazarin	Mieuxce / Boiarinia
		Miss Honor	Mr. Jinks / Bayora

953 **TARBES** 16 (b.c., April 22, 1968)

Bred by Mme. R. Canivet and Mme. G. Bridgland, in France.

Won 4 races, placed 6, 1,219,680 fr., in France, at 2 and 3 years, incl. Prix Lupin; 2nd Poule d'Essai des Poulains; 3rd Prix du Jockey-Club, Grand Prix de Saint-Cloud, Prix Morny and Prix de la Foret; 4th Prix Robert Papin.

TARQUIN (b. 1955)	Scratch II (ch. 1947)	Pharis II	Pharos / Carissima
		Orlamonde	Asterus / Naic
	La Taglioni (b. 1948)	Colombo	Manna / Lady Nairne
		La Truite II	Salmon-Trout / Quince
DJEIDA (b. 1955)	Djefou (b. 1945)	Djebel	Tourbillon / Loika
		Douce Folie	Monarch / Pure Folie
	Caida (b. 1947)	Mehemet Ali	Felicitation / Firouze Mahal
		Balaclava	Plassy / Ballili

954 **TARGOWICE** 16 (b.c., April 10, 1970)

Bred by Kerr Stables, in U.S.A.

Won 5 races, placed 1, 313,460 fr., in France, at 2 and 3 years, incl. Prix Eclipse, Prix Thomas Bryon.

ROUND TABLE (b. 1954)	Princequillo (b. 1940)	Prince Rose	Rose Prince / Indolence
		Cosquilla	Papyrus / Quick Thought
	Knight's Daughter (b. 1941)	Sir Cosmo	The Boss / Ayn Hali
		Feola	Friar Marcus / Aloe
MATRIARCH (b. 1964)	Bold Ruler (b. 1954)	Nasrullah	Nearco / Mumtaz Begum
		Miss Disco	Discovery / Outdone
	Lyceum (b. 1948)	Bull Lea	Bull Dog / Rose Leaves
		Colosseum	Ariel / Arena

955   **TARIM** 3 (br.c., April 6, 1969)

Bred by News of the World Stud, in England.

Won 3 races, placed 13, 433,390 DM., in Germany and France, from 2 to 4 years, incl. Deutsches Derby and Zukunftsrennen; 2nd Preis von Europa, Henckel-Rennen and Olympia-Preis; 3rd Aral Pokal, Grosser Preis von Nordrhein-Westfalen and Preis des Winterfavoriten; 4th Prix d'Ispahan.

TUDOR MELODY (br. 1956)	Tudor Minstrel (br. 1944)	Owen Tudor	Hyperion / Mary Tudor II
		Sansonnet	Sansovino / Lady Juror
	Matelda (br. 1947)	Dante	Nearco / Rosy Legend
		Fairly Hot	Solario / Fair Cop
TAMERELLA (b. 1961)	Tamerlane (br. 1952)	Persian Gulf	Bahram / Double Life
		Eastern Empress	Nearco / Cheveley Lady
	Ella Retford (ch. 1943)	Turkhan	Bahram / Theresina
		Prada	The MacNab / Pascaline II

---

956   **TARONA** 4 (b.f., March 25, 1975)

Bred by Citadel Stud Establishment, in Ireland.

Won 2 races, 235,000 fr., in France, at 2 years, incl. Criterium des Pouliches.

KARABAS (b. 1965)	Worden II (ch. 1949)	Wild Risk	Rialto / Wild Violet
		Sans Tares	Sind / Tara
	Fair Share (b. 1957)	Tantieme	Deux pour Cent / Terka
		Fair Linda	Fair Trial / Ortlinde
GRISCHUNA (b. 1959)	Ratification (b. 1953)	Court Martial	Fair Trial / Instantaneous
		Solesa	Solario / Mesa
	Mountain Path (b. 1948)	Bobsleigh	Gainsborough / Toboggan
		Path of Peace	Winalot / Grand Peace

---

957   **TEMPERENCE HILL** 4 (b.c., March 6, 1977)

Bred by Dr. A. F. Polk, Jr., in U.S.A.

Won 8 races, placed 4, $1,131,352, in U.S.A., at 2 and 3 years, incl. Belmont Stakes, Travers Stakes, Jockey Club Gold Cup, Arkansas Derby and Super Derby I; 2nd Withers Stakes and Dwyer Stakes.

STOP THE MUSIC (b. 1970)	Hail to Reason (br. 1958)	Turn-to	Royal Charger / Source Sucree
		Nothirdchance	Blue Swords / Galla Colors
	Bebopper (b. 1962)	Tom Fool	Menow / Gaga
		Bebop II	Prince Bio / Cappellina
SISTER SHANNON (b. or br. 1965)	Etonian (b. 1954)	Owen Tudor	Hyperion / Mary Tudor II
		Windsor Whisper	Windsor Slipper / Inkling
	Idaliza (b. 1957)	Princely Gift	Nasrullah / Blue Gem
		Pearl Fishing	Fair Copy / Brinda

---

958   **TENACITY** 9 (b.f., April 27, 1958)

Bred by W. H. D. Riley-Smith.

Won 3 races, placed 1, £6,413, in England, at 2 and 3 years, incl. Yorkshire Oaks, Princess Royal Stakes; 2nd Fred Darling Stakes.

WILWYN (b. 1948)	Pink Flower (b. 1940)	Oleander	Prunus / Orchidee II
		Plymstock	Polymelus / Winkipop
	Saracen (b. 1943)	Donatello II	Blenheim / Delleana
		Lovely Rosa	Tolgus / Napoule
ELA TENGAM (b. 1950)	Kingsway (b. 1940)	Fairway	Phalaris / Scapa Flow
		Yenna	Ksar / Yane
	Trixie from Tad (b. 1942)	Flag of Truce	Truculent / Concordia
		Tad	Tetrameter / Lemonade

---

959   **TENDER ANNIE** 1 (br.f., May 18, 1959)

Bred by National Stud.

Won 1 race, placed 3, £4,927, in England and Ireland, from 2 to 4 years, incl. Ribblesdale Stakes; 3rd Oaks Stakes, Hardwicke Stakes.

TENERANI (b. 1944)	Bellini (b. 1937)	Cavaliere d'Arpino	Havresac II / Chuette
		Bella Minna	Bachelor's Double / Santa Minna
	Tofanella (ch. 1931)	Apelle	Sardanapale / Angelina
		Try Try Again	Cylgad / Perseverance II
ANNIE OAKLEY (b. or br. 1952)	Big Game (b. 1939)	Bahram	Blandford / Friar's Daughter
		Myrobella	Tetratema / Dolabella
	Annetta (ch. 1941)	Fairway	Phalaris / Scapa Flow
		Caretta	Phalaris or Solario / Daumont

---

960   **TENNYSON** 1 (b.c., March 22, 1970)

Bred by F. W. Burmann, in France.

Won 2 races, placed 6, in France and England, at 3 and 4 years, incl. Grand Prix de Paris; 2nd Prix du Jockey-Club, Prix Ganay, Coronation Cup, Prix Niel and Prix Foy.

VAL DE LOIR (b. 1959)	Vieux Manoir (b. 1947)	Brantome	Blandford / Vitamine
		Vieille Maison	Finglas / Vieille Canaille
	Vali (br. 1954)	Sunny Boy III	Jock II / Fille de Soleil
		Her Slipper	Tetratema / Carpet Slipper
TIDRA (b. 1964)	Prince Taj (b. 1954)	Prince Bio	Prince Rose / Biologie
		Malindi	Nearco / Mumtaz Begum
	Djebel Idra (b. 1957)	Phil Drake	Admiral Drake / Philippa
		Djebellica	Djebel / Nica

961 **TEST CASE** 9 (b.c., January 31, 1958)

Bred by Sir Adrian Jarvis.

Won 3 races, placed 2, £8,143, in England, from 2 to 4 years, incl. Gimcrack Stakes; 3rd St. James's Palace Stakes.

SUPREME COURT (br. 1948)	Persian Gulf or Precipitation (ch. 1933)	Hurry On	Marcovil
			Tout Suite
		Double Life	Bachelor's Double
			Saint Joan
	Forecourt (br. 1943)	Fair Trial	Fairway
			Lady Juror
		Overture	Dastur
			Overmantle
TESSA GILLIAN (b. 1950)	Nearco (br. 1935)	Pharos	Phalaris
			Scapa Flow
		Nogara	Havresac II
			Catnip
	Sun Princess (b. 1937)	Solario	Gainsborough
			Sun Worship
		Mumtaz Begum	Blenheim
			Mumtaz Mahal

962 **TESTON** 1 (b.c., February 25, 1965)

Bred by Scuderia Mantova, in Italy.

Won 12 races, placed 19, 77,076,500 L., in Italy, from 2 to 6 years, incl. Gran Premio d'Italia and Premio Emanuele Filiberto; 2nd Gran Criterium and Derby Italiano; 3rd Premio d'Aprile.

RIO MARIN (ch. 1956)	Traghetto (ch. 1942)	Cavaliere d'Arpino	Havresac II
			Chuette
		Talma	Papyrus
			Tolbooth
	Cira (ch. 1942)	Cranach	Cannobie
			Chuette
		Cilea	Sans Crainte
			Calystegia
TONINA (b. 1956)	Fante (b. 1942)	Nesiotes	Hurry On
			Catnip
		Farnesiana	Michelangelo
			Flush
	Istriana (ch. 1947)	Arco	Singapore
			Archidamia
		Dalmazia	Bozzetto
			Talma

963 **THATCH** 5 (b.c., March 30, 1970)

Bred by Claiborne Farm, in U.S.A.

Won 7 races, placed 2, £40,277, in Ireland, England and France, at 2 and 3 years, incl. Vauxhall Trial Stakes, St. James's Palace Stakes, July Cup, Sussex Stakes; 4th 2,000 Guineas Stakes, Prix Morny.

FORLI (ch. 1963)	Aristophanes (ch. 1948)	Hyperion	Gainsborough
			Selene
		Commotion	Mieuxce
			Riot
	Trevisa (ch. 1951)	Advocate	Fair Trial
			Guiding Star
		Veneta	Foxglove
			Dogaresa
THONG (b. 1964)	Nantallah (b. 1953)	Nasrullah	Nearco
			Mumtaz Begum
		Shimmer	Flares
			Broad Ripple
	Rough Shod (b. 1944)	Gold Bridge	Swynford or Golden Boss
			Flying Diadem
		Dalmary	Blandford
			Simon's Shoes

964 **THATCHING** 5 (b.c., May 31, 1975)

Bred by Lyonstown House Stud.

Won 4 races, placed 2, £50,606, in Ireland and England, at 3 and 4 years, incl. William Hill July Cup, Cork and Orrery Stakes, Duke of York Stakes.

THATCH (b. 1970)	Forli (ch. 1963)	Aristophanes	Hyperion
			Commotion
		Trevisa	Advocate
			Veneta
	Thong (b. 1964)	Nantallah	Nasrullah
			Shimmer
		Rough Shod	Gold Bridge
			Dalmary
ABELLA (ch. 1968)	Premonition or Abernant (gr. 1946)	Owen Tudor	Hyperion
			Mary Tudor II
		Rustom Mahal	Rustom Pasha
			Mumtaz Mahal
	Darrica (ch. 1958)	Darius	Dante
			Yasna
		Erica Fragrans	Big Game
			Jennydang

965 **THE ELK** 11 (b.c., March 22, 1966)

Bred by D. and M. O'Brien.

Won 4 races, £23,745, in England, at 2 and 3 years, incl. Observer Gold Cup, Lingfield Derby Trial Stakes.

ONLY FOR LIFE (b. 1960)	Chanteur II (br. 1942)	Chateau Bouscaut	Kircubbin
			Ramondie
		La Diva	Blue Skies
			La Traviata
	Life Sentence (br. 1949)	Court Martial	Fair Trial
			Instantaneous
		Borobella	Bois Roussel
			Annabel
SAMBUR (b. 1959)	Big Game (b. 1939)	Bahram	Blandford
			Friar's Daughter
		Myrobella	Tetratema
			Dolabella
	Samaritaine (gr. 1949)	Maravedis	Massine
			Argentee
		Sarita	Biribi
			Lady Sarah

966 **THEIA** 16 (b.f., February 15, 1973)

Bred by Baronne S. de Lopez-Tarragoya, in France.

Won 5 races, placed 3, 714,229 fr., in France, at 2 and 3 years, incl. Criterium des Pouliches, Prix du Calvados, Prix Vanteaux and Prix de la Nonette; 2nd Prix Saint-Alary; 3rd Prix de la Cote Normande.

CARO (gr. 1967)	Fortino II (gr. 1959)	Grey Sovereign	Nasrullah
			Kong
		Ranavalo III	Relic
			Navarra II
	Chambord (ch. 1955)	Chamossaire	Precipitation
			Snowberry
		Life Hill	Solario
			Lady of the Snows
CAVADONGA (br. 1965)	Dan Cupid (ch. 1956)	Native Dancer	Polynesian
			Geisha
		Vixenette	Sickle
			Lady Reynard
	Edjele (b. 1957)	Djerik	Djebel
			La Tour Vesone
		Castel Amour	Chateauroux
			Djebel Amour

967   **THE MARSHAL** 10 (ch.c., May 1, 1962)

Bred by Col. W. M. E. Denison, in Ireland.

Won 6 races, placed 9, 415,505 fr., in France, from 2 to 4 years, incl. Prix Jacques le Marois and Prix de la Porte Maillot; 2nd Prix de Fontainebleau; 4th Prix Jacques le Marois and Prix de l'Abbaye de Longchamp.

MARTIAL (ch. 1957)	Hill Gail (b. 1949)	Bull Lea	Bull Dog / Rose Leaves
		Jane Gail	Blenheim / Lady Higloss
	Discipliner (ch. 1948)	Court Martial	Fair Trial / Instantaneous
		Edvina	Figaro / Louise
WAYFARER (ch. 1950)	Straight Deal (b. 1940)	Solario	Gainsborough / Sun Worship
		Good Deal	Apelle / Weeds
	Windway (ch. 1945)	Fairway	Phalaris / Scapa Flow
		Windfall	Windsor Lad / Miss Onslow

968   **THE MINSTREL** 8 (ch.c., March 11, 1974)

Bred by E. P. Taylor, in Canada.

Won 7 races, placed 2, £333,197, in Ireland and England, at 2 and 3 years, incl. Derby Stakes, Irish Sweeps Derby, King George VI and Queen Elizabeth Diamond Stakes, William Hill Dewhurst Stakes, Larkspur Stakes, Ascot 2,000 Guineas Trial; 2nd Irish 2,000 Guineas; 3rd 2,000 Guineas Stakes.

NORTHERN DANCER (b. 1961)	Nearctic (br. 1954)	Nearco	Pharos / Nogara
		Lady Angela	Hyperion / Sister Sarah
	Natalma (b. 1957)	Native Dancer	Polynesian / Geisha
		Almahmoud	Mahmoud / Arbitrator
FLEUR (b. 1964)	Victoria Park (b. 1957)	Chop Chop	Flares / Sceptical
		Victoriana	Windfields / Iribelle
	Flaming Page (b. 1959)	Bull Page	Bull Lea / Our Page
		Flaring Top	Menow / Flaming Top

969   **THREE TROIKAS** 1 (b.f., January 25, 1976)

Bred by A. Pfaff, in France.

Won 7 races, placed 5, 3,549,000 fr., in France, from 2 to 4 years, incl. Prix de l'Arc de Triomphe, Poule d'Essai des Pouliches, Prix Saint-Alary, Prix Vermeille, Prix Vanteaux and Prix d'Harcourt; 2nd Prix de Diane de Revlon, Prix Ganay and Prix du Prince d'Orange; 3rd Prix Dollar; 4th Prix de l'Arc de Triomphe.

LYPHARD (b. 1969)	Northern Dancer (b. 1961)	Nearctic	Nearco / Lady Angela
		Natalma	Native Dancer / Almahmoud
	Goofed (ch. 1960)	Court Martial	Fair Trial / Instantaneous
		Barra	Formor / La Favorite
THREE ROSES (b. 1968)	Dual (b. 1958)	Chanteur II	Chateau Bouscaut / La Diva
		Duplicity	Nearco / Doubleton
	Always Loyal (ch. 1963)	King's Troop	Princely Gift / Equiria
		Constant Worry	Torbido / Idle Curiosity

970   **TIDRA** 1 (b.f., March 19, 1964)

Bred by F. W. Burmann, in France.

Won 2 races, placed 2, 611,554 fr., in France, at 3 years, incl. Prix Saint-Alary; 2nd Prix de Diane.

PRINCE TAJ (b. 1954)	Prince Bio (b. 1941)	Prince Rose	Rose Prince / Indolence
		Biologie	Bacteriophage / Eponge
	Malindi (br. 1947)	Nearco	Pharos / Nogara
		Mumtaz Begum	Blenheim / Mumtaz Mahal
DJEBEL IDRA (b. 1957)	Phil Drake (b. 1952)	Admiral Drake	Craig an Eran / Plucky Liege
		Philippa	Vatellor / Philippa of Hainaut
	Djebellica (ch. 1948)	Djebel	Tourbillon / Loika
		Nica	Nino / Canalette

971   **TIERCERON** 6 (ch.c., April 8, 1969)

Bred by Razza Dormello-Olgiata, in Italy.

Won 9 races, placed 1, 110,375,000 L., in Italy, at 3 and 4 years, incl. Gran Premio d'Italia, Gran Premio del Jockey Club and St. Leger Italiano; 2nd Derby Italiano.

RELKO (b. 1960)	Tanerko (br. 1953)	Tantieme	Deux pour Cent / Terka
		La Divine	Fair Copy / La Diva
	Relance III (ch. 1952)	Relic	War Relic / Bridal Colors
		Polaire II	Le Volcan / Stella Polaris
TADOLINA (br. 1962)	Neckar (bl. 1948)	Ticino	Athanasius / Terra
		Nixe	Arjaman / Nanon
	Trevisana (b. 1945)	Niccolo Dell'Arca	Coronach / Nogara
		Tofanella	Apelle / Try Try Again

972   **TILLER** 3 (ch.g., April 14, 1974)

Bred by Claiborne Farm, in U.S.A.

Won 16 races, placed 13, $867,988, in U.S.A., from 3 to 6 years, incl. San Juan Capistrano H., San Antonio Stakes, Tidal H. (twice), Bowling Green H., San Marcos H. and Edgemere H.; 2nd Washington D.C. International, Santa Anita H., San Luis Rey Stakes, Man o'War Stakes, Manhattan H. and Turf Classic; 3rd Hialeah Turf Cup, Manhattan H., San Gabriel H., Brighton Beach H. and Bernard Baruch H.

HERBAGER (b. 1956)	Vandale II (b. 1943)	Plassy	Bosworth / Pladda
		Vanille	La Farina / Vaya
	Flagette (ch. 1951)	Escamillo	Firdaussi / Estoril
		Fidgette	Firdaussi / Boxeuse
CHAPPAQUIDDICK (br. 1968)	Relic (bl. 1945)	War Relic	Man o'War / Friar's Carse
		Bridal Colors	Black Toney / Vaila
	Baby Doll (br. 1956)	Dante	Nearco / Rosy Legend
		Bebe Grande	Niccolo Dell'Arca / Grande Corniche

973   **TIMANDRA** 12 (b.f., 1957)

Bred by Baron Guy de Rothschild, in France.

Won 4 races, 414,946 fr., in France, at 3 years, incl. Poule d'Essai des Pouliches, Prix de Diane and Prix Penelope.

COURT MARTIAL (ch. 1942)	Fair Trial (ch. 1932)	Fairway	Phalaris / Scapa Flow
		Lady Juror	Son-in-Law / Lady Josephine
	Instantaneous (b. 1931)	Hurry On	Marcovil / Tout Suite
		Picture	Gainsborough / Plymstock
BRIEF CANDLE (b. 1950)	Brantome (b. 1931)	Blandford	Swynford / Blanche
		Vitamine	Clarissimus / Viridiflora
	Lady Macbeth (b. 1944)	Teleferique	Bacteriophage / Beaute de Neige
		Anath	Massine / Ygerne

974   **TOM ROLFE** 9 (b.c., April 14, 1962)

Bred by Raymond Guest, in U.S.A.

Won 16 races, placed 10, $671,297, in U.S.A., from 2 to 4 years, incl. Preakness Stakes, American Derby, Arlington Classic, Chicagoan Stakes, Citation H., Aqueduct H., Salvator Mile and Cowdin Stakes; 2nd Belmont Stakes, Michigan Mile-and-One-Eighth H. and Washington Park H.; 3rd Kentucky Derby, Bay Shore Stakes and Futurity Stakes.

RIBOT (b. 1952)	Tenerani (b. 1944)	Bellini	Cavaliere d'Arpino / Bella Minna
		Tofanella	Apelle / Try Try Again
	Romanella (ch. 1943)	El Greco	Pharos / Gay Gamp
		Barbara Burrini	Papyrus / Bucolic
POCAHONTAS (br. 1955)	Roman (b. 1937)	Sir Gallahad III	Teddy / Plucky Liege
		Buckup	Buchan / Look Up
	How (br. 1948)	Princequillo	Prince Rose / Cosquilla
		The Squaw II	Sickle / Minnewaska

975   **TONNERA** 5 (b.f., April 14, 1963)

Bred by Francois Dupré, in France.

Won 4 races, placed 7, 481,392 fr., in France, at 2 and 3 years, incl. Prix Saint-Alary and Prix de la Grotte; 2nd Poule d'Essai des Pouliches.

WILD RISK (b. 1940)	Rialto (ch. 1923)	Rabelais	St. Simon / Satirical
		La Grelee	Helicon / Grignouse
	Wild Violet (b. 1935)	Blandford	Swynford / Blanche
		Wood Violet	Ksar / Pervencheres
TEXANA (ch. 1955)	Relic (bl. 1945)	War Relic	Man o'War / Friar's Carse
		Bridal Colors	Black Toney / Vaila
	Tosca (b. 1942)	Tourbillon	Ksar / Durban
		Eroica	Banstar / Macedonienne

976   **TOP VILLE** 8 (b.c., April 5, 1976)

Bred by Mme. F. Dupré, in Ireland.

Won 6 races, placed 3, 1,856,400 fr., in France, at 2 and 3 years, incl. Prix du Jockey-Club, Prix Lupin, Prix de Guiche, Prix Saint-Roman and Prix de Condé.

HIGH TOP (br. 1969)	Derring-Do (b. 1961)	Darius	Dante / Yasna
		Sipsey Bridge	Abernant / Claudette
	Camenae (b. 1961)	Vimy	Wild Risk / Mimi
		Madrilene	Court Martial / Marmite
SEGA VILLE (b. 1968)	Charlottesville (b. 1957)	Prince Chevalier	Prince Rose / Chevalerie
		Noorani	Nearco / Empire Glory
	La Sega (br. 1959)	Tantième	Deux pour Cent / Terka
		La Danse	Menetrier / Makada

977   **TOPYO** 7 (b.c., April 18, 1964)

Bred by Mme. Leon Volterra, in France.

Won 4 races, placed 8, 1,477,727 fr., in France and England, from 2 to 4 years, incl. Prix de l'Arc de Triomphe, Prix de la Cote Normande and Prix La Force; 3rd King George VI and Queen Elizabeth Stakes; 4th Prix d'Ispahan.

FINE TOP (br. 1949)	Fine Art (b. 1939)	Artist's Proof	Gainsborough / Clear Evidence
		Finnoise	Finglas / Unfortunate
	Toupie (br. 1943)	Vatellor	Vatout / Lady Elinor
		Tarentella	Blenheim / Andalusia
DELIRIOSA (b. 1956)	Delirium (ch. 1945)	Panorama	Sir Cosmo / Happy Climax
		Passed Out	Solario / Ambrosia
	La Fougueuse (b. 1950)	Admiral Drake	Craig an Eran / Plucky Liege
		La Foux	Vatout / Quick Change

978   **TOWER WALK** 8 (b.c., April 14, 1966)

Bred by Overbury Stud.

Won 7 races, placed 8, £40,480, in England and France, from 2 to 4 years, incl. Prix de l'Abbaye de Longchamp, Nunthorpe Stakes, Norfolk Stakes, National Stakes (Sandown), Greenham Stakes, Palace House Stakes; 2nd 2,000 Guineas Stakes, Middle Park Stakes; 3rd July Cup, Lockinge Stakes.

HIGH TREASON (ch. 1951)	Court Martial (ch. 1942)	Fair Trial	Fairway / Lady Juror
		Instantaneous	Hurry On / Picture
	Eastern Grandeur (ch. 1945)	Gold Bridge	Swynford or Golden Boss / Flying Diadem
		China Maiden	Tai-Yang / Bibi Sahiba
LORRIKEET (b. 1955)	Pearl Diver (b. 1944)	Vatellor	Vatout / Lady Elinor
		Pearl Cap	Le Capucin / Pearl Maiden
	Parakeet (b. 1950)	Colombo	Manna / Lady Nairne
		Lundy Parrot	Flamingo / Waterval

979   TRACK SPARE 3 (b.c., April 28, 1963)

Bred by Major and Mrs. Stephen Johnson.

Won 5 races, placed 10, £28,705, in England and France, from 2 to 4 years, incl. Middle Park Stakes, St. James's Palace Stakes; 2nd Queen Elizabeth II Stakes, New Stakes; 4th Sussex Stakes.

SOUND TRACK (ch. 1957)	Whistler (ch. 1950)	Panorama	Sir Cosmo / Happy Climax
		Farthing Damages	Fair Trial / Futility
	Bridle Way (b. or br. 1952)	Mustang	Mieuxce / Buzz Fuzz
		Straight Path	Straight Deal / Double Rose II
ROSY MYTH (b. or br. 1958)	Nearco (br. 1935)	Pharos	Phalaris / Scapa Flow
		Nogara	Havresac II / Catnip
	Rosy Dolly (br. 1950)	Bois Roussel	Vatout / Plucky Liege
		Rosy Legend	Dark Legend / Rosy Cheeks

980   TRANSWORLD 1 (ch.c., February 26, 1974)

Bred by Elmendorf Farm, in U.S.A.

Won 3 races, placed 1, £22,608, in Ireland and England, at 3 years, incl. Irish St. Leger; 2nd Blandford Stakes.

PRINCE JOHN (ch. 1953)	Princequillo (b. 1940)	Prince Rose	Rose Prince / Indolence
		Cosquilla	Papyrus / Quick Thought
	Not Afraid (b. 1948)	Count Fleet	Reigh Count / Quickly
		Banish Fear	Blue Larkspur / Herodiade
HORNPIPE (ch. 1965)	Hornbeam (ch. 1953)	Hyperion	Gainsborough / Selene
		Thicket	Nasrullah / Thorn Wood
	Sugar Bun (ch. 1946)	Mahmoud	Blenheim / Mah Mahal
		Galatea II	Dark Legend / Galaday II

981   TREE OF KNOWLEDGE 4 (b.c., February 10, 1970)

Bred by Pin Oak Stud Inc., in U.S.A.

Won 9 races, placed 11, $203,735, in U.S.A., from 2 to 6 years, incl. Hollywood Gold Cup; 2nd Bel Air H.

DR. FAGER (b. 1964)	Rough'n Tumble (b. 1948)	Free for All	Questionnaire / Panay
		Roused	Bull Dog / Rude Awakening
	Aspidistra (b. 1954)	Better Self	Bimelech / Bee Mac
		Tilly Rose	Bull Brier / Tilly Kate
BENT TWIG (b./br. 1959)	Nasrullah (b. 1940)	Nearco	Pharos / Nogara
		Mumtaz Begum	Blenheim / Mumtaz Mahal
	Pines of Rome (b. 1949)	Roman	Sir Gallahad III / Buckup
		Seven Pines	Haste / Zephyretta

982   TRELAWNY 1 (br.g., March 1, 1956)

Bred by Astor Studs.

Won 11 races, placed 9, £19,279, in England, from 2 to 10 years, incl. Chester Cup, Queen Alexandra Stakes (twice), Goodwood Cup. Also ran over hurdles at 10 and 11 years, won 3 races, placed 1, £1,952.

BLACK TARQUIN (br. 1945)	Rhodes Scholar (b. 1933)	Pharos	Phalaris / Scapa Flow
		Book Law	Buchan / Popingaol
	Vagrancy (b. 1939)	Sir Gallahad III	Teddy / Plucky Liege
		Valkyr	Man o' War / Princess Palatine
INDIAN NIGHT (br. 1946)	Umidwar (b. 1931)	Blandford	Swynford / Blanche
		Uganda	Bridaine / Hush
	Fairly Hot (br. 1939)	Solario	Gainsborough / Sun Worship
		Fair Cop	Fairway / Popingaol

983   TREPAN 26 (br.c., May 21, 1972)

Bred by Mme. J. Couturié, in France.

Won 9 races, placed 10, 1,055,105 fr., in France, from 2 to 5 years, incl. Prix Dollar, Prix Quincey and La Coupe de Maisons-Laffitte; also won Prince of Wales's Stakes and Joe Coral Eclipse Stakes in England, but disqualified from both; 2nd Prix Edmond Blanc; 3rd Prix Jacques le Marois and Prix de Ris-Orangis; 4th Prix d'Ispahan.

BREAKSPEAR II (br. 1961)	Bold Ruler (b. 1954)	Nasrullah	Nearco / Mumtaz Begum
		Miss Disco	Discovery / Outdone
	Pocket Edition (br. 1944)	Roman	Sir Gallahad III / Buckup
		Never Again	Pharos / Confidence
QUIRIQUINA (b. 1966)	Molvedo (br. 1958)	Ribot	Tenerani / Romanella
		Maggiolina	Nakamuro / Murcia
	La Chaussee (ch. 1961)	Tyrone	Tornado / Statira
		Flying Colours	Massine / Red Flame

984   TRIBAL CHIEF 19 (b.c., February 27, 1967)

Bred by J. R. Hindley.

Won 3 races, placed 1, £10,096, in England, at 2 and 3 years, incl. Norfolk Stakes, New Stakes.

PRINCELY GIFT (b. 1951)	Nasrullah (b. 1940)	Nearco	Pharos / Nogara
		Mumtaz Begum	Blenheim / Mumtaz Mahal
	Blue Gem (b. 1943)	Blue Peter	Fairway / Fancy Free
		Sparkle	Blandford / Gleam
MWANZA (b. 1961)	Petition (br. 1944)	Fair Trial	Fairway / Lady Juror
		Art Paper	Artist's Proof / Quire
	Lake Tanganyika (b. 1945)	Ujiji	Umidwar / Theresina
		Blue Girl	Gainsborough / Trustful

186

985   **TRILLION** 4 (b.f., April 15, 1974)

Bred by Nelson Bunker Hunt, in U.S.A.

Won 9 races, placed 18, 4,268,790 fr., in France, Germany, U.S.A. and Canada, from 3 to 5 years, incl. Prix Ganay, Prix de Minerve, Prix de Royallieu, Prix Dollar (twice), Prix Foy and Prix d'Harcourt; 2nd Prix de Diane de Revlon, Prix Royal Oak, Prix de l'Arc de Triomphe, Prix d'Ispahan, Grand Prix de Saint-Cloud, Prix Ganay, Prix d'Harcourt, Prix Gontaut-Biron, Prix Foy, Prix du Prince d'Orange, Canadian International Championship, Turf Classic, Oak Tree Invitational H. and Washington D.C. International; 3rd Prix Jean de Chaudenay, Preis von Europa and Turf Classic; 4th Washington D.C. International.

HAIL TO REASON (br. 1958)	Turn-to (b. 1951)	Royal Charger	Nearco / Sun Princess
		Source Sucree	Admiral Drake / Lavendula II
	Nothirdchance (b. 1948)	Blue Swords	Blue Larkspur / Flaming Swords
		Galla Colors	Sir Gallahad III / Rouge et Noir
MARGARETHEN (br. 1962)	Tulyar (br. 1949)	Tehran	Bois Roussel / Stafaralla
		Neocracy	Nearco / Harina
	Russ-Marie (b. 1956)	Nasrullah	Nearco / Mumtaz Begum
		Marguery	Sir Gallahad III / Marguerite

986   **TRIPLE FIRST** 1 (b.f., March 5, 1974)

Bred by Moyns Park Stud.

Won 7 races, placed 4, £46,350, in England, at 2 and 3 years, incl. Nassau Stakes, Sun Chariot Stakes, Musidora Stakes; 3rd Argos Star Fillies' Mile; 4th Oaks Stakes, Yorkshire Oaks.

HIGH TOP (br. 1969)	Derring-Do (b. 1961)	Darius	Dante / Yasna
		Sipsey Bridge	Abernant / Claudette
	Camenae (b. 1961)	Vimy	Wild Risk / Mimi
		Madrilene	Court Martial / Marmite
FIELD MOUSE (gr. 1964)	Grey Sovereign (gr. 1948)	Nasrullah	Nearco / Mumtaz Begum
		Kong	Baytown / Clang
	Meadow Song (b. 1953)	Nirgal	Goya II / Castillane
		Singing Grass	War Admiral / Boreale

987   **TROMOS** 3 (ch.c., March 10, 1976)

Bred by G. L. Cambanis.

Won 2 races, placed 2, £40,010, in England, at 2 and 3 years, incl. William Hill Dewhurst Stakes; 2nd Ladbroke Craven Stakes. Ran twice in U.S.A. at 4 years.

BUSTED (b. 1963)	Crepello (ch. 1954)	Donatello II	Blenheim / Delleana
		Crepuscule	Mieuxce / Red Sunset
	Sans Le Sou (b. 1957)	Vimy	Wild Risk / Mimi
		Martial Loan	Court Martial / Loan
STILVI (b. 1969)	Derring-Do (b. 1961)	Darius	Dante / Yasna
		Sipsey Bridge	Abernant / Claudette
	Djerella (ch. 1960)	Guersant	Bubbles / Montagnana
		Djeretta	Djebel / Candida

988   **TROPICARO** 9 (b.f., April 6, 1978)

Bred by Benjamin Coates, in France.

Won 2 races, 299,000 fr., in France, at 2 years, incl. Prix Marcel Boussac (Criterium des Pouliches).

CARO (gr. 1967)	Fortino II (gr. 1959)	Grey Sovereign	Nasrullah / Kong
		Ranavalo III	Relic / Navarra II
	Chambord (ch. 1955)	Chamossaire	Precipitation / Snowberry
		Life Hill	Solario / Lady of the Snows
TROPICAL CREAM (b. 1971)	Creme Dela Creme (b. 1963)	Olympia	Heliopolis / Miss Dolphin
		Judy Rullah	Nasrullah / Judy-Rae
	Tropic Star (ch. 1959)	Tropique	Fontenay / Aurore Boreale
		Patricia's Star	Prince Chevalier / Noah's Ark

989   **TROY** 1 (b.c., March 25, 1976)

Bred by Ballymacoll Stud Farm Ltd.

Won 8 races, placed 3, £450,494, in England, Ireland and France, at 2 and 3 years, incl. Derby Stakes, Irish Sweeps Derby, King George VI and Queen Elizabeth Diamond Stakes, Benson and Hedges Gold Cup, Sandown Classic Trial Stakes; 2nd Royal Lodge Stakes; 3rd Prix de l'Arc de Triomphe.

PETINGO (b. 1965)	Petition (br. 1944)	Fair Trial	Fairway / Lady Juror
		Art Paper	Artist's Proof / Quire
	Alcazar (ch. 1957)	Alycidon	Donatello II / Aurora
		Quarterdeck	Nearco / Poker Chip
LA MILO (ch. 1963)	Hornbeam (ch. 1953)	Hyperion	Gainsborough / Selene
		Thicket	Nasrullah / Thorn Wood
	Pin Prick (b. 1955)	Pinza	Chanteur II / Pasqua
		Miss Winston	Royal Charger / East Wantleye

990   **TRY MY BEST** 8 (b.c., April 28, 1975)

Bred by E. P. Taylor, in U.S.A.

Won 4 races, £48,389, in England and Ireland, at 2 and 3 years, incl. William Hill Dewhurst Stakes, Larkspur Stakes, Vauxhall Trial Stakes.

NORTHERN DANCER (b. 1961)	Nearctic (br. 1954)	Nearco	Pharos / Nogara
		Lady Angela	Hyperion / Sister Sarah
	Natalma (b. 1957)	Native Dancer	Polynesian / Geisha
		Almahmoud	Mahmoud / Arbitrator
SEX APPEAL (ch. 1970)	Buckpasser (b. 1963)	Tom Fool	Menow / Gaga
		Busanda	War Admiral / Businesslike
	Best in Show (b. 1965)	Traffic Judge	Alibhai / Traffic Court
		Stolen Hour	Mr. Busher / Late Date

991   TUDENHAM 21 (br.c., February 21, 1970)

Bred by Cleaboy Farms Co.

Won 1 race, placed 5, £16,323, in England, from 2 to 4 years, incl. Middle Park Stakes; 2nd Mill Reef Stakes.

TUDOR MELODY (br. 1956)	Tudor Minstrel (br. 1944)	Owen Tudor	Hyperion / Mary Tudor II
		Sansonnet	Sansovino / Lady Juror
	Matelda (br. 1947)	Dante	Nearco / Rosy Legend
		Fairly Hot	Solario / Fair Cop
HEATH ROSE (b. 1964)	Hugh Lupus (b. 1952)	Djebel	Tourbillon / Loika
		Sakountala	Goya II / Samos
	Cherished (b. 1955)	Chanteur II	Chateau Bouscaut / La Diva
		Netherton Maid	Nearco / Phase

992   TUDOR MUSIC 11 (br.c., March 2, 1966)

Bred by Mrs. A. King.

Won 6 races, placed 6, £27,353, in England, at 2 and 3 years, incl. Gimcrack Stakes, Richmond Stakes, Cork and Orrery Stakes, July Cup, Vernons Sprint Cup; 2nd Champagne Stakes, Challenge Stakes; 3rd Diadem Stakes; 4th Middle Park Stakes.

TUDOR MELODY (br. 1956)	Tudor Minstrel (br. 1944)	Owen Tudor	Hyperion / Mary Tudor II
		Sansonnet	Sansovino / Lady Juror
	Matelda (br. 1947)	Dante	Nearco / Rosy Legend
		Fairly Hot	Solario / Fair Cop
FRAN (ch. 1959)	Acropolis (ch. 1952)	Donatello II	Blenheim / Delleana
		Aurora	Hyperion / Rose Red
	Madrilene (ch. 1951)	Court Martial	Fair Trial / Instantaneous
		Marmite	Mr. Jinks / Gentlemen's Relish

993   TUMBLEDOWNWIND 4 (b.c., February 17, 1975)

Bred by Blandford Stud Farm Co.

Won 5 races, placed 9, £54,375, in England, Italy and France, from 2 to 4 years, incl. Gimcrack Stakes; 2nd Premio Chiusura; 3rd Mill Reef Stakes; 4th 2,000 Guineas.

TUMBLE WIND (b. 1964)	Restless Wind (ch. 1956)	Windy City	Wyndham / Staunton
		Lump Sugar	Bull Lea / Sugar Run
	Easy Stages (b. 1953)	Endeavour II	British Empire / Himalaya
		Saturday Off	Kiev / Mexican Tea
MISS PINKERTON (b. 1967)	Above Suspicion (b. 1956)	Court Martial	Fair Trial / Instantaneous
		Above Board	Straight Deal / Feola
	Igea (b. 1958)	Asterios	Oleander / Astarte
		Ischia II	Ticino / Yonne

994   T.V. LARK 9 (b.c., February 12, 1957)

Bred by Dr. W. D. Lucas, in U.S.A.

Won 19 races, placed 19, $902,194, in U.S.A., from 2 to 5 years, incl. Washington D.C. International, Arlington Futurity, American Derby, Arlington Classic, United Nations H., Washington Park H., Argonaut Stakes, Hawthorne Gold Cup, Los Angeles H., Knickerbocker H. and Philadelphia Turf H.; 2nd Hollywood Derby, San Felipe H., San Carlos H., United Nations H. and Round Table H.; 3rd Cinema H. and San Vicente H.

INDIAN HEMP (ch. 1949)	Nasrullah (b. 1940)	Nearco	Pharos / Nogara
		Mumtaz Begum	Blenheim / Mumtaz Mahal
	Sabzy (br. 1943)	Stardust	Hyperion / Sister Stella
		Sarita	Swynford / Molly Desmond
MISS LARKSFLY (br. 1948)	Heelfly (br. 1934)	Royal Ford	Swynford / Royal Yoke
		Canfli	Campfire / Flivver
	Larksnest (br. 1943)	Bull Dog	Teddy / Plucky Liege
		Light Lark	Blue Larkspur / Ruddy Light

995   TWILIGHT ALLEY 16 (ch.c., April 26, 1959)

Bred by Sassoon Studs.

Won 2 races, placed 1, £11,715, in England, at 3 and 4 years, incl. Ascot Gold Cup; 2nd Henry II Stakes.

ALYCIDON (ch. 1945)	Donatello II (ch. 1934)	Blenheim	Blandford / Malva
		Delleana	Clarissimus / Duccia di Buoninsegna
	Aurora (ch. 1936)	Hyperion	Gainsborough / Selene
		Rose Red	Swynford / Marchetta
CREPUSCULE (ch. 1948)	Mieuxce (b. 1933)	Massine	Consols / Mauri
		L'Olivete	Opott / Jonicole
	Red Sunset (b. 1941)	Solario	Gainsborough / Sun Worship
		Dulce II	Asterus / Dorina

996   TWO TO PARIS 2 (b.f., April 23, 1968)

Bred by L. P. Doherty, in U.S.A.

Won 1 race, placed 2, 173,410 fr., in France, at 2 and 3 years, incl. Criterium des Pouliches.

SIR RIBOT (b. 1959)	Ribot (b. 1952)	Tenerani	Bellini / Tofanella
		Romanella	El Greco / Barbara Burrini
	Monarchia (b. 1947)	Dante	Nearco / Rosy Legend
		Maintenon	Solario / Queen Christina
RUNNING ACCOUNT (b. 1963)	Tuleg (b. 1956)	Tulyar	Tehran / Neocracy
		E.G.K.	Rentenmark / Ardgo
	Bankline (b. 1946)	Debenture	Apple Sammy / Preference
		Veronica C	Master Charlie / The Minch

997   TYPECAST 13 (b.f., April 10, 1966)

Bred by Nuckols Brothers, in U.S.A.

Won 21 races, placed 21, $535,567, in U.S.A., from 3 to 6 years, incl. Hollywood Park Invitational Turf H., Sunset H., Man o'War Stakes, Long Beach H., Milady H., Santa Monica H. and Las Palmas H.; 2nd Vanity H., Santa Maria H., Manhattan H., Beverly Hills H., Ramona H. and Thanksgiving Day H.; 3rd Sunset H., Santa Margarita Invitational H. and Beverly Hills H.

PRINCE JOHN (ch. 1953)	Princequillo (b. 1940)	Prince Rose	Rose Prince / Indolence
		Cosquilla	Papyrus / Quick Thought
	Not Afraid (b. 1948)	Count Fleet	Reigh Count / Quickly
		Banish Fear	Blue Larkspur / Herodiade
JOURNALETTE (b. 1959)	Summer Tan (b. 1952)	Heliopolis	Hyperion / Drift
		Miss Zibby	Omaha / Fairisk
	Manzana (b. 1948)	Count Fleet	Reigh Count / Quickly
		Durazna	Bull Lea / Myrtlewood

998   TYPHOON 20 (br.c., March 2, 1958)

Bred by Mrs. M. Clarke.

Won 13 races, placed 14, £32,699, in England, Ireland, France and U.S.A., from 2 to 6 years, incl. Coventry Stakes, Richmond Stakes, Westlake H.; 2nd Prix Morny, Bay Meadows H., San Diego H.

HONEYWAY (br. 1941)	Fairway (b. 1925)	Phalaris	Polymelus / Bromus
		Scapa Flow	Chaucer / Anchora
	Honey Buzzard (ch. 1931)	Papyrus	Tracery / Miss Matty
		Lady Peregrine	White Eagle / Lisma
KINGSWORTHY (b. 1953)	Kingstone (b. 1942)	King Salmon	Salmon-Trout / Malva
		Feola	Friar Marcus / Aloe
	Sotades (ch. 1946)	Stardust	Hyperion / Sister Stella
		Springwell	Fairhaven / Springtime

999   TYRNAVOS 3 (b.c., February 17, 1977)

Bred by G. L. Cambanis.

Won 3 races, placed 3, £164,766, in England and Ireland, at 2 and 3 years, incl. Irish Sweeps Derby, Ladbrokes Craven Stakes; 2nd William Hill Dewhurst Stakes.

BLAKENEY (b. 1966)	Hethersett (b. 1959)	Hugh Lupus	Djebel / Sakountala
		Bride Elect	Big Game / Netherton Maid
	Windmill Girl (b. 1961)	Hornbeam	Hyperion / Thicket
		Chorus Beauty	Chanteur II / Neberna
STILVI (b. 1969)	Derring-Do (b. 1961)	Darius	Dante / Yasna
		Sipsey Bridge	Abernant / Claudette
	Djerella (ch. 1960)	Guersant	Bubbles / Montagnana
		Djeretta	Djebel / Candida

1000   UN KOPECK 5 (b.c., April 22, 1971)

Bred by Mme. J. Barker and J. Marx, in France.

Won 6 races, placed 10, 1,272,630 fr., in France, from 2 to 4 years, incl. Grand Prix de Saint-Cloud, Grand Prix d'Evry and Prix La Force; 3rd Prix Kergorlay, Prix Jean de Chaudenay and Prix Dollar; 4th Prix de l'Arc de Triomphe.

PIQU'ARRIERE (b. 1957)	Piqu'Avant (b. 1947)	Admiral Drake	Craig an Eran / Plucky Liege
		Providence	Vatout / Frivolity
	Garance (ch. 1945)	Teleferique	Bacteriophage / Beaute de Neige
		Alizarine	Coronach / Armoise
MACOPECK (b. 1962)	Pres du Feu (ch. 1955)	Prince Bio	Prince Rose / Biologie
		Proximites	Monarch of the Glen / Jenny Dee
	La Nievre (b. 1950)	Norseman	Umidwar / Tara
		Picardie	Goya II / Pereire

1001   VAGUELY NOBLE 1 (b.c., May 15, 1965)

Bred by Major L. B. Holliday.

Won 6 races, placed 3, £148,641, in England and France, at 2 and 3 years, incl. Observer Gold Cup, Prix de l'Arc de Triomphe; 3rd Grand Prix de Saint-Cloud.

VIENNA (ch. 1957)	Aureole (ch. 1950)	Hyperion	Gainsborough / Selene
		Angelola	Donatello II / Feola
	Turkish Blood (b. 1944)	Turkhan	Bahram / Theresina
		Rusk	Manna / Baby Polly
NOBLE LASSIE (b. 1956)	Nearco (br. 1935)	Pharos	Phalaris / Scapa Flow
		Nogara	Havresac II / Catnip
	Belle Sauvage (ch. 1949)	Big Game	Bahram / Myrobella
		Tropical Sun	Hyperion / Brulette

1002   VAL DE LOIR 5 (b.c., May 7, 1959)

Bred by R. Forget, in France.

Won 7 races, placed 6, 1,317,506 fr., in France, from 2 to 4 years, incl. Prix du Jockey-Club, Prix Noailles, Prix Hocquart and Grand Prix de Deauville; 2nd Prix Ganay and Grand Prix de Saint-Cloud; 3rd Prix de l'Arc de Triomphe and Prix du Prince d'Orange; 4th Prix Robert Papin and King George VI and Queen Elizabeth Stakes.

VIEUX MANOIR (b. 1947)	Brantome (b. 1931)	Blandford	Swynford / Blanche
		Vitamine	Clarissimus / Viridiflora
	Vieille Maison (b. 1936)	Finglas	Bruleur / Fair Simone
		Vieille Canaille	Zionist / Ficelle
VALI (br. 1954)	Sunny Boy III (b. 1944)	Jock II	Asterus / Naic
		Fille de Soleil	Solario / Fille de Salut
	Her Slipper (b. 1936)	Tetratema	The Tetrarch / Scotch Gift
		Carpet Slipper	Phalaris / Simon's Shoes

1003   VAL DE L'ORNE 11 (b.c., February 2, 1972)

Bred by W. Stora, in France.

Won 4 races, placed 1, 2,049,707 fr., in France, at 2 and 3 years, incl. Prix du Jockey-Club, Prix Noailles and Prix Hocquart; 2nd Grand Criterium.

VAL DE LOIR (b. 1959)	Vieux Manoir (b. 1947)	Brantome	Blandford / Vitamine
		Vieille Maison	Finglas / Vieille Canaille
	Vali (br. 1954)	Sunny Boy III	Jock II / Fille de Soleil
		Her Slipper	Tetratema / Carpet Slipper
AGLAE (b. 1965)	Armistice III (b. 1959)	Worden II	Wild Risk / Sans Tares
		Commemoration	Vandale II / Anne Comnene
	Aglae Grace (br. 1947)	Mousson	Rose Prince / Spring Tide
		Agathe	Amfortas / Melanie

1004   VALIANT HEART 26 (b.c., March 23, 1977)

Bred by Andre Michel, in France.

Won 2 races, placed 3, 491,500 fr., in France, at 3 years, incl. Grand Prix de Paris; 3rd Prix de l'Esperance.

MATAHAWK (b./br. 1972)	Sea Hawk II (gr. 1963)	Herbager	Vandale II / Flagette
		Sea Nymph	Free Man / Sea Spray
	Carromata (b. 1965)	St. Paddy	Aureole / Edie Kelly
		Carrozza	Dante / Calash
LA VIGERIE (b. 1967)	Buisson d'Or (b. 1950)	Coastal Traffic	Hyperion / Rose of England
		Rose O'Lynn	Pherozshah / Rocklyn
	Sylvania (b. 1959)	Sphinx II	Meridien / Sylla II
		Luz	Athos / Lamia

1005   VALORIS 5 (br.f., April 30, 1963)

Bred by R. Forget, in France.

Won 2 races, placed 1, £41,968, in Ireland and England, at 2 and 3 years incl. Irish 1,000 Guineas, Oaks Stakes.

TIZIANO (b. 1957)	Sicambre (br. 1948)	Prince Bio	Prince Rose / Biologie
		Sif	Rialto / Suavita
	Trevisana (b. 1945)	Niccolo Dell'Arca	Coronach / Nogara
		Tofanella	Apelle / Try Try Again
VALI (br. 1954)	Sunny Boy III (b. 1944)	Jock II	Asterus / Naic
		Fille de Soleil	Solario / Fille de Salut
	Her Slipper (b. 1936)	Tetratema	The Tetrarch / Scotch Gift
		Carpet Slipper	Phalaris / Simon's Shoes

1006   VALOUR 16 (ch.c., March 5, 1975)

Bred by Nelson Bunker Hunt, in U.S.A.

Won 5 races, placed 12, £103,704, in England, Germany and France, from 2 to 5 years, incl. Grosser Preis von Baden and Prix Jean de Chaudenay; 2nd Jockey Club Stakes and Geoffrey Freer Stakes; 4th Coronation Cup.

VAGUELY NOBLE (b. 1965)	Vienna (ch. 1957)	Aureole	Hyperion / Angelola
		Turkish Blood	Turkhan / Rusk
	Noble Lassie (b. 1956)	Nearco	Pharos / Nogara
		Belle Sauvage	Big Game / Tropical Sun
LOUISADOR (ch. 1964)	Indian Hemp (ch. 1949)	Nasrullah	Nearco / Mumtaz Begum
		Sabzy	Stardust / Sarita
	Louise Mason (b. 1957)	Count Fleet	Reigh Count / Quickly
		Kinfolks	Bull Lea / Aunt Chaney

1007   VARANO 1 (b.c., 1962)

Bred by Razza del Soldo, in England.

Won 7 races, placed 5, 27,240,000 L., in Italy, from 2 to 4 years, incl. Derby Italiano; 2nd Premio Emanuele Filiberto; 3rd Gran Premio d'Italia.

DARIUS (b. 1951)	Dante (br. 1942)	Nearco	Pharos / Nogara
		Rosy Legend	Dark Legend / Rosy Cheeks
	Yasna (b. 1936)	Dastur	Solario / Friar's Daughter
		Ariadne	Arion / Security
VARNA II (b. 1956)	Bey (br. 1945)	Deiri	Aethelstan / Desra
		Bourgogne	Blandford / Sherry II
	Vampa (b. 1942)	Pilade	Captain Cuttle / Piera
		Varsoviana	Cranach / Volage

1008   VARINGO 31 (br.c., January 23, 1977)

Bred by D. de Vere Hunt.

Won 3 races, placed 3, £48,954, in England and France, at 2 and 3 years, incl. Coventry Stakes; 2nd Richmond Stakes, Flying Childers Stakes, Prix Morny.

SAULINGO (br. 1970)	Sing Sing (b. 1957)	Tudor Minstrel	Owen Tudor / Sansonnet
		Agin the Law	Portlaw / Revolte
	Saulisa (br. 1963)	Hard Sauce	Ardan / Saucy Bella
		L.S.D.	Lighthouse II / Styrian Dye
VRAIMENT (ch. 1969)	Relko (b. 1960)	Tanerko	Tantieme / La Divine
		Relance III	Relic / Polaire II
	Oh! Do (ch. 1960)	Doutelle	Prince Chevalier / Above Board
		Oh My Honey	Honeyway / Oracion

1009 **VASCO DE GAMA** 3 (b.c., March 24, 1963)

Bred by M. Fabiani, in France.

Won 2 races, placed 7, 767,950 fr., in France and U.S.A., incl. Prix Royal Oak and Grand Prix du Printemps; 3rd Prix du Cadran; 4th Washington D.C. International.

BEL BARAKA (ch. 1955)	Worden II (ch. 1949)	Wild Risk	Rialto / Wild Violet
		Sans Tares	Sind / Tara
	Fleur des Neiges (ch. 1947)	Norseman	Umidwar / Tara
		Avila	Astrophel / Sevilla
PRINCESSE BALA (b. 1957)	Prince Bio (b. 1941)	Prince Rose	Rose Prince / Indolence
		Biologie	Bacteriophage / Eponge
	Bala (br. 1952)	The Cobbler	Windsor Slipper / Overture
		Mrs. Cidyns	Epigram / Fair Maid of Perth

1010 **VELA** 2 (b.f., April 26, 1967)

Bred by Lord Waterford, in Ireland.

Won 3 races, placed 5, 266,975 fr., in France, at 2 and 3 years, incl. Criterium des Pouliches; 3rd Prix Saint-Alary, Prix de Minerve and Prix de la Cote Normande.

SHESHOON (ch. 1956)	Precipitation (ch. 1933)	Hurry On	Marcovil / Tout Suite
		Double Life	Bachelor's Double / Saint Joan
	Noorani (ch. 1950)	Nearco	Pharos / Nogara
		Empire Glory	Singapore / Skyglory
CENERENTOLA (b. 1959)	Prince Chevalier (b. 1943)	Prince Rose	Rose Prince / Indolence
		Chevalerie	Abbot's Speed / Kassala
	Per Ardua (b. 1941)	Hyperion	Gainsborough / Selene
		Ad Astra	Asterus / Pyramid

1011 **VENETIAN WAY** 4 (ch.c., March 22, 1957)

Bred by John W. Greathouse, in U.S.A.

Won 7 races, placed 7, $359,422, in U.S.A., at 2 and 3 years, incl. Kentucky Derby and Washington Park Futurity; 2nd Belmont Stakes and Florida Derby; 3rd Arlington Classic.

ROYAL COINAGE (br. 1952)	Eight Thirty (ch. 1936)	Pilate	Friar Rock / Herodias
		Dinner Time	High Time / Seaplane
	Canina (b. 1941)	Bull Dog	Teddy / Plucky Liege
		Coronium	Pot au Feu / Bird Call
FIREFLY (ch. 1952)	Papa Redbird (ch. 1945)	Balladier	Black Toney / Blue Warbler
		Taj Bibi	Sickle / Black Queen
	Minstrelette (ch. 1933)	Royal Minstrel	Tetratema / Harpsichord
		Bannerette	Pennant / Meetme

1012 **VERONESE** 16 (ch.c., March 1, 1960)

Bred by Marquis de Talhouet-Roy, in France.

Won 16 races, placed 6, 85,378,000 L., in Italy, from 2 to 5 years, incl. Gran Premio di Milano, Premio Roma, Gran Premio del Jockey Club, Premio Presidente della Repubblica, Coppa d'Oro di Milano and Premio d'Aprile; 2nd Gran Premio d'Italia and Gran Premio del Jockey Club; 3rd Coppa d'Oro di Milano and Premio Roma.

LE HAAR (ch. 1954)	Vieux Manoir (b. 1947)	Brantome	Blandford / Vitamine
		Vieille Maison	Finglas / Vieille Canaille
	Mince Pie (b. 1949)	Teleferique	Bacteriophage / Beaute de Neige
		Cannelle	Biribi / Armoise
POINTE SECHE (ch. 1949)	Bozzetto (ch. 1936)	Pharos	Phalaris / Scapa Flow
		Bunworry	Great Sport / Waffles
	Spinella (ch. 1941)	Ortello	Teddy / Hollebeck
		Santaria	Santorb / Orangeade

1013 **VERVAIN** 12 (b.c., May 17, 1966)

Bred by D. McCalmont.

Won 3 races, placed 4, £8,058, in England, at 2 and 3 years, incl. King Edward VII Stakes; 2nd White Rose Stakes.

CREPELLO (ch. 1954)	Donatello II (ch. 1934)	Blenheim	Blandford / Malva
		Delleana	Clarissimus / Duccia di Buoninsegna
	Crepuscule (ch. 1948)	Mieuxce	Massine / L'Olivete
		Red Sunset	Solario / Dulce II
VERBENA (b. 1958)	Vimy (b. 1952)	Wild Risk	Rialto / Wild Violet
		Mimi	Black Devil / Mignon
	Val d'Assa (br. 1947)	Dante	Nearco / Rosy Legend
		Lapel	Apelle / Lampeto

1014 **VIELLE** 13 (b.f., March 15, 1977)

Bred by T. F. Blackwell.

Won 5 races, placed 6, £92,682, in England, at 2 and 3 years, incl. Nassau Stakes, Lancashire Oaks; 2nd Oaks Stakes, Yorkshire Oaks, Hoover Mile.

RIBERO (b. 1965)	Ribot (b. 1952)	Tenerani	Bellini / Tofanella
		Romanella	El Greco / Barbara Burrini
	Libra (ch. 1956)	Hyperion	Gainsborough / Selene
		Weighbridge	Portlaw / Golden Way
HURDY-GURDY (b. 1970)	Espresso (ch. 1958)	Acropolis	Donatello II / Aurora
		Babylon	Bahram / Clairvoyante III
	Street Singer (br. 1954)	Kingsway	Fairway / Yenna
		Record Serenade	Straight Deal / Columbia

1015 **VIENNA** 14 (ch.c., February 12, 1957)

Bred by Sir Winston Churchill.

Won 7 races, placed 8, £26,595, in England and France, from 2 to 5 years, incl. Blue Riband Trial Stakes, Prix d'Harcourt; 2nd Coronation Cup, Hardwicke Stakes; 3rd St. Leger Stakes, Champion Stakes (dead-heat) and Prix Ganay.

AUREOLE (ch. 1950)	Hyperion (ch. 1930)	Gainsborough	Bayardo / Rosedrop
		Selene	Chaucer / Serenissima
	Angelola (b. 1945)	Donatello II	Blenheim / Delleana
		Feola	Friar Marcus / Aloe
TURKISH BLOOD (b. 1944)	Turkhan (b. 1937)	Bahram	Blandford / Friar's Daughter
		Theresina	Diophon / Teresina
	Rusk (b. 1935)	Manna	Phalaris / Waffles
		Baby Polly	Spearmint / Pretty Polly

1016 **VIFIC** 5 (b./br.f., February 13, 1975)

Bred by J. Ternynck, in France.

Won 2 races, 235,000 fr., in France, at 2 years, incl. Prix Robert Papin.

RHEFFIC (b. 1968)	Traffic (ch. 1961)	Traffic Judge	Alibhai / Traffic Court
		Capelet	Bolero / Quick Touch
	Rhenane (br. 1961)	Tanerko	Tantieme / La Divine
		Rhea II	Gundomar / Regina IV
VIGOGNE (ch. 1966)	Sanctus II (br. 1960)	Fine Top	Fine Art / Toupie
		Sanelta	Tourment / Satanella
	White Heather (b. 1958)	Darius	Dante / Yasna
		Nyonda	Goya II / Canidia

1017 **VIMADEE** 4 (b.c., April 20, 1958)

Bred by T. McCairns.

Won 4 races, placed 13, £7,216, in Ireland and England, from 2 to 8 years, incl. Irish St. Leger; 2nd Desmond Stakes, Blandford Stakes; 3rd Blandford Stakes.

VIMY (b. 1952)	Wild Risk (b. 1940)	Rialto	Rabelais / La Grelee
		Wild Violet	Blandford / Wood Violet
	Mimi (b. 1943)	Black Devil	Sir Gallahad III / La Palina
		Mignon	Epinard / Mammee
UPADEE (b. 1950)	Fairfax (br. 1936)	Fairway	Phalaris / Scapa Flow
		Celiba	Bachelor's Double / Santa Maura
	Courine (b. 1941)	Coup de Lyon	Winalot / Sundry
		Rhine Wine	Flamingo / Rhinegold

1018 **VITIGES** 19 (ch.c., March 22, 1973)

Bred by H. de la Heronniere, in France.

Won 6 races, placed 7, £130,615, in France and England, from 2 to 4 years, incl. Prix Morny, Prix Robert Papin, Champion Stakes; 2nd Prix de la Salamandre, Prix Jacques le Marois (dead-heat), 2,000 Guineas Stakes.

PHAETON (gr. 1964)	Sicambre (br. 1948)	Prince Bio	Prince Rose / Biologie
		Sif	Rialto / Suavita
	Pasquinade II (gr. 1957)	Vandale II	Plassy / Vanille
		Mademoiselle Paganini	Loliondo / Mademoiselle Petitpas
VALE (ch. 1959)	Verrieres (b. 1953)	Palestine	Fair Trial / Una
		Serre Chaude	Pharis II / Vanda Teres
	Calliopsis (ch. 1954)	Prince Chevalier	Prince Rose / Chevalerie
		Calluna	Hyperion / Campanula

1019 **WAIDWERK** 5 (br.c., April 24, 1962)

Bred by Gestüt Ravensberg, in Germany.

Won 5 races, placed 6, 192,600 DM., in Germany, from 2 to 6 years, incl. Deutsches Derby, Deutsches St. Leger and Preis des Winterfavoriten; 2nd Zukunfts-Rennen and Henckel-Rennen.

NECKAR (bl. 1948)	Ticino (b. 1939)	Athanasius	Ferro / Athanasie
		Terra	Aditi / Teufelsrose
	Nixe (b. 1941)	Arjaman	Herold / Aditja
		Nanon	Graf Isolani / Nella da Gubbio
WINDSTILLE (br. 1949)	Avanti (br. 1926)	Fervor	Galtee More / Festa
		Abbazia	Dark Ronald / Adria
	Waldrun (b. 1943)	Alchimist	Herold / Aversion
		Walburga	Aurelius / Wally

1020 **WAJIMA** 3 (b.c., March 8, 1972)

Bred by Claiborne Farm, in U.S.A.

Won 9 races, placed 5, $537,837, in U.S.A., at 2 and 3 years, incl. Marlboro Cup, Travers Stakes, Governor Stakes, Monmouth Invitational H. and Marylander H.; 2nd Jockey Club Gold Cup, Woodward Stakes, Dwyer H., Saranac Stakes and Laurel Futurity.

BOLD RULER (b. 1954)	Nasrullah (b. 1940)	Nearco	Pharos / Nogara
		Mumtaz Begum	Blenheim / Mumtaz Mahal
	Miss Disco (b. 1944)	Discovery	Display / Ariadne
		Outdone	Pompey / Sweep Out
ISKRA (ch. 1961)	Le Haar (ch. 1954)	Vieux Manoir	Brantome / Vieille Maison
		Mince Pie	Teleferique / Cannelle
	Fasciola (br. 1946)	Fastnet	Pharos / Tatoule
		Foxcraft	Foxhunter / Philomene

1021   WALDMEISTER 6 (b.c., 1961)

Bred by Dollanstown Stud Establishment, in Ireland.

Won 6 races, placed 12, 638,061 fr., in France and England, from 2 to 5 years, incl. Prix du Cadran, La Coupe and Prix de l'Esperance; 2nd Ascot Gold Cup, Prix Hocquart, Prix de Condé and Prix Jean Prat; 3rd Prix du Cadran, Prix de Barbeville and Prix Gladiateur.

WILD RISK (b. 1940)	Rialto (ch. 1923)	Rabelais	St. Simon / Satirical
		La Grelee	Helicon / Grignouse
	Wild Violet (b. 1935)	Blandford	Swynford / Blanche
		Wood Violet	Ksar / Pervencheres
SANTA ISABEL (br. 1956)	Dante (br. 1942)	Nearco	Pharos / Nogara
		Rosy Legend	Dark Legend / Rosy Cheeks
	Shamsheeri (b. 1950)	Tehran	Bois Roussel / Stafaralla
		Benane	Big Game / Theresina

1022   WALE (b.c., March 26, 1974)

Bred by Dr. C. Vittadini, in France.

Won 3 races, placed 6, 55,700,000 L., in Italy, at 3 and 4 years, incl. Gran Premio d'Italia; 3rd Derby Italiano and Premio Principe Amedeo.

ARDALE (b. 1968)	Accrale (b. 1962)	Vandale II	Plassy / Vanille
		Accrued	Umidwar / Fair Emma
	Arandena (ch. 1962)	Worden II	Wild Risk / Sans Tares
		Aranda	Vatellor / Eyewash
WINDEN (ch. 1968)	Worden II (ch. 1949)	Wild Risk	Rialto / Wild Violet
		Sans Tares	Sind / Tara
	Wyndust (ch. 1954)	Nimbus	Nearco / Kong
		Just Wyn	Stardust / Wyn

1023   WATERLOO 1 (ch.f., May 4, 1969)

Bred by New England Stud.

Won 6 races, placed 4, £47,887, in England, at 2 and 3 years, incl. 1,000 Guineas, Cheveley Park Stakes, Queen Mary Stakes, Falmouth Stakes; 2nd Coronation Stakes, Lowther Stakes.

BOLD LAD (IRE) (b. 1964)	Bold Ruler (b. 1954)	Nasrullah	Nearco / Mumtaz Begum
		Miss Disco	Discovery / Outdone
	Barn Pride (ch. 1957)	Democratic	Denturius / Light Fantasy
		Fair Alycia	Alycidon / Fair Edwine
LAKEWOODS (ch. 1958)	Hyperion (ch. 1930)	Gainsborough	Bayardo / Rosedrop
		Selene	Chaucer / Serenissima
	Holwood (b. 1951)	Umidwar	Blandford / Uganda
		Beausite	Bold Archer / Orama

1024   WAUTHI 4 (b.c., March 21, 1977)

Bred by Gestut Rottgen, in Germany.

Won 5 races, placed 3, 308,500 DM., in Germany, at 2 and 3 years, incl. Aral-Pokal, Henckel-Rennen and Grosser Thier-Preis Deutsches St. Leger; 2nd Preis des Winterfavoriten; 3rd Grosser Preis von Berlin; 4th Deutsches Derby.

AUTHI (b. 1970)	Aureole (ch. 1950)	Hyperion	Gainsborough / Selene
		Angelola	Donatello II / Feola
	Virtuous (b. 1962)	Above Suspicion	Court Martial / Above Board
		Rose of India	Tulyar / Eastern Grandeur
WAIT AND TAKE (b. 1971)	Tamerlane (br. 1952)	Persian Gulf	Bahram / Double Life
		Eastern Empress	Nearco / Cheveley Lady
	Waverley (b. 1965)	Vimy	Wild Risk / Mimi
		Wallonin	Orator / Waffenart

1025   WAYA 1 (b.f., March 30, 1974)

Bred by Dayton Limited, in France.

Won 14 races, placed 11, $823,066, in France and U.S.A., from 3 to 5 years, incl. Turf Classic, Man o'War Stakes, Beldame Stakes, Diana H., Flower Bowl H., Top Flight H., Santa Barbara H., Prix de Royaumont and Prix de l'Opera; 2nd Prix de Malleret, Prix Chloe, Sheepshead Bay H., New York H., Bowling Green H. and Arcadia H.; 3rd Washington D.C. International, Ruffian H. and Prix du Prince d'Orange.

FARAWAY SON (b. 1967)	Ambiopoise (b. 1958)	Ambiorix II	Tourbillon / Lavendula II
		Bullpoise	Bull Lea / Alpoise
	Locust Time (br. 1955)	Spy Song	Balladier / Mata Hari
		Snow Goose	Mahmoud / Judy O'Grady
WAR PATH III (b. 1963)	Blue Prince II (b. 1951)	Princequillo	Prince Rose / Cosquilla
		Blue Denim	Blue Larkspur / Judy O'Grady
	Alyxia (ch. 1951)	Alycidon	Donatello II / Aurora
		Gold Lily	Gold Bridge / Wild Lily

1026   WEAVERS' HALL 19 (b.c., April 11, 1970)

Bred by McGrath Trust Co.

Won 2 races, placed 6, £67,757, in Ireland and England, at 2 and 3 years incl. Irish Sweeps Derby; 2nd Player-Wills Stakes; 4th King George VI and Queen Elizabeth Stakes.

BUSTED (b. 1963)	Crepello (ch. 1954)	Donatello II	Blenheim / Delleana
		Crepuscule	Mieuxce / Red Sunset
	Sans le Sou (b. 1957)	Vimy	Wild Risk / Mimi
		Martial Loan	Court Martial / Loan
MARIANS (ch. 1963)	Macherio (ch. 1941)	Ortello	Teddy / Hollebeck
		Mannozza	Manna / Moireen Rhue
	Damians (ch. 1942)	Panorama	Sir Cosmo / Happy Climax
		Thirteen	Bulger / Credenda

1027   WEIMAR 16 (b.c., February 5, 1968)

Bred by Mrs. G. Bullard, in England.

Won 13 races, placed 2, 144,270,000 L., in Italy, from 2 to 4 years, incl. Gran Premio d'Italia, Gran Premio del Jockey Club, St. Leger Italiano, Premio Emanuele Filiberto, Premio Pisa and Premio d'Aprile; 2nd Gran Premio d'Italia.

CANISBAY (ch. 1961)	Doutelle (ch. 1954)	Prince Chevalier	Prince Rose / Chevalerie
		Above Board	Straight Deal / Feola
	Stroma (ch. 1955)	Luminary	Fair Trial / Luciebella
		Whoa Emma	Prince Chevalier / Ready
WHOOPEE (ro. 1958)	Anwar (b. 1943)	Umidwar	Blandford / Uganda
		Stafaralla	Solario / Mirawala
	Sea Gipsy (b. 1951)	Ocean Swell	Blue Peter / Jiffy
		Wheedler	Umidwar / Miss Minx

1028   WELSH PAGEANT 1 (b.c., April 3, 1966)

Bred by H. J. Joel.

Won 11 races, placed 7, £53,527, in England, from 2 to 5 years, incl. Lockinge Stakes (twice), Queen Elizabeth II Stakes, St. James Stakes (Epsom), Queen Anne Stakes and Hungerford Stakes; 2nd July Stakes and Hungerford Stakes; 3rd 2,000 Guineas Stakes, Eclipse Stakes and Champion Stakes; 4th Sussex Stakes.

TUDOR MELODY (br. 1956)	Tudor Minstrel (br. 1944)	Owen Tudor	Hyperion / Mary Tudor II
		Sansonnet	Sansovino / Lady Juror
	Matelda (br. 1947)	Dante	Nearco / Rosy Legend
		Fairly Hot	Solario / Fair Cop
PICTURE LIGHT (b. 1954)	Court Martial (ch. 1942)	Fair Trial	Fairway / Lady Juror
		Instantaneous	Hurry On / Picture
	Queen of Light (b. 1949)	Borealis	Brumeux / Aurora
		Picture Play	Donatello II / Amuse

1029   WENDUYNE 1 (b.f., April 10, 1966)

Bred by J. R. Mullion.

Won 3 races, placed 2, £12,705, in Ireland and England, at 2 and 3 years incl. Irish 1,000 Guineas Stakes, Athasi Stakes; 2nd Yorkshire Oaks.

MOUTIERS (ch. 1958)	Sicambre (br. 1948)	Prince Bio	Prince Rose / Biologie
		Sif	Rialto / Suavita
	Ballynash (b. 1946)	Nasrullah	Nearco / Mumtaz Begum
		Ballywellbroke	Ballyferis / The Beggar
DJIDDA II (b. 1958)	Free Man (b. 1948)	Norseman	Umidwar / Tara
		Fantine	Fantastic / Sif
	Djebellica (ch. 1948)	Djebel	Tourbillon / Loika
		Nica	Nino / Canalette

1030   WEST COAST SCOUT 23 (b.c., May 12, 1968)

Bred by Oxford Stable, in U.S.A.

Won 9 races, placed 8, $543,191, in U.S.A., from 3 to 5 years, incl. Woodward Stakes, Amory L. Haskell H. (twice), Monmouth Invitational H., Gulfstream Park H. and Hobson H.; 2nd Travers Stakes, Suburban H., Widener H. and Nassau County H.; 3rd Brooklyn H.

SENSITIVO (b. 1957)	Sideral (br. 1948)	Seductor	Full Sail / Suma
		Starling	Noble Star / Feola
	Ternura (ch. 1947)	Embrujo	Congreve / Encore
		Bien Aimee	Parwiz / Aimee
DANDY PRINCESS (b. 1958)	Bull Dandy (br. 1941)	Bull Lea	Bull Dog / Rose Leaves
		Dandy One	Whichone / Dendera
	Harem (br. 1943)	Heliopolis	Hyperion / Drift
		Bourlon Reel	My Play / Tara II

1031   WEST SIDE STORY 1 (ch.f., February 12, 1959)

Bred by H. J. Joel.

Won 2 races, placed 4, £9,190, in England, at 2 and 3 years, incl. Yorkshire Oaks, Nell Gwyn Stakes; 2nd Oaks Stakes, Cheveley Park Stakes, Park Hill Stakes; 3rd 1,000 Guineas Stakes.

ROCKEFELLA (br. 1941)	Hyperion (ch. 1930)	Gainsborough	Bayardo / Rosedrop
		Selene	Chaucer / Serenissima
	Rockfel (br. 1935)	Felstead	Spion Kop / Felkington
		Rockliffe	Santorb / Sweet Rocket
RED SHOES (b. 1948)	Bois Roussel (br. 1935)	Vatout	Prince Chimay / Vasthi
		Plucky Liege	Spearmint / Concertina
	Picture Play (b. 1941)	Donatello II	Blenheim / Delleana
		Amuse	Phalaris / Gesture

1032   WHIP IT QUICK B3 (b.c., April 17, 1972)

Bred by A. B. Barraclough.

Won 7½ races, placed 10, £60,917, in England and Germany, from 2 to 6 years, incl. Coventry Stakes, Grosser Preis von Dusseldorf, Grosser Preis der Dusseldorfer Industrie und Wirtschaft, Grosser Preis der Stadt Gelsenkirchen; 2nd Champagne Stakes, Grosser Preis von Dusseldorf (dead-heat); 3rd King Edward VII Stakes, Grosser Preis der Stadt Gelsenkirchen (twice), Grosser Preis der Badischen Wirtschaft; 4th Observer Gold Cup.

PHILEMON (b. 1960)	Never Say Die (ch. 1951)	Nasrullah	Nearco / Mumtaz Begum
		Singing Grass	War Admiral / Boreale
	Winged Foot (br. 1949)	Big Game	Bahram / Myrobella
		Fieldfare	Bosworth / Molly Adare
MA GRIFFE (b. 1966)	Indian Ruler (b. 1951)	Sayajirao	Nearco / Rosy Legend
		Bright Hope	Craig an Eran / Bright Spot
	Yasmin II (br. 1960)	Gilles de Retz	Royal Charger / Ma Soeur Anne
		Firle	Noble Star / Versicle

1033   WHITE GLOVES 17 (ch.c., April 16, 1963)

Bred by Mrs. Marie A. Moore.

Won 5 races, placed 2, £17,660, in Ireland, England and Italy, from 2 to 4 years, incl. Irish St. Leger, Desmond Stakes (twice), Ballymoss Stakes; 3rd Coronation Cup, Gran Premio del Jockey Club.

HIGH HAT (ch. 1957)	Hyperion (ch. 1930)	Gainsborough	Bayardo
			Rosedrop
		Selene	Chaucer
			Serenissima
	Madonna (ch. 1945)	Donatello II	Blenheim
			Delleana
		Women's Legion	Coronach
			Victress
GALLAMOUD (ch. 1952)	Mahmoud (gr. 1933)	Blenheim	Blandford
			Malva
		Mah Mahal	Gainsborough
			Mumtaz Mahal
	Gallorette (ch. 1942)	Challenger	Swynford
			Sword Play
		Gallette	Sir Gallahad III
			Flambette

1034   WHITE LABEL 12 (b.c., May 19, 1961)

Bred by Baron Guy de Rothschild, in France.

Won 4 races, placed 3, 1,018,094 fr., in France; at 3 and 4 years, incl. Grand Prix de Paris, Prix de Barbeville and Prix Jean Prat; 2nd Prix du Cadran and Prix Berteux.

TANERKO (br. 1953)	Tantieme (b. 1947)	Deux pour Cent	Deiri
			Dix pour Cent
		Terka	Indus
			La Furka
	La Divine (br. 1943)	Fair Copy	Fairway
			Composure
		La Diva	Blue Skies
			La Traviata
ALBA NOX (b. 1951)	Coaraze (b. 1942)	Tourbillon	Ksar
			Durban
		Corrida	Coronach
			Zariba
	La Dame Blanche (br. 1943)	Biribi	Rabelais
			La Bidouze
		Nymphe Dicte	Diolite
			Nanaia

1035   WHITSTEAD 1 (ch.c., April 11, 1975)

Bred by Mayfield Stud Co.

Won 4 races, placed 2, £47,525, in England and France, at 2 and 3 years, incl. Great Voltigeur Stakes, Ladbroke Derby Trial Stakes, Classic Trial Stakes; 3rd Grand Prix de Paris.

MORSTON (ch. 1970)	Ragusa (b. 1960)	Ribot	Tenerani
			Romanella
		Fantan II	Ambiorix II
			Red Eye
	Windmill Girl (b. 1961)	Hornbeam	Hyperion
			Thicket
		Chorus Beauty	Chanteur II
			Neberna
TUDOR ROMP (b. 1968)	Tudor Melody (br. 1956)	Tudor Minstrel	Owen Tudor
			Sansonnet
		Matelda	Dante
			Fairly Hot
	Romp Home (ch. 1961)	Chanteur II	Château Bouscaut
			La Diva
		Rutherford Bridge	Sayajirao
			Rustic Bridge

1036   WINDMILL GIRL 20 (b.f., February 21, 1961)

Bred by Major L. B. Holliday.

Won 2 races, placed 3, £15,212, in England and Ireland, at 2 and 3 years incl. Ribblesdale Stakes; 2nd Oaks Stakes; 3rd Irish Guinness Oaks.

HORNBEAM (ch. 1953)	Hyperion (ch. 1930)	Gainsborough	Bayardo
			Rosedrop
		Selene	Chaucer
			Serenissima
	Thicket (b. 1947)	Nasrullah	Nearco
			Mumtaz Begum
		Thorn Wood	Bois Roussel
			Point Duty
CHORUS BEAUTY (b. 1952)	Chanteur II (br. 1942)	Chateau Bouscaut	Kircubbin
			Ramondie
		La Diva	Blue Skies
			La Traviata
	Neberna (b. or br. 1942)	Nearco	Pharos
			Nogara
		Springtime	Apelle
			Fancy Free

1037   WINDWURF 5 (b.c., January 30, 1972)

Bred by Gestüt Ravensberg, in Germany.

Won 11 races, placed 8, 1,315,640 DM., in Germany, from 2 to 5 years, incl. Preis von Europa (twice), Grosser Preis von Nordrhein-Westfalen, Grosser Preis von Berlin, Grosser Preis von Baden, Deutsches St. Leger, Union-Rennen and Grosser Preis von Dusseldorf; 2nd Grosser Preis von Baden, Henckel-Rennen, Grosser Preis von Dusseldorf and Grosser Preis von Dortmund.

KAISERADLER (br. 1957)	Nebelwerfer (br. 1944)	Magnat	Asterus
			Mafalda
		Newa	Arjaman
			Numa
	Kaiserwurde (bl. 1945)	Bubbles	La Farina
			Spring Cleaning
		Katinka	Biribi
			Killeen
WIESENWEIHE (b. 1962)	Birkhahn (br. 1945)	Alchimist	Herold
			Aversion
		Bramouse	Cappiello
			Peregrine
	Wiesenblute (b. 1956)	Neckar	Ticino
			Nixe
		Windstille	Avanti
			Waldrun

1038   WINTER'S TALE 6 (b.g., March 26, 1976)

Bred by Paul Mellon, in U.S.A.

Won 8 races, placed 1, $488,000, in U.S.A., at 3 and 4 years, incl. Suburban H., Brooklyn H., Marlboro Cup and Nassau County H.

ARTS AND LETTERS (ch. 1966)	Ribot (b. 1952)	Tenerani	Bellini
			Tofanella
		Romanella	El Greco
			Barbara Burrini
	All Beautiful (ch. 1959)	Battlefield	War Relic
			Dark Display
		Parlo	Heliopolis
			Fairy Palace
CHRISTMAS WIND (b. 1967)	Nearctic (br. 1954)	Nearco	Pharos
			Nogara
		Lady Angela	Hyperion
			Sister Sarah
	Bally Free (b. 1960)	Ballymoss	Mossborough
			Indian Call
		Fair Freedom	Fair Trial
			Democratie

1039   WISHING STAR 3 (b.c., February 14, 1969)

Bred by Hanstead Stud.

Won 9 races, placed 16, £24,091, in England, France and Belgium, from 2 to 6 years, incl. Gimcrack Stakes; 2nd July Stakes; 3rd Coventry Stakes; 4th Prix de la Salamandre.

REFORM (b. 1964)	Pall Mall (ch. 1955)	Palestine	Fair Trial / Una
		Malapert	Portlaw / Malatesta
	Country House (br. 1955)	Vieux Manoir	Brantome / Vieille Maison
		Miss Coventry	Mieuxce / Coventry Belle
SENTA (b. 1959)	Chanteur II (b. 1942)	Chateau Bouscaut	Kircubbin / Ramondie
		La Diva	Blue Skies / La Traviata
	Naval Patrol (b. 1952)	Blue Peter	Fairway / Fancy Free
		Filasse	Big Game / Filastic

1040   WLADIMIR 7 (b.c., February 26, 1972)

Bred by Frau A. Spaulding, in Germany.

Won 9 races, placed 18, 516,800 DM., in Germany, from 2 to 8 years, incl. Aral Pokal (twice), Grosser Preis von Dortmund (twice) and Preis des Landes Nordrhein-Westfalen; 2nd Grosser Preis der Stadt Gelsenkirchen; 3rd Aral Pokal, Grosser Preis von Berlin, Grosser Kaufhof Preis and Grosser Preis von Dortmund.

THIGGO (b. 1957)	Magnat (b. 1938)	Asterus	Teddy / Astrella
		Mafalda	Wallenstein / Madam
	Thilde (b. 1948)	Arjaman	Herold / Aditja
		Thuriswid	Avanti / Thurid
WASSIA (b. 1965)	Birkhahn (br. 1945)	Alchimist	Herold / Aversion
		Bramouse	Cappiello / Peregrine
	Wildmaus (br. 1958)	Mangon	Gundomar / Mainkur
		Whirlaya	Whirlaway / Zulaikhaa

1041   WOLLOW 22 (b.c., March 15, 1973)

Bred by Tally Ho Stud Co. Ltd.

Won 9 races, £200,790, in England, at 2 and 3 years, incl. William Hill Dewhurst Stakes, 2,000 Guineas Stakes, Sussex Stakes, Benson and Hedges Gold Cup, Joe Coral Eclipse Stakes, Laurent Perrier Champagne Stakes, Clerical Medical Greenham Stakes.

WOLVER HOLLOW (b. 1964)	Sovereign Path (gr. 1956)	Grey Sovereign	Nasrullah / Kong
		Mountain Path	Bobsleigh / Path of Peace
	Cygnet (b. 1950)	Caracalla II	Tourbillon / Astronomie
		Mrs. Swan Song	Sir Walter Raleigh / Donati's Comet
WICHURAIANA (ch. 1963)	Worden II (ch. 1949)	Wild Risk	Rialto / Wild Violet
		Sans Tares	Sind / Tara
	Excelsa (ch. 1949)	Owen Tudor	Hyperion / Mary Tudor II
		Infra Red	Ethnarch / Black Ray

1042   WOLVER HOLLOW 19 (b.c., May 5, 1964)

Bred by Gaybrook Park Stud.

Won 4 races, placed 12, £40,518, in England and France, from 2 to 5 years, incl. Eclipse Stakes; 2nd Queen Elizabeth II Stakes, Prince of Wales Stakes, New Stakes; 3rd Greenham Stakes; 4th Dewhurst Stakes.

SOVEREIGN PATH (gr. 1956)	Grey Sovereign (gr. 1948)	Nasrullah	Nearco / Mumtaz Begum
		Kong	Baytown / Clang
	Mountain Path (b. 1948)	Bobsleigh	Gainsborough / Toboggan
		Path of Peace	Winalot / Grand Peace
CYGNET (b. 1950)	Caracalla II (b. 1942)	Tourbillon	Ksar / Durban
		Astronomie	Asterus / Likka
	Mrs. Swan Song (b. or br. 1940)	Sir Walter Raleigh	Prince Galahad / Smoke Lass
		Donati's Comet	Flying Orb / Sunshot

1043   XERXES 7 (b.c., March 31, 1959)

Bred by Mrs. D. McCalmont.

Won 2½ races, placed 8, £6,403, in England, from 2 to 4 years, incl. Coventry Stakes, Woodcote Stakes; 2nd Dee Stakes.

DARIUS (b. 1951)	Dante (br. 1942)	Nearco	Pharos / Nogara
		Rosy Legend	Dark Legend / Rosy Cheeks
	Yasna (b. 1936)	Dastur	Solario / Friar's Daughter
		Ariadne	Arion / Security
LORELEI (b. 1950)	Prince Chevalier (b. 1943)	Prince Rose	Rose Prince / Indolence
		Chevalerie	Abbot's Speed / Kassala
	Rock Goddess (b. 1943)	Hyperion	Gainsborough / Selene
		Rockfoil	Felstead / Rockliffe

1044   YELAPA 16 (br.c., March 31, 1966)

Bred by Daniel Wildenstein, in France.

Won 4 races, placed 5, 1,031,411 fr., in France, from 2 to 4 years, incl. Grand Criterium and Prix d'Harcourt; 2nd Prix Ganay, Prix Jean de Chaudenay, Prix Exbury, Prix de Fontainebleau and Prix Henry Delamarre.

MOSSBOROUGH (ch. 1947)	Nearco (br. 1935)	Pharos	Phalaris / Scapa Flow
		Nogara	Havresac II / Catnip
	All Moonshine (ch. 1941)	Bobsleigh	Gainsborough / Toboggan
		Selene	Chaucer / Serenissima
YOUR POINT (br. 1955)	Nirgal (b. 1943)	Goya II	Tourbillon / Zariba
		Castillane	Cameronian / Castagnette
	Your Game (br. 1948)	Beau Pere	Son-in-Law / Cinna
		Winkle II	Windsor Lad / Cora Pearl

1045   YELLOW GOD 9 (ch.c., March 21, 1967)

Bred by Mrs. J. Alexander.

Won 5 races, placed 7, £41,305, in England and France, at 2 and 3 years, incl. Gimcrack Stakes, Prix du Palais Royal; 2nd 2,000 Guineas Stakes, Middle Park Stakes, Prix de la Porte Maillot; 3rd Cornwallis Stakes, Wills Mile, Prix Jacques le Marois.

RED GOD (ch. 1954)	Nasrullah (b. 1940)	Nearco	Pharos / Nogara
		Mumtaz Begum	Blenheim / Mumtaz Mahal
	Spring Run (b. 1948)	Menow	Pharamond / Alcibiades
		Boola Brook	Bull Dog / Brookdale
SALLY DEANS (ch. 1947)	Fun Fair (ch. 1940)	Fair Trial	Fairway / Lady Juror
		Humoresque	Walter Gay / Bar Sinister
	Cora Deans (b. 1932)	Coronach	Hurry On / Wet Kiss
		Jennie Deans	Buchan / Eleanor M

1046   YOUNG EMPEROR 22 (gr.c., March 6, 1963)

Bred by Mrs. Parker Poe.

Won 3 races, placed 3, £13,722, in England and Ireland, at 2 and 3 years incl. Coventry Stakes, Gimcrack Stakes; 3rd Richmond Stakes; 4th 2,000 Guineas Stakes.

GREY SOVEREIGN (gr. 1948)	Nasrullah (b. 1940)	Nearco	Pharos / Nogara
		Mumtaz Begum	Blenheim / Mumtaz Mahal
	Kong (gr. 1933)	Baytown	Achtoi / Princess Herodias
		Clang	Hainault / Vibration
YOUNG EMPRESS (b. 1957)	Petition (br. 1944)	Fair Trial	Fairway / Lady Juror
		Art Paper	Artist's Proof / Quire
	Jennifer (b. 1948)	Hyperion	Gainsborough / Selene
		Avena	Blandford / Athasi

1047   YOUNG GENERATION 13 (b.c., April 29, 1976)

Bred by Rathduff Stud.

Won 4 races, placed 8, £110,881, in England and France, at 2 and 3 years, incl. Richmond Stakes, Lockinge Stakes and Prix Jean Prat; 2nd William Hill Middle Park Stakes, Clerical Medical Greenham Stakes and St. James's Palace Stakes; 3rd Prix Morny and 2,000 Guineas Stakes.

BALIDAR (br. 1966)	Will Somers (br. 1955)	Tudor Minstrel	Owen Tudor / Sansonnet
		Queen's Jest	Nearco / Mirth
	Violet Bank (b. 1960)	The Phoenix	Chateau Bouscaut / Fille de Poete
		Leinster	Speckled Band / Garryard
BRIG O'DOON (ch. 1967)	Shantung (b. 1956)	Sicambre	Prince Bio / Sif
		Barley Corn	Hyperion / Schiaparelli
	Tam O'Shanter (br. 1959)	Tamerlane	Persian Gulf / Eastern Empress
		Madam Anna	Pappageno II / Outspan

1048   YOUR HIGHNESS 1 (ch.c., April 2, 1958)

Bred by Snailwell Stud Co. Ltd.

Won 3 races, placed 4, £10,611, in England and Ireland, from 2 to 4 years, incl. Irish Derby; 2nd Irish St. Leger, Coronation Cup; 3rd Princess of Wales's Stakes.

CHAMOSSAIRE (ch. 1942)	Precipitation (ch. 1933)	Hurry On	Marcovil / Tout Suite
		Double Life	Bachelor's Double / Saint Joan
	Snowberry (br. 1937)	Cameronian	Pharos / Una Cameron
		Myrobella	Tetratema / Dolabella
LADY GRAND (ch. 1943)	Solario (b. 1922)	Gainsborough	Bayardo / Rosedrop
		Sun Worship	Sundridge / Doctrine
	Begum (b. 1934)	Blandford	Swynford / Blanche
		Endowment	Silvern / Enrichment

1049   YOUTH 8 (b.c., April 12, 1973)

Bred by Nelson Bunker Hunt, in U.S.A.

Won 8 races, placed 2, 3,196,657 fr., in France, U.S.A. and Canada, at 2 and 3 years, incl. Prix du Jockey-Club, Prix Lupin, Prix Greffulhe, Prix Daru, Prix Niel, Canadian International Championship and Washington D.C. International; 2nd Prix Saint-Roman; 3rd Prix de l'Arc de Triomphe.

ACK ACK (b. 1966)	Battle Joined (b. 1959)	Armageddon	Alsab / Fighting Lady
		Ethel Walker	Revoked / Ethel Terry
	Fast Turn (b. 1959)	Turn-to	Royal Charger / Source Sucree
		Cherokee Rose	Princequillo / The Squaw II
GAZALA II (br. 1964)	Dark Star (br. 1950)	Royal Gem II	Dhoti / French Gem
		Isolde	Bull Dog / Fiji
	Belle Angevine (br. 1957)	L'Amiral	Admiral Drake / Hurrylor
		Bella II	Canot / Bayan Kara

1050   ZABARELLA 22 (gr.f., March 7, 1974)

Bred by Razza Dormello-Olgiata, in Italy.

Won 3 races, placed 1, 71,778,407 L., in Italy and France, at 2 and 3 years, incl. Oaks d'Italia and Premio Lydia Tesio.

CLOUET (br. 1964)	Hugh Lupus (b. 1952)	Djebel	Tourbillon / Loika
		Sakountala	Goya II / Samos
	Carminia (b. 1958)	Vimy	Wild Risk / Mimi
		Caspian Sea	Tehran / Sea Fret
ZANNIRA (gr. 1967)	Sovereign Path (gr. 1956)	Grey Sovereign	Nasrullah / Kong
		Mountain Path	Bobsleigh / Path of Peace
	Aimee (b. 1957)	Tudor Minstrel	Owen Tudor / Sansonnet
		Emali	Umidwar / Eclair

197

1051   **ZANK** 22 (b.c., January 30, 1961)

Bred by Gestüt Quenhorn, in Germany.

Won 4 races, placed 3, 127,100 DM., in Germany and Austria, at 2 and 3 years, incl. Deutsches Derby and Österreichisches Derby.

NECKAR (bl. 1948)	Ticino (b. 1939)	Athanasius	Ferro / Athanasie
		Terra	Aditi / Teufelsrose
	Nixe (b. 1941)	Arjaman	Herold / Aditja
		Nanon	Graf Isolani / Nella da Gubbio
ZACATECA (b. 1949)	Zuccarello (ch. 1938)	Ortello	Teddy / Hollebeck
		Flumigela	Michelangelo / Flush
	Katherine Roet (b. 1930)	Son-in-Law	Dark Ronald / Mother in Law
		Criseyde	Chaucer / Camlarg

1052   **ZAPOTECO** 5 (b.c., March 22, 1970)

Bred by Hurstland Farm, in U.S.A.

Won 3 races, placed 3, 465,697 fr., in France, at 2 and 3 years, incl. Prix de la Salamandre; 2nd Prix Morny; 3rd Prix Maurice de Gheest.

DELTA JUDGE (dk.b. or br. 1960)	Traffic Judge (ch. 1952)	Alibhai	Hyperion / Teresina
		Traffic Court	Discovery / Traffic
	Beautillion (bl. 1953)	Noor	Nasrullah / Queen of Baghdad
		Delta Queen	Bull Lea / Bleebok
MISS REMAID (ch. 1963)	Reneged (b. 1953)	Revoked	Blue Larkspur / Gala Belle
		White Samite	Gallant Fox / Ommiad
	Alamo Maid (b. 1958)	Brookfield	Bimelech / Knockaney Bridge
		Memsahib	Denturius / Mabama

1053   **ZAUBERER** 1 (b.c., May 6, 1975)

Bred by Gestüt Bona, in France.

Won 4 races, placed 6, 308,480 DM., in Germany, from 2 to 4 years, incl. Deutsches Derby; 3rd Aral Pokal.

SODERINI (b. 1961)	Crepello (ch. 1954)	Donatello II	Blenheim / Delleana
		Crepuscule	Mieuxce / Red Sunset
	Matuta (b. 1955)	Tantieme	Deux pour Cent / Terka
		Maitrise	Atout Maitre / Mabama
ZAUBERFEE (b. 1960)	Kilometer (b. 1953)	Alizier	Teleferique / Alizarine
		Kirschfliege	Brantome / Curl Paper
	Zauberflote (b. 1948)	Ticino	Athanasius / Terra
		Zakuska	Wallenstein / Numea

1054   **ZEDDAAN** 11 (gr.c., 1965)

Bred by H.H. Aga Khan, in Ireland.

Won 8 races, placed 3, 1,073,365 fr., in France, at 2 and 3 years, incl. Poule d'Essai des Poulains, Prix d'Ispahan, Prix Robert Papin, Prix d'Arenberg and Prix de Seine-et-Oise; 2nd Prix de l'Abbaye de Longchamp, Prix du Petit Couvert and Prix Eugene Adam.

GREY SOVEREIGN (gr. 1948)	Nasrullah (b. 1940)	Nearco	Pharos / Nogara
		Mumtaz Begum	Blenheim / Mumtaz Mahal
	Kong (gr. 1933)	Baytown	Achtoi / Princess Herodias
		Clang	Hainault / Vibration
VARETA (gr. 1953)	Vilmorin (gr. 1943)	Gold Bridge	Swynford or Golden Boss / Flying Diadem
		Queen of the Meadows	Fairway / Queen of the Blues
	Veronique II (b. 1937)	Mon Talisman	Craig an Eran / Ruthene
		Volubilis	Alcantara II / Polyflora

1055   **ZENOBIA** 9 (br.f., May 5, 1957)

Bred by Mrs. A. B. Biddle.

Won 1 race, placed 2, £2,614, in Ireland, at 2 and 3 years, incl. Irish 1,000 Guineas; 2nd Athasi Stakes.

SAYAJIRAO (br. 1944)	Nearco (br. 1935)	Pharos	Phalaris / Scapa Flow
		Nogara	Havresac II / Catnip
	Rosy Legend (br. 1931)	Dark Legend	Dark Ronald / Golden Legend
		Rosy Cheeks	St. Just / Purity
PERSIAN VIEW (br. 1951)	Persian Gulf (b. 1940)	Bahram	Blandford / Friar's Daughter
		Double Life	Bachelor's Double / Saint Joan
	Lady's View (br. 1942)	Panorama	Sir Cosmo / Happy Climax
		Girlish Fancy	Prince Philip / Graceful Girl

1056   **ZUG** 16 (br.c., March 15, 1968)

Bred by F. and E. de Brignac, in France.

Won 3 races, placed 2, 375,000 fr., in France, at 2 and 3 years, incl. Poule d'Essai des Poulains.

NASRAM II (b. 1960)	Nasrullah (b. 1940)	Nearco	Pharos / Nogara
		Mumtaz Begum	Blenheim / Mumtaz Mahal
	La Mirambule (b. 1949)	Coaraze	Tourbillon / Corrida
		La Futaie	Gris Perle / La Futelaye
LUCERNE (br. 1955)	Bolero (ch. 1946)	Eight Thirty	Pilate / Dinner Time
		Stepwisely	Wise Counsellor / Stephanie
	Wake Atoll (b. 1949)	Norseman	Umidwar / Tara
		Corsica	Brantome / Ephrata

198